T3-BLC-455

CENTRAL ISSUES IN CONTEMPORARY ECONOMIC THEORY AND POLICY

General Editor: **Mario Baldassarri**, *Professor of Economics, University of Rome 'La Sapienza', Italy*

Published titles include:

Mario Baldassarri, Michele Bagella and Luigi Paganetto (*editors*)
FINANCIAL MARKETS: IMPERFECT INFORMATION AND RISK MANAGEMENT

Mario Baldassarri and Pierluigi Ciocca (*editors*)
ROOTS OF THE ITALIAN SCHOOL OF ECONOMICS AND FINANCE: FROM FERRARA (1857) TO EINAUDI (1944) (*three volumes*)

Mario Baldassarri and Massimo Di Matteo (*editors*)
INTERNATIONAL PROBLEMS OF ECONOMIC INTERDEPENDENCE

Mario Baldassarri, Cesare Imbriani and Dominick Salvatore (*editors*)
THE INTERNATIONAL SYSTEM BETWEEN NEW INTEGRATION AND NEO-PROTECTIONISM

Mario Baldassarri, Alfredo Macchiati and Diego Piacentino (*editors*)
THE PRIVATIZATION OF PUBLIC UTILITIES: THE CASE OF ITALY

Mario Baldassarri, Luigi Paganetto and Edmund S. Phelps (*editors*)
EQUITY, EFFICIENCY AND GROWTH: THE FUTURE OF THE WELFARE STATE

Mario Baldassarri, Luigi Paganetto and Edmund S. Phelps (*editors*)
THE 1990s SLUMP: CAUSES AND CURES

Mario Baldassarri, Luigi Paganetto and Edmund S. Phelps (*editors*)
WORLD SAVING, PROSPERITY AND GROWTH

Mario Baldassarri, Luigi Paganetto and Edmund S. Phelps (*editors*)
INTERNATIONAL DIFFERENCES IN GROWTH RATES: MARKET GLOBALIZATION AND ECONOMIC AREAS

Mario Baldassarri and Paolo Roberti (*editors*)
FISCAL PROBLEMS IN THE SINGLE-MARKET EUROPE

Mario Baldassarri and Franco Modigliani (*editors*)
THE ITALIAN ECONOMY: WHAT NEXT?

Mario Baldassarri (*editor*)
MAFFEO PANTALEONI: AT THE ORIGIN OF THE ITALIAN SCHOOL OF ECONOMICS AND FINANCE

Mario Baldassarri, Luigi Paganetto and Edmund S. Phelps (*editors*)
INSTITUTIONS AND ECONOMIC ORGANIZATION IN THE ADVANCED ECONOMIES: THE GOVERNANCE PERSPECTIVE

Central Issues in Contemporary Economic Theory and Policy
Series Standing Order ISBN 0–333–71464–4
(outside North America only)

You can receive future titles in this series as they are published by placing a standing order. Please contact your bookseller or, in case of difficulty, write to us at the address below with your name and address, the title of the series and the ISBN quoted above.

Customer Services Department, Macmillan Distribution Ltd, Houndmills, Basingstoke, Hampshire RG21 6XS, England

Roots of the Italian School of Economics and Finance

From Ferrara (1857) to Einaudi (1944)

Volume 3

Edited by

Mario Baldassarri
Professor of Economics
University of Rome 'La Sapienza'
Italy

and

Pierluigi Ciocca
Vice Director-General
Bank of Italy

in association with
Rivista di Politica Economica, SIPI, Rome

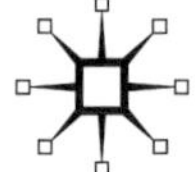

First published in book form 2001 by
PALGRAVE
Houndmills, Basingstoke, Hampshire RG21 6XS and
175 Fifth Avenue, New York, N. Y. 10010
Companies and representatives throughout the world

PALGRAVE is the new global academic imprint of St. Martin's Press LLC Scholarly and Reference Division and Palgrave Publishers Ltd (formerly Macmillan Press Ltd).

ISBN 0–333–92102–X

This book is printed on paper suitable for recycling and made from fully managed and sustained forest sources.

A catalogue record for this book is available from the British Library.

Library of Congress Cataloging-in-Publication Data
Roots of the Italian school of economics and finance : from Ferrara (1857) to Einaudi (1944) / edited by Mario Baldassarri and Pierluigi Ciocca.
p. cm. — (Central issues in contemporary economic theory and policy)
Originally published in Rivista di politica economica, June–July 1997, Aug.–Sept. 1997, and March–April 1998.
"[Published] in association with Rivista di Politica Economica, SIPI, Rome."
Includes bibliographical references and index.
ISBN 0–333–80205–5 (v. 1) — ISBN 0–333–92101–1 (v. 2) –
– ISBN 0–333–92102–X (v. 3)
1. Economics—Italy—History. 2. Finance—Italy—History. I. Baldassarri, Mario, 1946– II. Ciocca, Pierluigi, 1941– III. Rivista di politica economica. IV. Series.

HB109.A2R66 2000
330.15—dc21

00–066555

10 9 8 7 6 5 4 3 2 1
10 09 08 07 06 05 04 03 02 01

Printed and bound in Great Britain by
Antony Rowe Ltd, Chippenham, Wiltshire

Contents

Preface

Mario Baldassarri - Pierluigi Ciocca

In the period straddling the nineteenth and twentieth centuries the most significant and vital roots which had nourished the development and growth of what can today be defined as the fundamental framework of modern economic theory were extended and studied in depth. A significant number of Italian economists and thinkers furnished contributions of great originality and profundity to these foundations, so much so that, from many aspects, talk of an Italian school of economics and finance is wholly justified. Since the second half of the nineteenth century, this school has produced contributions of great importance and profundity of thought and analysis which undoubtedly include some of the most significant milestones of economic theory. The perspicacity of the analysis and originality of the intuitions assure these contributions are extremely stimulating and relevant even today.

Some of these important contributions enjoyed even then a wide diffusion thanks to their publication in English and French. For most of these works, however, their publication in Italian only was a serious impediment to their knowledge and diffusion in the broader European and international context.

Hence we believe it of considerable interest to collect some of the contributions we consider the most important and to publish them in full in both English and Italian.

The Italian version aims therefore to furnish, particularly to students and younger Italian economists, an overall reference which can outline the fundamental framework of the origins of the Italian school of economics and finance, i.e., the historical and theoretical origins of that which today appears to have become a diffuse and significant presence of Italian economists of the most recent generations, properly trained and in the international mainstream of contemporary economic theory and analysis.

The English version of an articulated and reasoned series of works hitherto unpublished in this language aims, on the other hand, to ensure broader knowledge of these works and make known some significant contributions of the Italian school to the foundations of the modern economic theory at the close of the nineteenth and start of the twentieth centuries.

In view of the size of the output of literature, we opted to select a relatively limited number of contributions. Hence these volumes do not aim to furnish the reader with a complete and exhaustive reference, but more simply to present a 'sampling' of that historical movement and those theoretical developments. We are certain, however, that this 'sampling' will not fail to confirm the saying that 'appetite comes with eating' and will stimulate in many readers curiosity and interest such as to induce them to continue their study and rediscover that strand of economists which Italy produced in these founding phases of the modern economic theory.

Although the contributions selected are necessarily limited in number, the breadth of the undertaking counsebled publishing the works selected in a total of seven sections, each dedicated to the more significant threads of analysis and debate, over three issues.

This first volume, presents, in six different sections, contributions on Value, Saving, Market, Trade *by Ricci, Einaudi, Pantaleoni, Barone, and Cabiati, on* Finance *by Einaudi, De Viti de Marco, and Del Vecchio and on* The Clash with Socialism and Analyses of the Labour Market *by Croce, Pantaleoni, Gramsci, and Demaria.*

Then, are collected works on Money and Banks *by De Viti de Marco, Del Vecchio, Bresciani Turroni and Cabiati, on* Income Distribution *by Pareto, Bernini, Bresciani Turroni, and Gini, and on the* Methods and Nature of Political Economy *by Ferrara, Labriola, Pareto, Croce, and De Finetti.*

The second volume hosts essays directly referred to the structure and development of the Italian economy of that period. This volume on the Italian economy, which will be published in the March-April 1998 issue, is divided into four sections.

The first section refers to some Contemporary Issues in Italy, *with papers by Pantaleoni, Montemartini, and Amoroso. The second and third sections refer to the age-old problems of the* North-South Gap *and* Emigration *and include papers by Ciccotti, Nitti, Franchetti and Sonnino, Beneduce, Coletti, and Pareto. The fourth and final section reproduces contributions by Amoroso, Barone, De Viti de Marco, and Montemartini regarding* Infrastructure, Public Works and Enterprises.

In chronological terms, the collection opens with a paper by Ferrara dating from 1857 and closes with one by Einaudi dating from 1944, at the threshold of that post-war reconstruction and period of heady growth which enabled Italy to leave the group of poor countries with a lagged development and rightfully gain a place among the leading industrial economies and democracies of the world.

I - WEALTH, LABOUR MARKET AND PENSIONS

On the Probable Amount of Private Wealth in Italy. From 1872 to 1889*

Maffeo Pantaleoni

1. - Why the De Foville Method is Chosen

It is my conviction, and I believe that of anybody else who has studied the statistics available to date in Italy, that none of the statistical methods used to measure the overall private wealth in a country in a given time can be applied to our country except that known as the De Foville method.

I am equally certain that there is no statistical material available in any other country on which the De Foville method can be applied with the same ease and certainty in results as the statistics for Italy.

It would be a lengthy undertaking to give proof of the first of these assertions, because it would necessarily have to be of what mathematicians call the indirect type.

As regards proof of the second assertion, I hope the considerations below will fulfil the task.

Under the present state of statistics, we can survey seventeen years of study of the probable amount of private wealth in Italy and reach three cornerstones, calculating this amount for three

---

* From: PANTALEONI M., «Dell'ammontare probabile della ricchezza privata in Italia», *Giornale degli Economisti, Rivista Mensile degli Interessi Italiani*, August 1890, pp. 139-76. [Cod. JEL: N 33].

successive five-year periods, namely for the periods 1872-1876, 1877-1881 and 1882-1887. In other words, we can take the five-year periods from 1873 to 1877, from 1878 to 1882 and from 1883 to 1888, or else, also chose the five-year period 1874-1878; that of 1879-1883 and the last one of 1884-1890. In any case we will have for every set of five years, three sets of data, each based on the five-year averages, which will indicate the probable overall amount of private wealth in Italy, and hence also its movement.

It may even be granted that a study of this type, given the reliability of its results, is not wholly devoid of interest, and is even somewhat opportune. Since many believe that in Italy wealth has increased, particularly in these last ten years, despite the impositions and debts and crises which it cannot be denied have taken place; others however believe we are on the edge of a precipice, indeed, already rolling towards the bottom of the stairs and complain of pains for every roll, due, they say to the bad air we breathe the further we descend. Who is right? In any case it is certain that we are not rich, and, then, we do well to count often, and exactly, the money to be found in our pockets.

2. - Overview of the De Foville Method

The De Foville method for estimating the probable amount of private wealth of a nation in a given age is of such an elegant simplicity that it can be compared to a mathematical theorem. Its fundamental tenet can be summarised thus.

Let us suppose that in a country in a year all the citizens, except the tax officers, died. The result would be that the latter would be charged with applying, during the year, the probate duty to the total amount of private wealth owned by all the components of that country and this would have given an estimate of all the assets of all the citizens.

Now, *de facto*, citizens never depart this world all together, but they do so, let us say, in sets, in waves. Hence, the tax officers who apply the probate duty and, therefore estimate the value of the assets handed down *mortis causa*, each year, only see and assess a fraction of the overall assets of the political society in which they operate. One asks: what is this fraction? Because, if we can know it, it is clear that, «given the value of the estate annually handed down to others, *mortis causa*, in a political society, it becomes easy to calculate the entity of the total private wealth owned, it sufficing to multiply the wealth handed down annually *mortis causa* for the reciprocal of the fraction it represents».

Now it is clear that if the political society in question is not subject to some force which profoundly modifies its demographic laws, or else, in other words, if we suppose that the sets which successively leave this life, have enjoyed it on average for equal times, the fraction sought will be found by calculating, «the amount of time needed for an individual who receives an inheritance, to, in turn, leave it to others, i.e., to his hiers». Hence, multiplying the inheritance of a set of individuals, i.e., of those who died in the same year, for the average number of years from the year in which they died and the average year in which the sets which inherited from the first will die, we will have done nothing other than repeat the value left *mortis causa* by the first set as many times as there are intermediary sets between them and that which inherits from them; in other words, as many times as the number of years required for the same succession to be handed down again. The result of this operation can only be that of having flash before our eyes all the sets which, in a given moment, were set out to tumble down in a long series of years, i.e., of providing us with the same effect that would be had in the grim first hypothesis of an entire nation inspected by the tax officers dealing with probate duty.

3. - The Lifespan of a Generation and What Net Estate should be Considered as Handed Down *Mortis Causa* Every Year

Like any other statistical method, that of de Foville, whose underlying idea is of a transparent simplicity, nonetheless encounters, as any other statistical method, a series of difficulties in practical implementation; and these difficulties in part differ according to how the statistical data to be used in the various countries were formed and recorded. Disregarding for the moment this second type of difficulty, we will dwell on that which can be called generic, i.e., on the question as to how one ascertains the average interval between the death of the deceased and that of his heirs.

This time, defined as we have above, has first and foremost a name which statisticians have at times employed to designate other average times, but which, since Rümelin, has been more properly reserved for this. It is in fact said in statistics that the duration of a generation is the average difference of age between father and children of both sexes. This average difference, between the age of the father and that of all the children, is obtained naturally, by counting from the birth of the father to the average time of birth of all his children of both sexes and this, in turn, is the same as counting from the death of the father to the average time of death of all his children of both sexes, on condition that the hypothesis, which conforms to the facts (when no transformations of the demographic laws take place) that the children live on average as long as the fathers, or else the equivalent hypothesis, which also confirms to the facts, that the probable life of the children at each age is of the same length as that the fathers had at the same age.

This problem was resolved by a double series of studies. On the one hand, Rümelin[1] calculated the average length of a generation starting in his statistical investigations from the average age of the fathers at the time of their wedding and adding the average of the time when they gave rise to offspring, i.e., which is almost[2] the same, the average of the difference of age between the firstborn and the youngest children, of whatever sex.

Thus he succeeded in determining the lifespan of a generation for the Aryan populations of the temperate climates based on the monogamous system within two limits, one minimum of 32

[1] See RÜMELIN Q., *Reden und Aufsätze*, Frieburg i. B. und Tübingen. Mohr. Vol. I, 1875, p. 285.

[2] It is not *exactly* the same, as the births could be subject to the law of greater concentration in some parts of the period of wedding fecundity than in others.

years, the other a maximum of 39 years, with a mean figure of 35 or 36.

On the other hand, De Foville himself had data for determining the survival of heirs of the deceased in a survey carried out in France, which showed that 45 years passed on average between two *inter vivos* transfers in the same property, while it was already known that there is a period of 20 years between two property transfers between the living or as a result of death. Given this, in 900 years there are 45 transfers of property between the living or *mortis causa* (900/20 = 45), of which 20 are between the living (900/45 = 20) and necessarily 25 *mortis causa* (45-20 = 25), which take place at an average interval of 36 years between one and the other (900/25 = 36).

Having thus ascertained the coefficient by which the values taxed for inheritance in a year should be multiplied, all that remains is to solve the problem of what should be considered as the patrimony handed down *mortis causa* each year. It was obvious that first and foremost this item should include the *net* successions effected; which, in France, for example, is not a easy item of data to obtain because the revenue authorities do not bother to ascertain the size of the inheritances net of liabilities before taxing them. Hence the data should be adjusted for this by means of a correction coefficient which can be applied to said succession values (multiplying them by a true fraction), or else reducing the figure of 36 years, ascertained for the span of a generation, to a smaller figure. In any case, some criterion or other has to be used to deduce the *ratio* between liabilities and gross successions. Now De Foville (in his most recent work on the subject[3]), reduces the length of a generation to 35 years, evidently to compensate for the amount by which he should reduce the succession values to take account of the liabilities. The reduction of the figure for the span of a generation from 36 to 35 years amounts to a correction coefficient of 2.78% (as 35 : 36 = 97.22 : 100; hence the correction coefficient in 2.78 = 100.00 – 97.22). This would appear to be lower than that

[3] See *La France Économique, Statistique, Raisonnée et Comparative*, Année 1887, p. 441. A more recent edition is now on sale.

actually encountered in real life if we compare the figures for France to those, certain, ascertained for Italy. As in Italy the revenue authorities deduct the liabilities from the successions, before levying the tax and naturally, do not tax at all those successions where liabilities exceed assets. For some three years now, the Italian tax administration publishes figures regarding the liabilities deductible from inheritances as a result of probate duty[4], and hence we can with perfect certainty say what the correction coefficient we should use should be, if in Italy the tax office had hit gross estates. Now for the fiscal years 1885-1886, 1886-1887 and 1887-1888, the figures for gross assets and inherited debts (without taking account of those estates where assets were absorbed by debts and hence not taxed) provide us with an average percentage of 11.33 of debts to gross assets, i.e., roughly we can hold that 1/8 or 1/9 of the gross estates consist of debts which have to be deducted. There is, a priori, no economic or statistical reason which leads us to believe that a different *ratio* exists in France.

Disregarding this first obstacle, which the legislation poses in France alone, and not here in Italy, to a rigorous application of the De Foville method, some legislations may put forward another, which consists in exonerating small estates from the payment of probate duty. A wholly similar difficulty is encountered in estimating national wealth using income tax statistics. And, as before, the remedy can only consist in seeking a new correction coefficient. However, this difficulty is encountered only in Belgium and the Netherlands, where estates of less than one thousand lire are exempt from probate duty, but not in France and not in Italy. We will not dwell therefore on indicating the formation of a correction coefficient with respect to this issue.

The most serious change to be made to the values taxed by way of inheritance by the revenue authorities consists in the addition of all the values handed down *inter vivos donationis causa*. Vacher, who even before De Foville thought of using inheritances

---

[4] See *Relazione dell'amministrazione del demanio e delle tasse sugli affari — 1887-1888*, allegato 9, p. 199 — 1886-1887, allegato 9, p. 225; *1885-1886*, allegato 9, p. 277. Vol. I, series 2.

to calculate private wealth, but who totally erred in seeking the coefficient with which it should be multiplied, overlooked the need for this correction until De Foville demonstrated it. It is in fact clear that gifts inter vivos are almost exclusively advances on estates made by relations for weddings or by entrepreneurs for their descendants and this is why the civil code makes their collation and charging mandatory. The error which would be introduced in the calculations if this item was omitted would be far from slight. In France, gifts inter vivos, account for, with insignificant annual deviations from the mean, 25% of inheritances, in Italy, with equal regularity, they account for an average 16.13% of inheritances[5]. Their omission would reduce the figure of national wealth by circa 6 and a half billion lire in Italy. At first sight the considerable percentage difference to which endowments and other advances on inheritances amount in France and Italy may strike one as a most singular fact. Why can it be that parents in France give 25% of their assets to their children before their death and those in Italy only 16%?

Given that these gifts are mainly dowries, we believe it very hazardous to suppose a diversity in customs, and say, for example, that in Italy, on the one hand, the bride and groom are less demanding as regards the dowry, and on the other parents are more reluctant to grant it; or else to suppose, that Italians are much better than the French in tricking the revenue authorities and circumventing the laws which require a public deed for dowries. On the contrary, we believe that the difference noted should be ascribed to the provisions of the Napoleonic Code on the one hand and of the Italian code on the other regarding asset relations between husband and wife. Section 1400 of the Napoleonic code, by *praesumptio juris*, presumes the sharing of assets if there is no marriage contract which stipulates otherwise. The Italian code, on the other hand, deems that the assets belong to the husband (section 1433)

[5] From 1877 to 1881, donations amount to 15% of successions; from 1882 to 1888 they are 17.08%; with a weighted average of

$$\frac{17.08 \times 15.00 \times 5}{11} = 16.13\%$$

if there is no marriage contract. Hence the need for the French to regulate their asset relations with the bride accurately with a marriage contract otherwise they lay themselves open to the risk of losing, on the day of her death, half of all the profits accrued during their marriage. Thence the more frequent and complete list of the bride's assets on her wedding day.

But, even when we have supplemented the estates with the addition of the gifts inter vivos, we will still not have the full figure we seek, as we have to take account of the fact that the revenue authorities are engaged in a continuous struggle with the taxpayer's astuteness and are far from being always the winner. Unfortunately, nothing is more uncertain than the correction coefficient for the schemes employed by taxpayers vis-à-vis the revenue administration. De Foville, whose administrative and statistical experience is universally known, dares to assess the amounts which elude the revenue authorities at 25% of inheritances, and we ourselves accepted this figure on another occasion. Then the tax administration[6] calculating only the personal property which eludes tax, estimated it at from 7 to 13% of the net estate, and we, on the basis of the surtaxes and fines, estimated at $1^1/_2$% or 2% of the net estate the wealth which in vain sought to elude the tax service, such that the error coefficient for this item can be left at 25% without concern that it is significantly vitiated[7].

Briefly recapitulating the operations that should be carried out to apply the De Foville method to the estimation of private wealth in Italy, except to explain below other small expedients to be employed in manipulating it when we analyse the statistics for Italy, we shall say that it consists in: 1) tracing back from the taxes, levied at the various rates which hit inheritances and gifts according to the degree of kinship between the heirs and the deceased, or be-

[6] See *Relazione dell'amminstrazione del demanio etc. per l'esercizio 1886-1887*, p. 54.

[7] Our argumentation, albeit approximate, runs as follows: if the tax administration acknowledges *for personal property alone* an error of from 7 to 13%, considered that the error in the assessment of land property should be much greater, and as regards its mass, and its *nature* (as shall be seen below), we should allow an *overall* correction coefficient, variable, of 14 to 26%, with a strong propensity for the upper limit.

tween the recipient and the donor, by simple proportions, the amounts subjected to taxation, when the administration itself, as sometimes it does and sometimes it doesn't, does not provide the amounts subject to tax alongside the amount levied by tax; 2) summing the values subject to probate duty with those subject to tax for free transfer between the living; 3) increasing this amount by a quarter by way of correction for wealth which avoids payment of tax; 4) multiplying it by 36. But then it is opportune to reason on five-year averages, rather than to operate on the data of a single year, or of each year of a series separately. The inheritance and gift statistics for a given year can every now and then be skewed because some extraordinarily large inheritance has been made or because some exceptional dowry has been donated[8]; hence using operating five-year averages, the effects of such an event disappear, or become inappreciably small. Moreover, it is to be feared that the inheritances of a given year can be affected by the effects of an epidemic; it is unarguably certain that to considerably alter even the data for a single year, the epidemic should truly be something exceptional, for example, the recent cholera epidemics which Italy has recently experienced and which, in every aspect, should be deemed events of the most serious nature, had only a very slight impact on the inheritance taxes, as there was an increase in the number of inheritances opened, but there was also a considerable increase in the number of untraceable items and of inheritances of the destitute[9] (Table 17); but, even of this disruptive cause every trace should remained submerged in the average of the five-year data. Finally, it is easy to comprehend, that from one year to the next, the zeal, activity, intelligence and success of the revenue administration, whose staff renew themselves gradually and which undergoes, as the individuals which comprise it, periods of discouragement and periods of energy, is similarly different; for this reason it is again better to work with the data for several years than with a single figure. Before leaving this argument, a final observation is in order. It has been at times believed that when one is talking only of appre-

---

[8] See *Relazione dell'amministrazione del demanio per il 1887-1886*, p. 52.
[9] See *Relazione del demanio per il 1886-1887*, pp. 53-4.

ciating the movement of national wealth, and it is of no importance knowing its actual amount in any age, one could resort not to the values taxed by way of succession increased by the values taxed by way of free transfer between the living, to the amounts collected for both these items, as the figure appears, at first sight, to be proportional to the figures for the amounts raised by each of said taxes, as the figures for the values appear, at first sight, to have the same movement. Now this is wholly erroneous, because while the values subject to inheritance tax (and the same holds for those subject to the tax for free transfer *inter vivos*) are subject only to the causes which modify the national wealth, the amounts collected by way of tax are subject not only to this category of causes, but moreover depend also on the nature of the succession which has taken place, i.e., on the degree of kinship between the deceased and his heirs. The same estate values give rise to wholly different amounts collected depending on whether the successions are direct or between collateral relatives or between spouses, etc., and the collections hence have from one year to the next differences which are increasingly greater that those encountered between the values taxed. The result is that the former are by no means an exact mirror of the movement of national wealth, and are in no way, translated into percentage figures, equal to the latter, which are the only ones which should be trusted.

4. - Presentation and Criticism of the Statistics for Italy

The statistical material for Italy which can serve for the application of the De Foville method has been perfecting itself since 1877 and more specifically since 1883. In 1882, one could not go back before 1875 for the values taxed *mortis causes* and also the data for 1875 and 1876 could not be used as they were not comparable with those for subsequent years and by virtue of their manner of presentation. In 1883, the administration[10] itself undertook to find the values subject to inheritance tax from 1872 onwards,

[10] See *Relazione del demanio*, allegato 13.

and in its report for 1885-1886 it attempted a calculation using the De Foville method[11]. It is only deplorable that the administration, roughly every year, invents some innovation in the manner or presentation of the data, often eschewing some good previous invention. Thus, for example (as can be seen in more detail in the Appendices) sometimes it publishes figures only on the collections made, sometimes it adds to these the values subject to tax, then re-abandons this system to return to the previous one, at times it groups the collection data in two distinct items (i.e., successions between brothers and sisters with successions in favour of charity institutes - which are taxed at the same rate — or else successions beyond the tenth degree of kinship with successions in favour of institutes other than charity institutes — which are also taxed at the same rate — or else, and this is worst, gifts, munificences and assignments between cousins-german with those between other relatives of up to the tenth degree of kinship — which are taxed at different rates —) and at times separates them, at times it supplies the data regarding the division of the assets taxed into personal property and real property, or better, other assets, and at times does not bother to do so, and one can see that it traces back to 1872 in the search for data on amounts taxed by way of inheritance and not do so for the data regarding gifts inter vivos. In short, it seriously lacks *espirit de suite* and forces those who wish to use its data to very complementary calculation and a constant vigilance.

As we shall now pass to a reasoned presentation of the official data and to their integration where they are lacking, we shall presuppose the reader is familiar with that part of the law on the registration fees concerning successions, and that it has not been amended in any part which concerns us since it was enacted in 1874, except for any greater means allowed to the administration to avoid being defrauded by the taxpayers[12]. We shall remind the reader solely to facilitate comprehension of Table 18, that the inheritance tax has eight brackets or categories which we shall denote with the let-

[11] See *Relazione del demanio per il 1885-1886*, pp. 85-9.

[12] See Law no. 2076 of 13 September 1874 and Laws no. 835 and 4702 of 29 June 1882 and 14 July 1887 respectively.

ters of the alphabet. Category *A*, which is taxed at 1.44%, covers direct-line successions between ascendants and descendants; category *B*, which is taxed at 3.60%, covers successions between spouses; category *C*, which is taxed at 6%, covers successions between brothers and sisters as well as successions in favour of charity institutes or charities, category *D*, which is taxed at 7.20%, covers succession between uncles and nephews, great-uncles and great-nephews; category *E*, which is taxed at 9.60%, covers successions between cousins-german; category *F*, which is taxed at 10.80%, covers successions between other relatives and collateral relatives up to the tenth degree of kinship; category *G*, which is taxed at 12%, covers succession beyond the tenth degree of kinship, relatives-in-law and collateral relatives, as well as successions in favour of institutions other than charities; finally, category *H*, which is taxed at 2.40%, on *half* of the value, covers the transfers of usufruct in favour of church institutions and services. And these same categories also apply for the tax on gifts inter vivos, except category *H*, which covers the establishment of dowries and munificences for marriage made by persons who are neither ascendants nor descendants of the spouses.

Now calculation of the values subjected to succession tax in these eight categories gives rise to no difficulty, and has, mostly, already been made by the revenue administration itself. Table 18 details the values taxed for each category from 1872 to 1889, with the sole exception of the data for first-half 1884, the half year which bridged the fiscal years conforming to the calendar year and those which, in accordance with the new law on public accounting, started on July 1st and ended on June 30th of the subsequent year. It is self-evident that the omission of this half year from the calculations can in no way upset them. If we wish to use these data to calculate the national wealth, however, we have to double the values ascertained in category *H*, as tax is levied on only half the asset's worth[13].

[13] Moreover, we have to calculate them for the years 1872-1873 and 1874 in which not even the amount collected by the administration is given in Appendix 13 of 1883. But this is easy, as from 1888 to 1882 the ratio of category *H* to the total of the other categories is 1.56% and in 1879 this ratio is 1.96%, while in 1876 it is 1.31%. We are therefore right to calculate this item for the afore-indicated three years at 1.60% of the other items.

We will then obtain the following picture (Table 1) of the values transferred *mortis causa* before any correction for tax evasion: (the following picture is also given in the second column of Table 19, while the first gives the overall figures of Table 18).

TABLE 1

Years	Amounts transferred *mortis causa* from 1872 to 1889	Years	Amounts transferred *mortis causa* from 1872 to 1889
1872	686,799,880	1881	914,668,400
1873	649,074,644	1882	931,403,400
1874	753,897,774	1883	994,593,400
1875	881,826,382	1884-1885	1,005,223,400
1876	830,389,816	1885-1886	987,161,300
1877	862,337,600	1886-1887	1,085,315,600
1878	878,069,600	1887-1888	1,092,062,400
1879	810,720,900	1888-1889	1,008,883,100
1880	957,072,500		

It is not easy, on the contrary, to estimate the wealth handed down through gifts inter vivos. First and foremost the data for the amount collected for said date not from 1877 but from 1872, so that they have to be reconstructed approximately for five years. This can be done, considering the constancy of the ratio between the amount of wealth handed down by gifts inter vivos and that *mortis causa* in the past eleven years, for which we have the data of the amounts collected; it is therefore legitimate to suppose that the ratio found in the eleven year period, for which gifts amount to 16.3% of successions, also holds for the preceding five-year period and we can use it to calculate the gifts. It should also be noted that only from 1886-1887 did the revenue administration not group in a single figure the amounts collected by category *E* at 9.60% and those by category *F* at 10.80%. Now to trace back the values taxed from the amount raised, we have to assume an average rate of between 9.60% and 10.80%, namely 10.20%, which is feasible only in the hypothesis that the assets hit by one and the other rate are more or less equal. If they were considerably different we should have to use a weighted average to obtain a more truthful figure. However, the only two years the revenue administration distinguished between the amounts collected for these two rates do not allow us to form a weighted average, while they leave us in doubt as regards the equality of the amounts hit by tax. Fortunately, these are very small quantities of wealth which cannot alter the overall data, whenever the actual truth of the matter. But there is a more serious difficulty in calculating the values of category *H* as the amounts raised by this rate is due to the application of half of one or the other of the various rates of tax of the foregoing six categories according to the donor's degree of kinship.

Now, in this emergency, we could once again take the average of the six preceding rates (categories *B* through *G*), i.e., assume the amount raised by category *H* was all obtained at the rate of 4.16% or double the values which correspond to such. Except that it is certain in this case that the various rates of tax are not applied by the revenue administration with the same frequency, but those of the first two of the six categories should be the most frequent; hence, to correct the amount the rate of 4.16% would be exaggerated, we have preferred to calculate the values of this category at 3.36%, the average of all the seven preceding rates (categories *A* through *G*), naturally doubling the values which correspond to the amount raised. Details of the calculations of the various amounts taxed by way of gifts inter vivos are given in Table 20 and reproducing the overall figures in column 3 of Table 19 while Table 2 gives the total values of wealth annually handed down free inter vivos.

TABLE 2

Years	Amounts transferred by donation *inter vivos* from 1872 to 1889	Years	Amounts transferred by donation *inter vivos* from 1872 to 1889
1872	109,167,821	1881	180,961,900
1873	104,695,740	1882	181,491,800
1874	121,603,711	1883	177,337,400
1875	142,238,595	1884-1885	182,309,600
1876	133,941,877	1885-1886	185,658,400
1877	205,043,220	1886-1887	177,850,800
1878	155,815,670	1887-1888	173,963,000
1879	149,634,525	1888-1889	178,601,600
1880	150,860,278		

All we now have to do is add, year by year, the figures of the previous two tables, to increase them by a quarter and to multiply them by 36, which is the average span of a generation. These three operations are found completed in detail in the last two columns of Table 19 and in the first two columns of Table 21. Table 3 shows only the final figures which express the national private wealth estimated for each year from 1872 to 1888, on the basis of the data for each year:

TABLE 3

Years	Total private wealth	Years	Total private wealth
1872	35,369 million	1881	49,303 million
1873	33,920 »	1882	50,080 »
1874	39,398 »	1883	52,737 »
1875	46,083 »	1884-1885	53,439 »
1876	43,395 »	1885-1886	52,777 »
1877	48,032 »	1886-1887	56,842 »
1878	46,525 »	1887-1888	56,971 »
1879	43,216 »	1888-1889	53,437 »
1880	49,857 »		

5. - Estimation of the Probable Amount of Private Wealth in Italy and its Movement

5.1 *Movement of Public Debt Compared with That of Private Wealth. Classification into Rural Land, Buildings and Personal Property. Overview of the Distribution of Wealth by Regions*

From the figures given in the foregoing section we obtain the five-year averages, which alone are reliable. We can do this in three ways, as we have available data for 17 and not 15 years. We can start from 1872 and go to 1887, or else we can start from 1873 and go to 1888, or else we can span from 1874 to 1889. Placing this triple set of data in a framework and translating similarly the absolute figures into percentage figures, gives us Table 4:

TABLE 4

Years	National wealth in absolute figures	Figures
1872-1876	39.6 billion	100.0
1877-1881	47.4 »	121.5
1882-1887	53.1 »	134.1
1873-1877	42.2 »	100.0
1878-1882	47.8 »	113.3
1883-1888	54.6 »	129.4
1874-1878	44.7 »	100.0
1879-1883	49.0 »	109.6
1884-1889	54.7 »	122.4

Hence, according to Table 5, from the first five-year period to the second, the national wealth increased in absolute terms by 7.8 billion lire and from the second to third five-year period by 5.7 billion lire. According to Table 6, from the first five-year period to the second, national wealth increased in absolute terms by 5.6 billion lire and from the second to third five-year period by 6.8 billion lire. Finally, according to Table 7, for the second five-year period it increased by 4.3 billion lire vis-à-vis the first and for the final five-year period by 5.7 billion lire on the second. The discrepancy between these results according to whether one uses one or the other table, should be no surprise, as the starting and end points of the comparisons and the years which comprise the five-year periods are adjusted for this fact. On the contrary, what should attract our attention is the fact that both one and the other estimation show, albeit in differing measure, that the last five-year period was much less favourable to the movement of national wealth than the previous such period.

The measure of this deplorable fact is aggravated if we take account, as indeed we should, of the movement of the population in the three five-year periods in question. Such that it is evident that the data become truly comparable only if we equate the national wealth of each five-year period to *its* population.

Now, adjusting the three foregoing tables by employing this criterion, and taking the probable population of the last year of the five-year period[14], we obtain the estimates in Tables 5, 6 and 7:

TABLE 5

Period	Population	Absolute wealth	Per-capita wealth	Difference	As %
1872-1876	27.7	39.6 billion	1,429.6		100.00
1877-1881	28.4	47.4 »	1,669.6	+239.4	116.74
1882-1887	30.2	53.1 »	1,758.0	+ 89.3	122.99

TABLE 6

Period	Population	Absolute wealth	Per-capita wealth	Difference	As %
1873-1877	28.0	42.2 billion	1,507.1		100.00
1878-1882	28.7	47.8 »	1,665.5	+158.4	110.51
1883-1888	30.5	54.6 »	1,790.1	+124.6	118.78

TABLE 7

Period	Population	Absolute wealth	Per-capita wealth	Difference	As %
1874-1878	28.2	44.7 billion	1,585.1		100.00
1879-1883	29.0	49.0 »	1,689.6	+104.5	106.59
1884-1889	31.0	54.7 »	1,764.5	+ 74.9	111.32

It can be seen that, according to Table 5, national wealth increased from the first to second five-year period by 239 lire per

[14] See *Annuario-statistico italiano*, 1890, p. 72, Table VII.

inhabitant, while from the second to the third five-year period, it increased by only 89 lire per inhabitant, i.e., the rate of increase of national wealth diminished considerably.

According to Table 6, national wealth grew from the first to second five-year period by 158 lire per inhabitant, while from the second to third five-year period it increased by only 125 lire per inhabitant. Finally, according to the third table, we see that wealth increased from the first to second five-year period by 104.5 lire per inhabitant and from the second to third such period by only 74.9 lire per head. Hence these three tables confirm and compound the fact already indicated by the previous tables, namely that the upward movement of wealth was considerably less in the five-year period closest to us than in the preceding five-year period.

6. - Comparison between the Wealth of France and That of Italy

Nonetheless, the importance of this fact, despite its gravity, should not be overstated, and, before proceeding to the considerations which it suggests, it should be noted that the movement of wealth, even slowed, is probably no less than that which took place in France. To give us an approximate idea of the reality, we shall compare the values taxed by way of succession and gifts in France with the same data for Italy and will translate both one and the other into percentage figures starting from 1876[15]. We will obtain Table 8, in which we omit the final three zeros:

[15] The data for France are taken from DE FOVILLE's *France Économique*; those for Italy are the same as in the fourth column of Table 19. The dual scale for the years to which the data refer was made necessary by the differing fiscal years in France and Italy. The years prior to 1876 cannot be compared because only after 1875 was the inheritance tax not amended by the legislator in France.

TABLE 8

Years	France absolute figures	Italy absolute figures	France percentage figures	Italy percentage figures
1872	5,079	786	—	—
1873	4,745	754	—	—
1874	4,928	875	—	—
1875	5,321	1,024	—	—
1876	5,770	964	100	100
1877	5,466	1,067	94	110
1878	5,802	1,033	100	107
1879	6,107	960	106	99
1880	6,383	1,108	110	115
1881	6,001	1,096	104	113
1882	6,073	1,112	105	115
1883	6,305	1,172	109	121
1884 1884-1885	6,101	1,188	106	123
1885 1885-1886	6,429	1,173	112	122
1886 1886-1887		1,263		131
1887 1887-1888		1,266		131
1888 1888-1889		1,187		123

We are struck by two facts in Table 8: on the one hand to the detriment of Italy, the enormous absolute difference between the values taxed by way of succession and gifts in France and the same data for Italy; on the other, the much quicker progression of wealth taxed in Italy than that for France.

We shall return to the first fact in a while; on the second there are some observations to be made. First of all, it would be erroneous to believe that wellbeing, insofar as it is due to wealth, is growing in France and Italy at the rate given by the percentage figures of the last columns, as the increase in wealth in France goes to benefit an almost stationary population, while that in Italy leaves us more or less in the poverty in which we live as the population increases almost at the same rate as wealth, as was seen in the preceding tables. It is therefore obvious that equal absolute increases give higher percentage figures where the initial absolute figure was less. Nevertheless, the fact remains that we will soon have doubled the values of 1872 and if we are now badly off, then we were worse, while of France it should be said that they were well off already in 1872, and that they are less notably better off now than we are less worse off; and that, in any case, the opinion that wealth is increasing in Italy at a rate which is no less than that recorded in France is judicious.

Returning to the tables on private wealth per inhabitant, we will compare it with the Italian public debt, whose guarantee lies precisely in the amount of private wealth, in states which, like Italy, have almost consumed its state assets and do not own railway industries or others, or have, for this item, heavy losses in every year[16].

---

[16] When part of the national debt corresponds to a state asset in the form of railways and more specifically, when these railways have been built, or bought, with money raised by the disposal of state assets, it appears easy to that part of the public which is unfamiliar with business that one can undoubtedly compensate part of the national debt having that origin with the railway assets, or view it as a mere transformation of of capital. And yet it is evident that from the viewpoint of public finance one should take into account, on the one hand, the real interest paid to the debt incurred, i.e., the nominal interest equalised to the rate of return at the act of disposal, and on the other of the net income of the railway industry. If this net income, whose calculation should entail much caution and which is quite a complicated matter, turn out to be less than the interest on the debt, one cannot, in view of the difference between interest and income, speak of compensation or transformation of capital. From the viewpoint of the national economy, comparison between the yield of a similar state asset and the weight of the national debt which derives from it, gives rise to calculations which are even more difficult to make, as on the one hand they have to take account of the savings of cost earned directly and indirectly from many private economies, for the fact that a railway exists, and, on the other, one should include the greater profit which the country would have obtained if the private economies had administered, and not seen subtracted, the capital needed to pay the interest on the national debt.

There are also some quite widespread illusions regarding the returns from railways in Italy and the capital which they represent, or would represent, for the state. More specifically, now that the concession regime is in force, they have forgotten some figures ascertained before and which are worthwhile recalling briefly. Hon. Grimaldi (Parliamentary sitting of May 5 and 6, 1879), on the basis of official data for 1877, pointed out that the product of the railways, adjusted per kilometre, and deducted the operating costs, was in the following ratio to the building cost:

3,449 km. of northern Italy amounted to 3.26% of the building capital
1,638 km. of central Italy » » 1.41% » » »
1,443 km. of southern Italy » » 1.62% » » »
181 km. of private railways » » 1.78% » » »
1,333 km. of the Calabrian and Sicilian railways produced a loss of 358 lire per km.
198 km. of the Sardinian » » » » » 2,609 » » »

Hon. Baccarini (Parliamentary sitting of May 2, 1879) gave the following data: 14 lines of northern Italy and one of central Italy produced a product equal to 4% on the starting capital; 26 lines of northern Italy, 13 of central Italy and 6 of southern Italy and 3 of Sicily produced a profit of less than 4% of the starting capital; 13 lines of northern Italy, 2 of central Italy, 7 of southern Italy, 1 of Sicily and 1 of Sardinia produced a gross product which did not cover the operating costs.

Naturally, the national debt to be taken into consideration will be the perpetual and redeemable debt and should also be proportioned to the population.

We shall therefore make a table (Table 9) which includes not only columns for the years and population for each year, but also the private wealth per inhabitant, the differences, positive or negative, which private wealth shows from one five-year period to another, the percentage figures with which it can express the five-year differences between the percentage figures for private wealth; the national debt per inhabitant, the differences from one five-year period to the next, the percentage figures which express its movement, the percentage differences of the movement of national debt; the remaining private wealth per inhabitant, the five-year differences to which it gives rise, the percentage figures which express its movement. We shall do this in Table 10, for the five-year periods, calculated in a dual manner, as above.

Some unexpected facts now clearly reveal themselves. According to Table 9, although the weight of Italy's national debt has increased per inhabitant, it has not done so by much, in other words, in percentage terms, from 100 to 103 to 108: according to Table 10 it has recently even fallen vis-à-vis the previous five-year period and overall has increased by very little, in other words, it has increased in percentage terms from 100 to 106 and 103. In any case it is certain that the national debt, adjusting its movement to that of the population, cannot be said to have significantly increased.

If we proportion the movement of national debt to that of total private wealth, we have to say that the latter has increased significantly more quickly than the former, as, according to Table 9, wealth has increased from 100 to 117 to 123, while national debt has increased from 100 to 103 to 108. And according to Table 10, wealth has increased from 100 to 111 to 119, while national debt has increased from 100 to 106 to 103.

Net wealth, namely that which remains after having subtracted the national debt from total private wealth, therefore shows quicker progression rates than those for what we can call gross

TABLE 9*

Data	Population	Private wealth				Public debt				Remaining private wealth			
		per inhabitant	differ.	% figures	% differ.	per inhabitant	differ.	% figures	% differ.	per inhabitant	differ.	% figures	% differ.
1	2	3	4	5	6	7	8	9	10	11	12	13	14
1876	27.7	1,429.6	—	100.00	—	347.9	—	100.0	—	1,081.7	—	100.00	—
1881	28.4	1,669.0	+239.4	116.74	+16.74	358.2	+10.30	103.3	+3.0	1,310.8	+229.1	121.18	+21.2
1887	30.2	1,758.3	+ 89.3	122.99	+ 6.25	374.7	+16.50	107.7	+4.7	1,383.6	+ 72.8	127.91	+ 6.7

* (See the anonymous work, commissioned by GENALA *L'Ordinamento delle ferrovie italiane*, Roma, Bencini, 1884, p. 46).

With the *Annuario di statistica* for 1887-1988, pp. 1042-3, it is easy to determine the percentage product of railways on starting capital for 1884. The cost of the lines, tracks and rolling stock, was estimated to be worth 2 billion 875 million lire at end-1884. Per kilometre, the starting costs were 271,766 lire. The operating costs at the same date averaged 16,164 lire per km., while the gross product per km. was 21,467 lire which compared to the starting capital of 2,875 million gives a profit of 1.81%.

TABLE 10

Data	Population	Private wealth				Public debt				Remaining private wealth			
		per inhabitant	differ.	% figures	% differ.	per inhabitant	differ.	% figures	% differ.	per inhabitant	differ.	% figures	% differ.
1	2	3	4	5	6	7	8	9	10	11	12	13	14
1877	28.0	1,507.1	—	100.00	—	361.1	—	100.0	—	1,146.0	—	100.00	—
1882	28.7	1,665.5	+158.4	110.51	+10.51	381.6	+20.5	105.7	+5.7	1,283.9	+137.9	112.03	+12.0
1888	30.5	1,790.1	+124.6	118.78	+ 8.27	371.3	+10.3	102.8	–2.9	1,418.8	+134.9	123.80	+11.8

TABLE 11

Data	Population	Private wealth				Public debt				Remaining private wealth			
		per inhabitant	differ.	% figures	% differ.	per inhabitant	differ.	% figures	% differ.	per inhabitant	differ.	% figures	% differ.
1	2	3	4	5	6	7	8	9	10	11	12	13	14
1878	28.2	1,585.1	—	100.00	—	357.0							
1883	29.0	1,689.6	+104.5	106.59	+ 6.59	389.5							
1889	31.0	1,764.5	+ 74.9	111.32	+ 4.73								

private wealth. In fact, private wealth increased from 100 to 117 to 123 according to Table 9 and net wealth from 100 to 121 to 128; or else, according to Table 10, while wealth has increased from 100 to 111 to 119, net wealth has increased from 100 to 112 to 124.

Except that, and here the fact repeats itself, the last five-year period has been less propitious for Italy than the preceding one. This can be seen from the columns regarding the absolute and percentage differences of private and net wealth. In fact, giving here only the percentage figures of Tables 9 and 10, we see that private wealth grew from the first to the second five-year period by +17, while, on the contrary, from the second to third only by +6, and we see that net wealth grew first by +21, then by only +6.

This is according to Table 9: according to Table 10, the figures are different, but the fact is the same. Private wealth increased in the first five-year period by +10, and in the second by only +8; net wealth increased first by +12 and then only by +11. And the worst is that there is reason to fear that, in the new five-year period already under way, this state of affairs will not improve unless there is a rapid change of mind.

The national private wealth we have estimated for the three successive five-year periods in 42, 48 and 54 or 55 billion lire probably comprises 60.5% real property and 39.5% other assets. Nonetheless, these figures are quite uncertain, as we know only for the last four years the division between real property and other assets in successions and moreover, the deviations from the average of the ratio of the other assets to real property is quite substantial[17]. Moreover, we understand as real property and other assets those which are such under the provisions of the law. But, operating with these figures as the only ones we know, we should say that the division between real property and personal property is, for the three five-year periods, as shown in Tables 12 and 13:

---

[17] In fact, for 1885-1886, the deviation is +2.77; for 1886-1887 –8.27; and for 1887-1888 +5.49.

TABLE 12

Years	Property	Other assets	Total
1873-1877	25.5	16.7	42.2 billion
1878-1882	28.9	18.9	47.8 »
1883-1888	33.0	21.6	54.6 »

TABLE 13

Years	Property	Other assets	Total
1874-1878	27.0	17.7	44.7 billion
1879-1883	29.6	19.0	49.6 »
1884-1889	33.1	21.6	54.7 »

Now, the figures for 1878-1882 are quite different from those we calculated, on another occasion, with wholly different method and bases. Then, as now, total wealth was estimated at 48 billion lire; but, then, we estimated land assets alone at 60.57% of the total, namely at 29 billion lire, and buildings at 18.77%, namely at 9 billion lire, and the rest at 20.87%, namely 10 billion lire. In other terms, real property therefore amounts to 79.3% of total wealth and not 60.5%.

How can this difference be explained? There are two explanations which support one another, in other words they both serve to explain a part of the difference. Firstly, it should be borne in mind that the value of rural real property is the most difficult to estimate for the revenue administration and that which can most easily give rise to a controversy with the taxpayer, a controversy which usually ends to the detriment of the revenue administration. Everyone knows that the value of a plot of land can be estimated only approximately and uncertainly, by means of the most complicated and difficult of calculations, and that there are as many experts as there are opinions. On the contrary, every year a house has a rental value, regarding which anybody who lives in the same area can have a almost exact concept. Similarly, shares, bonds and stock-market securities in general have a specific quotation, every day. Hence, we believe we can state firstly that the revenue administration is defrauded even more on rural property in the estimate than on personal property by subtractions and untruthful returns. Secondly, our faith in the De Foville method to estimate total private wealth is matched by our lack of faith in the revenue administration's division of successions into real property and personal property, and not because the administration makes mistakes in making these divisions, but because the term 'other assets' includes conspicuous items of real property. In fact, if the administration finds land-credit securities, land certificates, shares and debentures of railway companies, shares of building companies, shares of factories, etc. in a succession, it will classify these assets as personal property. Now it is evident that if for example all the owners of shares in a railway company were to die, the largest part of this patrimony, registered as a moveable asset, would instead consist of the ownership of stations, roads equipped with track, the so-called structural works, bridges and viaducts, land, manufacturing and repair works, etc. i.e., by property which is as immovable as a plot of rural land. And if we should call a part of this inventory personal property, to distinguish it from rural real property and urban real property, however a part should be deducted and included in these two categories. Similarly, the owners of land certificates have a *jus in re aliena* which is nothing other than co-ownership of real property, if one looks behind the juridical façade and focuses on the economic aspect of the relations. Hence it should be considered that the category of 'other assets' includes a large part of the nation's real property, i.e., of the property which other methods of assessment would register as real property; hence the apparent contradiction of the facts.

In the period 1878-1882 rural real property alone amounted to circa 29 billion lire, i.e., 60.5%, — while according to the division of the state property and business tax administration, total real property amounts to only 60.5%, — can be demonstrated with a most certain estimate made using the real method, neither can one cede on this point for any reason whatsoever. We therefore believe that we should redo the preceding table of the division of total wealth into rural, urban and personal property, as more or less shown in Tables 14 and 15.

TABLE 14

Years	Land		Buildings		Personal property		Total
	%	real figures	%	real figures	%	real figures	
1873-1877	60.5	25.41	18.7	7.85	20.8	8.74	42.0
1878-1882	60.5	29.00	18.7	9.00	20.8	10.00	48.0
1883-1888	60.5	32.97	18.7	9.79	20.8	11.74	54.5

TABLE 15

Years	Land		Buildings		Personal property		Total
	%	real figures	%	real figures	%	real figures	
1874-1878	60.5	27.04	18.7	8.36	20.8	9.30	44.7
1879-1883	60.5	29.65	18.7	9.16	20.8	10.19	49.0
1884-1889	60.5	33.09	18.7	10.23	20.8	11.38	54.7

At first sight, it will perhaps appear arbitrary, and contrary to some obvious claims that we hold the division percentage figures calculated for the second five-year period stable for the first and third such periods, and it will be said, for example, that the value of rural property has fallen considerably or, in any case, it has not increased, at the same rate, as personal property and one will think of the bugbear of American competition and the crisis in which the owners of vineyards and suchlike find themselves. More specifically, since 1884-1885, the state property and business tax administration has adopted the deplorable habit of extolling the increase in personal property values which elude it and to lament the depreciation of real property which it asserts cannot be hidden away. Except that, disregarding the fact that it is of little importance that real property cannot be hidden, while their value can be, and the other fact that shares, securities, debentures are ways of sharing out things, which are as visible as a rural property, this is a calculation which has not been made, whether rural properties or securities have depreciated the more, and it is not known what the result would be if one were to compare the quotations of the principal securities of the previous five-year period to those of the five-year period which ends in 1888, multiplying each category of securities by the number of securities of which it consists. One would then see hundreds and millions or lire disappear, just as in the depreciated rural real property. And if despite the land crisis and the collapse of the personal property values, the total mass is now worth more than before, this is explained easily, considering that in the rural real property, millions on millions of lire have been invested in reclamation and that in personal property, where there was one enterprise, there are now three.

Nonetheless, this is a part of our argument which is conjecture, just as the figures we offer are a mere *faute de mieux* conjecture.

The reader will perhaps be curious to know how Italy's wealth is distributed among the various regions which comprise Italy. It is common knowledge, vaguely, that Lombardy is more affluent than Sardinia, and Piedmont than Naples. But, who could say, at first sight, which is more affluent: Tuscany or Veneto? Marche or Umbria? Or Sicily? Piedmont or Liguria, or Lombardy? The argument is quite subtle and we will deal with it, shortly, in another paper. A few data will suffice here, presented without justification, albeit thoroughly considered.

Let us proportion the wealth of each region to the population each had in 1880 and assume that total private wealth in Italy in 1880-1884 amounted to 100. We would then have Table 16 in round figures:

TABLE 16

Region	Wealth per inhabitant as % of total	Region	Wealth per inhabitant as % of total
Piedmont and Liguria	16	Veneto	9
Lombardy	14	Naples	7½
Lazio	13	Marches and Umbria	7
Tuscany	12	Sicily	6½
Emilia	10	Sardinia	5

Hence: we can say that if a minister of finances viewed the Italians as a herd of cows to be milked, a Piedmontese is worth two Neapolitans or three Sardinians; a Lombard is worth two inhabitants of the Marche; two Tuscans are worth three Neapolitans; two Lombards are worth three Venetians, and so forth.

However, this picture relates other stories, which are far from funny.

Before concluding this paper, let us make another cursory comparison between the total wealth of France, estimated using the same method, and that of Italy. Elsewhere, we estimated the private wealth in Italy at 48 billion lire for the five-year period 1877-1881, De Foville estimated that of France in 215 or 220 billion, and many believed our estimate excessively small. We have to re-affirm the accuracy of that estimate for that period because the figures from which it is deduced allow no further increase. De Foville, then, having repeated his calculations, for 1887, believes that wealth in France should amount to a maximum of 200 billion, to which correspond, for Italy, the new figure of 54 or 55 billion lire.

This inferiority of Italy will make some sense to many. Indeed, it appears certain. Let us reason a little.

In 1888, France had a population of, probably, 38.2 million, calculating on the base of an annual increase of 2%; that of Italy was 30.5 million, as we have seen. Hence, the population of Italy was 79.84% that of France, while wealth in Italy was only 27% of that in France: or else, succinctly, the population of Italy is almost 4/5ths that of France, while wealth in Italy is just over 1/4 of that in France.

Now, do all know the ratio, for example, of Italy's special foreign trade with that of France? France's foreign trade was in 1885 more than seven billion, while Italy's trade did not reach two and a half billion. The ratio between France's and Italy's trade was therefore 100 to 33.4; in 1886, France's trade exceeded seven and a half billion while that of Italy remained less than two and a half billion: hence the ratio between the two of 100 to 32.87[18].

---

[18] The figures for France are now taken from De Foville's *France économique* for 1887 and those for Italy from the *Annuario di statistica per il 1887-88*. Hence the figures are not always the most recent available; but the most recent give the same results and I therefore preferred to recall those to be found in sources which everyone can consult.

In short, while the population of Italy is almost 4/5 that of France, Italy's international trade does not even reach, or only just does so, a third that of France. Now, why does this fact not engender as much surprise as the other, that total wealth in Italy is between a quarter and a third that of France? Does it not perhaps confirm the proportion between the two countries' foreign trade, that which we maintain is the ratio between the capital of the two countries?

But let us see what some other semiological data say of this ratio. In 1883, railways in France carried 207.2 million passengers; those in Italy, for the same period, 36.8 million. Hence, the ratio of the movement of passengers in Italy to that in France is 17.76 to 100, in other words the movement of passengers in Italy is not even 1/5 that of France. But, if this is a certain fact, what is there improbable in the probable fact that wealth in Italy is between 1/4 and 1/3 that in France? Passing from rail passengers to freight, it is easy to persuade oneself that the tonnes transported at low speeds in Italy in 1883 represented only 13.35% those transported in France, i.e., 11.9 million in Italy against 89.1 million in France. In 1885, the length of Italy's rail network was circa 31.8% that of France, i.e., more than a quarter, but less than a third of it, precisely as we maintain is the case for national wealth. Yet another data item: the amount of tobacco consumed in France in 1885 was 36.2 million kilograms; in Italy in 1886-1887 16.77 million kilograms of tobacco were consumed, i.e., circa 46.4% of the amount consumed in France a year earlier. It is clear that the consumption of tobacco depends on the spread of the taste for it and the prices. But the prices in question are higher in France than in Italy, and considerably so, precisely because of the large amount of pipe tobacco[19]. Hence the fact that the consumption in Italy is not proportionate to that in France according to the population of the two countries should be explained either by the difference in the diffusion of taste, or by a lesser quantity of the means of pleasure among the inhabitants of Italy.

---

[19] The selling price of ordinary tobaccos in France is 12.50 lire per kilogram. Here in Italy, second-grade pipe tobacco costs 7.60 lire per kilogram and first-grade pipe tobacco 11.40 lire per kilogram.

Let us now conclude this argument with a final item of data. It is known that in Italy post-office savings banks were established six years before they were established in France; it is also known that in Italy, in absolute figures, the number of depositors is circa double that in France; it is also known, that the organisation of our ordinary savings banks is deemed much superior to that of their counterparts in France, and that the savings that accumulate there do not meet with the Caudine Forks of the French law; it is also known that the inclination of the lower sections of the population to invest their savings in public interest-bearing securities or industrial equities is more common in France than in Italy; finally, it can in no way be claimed that the population of France is more moderate and thrifty than that of Italy. And yet, despite all these factors which are advantageous for our savings banks and post-office savings banks, savings in France, held at savings banks and post-office savings banks, amounted in 1886 to at least 2 and a half billion while, at the same date, savings in Italy amounted to only 1 and a quarter billion, i.e., 50% that in France. Now, as a ratio of the population, it should have been 80% of that in France, i.e., 2 billion. But the fact of the matter is that we are considerably poorer than our blood-brothers and there is no reason for mistrusting the measure of this lesser economic potential furnished by the calculations of total private wealth as we have illustrated.

TABLE 17

TABLE OF INHERITANCE

	1879	1880	1881	1882	1883	1884-1885	1885-1886	1886-1887	1887-1888	1888-1889
Inheritances still to be ascertained at the end of previous year	153,927	128,458	129,152	105,402	123,360	97,624	92,603	79,166	85,330	
New inheritances recorded during year	773,935	860,805	788,830	790,204	774,925	756,545	802,085	848,663	849,014	783,875
Total	927,862	989,263	917,982	895,606	898,285	854,169	894,688	927,829	934,344	
Inheritances annulled as heirs untraceable or decreased was property	674,362	717,597	682,640	642,015	649,808	626,692	681,211	695,470	688,664	
Balance	253,500	271,666	235,342	253,591	248,477	227,477	213,477	232,359	245,680	

Table 18

AMOUNTS SUBJECT TO INHERITANCE TAX FROM 1872 TO 1889

Category	Tax rate (%)	*1872*	*1873*	*1874*	*1875*
A	1.44	441,674,000	417,410,400	502,511,300	588,450,500
B	3.60	53,993,900	57,856,600	60,498,300	70,638,700
C	6.00	72,133,900	70,356,200	74,484,600	90,615,400
D	7.20	55,861,100	53,122,300	59,478,200	73,020,200
E	9.60	6,170,000	3,366,200	3,563,900	4,823,800
F	10.80	4,266,700	3,662,000	5,373,400	4,898,100
G	12.00	21,714,200	23,174,600	24,611,400	25,591,600
H	2.40	10,493,040	10,063,172	11,688,337	11,894,041
	total	666,306,840	639,011,472	742,209,437	869,932,341
		1876	*1877*	*1878*	*1879*
A	1.44	560,812,200	563,348,000	555,429,400	519,186,000
B	3.60	75,307,900	70,961,000	71,962,600	69,116,600
C	6.00	75,638,500	83,413,200	89,902,900	86,454,900
D	7.20	64,063,600	78,273,300	87,119,100	75,042,700
E	9.60	4,557,900	3,888,700	4,366,400	3,308,300
F	10.80	3,675,000	12,597,300	7,745,500	3,381,700
G	12.00	25,038,800	24,512,100	31,572,700	25,452,500
H	2.40	10,647,958	12,672,000	14,985,500	14,389,100
	total	819,741,858	849,665,600	863,084,100	796,331,800
		1880	*1881*	*1882*	*1883*
A	1.44	602,388,500	590,013,700	608,231,800	650,797,100
B	3.60	75,613,400	73,374,400	77,016,800	82,582,000
C	6.00	97,306,200	95,225,000	91,700,000	100,824,400
D	7.20	92,572,300	87,098,900	85,700,000	90,660,800
E	9.60	5,647,200	2,376,000	6,942,900	3,032,600
F	10.80	10,824,800	5,303,700	6,725,600	8,100,400
G	12.00	40,369,700	26,729,700	29,345,500	29,341,300
H	2.40	16,175,200	17,273,500	12,870,400	14,627,400
	total	1,940,897,300	897,394,900	918,533,000	979,966,000

Table 18 *continued*

AMOUNTS SUBJECT TO INHERITANCE TAX FROM 1872 TO 1889

Category	Tax rate (%)	*1884-1885*	*1885-1886*	*1886-1887*	*1887-1888*	*1888-1889*
A	1.44	638,249,200	602,504,100	704,824,200	675,851,300	617,807,600
B	3.60	87,030,600	80,668,400	94,664,800	95,452,600	97,247,800
C		96,164,600				
	6.00	15,039,100	118,098,200	108,859,700	116,860,400	118,095,300
D	7.20	91,706,600	83,672,100	100,593,000	105,382,300	95,665,400
E	9.60	8,304,400	8,782,300	5,353,100	6,473,300	4,137,700
F	10.80	5,067,900	16,743,600	6,027,800	12,288,700	10,924,800
G		35,146,000	33,598,800	32,546,900	47,115,700	33,689,100
	12.00	1,247,600	2,579,600	1,869,300	2,031,100	1,448,800
H	2.40	13,633,700	20,257,100	15,288,400	15,303,500	14,933,300
	total	991,589,700	966,904,200	1,070,027,200	1,076,758,900	993,949,800

Table 19

Years	Inheritances		Donations *inter vivos*	Total inheritances and donations	Total increased by a quarter
	amount subject to tax	with doubling of cat. *H*	amount subject to tax		
	column 1	column 2	column 3	column 4	column 5
1888-1889	993,949,800	1,088,883,100	178,601,600	1,187,484,700	1,484,355,875
1887-1888	1,076,758,900	1,092,062,400	173,963,000	1,266,025,400	1,582,531,750
1886-1887	1,070,027,200	1,085,315,600	177,850,800	1,263,166,400	1,578,958,000
1885-1886	966,904,200	987,161,300	185,658,400	1,172,819,700	1,466,024,625
1884-1885	991,589,700	1,005,223,400	182,309,600	1,187,352,000	1,484,415,750
1883	979,966,000	994,593,400	177,337,400	1,171,930,800	1,464,913,500
1882	918,533,000	931,403,400	181,491,800	1,112,895,200	1,391,119,000
1881	897,394,900	914,668,400	180,961,900	1,095,630,300	1,369,530,375
1880	1,940,897,300	957,072,500	150,860,278	1,107,932,778	1,384,915,972
1879	796,331,800	810,720,900	149,634,525	960,355,425	1,200,444,281
1878	863,084,100	878,069,600	155,815,670	1,033,885,270	1,292,356,587
1877	849,665,600	862,337,600	205,043,220	1,067,380,820	1,334,226,025
1876	819,741,858	830,389,816	133,941,877*	964,331,693	1,205,414,616
1875	869,932,341	881,826,382	142,238,595*	1,024,064,977	1,280,081,221
1874	742,209,437	753,897,774	121,603,711*	875,501,485	1,094,376,856
1873	639,011,472	649,074,644	104,695,740*	753,770,384	942,212,980
1872	666,306,840	676,799,880	109,167,821*	785,967,701	982,459,626

* Calculated at 16.13% of inheritances.

TABLE 20

AMOUNTS TAXED FOR FREE TRANSFERS BETWEEN LIVING PERSONS

Category	Tax rate (%)	1872	1873	1874	1875
A	1.44				
B	3.60				
C	6.00	calculated	calculated	calculated	calculated
D	7.20	at 16.13%	at 16.13%	at 16.13%	at 16.13%
E	9.60	of	of	of	of
F	10.80	inheritances	inheritances	inheritances	inheritances
G	12.00				
H	varies				
	total	109,167,821	104,695,740	121,603,711	142,238,595
		1876	1877	1878	1879
A	1.44		174,418,700	144,074,600	139,354,400
B	3.60		1,251,500	1,289,700	1,172,000
C	6.00	calculated	1,973,400	1,719,000	1,839,000
D	7.20	at 16.13%	2,200,200	2,438,800	2,083,000
E, F	10.20	of inheritances	10,016,220	280,000	220,255
G	12.00		10,016,100	875,100	1,050,900
H	varies		5,167,100	5,138,470	3,914,970
	total	133,941,877	205,043,220	155,815,670	149,634,525
		1880	1881	1882	1883
A	1.44	138,408,500	166,457,100	166,464,100	162,945,800
B	3.60	1,129,200	1,540,600	1,666,700	1,601,500
C	6.00	2,342,200	2,845,300	2,002,600	3,181,800
D	7.20	2,925,200	2,463,800	2,749,400	2,477,100
E, F	10.20	256,378	251,200	172,000	231,600
G	12.00	1,183,900	1,599,000	1,024,500	1,014,400
H	varies	4,614,900	5,804,900	7,412,600	5,885,200
	total	150,860,278	180,961,900	181,491,800	177,337,400

TABLE 20 *continued*

AMOUNT TAXED FOR FREE TRANSFERS BETWEEN LIVING PERSONS

Category	Tax rate (%)	*1884-1885*	*1885-1886*	*1886-1887*	*1887-1888*	*1888-1889*
A	1.44	168,039,500	166,486,700	157,634,800	154,993,600	161,287,300
B	3.60	1,884,800	1,917,800	2,695,200	2,371,400	2,128,100
C	6.00	2,299,300	4,840,500	3,607,800	3,075,900	1,738,900
D	7.20	2,507,700	2,500,700	2,154,400	2,242,900	3,128,000
E } *F*	10.20	207,300	387,500	110,300[1]	108,300[1]	46,100[1]
				97,300[2]	172,500[2]	203,800[2]
G	12.00	1,091,000	1,340,400	1,474,500	1,408,300	1,058,200
H	varies	6,280,000	8,184,800	10,076,500	9,590,100	9,011,200
	total	182,309,600	185,658,400	177,850,800	173,963,000	178,601,600

[1] For these three years 1886-1887, 1887-1888, 1888-1889 they are calculated at the tax rate of 9.60%.

[2] *Idem* at 10.80%.

TABLE 21

	Total inheritances and donations increased by a quarter	Total inheritances and donations multiplied by 36, i.e. the average span of a generation	National capital for average five-years periods	*Idem* for other five-years periods	*Idem* for other five-years periods
	column 1	column 2	column 3	column 4	column 5
1888-1889	1,484,355,875	53,436,811,500			
1887-1888	1,582,531,750	56,971,143,000			
1886-1887	1,578,958,000	56,842,488,000			54,693,259,200
1885-1886	1,466,024,625	52,776,886,500		54,553,274,100	
1884-1885	1,484,415,750	53,438,967,000	53,175,102,300		
1883	1,464,913,500	52,736,886,000			
1882	1,391,119,000	50,080,284,000			
1881	1,369,530,375	49,303,093,500			49,038,646,522
1880	1,384,915,972	49,856,974,992		47,796,236,748	
1879	1,200,444,281	43,215,994,116	47,386,607,328		
1878	1,292,356,587	46,524,837,132			
1877	1,334,226,025	48,032,136,900			
1876	1,205,414,616	43,394,926,176			44,686,478,196
1875	1,280,081,221	46,082,923,956		42,165,444,226	
1874	1,094,376,856	39,397,566,816	39,632,726,153		
1873	942,212,980	33,319,667,280			
1872	982,459,626	35,368,546,536			

Source, Relazione sull'ammin. del demanio e delle tasse sugli affari:
— 1887-1888, Appendix 9, pp. 201-9.
— 1886-1887, Appendix 9, pp. 227, 228 and 235.
— 1885-1886, Appendix 9, pp. 280, 281 and 287.
— 1884-1885, Appendix 10, pp. 371-2 and 379.
— 1883, Appendix 9, pp. 256-7 and 245
— 1883, Appendix 13, pp. 286-187.
— 1882, Appendix 7, pp. 163-4 and 153.
— 1881, Appendix 3, pp. 586 and 577.
— 1880, Appendix 3, pp. 146 and 130.
— 1879, Appendix 3, pp. 848 and 841.
— 1879, Appendix 3, pp. 124 and 117.

The Labour Market*

Giovanni Montemartini

1. - Methodological Notes[1]

We too are confident we can represent in numbers and tables the concrete phenomena encountered in the labour market. This is the ideal of all the economic observatories which go under the name of Labour Offices. Alongside the stock-market lists, the market lists of products which record values and prices, we are talking of erecting the statistics of the price of the labour good, the universal good par excellence. Systematic surveys of data on labour are last in statistical theory and practice; but as soon as they cross the threshold of political and administrative life, they acquire an impressive and imposing importance.

2. - The Labour Market

How we should understand the so-called labour market is still controversial. Even Dr. Jastrow, perhaps the most competent theoretician and competent organiser of labour statistics, is uncertain as to the limits which bound the special market we are studying[2].

---

* From: MONTEMARTINI G., «Il mercato del lavoro», *Giornale degli Economisti*, April 1904, pp. 326-35. [Cod. JEL: N 33].

[1] From a study forthcoming in *Bollettino del lavoro*.

[2] See JASTROW J., *Sozialpolitik und Verwaltunswissenschaft*, Band I. *Arbeitsmarkt und Arbeitsnachweis. Gewerbegericte und Einigungsämter,* Berlin, 1902, p. 62 ff.

Nonetheless, if we proceed with the same scientific criteria adopted to date for other goods, the outline and contents of our study are clearly evident. On the one hand we are talking of fixing the value of a good, determining its variations as a function of the supply and demand of the good itself, which in this case is labour. We are also talking of ascertaining the market conditions within which the value being sought is determined; these conditions could be the working hours, the protective laws, the organisation of the contracting forces. Finally, we are talking of ascertaining the final effects to which the relations between labour supply and demand give rise and to which the very valuation of the labour itself gives rise; the most important effects are expelled by the level of employment or unemployment experienced by the working class and by the entity and speed of the migratory phenomena of workers who are expelled or re-absorbed by the oscillations in demand in the various parts of the labour market.

The labour market is then numerically determined by surveying the following principal elements: wages, labour supply and demand – specifically the number of employed and unemployed – working hours, organisation of the contracting forces, migration.

All these elements are interdependent with each other, as variations in one are a function of the variations of all the others. These interdependencies are revealed as soon as one progresses from a survey regarding a specific moment in time – as is the case with all surveys – to a continuous, successive survey, which attempts to trace the evolution of the economic phenomena in the labour market over time. The continuous survey is the task of the *Bollettino del Lavoro (Labour Bulletin)*. We are talking not of historical statistics as Dr. Jastrow would have it[3], but of current statistics, which have the dual purpose of illuminating the most recent conditions of the market studied and to also assist the attainment of new equilibria every time the market conditions themselves shift or modify themselves vis-à-vis each other. Knowledge of the variations in a wide area and in increasingly distant areas helps reduce the risks of imbalance, di-

[3] See JASTROW, *op. cit.*, p. 64.

minishes the frictions of the economies which are thrown onto the market thus achieving the levelling of the values which is the final result of the knowledge of the market and of the freedom of movement.

3. - Methodological Procedures

Now that we have delimited the field of our statistical survey, we believe it appropriate to trace some methodological procedures to indicate the sources to which we resorted, the criteria followed in the choice and distribution of the data, the systems adopted in the representation of the phenomena. We will examine separately the various elements which contribute to determine the labour market.

3.1 *The Supply and Demand of Labour*

The most studied phenomena which expresses the index and most painful exponent, in its economic effects, of the relations between the supply and demand of labour is that of unemployment. If one thinks of the serious repercussions, not only economic, but also moral and political, which a mass of economies wholly without income entails, because they cannot sell the sole good they can supply, the labour good, - one can also understand why the phenomenon of unemployment has been so studied by all the social laboratories which deal with questions of labour and workers.

Abstracting for the moment from the technique to be followed in statistical surveys regarding the phenomenon in question, and dealing here only with the systems used to determine the number of unemployed, there are two methods available - which we can call the German method and the English method after the Labour Offices which generally employ them. The German method studies the labour supply and seeks to calculate the number of unemployed from the state of this supply; the English method on the other hand uses the labour demand to calculate unemployment. However, both methods should theoretically yield the same results; only the survey bodies used are different.

The German method was first used by Dr. Jastrow in his monthly journal *Arbeitsmarkt*; it was embraced by the Austrian Labour Office, as can be seen from its bulletin *Soziale Rundschau*, and also adopted by the Labour Bulletin of the German Empire, *Reichs-Arbeitsblatt*. The method consists in registering the number of unemployed who present themselves at the labour exchanges for each market and industry. Alongside the number of jobs requested by workers, the number of jobs offered by industrialists is also recorded, the difference between these two figures indicates the level of unemployment. The labour supply is thus followed from close up and is used to obtain the data required.

It is undeniable that the validity of this method depends on the labour mediation system being almost perfect. The German labour exchanges, which have long since transformed themselves from offices of class into mixed offices and even into offices administered by public bodies with their admirable internal organisation and federal organisation, are the bodies most suited to such a system of survey. Nonetheless, the system is not without its shortcomings. As the picture is not complete for all industries, one can never, particularly in the unskilled trades, ascertain from where the labour supply comes. Neither, moreover, can one classify as real unemployment that represented by those requesting work at the counters of the labour exchange, as the request could be made when the worker already has a job, but hopes in and seeks a better job.

The English method is based on study of the demand; one determines the contractions, expansions and trends of the various industries. Knowing the various workshops of a region, one asks the entrepreneurs every month how many workers they employ. Comparing the various periods to a base period gives the number of unemployed at each contraction of the industry.

This method, which ascertains unemployment indirectly, by establishing the data regarding employment, is feasible only when the industrialists are intelligent and willing or better with strong associations of industrialists, as is the case in England. For the rest, the method is surprisingly simple and has proved itself valid in practice. It was also adopted by France, as can be seen in the *Bulletin de l'Office du Travail*, and by Belgium in the *Bulletin*.

One can ask which of the two methods described above should be used in Italy. The terrain here is still virgin, no survey has yet been made to establish the oscillations in labour supply and demand and the consequent phenomenon of unemployment. In view of this virginity of the terrain, given the absence of any source of information, the question of preference for one or the other of the systems would appear feasible, this question has been rendered superfluous in the other countries because it was resolved in advance by the existence and development of bodies which served to provide the necessary information.

Nonetheless, in Italy too the question is resolved by the de facto conditions found in the country; and the resolution is eclectic. We seek to determine the phenomenon following the two systems described and simultaneously to develop the bodies which give rise to one or the other system. This is because we wish to exploit the local elements offered by the few labour exchanges which operate in Italy, and because we believe we can discipline the employees' and workers' organisations which are starting to assert themselves also in Italy, particularly in northern Italy.

The labour exchanges in Italy are either in the hands of private intermediaries or are class offices, whether this class is that of the employees or that of the workers. The superior type of mixed exchanges has not yet taken form. There is a strong dislike of offices exercised by public bodies and perhaps our political conditions justify the opinion that the functioning of labour exchanges should be left to those concerned without the intervention of the political body. As regards the few existing and operating offices, offices of labour chambers, or those of workers' or industrialists' federations, we have asked and will ask a technical framework and working which allows us the most complete and reliable statistics. Thus, for example, we will ask our correspondent offices for records which will not only give us the number of unemployed, but the number of days of unemployment of those who present themselves at the counters, dividing then this number into days of unemployment preceding the employment application and days of unemployment following said application[4].

The adoption of the English method to study labour demand can be successfully applied with success in some of our industries, in which the organisation of the entrepreneurs is quite developed. Naturally, it can never embrace from an association of industrialists, an entire branch of an industry for all the various regions of Italy. Nonetheless, the oscillations of demand calculated on a group of industrialists that encompasses and controls thousands and thousands of workers can yield a sure index of the trends experienced by an industry. Thus, for example, the data that came from the Association of Cotton Manufacturers which consists of 107 members and which currently controls 59,630 workers; from the Association of the Silk Industry and Trade with 548 members encompassing 1,005 plants and 127,864 workers; from the Consortium of Engineering, Steel and Shipbuilders and similar in Liguria consisting of 11 members with 20 plants and 13,474 workers, from the Federation of Monza Industrialists consisting of 63 members with 57 plants and 9,330 workers. The data of these strong nuclei of industrialists, to cite those which first spring to mind, are admirably suited for fixing, at regional and at times national level, the oscillations of labour demand in the various industries and consequently the level of unemployment of the working class.

3.2 *Labour Statistics in the Agricultural Industry*

Statistical surveys of the agricultural industry have distinctive features. The phenomenon of unemployment, for example, cannot be understood in agriculture as one understands it for the manufacturing industry. In the latter, generally, the work is continuous, and the ending of the work means unemployment. In agriculture on the other hand, there are long periods of rest; the number of days of employment in any month differs from that in previous or subsequent months. To establish whether we are faced with a

[4] See MONTEMARTINI G., *L'industria delle calzature in Milano*, 1904, pp. 20-4.

period of unemployment, the given period should be compared to previous, similar periods; hence it is necessary to have statistically recorded, as regards labour demand, a base period which serves as a comparison for subsequent surveys.

Moreover, theoretically, the phenomenon of unemployment does not differ whether one examines it in the agricultural industry or in another industry. For us, unemployment is but a variation from previous conditions of income, of productive and consumption activities[5]. The unemployed worker experiences a consequential loss as a result of the reduction in the demand for labour, which entails a slackening in consumption. All these acts of the entire cycle are interdependent on one another, and entail far-reaching repercussions on the entire economic system. But if unemployment is conceived thus, there is no difference in the phenomenon whether it manifests itself in agriculture or in the other industries; in the first hypothesis the periods of comparison for determining the afore-mentioned variations in income, productive activity and consumption are long, in the hypothesis of manufacturing industry these periods are of short duration.

There are two types of labour demand surveys in the agricultural industry: qualitative or quantitative. The qualitative survey regards the type of workers requested in a given region and at a given time, which is the same as reporting the specific agricultural works of a given period and time. The quantitative survey on the other hand seeks to fix the number of days of work actually requested in a given period and place. Both surveys are receptive to considerable development and to a broad range of applications.

Up to now, we have accepted the qualitative survey arrangement. Resorting to technical bodies, such as itinerant agricultural chairs and agrarian schools, will make it be easy to gather in a short time rich material from which we can deduce which are the workers requested by the agricultural industry or rather, which are the agricultural operations normally carried out by our agriculture. In a year's time we can have before us, month by month,

[5] See «La disoccupazione nel basso emiliano - Inchiesta dell'Ufficio del lavoro della Società umanitaria», Milan, 1904, *Preface* and p. 12 ff.

the picture of the agricultural operations of the various regions of Italy, and the economic conditions under which these operations are carried out. These conditions are the average working hours and wages for each operation and for each region. These latter data, and the number of working days which for atmospheric reasons can be performed, month by month, in the various regions, already draw our qualitative statistics close to the quantitative statistics of which we shall now speak.

We are preparing the sources for the quantitative survey of labour demand. This survey can be divided into two levels, each with various difficulties. In all agricultural concerns, in fact, we have a labour demand which we can call fixed, and which resolves itself in the use of the so-called 'bonded' workers (obbligati). The survey of the amount of the use of this labour, continually bound to the agricultural concerns, presents no particular difficulties, when however one can draw on local bodies for the gathering of data, or when one can count on the support of organisations of land-managers or workers as is the case of northern and central Italy. But in addition to this fixed force, the concerns demand from time to time, for each work and each season, temporary workers, free and independent farmhands who sell their services by the day or by work. Surveying the demand for this workforce, which is very variable and fluctuating, is very difficult. Nonetheless, in view of the size of day labour demand's importance with regard to the phenomenon of unemployment, no statistics of agricultural labour would be complete without also fixing the oscillations of this specific demand.

3.3 *Domestic Migrations*

Labour supply cannot be exhaustively studied without taking account of the migrations which take place within the labour market in question at every season, shifting the workforce, attracted by higher wages from one to the other of the centres by higher wages. This attraction of labour towards a given place can be constant, or occasional and seasonal. In the former case we have the attraction the big urban centres exercise on the neighbouring minor centres, and which goes under the name of urbanism. Here, in Italy, there are only a few of such centres; and it was easy to start a systematic survey which cast the correct light on the entity of the various urban attractions. The case of seasonal migration encompasses all these movements of workers who are related to agricultural works. The framework of an appropriate survey system has cost us and continues to cost us considerable effort, but we have already succeeded in attaining a good level. Month by month we seek to record the number of temporary emigrants, who leave one centre for another, taking account of the occupations for which the emigration takes place. This first record is controlled by the contemporaneous survey of the number of immigrants in the places where the migratory movement heads. After a year, we will have a complete picture of the main migratory flows of Italy, a picture which will be revised every year to determine which are the usual movements and which are the quantitative oscillations in the movements themselves. And as the scope of our records is not merely theoretical, but aims at immediate utility, thus the surveys are not made for the past months, by way of final balances, but are given by way of estimate, also for the months or month to follow, indicating the numerical data which are deemed the most reliable on the basis of experience. This survey is of the maximum importance, because knowledge of the conditions of habitual or approximately foreseeable supply and demand of labour, in upcoming periods, helps avoid an oversupply of labour in specific places and helps to level the price of the labour. Only with this knowledge can one economically regulate the migratory movements.

3.4 *Wages, Working Hours*

The most important item of data regarding the labour market is unarguably that of wages, which represent the value of the labour good, the ultimate expression of the relations between demand and supply. And when recording the wage, it is contemporaneously necessary to record the working hours as this latter item represents the labour as a function of time, and the time of labour is an indispensable element for establishing the entity of the economic results of a given use of a productive force.

But when we wish to draw up wage statistics, the creation of the sources which should provide the data in question is of great difficulty.

Here, in Italy, there are not only no wage statistics — and hence the very technique of this part of statistics has not received broad development — but attempts to achieve this are also rare and deficient. This shortcoming has been felt for some time now, and back in 1855 Bodio, that great organiser of Italian statistics, sought to furnish norms and rules for the ordering of wage statistics. After Bodio's excellent report on the issue and after the ensuing discussion at the Higher Statistics Council[6], there have been no further theoretical attempts to study and investigate the problem in more detail. Practical attempts have been seen, it is true, but they were few and far between and could be counted on the fingers of one hand. In 1885, there was a contribution for wage statistics, including some data on the wages of workers employed in some of the principal industries of Lombardy in 1847, 1859, 1866, 1874, data due to Professor Pietro Rota, and other data furnished directly by some owners or heads of industrial plants[7]. But the data provided by Rota wholly neglects the technical part of the survey; thus, for example, it speaks of summer and winter wages for hired farmhands, without thinking that in agriculture the price of labour for specific work, particularly for harvests, undergoes strong variations; which is moreover proven by some records of the author himself, which specify the various seasonal works. Thus also for the industrial workers a maximum and a minimum wage is almost always recorded, without reference to the various categories of skills which are found in a single industry and the number of the workers surveyed. As regards the data provided by the plants, we are talking of a few plants which can

---

[6] See *Atti del Consiglio superiore di statistica*; sessione dell'anno 1882. - «Relazione e discussione del programma di una statistica dei salari» (*Annali di Statistica*, series 3, Vol. VII, pp. 50-83).

[7] See «Contribuzione per una statistica delle mercedi», *Annali di statistica*, series 3, Vol. XIV.

in no way provide us with a certain index of the general conditions of the market: it suffices to bear in mind that for hundreds of cotton-mills, the data of only two plants are recorded, for the large number of silk plants, the data for only four plants; and thus the data for a hemp mill, of four wool mills, and of four paper mills. These are all surveys whose value is merely monographic.

The wage statistics paper which was published in 1888 and concerns 44 engineering and iron and steel plants, adopts, from the technical point of view, an incisive and correct analytical procedure[8]. As these are surveys in a single industry, one can say that this time the attempt to provide a certain index for the industry studied has been successful. Nonetheless, here again the system of survey is akin to that of the monographic method, such that each plant represents a small monograph.

Official statistics, until quite recently, have not shed the initial method, and limit themselves to surveying a few isolated plants, as can be seen in the series of our *Annuari* from 1886 to 1900. It is therefore no surprise that in foreign publications referring to international wage statistics, information regarding wages in Italy is brief and cursory. In the *First Annual Abstract of Foreign Labour Statistics* published by the English Department of Labour, the data for wages in Italy are recorded on one page which contains a table of wages in mines excerpted from our *Annuario statistico*, and a table on wages in the silk manufactures of northern Italy excerpted from a report by Mr. F. Armstrong, the English consul in Milan, published by the Silk Association of Great Britain and Ireland[9].

In the broad study of wages in all commercial countries which surveyed 714 official sources started by the Washington Labour Office in 1894 and completed in 1900, Italy is mentioned only for the works cited included in the *Annali di statistica* and for its *Annuari statistici*, thus offering insignificant data[10].

---

[8] See «Saggio di statistica delle mercedi», *Annali di statistica*, serie IV, vol. 26.

[9] See *First Annual Abstract of Foreign Labour Statistics* (1898-1899), London, 1899, p. 53.

[10] See *A Compilation of Wages in Commercial Countries from Official Sources*, vol. II, «*Fifteenth Annual Report of the Commission of Labour, 1900*», Washington 1900; Chapter 1, *Introduction*.

The shortcoming of our wage statistics consisted in continuing to rely on the monographic method, on isolated and atomistic surveys of specific plants, without attempting to progress to broader and more comprehensive sources. From the smaller units of plants it is worthwhile passing to increasingly larger statistical units including the largest possible number of plants. The survey is made by taking as a source a group of units, starting from the fact of an organisation of similar forces.

This is the method which has been followed for considerable time, because the conditions of the environment allowed such, by the more advanced countries. The English Department of Labour compiles statistics on wages and hours of work receiving the information from entrepreneurs' associations, from trades unions and thus overcomes the many difficulties of survey, because it has been noted that where organisations of the contracting bodies exist, there are also important agreements on the tariffs established by the representatives of said parties[11]. The same method is broadly followed in France and in the labour offices of the United States. Neither should one believe that the system of resorting to single plants and establishing the statistical bases of wages on the averages of thousands and thousands of single observations has been abandoned; to do this a general, methodical and scrupulous correspondence is necessary between the office gathering the data and the mass of industrialists who have to supply the data. Nonetheless, the system serves more for historical surveys than for continuous surveys, entailing otherwise a work of sorting and processing which is too long to be done in a short period of time. Thus, for example, the statistics on wages gathered in the United States for the 12th census (1900) are based on the transcription of the paysheets of plants representing the main industries for the corresponding months of the year from 1890 to 1900[12]. Thus also the survey by the Department of Labour of the United States on American and European wages from 1870 to 1898 was carried

[11] See *Report on Changes in rates of Wages and Hours of Labour in the United Kingdom in 1902*, pp. ix-x; *idem* in 1900, p. xiii.

[12] See *Employees and Wages*, Washington, United States Census Office 1903, (*Twelfth Census*, 1900). See *Labour Gazzette*, March 1904, p. 678.

out on data supplied by the companies which in the United States, Great Britain, France and Belgium continued to exist in the ten-year period surveyed[13].

3.5 *The Organisation*

We have drawn on our relations with the organisations of industrialists and workers to start out along this path of the collective survey of data. The statistical data is less precise, but better reflects the movement of the economic aggregate and furnishes a broader index of the real conditions of the environment. The greater reliability of approximation of this index in reflecting the environment, derives from the extension of the organisation, i.e., from the breadth of the source which offers us the information. This is why the data on the organisation is not only important, but necessary for determining the weight of the single surveys. If the wage of a given market is provided to me by a category of organised workers, it is indispensable to know the numbers of these organised workers to assess the importance of the data. These organisations, it should be noted, represent as many units as enter in various plants, and contribute to determine a broader field of observation and survey.

When the data derive from two sources assumed to have opposing interests, the survey is also controlled automatically. This gives rise to that statistical confrontation which is most useful for an efficient determination of the truth.

The fact of the organisation is moreover of such importance in itself as to induce us to an accurate recording of the phenomenon. The organisation is the most fecund force for reducing the frictions between the antagonistic interests and for taking the competition to superior and more comprehensive units, thus eliminating the waste of the small forces and small energies. It is there-

---

[13] See «Wages in the United State and Europe, 1870 to 1898», *Bulletin of the Department of Labour,* no. 18, September 1898.

For all the other publications made by the various Labour Exchanges, on wages, consult the most recent and valuable monograph of the German Office: *Die Fortschritte der Amtlichen Arbeitsstastistik in den Wichtigsten Staaten. Beträge zur Arbeitsstatistik*, no. 1, Berlin, 1904. Erster Teil, pp. 35, 68, 107, 138, 164, 198.

fore of interest to establish the size and development of the organising force in every moment of the country's economic life.

3.6 *The Difficulties of Collective Surveys*

The data we are gathering are never an absolute representation of reality – which cannot and never can be achieved – but are approximate indexes which express the reality itself. Hence we should adopt the maximum caution to ensure the best of approximations.

For wages and hours of labour it is necessary first of all that the survey be made industry by industry and by categories of trades in each single industry. Mass and generic surveys have no technical nor practical value. Moreover, the numerical data expressing the phenomena studied should represent that normal value around which all the similar values of a specific market oscillate. This normal value cannot be the arithmetical average of the various terms recorded.

In determining a market's normal hours of labour and wage, we have followed the method adopted by the Belgium Office of Labour in the general census of industries and trades of 1896. Given a statistical series expressing the various wages for the various groups of workers, one calculated 75% of the workers surveyed by the entire series, then if the highest partial number of the series was less than the 75% one added the closest higher number and so forth for the other numbers until one achieved the three quarters of the workers observed. Then one concluded that the most frequent wage was that included within the limits marked by the various groups summed to obtain the 75% of the total, and then determined the dispersion of the other wages around the limits thus determined.

We deemed this the best method to adopt in surveying wages and hours of labour; and we always asked the organisations corresponding with the Office for the most frequent wages and hours of labour, those which correspond to the mass of workers which was the equivalent of a typical average worker who supplies work in a given market.

3.7 *Labour Conflicts*

To complete the picture representing the life of labour and of the workers, we had to survey the struggles between capital and labour, which manifested themselves in the form of strikes, disputes and lock-outs.

Strikes can be political and economic. The political strike is related to the worker's entire political behaviour. The economic strike should be conceived as a special undertaking exercised in specific moments by groups of workers, who undertake the industry of strike with the specific use of capital, incurring specific risks and costs with an eye on future improvements. Hence, all the elements which participate in the strike should be illuminated; and the data can only be given by those concerned. Hence the framework for statistics on strikes becomes very complex, particularly as we are talking of present information of the movements and not the usual historical data. The office hopes, judging from the results already achieved, to be able to obtain from the parties directly concerned information referring to the struggles between capital and labour. Only thus can one represent the conflict with specific data and not with the usual generic and inadequate data.

In expounding the results, the *Bollettino* will seek to give as much material as possible, disregarding the classifications and elaborations which may be made a posteriori for long periods, both by the Office and scholars or those concerned.

On the Reform of Civil and Army Pensions*

Luigi Amoroso

1. - Introduction

Legislation regarding the arrangements for civil and army pensions in Italy is extremely varied and complicated. As is known, it dates back to 1864 for civil pensions, and to 1850 for army pensions and comprises a very large number of special laws, which it would be a waste of time to enumerate here. What it is basically important to note — and moreover is well known — is that the system currently in force is not a scientific system, there being no relation between the size of the pension and the amount of contributions paid, the size of the pension being related not to the contributions paid, but rather to the wage of the last five years of working life and the number of years of service.

The danger of a system which obeyed not so much reason as, we can say, chance, was intuited by the first statesmen who formed the government of the new Kingdom of Italy and the studies to achieve a rational reform, which ensured the state treasury was secure from the blindness of destiny, started in earnest in the very first years of the establishment of the Kingdom. In 1886 the question was, scientifically, already mature: and the famous Commission of Fifteen already indicated in that year the reforms which

---

* From: AMOROSO L., «Sopra la riforma delle pensioni civili e militari», *Giornale degli Economisti e di Rivista Statistica*, Roma, Athenaeum, 1913, pp. 361-85. [Cod. JEL: N 43].

in more or less similar form — were then invoked by all (officials, parliamentarians, scholars, ministers) when they had to, spontaneously or not, deal with the question.

However, if in the subsequent 47 years — the number of years which have passed since 1866 to the present — the question has still not found a concrete solution, such that matters are at precisely the same point, this was by no means due to lack of study. There were in fact in this period of time, to cite only the principle of these studies carried out:

1) in 1880-1882-1886, the three bills by Magliani, of which only the first became law. The bill set up a national insurance fund (Cassa di previdenza) destined to effect a financial operation regarding the pensions paid to that date. The fund was abolished in 1889;

2) Grimaldi's bill of 1892 (which was passed by the Lower House but withdrawn by the Senate) set up - for new employees - a national insurance fund; the bill was conceived with breadth of vision and a refined scientific criterion;

3) in 1893 the studies of the Finali Commission, whose members included illustrious figures such as the mathematicians Francesco Brioschi and Luigi Cremona. The contribution of this commission's studies was truly important, particularly from a statistical point of view. Even today, its report is the most complete and precious collection of statistical elements regarding the demographic conditions of state employees and pensioners;

4) the Rubin Commission of 1898, whose studies led, moreover, to no new essential contribution;

5) the Pavia Commission appointed in this year 1913, which proposes to repeat the demographic survey on state employees and officials, previously carried out in 1892 by the Finali Commission. This commission's studies are still in progress.

Will success be achieved this time? We have seen four commissions over the course of 47 years, and the results of their studies — whatever their scientific worth — were in practice zero. There must therefore be something stronger than the will of man (it is the financial question, as we shall see), which opposes the proposals becoming reality: the experience of the past therefore induces us to conclude that no results will be seen this time either. But, this time all know that the question is related to a broad plan of organic reforms of national savings, whose cornerstones are the establishment of the Istituto Nazionale delle Assicurazioni (National Insurance Company) and the development of the Cassa Nazionale di Previdenza (National Insurance Fund). In an article published recently (on October 14, 1913 to be precise) in *Corriere della Sera*, Einaudi drew attention to these facts. Hence, this attempt may even be crowned with success. It is therefore worthwhile enlightening public opinion and seeing in what this vexed question consists in substance: what essential reasons have prevented the reaching of a final solution in these fifty years: whether the present conditions allow such a solution to be reached. This is what we propose to do in this paper in the briefest and clearest of manners possible.

The problem involves and embraces various questions which we should distinguish and enunciate clearly from the outset.

Question l: in the hypothesis that no essential reform in the pension system takes place, to determine what will be the development of the state's annual annuity debt in the near future, for example in the next twenty five years.

Question II: in the opposite hypothesis that the pension system changes in the direction of reducing the future annuity debt, to determine the future annual burden required to form the necessary reserves. Moreover, to determine what deficit has accrued because such reserves were not accumulated in the past. On the basis of these two elements, to study how this should be implemented.

Question III: leaving aside the financial (II) and administrative (IV) questions, and considering the relations between the state and its employees, to study what should be the guidelines for the state's action in respect of these relations.

Question IV: discussing to which body the management of pensions should be entrusted.

The first question is an actuarial question, the second is simultaneously an actuarial and public-finance question, the third is a political question and the fourth is an administrative question.

2. - The First Question. The Development of the Annuity Debt in the Next Twenty Five Years

Let us suppose that no essential modification is made to the present legislation on pensions in Italy: what will then be within the near future, twenty or twenty five years for example, the development of the annual annuity debt? This annuity debt — i.e., the sum of all the civil and army pensions, ordinary and extraordinary, paid annually by the state — has risen in the last financial year to the figure of circa 105 million lire. Will this figure increase in the coming 25 years? and by how much? Will it reach 150, 200, or instead not exceed 130 million lire? This is the first (financial) question to be resolved.

Below is an overview of the development of this debt in the past twenty five years:

Disregarding the extraordinary pensions, whose development depends on political causes (in the fiftieth anniversary year they more than doubled), and confining ourselves to considering the ordinary pensions, Table 1 shows that the period considered can be divided into three periods of more or less equal length. A first period from 1888-1889 to 1895-1896 in which the annual annuity debt increased from circa 65 to circa 77 million lire; the total of new pensions paid in each fiscal year exceeded the total of pensions which ceased to be paid in the same year, the difference was highest in the first year, namely around 1888 and gradually decreased until it became minimal around 1895. A slight oscillation was recorded in the fiscal year 1895-1896, due to the large number of new invalidity pensions paid out following the African war.

The second period runs from the fiscal year 1896-1897 to 1903-1904; in this period the annual annuity debt remained more or less stationary, growing in seven years by barely one million lire, namely, increasing from 78 to 79 million lire. In each fiscal year, the amount of new pensions more or less equalled the amount of pensions which ceased to be paid.

Finally, there is a third period which runs from 1904-1905 to 1911-1912, in which the annuity debt shows a significant increase,

TABLE 1

PENSION TOTALS

Fiscal year	Ordinary pensions (thousand of lire)			Extraordinary pensions (thousand of lire)
	New during year	Eliminated during year	Balance at year-end	
1887-1888			64,129	
1888-1889	4,770	3,937	64,962	2,512
1889-1890	5,949	4,198	66,713	2,382
1890-1891	5,464	4,284	67,893	2,261
1891-1892	6,688	4,752	69,829	2,283
1892-1893	7,874	4,618	73,084	2,261
1893-1894	7,049	5,326	74,807	2,171
1894-1895	5,186	4,560	75,433	2,095
1895-1896	5,742	4,586	76,589	2,051
1896-1897	5,648	4,491	77,746	2,421
1897-1898	4,624	4,487	77,883	2,531
1898-1899	5,162	4,554	78,491	3,329
1899-1900	5,041	5,217	78,315	3,411
1900-1901	4,679	4,871	78,123	3,416
1901-1902	5,238	4,628	78,733	3,159
1902-1903	5,399	5,259	78,873	2,871
1903-1904	5,400	4,573	78,670	2,600
1904-1905	5,580	5,391	79,889	3,318
1905-1906	5,950	5,187	80,652	3,534
1906-1907	6,396	5,550	81,498	4,256
1907-1908	7,055	5,036	83,517	4,869
1908-1909	6,674	5,695	84,496	5,289
1909-1910	7,547	5,325	86,718	5,424
1910-1911	8,021	5,819	88,920	5,274
1911-1912	8,435	5,273	92,082	10,692

rising from 80 million to circa 92 million lire; the amount of new pensions increased considerably and jointly, becoming greater than that of pensions which ceased to be paid in each financial year; while the latter oscillated between five and six million, the former (the new pensions) increased from five to eight million.

To explain the significance of this fact, we should bear in mind the general development of the function, representing the amount of annuity debt, formed by pensions to a continuously renewable group. As is well known, this function starts from the value zero and gradually increases until it reaches a limit. This limit is constant in time, and around it the annual values of the function oscillate if the number of individuals comprising the group is constant in time. If on the other hand this number varies in time, i.e., it increases, but its increase in every moment is small vis-à-vis the total number of individuals comprising the group, even the limit value does not remain constant in time but rises slightly. In both cases, when this value limit has been reached, it is said that the annuity debt has reached normal regime. In the concrete case we are examining, the regime was reached in the period which roughly runs from 1896 to 1904. However, that the function subsequently recommenced increasing significantly indicates the existence of an occasional disruptive cause on the normal trend of the phenomenon. This disruptive cause exists in reality and is well known to us; it consists in the improvements to the wages of state employees, improvements which have come into force precisely in the last ten years. As the pension of state employees is fixed according to the wage of the last five years, an increase in their wages immediately leads to an increase in pensions.

The problem we posed therefore involves the following: When will the disruption produced by this occasional cause be eliminated? In other words, when will we reach a new period of regime? As can be immediately seen, this problem is wholly determined if we confine ourselves, as we indeed intend, to consider what will happen in the next twenty five years. A state law in fact lays down that ordinary pensions can be paid only to those who have a minimum of twenty five years of service: the ordinary pensions which will be paid in the next twenty five years will therefore be paid either to the present pensioners or to the present employees, any future change in staffing levels will have no influence on the development of pensions in the next twenty five years. The elements which determine the configuration of the regime are therefore demographic and financial regarding groups which exist today: present pensioners and employees. Hence the problem is determined.

Let us now see to resolve it, we can therefore calculate the real capital value of all the pensions which will be paid in the next twenty five years[1]. We therefore have to distinguish between the pensions which are in force today, and which will therefore be paid in the coming twenty five years to the present pensioners, and those which will mature in the twenty five years and hence be paid to the present employees.

We would point out — once and for all — that all the calculations in this paper have been made using an interest rate of 3.50%[2].

A) Present pensioners. According to Appendix D to Magliani's bill of 1880[3], the elimination of one lire of current pension within twenty five years takes place as indicated in the following table:

initial value			1.0000
value after	5	years	0.7326
" "	10	"	0.5152
" "	15	"	0.3461
" "	20	"	0.2212
" "	25	"	0.1343
average value over	25	years	0.4916

This means that 100 lire of current pension in a given instant becomes 73.26 lire after 5 years; 51.52 lire after 10 years, etc. Their average value over the twenty five years is 49.17 lire. One hundred million lire of pensions now being paid — and this is more or less the amount paid for ordinary pensions in the financial year

[1] We would point out — once and for all — that this calculation, as indeed all subsequent calculations, are perfunctory and schematic. The nature of this journal does not allow detailed calculations, which, moreover, would be useless for our purpose.

[2] This hypothesis — that the interest rate is 3.50% — has no influence as regards the solution of our present problem, i.e., on the determination of the future development of the annuity debt. In fact, first we capitalise the present debt, then we transform this capital value into an annuity.

[3] As we are dealing with pensioners, the present elimination can differ little from that adopted in Magliani's report. This does not mean that it would not be desirable to apply figures founded on more recent observations. The Finali Commission's *Report* (1893) contains the statistical elements necessary to construct similar tables founded on observations for the decade 1882-1892. Making the calculations, which are easy, but long and laborious, is not the work of a private individual: why has the Technical Department of the General Direction of the Treasury not done so in 20 years?

1912-1913 — are therefore equivalent, in capital and over 25 years, to a constant annuity of 49.16 million lire. But the initial capital value 0.1343 of an annuity of a lira for twenty five years at the rate of interest of 3.50% is 16.4815: the capital value that we are looking for will therefore be:

$$16.4815 \cdot 49.16 = \text{circa } 810 \text{ million}$$

As the ordinary pensions currently recorded amount to circa 100 million, we can conclude that the real capital value of all the ordinary pensions which are currently recorded and will be paid within the forthcoming twenty five years is, in round figures, at the rate of interest of 3.50%, circa 800 million lire.

B) Present employees. There are currently circa 155,000 state employees; of these a part will retire and will enjoy the pension during a more or less long period of the forthcoming twenty five years. We have to determine the present capital value of all these pensions.

In the absence of more recent figures, we have to avail ourselves of data obtained from statistical elements published in the Finali Commission's *Report*. Schedule 1 which is part of Appendix 2 on page 166 of this report (regarding the distribution of employees by age), and the elimination table drawn up by Toja[4] on the preceding data (regarding the probability of retirement) produce Table 2 which gives us an idea of the demographic structure of a typical group of 10,000 employees.

TABLE 2

Age limit	Number of persons	Average age (years)	Probability retirement within 25 years	Age of retirement versus probability in foregoing column
Less than 43	5092	34	0.2357	52
More than 43	4908	53	0.6533	63

[4] See the technical-financial study of the pension regulations currently in force for Bologna town council employees in COMUNE DI BOLOGNA, *Studi sulle pensioni e loro ordinamento*, Bologna, Regia Tipografia, 1901, p. 102.

Let us call I the first group, i.e., the group of individuals aged less than 43, Il the second group, and carry out the pension cost calculations separately for the two groups.

TABLE 3

		I	II
Initial year		1913	1913
Probable number of pensioners		5.092 · 0.2357 = 1.200	4.908 · 0.6533 = 3.206
Years of pension in twenty five year period		7 years from 1931 to 1938	15 years from 1923 to 1938
Capital value of 100 lire of recorded pensions, according to Magliani's table	at year of commencement[5]	Capital value in 1931 of 7 deferred annuities of 80.67 lire each = 548.3 lire	Capital value in 1923 of 15 deferred annuities of 69.04 lire each = 795.3 lire
	at the initial year 1913	295.2 lire	563.8 lire
Cost in capital at initial year 1913 of pensions, assuming an average pension of 100 lire		295.2 · 1,200 = 35,400 lire	563.11 · 3,206 = 180,000 lire

Overall, therefore, an average pension of 100 lire for a group of 10,000 current employees in the forthcoming twenty five years has a current capital value of 35,000 lire plus 180,000 lire, in round figures, more than 250,000 lire. Valuing the average pension which will be paid in the forthcoming twenty five years at 2,000 lire[6], as

[5] See Schedele E to the cited bill of 1880.

initial value	1.000	initial value	1.000
value after 2 years	0.9391	value after 5 years	0.8237
value after 4 years	0.8617	value after 10 years	0.6415
value after 6 years	0.7862	value after 15 years	0.4774

[6] The average value of a pension recorded was circa 1,100 lire around 1900. Subsequently it increased rapidly, mainly as a result of employees' improved conditions. In the last financial year it ranged from 1,500-1,600 lire. The figure of 2,000 lire we have applied in our calculations takes account of the fact that the effects of the afore-mentioned improvements are still incomplete: it is therefore founded principally on the hypothesis that there is no new improvement as regards wages, and hence of employees' pensions.

155,000 is the number of current employees, the cost of pensions for the real group we are considering will be:

$$250{,}000 \cdot 15.5 \cdot 20 = \text{circa } 800 \text{ million lire}$$

All the ordinary pensions which will be paid in the next twenty five years to the current employees amount therefore today to a capital value of circa 800 million lire.

Overall, therefore, the pensions of the present pensioners today represent a capital value of circa 800 million: adding, we obtain in round figures 1,600 million lire as the present capital value of all the ordinary pensions which will be paid in the next twenty five years.

Suppose we wish to settle this debt by a constant annuity for the entire twenty-five year period. As a lire of capital corresponds to an advance annuity of 0.0607 lire (amortised in twenty five years, interest at 3.50%), the constant annuity which pays off the total preceding annuity debt, can be assessed at circa:

$$0.0607 \cdot 1600 = \text{circa } 100 \text{ million}$$

Again allowing an error of 10%, this means that if we assume to wish to satisfy the total annuity debt (for ordinary pensions alone) that will develop in the coming twenty five years, with a constant annuity, said annuity will be valued at circa 110 million lire.

This shows — as today the annuity debt of ordinary pensions totals almost circa 100 million lire — that we are quite close to the normal period of regime. It is therefore logical to admit that the limit around which the function will oscillate in the coming twenty five years will be at the most around 110 million lire. Moreover, estimating at the most 15 million lire for extraordinary pensions, we obtain the figure of 125 million lire as a maximum for the development of the total annuity debt in the coming twenty five years.

It should therefore be noted:

1) the preceding figures hold in the essential hypothesis that the wages of employees and hence pensions see no new improve-

ment. Moreover, no essential modification should take place in the pension arrangements, they should always be paid in accordance with the present formula according to the years of service and wages of the last five years of work;

2) that the figures themselves represent — in the afore-indicated hypothesis — an approximate value by excess. Moreover, this approximation has always a relative value, as the general development of the annuity debt depends on technical conditions, but also on political and financial conditions, as the government in part decides the number of retirements in each financial year.

Nonetheless, what is clearly evident from all the above is this: concern that the annuity debt — assuming no essential variation in the present pension arrangements — can reach 140 or 150 million lire or even higher in a near future is therefore wholly unfounded.

3. - The Second Question. Burden of Future Reserves

All our foregoing considerations refer to the hypothesis that no essential modifications were made to the present pension arrangements. Let us now pose the opposite hypothesis, i.e., that one wishes to bring order to the pension system and no longer settle them year by year with the funds of the Treasury Ministry, but rather with reserves accumulated during the employees' years of service. Let us first of all seek to give ourselves an idea of the size of these reserves, i.e., calculate roughly what sums would have to be set aside each year. Hence we shall: 1) disregard in this moment any deficit accumulated in the previous years (this question will be dealt with in the next section); 2) maintain for the future pensions (by means of allocation of reserves) more or less the same figures which would be paid out under the present arrangements should these not be modified.

The ordering of pensions is already an accomplished fact for many groups of employees in Italy. Without taking account of the minor such groups, the most important are: the railwaymen, primary-school teachers, town-council secretaries and notary-archive clerks. For all these groups the actuarial reserves needed to form the pensions are calculated in percentages of the their wages, which vary from 11% to 20% circa of said. More specifically[7] for railwaymen they are 19.25%; primary-school teachers 11.1%; town-council secretaries and notary-archive clerks 12%.

These percentages were calculated on the basis of the following elements: size of the pension; elimination curve of beneficiaries in service; size of the burden formed by reversion to the surviving spouse; extraordinary revenues provided to the pension fund by sundry bodies.

Of the groups considered, the railwaymen are those which eliminate themselves significantly quite early: moreover, the size of the pension — relative to wages — is higher for them than for the other groups, which explains why they have the highest percentage. On the opposite hand, primary-school teachers, which is a group composed of many women, has a minimum burden of reversion to the surviving spouse.

For mid-ranking state employees, the Finali Commission[8] in 1893 calculated a percentage of 13%. Nevertheless, given the improvement in wages which has taken place since 1893, — the pension now being paid on the wage of the íast five years, the average pension has increased more than the average wage has increased proportionally — this figure appears excessively low. It would not be suffice to conserve, after the reform, approximately the same pensions which would be paid if the reform had not been implemented. It should be raised to between 14 and 15% of wages.

A summary calculation will suffice to confirm this forecast. Paying one lire per year, from 27 years (the average age of hiring) to 60 years (the average retirement age) gives an income of 7,830 lire (compare the tariffs of Cassa nazionale di Previdenza, Assi-

---

[7] The increase in railway reserves from 18 to 19.25% of wages is the work of the Sacchi law of 1911. For information regarding the primary-school teachers, town-council secretaries, etc., refer to the monograph presented on the fiftieth anniversary at the Turin fair by the General Direction of the National Insurance Institutions of the Treasury Ministry.

[8] See the *Relazione* often cited above, p. 44 ff.

curazioni popolari, calculated at the rate of 3.50%, transferred capital paying-in).

To form 2,000 lire of pension, the annual paying-in therefore has to total:

$$\frac{2{,}000}{7{,}830} = 255.4 \text{ lire}$$

Estimating, as is known, the reversion to widows and orphans at 30% of the pension, we should add to the preceding figure a further 30%, i.e., another 76.6 lire.: in all, we therefore have the round figure of 330 lire.

It follows that the sums which should be set aside at 1 July 1912, as there were 155,000 employees at this date, should have been circa:

$$330 \cdot 155{,}000 = 51.15 \text{ million lire}$$

On the other hand, the wages at the same period amounted to 361.7 million lire, hence the wages necessary to establish the reserves can therefore be valued at:

$$\frac{5{,}115}{3{,}617} = 0.1415$$

i.e., equal to 14.15%.

It is worthwhile carrying out the following calculation again. Let us suppose that one wishes to award the employee the right to not lose the capital accumulated on his behalf (with his payments and the state's contributions) in the event of voluntary abandonment of service or death prior to retirement, and we calculate what the approximate cost of this right would be.

An immediate income of 100 lire per year at the age of 60 costs 1,079.91 lire in capital (according to the afore-cited tables of the Assicurazioni Nazionali at the Cassa di Previdenza). We refer this amount to the time when the employee commenced service, i.e., in the hypothesis already made, that he commenced service at the age of 27, we refer it to 33 years earlier. As the present value of a lire in 33 years, at the rate of 3.50%, is 0.3213, the present value of 1,079.91 lire will be:

$$0.3213 \cdot 1079.91 = 346.9$$

We form this sum with 33 advance annuities: as a lire of capital is equal to 33 advance annuities of 0.5156 each, we will form 347 lire with 33 advance annuities each of one lire:

$$0.5156 \cdot 346.9 = 17.90$$

Estimating, as earlier the average pension at 2,000 lire, and at 30% the reversion to widows and orphans, we obtain:

$$17.90 \cdot 20 \left(1 + \frac{3}{10}\right) = 465 \text{ lire}$$

per employee, in other words circa:

$$\frac{465 - 330}{330} = \frac{135}{330} = 0.41$$

of the original figure of 330 lire.

Hence: all other conditions being equal, the right to not lose the capital paid on one's behalf, either by reason of death or voluntary abandonment of state service, costs 135 lire per average employee, at also circa 40% of the amount of the present pensions.

3.1 *The Second Question Continued. The Present Deficit*

The figures considered above provide for the establishment of reserves for the future. However, we still have to make good the deficit which has come into being because such payments were not made in past years. Let us now calculate the approximate present capital value of this deficit.

Hence we have to calculate separately the sums which refer to present pensioners and those which refer to present employees.

In one of the previous tables we indicated how one eliminates a lire of current pension in a given instant in a period of 25 years: a similar calculation has now to be carried out, abandoning the limitation of 25 years. It therefore suffices to apply Magliani's table in full, rather than stop at the twenty-fifth year of age. The present capital value of all the pensions which are currently being paid thus amounts to circa 850 million lire (we previously found 800 million for the part which will cease being paid in the coming twenty five years).

Let us turn to the present employees. The group they comprise can be substituted by an abstract group, formed by the same number of persons, who are all now aged 43 (the average age of employees), who one assumes all commenced service at the age of 27 (average age of hiring), i.e., 16 years earlier.

As these are reserves which should have been accumulated in past years, we have to refer them to a number of average employees in the period of time considered, in round figures we therefore have to assess 330 lire per employee for 16 years and an average number of 125,000 employees. Sixteen annuities of one lire, at the interest rate of 3.50%, form an advance capital of 20.96 lire. The present value of the reserves which should have been paid for the present employees can therefore be estimated at:

$$330 \cdot 125{,}000 \cdot 20.96 = \text{circa 850 million lire}$$

Above, we calculated in 800 million lire the present overall capital value of the pensions which will be paid to the present employees, in the next twenty five years only. It is worthwhile pointing out that the meaning of this figure is essentially different from the present figure (850 million) which represents a part of the capital value of all the pensions which will be paid to the present employees without limitation of time.

If we add the two figures regarding the deficit for pensions for present pensioners (850 million) and present employees (also 850 million) we obtain a round figure of 1,700 million.

The deficit which has accrued because we did not accumulate in the past the reserve corresponding to the services rendered in the past by present employees to pensioners amounts in round figures to 1,700 million lire.

Let us suppose we wish to pay off this debt, paying it as late as possible, i.e., transforming it into a constant and perpetual annuity. At the interest rate of 3.50%, this transformation leads to a perpetual annuity of circa 60 million lire per year. The deficit accrued for not having accumulated in the past the reserves corresponding to the services rendered in the past by present pensioners and present employees amounts to a constant perpetual annuity of 60 million lire.

3.2 *The Second Question Again. Bring Order to the Annuity Debt*

To summarise, to order the annuity debt, the state should simultaneously:

1) pay off the debt accrued to date. According to our calculation, it can be estimated at equal to a perpetual annuity of 60 million lire:

2) allocate reserves to prevent this debt forming again in the future. According to our calculation, this burden today amounts to 51 million lire, of which circa 8 million are deducted, as employees' contributions (on average little more than 2% of wages), the state remains with a burden of 43 million lire. This amount will increase in the future years, proportionally to the increase in wages.

Overall, the state would settle the annuity debt, for ordinary pensions alone, by paying a sum which today would amount to 103 million, and which would increase in subsequent years. Already today it would be more and would remain in the near future higher than the amount which the state would have to pay if things were to remain as they are at present: today in fact the annuity debt (for ordinary pensions only) totals less than 100 million lire. In the near future — as we have seen — it will consolidate around this figure or at the worst around the figure of 105 or 110 million lire[9].

Moreover, this is easily understandable: under the present system, the state pays the pensions as late as possible; if settling means paying off the past and at the same time making arrangements for the future by means of the setting aside of reserves it is quite evident that if one wishes to set aside, one has to spend more today. This is the essential reason which for fifty years now has prevented any concrete settling. Indeed, if the difference is not so great today, this is because the state simultaneously carries out two opposing operations: in other words at the same time as it sets aside the reserves to meet the debt which will form in the future, it transforms the debt contracted in the past into a perpetual annuity, in other words it places as a burden on the future all the outlays which have been contracted to date regarding the past.

We thus reach the crux of the question. What is therefore the purpose of carrying out these two opposing operations? Would it not be simpler to pay out those sums which one wishes to set aside today for the future to pay the debts of the past?

This is basically what is being done today, reserves for the future are not set aside and the debts of the past are paid by charging the present pensions to the Treasury. But that which today is being done blindly could be done tomorrow rationally. In other words, while there is no relation between pension and pension contributions today, such relations could exist tomorrow: and the two items — paying off past debt and reserves for the future — which are in accounting terms two distinct items — could instead constitute a single item.

Past experience indicates this is the path to follow. The actual establishment of actuarial reserves is the pivot on which the life of free insurance, which is by its nature limited and discontinuous in time, hinges. But when we are speaking of compulsory insurance, however, i.e., when we are talking of groups of insured

[9] It is understood that the amount which would be paid in the next twenty five years would be saved in the future. The present debt is that which it is; neither can its present capital value vary because of the fact that it, the debt, will be paid today or tomorrow.

persons which renew themselves continuously in time, such that a certain number of pensions which cease to be paid is matched every year with continuity by a certain number of new pensions to be paid, experience shows: 1) that the reserves can de facto be limited to the measure in which the difference between the liabilities (pensions) and the assets (contributions) is the maximum possible; 2) that on the other hand the integral actuarial reserves would total enormous amounts which would be quite difficult to raise, if a certain deficit was allowed to accumulate during a certain period of years. This is the experience of Germany, where compulsory insurance of workers has been carried out with these criteria since the time of Bismark; and also — not to mention others — of railwaymen's pensions in Italy.

We will now dwell on the question of railwaymen's pensions in Italy. During the entire period of private operation, the public was accustomed to hear talk of the question of the railwaymen's welfare institutions as an important question, involving a large debt for which the managing companies and the government shuffled responsibility. When the railways were nationalised, this question disappeared as though by magic, indeed, the state was able to introduce in railwaymen's pensions those improvements which the railwaymen had asked the state for in vain for twenty years; all this, it should be noted, without asking the Treasury for a lira.

What is the explanation of this which might appear a miracle but which is not one at all? The companies act in accordance with industrial criteria: concerned that one day they would have to settle the dues, they could not allow the formation of a deficit, for which a still uncertain legislation might one day make them responsible. The pensions were therefore formed by the accumulation of integral reserves: and as de facto — disregarding whether the government or the rail companies are to blame — deficits had been formed, the company continually did all it could to eliminate or at least stem the deficit. Consequences: 1) impossibility for the companies to increase the pensions, which were gradually paid (as they were paid on the basis of the size of the reserves accumulated — de facto — for each person); 2) continuous increase — by virtue of the compound interest accrued — of the initial deficit.

In short, all the state did was to substitute the system of integral reserves with that of partial reserves, i.e., of reserves which could annually pay off the balance of the pensions. This was made possible because the railway management is a continuous management, which one does not envisage — at least today — ending one day. In other words the money of the young was used to pay the pensions of the old. The accumulated capital, which was insufficient to constitute the integral reserves of the present railwaymen in service, was instead more than sufficient to bridge the difference between income and outlays to the regime period, and moreover, to give the railwaymen those pension improvements they had previously asked for in vain.

It is worthwhile recalling that this righting was made — modestly — without setting up an autonomous pension institution, indeed by reducing the staff which previously existed for the pension fund; and the illustrious man who was the promoter of all the state's policies regarding the railwaymens' pensions of the last decade, whom the state has to thank for resolving the question, and 150,000 railwaymen should for having seen the acceptance of one of the most oldest desires, was satisfied with having rendered a service to his country.

4. - The Third Question. Pension Policies

Lack of space permits us only a cursory overview of the principal points of the economic relations between the state and its employees as regards pensions. These relations regard the following points:

1) Forecast of future outlays regarding any improvements in employee's conditions. The conditions of human society are today dynamic conditions in the sense that they vary continuously in time. On the other hand, the bureaucracy — and everyday experience proves this — is acquiring an increasingly intrusive and prevalent part in all the affairs of state, and the state in turn — again as a

result of the trend of modern life — invades an increasingly larger part of the nation's economic life. Hence the forecast that in a more or less long period of time the conditions of state employees will see further improvements is by no means unreal. Now, it is in the supreme interest of the state treasury to consider, should these improvements be granted, their repercussions on the increase in pensions: and make provisions from the very outset for the means with which to pay the future outlays. If this policy is not followed, the question of the ordering of the pensions will never — de facto — be resolved, but there will be subsequent periods of equilibrium, and then shifts from this equilibrium, and then once again equilibrium, etc. Experience confirms this result: as in the decade which roughly runs from 1895 to 1905, we developed an annuity debt which had reached the state of equilibrium or regime: subsequently, as a result precisely of improvements in wages, the function started to rise again. If a pension reform question exists today, this is precisely because no provision was made in time for the outlays which it was easy to envisage would accrue in a near future. Let us vow that a similar error will not repeat itself in the future.

2) Change in the employee's contribution to the formation of the pension. Today this contribution is slightly higher than 2% of wages, but it is known that there is a current of opinion in government circles favourable to increase it, at least for future employees, who as yet have no entitlements in such respect. There is talk of a quota — on the part of the employees — which should be a third of the total quota, to thus rise to circa 5% of wages. We do not believe that such a current of opinion can produce good fruits: the present trend — as we noted above — leads to an improvement rather than a worsening of state employees' economic conditions. If also the government's concept was to prevail, it is easy to foresee that sooner or later some compensation would have to be furnished, and perhaps that which the state would be forced to grant in a near future would be higher than that it was thought to obtain from the increased contribution today. In short, from a general point of view, the conditions of state employees depend on a series of economic and political forces which the state is powerless to vary at its will.

3) Choice between the individual account system and the collective account system. The individual account system consists of balancing for each single item at the moment of the payment of the pension the capital value of all the payments and the capital value of the pension itself at the same moment: with the collective-account system, this balancing takes place only for all the items. Nonetheless, in all the compulsory insurance systems — and the pensions of state employees are all said and done compulsory insurance, formed with the contributions of the state and employees — the individual account does not exist in itself, but rather flanks the individual funds, a common mutual-aid fund for which the capital value of each pension is not exactly equal to the capital value of the payments: hence the difference between the two systems is more quantitative than qualitative. It should also be noted that, contrary to common belief, there is no financial difference between the two systems, integral reserves can exist in the individual account system. The only essential difference which derives from what we observed above, consists instead in the greater or lesser inequality of the various pensions between one another, this inequality being all the less the more the system takes the form of the collective account system.

The collective account system is that which is currently in force for state employees' pensions.

Neither do we believe that innovations would be opportune, as they would lead to a lowering of the minimum pensions. Given the tendency of the present state's policies to always support the small and humble, as the many new Saint Francises of our time like to repeat, a reform in the direction indicated would have as a consequence, sooner or later, direct state intervention in favour of the small and humble; and the effect of this would be to destroy in substance, if not formally, that which had previously been modified.

To create and destroy is not the work of serious men.

We believe it appropriate — given the conditions of present-day life, which unfortunately all too often tend to suffocate rather than develop feelings of individuality — to allow these feelings to develop; but we believe that — in the present case — they can have a more practical and important manifestation in the reform we will propose in the next section.

4) Introduction of the right to not lose the capital accumulated in one's name in the event of death or voluntary leaving of state service. Above, we have made an approximate calculation that the cost of this right can be estimated at circa 40% of the present cost of pensions. If it was to be borne by the employee - with the choice to accept or refuse the new credit, and hence the new right, the overall withholding from wages would amount to circa 8%.

The consequences of the introduction of this new right could be of supreme importance. It would in fact make state employees freer and more independent men: it would place many in the condition to develop activities and energies which are bridled in their current condition. It is free and enterprising men — and not bureaucrats — who form the nation's backbone.

But from another angle too the reform we indicate could bear excellent fruit. It would allow the introduction — which with the present arrangements is in practice absurd — of temporary service in the state administration. This trend of contemporary life we which have mentioned on several occasions on these pages, namely that the state is acquiring an increasingly important role in the nation's economic life, and the bureaucracy an increasingly important role in the government of the state, means that the qualities demanded today from state employees are no longer those which were once demanded: seriousness, order, discipline, etc. The state today needs men with broad views, with initiative, who have a profond knowledge of the conditions of the world market. Such men can be much more easily found for a limited period of time than if they were to be employed for all their life. Ambition, the feeling of public respect, the pleasure of commanding are in reality forces which act as do electrical forces or the forces of gravity. Experience shows that only madmen seek to alter the forces which act in a given social configuration, and that the wise man is he who does not attempt to alter the forces which exist, but knows how to use them all to achieve the end he has put forward.

5. - The Fourth Question. The Administration of the Pensions

The men who are today at the head of the movement which aims to reform pensions tend to separate in this management the present employees on the one hand and the future employees on the other: separation in the sense that the two managements are entrusted to different institutions. Let us categorically state that we believe this tendency is dangerous, as it can produce serious damage.

Indeed, when we dealt with the financial question regarding the ordering of the pensions, we recognised the continuousness of the function which represents the trend of the annuity debt as characteristic of every compulsory insurance. By virtue of this continuity, the financial ordering of the insurance is easier when the insurance is compulsory than when the insurance is free. It then allows the sole solution which makes it possible to tackle the deficit accumulated in the past, without resorting to the state treasury: a solution which consists — in substance — in paying the pensions to the old with the money of the young.

Separating the two managements as indicated above, this continuity would be lost. It is no longer possible to adopt the foregoing system; reserves will have to be set up at least for the period necessary for the group of present pensioners and present employees to be practically eliminated (in practice at least 40 years). The state should simultaneously carry out two opposing operations: in one of the two institutions, that which is to administer the new employees, set aside money, and in the other, that which will pay the pensions to the present pensioners and present employees, borrow money. All this without any purpose, but merely for the pleasure of complicating things considerably from both the financial and administrative points of view. There is no reason of public interest which supports this separation.

Having clearly stated this, and supposing it has been decided to concentrate everything in a single institution, let us now discuss the choice of the insurance institution. Should it be an new autonomous institution or the already existing Istituto delle Assicurazioni or the General Direction of National Insurance at the Cassa Depositi e Prestiti?

Fortunately, nobody talks of a new autonomous institution so that discussion is practically limited to the Istituto delle Assicurazioni and the Direction General of National Insurance. We would therefore note that Instituto delle Assicurazioni superintends voluntary insurance; the Direction of National Insurance on the other hand arranges for the pensions to primary-school teachers and town-council clerks, medical officers, notarial-archive clerks, etc. If it is useful — and who could argue the opposite? — if it is useful we say, that the management, concentrated in the same institution be, as far as is feasible, similar and homogeneous, it is certain that the choice should not fall on Istituto delle Assicurazioni.

This institution on the other hand has already a broad and grandiose task ahead of it — to develop voluntary insurance, which in Italy is very underdeveloped. Entrusting it with servicing state employees' pensions, which is essentially different as regards techniques, administrative structure, etc., would merely distract the institution from its natural function, and hamper its growth, which all — those who did not greet its foundation with joy, as the others — desire prosperous and flourishing for the sake of Italy. Of the many things that were written and said when the institution was established, two were repeated more insistently than the others: and they were two manifestations of scepticism — the first regarding the capacity of the state, as voluntary insurer, — the second concerning the accuracy of the mortality tables on which the advance calculations were carried out regarding the institution's balance sheet. Those who wished the foundation of the institution and are today at its head, have therefore a dual commitment of honour to absolve, to demonstrate that the state is capable of giving voluntary insurance with that increase which, we should honestly acknowledge, the private companies have not managed to give in Italy; and to demonstrate that the tables on which the calculations were based corresponded to reality. These men are undoubtedly suited for their task; but their obstinacy in wishing this new service, if such obstinacy was to be realised, could engender a widespread suspicion — undoubtedly unfounded, but it is good that there are no reasons for it to arise — that there is fear of the future and hence one is today seeking to muddle up everything such that tomorrow it is impossible for anyone to understand anything.

Finally, — and let this be said without wronging anyone — Instituto delle Assicurazioni has to date produced only hope; the news which comes from it and which a press, today perhaps excessively indulgent, hastens to spread, has not regarded to date the essential parts of the institution's management. the figure of one billion lire as the size of the institution's business, appears to the technicians as purely fictitious, as the solidity of insurance institution is measured not by the size of its business, but by the size of its actuarial reserves: the latter are the 'hard cash', the former is merely hope. Moreover, it is easy to increase the amount of business when a law facilitates, if not indeed imposes, the disposals of the portfolios of the past insurance companies: neither do we yet know — we repeat that this is said without any allusions— the cost of said disposals.

To summarise, we have on the one hand an old institution, the Cassa Depositi e Prestiti, whose glorious history can be summarised thus that in fifty years of life in which it become the strongest of the national banks, even stronger than Banca d'ltalia, it never engendered any gossip. On the other we have a new institution, which was established very recently, for whose future we have only hopes. The service in question to be provided is very similar to others which the first institution already provides, and is completely different from those which the second institution carries out. Under this order of things, the choice could not be clearer, and if a powerful government succeeded in imposing the other solution — contrary to logic and common sense — many would start to doubt that the interests of the state do not always guide the actions of the men of government.

6. - Conclusions

We reply to the questions we posed at the start of this paper.

As regards the first question: the annual annuity debt of the state formed by the ordinary pensions, has almost reached the state of regime. If no essential modification is made in the pension system, one can hold that in the coming twenty five years these will not exceed 105 or 110 million lire. Adding the extraordinary pensions gives a maximum of 120 or 125 million lire.

As regards the second question, the ordering of the annuity debt can be achieved either by transforming into a perpetual annuity the debt which has accrued to date and simultaneously setting aside every year reserves for the future, or else more simply by adopting the individual account system, setting aside these reserves in accounting terms only, and drawing on them to pay off the debts of the past. The nature of the management of state employee pensions shows that the second is the natural path to follow.

In respect of the third question:

1) as regards any improvements granted in the future to state employees, account should be taken of any repercussions they will have on pensions;

2) it is not worthwhile increasing the employee's pension contribution, as otherwise the state would have to give provide some compensation sooner or later which could result in a greater burden for the state itself;

3) the collective-account system is the most convenient for the determination of the pensions themselves;

4) should one wish to provide an outlet for individual initiative, one could grant state employees the right to not lose their pension should they voluntarily leave state service. The outlay for this right could be borne by the employee himself.

As regards the fourth question: it is not worthwhile separating the management of pensions (future employees, present employees, present pensioners). All the pension managements should be concentrated in a single institution and the natural seat is the General Direction of the National Insurance Institutions at Cassa Depositi e Prestiti.

II - NORTH AND SOUTH

The Mezzogiorno and the North of Italy*

Ettore Ciccotti

1. - First Part

1.1 As envisaged, Francesco Crispi was re-elected in the city of Palermo on April 17th. His friends had prophesised a landslide; demonstrations of joy were expected at the announcement, There was neither the landslide nor any celebrations. The senators and deputies and lawyers who had acted as trumpeters should have felt quite humiliated by the result; but they do not confess this and they console themselves, — now, when the game is over — by noting that despite the relentless opposition, Crispi obtained after the censure of 1898 the same number of votes as in 1895 when he was Prime Minister. «Hence, — they conclude, — he has not lost his constituents' trust». And who doubted this?

The statement is exact, but should be clarified. Was there a fierce battle in the second constituency of Palermo? Not in the least! There was not even the candidate, as Barbato in his much-publicised letter to *Giornale di Sicilia* had disdainfully renounced the candidature: his words were such that they were skilfully exploited and interpreted as a homage to Crispi! An erroneous and malevolent interpretation, which did not even need the denial sent

* From: Ciccotti E., «Mezzogiomo e settentrione d'Italia», in Colajanni N. (ed.), *Settentrionale e meridionali. Agli italiana del mezzogiorno*, vol. III, Milano-Palermo, Remo Sandron; Roma, Rivista Popolare, 1898, pp. 1-40 and 69-101. [Cod. JEL: N 33].

by Barbato himself to *Avanti* and the full and complete solidarity of the socialists of Palermo. Hence, no fierce battle. Against the ex-dictator there went to the ballot box some republicans and not all the socialists. And yet, despite the uncertainties and contradictions and the abstentions, without a candidate, Crispi's opponents succeeded in scraping together circa 300 protest votes in a constituency which the elected member had represented for many years. The few sincerely progressive monarchists and moderates abstained: if they had voted, there would probably have been a second ballot, in other words the clamorous defeat of he who was to have received an unopposed landslide of admiration!

What is the significance and reasons for the re-election of Francesco Crispi? We shall disregard the swagger and audacious assertions of Commander Marinuzzi. He is a valorous criminal lawyer and his speech to the notables who supported the candidature of the former Prime Minister should be viewed as a defence address worthy of the Court of Assizes. As he presents the accused he defends as honest men to the jury, so he presented the candidate to the electors as an honest man.

The posters and famous telegrams of the senators of the Electoral Committee of Palermo have a quite different importance. Let us examine them.

Scrupulous silence on all this — a truly eloquent silence. The senators speak of the fifty years of services rendered to the homeland, they speak of national unity, of the stature of the candidate; but they do not recommend him at all for his honesty.

Even Crispi's telegram to the Duke of Verdura, the day after the vote, is a masterpiece of grotesque megalomania and confuses his own cause with that of the Unity and Monarchy… and very prudently says nothing about the moral question and the *Report of the Five!*

Given the causes of the resignation, given the precedents and the conditions of the battle, if the senators had believed in Crispi's honesty, they would have had the courage to say so: those who know them know they are plucky. This omission becomes even more significant, later, with the telegram which explains the words «before the contemptible effort of a few irresponsible persons» in which Hon. Engel saw an outrageous insult to the Chamber of

Deputies. And the Parliamentary question of the member for Treviglio was very timely in that it provoked the reply of the senators and of Marinuzzi, which absolutely excludes the moral significance of Crispi's reelection and reduces to miserable dimensions the previous protest against unjust attacks to which the candidate was subject.

This is the fundamental point whose importance has eluded the socialists and republicans of the mainland, inducing them to inexact, unjust and slanderous judgements.

These words should not offend our politician friends; they reflect my sincere conviction, and I have the habit of speaking my mind to both my enemies and friends.

Republicans and socialists of the Italian mainland, particularly of northern Italy, inspired by hate and resentment — understandable, indeed very justifiable against Crispi, are mistaken and have overstepped the mark in judging the Palermo vote: they have slandered an entire region, and have gradually extended the judgement to half of Italy. Let it be clear, however, socialists and republicans, sincere and impetuous as they are, have said in public what they think; but the mass of people of their regions do not dissent from them in the least. If the press which reflects their currents has not repeated their accusations, this is due to elementary political prudence, which should not and cannot lack in political parties which are charged with governing public business[1].

---

[1] *Resto del Carlino* of Bologna, *Il Corriere della Sera* of Milan, *Adriatico* of Venice and other serious and authoritative monarchist newspapers have more or less repeated the considerations published in the republican and socialist newspapers, albeit more moderately. This was noted by *Corriere dell'Isola* of Palermo. Moreover, I could prove that the thought of the republicans and socialists, sincerely expressed, is that of the large masses of northern Italians with an infinite number of documents which I have collected for some twenty years now and which, as I write, I do not have at hand. I will recall three very famous men and three distant dates: 1) in 1862 General Govone insulted Sicily publicly; 2) several years later Hon. Gabelli called southern Italians sudici (a play on words, a combination of sud, meaning south and sudicio, meaning dirty, unclean, dishonest — translator's note); 3) in 1889, Hon. General Corvetto — Under-secretary of War in Crispi's government: qu'on se le dise! — repeated Govone's and Gabelli's insults in a private letter which was, however, published by *Arena* of Verona.

Felice Cavallotti, always noble and generous, defended Sicily and fought a duel with Corvetto. It is more appropriate than ever to recall these events now.

It is not in the least exaggerated to attribute unjust and slanderous excesses to the socialists and republicans of northem Italy — the collaborators of *Avanti* of Rome are from northern Italy. *Avanti* ascribes the victory to the mafia and speaking of Barabbas's Easter asserts that there is little moral sense in the Mezzogiorno. *Emancipazione* of Livorno notes the moral perversion of the great majority — not even a third of socialist party members turned out to vote! — of Palermo's electors. *Uomo di pietra* of Milan in *Risurrezione* (16 April) gives certain norms for voting which are an atrocious insult to Palermo's voters; and in a cartoon entitled *Southern Italian Taste*, the Palermitan voter wears the traditional bandit's hat. *Italia del popolo*, again of Milan, dedicates an article to the two morals — to those of northern Italy and those of the Mezzogiorno. *Giustizia* of Reggio Emilia reproduces the contemptible *calembour* which Hon. Gabelli once made at the Chamber of Deputies, and speaks of the northerners and the *sudici... Italia del popolo*, wishing to praise the citizens and associations of Marsala who had protested against Crispi, finds no better way to describe them than with this phase: Sicilians of northern honesty...

We are in the throes of derangement and slander; and Cammareri-Scurti is justified when he notes that those who are unable to explain the preference of Palermo's bourgeoisie for Crispi resort to insult.

We would add this, however much it may wound the arrogance or special megalomania of the Italian socialists, that without the avalanche of insults and slander hurled against Palermo and the Mezzogiorno, one can be sure that Francesco Crispi in the last election would perhaps not have succeeded in scraping together half of the votes he obtained. Against the language and action of the socialists, Palermo, which tolerates arrogance from neither above nor below, reacted violently. They would have fought better, much more profitably, — not having a candidate who accepted and entered the fray; there being no candidate who could have obtained the votes of the honest and of all the parties without having one growing proud to the detriment of the others — if they had confined themselves to illustrating the life of Crispi and to carefully watching the ballot boxes to prevent his friends, enterprising and experts in the trade, from gerrymandering.

This is the truth; and it should not be denied by the socialists of Palermo, who should see clearly and not be influenced by the inebriation which repeated successes have induced in their northern comrades.

1.2 I would not take up my pen and write what I am about to if I did not feel myself above and immune to offensive suspicions. An old, constant and inexorable critic of Francesco Crispi, never blinded by love for the native parish — my books on the *Events in Sicily*, on *Crime in Sicily* and one hundred articles in Italian and foreign newspapers and journals, testify to the truthfulness of both assertions — I can speak freely.

An open and sincere federalist — not regionalist in the common sense of the word — because I know the intellectual, economic and moral differences between the various regions of Italy — I am fully convinced — as I have repeatedly stated quite publicly — that the present absolute uniformity in the laws is dangerous for that true and beneficial unity which should be interior — in the souls of the Italians — and not in the artificial external scaffolding, which lets moral disputes and conflicts of interest which can be at times fatal smoulder, arise and mature in the shadows.

Given this, let us return to the present argument. Since the time of the celebrations of January 12th, when the anger of the socialists and republicans started to break out against Palermo, in an article which the bestial treasury of Rome seized, I asked «How can one explain Palermo's welcome of Crispi? The simplistic explanation would be that put forward by *Giomale di Sicilia* and *Idea liberale* (of Milan): the country is worse than the government and Parliament; Crispi is the representative of the country. Hence the two should understand one another. But this would be an incomplete and flawed explanation.

«First of all let us eschew petty expedients and not diminish the importance of the demonstrations, taking note of some catcalls and blowing them up out of all proportion. The number of personal friends and of beneficiaries and of those who hope in his resurrection tells us little: Palermo would have beaten the demonstrators, however numerous, if it had not wished to show its benevolence toward Crispi. The truth is that the city was behind him. In extolling the moment — and the reason for the celebrations explains it — one was admiring the ancient eighty year-old, who recalled two glorious revolutionary events and who conserves as much energy as a youngster of twenty years. The cause of legitimate regional pride, and a false concept of justice may also have not been absent.

«Many have asked why try only Crispi, and not also many other guilty politicians? Let us not bother ourselves with whether the others are as guilty as Crispi: certain subtleties are not for the masses. The masses of Palermo — the most regionalist in Italy, after, or at least alongside those of Lombardy — have instead understood that Crispi is being persecuted because he is Sicilian.

«Although the reasoning is wrong for many reasons, it has been made.

«But as this wrong reasoning has been made, the *Tribuna* fails to comprehend that the acclamations of Palermo derive from the judgement of a purifying people —; and it is a people because it applauded; it would have been a rogue if it had catcalled!

«The authors of the Roman newspaper would have done better to note that many in the city of the Vespers applauded because they were invoking pardon, even though this author believes that Crispi awaits justice from the Committee of Five, that it will rehabilitate him and quash the request for money from Banca Romana to pay for the speech of 20 December 1892, the repressions in Sicily, the Herz cordon, Abba Carima... !

«On the one hand, as this wrong reasoning has been made in good faith, the unpleasant paragons, which cannot hit a city such as Palermo, disappear.

«Just think. The impressionability and nervousness of Palermo reminds one of Paris; and its chivalry is measured by the very revolution that was being commemorated. And quite inopportunely Milan, which catcalled Crispi when Prime Minster, was recalled on this occasion. He dared to go to Milan; not to Palermo, where then he would have engendered something rather more serious than catcalls. *Consul Crispi*. Palermo showed itself to be noble and proud toward him, Palermo poisoned his most purest domestic joy with the Bosco election; and Crispi, furious, could only revenge himself by kicking out Prefect Cavasola after a few days, as he had sworn to do; Crispi the minister narrowly risked succumbing before Barbato prisoner — and only trickery saved him. Crispi the minister could not even set foot in Palermo, but this was done by Cavallotti, who could never forget the enthusiastic welcome of the Bellini Theatre, where beautiful, elegant ladies rushed to welcome him frenetically, even though sinister rumours circulated of tumults and repressions confirmed by the provocative presence of soldiers and carabinieri. Palermo may have been too generous, not too servile. Those who believe otherwise do not know the city and unconsciously slander it».

Thus I wrote on January 30th in the 14th issue of the *Rivista*; and I would not change a single letter of what I wrote then. I would however add only this. On March 13th, commemorating Cavallotti at Palermo's Politeamo Theatre, before many thousands of citizens, I pronounced these precise words:

«My physical and moral conditions should not have allowed me to come here; but I came because I wished to attend this great event in honour of Cavallotti, here in Palermo, where it has a high political and moral significance, which it would not have, I would dare to say, at Rome and Milan». And my words, which need no gloss, were met with an outburst of thunderous applause...

Let us now discuss the value of the April 17th election and what the sponsors and electors proposed to do: precedent tells us that we will not rummage through the intentions and not expound arguments founded in thin air.

Was the election an expression of the mafia of Palermo sic et simplicitur? This is anything but serious and in no way honest. It suffices to point out that Crispi's sponsors included Professor Gemmellaro, Prince Niscemi, Biagio La Manna, Olivieri, etc., from whom one can dissent politically, but whose personal honesty and meek soul, wholly alien to that criminal and violent spirit which characterises the mafia, one can only recognise.

The supposition that in a single constituency of Palermo there are circa 1,200 mafiosi, and in the class which enjoys a certain culture and a certain affluence — the class which in Sicily gives least followers to the mafia — is the same as claiming that Palermo is not a civil city, but a prison populated by dangerous criminals.

Let it not be objected that one is exaggerating the conclusions of some political philosophers in order to better and more easily oppose them with a convenient *reductio ad absurdum*. This is not my style. The exaggeration, the unilaterality of the explanation of the phenomenon lies wholly with the socialists and others who have explicitly posed the problem in these terms: on the one hand the mafiosi for Crispi, on the other the honest people for Barbato! I would also warn that it is not the first time that the socialists ascribe to themselves alone not only logic, but also rectitude and all the other political and civil virtues.

If the mafia does not suffice to explain Crispi's election, will it be said that Sicily and the entire Mezzogiorno have moral criteria which differ from those which prevail and regulate life in northern Italy? *Italia del Popolo* must have missed a contemptible article by Scarfoglio which spoke of the narrow-minded morality of the Longobards and of the broad and grandiose morality of the Greek-Latins, otherwise it would have noted it to triumphantly exclaim: see, we were right?

I am certain that dear Chiesi would not be satisfied to find himself in the company, even in a simple statement, of Scarfoglio. It would not be misplaced however to recall that the Scarfoglio's cynicism is nothing new. He showed it with similar brutality in 1893 in defence of Giolitti, who is, if I am not mistaken, from northern Italy just as today he deploys it in defence of Crispi who is from southern Italy.

Furthermore: Scarfoglio's cynicism in 1893 found a enthusiastic exponent, if not a photographic reproducer, in Parliament, in Hon. Mario Panizza, who, if I am not mistaken is from northern Italy.

Let us recall certain precedents: this is useful for a correct interpretation of the facts. The moral question has not arisen today;

and before Felice Cavallotti posed it before the Lower House with *Lettera degli onesti* in his splendid speech of 25 June 1893, which started with the famous phrase: A disreputable figure, suspicion, has entered the Chamber and lingers there!

Well, in the name of the morality which should be of the south Mario Panizza replied to Cavallotti with a speech which was an unrestrained explosion of scepticism and cynicism, in which he deplored the appointment of the Committee of Seven, supported the unchallengeability of members of Parliament, recognised the uselessness of attempting to moralise the environment; a speech, finally, which was a true hymn ... to immorality.

After having read it, Scarfoglio will, I am certain, have sent his best and most sincere congratulations.

I shall return later to this distinction between the morality of the south and that of the north, noted a hundred times by those from northern Italy and also by *Critica sociale* which represents scientific socialism; I now believe it time to summarise my thought on the factors behind Crispi's election.

I speak of factors and not of a single cause. The uniqueness, the simplicity of explanation of political-social phenomena leaves behind reality, positivism and also historical materialism as properly understood to become true metaphysics in the philosophy of history, a sectarian expedient in politics.

Given this, here are the elements which I believe acted to give the result of the election in Palermo.

There will have been mafiosi in action on the 17th, but they could only be a very small minority. If Hon. Di Rudini's aversion toward Hon. Crispi was not common knowledge, one would suspect that he intended to protect those mafiosi by putting, or maintaining, the Prefecture, Banco di Sicilia, the mental hospital, etc., in the hands of the most well-known and enterprising friends of Crispi. There are those who harbour gratitude to the former Prime Minister for benefits received; while only a very few hope in future benefits, because all have lost any illusions about Crispi's possible return to power.

Many were overcome by pity for an old man of eighty whose last days it was not desired to embitter. Everyone undoubtedly harboured admiration toward a great statesman. In view of his political merits, many forgave him his immorality and even his private sins.

It was these merits that Marinuzzi sought to underscore with the reading of a missive of G. Garibaldi to Dear Crispi in 1880 in which the great man of Caprera acknowledged the generous cooperation of Crispi in the realisation of his sacred duty.

A phenomenal ignorance is manifested in neglecting this latter factor, which is by far the most preponderant over all the others and which absorbs them all and pushes them to the background. Faced with this factor, there arises great disagreement regarding the criteria which should be employed to judge conduct in public and private life and which can be applied in various ways and to a varying degree of approximation.

Those who admit the distinction between public and private life will forgive, I repeat, the turpitudes of the latter when they find the former useful and radiant.

The distinction is deplorable and deleterious and poisons the sources of both public and private life which should be most pure.

Is this distinction, which I do not hesitate to condemn as a political, intellectual and moral aberration, characteristic and unique to the voters of Palermo? If this were the case, the wave of indignation of northern Italians for Hon. Crispi's re-election would not only be explained, but also wholly justified. And if this was the case, I add, we would be quite satisfied because it would be a sign that the flaw is circumscribed and limited, and hence easy to right.

Unfortunately, the ill has invaded the entire Italian body, or rather, this has never been immune from it for centuries. It is therefore mistaken to invoke the foregoing distinction as a characteristic of the south's moral inferiority. I recall that a very liberal application, but in the opposite sense, was made of this distinction at the time of Giolitti. It is desired to forgive Crispi's private sins in view of his political merits, while one desired to forgive Giolitti's serious political errors in view of his irreprehensible private life — an irreprehensibleness which I explicitly acknowledged in *Banche e Parlamento*.

It is clear that the second case should be less disagreeable to honest men; but it cannot be denied that basically it is but a variant in the application of the same false and damaging principle.

Our friend Ferrero, sneering, might note that this moral dissent is characteristic of Latin decadence. But France, which proclaims itself, — and wrongly — as the most corrupt of the Latin nations, excluded from public life two famous persons: Clemenceau and Floquet for a suspicion and act whose *object* was most high, even though the means were dishonest; it also saw sentenced a former minister and Lesseps: he who was rightly called the Great Frenchman. And the resignation which Grevy was forced into tendering can be said, when relative comparisons are made, to have taken place for a prank of little import, for a trifle. This, at least in those cases, testifies to a high moral sense which wishes to apply the same criteria in public and private life in the neighbouring republic, and victoriously excludes racial prejudice concerning which a certain school in Italy is working hard. Moreover, the memories of the turpitudes of Walpole and of other indecencies, not very old, of the English parliamentary regime are even more convincing in reinforcing the impression that the malaise is not a *Latin* monopoly and not even a *sudern* fatality, namely of the Mezzogiorno.

I wish on this matter to quote this excerpt from an article by Cammareri-Scurti, by debt of loyalty, and to show that there are some socialists also in Italy who see clearly on this question.

He writes in his *Lotta per la vita*: «Could not Mr. g. z. who, in issue 615 of *Giustizia* of Reggio Emilia, on the issue of Crispi censured, compares the morals of the northerners with those of the 'suderners', have employed a less defiled word to designate the peoples of the south of Italy? — That the middle class use that type of language towards the lower classes is natural; but it is painful that the socialists, instead of seeking the causes of the most characteristic social ill in those provinces, and implementing remedies, confine themselves to insulting those affected by said ill. It is like a doctor who does not cure an ill person, but dispenses insults and slaps instead.

«But Mr. g. z. allows one to believe that the lesser sense of individual morals is the effect of a real and marked difference of race which persists and resists, and effect of the enervating climate which induces hatred and hence theft in all forms, as a means of living without exertion.

«Let us draw the consequences from these premisses.

«Hence the Sicilians are a race different from the other Italians of the mainland? One could prove that this is an error or at least an exaggeration; but this will not help us. We wish to know: in what consists the physiological difference for one race to have a less developed moral sense than another? How does this supposed difference fit in with the variety of races which many observers believe they see in the peoples of Sicily? How could the Greek-Sicilian civilisation end up with such an organic inferiority when the Northerners were barbarians? Why, while it is denied that there exist races fatally condemned to inferiority and one sees in every people a part of the great human family, does one then wish to find some *pus* or some microbe of immorality in the organism of the Sicilians?

«There is also the question of the enervating climate which induces to laziness and theft. Mr. g. z. should tell us if the climate of northern Europe was also enervating when until a few centuries ago those peoples lived by plunder? Is that popular consensus indicated by George in *Progress and Poverty* for the plundering of Tweed and Tammany Hall of New York also the effect of an enervating climate?»

Furthermore, more could be added on the morals of the Northerners and Anglo-Saxons such as they currently manifest themselves in the United States, as recently described by a popular book by Stead.

The wise words of our friend from Marsala underscore that which I have proven in broad daylight in many volumes and most recently in the pamphlet *Per la razza maledetta*. But there is a contemporary case which settles things once and for all and proves the absurdity of the explanation with the intervention of race and climate of political and moral phenomena and the brazen and grandiose triumph of immorality and the distinction between public and private life in a nation dearest to our Latinophobes and in the most northern latitude of Europe.

While I write I have before me on my desk a book which I have read with malicious satisfaction and which bears a very long title[2]. It is an appeal to true German patriots and bears this motto: historical truth is harsh and painful, but necessary and healthy. The author Mr. Diest-Daber — a former colonel — tells of Bismarck and his banker Bleichröder.

The colossal political cynicism of Prince von Bismarck was no secret; and I mentioned it in another work. As regards vanity, it would appear that he was on a par with Crispi if it is true that at Sedan he thought his the applause by the victorious troops for Marshall Moltke. The series of his lies is as infinite as God's mercy and almost makes one forget Crispi's *firmatissimo* and his *Treaty of Bisacquino*. His relations with the police were always scandalously close, the pressures on the police and judges, narrated on pages 98, 102 and 103, put to shame the statements of Senator Calenda dei Tavani on the wise preparation of the judicial ambit and the suspension of the inspection of Bologna Crispi ordered the Royal Commission at Banco di Napoli. The scandalous privileges which were accorded, for personal purposes, to the Prussian Central-Baden Kredit Aktien-Gesellschaft of which Bleichröder was the auditor (pp. 88 and 89) reduces the purchase of the vehicles, in which it has not been proven that any person truly close to Crispi participated, to the size of a trifle.

The foreign currency operations made by Bismarck through Bleichröder and his interested and premeditated statements contrary to the bimetallic regime (pages 162, 163 and 164) explain the rapid and colossal enrichment of the Iron Chancellor and exceed, in their social consequences and turpitudes, Crispi's relations with Banca Nazionale, Banca Romana and Banco di Napoli.

And yet: no Committee of neither Seven nor Five, nor Three has investigated the life of Prince von Bismarck and even less have they attempted to drag him before a court charged with a common offence!

---

[2] See *Bismark und Bleichröder. Deutsches Rechtsbewusstsein und die Gleichheit vor dom Gesetze. Lebenserfahrungen aus Acten, Tagebuchern und Briefen*, Munich, Verlag des Deutschen Volksblattes, 1897.

Why this lack of equality before the law, strongly deplored by the historian of the enlightened relations between Bismarck and Bleichröder, even though they have been reported and documented in a book and sharply commentated by German socialists? Because the enormous political merits of the Iron Chancellor have exculpated his private misdemeanours.

Bad, very bad in truth! But this gives us at least this consolation: judgement in the extreme North is as in the extreme South; dissent on the criterion for judging public and private life exists among the very elect and young German people as among the degenerate and old Latin people. This dissent is so universal, without exception of race and climate, that Scipio Sighele has dedicated a book rich in brilliant paradoxes to oppose it, explain it, and almost justify it. I refer all those who wish to know more on the argument to this book.

But Prince von Bismarck, despite his satanic dishonesty, remains a political giant; can his friend Crispi match him? Denying Crispi any merits — even that of his decisive participation in the expedition of the Thousand — was an error made by Cavallotti in his last splendid, well-deserving and unforgettable campaign in favour of public and private morals, an error which I did not await his death to indicate; but the desire to make Crispi a great statesman, who rendered great services to Italy, is a political and intellectual aberration, which does a grave injustice to the homeland of Machiavelli. A dispassionate and diligent examination of his three governments leads to the inexorable conclusion that «Crispi lacked the qualities of a great statesman». He lacked that energy which many agree is the extraordinary gift among many weak ones and which I also — *mea culpa!* — attributed to him for a moment. He did not render services to Italy as a minister, as those which are ascribed to him, such as those rendered to the monarchy and to the conservative party, which always extols him for crushing the uprising in Sicily, for any other healthy and vigorous people could change into bad services, which should be atoned for with the tears of blood of the blind and foolish who extol them.

Hence, does the fault, the responsibility of the voters of Palermo, who forgot or forgave the true errors and real misdeeds of he whom they elected in the name of a nonexistent political stature, therefore reappear under the form of political and intellectual inferiority?

Let us not rush. Let us not forget very recent, contemporary history. Not only Palermo, not only Sicily, not only the Mezzogiorno err when they ascribe to Crispi merits and stature which he does not have. Unfortunately, most of Italy made that very same error. Crispi the minister had four-fifths of the Lower House on his side, they approved him, they praised him, they glorified him treating Cavallotti and all the other adversaries and accusers as enemies of the homeland and slanderers. And he found foolish and enthusiastic apologists not only in Parliament; but also, and perhaps even more, in the press and in the country. The newspapers *Nazione* of Florence, *Gazzetta dell'Emilia* of Bologna, *Gazzetta di Venezia*, *Gazzetta di Parma*, *Sera*, *Corriere della Sera* and *Perseveranza* of Milan and even *Gazzetta del Popolo* which in Turin represents the most genuine current of Piedmontese public opinion — not citing the secondary newspapers and those of the Mezzogiorno — daily extolled and vigorously supported Crispi when he was in power. Some even stood by him after Abba Carima!

Even Gustavo Chiesi, always a noble and generous soul, indigant at certain quite cowardly turncoats the day after Crispi's fall, wrote a fierce article — an indictment against *Corriere della Sera* of Milan reminding it that it too had been among the fanatic supporters of the deputy from Palermo and stating, also, that if the friends of *Corriere* had to chose between Crispi and any other gentleman they would not have hesitated in preferring the former («Non confondiamo», *Italia del Popolo*, 17 April 1898).

Yes, Guglielmo Ferrero, who did not wait his fall to pillory F. Crispi, was right, to reproach the Italian and not only Sicilian bourgeoisie for its blind and obstinate admiration for the great lamented (*Secolo*, 22-23 April 1898).

Abba Carima raised Italy up against him and it is a lie or illusion — as Hon. Nasi justly noted — to wish to deny that if the African defeat had been a victory, Crispi would have still been an omnipotent and venerated minister.

But Favilla... Favilla and the Bologna trial, it is said, were such a revelation, which deluded, enlightened the honest men in every party and changed the current of public opinion.

Untrue, untrue, untrue. The Herz cordon, Banca Romana, the criminal delay of the bills of exchange on the desk of Grillo, the massacres, the state of siege, the thousands of years of prison distributed to the poor peasants of Sicily and many other errors and many other responsibilities would have had to weigh a hundred times more for general execration to descend on the head of the elected member for Palermo. Which is what Chiesi pointed out in the afore-cited article.

This is the point to rebut for those who return to the difference between the morals of the south and those of the north to write: «Honest and outraged voices were also raised in the Mezzogiorno against the spreading current of immorality: but they remained and remain unheard, solitary — and hence much more remarkable in their exception — amidst the tumult of the other acclaimers. Did Imbriani, for example, who is one of these voices, ever have a following, ever have a strong determining influence on the public opinion of these regions? The very same could be said of Bovio and other very upright persons. And why was this? Because theirs was a voice which spoke in the desert: which found a way to the heart and reason only among a very limited and chosen minority. But in the great dominating mass, their word never aroused any interest, their virtuous example never found imitators». (*Italia del Popolo*, 24 April 1898).

The moment for reproaching the south for the inanity of the campaign of its honest men couldn't have been better chosen!

What were the fruits of Cavallotti's five months of strenuous opposition to Crispi, from December 1894 to May 1895? Only this: the dictator whose shortcomings were all too well known, obtained an overwhelming majority in the general election. Not only this, but something worse: Crispi succeeded in getting passed the unprecedented order of the day of 24 June 1895 which cynically denied the moral question had any importance! It was voted for by men of the south, the centre and north with an immorally astounding harmony of intent. And the northerners haven't even the consolation of being able to foist that order of the day off to a suderner. Oh! no: it was proposed by the Tuscan ... Torrigiani.

And, I repeat, the moment for launching a bitter rebuke to the Mezzogiorno has been well chosen, because it lets the word of its honest citizens fall unheeded in the moment when the constituency of Corteolona — which is not in Sicily — showed it had much benefited from twenty five years of moralising propaganda with the second ballot of 24 April ...!

The conclusion that clearly emerges from all this is that those who exalted Crispi the minister and then kicked him as soon as they knew he had irremediably fallen committed an act of true political cowardice. And the most clamorous example of this political cowardliness — it pains us to point out — came from an illustrious scientist. Cesare Lombroso proclaimed Crispi as an example of the genius of Sicily in 1894 and realised only in 1898 that he was dealing with a madman and a scoundrel[3].

A serious error, a serious wrong was committed by the Palermo voters when they elected Francesco Crispi; but their error and their blame should be shared by a overwhelming majority of Italians. At least they were not cowardly when they saw their idol had fallen down!

1.3 Having cleared the air of the Crispi phenomenon, which currently represents a digression in any discussion, we can return to the discussion on the morality of the south without anger, without political concerns and, above all, without local prejudices.

I reaffirm what I have said and written so many times. In the south and on the islands there prevail: agriculture, big landowners, extensive farming, the agglomeration of the population, illiteracy, the lack of roads and of other means of communication — between regions, between provinces, between

[3] In a brief rectification published in a Turin journal Professor Lombroso wishes to point out that since 1878 he had indicated Crispi as a criminal. I had taken account of the last manifestation of his thought which was contained in his excellent book on anti-Semitism which dates from 1894.

towns; — there prevail feudal relations between the various social classes, mechanical respect under the political aspect to the impositions of the government, economic misery, the lack of technical and commercial education, indifference. In the north, on the other hand, one finds: predomination of industry, small and medium-sized land ownership, sharecropping, low-density population, literacy, roads and means of communication of every type, intensive farming, ordinary civil relations between the various social classes, a certain independence from the government, prosperity, a technical-commercial culture, individual and collective initiative[4].

I have drawn up, at random, these conditions which characterise the two great divisions of the Italian peninsula which so many years ago were designated by General Marselli as one finding itself in the military phase and the other in the industrial phase, as I wish to eliminate even the appearance of any intent to establish or attempt between said any causal connection. I wish only to state the de facto conditions, nothing else. I have kept quiet about crime, as I shall deal with it last at length. It is also understood that when I speak of intensive farming, of industry, of prosperity, of misery, etc., I hint at prevailing gradations of said phenomena and nothing else; — gradations which vary from region to region and from province to province.

With this premiss, let us turn our attention to the morals of the north and those of the south: let us do so as good friends, so as to better get acquainted and appreciate one another and in the hope also of being able to mutually correct and help each other in the transformation.

Speaking of the general moral differences between the parts of a same state one should confine oneself to a quantitative and not a qualitative difference; one should ascertain that there are

---

[4] The figures on most of these conditions can be profitably read in a dear and synthetic work by Groppali: *Le Mouvement Social en Italie*, Paris, 1897. I heartily recommend this brief work rich in content and thank the author for having dedicated it to me. He thus wishes to show his affection, which I cherish particularly because it comes from Lombardy, where it is known and acknowledged that for some time I have been on the right path for studying Italian phenomenology.

a greater number of honest persons in the north and of rogues in the south, but not that, according to the difference Montesquieu found this and that side of the Pyrenees, the honest men and rogues differ in quality if observed in Sicily or in Lombardy.

I am even prepared to recognise some qualitative difference, Aversion to blood crimes is less in the Mezzogiorno and in Sicily, although it is not very large in northern Italy; the arbitrary exercise of one's own reasons, the so-called penal individualism which leads to the vendetta is also quite diffuse in Sicily and much more on the mainland. These characters of the psychomoral constitution of the Mezzogiorno indicate a reversion in the development of morals. But Gustavo Chiesi, who has travelled Sicily and the island, has written with love equal to intellect, he has acknowledged many other good qualities which go to compensate the difference noted. *La Sicilia illustrata*. And, in my opinion, the high consideration in which the family is held in the Mezzogiorno alone would suffice to forgive the considerable serious defects characteristic of a people which is still in a different stage of development.

Today, as they can no longer seriously speak of a true inferiority of race for the inhabitants of the Mezzogiorno and the islands, with the ability of jugglers they eschew the theories proclaimed yesterday and maintain that there has been a halt in development; but the truth is that we are dealing with changes or varying degrees of speed which can lead to reversion. Which does not exclude subsequent improvement, but makes the inferiority which can be noted in a given moment fatal and instils an active faith in those who do not feel themselves perpetually condemned to illiteracy and to a high level of crime.

In fact, in present-day politics, one admires in the north greater correctness in the electoral battles, clear and more decisive characters; the prevalence of programmes and not of men and cliques; greater independence from the government, a certain pride and sincere love for freedom. However, the times when the roles were reversed are not all that far away. Poerio, Spaventa, Natoli, Settembrini, Conforti, Pisanelli, Imbriani, Savarese, De Sanctis,

Zuppetta, names of a rigid morality and of clear and marked political colour, all lived in the Mezzogiorno. Precisely in those times in the Mezzogiorno and in Sicily the best elections were fought in the name of the liberal principles and it was the deputation of those regions which provided the biggest and best contingent to the Left, which embodied those principles. The fact was so well known that then — see how the criteria of the wise northerners change! — it was seen as a sign of inferiority of the Mezzogiomo and of Sicily. It aroused the admiration of those who love freedom, the selfless protest of Milan, which elected Barbato. But only the Italians' phenomenal liability of memory has made it possible to forget that Filippo De Boni for many years represented the constituency of Tricarico and Alberto Mario was elected at Noto; and both were northerners, who at that time did not pass for more tepid revolutionaries than Barbato. But can the struggle of Milan be compared as regards its historical and political importance to that of Messina, which continually elected Giuseppe Mazzini and annulled the death sentence which the monarchy had inflicted, and gave Italy its greatest son?

Today great sensation is aroused by the diffuse corruption in the south. The Giarre case has furnished material for light-hearted comments in the Lower House and in the country and, with a phenomenal lightness, one wishes to make electoral corruption one of the many signs of the Mezzogiorno's inferiority.

Nothing could be more untrue and arbitrary. Turin's *Germinal* had honestly protested noting that the surprise at the Giarre case was undeserved because that the ballot of Giarre was typical of three quarters of those in Italy and that government pressure, the buying and selling of votes, and getting the voters drunk were common practices everywhere.

Moreover, the reports of the Election Result Commission for the last twenty years or so show that if the ballot box response has been adulterated, in the Mezzogiorno and in Sicily the phenomenon has mainly taken place as a result of government pressure and in northern Italy as a result of corruption.

The very same reports appear to indicate that corruption in the north is uglier: the good peasants of Veneto, of Lombardy, of Piedmont have sold their vote for a pittance: for some tripe and half a litre of wine. In 1892 the voters of Corteolona kicked Felice Cavallotti out for a few lire; and the same voters today to Romussi, the bosom friend of the unforgettable victim of Villa Cellere, of that man who gave that constituency prestige and fame, have preferred a Dozio, whose exploits we will soon hear about.

In the heart of Lombardy, in the same province of Milan there is a constituency in which republicans, progressives and socialists have been unable to make a single statement, a single protest, although they appointed as their deputy — I refer their opinion without any valuation as to its propriety — one of the most contemptible persons who sits in the Lower House! And not even the socialists, who have a large stock available, and who are to the fore when an honest democrat is to be slurred, have been able to find a candidate, any candidate to stand against him!

And what about Pietrasanta? It is worth all the cases of corruption in the Mezzogiorno together. The excellent Prince of Carovigno has immortalised that constituency; Pietrasanta, for notoriety..., he has outdone even that corrupt town of England where an irritated lord promised to have his footman elected...

In the Mezzogiorno there are still some zones where the shady goddess which degrades Parliaments has never penetrated: in Basilicata securities and millions count for nothing; only intellect and culture count: Giustino Fortunato and Ascanio Branca would not have been elected if they had no merits other than their wealth. Hon. Greppi, who both radicals and socialists indicate as a complete jackass — and here again I give their opinion without judging its propriety — was instead elected at Milan, which is rightly called the moral capital, while he would have undoubtedly have lost in Basilicata.

On the other hand there is a entire zone of northern Italy where the various gradations of democracy have no hope of engaging battle with the probability of winning: in some constituency they have to date renounced any attempt. During my last visit to the constituency of Corteolona I asked some very dear friends of mine the reason for this phenomenon. Humiliated, they replied that any attempt to fight for democracy is useless because in those constituencies the voters are wholly and long tamed[5].

All this proves that the voters of the Mezzogiorno are less soiled than others than one attempts to paint; it also shows that the political decadence of the Mezzogiorno is recent, therefore it is a product of neither race nor climate.

The latest, distressing events have shown that also the masses

---

[5] If I wished to give this paper the size of a volume the reports of the Electoral Commission from years back would furnish me with precious material on corruption in the north. At the time, there was much talk of the election of Weill-Weiss in a constituency of Lombardy which cost the millionaire banker a fortune. I cannot be silent, however, of three elections which the Commission investigated after these articles were published in *Rivista popolare*.

Hon. Callaini presented his report on the election of Gavotti in the constituency of Nizza Monferrato on 25 June 1898 and proposed the annulment of said election by virtue of the brazen corruption exercised by friends of Gavotti. «Who, on the eve of the election in the constitutency of Nizza, where he does not reside, has exercised such a generous philanthropy that it engendered the suspicion that it did not derive from the disinterested sentiment to do a good deed». The Lower House annulled this election.

Hon. Coppino reported on the election of Massa Carrara on 4 July. The report of the venerable man includes the following:

«Of the deadly action of money the traces are more profound and dearer. It is not that one can find the many thousands of lire that it is said were distributed to prepare the ground. He who distributed, denies the fact, and he who received is silent. The shameful market even there, and perhaps more there than elsewhere, caused no scandal; the vote is offered and given if one asks the price, it being wholly natural that the friends of the candidate have money for said purpose, and the ways of asking are courteous such that two respectable supporters of Binelli sought refuge in the police station». As the corruption did not suffice, even the dead and absent went to vote and the votes often were written by the same hand. The Lower House annulled this election.

More upbeat than all the others was the election in the constituency of Fossano on which Hon. Giusso reported in 4 July. Here everyone corrupted — the winner and the loser. Let us hear the severe and official words of the report: «The true struggle was fought between three candidates, all three being wealthy men; and all three little known in the constituency. And as all three were of the same political colour to ensure victory they resorted to generous gifts and corrupted almost the entire constituency. There were those who distributed generous subsidies and gifts, those who were thrifty in this sort of electoral charity and those on the other hand who merely promised to give... Thus we can undeniably state that he who spent more gained more votes. This election is viewed by the honest men of the constituency as an unheard of disgrace!»

Now is it not legitimate to conclude that Giarre's constituency was truly slandered when presented as a constituency typical as regards corruption and fraud? What can we say, then, of *Avanti!*'s insistence in continuing to cite the constituencies of Giarre and Regalbuto as typical examples of electoral fraud and corruption? It can only be explained by regional passion.

of Milan, for whom I nurture the greatest admiration, are equally impulsive as those of the Mezzogiorno. On the other hand, the ruling classes of Lombardy have revealed themselves on this occasion more dishonestly reactionary. During the time of the Sicilian fasci the barons, knights and senators meeting in the Ragona Hall, after proclamation of the state of emergency, discussed economic questions, calling for economic measures — without overlooking their own interests — and as regards reactionary spirit they confined themselves to manifesting their dislike for the school. But let us be fair, they did not invent the plundering, fires, devastations and barricades seething with armed defenders out of thin air; they did not act as informers and spies; they mitigated, when they did not openly defend, the accused before the military courts; they did not shout against those who bore among them the voice of reason and justice. Instead the upper middle classes and the Lombard aristocracy had the sad privilege of having sent to Rome its representatives to consciously mislead, to falsify public opinion on the cases of Milan, to have called for the sternest reaction; to have sent indecent missives to General Bava Beccaria, perhaps to commemorate those which he had once sent to the Emperor of Austria. And what of the press? Sicily comes out of this comparison with its head high. In Palermo *Giornale di Sicilia*, although a long-standing fanatic admirer of Francesco Crispi, openly and courageously condemned the government's methods during the state of emergency; it did not wish to disarm before the threat of suppression and protested against the suppression of the socialist journals; it printed accounts of the trials which had taken place before the Palermo military court which were not only truthful, but also justified those accused. And what happened in Milan? The behaviour of *Corriere della Sera* during the tumults was such that it could be accused by a Rome newspaper of having caused the suppression of *Secolo* and *Italia del Popolo* and other socialist and republican newspapers. It then resigned itself to the state of emergency and rather than raise its voice loudly and indignantly against a Bava Beccaria thus announced its acquiescence to the system of violence and lies: «Since yesterday (May 25th if I am not mistaken), the reports from the War Tribunal are reviewed by a public security official who naturally has the authority to censure that which he deems is useful not to publish».

That 'naturally' represents the entire poem of faintheartedness. And this should have been understood by Torelli-Viollior, its long-standing owner and director, who was nauseated and requested hospitality on the pages of Turin's *Stampa* for his dignified but noble and memorable protest.

1.4 Let us turn now to the subject of crime. The Mezzogiorno's sad statistical superiority is undeniable. We will not seek in the lesat to attenuate it with the figures for Rome, Livorno, Treviso, etc. I shall not evoke again the deeds of the action squads which were not below those of the mafia. Neither the frequency of murders in Romagna, which joyously induced the anthropological school to claim brachycephaly as the cranic form which fatally predisposed to said crime; I shall not recall that the theft of millions from the banker Parodi in Genoa presupposes a wise preparation and such a broad complicity as to throw a sinister light on all the city; I shall not insist on the most famous Ceneri trial in Bologna — for which an immense cage had to be built. No, I shall pass over all these; but it is right, indeed, my duty, to take account of them when speaking of crime, of the distinction made by Lacassagne, generalised and developed by Scipio Sighele. The illustrious professor from Lyons says: the cities are no longer more moral than the villages; but one and the other have their own specific crime. Roughly, Sighele repeats the same thing, shifting the distinction from space to time and stating that the morals of civil peoples are no greater than among barbarians, but that there is only a different type of crime: based on fraud and cunning among the former, and on violence among the latter[6].

[6] Professor Pullé was eminently clear. He also wished to join the school of criminal anthropology, embracing the vices of facile generalisation and exaggeration with regard to the criterion of the determinant and particularly of the psychological factors of delinquency. He divides Italy into two parts the background of one, the north, is dominated by greed, the other, the south and islands, by the passion which generates the crimes deriving from impulsiveness. (*Profilo antropologico dell'Italia*, Firenze, 1898, p. 112). I shall repeat my reservations on this distinction, which is not new; but if it was exact would the conclusion not be that northern delinquency is more despicable?

I have several reservations about Sighele's ideas and I shall not hesitate to say that I believe preferable — if one can speak of preference with regard to evil — civil crime to barbarian crime: without this preference leading to one of the habitual exaggerations of Lombroso, who for the convenience of his theory views famous bank robbers as only delinquents and not criminals true and proper.

Now it is undeniable that barbarian crime predominates in Sicily, in Sardinia and in the Mezzogiorno, while civil crime is rampant in the North. We should be alarmed by the former and seek remedies: but we cannot concern ourselves less about the latter whose economic and social consequences are broader and more disastrous than the former. We should be even more concerned as statistical appearances can mislead. It goes to embody the numerous category of artful and lucky delinquents illustrated by Lino Ferriani, who knows them. In fact, the form of so-called mitigated delinquency often escapes the investigations of justice and does not give rise to trials, but to ignominious accommodations and transactions which indicate a fearful moral shortcoming: fearful even though it is not translated into figures. And because it is not translated in figures, because there is not statistical survey of this immorality, the northerners, wrongly, brim with pride.

The readers of the *Rivista*, and those who know me know that I do not resort to certain observations for commodity of polemic: what I write and say is the result of serene study and the expression of my most sincere convictions. In this case I can prove that I do not resort to these distinctions to defend the mistreated Mezzogiorno by pointing out that I stated them, and nobody challenged them, before the present controversy arose.

I wrote in 1893: «At the Banca Romana trial, alongside the two principal accused, one of whom is a native of Genoa, there also stand a member of Parliament and two officials from the southern provinces. Among the ministers and members of Parliament suspected there is an abundance of those from the Mezzogiorno. From this one infers how large is the distance between the delinquency of upper, central and lower Italy with the islands just as there is the same distance between the manifestations which are just inside the law and which fall in the field of immorality.

«The different phenomenology is undeniable; but anyone who rushed to draw an optimistic induction in favour of the northern provinces in the matters which this book deals with would err considerably.

«If the exploits of the rabble and the scoundrels are not as numerous and clamorous as those of the camorra and mafia, well studied and well known criminal associations, other deeds which are no less socially dangerous and which the law still does not punish, but which in the future will undoubtedly be punished, prevail in northern Italy, where the customs of bankers and shareholders are more common and are near in number and quality to those of countries where the capitalistic regime is more developed and powerful.

«Who will write the history of the stock-jobbing, usury and theft in yellow gloves, which is perpetrated daily in the stock markets and with the establishment of joint-stock companies, will see confirmed in full this assertion which is not suggested by regional passion: I have been reproached even by northerners for worsening the hand of my native southern provinces in criminological studies. He who carries out such a study will realise that there descended to Rome from the hamlets near the Alps a swarm of unscrupulous businessmen who went to organise the skilful depredation of the credulous which still eludes the quest for justice and the action of the penal code. And these depredations, which still do not arouse the repugnance of vulgar theft, nonetheless escape the code and justice because one was done and the other administered by the middle class of whom such actions are characteristic, if not legally criminal, certainly quite dishonest and harmful».

These observations of mine were written in summer 1893 for the book *Banche e Parlamento* and would have been even more severe toward the North if then I had full knowledge — I knew something and had mentioned it in the Lower House — regarding the amazing deeds of the Tiberina, the Mobiliare, the Immobiliare banks ...

The Luraghi trials had not taken place and Cavallini was still considered a gentleman, indeed, he was member of Parliament for the north. Then Attorney Bo had still to denounce — or at least I did not know of any denouncement — the Veneta.

The Committee of Seven, which could go through the books and accounting of Banca Romana, Banco di Sicilia and Banco di Napoli, had the door slammed in its face by Banca Nazionale and only the formal denouncement of Hon. Giolitti, prime minster, led to the discovery of Crispi's bills of exchange, jealously hidden in Grillo's desk; but in this case too, the northern corrupter cannot be denied the censure of the corrupt southerner. And if the Committee of Seven had come to the Lower House to ask powers sufficient to carry out accessory investigations of Banca Nazionale, what and how many turpitudes would have come to light to the great dishonour of the northerners![7]

In that shadowy bank business it was the interference of politics which engendered everything. But, unfortunately, in latent or manifest delinquency, the wise and prodigious activity, dishonesty of the northerners can offer wonderous pages for a history which could have been written only by the late Felice Cavallotti. By him alone, who was a true and sincere supporter of unification and knew how to write the *Storia meravigliosa* of the northerner Chauvet and of the southerner Crispi. In the wonderously shameful history of the jointly-interested tobacco monopoly, of the forced circulation, which was proclaimed in 1866 with almost criminal procedures — those who do not believe so should read the Seismit-Doda report — of the railway construction, of the supplies, of the

[7] Someone, having read the articles in *Rivista Popolare*, said to me that the disappearance of Banco di Napoli's capital spoke against the morals of the south. But it should be noted that the much greater the capital of Banca Nazionale, as is shown by the speeches by Sonnino and myself on the discussions of June-July 1893, had also vanished and in large part the responsibility lies with vampire banks (Tiberina, Mobiliare, Immobiliare, etc., etc.) all owned by northerners. Banca Nazionale made heavy losses in the Mezzogiorno, particularly on land credit transactions. But one can say that it was justly punished by the unfair competition organised against the southern banks to make them disappear and to realise Grillo's dream: the single bank. The millions lost by Banco di Napoli in Bologna were all eaten away by northerners. We will see this at the trial of Favilla... if it is ever held!

trade treaties... — the list is not complete — the southerners either do not figure at all or only in the smallest proportion. The choir and protagonists of these storms came from the north!

And all these affairs cost the Nation hundreds of millions which reached billions of lire.

The painful conclusion? The Mezzogiorno and islands abound and swarm in petty thieves, but the giants of theft lord it in the north!

Is there any difference? Yes there is! The Sgadari barons have been pilloried at the Milan Court of Assizes, but ten Sgadaris are needed to equal a big northern thief! And the able croesi of the railways, of the banks, do not sit on the bench of the accused, but are living it up in splendid villas on Lake Maggiore and, if they wish, go out to amuse themselves to Montecitorio or Palazzo Madama[8].

1.5 The ill person whom one wishes to diagnose and cure at this moment is the Mezzogiorno, it is Sicily. We know the symptoms of the illness; but we cannot proceed successfully against them if we do not know what cause or causes allow them to persist. It is wishful thinking to hope to cure a suppuration maintained by a extraneous body if one does not remove the extraneous body.

No climate! No race! Filippo Turati rightly exclaims regarding the moral ills of the Mezzogiorno and Sicily (*Critica sociale*, 15 April). And this is what I have been shouting for circa twenty years against the school which calls itself positive and which is merely metaphysical and seeks to condemn half of Italy to a fatal and perpetual inferiority[9].

---

[8] An honest moderate of the old sort, former member of Parliament Morini, in the book on electoral corruption, severely deplored that the «criminality in the Upper House exceeds the average of ordinary criminality...». For reasons which are easy to understand, I can only gloss over this point. But if there is criminality in the Upper House, rumours suggest that the majority of the criminals belong to the north.

[9] In *Delinquenza della Sicilia e le sue cause*, in *Alcoolismo*, in *Sociologia criminale*, in *Razza maledetta*, etc., I showed the non-existence of this relation between race and criminality. My adversaries — often able, and very rarely loyal — have either modified their theories without ever indicating they were forced to do so by me, or they have continued to repeat the old errors without ever replying to my criticisms.

No climate! No race! I can also today proudly repeat to the audacious assertions of Pullé who had fun finding the somatic types — en bloc and not in the single cases! — of delinquency in the Mezzogiorno and on the islands; who ascribes the illiteracy of the Mezzogiorno and the islands to race; who bizarrely interprets the figures, which he himself gives, of the number of illiterates and relates them to illiteracy and crime!

Cammareri-Scurti, rigidly applying historical materialism in studying the genesis of Crispism, summarises all the factors of the phenomenon under a common denominator: the latifundium.

Here is the exclusivistic one-sidedness of the systematic person. If by latifundism in the broad sense one wishes to indicate the series of political, economic and social causes which have acted and consolidated and reinforced their action in the regions in question for several centuries, we are still faced with a metaphor which imposes analysis and discrimination of its single component elements to be able to efficiently and surely obtain a good result.

In the specific and concrete case, latifundism was only very slightly the sole and direct cause of the deplorable moral phenomena we are talking about, as we see the greater and more general veneration of Crispi deplored in the coastal zones of the provinces of Messina and Catania, where there is no trace of latifundism and where small and medium-sized estates, proper sharecropping and magnificent intensive farming predominate. And these are — it should be noted — the zones with the lowest levels of crime in Sicily. The same unbounded admiration for Crispi exists in many points of Tuscany which know neither the mafia nor latifundism.

Undoubtedly the economic factor is of great importance; and acts in a hundred different ways, which at times hide its intimate nature; but the political factor in the Mezzogiorno and on the islands had a no less energetic and undoubtedly more continuous and constant influence for many centuries. The political factor eliminated justice in social relations; it cultivated obsequiousness and arrogance; it made rebellion fatal and vendetta the sole corrective; it halted any development of the intellectual culture; it reinforced or created, where it did not exist, the influence of the economic factor. This action of the political factor is so certain that its effects are to be found throughout the Mezzogiorno, even there where the conditions of land ownership are different; and we find them in Romagna, whose action squads — at times a mere degenerative transformation of Carbonarism — bear a close resemblance to the mafia[10].

The ills, and the causes which generate them, have been known for many years. They were studied by the special Parliamentary Commission of Inquiry whose report was written by Bonfadini, by Damiani in his *Inchiesta agraria* dedicated to Sicily, by Villari in his *Lettere meridionali*, in many other later articles, by Turiello in *Governo e governati*, by Sonnino and Franchetti in two truly masterly volumes. For the mainland south, in addition to the works of Turiello, Pani-Rossi, Santa Maria, Winspeare and of a hundred others it suffices to recall, so as not to excessively lengthen the list, the Parliamentary Inquiry into Banditry, the speeches which for many years in succession members of Parliament of every political hue from Lazzaro to Castagnola, from Miceli to Massari, etc. — made in the Lower House on banditry, etc. Well then, what has been the purpose of so much precise indication of the ills, causes and remedies?

Nobody can call into question that something has been done, that, from certain aspects, much has been done, for example, as regards roads. But there was much more to do, there was a host of tasks to do from the political, economic and intellectual aspect.

In 1860, when Garibaldi landed at Marsala, and after he had triumphantly marched through all the Mezzogiorno, the populations saw in the legendary red-shirted soldiers brothers, and moreover they admired them as older brothers, brothers

---

[10] In *Delinquenza della Sicilia e le sue cause* as early as 1855 I noted that the political conditions had exercised a similar disastrous action in Sicily and in Romagna; and since then I noted that the greater poverty of the Lombard and Veneto peasants did not lead to more crime because the actions of the political and social factors was lacking. I recently saw from close up the economic condition of the land workers of the affluent Lombardy and find my judgement wholly justified.

who were more cultured, richer, more educated in the ways of freedom[11].

This they were; and as such they should have carried out a truly fraternal work, an educating and redeeming work. They failed in this. This is the harsh truth which does not fear rebuttal.

The liberating brothers arrogantly and foolishly called themselves conquerors. And the harsh polemics which raged after 1860 between Sicilians and northerners testifies to this; Guerzoni also fanned the flames of these fierce polemics. They not only called themselves conquerors, but they also acted as such. They looked down with supreme contempt on their younger brothers, they called him a barbarian, they treated him as a barbarian and they showed themselves, they themselves, to be the true barbarians. In the proud soul of the islanders they aroused a terrible reaction and an accumulation of hatred toward so-called Piedmontesism, which then exploded terribly with the uncontrolled scenes of Misilmeri and with the uprising of Palermo in 1866.

From then to the present, the northerners' attitude toward the Sicilians and southerners has changed a lot and improved; and I would recall that the mainland journalists who followed King Umbert in Sicily and the Mezzogiorno in 1881, wrote true hymns in favour of those regions and their inhabitants, and confessed — note well — and deplored the fact they had not known them earlier. The confessions and admiration were renewed on the occasion of the National Exhibition of Palermo in 1892.

---

[11] Those ignorant or malicious persons who falsify history speak or write of the legendary expedition of the Thousand and of the liberation of Sicily, as though this took place thanks to the miraculous work of Garibaldi, without the effective participation of the populations, indeed almost against them. But the great man of Caprera, who did not need to alter the truth and to lessen others to seem what he was, a giant, saw things differently. Gustavo Chiesi with healthy patriotism noted the fact in his splendid *Sicilia illustrata* with these words: «Catania — Garibaldi himself wrote in his *Frammenti a matita*, quoted by Guerzoni, showed itself worthy of Palermo and Sidly. Men, money, victuals and clothes for my nude men»... A volcano of patriotism! Garibaldi's judgement of Catania could not be neither more just nor more synthetic in its sculptural simplicity. It reflects the heart of this great, noble and beautiful city, which extends from the flowered slopes of Europe's biggest volcano, like a woman in love would lean on the shoulder of the bridegroom, loving and proud!

If a significant and beneficial change has taken place in the relations between men of the various regions, and the mutual esteem which has induced them to a reciprocal respect has increased — a change I hope is not stopped by the recurrence of insults and erroneous judgements which gave rise to the sad phenomenon of Crispi in the north — in substance and in form progress has been scant.

Let us see. In the mainland south the task included eliminating the causes of banditry, but these causes have been dusted, painted and smoothed over while leaving them unchanged. They could in no way be eliminated by the ferocity of Colonel Fumel and General Pinelli, with acts of cruelty and summary executions[12].

Arrangements should have been made for popular education throughout the Mezzogiorno; but the Italian state spent most of the small amount set aside for this purpose in northern Italy.

This failure of the Italian government in its reparative work is such that as regards illiteracy of the island it forced from Gustavo Chiesi this vibrant page of love for Sicily which, as a sign of true recognition, I feel bound to reproduce: «It is not a reproach I wish to make to those populations, over which so much ignorance casts its shadow, but a regret for the good which has been lost as a result; it is a protest, an invective, almost a curse against the set of those systems which, from the domination of Rome onwards, allowed Sicily to be considered not as Italian soil, but as a land to conquer, and sent there over the course of the centuries proconsuls and lictors, vicars and tutors, viceroys and cut-throats, intendants and cops, prefects and policemen, to levy taxes and deprive them of their wealth, and to force them to inaction and in the shadows the thought, the genius of its people — who twice have raised, first in Europe, the luminous light of civilisation —

[12] In the interesting discussion on banditry of 31 July 1863 in the Lower House, General Avezzana said that he had seen nothing more criminal than the Italian government had committed in the Mezzogiorno during the civil wars in Mexico. During the same session, Hon. Lazzaro and hon. Miceli told of the horrors committed, and Stefano Castagnola concluded by stating that the local population was contemptuous of the summary executions and considered those executed as martyrs.

and was the first even in this century to give the precursory signs of the Italian renaissance.

«...And in the last thirty years which have now passed, the national government has given itself, for a set of reasons which it is useless to analyse here, less than poorly the thought of uprooting with education and schooling the bad plants of prejudices and of the ancestral customs which negligence and the culpable amenability of past governments — drawing all their force, their raison d'etre from the increasingly greater moral depression, if not indeed dejection, of the subject populations — had allowed to grow and take strong root in every class of society».

Siciliy did not have the draft and conscription was hated and feared. The government imposed it with an incomparable and unsurpassed violence, made all the more odious and unpardonable by the state of emergency, by the torture against the deaf-mute Cappello whom it was sought to make speak at whatever cost, by the death by suffocation inflicted in Petralia Soprana by Lieutenant Dupuy to a whole peaceful family, by the assault by night to the sound of the bugle of tranquil citizens to seek out and arrest the draft-dodgers.

In Sicily there was a desire for justice and the rule of law. Colonel De Villata ensured both one and the other were known and appreciated with the executions at Fantina; with the mysterious and unpunished assassination of General Corrao; with the military prefecture of General Medici, whose horrors were denounced and documented by Tajani, then attorney general in Palermo. And even today, in the year of grace 1898, appreciation of the honest and correct judicial proceedings is furthered by the execution of Castellano on mere suspicion of being an accomplice; making two new crimes necessary in Siculania to induce *madame* justice not to find the true author of a previous murder, but to free at least a hundred innocent persons unjustly accused of that crime, and guilty of nothing, in fact, other than of suspected fascism!

Sicily needed capital to ensure the development of its enormous natural resources and the Italian state, not satisfied with impoverishing it with an exorbitant tax system, which weighed down on all inhabitants like a curse, has stolen hundreds of millions of the Church estate which was its own only. The indifference of private citizens was already a calamity; it was compounded by the indifference of the state.

In Sicily and the Mezzogiorno political education had to start from scratch; and the great educator was Depretis, who implanted fraud, corruption and violence as suitable electoral methods — the same Depretis whose disciples and continuators include Crispi and Giolitti, Codronchi and Di Rudini.

In Sicily, there was the serious agrarian question to be resolved, there were social relations to be corrected. The initiators of the solution and correction were General Bixio with the shootings of Bronte; Depretis continued with the shootings of Catalabianco; Crispi and Giolitti perfected the system with the massacres of 1893-1894, which have not ceased under Hon. Di Rudini. It should not be objected that the latter two are Sicilians: it should be recalled that Crispi's claim to fame in Parliament and in the country was precisely that of having energetically repressed the agrarian unrest. He was the faithful agent of all the Italian middle class, as Ferrero excellently put it in the cited article.

And just think that as early as 1876 Hon. Sonnino — yes he! acknowledged that left to themselves, without the oppressive intervention of their mainland brothers, the peasants wouldn't have succeeded in resolving the agrarian question![13].

The conclusion? Clear and painful. The northern brothers have sought to remedy the economic ills of the Mezzogiorno and Sicily by considering said regions as a colony populated by barbarians — a colony where there was only a good market for their industrial products. The northern brothers have dealt with the political, intellectual and moral ills of Sicily and the Mezzogiorno by viewing them haughtily, treating their inhabitants brutally and contemptuously. When they allowed the handcuffs and carabineri to rest; when

---

[13] In his famous speech of 1863 replying to General Govone's abuse and slander on the government's task in the Mezzogiorno and in Sicily, Filippo Cordova said «I believe the government, when it receives a country not by conquest, but from the hands of the revolution, should ask itself what brought about this revolution, what did the people who rose up seek and do everything possible to satisfy these needs».

the cannon felt silent, the Govones, Gabellis, Corvettos spoke with insults and slander calling them *sudici* and barbarians... And, it would appear impossible, republicans and socialists, vexed and sorrowed at seeing that their theories still had not worked in these regions — as a result of historical causes, which cannot be changed by a wave of the magic wand, not even by the magicians of Marxism — at this end of century they joined the choir of the denigrators of regions which should gain from their cause with love and persuasion! Moreover, in the year of grace 1898, when the constitutional regime is said to be extended also to Russia, a columnist, moreover conscientious, such as Adolfa Rossi, in Milan's *Corriere della Sera* — that is to say in the great organ of the northern ruling classes — to give Sicily a political education and to help it set out toward a better future, can proffer only this recipe: suspend there for fifty years at least the constitutional safeguards and administer it with a governor, with prefects and with local commissars chosen from among the most honest and capable of the mainland...[14]. Ah! So you want to send the most honest and capable administrators of the mainland to the island! Why then were the most dishonest and incapable officials sent to Sicily for 38 years as though to a place of punishment?

I have noted the unjust judgements and iniquitous accusations not by way of impetus of a indignant soul, not by way of reaction based on resentment and regional passion; but by way of a true sentiment of Italian spirit, to remind of the truth and reality those who have strayed from them in good faith. I did so because I believe the two conditions of arrogance and ignorance equally disastrous. Now the northerners are excessively proud of their good and undeniable qualities; and in this mood there is already a seed of decadence, of degeneration which has to be pitilessly uprooted and not lovingly cultivated. I would add that in the growth of this unhealthy pride of the northerners, part of the blame — and mine is great — belongs to the southerners, who, if they showed both in and outside Parliament their defects, they ad-

---

[14] I read this absurd proposal in a satirical article in *Italia del popolo* (1-2 April 1898).

mired the former too much and with rare ingenuity praised them, thus laying it on thicker about their inferiority[15].

Ignorance of the true conditions of the single regions of Italy lies in everyone, but it is greater in northerners about the Mezzogiorno and Sicily on which they express judgements which are extravagant if not even slanderous. For example, I have seen that several newspapers of northern Italy deplore the sharing out of the land to the peasants of the Mezzogiorno and of the nearby island with a sense of envy and denounced as an injustice committed to the detriment of the northerners. They ignore the fact that these famous and derisive parcellings out did not take place free of charge, but entailed exorbitant fees — as at Mistretta, Caltavuturo, etc. — which led to abandonment. Moreover — the critics should bear this well in mind — even the fees are unjust, because the division into lots took place for land which rightfully belonged to the local peasants; for lands which belong to the local council, on which the state has no rights. Hence, by assigning them to the peasants of the Mezzogiorno, the state is not stealing them from the peasants of Veneto or Lomellina.

Individuals of rare culture and exceptional intelligence have stated vulgar howlers as a result of their ignorance of local con-

---

[15] To the Sicilian socialists Loncoao and Bonagiuso, moreover worthy men and scholars, who for political subjectivism, exaggerated the hues of the characters of the people of Italy Cammareri-Scurti replied «In Sicily there is undoubtedly people such as those described. It is natural that the sad conditions of life, of the Sicilian rural masses through a long series of centuries, have impressed profound marks on the subjected classes; but that the majority of Sicilian workers, or all of them, as is claimed, consists of debased, vile and criminal persons is not in the least true and does not ring true. It is true that such people abound in any district, but they do not equally abound in all».

«A people which speaks in a vigorous dialect rich in voices, phrases and lively ways of saying things, which boasts a great heritage of traditions; which dedicates to citrus fruit and vibrant proverbs all the errors and all the moral truths; whose history includes the Greek-Sicilian civilisation, the monarchy of the Normans and of the Swabians, alongside the glorious Italian comunes, the renaissance of the XVI century which is worthy of comparison with that of other regions, which can boast a long series of uprisings against oppression; which made possible Garibaldi's epic deeds of 1860; and which always engenders talk of itself when one speaks neither of Sardinia, nor of Veneto, nor of the other regions which are famously as poor or even poorer than Sicily, oh, no! such a people — if a collective psychology exists — can be neither vile nor obtuse, as some qualify it».

ditions. Thus, for example, Filippo Turati could write that that the Barons of the Mezzogiorno in 1895 had managed to suspend operations for a new land register another means of plundering to the detriment of the Mezzogiorno which will cost the state 500 million lire! Now the latifundists of the Mezzogiorno, who have numerous real sins on their conscience, are attributed another for which they have none at all. In 1892, the serious question of the land register was raised in the Lower House by me who — to my shame — owns not a plot of land. The legislative measure was proposed by the Tuscan Sonnino and the Ligurian Boselli. And it was a southern latifundist, Hon. Di Rudini, who satisfied the northern watchdogs resuscitating the implementation of the inauspicious Law of 1 March 1886!

It has also been the case that some who have studied and known the Mezzogiorno forget this at times. Sonnino did so when minister; and it would appear that our dear friend Gustavo Chiesi wishes to forget it when a journalist.

This ignorance is a most serious ill. No political and material unity of the nation can give it true power if there is no moral unity. There can be no moral unity if the united parts do not know each other and, when they do, do not learn to esteem and respect one another and to amend and improve themselves reciprocally. But given how Italy has been made, moral unity cannot and will not exist. It exists only in the laws and sufferences, but not in the customs and good usages. Naples and Milan, Palermo and Turin exchange some culinary taste; the soldiers of one region learn perhaps the vices of those of another; but the matter goes no further. And it cannot, because the best patriots believed that the best education of unity should be carried out in the army. The educational barracks!

There can be no true education where there is coercion or fanatic and reckless imitation without knowledge of the necessary proportion between the means and the end.

We are on the wrong path and we have to change tack if we do not wish to arrive at the necessary and irremediable perdition. We cannot start out on a right path if we lack the courage to tell the truth to the northerners and the southerners, the truth and nothing but the truth. We cannot correct and improve ourselves if we do not acknowledge that the country as a whole is ill — at one point with anaemia and scrofula, in another with epileptic convulsions or infectious fever — but still ill. We will not have true unity which is a producer of healthy energy if we do not respect the natural and historical conditions of the single regions.

One can only achieve moral unity with time, with training, with education, with spontaneous consent which engenders imitation: ethnic elements of advanced civilisation lack that plasticity of amorphous substances which allows unification by means of force as takes place in France. Those who love the true greatness of the homeland should pursue and achieve this moral unity, based on culture and prosperity equitably shared among the single regions of Italy, dedicating their works and thoughts to it; but all the sincerely democratic elements which prevail in the north and which in the Mezzogiorno and the islands will always find a mass which will crush them, if well used by the rulers, until such time as their lack of culture and political education persist, should dedicate themselves all the more to this task.

2. - Second Part

... *rerum cognoscere causas* ...
... *et vitam imprendere vero.*

2.1 In the north of Italy there is advancing, every day slightly more, a sentiment toward the Italy of the Mezzogiorno which consists not only of diffidence, but of rancour; and at times, and indeed increasingly frequently, as soon as something happens which would appear to legitimate it, it manifests itself in a more open and virulent form. The re-election of Crispi at Palermo was one of such occasions; and it is unnecessary to repeat the fervour with which old and new charges were re-evoked, the old and new scorn revived.

The worst is that this hostile sentiment does not incarnate any clear and determinate proposition which intends, in any case, to put an end to the sorrowful state of affairs or to accept the final consequences, whatever they may be, of a condition with remedies. One examines things little, even less the remedies and even less the case of having to put an end to a coexistence deemed no longer neither useful nor pleasant. This open hostility would appear to flourish and spread itself in that part of the middle class which professes to care for and probably does, for the unity of Italy; and thus everything ends with the sigh of the unhappy lover: *Nec tecum vivere possum, nec sine te*, and in a fresh blossoming of anger and offence, fermented by rancours which are increasingly profound and increasingly sterile, or fecund only with evil.

It should be added that, for a false habit of mind, one considers by the same standards a part of a country which is so vast and distinguished by so many and so characteristic differences; and, as though this did not suffce, every individual is regarded as the immediate and complete incarnation of that presumed regional type, which would be, in any case, the result of a long process of formation and would constitute an abstraction, realised and reflected only fragmentarily in real and true persons and in specific ambits.

It is a sort of Italian anti-Semitism, of which in turn Italians of the south and Italians of the north feel then the injustice and damage, when as a result of the same methods they see abroad the typical Italian summarised in the forms and nature of the traditional bandit and every Italian, whatever he is like, saddled with that characteristic.

At this juncture, it is more necessary then ever to look at the situation without reticence and without feigning to see how much it is justified and how much exaggerated and where are the causes of the real ills and sentiments which concur and if and what way out of this state of affairs might offer.

Under the unitary regime, the Mezzogiorno, which is a large part of Italy, can exercise and exercises quite a significant action on the entire life of the nation, such that no other region can be indifferent to what concerns it, and, in such a weft of interests, in so much communion of institutions and representations, the interest of the Mezzogiorno is that of Italy.

Several years ago, I had occasion to write about a region of the Italian Mezzogiorno; and, deploring the ills it had in common with many others of the Mezzogiorno, it treated it with the bittemess with which one speaks of a stray brother. I have had frequent occasion to reflect on the argument; and, as my experience of the towns of Italy and of some social concerns has increased, and I have understood the causes of many things, I looked at the conditions of the Mezzogiorno with a sense of pain more than indignation, and I believe it not only interesting from the theoretical point of view, but also, and above all, a civil duty, to say that which I believe is true and just.

Perhaps it will be worthwhile it be spoken about particularly by he who can escape the prejudice and charge of regionalism for the frankness used in denouncing the ills of his own region, for the possibility of being able to live alternately both this and that side of the Tronto, participating also in the political life of the more advanced northern towns and, still more, advocates an order of ideas which co-ordinates, rather than subordinates, the regional and national interests and phenomena to universal interests and phenomena.

2.2 First of all one should note that he who wishes to confine the most recent degeneration of Italian public and social life, particularly in its last phases, to the Mezzogiorno, and wishes only to trace the causes in it is committing a grave error.

A mere cursory look at the latest events more than suffices to reveal the fallaciousness of such a manner of viewing things.

Starting with electoral corruption, the elections of Fossano, Nizza Monferrato, Pietrasanta, Gavirate Luino — not to mention others where corruption was not officially declared — have shown and show how electoral corruption, in its most immediate and open form of buying votes for cash, flourishes and prospers in northern Italy much more than in the Mezzogiorno.

Irony would have it that at the head of Banca Romana, the typical phenomenon of its kind, there was a Ligurian and that the management of Banco di Napoli gave some of its worst fruits in the lands of Lombardy and Emilia, and that the trials of Como and Bologna represent not the moral unity, but the immoral unity of Italy.

And when in a profound crisis of Italian life engendered by the most intimate causes, the traditional political parties broke up and dissolved into groups and fractions which joined forces in groups bound together only by political and personal opportunity; when, in the most perspicacious form, our entire political life appeared no longer as a struggle of general interests reflected in ideas and sentiments, but as a no-longer dissimulated game of specific and private interests, and of that new phase of life one wished to see not the index and the instrument, but the author in a man; a city midway between Piedmont and Lombardy gave the man who was the representative and centre of this initial period of chaos; and, while the ancient moderate political cliques went to him with the olive branch as a crowd, a southern moderate, Silvio Spaventa, withdrew with a contemptuous rebuke.

Then came another period, whose responsibilities and errors — incredible responsibilities and errors, did not succeed in cancelling those of the past from the Italians' memory; a period in which lie spoke from the government benches without the mitigation of passion and without care to feign, and corruption, a cynical fact, appeared to spread quite tranquilly, inexorably, like a gangrene which advances; and, this time too, the irony of fate had it that this period and this system of govemment took the name and direction of a politician from Piedmont.

But when Crispi came to administer and crown these systems of government which had been made more diffuse by the pressure of time and made more sadly active by the nature of man, it was sought to localise this arrangement, which had found impetus and consensus in so many parts of Italy, in a single region. And when the baptism of the purification wrongly asked of the Palermo voters came, — no matter how it came, it came — there was no stemming the complaints.

And yet it was forgotten that Crispi had been for the Mezzogiorno that which journalists call a return horse; greeted and cherished perhaps only after from on high he had been proclaimed the country's sole statesman and saviour. It was forgotten that he had been supported and upheld by many representatives of northern Italy in the most baleful part of his work — much sadder in the eyes of humanity and history than the fraud at Bologna and the afore-mentioned market of votes — in the bloody repressions of Sicily, in the violations of freedom, in the African policy. Finally, it was forgotten that not only in the Mezzogiorno, and perhaps more in the north than in the south, had Crispi found the bankers to subsidise him, the pens to laud him, the tongues to extol him, the votes to incite him; and it was forgotten for what common amenabiiity, for what hidden thought of distant solidarities and of inevitable complicities Crispi had eluded the judges with a half term which simultaneously offended both the law and the accused, and spurred him to attempt a come back.

Hence our political corruption is no more a southern ill than it is a northern ill, and it is not in it that one should seek the true distinctive character of the opposite parts of Italy; this is not to say that there are differences and there are many of them, and such that they put the Mezzogiorno in a condition of evident inferiority. Whatever the potential habits of one and the other part of Italy are or may be, he who looks at the statistics and principal indices of social life — and the atlas of the anthropological profile of Italy just published by Pulle facilitates its verification with its graphical representation — immediately sees the imbalance which exists between the towns of the Po plain, particularly, on one hand, and most of central Italy and the Mezzogiorno on the other, in the level of culture, in the figures for crime, in the level of economic affluence. Faced with these manifestations of a life of a higher order, such as is lived particularly in the principal centres of the Po plain, one notes in the Mezzogiorno manifestations of a backward social life and a state of persistent and diffuse hardship which is found under many material and moral aspects: in the rooted illiteracy, in a broad and primordial current of emigration, in the litigious spirit which spawns civil-law suits, in the lack of restraints and in impulsive spurs which develop certain forms of crime, in the lack of a true collective intellectual life and, in general, in the absence or in the poverty of all those manifestations of collective life which testify to a people's progress.

Now, although this diversity of social characteristics is confirmed by some anthropological characteristics, the hurried tendency to explain and generalise has easily led more than one to espy in a diversity of race the true and permanent cause of the different degree and diverse forms of social life.

I shall not concern myself here with ascertaining whether and to what extent the forms and degree of social life depend on ethnic diversity, particularly when history shows us that the peoples have mixed and how civilisation has proceeded, promoted by peoples of different race, who has handed it down as a heritage to which each has made his own contribution.

I shall not even inquire whether it has been proved that each and every diversity of anthropological characters corresponds to a diversity of moral character and social life.

These are questions of a general order which could not be easily discussed here even by he who feels the capacity and desire.

Colajanni has now summarised and quite lively discussed the question in a brochure of his on *La razza maledetta* which, even for those who do not wish to further their studies and investigations, can give an idea of the many difficulties faced by the anthropological interpretation of history[16].

In any case, those who believe in an incurable degeneration of the race can only, for love of logic and humanity, preach a war of extermination; which is something I am unable to resign myself to on the basis of quite dubious theories.

Since, to show the fallaciousness of the latter, the study which substitutes them is even more important than the criticism which demolishes them, it is perhaps worthwhile to see whether the specific conditions of the north and the south of Italy do not yield a less precarious and more plausible explanation of the causes which history has matured and which history can render inactive and correct.

---

[16] In *In Sicilia. Gli avvenimenti e le cause*, Roma 1894 (p. 32 ff.) and in other preceding publications (*La delinquenza della Sicilia e le sue cause* of 1885), Colajanni had fought the anthropological point of view and indicated the importance of the sociological factors of southern life; subsequent events have confirmed the conclusions of his honest study of the facts and his acute spirit of observation.

2.3 Anyone who has glanced at the map of Italy, first sees it as a flat, open country, furrowed by great rivers in the north, which gradually lengthens and narrows; the Apennines, which follow the country's extension, increasingly branch out into mountain ranges and spurs, which particularly on the western side, make the mountainside narrow, the slopes craggy, the region rugged and with frequent gorges and valleys which are difficult to cross.

Following this different oro-hydrographic configuration of the landscape, the inhabited centres, more or less populous, which abound in northern Italy, become increasingly rare as one proceeds toward the Mezzogiorno, where the village (*borgo*) characterises the aggregations of the population and gives its mark to the larger aggregates, even when they bear the name and qualities of the city.

The formation of the city was fostered and encouraged in the north by the facility of communication, by the fertility of the land, which had already maintained and kept flourishing the Roman colonies, while elsewhere, the lack of a middle class led to latifundism, languor and desolation. As the centre of gravity of the civil world gradually shifted from the Mediterranean to the Adriatic, northern Italy found itself on the new, important trade routes; and, situated as it was at the passes of the peninsula and an intermediary between Italy and the foreign countries, it monopolised the trade, it assimilated some industries and rose to increasingly great fortunes despite the wars of which it was a frequent theatre and contended prey.

Milan, the largest and most flourishing inhabited centre of northern Italy and basically a modern city, flourished with the collapse of the Roman Empire and with the propagation of civilisation in the west and north of Europe.

Now intensive farming, made possible not only by irrigation but also by the proximity of densely-populated cities, flourishing trade, the industries fostered also by an outlet such as the port of Genoa, the relative proximity of the coal regions: all these factors created an environment of economic prosperity. The inhabited centres which were the stimulus of this, were, by way of reaction, extended in turn, and gave rise to better realised forms of political and moral life.

The clash of interests which in the village creates the factions and degenerates into personal strife, here took on proportions such as to find a theoreticai reflection in opposing directions of ideas and action and determined the formation of political parties true and proper. A true middle class, which arose from trade and industry and necessarily more enlightened by virtue of its broader and more varied field of experience, arose with the tendency to rid itself of constraints and fetters, often supported by a more advanced proletariat which in turn would have then acquired reasons of autonomous political life, thus making the already liberal middle class into a conservative party, but by dint of things albeit within certain limits, less averse to reform.

The school, which in solely agricultural areas is a luxury and a reflected need, was instead in northern Italy a felt need, destined to exercise a function of practical and immediate utility.

The habits and customs of reading, the force of the political contexts were then propitious terrain for literary production, particularly journalism, which arose there more vital than elsewhere; and the newspaper and the existence of the political party were an element of control and a brake on arrogance, exorbitance and public and private misdeeds.

Naturally, this more developed social life did not lack pathological manifestations which were inherent to it. The association of petty pickpockets of other countries here took the form of associations of smugglers; the small cliques of petty swindlers here took the form of the black gang, which served disasters to the nation and was ready to speculate from them. Blind impulse and violent aggression, where the need demanded and opportunity suggested, were replaced by pondered perfidiousness and the armoured prudence of hypocrisy; and criminality, more limited in number, appeared to compete with the more frequent of other countries in greed, in the quality of the criminal motive. But in any case there disappeared that fastidious bramble of crimes to which hardship gives rise, encourages and feeds; and, with the possibility of a higher standard of living, with the assured expansion of normal energies, every disruption of the social order by crimes consumed in the legal orbit up to the mob and villains appeared as an exception and almost like a shadow destined to better emphasize the luminous part of the picture.

That the diversity of moral life was due, in the meantime, to the different material conditions of life, is better proven by the fact, that in northern Italy itself, when the former changed, so did the latter. In Lombardy itself, much of the countryside obtained, from the political point of view, the name Lombard Vandea. The less accessible and poorer regions of Veneto have, from many aspects, i.e., from the point of view of emigration and criminality, similar characteristics to those of the Mezzogiorno.

2.4 The Mezzogiorno has wholly different characteristics. Not irrigated and largely not irrigable, intercepted by the new centre of gravity of the civil world, the Mezzogiorno has little developed intensive farming, trade is scarce and industrial development even less so. And — cause and effect simultaneously of these conditions — lacks big inhabited centres. The few which did come into being, disproportionate and excessive as hydropic excrescences rather than as organs of normal functions, rather than laboratories of production, were the shelter and playground of parasites, attracted by the pleasant aspect of the places and by the ostentation of the courts; braided rabble for the most part, around which there grew and multiplied a ragged and more numerous rabble of minor parasites.

It was parasitism elevated to a system: he who, such as the feudatory and the absent landowner lived from the rent produced and reproduced automatically by distant lands; who lived with their luxury and off their luxury, who off their corruption; and almost the sole and better understood industry, and that more in fashion, was the foreigner, and, above all, the province, the full breast from which from all, either directly or indirectly, sought to suck. Hence not aristocracy emulous of the royal power, but courtesan and eager to dominate by serving; not the industrial middle class, but pettifoggers, secondhand dealers, go-betweens of every degree and measure; not people, but rabble; no contrast of living forces which would lead to an intellectual and moral elevation; no open resistance, but divergent adaptation; and from all this degenerative process there emerged, naturally, as a poisoned flower, the camorra or the mafia, crime and reprisal, emulous and avenger of every other parasitism.

Such cities, which in actual fact can be defined from the qualitative point of view as gigantic villages, often separated from the rest of the country by the impervious nature of the places, were even farther separated from the various ways of life, from the deaf rancour and the reciprocal contempt there exists between the parasite and who he lives off, by the town's arrogance and the rustic clumsiness. They only kept in contact with the provinces to feed off them. They gave rise to no innovative current; at the most, at times, a whiff of corruption; and the provinces, over which it appeared the assiduous work of centuries had passed in vain, lived a rudimentary and unchanging economic and moral life, conserving the village and the latifund, which was now halfway between scant pasturage and small-scale farming, as characteristic traits of their productive and civil life.

How much breath has been wasted in the ingenuous faith that the latifund could be transformed and broken up with good words, said or written, perhaps in the form of laws! And how it has persisted unperturbed against these assaults of the wind and how it has continued to expand with its drowsy manner of one who yawns and stretches out!

Nitzsch, the historian of the Gracchis, saw it arise, when the Romans had completed their conquest of Italy and succeeded in alternating mountain pastures with those of the plains, transhumance found the conditions for its growth and replaced the growing of cereals which were now supplied by ever growing imports. Under this stimulus, the latifund grew, propagated itself, extended on the ruins and to the detriment of the middle class, stamping its mark and its countenance on the agricultural economy. The feudal age accepted it, conserved it, immobilised it in the form of feud and fidei-commissum; and when the feud and fide-commissum disappeared from the political and legal order, the latifund persisted, maintained and favoured by the very economic environment of the country.

That type of sheep-farming, which did not have the irrigated Lombard plains at its disposal and, given the lack of chemical fertilisers, reintegrated the fertility of the lands used for crops, required a latifund which extended as far as the eye could see on the often malarial plain and on the mountains covered with woods.

Every now and then, the city started to merge, like a crucible, the heritage of some absentee wealthy person, but here again the heritage changed name and owner rather than size and nature; and, in general, the family, still constituted on a patriarchal basis, rigidly conserved the ancestral heritage with celibacy imposed on the younger sons which lead to an accepted and habitual common law marriage, with the absorption now occasional, now overbearing of every field which served to round it up and extend it. The non-profit corporations, the mortmain concentrated and extended it on the other hand; and, when the assets of the church estate were sold, they usually served to extend the latifunds or to create new ones.

Generally, will and capacity were lacking to change farming from intensive to extensive, more often the utility and impulse.

As noted, sheep-farming was common and was a traditional, easy and flourishing enterprise.

The low price of labour excluded the use of machinery, even there where nature made such possible. The lack of any outlet, except for the limited local market, made it impossible to sell intensively farmed products; and the prices of cereal production, regulated by the small market closed to foreign imports, were remunerative in years of both good and bad harvests.

Where these impediments did not exist — as around Naples, in Salerno, in Campania, where the soil and the market conditions favoured intensive farming — the land was broken up and farming became more intensive. Not so elsewhere, except perhaps in the zones immediately adjacent to the inhabited centre.

The attempt to create or reconstitute a class of small landowners with the division of the state owned land was completely aborted; and perhaps not only as a result of the methods employed by way of implementation.

Then, when sheep-farming, made difficult by the spread of banditry, threatened and eliminated by foreign competition, disappeared or almost so, and the open roads and the very consequent new conditions of the cereal market engendered the impulse to transform the crop, it was too late; the capital which had for so long been hoarded, now dissipated or invested to buy other land, was no longer, and time pressed, maturing ruins at every moment, and the water rose without any way of escape in sight.

The small tenant, as a surrogate of the ancient serf and, on a level with him, characteristic of countries and periods poor in capital, increasingly became if not the sole, the most diffuse means of farming; until, himself threatened by the competition of foreign cereals, he too exhausted himself, and the peasants were forced to emigrate, far away, across the ocean, to seek escape and subsistence.

Sharecropping, preached and instilled as a means of salvation — as though the forms of agricultural contracts could be imported at one's pleasure and not germinated by the very conditions and concrete ways of production — put an appearance in now and then; and retreated rather than advanced, spurned and hindered by the poverty of the sharecropper, by the lack of that intensive farming which provides the sharecropper with a continuous employment of work and the restoration of the returns; which is what takes place in Tuscany and maintains and spreads that type of contract.

Thus the latifunds not only persisted but became sadder, more desolate; deserted even by those animals which browsed on it, by those human animals who rasped it. Like an unpleasant scab they grew and on them the nettles and thistles spread, and the monster, dull as an idiot, inert as a paralytic, basks in the sun waiting for something which releases it and lets it become green again and reflower with crops, vegetables and plants!

And between one latifund and another, as though interrupting the solemn sadness and testifying to the presence of man, some village perched on a crest, closed in a gorge, and one distant from the other, often one hidden by the other. Separated by rivers and torrents long deprived of bridges and frequently uncrossable because of the frequent spates, these villages often have lived wholly extraneous from one another, almost without being able to understand one another, at but a few miles distance, with their different dialects, often also in natural and moral conditions. Here amidst the orange groves, in an inlet of the sea, and there among the chestnut and beech trees, confined for several months of the year by the snows, with the inhabitants of a place dulled by malaria, in another made bold and ready for the mountainous air and with some glimmer of civil life; here jealous of their women with a jealousy of Moors, there haggling the *jus primae noctis* to make the layette for the offspring; an infinity of types, here Saracens, there Greek and Albanian colonists, there vigorous and Junoesque, there disfigured by progressive degeneration.

He who espies these human remains from the quickly fleeing train or from the slowly crossed valleys immediately understands the importance of these solutions of continuity of the social aggregate; how, entering in one of those villages, one senses their political and moral life, if it can be called such.

Around the houses or the houses of the important people of the place there gather the hovels and more than once one could say the dens of the poor, crossing the alleys which often turn out to be twisting mazes, which the long and stagnant rains turn into mud for many months of the year.

Probably those peasants used those hovels as their first shelter when the village first came into being; then the village grew and they stayed, detained by the little security of the countryside, by malaria, by the interest of the owners of those hovels, by the little expediency or impossibility of building farmhouses, by the impossibility of providing for the necessities of life in the desert of the latifund, by the habits of which those rough creatures are slaves; they have remained, to their curse and that of hygiene, dwellers of neither the town nor the countryside, deprived of all the benefits of country and town life and saddled with all the drawbacks of one and the other.

Meanwhile those few houses, sometimes yearning of palaces, which tower above that mass of hovels, the image and reflection of the latifund which flaunts itself to the outside world, clearly indicate that feudalism has disappeared in name more than anything else. This is indicated even more clearly sometimes by the glimpse of a castle, half ruined but still inhabited by the steward or restored by the middle class which has taken the place of the feudatory.

And the feudal usages and abuses persist, naturally transformed and remodelled differently, as the new environment has desired.

The new feudatory is called the mayor, his court is called the town council, and his men are called councillors, country wardens and so forth. The lower court judge has for the modern Don Rodrigo the same respect Dr. Azzeccarbugli had for the old one; the local capital has a Count Uncle, and there is another at Rome; state property is usurped as before, marriages are arranged as before, others go wrong: everything precisely as it was before.

But to tell the truth there is something different.

Quite often, there are several new feudatories and, as they do not always succeed in agreeing, the town, the village, the hamlet and the countryside become the theatre for their rivalries, which remain traditional in the families and employ for their struggle all weapons, often excluding none. As a rule, the member of Parliament is the emanation of these petty disputes, for which he serves as an instrument and which serve as an instrument for him, and which he speculates and exploits.

The overwhelming mass, slave of need, slave of ignorance, has no say; and if part of it has the right to vote, its role is that of the pawns in the hands of a chess player, who uses them and discards them as he sees best in order to achieve a checkmate.

The exercise of the right to vote is, usually, for those common people, another sort of service, which they render to the houses of those on whom they depend, directly or indirectly; and it is they who end up paying for the ups and downs of the game. They lose the state lands, they pay taxes, but this would appear to now be part of the normal order of things. And yet, from time to time, their patience runs out; they rise up somehow, they rebel, they attempt to set fire to the town hall, until the tumult exhausts itself in its own improvised letting off of steam; and the hottest heads go to prison or to forced exile and the others return to crouch down with the feeble and distant whimpering of a beaten dog who obeys his master once again.

In this environment, with these elements and on this field of action, it is naturally not the case to speak of political parties and of great currents of ideas.

The big and common interests are too fragmented and overwhelmed by the town, local and individual interests for them to appear and operate in such a manner as to constitute the base of strong aggregates intent on ensuring they count.

There is no terrain for this activity, just as there is none for any other form of collective, intellectual and moral life.

Hence the Mezzogiorno is the land of the solitary; and its big intellectual manifestations have been and are personal, intermittent, in contrast with the present and with the environment, and prophetic of the future.

The newspaper is starting to penetrate there, but does not spread; one can say that the book does not penetrate there at all.

The school does not arise there spontaneously, as in a more advanced industrial country, where it satisfies an urgent need and an immediate utility; but it enters there imported as a reflected need; and, in this its first stage, if it has a result, in addition to the purely technical one, naturally, it can serve only to instil in the conscience a seed of uneasiness, to recall, compared with other horizons, the misery of one's own state to who is depressed. This same imbalance is an inevitable fact and is a lever to the movement of progress and redemption, such that he who does not assess the far-reaching consequences or allows himself to be concerned more by the closer and more personal consequences, views the school with a sense of ill-concealed disapproval.

Religious faith, on whose efficiency — degraded as it is to superstition and formal practice of worship — one harbours many doubts, is also lacking, imperceptibly but continuously eroded by the fatal work of time, and there is not even, as in the north, a clerical party which, with promises and occasions of immediate profit, seeks to hold up on it at least the external apparatus, the base of the church hierarchy and the interests to which it is related and participant. That fragmentation of the social aggregate into numerous small closed groups, that age-old particularism have shattered or weakened also the church hierarchy, and the church ministry has become a sort of revival of the priests who, indulging in all the stimuli and tendencies of their human nature, wholly conform themselves to the environment and become incoercible by discipline and rebellious to the bishop's authority.

The ancient simplicity of usages, the country life, which so many times absorbed the landowner's time with the needs of a more complex agricultural economy and created for him an environment of relative affluence, often gave rise to truly patriarchal systems of life and characters of probity which were indeed rural, but also solid and limpid, of which, to tell the truth, traces can still be found. But when, for so many of the reasons mentioned above and which will be mentioned below, those forms of agrarian and pastoral economy declined and disappeared, the owner became the true parasite, who remained only to see the harvest grow from afar and who, under the action of idleness and the impetus of new needs, dissipated along with his wealth, already compromised by the new economic environment, also the good name and traditional rectitude of his family. Then taking to drink, siring a bastard child, exercising all the deleterious action a dissolute and idle life can have in an environment enfeebled by poverty and subjection: this is what the life of the gentleman of the village, as he is continued to be called with an unconscious irony of language, often comes to.

The narrow circle of the village only multiplies the nasty effects of this state of things with the sad virtue of the examples, the frequency of the contagions, the grudges which agitate and maintain and which corrupt the character.

Some forms of criminality are due, perhaps mainly so, to the type of life determined by that narrowness of environment. Closed in the small town as in a trap, with that discomfort that is the ferment of contrasts and the forced idleness which augments them, from those continuous and inevitable meetings there arise insurmountable aversions, suggestions of hatred which seethe and rage and the only remedy to that compulsory and intolerable cohabitation lies in violent elimination, in crimes of blood. Where then, as is the case there, the law is often a hollow word or else bends under all the interferences, individual violence is easily confused with self-esteem and becomes a normal means of protection. It is the Selbst-Hulf, private justice which persists or rises again.

Banditry was a way of escaping punishment for he who had thus put himself outside the law and, also, a way of continuing the struggle, discharging the rancour accumulated for years in the heart, opposing all of society as power to power, between a matter of generosity and baseness, of heroic deeds and cruelty, suited to enable one to conceive of a soul's entire abyss.

The very narrowness of the intellectual and moral horizons and the rudimental state of their experiences, means that all the facts of life are conceived in backward forms. Glory appears still to them as arrogance; the good outcome a legitimation; political life a mere reflection and an immediate extension of private relations. The mad violence of a politician is for them energy, and, if necessary, heroic virtue. National prosperity is not conceived — and cannot be conceived by them — as a normal development of fertile energy, but, as a great raid, like that of the Romans, or like the fortunate discovery of mines, which is for the country that which the lottery jackpot is for each of them. Hence certain enthusiasms, fatuous moreover, for undertakings such as those of Africa and for their sad architects.

2.5 These two Italys, as they have been and are called, have been welded together rather than merged by unity.

And unity has had different precedents, different meanings and different effects for one and the other.

For northern Italy unity meant a more vigorous and compact nucleus of forces suited to resist foreign powers which pressed from both sides of the Alps; it meant independence and the necessary premise for a considerable commercial and industrial development, necessarily rendered difficult and suffocated by the shackles of foreign domination and little promising in the closed confines of a single autonomous region, or of a province open to the competition of the more industrially advanced regions. The great ideal of independence, germinated by centuries-old sufferances and struggles against foreign theft, as index and standard of all antagonisms, was fed, now consciously, now unconsciously, by these needs and hopes, and became an increasingly common and overbearing movement which succeeded in defeating and dominating the federalist and republican tendencies.

In the Italy of the Mezzogiorno on the other hand, the aspiration and the movement for unity progressed slowly and uncertainly, until the Bourbon principality appeared as an insurmountable obstacle to the introduction of those freedoms and civil reforms which responded to a reflected, but deeply felt need, of the middle class which had arisen alongside decadent feudality and risen even higher on the latter's ruins.

The effects were equal to the different intensity of the desires and different hopes.

I am not the first to say that the unity of Italy did not turn out to the benefit of the southern part.

In its best period, the Bourbon principality had sought to introduce and acclimatise in the kingdom some industry; it was one of the first, if not actually the first, to build short sections of railway whose extension was then prevented by dynastic reasons.

These industries died immediately or lived a difficult life under the competition from northern Italy, whose easier supplies of raw materials, better road network, and more strategic position vis-à-vis the port of Genoa and the great trade routes were invincible elements in its victory; and it also enjoyed the proximity of the industrially more advanced states, assimilating their progresses and defending itself from their competition with a protectionist barrier imposed to all the rest of Italy.

United Italy became the great market of its industrial region; and Milan particularly, which was its emporium, saw its population double and accumulated in itself the energies from every part of Italy.

Those who speak of a 'state of Milan' to juxtapose it to the rest of Italy, if they assume as their starting point the conditions found in the city and the region, fall, without realising it, into the error of supposing — separating two indissoluble terms — that Milan would have become what it was without the unification of Italy.

What on the other hand were the effects of the unification of Italy for the Mezzogiorno?

First of all the development of military force, always increasing, and the bigger the worse supplied.

The extreme southern strip was not joined to the rest of Italy before 1881.

The tax contingent is not proportionate to the country's wealth.

In the Kingdom of the Two Sicilies, as is the case in countries whose economies are still rudimental, the tendency to accumulation had taken the form of hoarding, and was considerable in size.

Now, under the regime of united Italy, the increasing taxes, the sale of church assets, the growth of the public debt brought about in the Mezzogiorno a veritable draining of capital; such that that part of Italy, least suited to restore its capital, found itself deprived of it precisely when it needed it most.

Instead, the more the capitalistic economy developed in the North through the growth of industry and trade, the more there increased the desire and need for new employment and investment.

If this investment had been made, compatible with the conditions of the Mezzogiorno, in the form of industrial and agricultural investment, it would have benefited from said. But these investments, even where they were possible or forthcoming, promised more distant and more modest profits. Speculation advanced in the Mezzogiorno in the most plundering and sterile forms for that region; in the form of bank and contract speculation.

Public debt, offering an easily convertible investment, safe, advantageous particularly in long and frequent periods of depreciated currency, had ended up attracting capital which was surplus to the Mezzogiorno, neither contended by any industrial development; and it had been definitively lost to agriculture, where the investment would have been in any case less remunerative and above all more uncertain.

Thus, when the vicissitudes of European wine production engendered a transformation of farming in the Mezzogiorno, particularly a diffusion of vineyards and tree crops, there was a lack of capital and it appeared appropriate the banks should supply it, taking advantage of the opportunity to extend their own activities. In truth, this was not the task of banks of issue, it could have been realised merely by a rationally constituted land or agricultural credit. What is beyond dispute is not only that the occasion was taken, but that the occasion was used as a pretext for organising a bank speculation based on a vacuum and which assumed the form of a true and colossal fraud. Credit was granted with a hitherto unheard of largesse and was principally granted to those who owned nothing and the captains of industry, who, acting as heir apparents, should have caught, as was indeed the case, as many rash and badly advised persons as let themselves be attracted by the bait.

If the shareholders of the banks of issue, which often, thanks to illegal circulation, gambled without risking the stakes, were damaged, it is no concern of ours to examine it here. What is certain is that that bank carnival, as it was correctly called, gave rise in the country to a long and painful Lent, whose end is awaited in vain. That mob of few speculators brought about the complete ruin of the Mezzogiorno's economy. The enormous credit vanished without having realised anything worthwhile and left behind it all the land property encumbered with an exorbitant mortgage debt paralysed in the present and compromised for a long future. Any hope of reproducing a rational form of credit and reviving the agricultural economy, by transforming it and intensifying its crops, was lost, perhaps for ever, and uncertainty, more than of tomorrow, of today, in those owners who had become precarious owners of land, compounded their previous sad condition.

The moral counterblow was the most visible and prouder than ever.

The mirage of deceptive wealth created by that fictitious circulation gave rise to dissipation and luxury, corrupting all that remained of the simplicity of the old way of life. The sudden collapse undermined any good faith, evoked every kind of expedient and profoundly perturbed public and private life.

Anyone who has lived in the Mezzogiorno in the last twenty years will have seen pass before his eyes, in a very short period of time, two distinct eras, marked by different ways of life and morals.

A truly historical experience!

As in a shipwreck, the instinct of one's conservation led to the resuscitation of egoism in all its power and armed it with all its weapons.

At the same time the empire of money arose and loomed as never before, and a crushing slavery, as perhaps had not been seen even under the tyranny of the Bourbons[17] weighed down on that mass of debtors, suspended between life and death and reduced as the mouse between the claws of the cat who plays with it before deciding to devour it.

Political life was naturally also polluted and, rather than make a step toward the formation of parties inspired by general criteria and interests, several steps back were taken.

In other times, in periods when the right to vote was limited, the bourgeoisie, independent in their home as in a fortress, had elected, in an outburst of protest and opposition, persons such as Saff, De Boni, Campanella, in spite of prefects and ministers. Now they voted as the director of the bank wished, or as the government wished said wished.

A popular, educated and organised class could have stemmed and corrected this political degeneration; but the entire direction of domestic politics of the new Italy, narrow and suspicious, as a result of a vicious circle made possible by the very condition of the masses, was always aimed at preventing any form of organisation and every step with which the popular classes of the Mezzogiorno started to participate in some manner in the civil life of their country. It was said that one should only depend on that which resists; and here, having eliminated all the possible resistances, the abuses persist and spread ever more as a normal fact; and the people has become accustomed to live, alternatively, be-

---

[17] I should apologise once again to the Bourbons if, speaking of tyranny, I have employed their name as a term of comparison instead of another; but long habit has betrayed me; and then this paper, I repeat, predates certain other recent events.

tween everyday supine acquiescence and the rebellion attempted and cherished for the holiday.

The beneficiaries of the patronage diffused from the bottom to the top, and from the top to the bottom, in a closed circuit, constituted the base and aspect not only of political life, but of everyday life, cementing with stimuli and the constraint of interest, the power gained and with the exercise of the power the network of the shady interests. And the ministers of every part of Italy, reduced so often to living off expedient and petty artfulness, exploited this fount of factions and cliques to their advantage, being generous with obligingness, tolerances, support, interference in the function of the banks, in that of justice. Magistrates, publicly indicated as corrupt, were tolerated and, when necessary, rewarded; and one often hears recalled with a sense of nostalgia the Bourbon magistrates who, prone before the prince in matters of politics, showed their rectitude and impartiality — as was the interest also of the sovereign — in private matters.

All this explains better the fact that in the Mezzogiorno overall life is worse than its elements would lead one to suppose. Considered individually, the great majority are not bad, but lacking in civil education, lacking, because of the conditions of the environment and long-standing custom, of any force to resist; such that a few crafty persons, powerful or violent, easily manage to dominate under the form of mafia, specific to Sicily, of camorra, specific to Naples, of clique, extended to the rest of the Mezzogiorno and, one could say, of Italy; and succeed in moulding and directing social life.

Meanwhile, under the action of the forces of organised evil against the disorganised forces of good, chaos increases and spreads; and everything which is impure ferments like a sad leavening, and the wind sown generously hides beneath the ground to put forth in the form of storm.

2.6 And what do the astrologers say? This issue of the Mezzogiorno was for a certain time a favoured issue which has given credit of profundity to who has described, pruning, its such visible ills, and has given credit of courage to he who with the cheap abundance of hyperbole and epiphenomena has flaunted a pity and civil indignation which under that general form lead to nothing nor ever offended anyone.

But to study the issue in depth, to reach the root of the ill, this no!

There has been mild criticism of the Mezzogiorno's ruling classes, as though they had reached the deplorable state they have because of some fault of their own and not as a result of overbearing actions!

But throwing some of the cargo overboard sometimes saves the ship, while blaming men leaves things intact.

Then there came the question of the race, this too very generic and very distant which, competing with the explanation of the plague given by Don Ferrante, compromises nothing and nobody.

And as for the remedies, everything boiled down to some adjustment, or to the Sisyphean task of changing the effects of the unchanged causes; even if the eloquent speeches of the revealers of the scourges of southern Italy did not suffice, cautiously whispered to the ears of the middle class as one of the great men of the new Italy[18], with incredible ingenuousness, was very careful to warn.

Decentralisation is now fashionable, a generic and ambiguous word which can mean something and can also mean nothing.

If understood, as it is, in the form of simple administrative autonomy, under the same political organisation, which represses

[18] One of these great men, after the tumults in Sicily, and several times after, blamed the law on compulsory education, which is moreover so little compulsory in its application. I have always believed and believe that more than words — remote and pallid images of things — things have operative virtue. But, if anything is ever capable of arousing in a dull, incurious and largely illiterate people class hatred, this merit should be ascribed to the rhetorical outbursts — at times even official — of the type of the *Lettere meridionali* where, neglecting an investigation of the objective causes, men take the blame for much of what is that of things, and one preaches, with Jacobin conception, the wholly voluntary nature of facts and social reforms. I called the *Lettere meridionali* rhetorical outbursts, a convenient name for all the writings of the same type; and do not repent of this. The author, subsequently a member of Parliament, minister and senator, has never known, nor sought to do anything to eliminate or mitigate the ills deplored; that which, added to the others, is not a negligible argument to judge the sincerity or inanity of that and of other similar such works.

and discourages any resistance, decentralisation would lead to the reforging of the local political cliques and would be akin to the work of he who intervenes between the two parties to an argument to tie the arms of one and give the other an advantage to beat him. Even though central power often does not prevent or support the arrogance of local groups, it sometimes, to obey broader needs, for the moral responsibility with which it is publicly ascribed, for party affairs, is obliged to do something which helps restore the empire of the law. The bastard decentralisation in question would eliminate even this escape, without replacing it with anything equivalent.

I either delude or deceive myself to have not fully shown, but at least outlined the seriousness of the question of the state of the Mezzogiorno and the vast, enormous and complex causes which have led it to its present juncture.

The bourgeoisie of united Italy, less mature than that of other countries and which arrived later in power in a poorer country while the world markets were already occupied or strongly contended, has done that which unfortunately was to be feared in these conditions: more unprepared, more hurried and impatient to get rich, more pressed by foreign competition and reduced to having much fewer scruples, the more it had to live of expedient, it has not succeeded in attenuating some of the ills of the Mezzogiorno and it has often aggravated them. But it too has been that which has made history; and it is pointless rewriting the past on one's own behalf with the benefit of hindsight and believing that the Mezzogiorno could have been substantially different, given the substratum of its life.

I am not saying that something useful could not have been and could not be done, even with the pressure of time which makes it more difficult to implement, today, in a timely manner, some of those remedies, even if there was the way. There would be quite a lot to do; but it is vain to hope in a true and complete resolution of the question in our economic environment.

The Mezzogiorno, more than the rest of Italy, suffers, at the same time from the development of the capitalistic economy and the insufficiency of this development.

This has engendered its economic hardship and the consequent abnormal moral and political phenomena.

While a state of affairs which prevent a true industrial development continues and the capitalistic economy lasts, its essentially village life will conserve almost all the characteristics it currently has.

While the exercise of agriculture and the production of food remain entrusted to private initiative and benefit, the zone of uncultivated and desolate land will extend, as a result of the competition of more fertile countries with more capital to invest in the land.

This type of economic state will be flanked by an equivalent moral state.

The condition of the Mezzogiorno is that which the capitalistic economy imposes on the defeated in the struggle of competition.

Called to produce for consumption, it feeds and educates a strong issue of sons called to produce for speculation, necessarily regresses and succumbs.

Its destiny is therefore decided where the great struggle for socialism is fought, as even its very conditions prevent it from understanding it and co-operating.

Meanwhile, as is the case, its revenge lies in its very degenerative process, given the arrangement and mutual weft of world relations.

Put to compete against the strongest, what surprise is it if it does as all those who are slower and seeks a shortcut to reach the finishing post with the others or throw a stick between the legs of the emulators?

Its helots which spread through the world, like western Chinese, to compete with the other workers; the bad examples it offers, the sad instruments it furnishes to the forces of evil; these are its deaf, objective and inevitable reaction.

One can only demolish well that which is to be replaced.

Banditry has disappeared, where it has disappeared, not by virtue of the eloquent passages of literary men who have written, neither of the anthropologists who — a work which is undoubtedly useful from another aspect — have classified the craniums of its soldiers. It has disappeared because of the railways, which have made it difficult to exercise, and because of emigration, which offer criminals the escape once offered by the mountains and woods.

With the decline of the capitalistic era the degenerative characteristics of the Mezzogiorno will also disappear.

But, until such time, it will be a danger and a threat, just as the hovels where the poor irradiate the microbes of the epidemics which they maintain and feed are a threat to the city.

At times, crossing Italy, while the express train rushed between the gorges of the Apennines, I watched these last peaks which were still crowned with ancient flourishing woods; and, thinking of a fire which, from peak to peak, propagated along the ridge of the Apennines, pondered that it would be a child's flame compared with the great fire which secretly spreads and could burst from suppressed anger, from the brutalisation of those populations.

While I write, the echoes of the tumults provoked by the increase in the price of bread are like an antiphony.

But the beautiful moonlit bays of the quiet sea, the orange groves, the arid slopes which, almost by way of example and rebuke, are in some place being covered with olive trees, reconciled me to more upbeat forecasts; and said to me that nature cannot have made a paradise for men to make an inferno of it for ever.

Courage, brothers of the north and the south, leave your logomachies and regional rivalries to those who need to deceive themselves as to the real reasons of the evil to live off the fruits of the evil of all, making the different language or the different dialect or the different latitudes reasons for disagreement.

We have a great work to achieve together; we have to redeem ourselves, to oust privilege and injustice, its mother and its daughter, with peaceful and unremitting everyday work; we have to fight against the forces of evil.

It is a slow and laborious work of civilisation, which time, the corrector and dissuader of all violence and impatience, is called to achieve; and it is a blessing to watch it, even from afar, and it is useful to present it and to understand it to help it with an ordered, prudent, enlightened and civil cooperation.

To the Italians of the Mezzogiorno*

Ettore Ciccotti

1. - The title of this short paper which I add to the articles published in *Rivista Popolare*, now published in one pamphlet, will arouse the indignation of the bigots of unity. I employ this phrase because it is convenient and synthetic, but append no disparaging meaning; and I will be believed when I have said that the bigots of unity include Felice Cavallotti and Matteo Renato Imbriani; one dead and the other alive, for whom I nurture affection and admiration. I in no way include them among those miserable persons for whom the unity of Italy such as it is now, is and was a speculation and of which they speak and write knowing they lie, expressing sentiments which they will never harbour in their soul or are not part of it following the bitter lessons of experience.

Both in and outside Parliament I have experienced the anger of these fanatics of excessive unity, which has turned out to be a veritable bed of Procrustes for the single regions of the peninsula and for the bigger islands and which has yielded bitter fruit for all. I laughed and scorned when the abuse was hurled against me by the hypocrites; I was pained when it gushed out, spontaneous, sincere, generous from those who have a true cult for the motherland and who for it were or are ready to sacrifice everything: from their possessions to their life.

---

* From: Ciccotti E., «Mezzogiorno e settentrione d'Italia», in Colajanni N. (ed.), *Settentrionali e meridionali. Agli italiani del mezzogiorno*, vol. III, Milano-Palermo, Remo Sandron; Romes, Rivista Popolare, 1898, pp. 41-68. [Cod. JEL: N 33].

The strong regret caused me by disagreement on the means to achieve an intent common to all — the well-being and greatness of the nation — did not, however, for a moment distract me from achieving what for me represented a sacred duty. And for a man who is in public life and is so as a mere soldier, without ambitions and without aspirations to attain whenever and whatever, the first and principal duty I believed that of telling the truth. Disregarding the interests and sentiments and also the prejudices, which might have offended, disregarding the derision, the abuse and accusations which may have come from those offended.

I said the truth on the Banca Romana scandal, setting off against me all the silent anger which wished to protect the credit with deceit and false accounts; I said it portending, unheeded, the disorders of the Fasci in Sicily and causing the resentment of most dear friends, who did not have an exact conception of the reality; I said it praising those who, such as Sonnino, expounded the truth of the conditions of our budget, attracting reproaches from dear colleagues who judged my conduct parliamentarily impolitic, I said it warning friends and adversaries that we should pay more attention to the unwholesome conditions of the country which remains, rather than to Crispi, who passes; and I repeated it announcing that at a given hour we would have seen appear at the gates of the cities of the Mezzogiorno the hordes of Cardinal Ruffo. And one can image what recriminations and protests were aroused by words which were judged inspired by a gloomy pessimism, which led to the painting of the new Italy in sombre colours, thus slandering it. And what if I were to say that my temperament is fundamentally optimistic. In any case, the warnings, to my great regret, will not belie me: never.

I received the biggest and most felt reprobations precisely when without euphemisms and feigning I insisted on the regional contrasts and on the damage which derived from the present centralisation and on the dangers which said posed — for wanting it when nature and history did not allow it — to the unity, which was, or so was claimed, uppermost in everybody's thoughts. Since my first speech in the Lower House in January 1891 — I have not failed to state what I am and remain, what I professed myself in my speeches so as not to steal votes, hiding and disguising myself under false pretences, namely: a convinced disciple of Cattaneo and of Ferrari, of Rosa and of Mario, and even then causing a stir and protests, I stated that the agricultural Mezzogiorno had been sacrificed to the industrial north. Barely a year after this first speech, discussing the trade treaties with Austria and Germany, I forced Hon. Ellena, who was reporting on said, to admit that I was largely in the right. The reply to the stir and protests of the northerners came therefore from he who could give so on great authority — from the manipulator of the general tariffs of 1887 — procuring me indescribable satisfaction. As I had several other occasions to illustrate my thought; and more than my thought I expounded facts from which one should have learnt that the path followed to date is wrong. I did this dealing with: the set-up of the army, which had been retained as national and not regional, and is the cause of economic and military weakness; the institution of the Royal Civil Commission for Sicily; the national holiday of 20 September; the bringing forward of the holiday of the Statuto to celebrate its jubilee in 1889, etc. And I insisted on this point: the Italians are different among themselves, more than the French and Germans are — even though they maintain a federal arrangement —; and being different cannot live well and develop quickly under the present colossal unity. My parliamentary speeches were flanked by the propaganda in the *Rivista popolare*, where among other things, once examining the great equivocation — the unity of Italy — I concluded thus: «The Italians differed by anthropology, interests, culture, morals, tendencies, industrial development, traditions and one wishes to unite them under a rigidly unitary regime. Necessarily disquiet did not take long to rear its head and today everyone complains of the unity, to which they also ascribe consequences which are not its ... In any case, today, perhaps we cannot undo what has been done, but the temperaments assert themselves and if we wish to save Italy we should concern ourselves with unitary decentralisation and not make it, as it is, synonym of harmful uniformity; if we wish to save the union of the Italian forces we will have to give up a lot and embrace the federal idea» (year 3, n. 14). Was this discovery of the great diversity between the Italians of the various regions mine? Not in the least. In the conclusions of his *Inchiesta agraria*, Iacini noted that in Italy there was a broad range of crops caused by the variety of the natural conditions as one could observe travelling south from Norway to Andalusia; Aristide Gabelli stated that the anthropological differences were more marked between the Piedmontese and Sicilians than between the Italians and Scandinavians; General Marselli, finally, found that two civilisations lived simultaneously in Italy: the military and the industrial tradition; and that in the Mezzogiorno there persists the monarchical tradition, which is lacking in northern Italy. Marselli took heart in this, espying in this tradition a guarantee for the Savoia Royal House ; but he should have borne in mind that the maliciously minded could find a causal nexus between the centuries-old monarchical tradition and the present social conditions of the Mezzogiorno! The pernicious consequences of an order contrary to nature and history have been clear and obvious: the disquiet, engendered not only by economic reasons but also by centralisation, has continued to increase and taken the form of aversion to unity. Such that maintaining the rigid unity and stemming the spread of the loathed regionalism succeeded only in mitigating rather than augmenting the support for unity. The bigots of unity, whether or not they are in the government, have never realised the existence this vicious circle.

And this was no small responsibility of their part.

Such things said with firm conviction but with little authority by me alone should not have produced any considerable effect among politicians who are not in great favour of experimentalism in politics. But certain statements, which came from persons above suspicion for their love of a single Italy, should have induced meditation.

Meanwhile, the men who saw things right, as the signs of the profound and general disquiet augmented and became all the more evident, increased in number and value.

Firstly, I am pleased to cite Ruggero Bonghi, who in writing with impartial and noble synthesis of the silver anniversary of the marriage of Rome with Italy, dejectedly confessed that instead of increasing, the sentiment for unity after the nation had acquired its historical capital diminished significantly. He confessed the fact, but did not investigate the precise reason: the excess of unity.

The increased awareness of the disquiet regarding unity is due to the establishment and action of the regional committees of Lombardy, Piedmont and Veneto for decentralisation. These committees' members included fanatical monarchists of all gradations — from the most rigid conservatives to the most advanced democrats. Alongside and complementing the propaganda of these men of order a parallel movement — among the so-called subversives — started to take shape in another field: among the fanatical socialists of the German mould, who always want the rigorous singleness of method and tactics there was a reaction in favour of federalism.

Filippo Turati was among the first to raise the new banner with all the authority which derived from his culture, great intellect and practical sense.

His ideas did not triumph at the party congresses; but undoubted and numerous signs allow one to state that they are gaining ground with the speed which the painful experience imposes on sincere and intelligent persons[1].

This painful experience has lately led to the explosion of a series of manifestations which have proven me right and confirmed that my stance was right when I indicated the dangers of a centralising unity and the opportune measures to remedy it.

It was the unrest in Milan, which has led to a diligent psychological examination of that which was called the State of Milan by way of derision — and which for me was the object of admiration: not diminished by the unjust judgements, which in a spur of impetus and through imprecise knowledge and valuation of men and things were pronounced against my native region —; and this examination led many, who in the past had ei-

---

[1] With regard to the article of *Don Chisciotte* which I will deal with below, the socialist newspaper *Avanti!* acknowledges the need for the tactics to be followed in the Mezzogiorno and on the islands to be such as to favour the republicans and radicals. When I pronounced such a blasphemy, I was the recipient of insults and derision from the mouthpieces of Italian socialism.

ther not realised or had not said it, to recognise that the Italians differ from one another and do not live in harmony under the pall of gloom of unity.

It is thus that in Turin *Riforma Sociale* (in its issue of 15 May 1898) could write: «In Lombardy the Mezzogiorno is not loved, because it is wrongly believed that the policies of Crispi and of other similar persons emanate from the South; Lombardy is not loved in the Mezzogiorno, because it is known that the economic constitution of present-day Italy, above all as regards customs tariffs, is made solely for it, with serious damage to the agricultural regions. In Tuscany, in Piedmont, in Veneto, the separatist traditions — the cause of all misfortunes — are rearing their head again».

It is clear here that the statement of the phenomenon is precise, although no mention is made of the cure for the ill. The anonymous author would have done better to confess that separatism has revived because unity has brought about fatigue and delusion rather than to indicate these separatist traditions as the cause of all the misfortunes. By presenting the former as in the ordinary and general meaning one resorts to chauvinistic rhetoric and incurs in a historical error of no small import.

Even more explicit was Nitti, in an excellent article on the «Uprisings of Yesterday and the Repressions of Today» in said *Riforma Sociale* (15 June) when he concluded: «The bond of unity has slackened, it has weakened to such point that the dissent between the north and south manifests itself in every possible manner. Already the rebirth of the separatist tendencies is worse than a threat, a most serious ill ... The separatist ideas are common and they should be fought, not by condemning, rightly or wrongly those who interpret them, but by eliminating the causes of conflict and aversion, by doing the opposite of what has been done to date and introducing a note of greater nobility and greater disinterest in every act of national polity».

Our friend Nitti also overlooks or errs on the aetiology after having made an attentive description of the symptoms; and a partial, but exact, statement of the phenomenon is also made by the *Rivista Politica e Letteraria* of Rome which in «Psychology of the

Revolt» (1 June 1898) admits the regional exclusivism of Lombardy.

These other confessions which I chose from many, suggested by different reasons, are truly symptomatic. Regarding the different concept of the state's task held by southerners and northerners, *Don Chisciotte* of Rome writes: «A tendency of the Mezzogiorno is opposed by one of northern Italy, and particularly of Milan. And these opposing tendencies are not passing and arbitrary; they respond to two differing ways of being, to two contrary conditions of fact.

«Lombardy, having attained almost the peak of prosperity with labour, is concerned only with lightening the taxpayers' burden; and so any threat to the arithmetical, if nothing else, stability of the budget frightens it, whether this takes place because of foreign policy or the needs of domestic policy.

«The Mezzogiorno – and one should always bear in mind that Naples is a separate case – which has lacked the vigour, virtue, subsidies or fortune to redeem itself economically from its long abjection, asks to be helped and understands the functions and duties of the state differently.

«It is unnecessary to ascertain which of the two parties is abstractly right; indeed, in concrete terms, both are right, because both expound and summarise their state as it is.

«What, on the other hand, I do believe serious is precisely that that state is thus, namely so dissimilar as to threaten to openly become more acute in antimony with the manner of conceiving the government between the two parts of the peninsula. This is permanent conflict.

«Neither can talk, whether calculating or civilly compassionate, sweep aside the fact that it exists, indeed it becomes more strident with every day.

«And this conflict, from the economic causes, from the conditions of the land and of the workers, invades the local administrations and their mechanisms, reaches Parliament and makes its effects felt there. While the generation of whose who fought and suffered for unity was alive and strong — may God bless them — generous effort ensured that the conflict was less apparent. But the disappearance of the few, the increase in prosperity for some, of poverty for others has led and will lead to very significant changes.

«Here lies — and I am certain I am saying nothing foolhardy — the greatest problem for Italy» (year 1898, no. 215)[2].

The Neapolitan newspaper *Mattino* (in its issue of 30-31 July 1898) in turn confesses that the Neapolitans live in a violent antagonism of interests and ideas with Milan.

But the existence of the regionalist movement, which I would never wish confused with the separatist desire, which can lodge only in some spirit won over by atavistic reversion, which will be a case of individual aberration rather than a collective aspiration, is now so accepted that we have reached the situation where the *Daily Chronicle* and other German newspapers and magazines are exaggerating its importance and altering its meaning, ascribing to it solely the genesis of the more recent movements; this explanation is very convenient for those who governed Sicily from 1892 to 1894 and did not displease those of 1898 who sought, in said manner, to whip up public feeling against those who out of hunger or aversion had risen against the misgovernment which had come from Italy for circa forty years. It is significant that a Lombard, the former member of Parliament Siliprandi, can acknowledge that the discontent for the regional antagonism developed in the provinces of Lombardy, Veneto and Emilia and had its epilogue in the rebellious stance of the city of Milan. He boasts — and not without reason – that he foresaw the movement in a speech at Mantua in 1889[3]. Who did, finally, make a right and direct relation between causes and effects — centralising unity, misgovern-

---

[2] I feel bound to state that the same *Don Chisciotte* signed by Saraceno (L. Lodi) who is from northern Italy, published an article (*Rivendicazioni*, 1898, no. 213) in which regarding the election of Gavotti in the constituency of Nizza Monferrato he reveals that northern corruption is much ahead of that in the South. He repeats the concept I developed. Now, there is only *Avanti!* which ascribes the southern Italians with a monopoly in electoral immorality and works itself into an outrage when the trickery of Giarre and Regalbuto can take place in Piedmont (*Avanti*, 20 July 1898).

[3] See *Capitoli teorici-pratici di politica sperimentale*, Mantua, 1898, Vol. 3, p. 223.

ment and discontent, whatever its form — was Castagnino, who after the tumults made the diagnosis and proposed the remedy for the Italian disquiet:

«In this bedlam of Italian political life, he observes, the regional antipathies and diffidences, the contrast of the regional interests are the mysterious force of those who agitate disorderly elements; according to whether one or the other of them prevail, one believes or it is sought to have one believe in a manifestation of national public opinion — which does not exist; and consequently that a given government programme is requested and approved, said responding solely to specific party or personal interests». Well said[4].

Another citation which is worth a hundred comes from Italy's most prestigious journal and is provided by Ercole Vidari — an illustration of Italian juridical science.

«In a country, the professor from Pavia notes, for so many centuries divided into seigniories, with different legislations, with different customs, attitudes and tendencies, the need for a town, provincial or regional life, free from the fetters of the central power, is most evident. To force it instead to an absolute and invariable bureaucratic uniformity is to wish to spread it on Procrustean bed, to force it to wear a shirt of Nessus. To think that a town of northern or central Italy can be administered with the same norms as a town of southern or insular Italy implies total ignorance of the social and moral conditions of each of these lands, it is the same as giving a weapon to someone who knows how to use it rather than to someone who is wholly ignorant of such matters.

«... With true and broad local autonomies, Italy will perish in the suffocating embraces of a legislative unity which initially thought it necessary to maintain steadfast the uncertain structure of the new state, and instead throttled every energy of local and regional life. ... If the force of things had not imposed on us the unity of state, perhaps no other state more than ours, and by tra-

[4] See *Il disagio italiano. Diagnosi e rimedio*, Roma, E. Loescher, 1898. (One lira) Many good pages are dedicated to the economic differences between north and south, to the economic crises of the Mezzogiorno to which the north gave no thought, etc., etc.

ditions and by customs and by tendencies and by aspirations, would be more suited to the federative life. Fortune, whether good or bad, had it otherwise; and the matter was settled. Anyone who sought to modify it today would run the grave risk of having the entire national structure collapse on him» («Delle presenti condizioni d'Italia», *Antologia*, no. 1, August 1898).

Would it be right for me to point out that the premises and conclusions of the moderate Professor Vidari are perfectly similar to those of the article on the «Great Equivocation» which was published in *Rivista Popolare*, arousing Fisco's anger?

Hence, there is no longer any doubt concerning the principal cause of our ills: they derive from the centralising unity. This is acknowledged by men of various regions and colour, whether famous or obscure. It is remarkable that it is also acknowledged by Siliprandi who professes himself averse to any federal tendency (*loc. cit.*, p. 221). It was acknowledged by Ottonieri — another sincere supporter of unity — who deplored the excessive haste of uniform unity[5]. And this was courageously reiterated by Castagnino. To the ills of every kind one should add that of the bigotry of unity which forbid the regional recruitment of the army with serious economic consequences for the nation and considerable decrease of the motherland's defensive force. All the ills deriving from the centralising unity have justified Carlo Cattaneo's prophesies.

If this unity without articulations, without joints, all ankylosis, which hamper its movements and make them painful, as Alberto Mario put it so well, was the principal, not sole, cause of our ills it is incomprehensible how men eminently familiar with the use of the inductive method — such as allowed in the social sciences — such as the illustrious Professor Carlo F. Ferraris, can be alarmed by the regional arrangements[6]. When an arrangement has given a bad result — and the period to obtain this result has lasted some forty years — does healthy experimentalism not advise it be changed?

---

[5] See *L'Italia presente e I suoi fatti*, Rome, E. Loescher, 1898, p. 37.

[6] See *La nozione scientifica del dicentramento*, Venezia, 1898, p. 32.

The doctor who wished to insist in the use of a drug which had been proven dangerous would kill the patient; it is no different for the politician, unless one wishes to apply a specific homeopathic remedy which boils down to the following formula: the ills of unity are remedied by continuing with unity.

The diagnosis, as seen, is made by many and precisely; but most still shun that which in medicine is called causal indication: the only efficacious one, as it aims to eliminate the cause and consequently eliminates the effect. The fear of seeing Italy return to a geographical expression still deters the Imbrianis, the Fortunatos, the Sonninos and many others whose rectitude of intent is unquestionable, from the right path; there are still but a few who courageously indicate the remedy: Gobbi is unhesitant in suggesting the constitution of regional councils as they were proposed in 1861 by Mighetti, as they were cherished until recently by Bertolini; Castagnino wishes to balance the economic conditions of the two big subdivisions — North and South — and prefers federation in the economic field and unity in the political field.

I do not question the formula, which I do not believe exact; it is unarguable however that he is right when he states that the nation lacks any real unity and that instead we have two real Italies in contrast and that if we are unable to harmonise them we will never have a single Italy in the noble and patriotic sense of our martyrs and thinkers — we will not have that unity which should be the source of strength and prosperity.

In any case, I would close these citations and brief considerations stating with legitimate pride that mine is no longer a sole voice, but finds a loud and powerful echo in the country. The appropriate measures may be late in coming; but they will come because they are fatally and quickly maturing in the public conscience. The problem has been posed and will have a solution.

2. - If the ill described is not of this or that other region; if the disquiet is general, is Italian: why, somebody may ask me, do I appeal to the Italians of the Mezzogiorno and not to all the inhabitants of the peninsula?

The reasons are clear and evident. In northern Italy there is full and complete awareness of the need to change course; if nothing else, it would be proved by the existence and propaganda of three committees — of Veneto, Piedmont and Lombardy — for decentralisation. Such an awareness is wholly lacking in the Mezzogiorno, where there live and reign the most obstinate centralisers, who have lost and make one lose the precise perception of the interests of one's own regions which the Ligurian deputies always had so prodigiously clear. This perception of the regional interest has been so lost that the denouncement of the trade treaty with France in 1887, which was to have heralded the great economic ruin of the Mezzogiorno and the islands, was greeted with the signs of the liveliest of exultation, with fanaticism - propagated by the deputies to the press, and from this to the masses. In this respect, I will always remember with painful regret I managed only a lively polemic in the newspapers of Catania and Messina and in the *Giornale di Sicilia* of Palermo against the inauspicious measure and that my opponents included also very dear political friends.

Not only this, but the southern apathy, the tacit, understood, if not explicit, acquiescence in the ill, in the damage experienced, the social phenomenology of the Mezzogiorno and the islands due to historical causes, whose action has accumulated for centuries and which the reparatory government of the single Italy should have mitigated, if not wholly eliminated in forty years — as the centralisers, who are inspired by the seductive doctrines of Dupont-Whith, in vain still hope — have ensured that the northerners hurled against the southerners and against the islanders prejudices and exaggerations which one should combat and correct in the vital interest of those who are their victims.

To contribute with my forces to the re-awakening of this conscience of the south and the islands and spur it to recognise the reality in its entirety, but to reject the slanders or errors, I address my appeal only to the Italians of the Mezzogiorno, only deploring that my words do not have the regenerating effectiveness of the fire applied to unhealthy vegetation.

The exaggerations, the mistaken interpretations of real facts and the wholly erroneous judgements of the northerners regarding the southerners and islanders are of both an economic and moral order.

From the economic point of view on the one hand the lesser wealth of the Mezzogiorno is not believed — it is still suspected that if the revenue service auctions the assets of taxpayers, this is because of the latters' bad intent and not because of their impossibility to pay! — and it was whispered by a northerner while I attacked the inauspicious equalisation — it is swore that the northerner pays more, unduly than the rest of Italy and it is concluded that roads, schools, bridges, etc., are built in the lower part of Italy with the contributions of the upper part of the peninsula. In short, the southerners are nothing more than mendicants, or almost, maintained at the expense of the northerners.

On the other hand, again in the north, it is maintained that the statistically provable higher level of crime, illiteracy, political corruption, and barbarities found in the Mezzogiorno are the fatal product of the race and climate. The present inferiority, undeniable in many things, of the southerners lies in their nature; and is hence fatal, unchangeable, eternal!

In respect of the economic question I have already published several articles in *Rivista Popolare*; I will continue with the hope of demonstrating in broad daylight that the Mezzogiorno — against the tacit provision of the Statute — pays more than it should and that the state spends for it much less than it should; while the same Mezzogiorno functions as the principal market, as the colony which serves marvellously for the increase of the wealth of the industrial regions of the North[7].

Some will find disagreeable this account of credit and debit; disagreeable and antipatriotic. Perhaps it is. But what blame have the southerners if they intend to revise the accounts which were to their detriment, which since 1863 the deputations of Lombardy, Veneto and sometimes of Emilia have openly and solemnly presented a hundred times in Parliament? Was it not they who im-

---

[7] Castagnino rightly observes: «The people of the north should bear in mind that their prosperity is due not only to their industriy, but also to the circumstance that they found in two thirds of Italy a large and most favourable consumption market for their manufactured products. Its wealth derives from the Mezzogiorno of Italy».

posed on the Nation the Abba Carima of Italian finances, which is called the establishment of a new land register, compounded by that devilry which responds to the name of acceleration?[8]. If the southerners have any blame it is this alone: to have proven themselves impotent, incapable to obtain rectification of the north's fantastic accounting system[9].

On the moral question the Mezzogiorno would be wrong if it did not acknowledge its own shortcomings; but this would not be to its detriment because one can only put things right when one is conscious of the danger. These pages aim to re-awaken said conscience.

However, one should prevent the exaggerations and erroneous explanations of true facts from gaining currency. Talk of an absolute inferiority of the civilisation of the south and the islands is an exaggeration; often it is nothing more than a difference which entails and implies that there are as many good and bad sides in the set of social conditions of the Mezzogiorno as in that of the north.

Whatever the case, this civilisation of the Mezzogiorno is a historical product which can and should disappear just as it has appeared, and we should co-operate to ensure its disappearance as soon as possible as regards that which is bad.

But neither the race nor the climate have anything to do with the present phenomenology and more than the right there is the duty to rebut the errors which were earlier the legacy of only the criminal anthropology school, but which have gradually gained ground in the daily newspapers and among the masses, conquering even some southerners, who are not ashamed to apply to themselves the stigma of inferiority and degeneration.

I have fought and will continue to fight this prejudice, this error; I am even more aware of the need to insist in the fight now that it is deployed, dangerously, to explain political phenomena.

---

[8] The apathy and recklessness of the southerners did not allow the provinces of Caltanisetta and Girgenti to demand acceleration. A formal proposal for such was made in the provincial council of the former to no avail.

[9] During the discussion of that which became the Law of 1 March 1886 on the establishment of the new land register, the deputation of southern Italy was energetic and unusually compact in defending the interests of its regions. One of the best speeches was that of Hon. Di San Giuliano: justice should be rendered above all to one's adversaries.

I shall not repeat myself here on the influence the climate and race exercise on the development of civilisation, which I expounded in great detail in *Sociologia criminale* (Vol. 2, Chapters V, VII, VIII and IX). The facts and considerations I expounded there have never received an exhaustive reply; this phenomenon having manifested itself; the scientific adversaries mitigated their primitive papal dogmatism and quickly accorded the maximum preponderance in the genesis of social phenomena to the so-called physical and anthropological factors, then gradually shuffled the cards until it reverted to the social factors.

After Sergi's studies on the Mediterranean race which were excellently summarised as regards Italy in the volume *Ari ed italici* (Torino, Bocca, 1898), I believe one has to be quite impudent to claim that the race or races — and it would be no bad thing if the anthropologists were to agree amongst themselves on the concept of race — which populate the Mezzogiorno and the islands are inferior to those which live in the north of Italy. These inferior races have given the Egyptian, Carthaginian, Greek and Latin civilisations. Here is a merit which can proudly compete with that of the Anglo-Saxon race. The civilisation of the Anglo-Saxons, which will never have that special mark and originality of those passed down to us by Athens and Rome, have drawn most considerably on the most genial heredity of that Mediterranean race which today one wishes to foolishly pass off as inferior. The unchallengable merit of the Mediterraneans will always remain that of the priority. Siracuse, Agrigento, Selinunte, Enna, Sybaris, Taranto, Crotone, etc. were most civilised while London, Berlin, Milan, Turin, Venice had not even been founded and the inhabitants of their regions lived in the darkest of barbarisms[10].

---

[10] It is undeniable that there are considerable anthropological differences between the north and the Mezzogiorno in Italy; but difference does not mean inferiority. This is proven by the history of southern civilisation. moreover, he who wishes to gain an appropriate idea on the one hand of the lack of correspondence between race and nation and on the other on the relation between the shape of the skull and the development of civilisation only has to read, in addition to the masterly studies by Sergi, those by Renan, Fouillée, Gumploviez, among the more famous and among the more recent AUERBACH, *Les Races et Les Nationalités en Autriche-Hongrie*, Paris, Alcen, 1898.

The flourishing of the civilisation of Sicily and of the Magna Graecia was splendid by intensity, quality and variety; the inhabitants of those regions excelled themselves in art and politics, in science and in poetry.

I am unable to understand, therefore, the observations on the diversity of the nature of the Mediterranean peoples and Indo-Europeans: the greater sociality ascribed to the latter by Sergi; less still the characteristic quantities of genius among the northerners and the southerners of Italy, which Pullè assigns: «In the genius of upper Italy, he writes, there are more solid qualities, implementary energy, more plastic and concrete forms: this is what makes it more suited to the figurative arts, to the methodically disciplined positive studies, to the continuous conservation of the intellectual heritage». (*Profilo antropologico d'Italia*, Firenze, 1898, pp. 128-9).

One thinks one is dreaming when one reads such things, which are written by eminent writers familiar with the history and monuments of the Magna Graecia and Sicily!

Do the temples of Agrigento, the ruins of Siracusa, of Taormina, of Selinunte, of Segesta, etc., really testify to the artistic genius of the north? Were Pythagoras, Philolaus, Lysis, Archytas, Osello, Archimedes, Caronda, Dion, Euhemerus, Petrone, Dicaearchus, Empedocles, etc. who for their times were masters of positive studies, really born on the banks of the Po and at the foot of the Alps and did they attend the University of Pavia or Pisa?[11] And what about sociality? It prevailed in Rome and in Greece, so

[11] The school of Pythagoras was a nursery of philosophers, scientists and statesmen; Philolaus discovered the two motions of the earth; Lysis of Tarentum was the teacher of Epaminondas and Philip the Macedonian, Archytas a major mathematician and philosopher, greatly admired in Greece as a scientist and moralist followed and fought by Aristotle. Osello proved the eternity of the world before Stagirita, Caronda was a great legislator and the founder of the first public school, Petron of Imera was perhaps the first to think of the plurality of worlds; Dion of Syracuse was an eminent thinker and statesman; Euhemerus considered the gods as primitive heroes and sovereigns of peoples; Dicaearchus of Messina, materialist, preached the eternity of the human kind. it is perhaps superfluous to recall who Archimedes was. To the divine Empedocles our Rapisardi dedicated a idyll and also splendidly mentioned him in the third tercet of *Giobbe* and in the ode on the *Volunteers of charity*.

much so that they were reproached for their scant account of the individual: until very recently individualism was believed the principal character of the Anglo-Saxons. Did those giants who honoured the inferior races of the Mezzogiorno lack the method? But the method — which is still being discussed — was born yesterday: it is simply absurd to wish to pretend that the predecessors profit from the discoveries and progresses which subsequently — many centuries later — take place. And as regards the spirit of continuity of these inferior Mediterranean peoples I believe this circumstance alone suffices to appropriately appreciate certain fantastic distinctions: when one wishes to praise contemporary England for the sagacity and perseverance with which it extends and governs its dominions it is compared ... to Rome.

That is as regards race. As regards the climate, history is there to show that not one single, but several civilisations succeeded in taking root and flowering in the soil of Sicily: the Greek-Sicilian civilisation, the Arab civilisation and the Norman Swabian civilisation. And so: under what climate and on what soil could the succession of so flourishing civil flowerings take place?[12]

3. - All this, it is replied, is the past, it belongs to history; the present is different and the rosy hues of the past make the contrast with the gloomy hues of the phase we are experiencing all the more painful.

The present may indeed be most sad; but to judge a race or a physical environment should the past not count as much as the present? Where is the logic which arrogantly cancels history to legitimise the capricious sentences of those who condemn to inferiority a race and claim a given climate is unsuited to civilisation?

---

[12] On this succession of various civilisations in Sicily, read the brilliant conference by ARCOLEO G., *Palermo e la coltura in Sicilia*, Milano, Fratelli Treves, 1898. Those who speak of the inferiority of the race which populates the Mezzogiorno would do well to read it. Arcoleo was mistaken in not having allowed an autochthonous civilisation of Sicily, which was eminently recognised and demonstrated by GUSTAVO CHIESI, *La Sicilia illustrata*, Milano, E. Sonzogno, 1892. One can and should not forget the afore-cited masterly speech by Filippo Cordova at the Chamber of Deputies in Turin on 9 December 1863 in reply to General Govone's charges. One of Cordova's observations is still topical, namely: «the idea of civilisation is too civil an idea ... to be military».

In several places in *Sociologia criminale* I showed the absurdity of the school which takes account only of one given phase; which chooses a single moment of the life of a people to judge its greatness or low level.

Giacomo Novicow, more recently and for his part, has insisted in demonstrating the extreme fallaciousness of such a criterion, thanks to which a people, according to the moment in which one observes it, can appear great or small, superior or inferior. And it is the most amusing thing in this world to at times observe the speed of the succession of the conditions from which one deduces its superiority or inferiority (*L'avenir de la Race Blanche*, Paris, F. Alcan, 1897).

It is not the case to expound here for what reasons are the conditions such at present in the Mezzogiorno and islands to admit their inferiority: one would need volumes, to narrate the historical vicissitudes and above all the succession of increasingly worse governments which history mentions: action of bad governments, which in the moments of sincerity are not disregarded by the monosyllabisms of race and climate[13]. Now it suffices to

[13] I shall confine myself to recalling two young writers; who on the one hand resort to race to explain the present inferiority of the Mezzogiorno and the islands, while on the other they themselves furnish the proof, and numerous at that, of the social origin of the present phenomenology. Of the two, CIRAOLO HAMNETT, *Delitti femminili a Napoli*, Milano, Kantorowicz, 1896, is much more prudent. Niceforo who had ventured too far in stating the influence of the race in studying Sardinia's crime, a few months later modified the theory to substitute it with the more acceptable one of degeneration and the halt in development due to social causes as can be deduced from this brief judgement: «Bourbonism and the misgovernment barbarised southern Italy: the present governments destroy and kill all of Italy». This is the right way followed with so much success and for so many years by men of the worth of PASQUALE VILLARI, *Lettere meridionali*. Giustino Fortunato, who studied with much love the economic and social conditions of his towns, also sacrificed a little to the prejudice of the race and climate, and in his justification triumphantly reminded me another time that banditry and the question of state property have been mentioned in the Mezzogiorno since Titus Livy. He found the explanation of the persistence of the two phenomena over the centuries in a brochure he himself sent me — and for which I am grateful — and which he rightly appreciates (GOYAN G., *Il regime della grande proprietà nelle Calabrie*, Trani, V. Vecchi, 1898). In any case one should not forget that banditry has disappeared, thanks to the roads and schools — few and badly organised. Why should the question of state property not disappear and with it that of malaria, which today afflicts where there once flourished those centres of splendid civilisation which go under the name of Sybaris, Crotone, Metapontum?

recall only that that England, which is the object of unbounded and deserved admiration for its superiority in many fields of social activity, would be judged absolutely inferior if we wished to judge it from the manifestations of the last century and — from certain aspects — also of the early years of this century. The phase of splendour is that which is represented by the so-called Victorian age. But has not each people had its own? And who can guarantee that the moment of decadence will not arrive for England, as it has for France which had the Encyclopaedia and 1789? Our descendants will perhaps listen to the future philosophers of history who will boast the superiority of the Slavs and will include the Anglo-Saxons among the degenerates, among the inferiors, among the races which have seen their development come to a stop.

Whatever the present of the Mezzogiorno and Sicily, moreover, one should reflect that exaggeration which borders on slander has often described one and the other completely different and worse than they actually are. Even Gustavo Chiesi, who in a moment of anger and indignation, wished to ascribe Sicily with the stigma of inferiority, in calmer moments, after having studied with love and acknowledged *de visu*, protested scornfully against the slanderous information which was and is being spread about the beautiful island with audacity verging on recklessness:

«We have read, writes the good and generous recluse of Finalborgo, in a foreign book, translated into Italian, wholly false portraits of Sicilian society; reconstructions of a Sicilian society which might perhaps have existed a century of two ago, which perhaps has some sucker, here and there, in some noble family, of some almost ignored small provincial town. But in the overwhelming majority, in the big cities, if some anomaly, discordant with the usages of the time still rears its head, the wind of progress works assiduously around it to smooth it out, and it, almost ashamed of itself, hides from the bright light of modernity.

«The ideas which are generally held on Sicilian society, propagated by people who hurriedly passed through in a railway carriage or with a Baedeker in their hand, as we have already said, refer to a society of one or two centuries ago, when Sicily was bereft of freedom and common reason between cities, neglectful of education, squeezed and exploited on the one hand, abandoned and maintained by force in the greatest ignorance possible on the other».

And Chiesi — who with regard to the ambit acknowledges the island has a special and noble indigenous civilisation, with its own specific character — after having smiled at the fancies narrated by Schneegans, adds: «these things would make one only smile, if together with other little truthful rehash of old stories concerning banditry, the mafia, the camorra, mendicity, they did not make one indignant at the thought that they help establish around the Sicilians an opinion which is completely different from that which one should have, and hence damagingly contrary to the truth. We have seen, if not indeed considerably patronised, the good society of the big cities of Sicily, at parties, in theatres, in clubs, in public meetings and we have seen no significant differences from the society of the mainland cities worthy of note: moreover, we have easily seen that in the relations of the educated classes in Sicily, there exists an exquisite courtesy of manners and between the popular classes an unostentatious sincere cordiality and we would wish both one and the other were similar in other regions of Italy where, on both sides, there should be a greater tolerance of customs» (*La Sicilia illustrata*).

These statements and these judgements of the worthy Lombard republican can be better supplemented only with the statements and judgements of a Sicilian monarchist.

Hence Arcoleo — the Sicilian monarchist in question — said that Sicily «boasts the treasure of traditions which can make it more solicitous and steady in the cult of the parliamentary institutions in which the other regions of the mainland preceded it.

«But every other part of Italy should also contribute something for the development of the island. Culture, the true national culture, which is not only a book or newspaper or compulsory education or university, but refinement of all the social aptitudes, so that they become industrious and fecund, can do more than railways, industries, trade, political life and laws; that culture which, like the soul of the school pupil, is wholly the organism of a people, and circulates and palpitates equally intensely in its various parts».

On the way of fostering the increase of this culture, Arcoleo adds: «Few during dark and sad centuries, many in the last century, very many in this century, came from Sicily seeking in the sister regions hospitality of sentiments and doctrines. We had from the last century eminent exiles in science, art, politics, refuges of the land saddened by so many tyrannies, who returned with the baptism of Italianity. But those currents which came from the island were not matched by those from the mainland. There came the army, the bureaucracy, they wished to know us through investigations, trials, official reports or statistics which reported with scientific irony that primary education and crime had increased twofold!

«The true Sicily is still largely undiscovered and it cannot be understood with a clinical study or landscape. In periods of indisposition, the diagnosis sees only illnesses; the aesthetic vision of the landscape and monuments sees only nature and art. A work of integration is needed, to remove not the innate differences of climate, race, traditions, but the anachronisms which exist not only in Sicily».

The intelligent reader will understand all the bitterness contained in the regret for the intellectual exchanges between Sicily and the mainland when he recalls that the orator and writer was bound to a great discretion not only because he was speaking in Milan to a public — however elect — whose regional susceptibilities he had to respect; but also because at the time he was a member of the government. And it would have been a unheard of scandal indeed for a member of the government to be accused of having fermented regional disagreement. This necessary reserve, however, did not prevent him from noting that Sicily was not so much judged as slandered by the northerners and he noted: «For no other reason than this is it difficult to find the right note: Sicily is slandered several times most viciously, legislators, historians, travellers. Sociological, economic, political criticism made even more reckless by the ignorance of the majority, took delight, like art, in the exceptions; on isolated facts not dissimilar from many which took place elsewhere, it formulated systems and sentences, decimated entire social classes, landowners, peasants, workers, created types, invented a wild, ill, separatist Sicily. Thus in the midst of positive studies and documents there still persists in the minds and imaginations a gloomy epic, which are sadly framed by exceptional laws, states of emergency, inquiries. It is a false perspective which distorts sight and intelligence».

The agreement between Chiesi and Arcoleo, between two men essentially different by origin, political conventions, culture and social condition is no coincidence; it arises spontaneously, necessary, from the depth of things, from the mere observation of reality!

This agreement on the past civilisations of Sicily, on the possibilities of seeing the island arise again and on the present slander of which it is victim, dispenses me from further insisting on the claimed ethnic inferiority of the inhabitants of the island and counsels that I close this appeal to the Italians of the Mezzogiorno which, more or less, are all of the same race as that of Sicily and to which all the foregoing and subsequent considerations apply.

The Italians of the Mezzogiorno, if they wish to be respected should feel themselves potentially intellectually and morally equal to those of the North: they should be fully and wholly conscious of said equality, banishing from their minds any concept of inferiority. Even mere doubt is fatal, as it paralyses us, and we believe ourselves damned to perpetual inferiority by the fatality of race and climate.

This consciousness will restore to us the energy and initiative we have lacked of late and will have incalculable practical value in making our brothers — and we call them that without any irony — of the north understand that they have towards us economic and moral duties, as toward equals. They will not feel them while they believe we are inferior beings, who live at their expense.

We should demand the respect of our rights: we should defend our economic and moral interests. But to succeed in doing so with the maximum of utility for all and with the greater manifestation of the collective forces in favour of the true greatness of the motherland, the Italians of the Mezzogiorno will have to get it well into their minds that they have duties alongside their rights.

They should, principally, not hide, not mitigate the truth by an ounce; but they should scrutinise it to its very depths and harshly expose it naked.

To be respected they should henceforth make themselves more respectable; and they will not wholly succeed in this until they have triumphed over the scourges of illiteracy and that of crime and ensured the better functioning of the wheels of the representative mechanism in matters which are of their competence. I say: for matters which are of their competence, because to obtain a significant improvement not everything depends on them, and the central power should also make a considerable contribution to ensure their efforts are efficacious. Local action, however, represents a valid spur and will force the government to do the rest.

Now the southern Italians in the local administrations should start to put illiteracy to flight, not look on the school as an evil; not have it serve solely as a source of jobs for friends, relatives, clients; but instead supervise it, make possible the observance of primary education with the administration of means to those, and they are not few in number, who have none. They should not blame financial difficulties: paring down the spending on luxuries — banquets for the visiting Member of Parliament and Prefect, big and small theatres, scandalous bureaucratic sinecures, etc., — they will find sufficient to reinvigorate the school and the pupils. They should not be afraid of the spread of education, which the ruling classes consider as the poisonous vehicle of socialist ideas. Oh, no! It is not the school, nor education which threatens it. The hordes of Cardinal Ruffo were illiterate; the enraged peasants of Bronte and Nissoria in 1860 who cut the *cappeddis'* throats, had not attended school, the peasants of Minervino Murge who committed the excesses of 1898 could neither read nor write. These events differing in time, place, nature which would have been adverted had the ruling classes thought to economically, intellectually and morally better the classes hitherto held in subjugation and in mediaeval brutality.

A refined culture ennobles and gives a civil, human imprint to those same inevitable conflicts which constitute the backdrop of history and which exploded and will always explode, with or without education.

The struggle against crime should be intense, unceasing, above all intelligent. In this field the government should do much and much also should be expected from the economic and intellectual improvement; but much more from the moral propaganda, particularly to stem the sea of bloody crime which dishonours the Mezzogiorno and the islands.

Many years ago in Romagna murders and unrest were much more frequent than they are today; the causes which generated them and the circumstances which accompanied them made that region very akin to those of our Mezzogiorno and as these this incurred the derision and horror of men of order. Rigour and exceptional measures were to little or no avail; much, on the other hand, the holy propaganda against crime which was led by Aurelio Saffi. In the Mezzogiorno and on the islands more than elsewhere the good and intelligent men should mobilise themselves to destroy all the prejudices which are a sad legacy of the cursed Bourbon regime; the police should not been viewed as an enemy — and such unfortunately those in government would appear to wish to continue to be the case by not making it respectable, by not keeping it extraneous to the political persecutions and intrigues; one should not always see the criminal as a victim worthy of compassion, one should not look with indifference at one's neighbour's misfortune, but instead develop and cultivate the natural sentiment of social solidarity.

A longer speech would have to be dedicated to the correction of the political function among the southern Italians; but as it is not my intention in this appeal which I address to them neither to give moral lessons which are of a general nature and of which the northern Italians have equal need, nor to suggest the political criteria to which preference should be given — which would lead me into a field which I do not wish to enter — I shall confine myself to drawing attention to that which is specific or prevalent among the active political elements of the regions of the Mezzogiorno.

First and foremost, the voters should cease blubbering over the exorbitant taxes while they grant all their support to the policy which makes them necessary, and that they should get into their heads the concept of responsibility and the cause-effect relation; they should stop shouting against the government while giving their votes to the members of Parliament who systematically support each government; in the elections a, any, political criterion — clerical or liberal, monarchic or republican, individualist or socialist — should prevail and should not be subordinate to the advice of Tizio or Sempronio; political criteria should count when choosing a candidate, but they should not suppress the indications which derive from the personal qualities — for my part I would not hesitate to banish anyone who displayed a bright sign to cover a shady trade in smuggled goods; one should support a government when it fulfils its programme, but one should not invoke the illicit use of its forces to fell adversaries, whom should be fought in another way and by other means and who at a given hour pay one back in kind, substituting the vendetta for political struggle; one should emancipate oneself from the body government — not show oneself timid or servile vis-à-vis said, but never ask it those dishonest and illicit acts which require a payment by way of remuneration; finally, to maintain in the person elected that independence which should be the supreme guide of the electors, who place him in the condition to exercise it and not ask him favours of every nature, which lie outside his mandate and create and develop between members of Parliament and ministers those relations and ties which eliminate the necessary control the former should exercise over the latter and end up in the degeneration of the representative regime and general political corruption[14].

From a representation which derives from the foregoing indications one can demand that the natural hierarchy of interests be respected so as to end the all too oft deplored indecency whereby the interests of a town or a province are sacrificed to the ambitions and inappropriate interference of an important voter, or of a local clique; similarly the interests of the entire nation should not be sacrificed to those of a region.

---

[14] Castagnino gives an efficacious description of the nature and action of the members of Parliament for southern Italy.

Respect of the hierarchy of these interests will allow the union, outside any political distinction, of the members of Parliament of a region to ensure the legitimate regional interests prevail; and the very control which the various regional representatives exercise among themselves will eliminate the dishonest contracts which lie at the base of the *do ut des* which have opened several times at Montecitorio and which represent the abuse of power of a class or a region to the detriment of the general collective interests.

Political renovation, finally, will not be possible in the Mezzogiorno and also in the rest of Italy — although the ill of which I shall speak last is more pronounced in the South and on the islands — it will not be possible, I repeat, while Guicciardini's typically egoistic man remains the model to be imitated by the mass of the populations and in particular by those which, ironically, are called the ruling classes. The lack of social solidarity encourages the spread of the poisonous plant of delinquency; the lack of political solidarity in the defence of the fundamental rights produces the de facto humiliation of all the Statutes and of all the written laws. I am comforted here by an opinion by Spencer, who judged the Americans inferior to the English solely because the former did not attach sufficient importance to the abuses of authority, whether large or small. «Freedom, he added, can only be maintained by citizens, each of whom is ready to oppose every illegitimate act, every attempt to dominate, every official abuse of power of however little importance it may seem. Freedom is the prize of an eternal vigilance; and this vigilance is necessary above all against the insidious repetition of domestic interventions against personal freedom»[15]. Now in Italy in general and in the Mezzogiorno in particular this vigilance to defend freedom is totally absent; its violation is encouraged to the detriment of others and thus one prepares the very arms which at a given hour shall wound one's own freedom. Such a condition ends up by reducing the representative regime to a great lie.

---

[15] *Les americains. Problèmes de Morale et de Sociologie*, Paris, Guillaumin, 1894, p. 117.

This is my thought, these my wishes which I submit to the Italians of the Mezzogiorno. Let them discuss them, approve or reject them, but at least shake off the lethargy in which they have lain for years and which will be of incalculable damage for the common motherland.

The Italians of the Mezzogiorno should rouse themselves, and place themselves in a position to reject with contempt the most serious charge which has been made against them: namely that of being one of the principal causes of Italy's present decadence[16].

---

[16] Professor Ercole Vitali, in the cited article in *Nuova Antologia*, includes among the causes of the present situation: «the preponderance, first slight, then overwhelming, of the southern element, i.e., of the least healthy element of our country» (p. 536). I would be interested to know how the illustrious professor can prove this preponderance of the southern element.

North and South. Preliminary Study of the Distribution of State Revenues and Spending in Italy*

Francesco Saverio Nitti

1. - Introduction

To Dr. Luigi Roux, Senator of the Kingdom
Naples, Easter Sunday 1900

My dear Roux,

I dedicate to you this my book to fulfil an old vow of recognition. You have always been my courteous publisher and you welcomed me in your journal many years ago, when I was almost a young lad and unknown. I have never forgotten your affectionate kindness at the start of my working career (how coarse this sounds!), your advice and your words and I shall not forget them in the future.

But this book is dedicated to you for a less noble reason: because I believe it should benefit from your name.

You who are play a leading role in the life of your noble Piedmont; you who in politics, in the press and in trade admirably represent the activity of your people; you know what ideal has guided me to seek the causes of the present imbalance.

---

* From: NITTI F. S., *Nord e sud. Prime linee di una inchiesta sulla ripartizione territoriale delle entrate e delle spese dello Stato in Italia*, Torino, Roux e Viarengo, 1900, pp. 209. [Cod. JEL: N 43].

All the times I spoke of it to you, you who love the truth, you who are good and strong, you never appeared neither sceptical nor diffident.

You were born in the extreme north of the peninsula and I in the extreme south: as you are above suspicion, do you wish to help me in a work of truth which aims to show a true danger, but also that one should always have faith in the future?

How could one not have faith?

From 1860 to the present Italy has achieved marvellous progresses: perhaps no other country has achieved so much in the same period of time.

We, who were born after that time, do not recall how little those things we now extol with excessive thoughtlessness were worth. The only true ill present-day Italy has is lack of faith in itself: as it unjustly exaggerates the past and does not view the present with the necessary serenity.

Except for Germany and Hungary, no country compared with what it was, has made as much progress as Italy.

Forty years ago Italy almost had only its enthusiasm and its hopes: it was a lot because they prepared the national conscience, but it was a little because it did not translate into material assets.

From 1860 to date, Italy's population has increased by 44.40%; but the general wealth has perhaps tripled. We had nothing and we had to do everything. We built more than 13,000 kilometres of railway, an extensive road network; we have created an army and a navy which, if they have not given us military victory, have at least furnished a powerful contribution to cementing the unity and they ensure we are not isolated and undefended in the world. Before 1860 there was almost no trace of big industry anywhere in the peninsula. Lombardy, now so proud of its industries, had just its agriculture; Piedmont was an agricultural and thrifty country, at least in the customs of its citizens. Central Italy, southern Italy and Sicily were in conditions of quite modest economic growth. Entire provinces, entire regions were as though closed to any civilisation. The new Italy has given 50,000 primary schools and 1,000 secondary schools to a country whose people was at a very low intellectual level. International trade is not the sole, nor always the greatest expression of a country's wealth. And yet in it too, even through errors, much progress has been made. A French senator, Siegfried, recently stated that from 1860 to 1897 Italy's trade increased by 99%, exports by 120%. There is no remote corner of Italy which is isolated from civilisation in the way all too many provinces were previously. Except for some luminaries — perhaps excessively cited and never read — Italian science was of scant importance: and now in the silence of the laboratories and schools an industrious youth is coming into being. There is no discipline in which considerable progress has not been made; in some, without dreaming of Gioberti's hypothetical supremacies (how illusory they are!) the new Italy has a place of honour.

At the start of this century France's population amounted to a sixth of Europe's and Italy less than an eleventh. Despite the extraordinary increase of the new countries, Italy has maintained its position and France on the other hand now represents less than a tenth.

Our poverty did not allow us to export capital; and our lack of progress meant that until just a few years ago we sold only products from the industries of the land; but without capital and organisation we have exported men. This emigration, which was not understood, hindered, neglected, has allowed a new Italy to arise. The poor peasants of the north and south, united at least in this good work, have created the civilisation of Argentina; they have opened a vast new consumption market. Later we will see what immense work these illiterate pioneers have achieved and how they have created, on the other side of the ocean, a new and greater Italy.

Italy is the sole country which in the history of civilisation gives an example of true resurrection, after a slavery and a decadence which lasted centuries. Greece, Spain have been unable to rise again.

And yet in Italy everyone is dissatisfied. Before there were — a most perceptive writer has noted — papalists in Rome, supporters of Austria in Milan, supporters of the Grand-duchy in Tuscany, those of the Bourbons in Naples; now they are all united in one activity — speaking ill of the present government.

Disregarding any paradox, this too is a very great progress: because for countries which are coming into being, nothing is more useful than a spirit of intolerance. Those men who liked tranquillity, who satisfied themselves with a tranquil hypocrisy the absolute governments gave them, and who were supporters of the grand duchy, or Bourbons, or Austria, belonged to a species which is disappearing in Europe. It should be said that intolerance, within certain limits, is the first condition of growth. Many injustices which now offend us, previously passed unobserved. Even the growth of socialism and the popular parties is proof of a more diffuse conscience, of an ascending tendency in the people. There is a lot of discontent not because one is worse off, but because we have become better and our intolerance has increased.

We have inherited from the past a dangerous conception: we have believed (can one say that we do not believe?) that the history of civilisation is but the history of man's emancipation, when it is but the history of his education.

It was said: when Italy has been emancipated from its tyrants, this most fertile land of Europe, too favoured by nature, this land to which God has given all his gifts (alongside each of these phases one can write the names of the leading authors of the unity and of our most eminent politicians) will become the first in Europe.

How many still do not believe that Italy is naturally a very rich country? How many do not believe that if we had a good government we would be rich?

There is nothing more revolutionary than this belief. It should be repeated to all that Italy is a naturally poor country, such that even if well governed (and it would not be difficult to do better than that which has been done in these many years of errors) it would still be poor. It should be taught also in the schools that our economic prosperity can be acquired only through a harsh struggle and in far from easy conditions.

But all the progresses which have been achieved to date are but the effect of unification. I do not mean by this that our distressing administrative uniformity is always an asset: nor that the weight of our political mechanism cannot be eliminated. But I mean only that political unity has given us all the best things we have: the supremacy of civil power, the re-awakening of the individual conscience, the desire of expansion which is now starting to be felt in all the nation and which will be our fortune.

If Italy is to be anything in the world it has to be united. An autonomous Lombardy or Sicily would be nothing, even if we allowed this historical nonsense only for the sake of hypothesis.

And so why this study, which appears carried out with the intent to re-awaken those regional disputes which time would appear to have soothed?

This book, whatever significance one wishes to give it, is but the defence of unification against a danger which overhangs it and which we should eliminate.

The unity of Italy could only be achieved with the sacrifice of some regions, above all of the mainland Mezzogiorno. This extensive zone, while at the time of the establishment of the Kingdom, had lower debt and greater public wealth, was placed at the farthest distance from the border by its very geographical position. The configuration of Italy — which is not encountered in any other country in Europe — led, in an initial period, to a vast exodus of wealth from south to north.

Southern Italy was the kingdom, the kingdom par excellence as the historians said: northern Italy was divided into many states and each of them had its own institutions. The latter were carefully conserved; and when they were small they were enlarged. The south lost its army, its extensive and poor bureaucracy: and saw, when the wealth had not grown, the taxes increase disproportionately over a few years.

Everything was done with ill-intent; indeed, it was the effect of necessity.

After the border had moved, could the south continue, as in 1850, to have almost 100,000 soldiers?

The impelling needs of the years subsequent to 1860 made it necessary to increase revenues. Could a country in transformation really have adopted the fiscal regime of Naples, so bland and unsuited?

The southern bureaucracy was Bourbon: what alternative was there to dismissing them en masse?

Unification still had to be completed and the wars had to be fought in the north. How could one avoid providing Lombardy, Piedmont, Liguria and Veneto with roads, railways and forts? The supreme need of defence brooks no discussion.

There was a difference in the public debts, a enormous difference in the assets of each state: but in the moment of enthusiasm, in the joy for the dream come true would it not be strange to do the accounts?

When the capital has grouped in the north, it was possible to attempt the industrial transformation. The protectionist movement did the rest, and two thirds of Italy have functioned as a consumption market for at least ten years.

Now the industry has formed, and Lombardy, Liguria and Piedmont may even, in a short time, not recall the reasons for their present prosperity.

Without any hint of irony — it is neither the case, nor would I wish so — the North is to blame for all this: the present imbalance which has placed the regions of the same country at such different levels was the fruit of political and historical conditions.

But the North of Italy has already forgotten: it has also sinned of pride. It no longer remembers the billions the South has given: it is blind to the sacrifices made.

Some author has even said that in Italy there are superior and inferior races. The southern Italians belong to the latter. There exists a science, indeed a half-science, which foresees without difficulty the future of the peoples and which can predict which will progress and which not. This half science has a predilection for saying that the southern Italians are an obstacle to any progress; even that every reaction comes from the Mezzogiorno.

Now the truth should be said: it will render northern Italy less proud and southern Italy more hopeful. When one realises what the latter has given and how much it has sacrificed, albeit without wishing to or knowing, the cause of unification will only benefit.

It is not uncommon to read in Milanese newspapers that an election in Lombardy is politically worth ten in the Mezzogiorno: that the southern Italians are the cause of the disorder of Italian public life. It is not rare to hear said that things have got worse since southern Italians have increased their participation in Italy's political life. Southern Italy appears as a Vandea of absentee barons, of ignorant plebs and of corrupt politicians. The Mezzogiorno's railways are the cause of the budget difficulties; the southern Italian state employees of the administrative disorder; the southern Italian politicians of militarism. These things are said in half of Italy, but in a low voice, in that discrete way of speaking which is our ill. And so, let us tell the whole truth, let us let it be heard openly, as is our duty.

Who has not heard talk in Milan of the barons of the Mezzogiorno?

If bread is expensive, it is to pay enormous benefits to the barons of southern Italy; is the state is in disorder, it is again the barons of the Mezzogiorno, such that southern Italy has not only the latifundium, but is itself a political latifundium.

The barons of the Mezzogiorno are nothing more than an unhappy expression. If the oldest catalogue of the southern barons is, they say, that of Roger the Norman, and cannot be found anywhere, the most modern catalogue can always be found and it is in the registers of those who have not paid their land credit.

However harsh it might be, the truth is always preferable.

And the truth is that southern Italy has given since 1860 much more than any other part of Italy in terms of its wealth, that it pays more than it can (the high tax-collection figures are the tragic prelude to innumerable expropriations); that the state has spent for it, for everything, much less, and that there are some provinces in which it is absent at least as much as the landowners. The truth is — and it jumps out of every page of this book — that the Mezzogiorno is reproached for all the things for which it has no blame. All the important institutions of the state are concentrated, at least like the army, in the zones which were already the most affluent.

For a variety of causes (union of debts, sales of public property, privileges to trading companies, issues of bonds) the Mezzogiorno's wealth, which could have been the nucleus of its economic transformation, has immediately transmigrated to the north. The onerous taxes and the concentration of state spending outside southern Italy have merely continued this bad work. There is now nothing, except the taxes, in which the Mezzogiorno does not come last.

And yet up to 1860 no authoritative voice had ever been raised from southern Italy to note this striking imbalance: this ugly word was invented in Lombardy and Piedmont when it was believed that the southern Italians paid little for the land and it was desired to force them to pay more.

It is said that the southern Italians pay little, yet anybody who has even merely glanced at the question knows they pay more; they that ask much of the state, and vice versa one knows that the state spends very little in and for almost all the Mezzogiorno; that they have invaded the public administration, and vice versa that they are a slender minority.

At the moment of union, southern Italy had all the elements needed to transform itself. It had a considerable amount of state property, an enormous monetary wealth, a very solid public credit. What it did lack, however, was any form of political education: what should have been done was to educate the middle classes and form above all the political environment.

However, the opposite path was followed: somewhat out of necessity, somewhat out of irresponsibility; above all the southern Italians themselves are to blame for this state of affairs.

Southern Italy, which had united unconditionally, was intellectually at a much lower level than Tuscany and all the regions of northern Italy. As a result of the centuries-old domination one noted then, and still does, a great contrast between public and private morals. The latter, above all from the family point of view, are higher, in general, than in another other land of Italy. The former were — and who can deny that they often are? — very lacking. The absolute governments had almost prohibited the citizens from taking an interest in politics: and often politics meant corruption or abuse of power.

It is unarguable that politically the southern Italians have represented an element of disorder. There local administrations function, as a rule, badly; their politicians do not concern themselves, in the majority of cases, than with local concerns. A trade treaty has nearly always for them less importance than the stay of a public order official. Agreeing in requesting special laws, a subsidy, grants for often imagined political damages, they disagree in every large collective work. Taken individually they often are worth a lot, singly, little.

Politically, southern Italy is absent: it is neither conservative, nor liberal, nor radial, it is apolitical. It has been too tormented, it has given too much, it has suffered too much. It asks only some equilibrium and order, the possibility to breathe and live.

In 1860, above after 1876, southern Italy was considered as the country destined to form the ministerial majorities. The prefects' only function would appear to be that of administering elections. A former minister told the Lower House that a prefect had stated that he was the arbitrator of the elections, because he could send all the mayors of his province to prison. Every party has speculated on the ignorance and suffering. Where the ill was to be cut, it has become harsher. Entire regions have been abandoned to infamous electoral cliques.

Thus the southern country has seen followed in politics, in tariffs, in finance, in administration, the most opposite direction to its interests, it has become sceptical. It would renounce half the Statute just not to pay half the land tax. The Mezzogiorno is viewed as a legitimist Vandea, as the bulwark of the institutions; and instead it is neither loyal nor unfaithful, it is indifferent. The Bourbons were much loved by the people whom they kept in ignorance and happiness: they year before they left they made triumphant journeys. And yet they lost the kingdom from one day to the next. The countries which do not engage in politics are the most revolutionary: the hatreds nursed in silence, the blind dominations, are much more revolutionary than one might imagine. In this sense there is nothing more conservative than parliament and electoral systems.

The southern Italians have many political wrongs! But not even the wrongs should be exaggerated! Of the 174 persons who have been ministers once or more, from the first national prime minister to the last government of Pelloux, 47 were from Piedmont, 14 from little Liguria, 19 from Lombardy, 41 from all of southern Italy, 14 from Sicily. Southern Italy would have had 119 ministers if it had had them in the same proportion as Liguria! The government of the provinces, prefects, finance superintendents, generals, etc., is still now to a large part in the hands of officials from the north. There is no sense of envy in our statement. We wish only to say that if the governments had been more honest and had not wished to make the Mezzogiorno work, i.e., corrupt the middle classes even more for electoral purposes, much could have been done, and, in any case, responsibility lies not only with the southern Italians.

The problem of the Mezzogiorno is the biggest current problem: freedom and the future of Italy rest on the solution of this problem.

The landowners of the south, often forced to live a life the workers of Milan would not accept, are described as the feudatories of a political Vandea. Now it is curious that in 1799, 1820, 1848, 1859, albeit in a disordered manner, the ideologues of this Vandea sought insurrection before any other land of Italy. In this country, which pays as though it were rich, and is treated as a nursery of parliamentary majorities, the state has often showed itself only in the form of the tax agents and carabinieri.

There is no doubt that the national bourgeoisie is quite dull; but the lack of initiative is more than one would think the fruit of the difficulties. One can try when the primary needs are assured; but he who lacks this security, does not even try. In Milan, there is no doubt that the millions needed for an industrial enterprise are raised in a few days, but in Naples no. But first of all the wealth has already been formed, and the first formation was the result of the general policy, and then the existing or created conditions assure a remuneration of capital easier. When there is a capital which is seeking investment one can be more daring than when there is an unsatisfied demand for capital.

It cannot be denied that after 1860 southern Italy has made much progress: the provinces have opened to civilisation, the general conscience has risen: the population above all is freer and has felt the need for a better life. As in the old Vatican maps the inland of Africa was blank and bore only the mysterious wording: hic sunt leones; the map of civilisation had in the Mezzogiorno big blank spaces which are increasingly diminishing.

With all its faults, this unity, which was the aspiration and goal of centuries, has led to too many good things for one to speak only badly of it. But the good things it has achieved have been quite unequal; hence the present contrast.

And so the origins of the prosperity of some regions have been sought not where they were, in the tariffs, in the public finance, in politics, but in an ethnic superiority which has never existed. And it has also been the case that who has given most has also appeared as an profiteer.

I was born in Basilicata, in the poorest land of the Mezzogiorno, and the memory of it, albeit distant, lies in my soul. The inhabitants of that region are considered capable, because some of them have been prefects, others ministers: it was said they had received much from the state. But every time I crossed this land, sad, solemn, poor, I asked myself: in what has it been capable? This word, which is a praise and an offence, this word, which is pronounced with respect and diffidence, how has it deserved it? I had heard it said in Lombardy that the southern Italians do not pay, and in my eyes and heart I imagined the hundreds of families hounded from the land, because they could not pay the taxes; I had heard it said that they do not work, and I had seen the poor rural peasants work to exhaustion as in no other place on earth; I had heard it said that there is a bourgeoisie which hides its savings, and I saw only insolvent debtors, persons who begged with banks and the few rich people so as to avert expropriation. Finally, I had been told that the children of the middle class had invaded the public administration: and yet in the army I found less of them than from those regions which hate militarism.

What is it then which maintains his iniquitous legend? and why shouldn't we destroy it? why should the new generation, which should honour the truth, have to lie as well?

And yet another new problem! As though Italy didn't have any others, yet another one!

And why should there not be another problem? Peace is not the purpose of life and it is only in difficulties that a people's energy is measured.

On the other hand, the problem in all of this is only of a moral nature.

What is done cannot be undone, says Shakespeare's tragic woman: what is done is done and let's not speak about it again. Southern Italy have given what it has for an important work of good: for its own future; it, which is so little advanced (and this should be loyally acknowledged) has paid for its entry into civilisation. It is something of a high entry fee; but it is not disproportionate to the work.

Now southern Italy should ask neither hurried public works, nor grandiose concessions and perhaps not even new institutions. These things serve sometimes more for speculation than industrial development; more to create jobs than to enable a country's economy to rise up.

But the past should be a great school.

Those who are higher up, the richest, the most fortunate should the loudest. I dare not even broach institutions or reforms useful to the middle classes.

Before creating new institutions for the same workers of Lombardy and Piedmont, who already receive the wages of civilised countries, it should be recalled that these wages would not be such without the Mezzogiorno; and that there are still even now in the Mezzogiorno vast plains where malaria kills.

Before doing anything which might increase the taxes by even one lira, one should recall that there are lands in which the state appears more cruel than the cruellest of landlords in Ireland.

Violence is sometimes the case of good: each act of creation often derives from violence. Now, having forced the country's conscience, one should also with violence fight all those systems which are based on the criterion that southern Italy should provide the ministries with their praetorians.

Southern Italy has little wealth and little industrial education: even the state when it has spent for it has spent more to maintain the parasitism rather than fight it. It is instead industrial education which should be formed.

During the revolutions of 1820, 1848 and (why not say it?) 1860 there were innumerable masses in the Mezzogiorno which demanded state investment. Even now the otium cum dignitate of a state employee is seen as happiness: and a mother's aspiration is a son employed by the state.

In two studies on 1820 and 1848 I had occasion to say the numerous masses invaded in Naples the offices demanding jobs. The same thing happened in 1860, and Garibaldi in his heroic ingenuousness, believing Italy very wealthy, wanted the officials of the Neapolitan army who had fought alongside him recognised: one official for every six soldiers. Southern Italy has perhaps few employees because it has wanted too many of them. Now it is the education which should·be changed, indeed, which has to be refounded. The Mezzogiorno of Italy, if it is destined to a big reawakening, can only be conquered slowly, purging its administration and assuring it an economical education.

Every now and then muddled reform projects are presented, more or less fortunate attempts, where illusion helps the error. In future, in any reform project, one should think of southern Italy which nature did not make rich and which has given everything for unity.

The tendency of modern peoples does not tolerate fragmentations, and it is not possible, not even by baleful hypothesis, to conceive of a divided Italy. For the greater good of all, unity is necessary and should be placed before everything. Germany, France, England, how many highly civilised peoples in Europe have attempted also with violence to reforge the unitary bonds. Political unity, customs unity should therefore not be called into question, not even if some region might think more useful a separation which, given the struggles of the modern peoples, would end up being fateful for it.

The discussion which is opened may harbour a danger. In the south of Italy where there is little wealth, the difficulties are many and the middle class is poor, there is an innumerable mass which seeks jobs or positions and wishes instead to instigate rather than destroy parasitism. Well then, we should not bother ourselves with them.

Southern Italy, suffocated by the tax burden, needs breathable air, above all to expand its horizons, to form its own collective conscience, to eliminate any antisocial features which might still persist.

If the budget cannot tolerate new spending, nothing is asked on condition that nothing be given to those more rich and less tormented.

But if a financial reform should be attempted, before thinking of other things or of others one should remember the many provinces where the taxes cause ten times more damage than hail and plagues. If new institutions are to be created, and they do not necessarily have to be at the border, one should remembers that administrative land which is the Mezzogiorno.

Above all, the spirit of Italian politics should change. When one sends to southern Italy not the worst officials, but the best because their work is the most difficult; when the present forms of parasitism will be fought and not fostered, and the Mezzogiorno not considered as a field of conquest for every leader, sometimes of every parliamentary adventurer; when one facilitates the formation of wealth and now new tax will depress it; then one will help the industrial transformation of the Mezzogiorno and the problem will be resolved.

If the name of Italy has come from the extreme south of the peninsula, so also did much of its history. The problem of liberty and the future of unity lie now in the solution of the problem of southern Italy.

O Italia Diis sacra: o sacred Italy to the fight!

Dear Roux, do you wish to help me spread the truth and free Italy of a prejudice which harms it more than its poverty?

Your friend,
NITTI

2. - The Composition of Italy's Budget

2.1 - *The Situation of the Old States Prior to Unification*

The aim of this study is to establish the situation of each Italian region vis-à-vis the state budget.

It is common belief, generally if not solely rooted in northern Italy, that the south profits from the national budget, contributing, vice versa, to a lesser extent. It is said that while the southern Italians pay less, they have demanded and obtained a large number of unproductive railways, they have demanded and claim increasingly broad concessions. It is believed (and such an opinion has found fertile ground in Piedmont and Lombardy) that southern Italians, while they find ways to evade many taxes through the old land registers, as in the land tax, or by not investing, but simply hoarding their wealth, as in the taxes on personal non-property income, continued to demand new concessions from the state. It is noted that the number of southern Italians in the public administration increases: and this fact engenders unease.

On the other hand, the Mezzogiorno which before 1860 had more savings that almost all the regions of the north; where savings, albeit in the primitive form of accumulation and hoarding of money, were huge; where life was very shabby, but where consumption was considerably high, shows all the symptoms of depression and stagnation. Even between 1880 and 1888, the agricultural wealth of Veneto did not exceed that of Apulia, and between Genoa and Bari, between Milan and Naples there was a much smaller gap in economic and industrial development than there is now. But now, together with a reduction in the capacity to consume, one espies the alarming symptoms of a halt in saving, of the growth of poor emigration, of the sluggish formation of industry in the face of a growing demand. Between 1870 and 1888, the Mezzogiorno's importance in Italy's social and economic life was much greater than is the case today. All these things, even though not known, but felt by the population of the Mezzogiorno, determine a state of disquiet.

Many reasons have been adduced to explain this difference and many facts have been put forward: there has even been talk of different races, of superior and inferior races; as though that which is produced by races, i.e., by nature, can change from one decade to the next.

To study the state's action vis-à-vis each region it is necessary to examine: *a)* the financial policy — i.e., the distribution of the receipts and public expenditure in each region; *b)* the customs policy; *c)* the economic policy.

This study confines itself to studying only the state's financial policy. It aims to investigate how much wealth the state collects in each region every year and how much it spends there. It aims to examine how the present financial system has come into being: and how the taxes weigh in proportion to each region's wealth. Finally, it intends to see how the state has spent in terms of geographical distribution the receipts from ordinary and extraordinary taxes, and what is the distribution of all the state institutions, whether they be inspired by civil, welfare or military purposes.

The movements of wealth brought about by the financial policy are enormous. Several billion lire move in a series of years, as a result of said, from one region to another: the phenomenon has been noted everywhere, in France, in Russia, in Austria, in Germany. But in Italy it has acquired an even more intense form and hence should be studied in greater depth.

Yet the movements of wealth brought about by the financial policy are small compared with those engendered by the economic and customs policies. The distribution of private wealth in Italy has changed significantly since 1887: and southern Italy initially acted as a consumption colony and thus allowed the development of big industry in the north.

The history of the national economy with regard to the changes the customs policy has brought about in the wealth of each region would be a work of considerable importance.

This study however confines itself to examining the action of public finance on the life of the single regions: the results of economic and customs policies on each region can only examined by those who have much comprehensive elements than those currently available.

However, this limitation in no way diminishes the extreme importance of the study.

The author of this study has traced only the outline: he who can conclude it with more comprehensive means and greater preparation will render a true and great service to science and history.

It is obvious that in a unitary state each province or region should contribute in equal measure, or, to put it better, in a proportionally equal measure. But it is equally evident that this is not nor can it ever wholly be the case.

There are towns which, proportional to their wealth, pay less, and there are towns which receive a greater number of benefits. The military and cultural institutes are unequally distributed; this inequality is almost always the result of neither ill-will nor bad arrangements, but rather of historical traditions and political needs.

As regards the revenues, it is, albeit roughly, possible without serious error to indicate the participation of each province or region in the life of the state; but it is not easy to calculate the real contribution without bearing in mind a series of variations of considerable importance.

In general, those writers who have dealt with these arguments have not taken account of the particular constitution of Italy's public finances; it is not only Rome that pays the taxes of other regions. In Milan, Florence, Naples, Palermo, the taxes and contributions of the province include contributions from throughout Italy.

In Milan, the Società mediterranea delle Ferrovie pays 6 or 7 million lire per year of taxes; in Florence the Società Adriatica circa 10 million lire. The contributions of Naples include 11,500,000 lire, those of Rome 14 million lire for sales taxes which are in fact collected by the state on behalf of the local council. The Banca d'Italia pays its taxes in Rome, the Banco di Napoli in Naples; now these two institutes operate throughout Italy, and the millions they give every year to the state are generated only in minimal part by the provinces of Rome and Naples.

The state's spending is modified by causes of the same nature. At Florence every year the state pays from 40 to 50 million lire for kilometre subsidies, construction of rail track and operating expenses for the complementary networks of Società Adriatica delle Ferrovie. Florence province has hardly anything to do with this spending by the state. So those who attribute such an enormous sum to it are necessarily obtaining erroneous results.

The studies carried out to date by numerous authors have not taken any account of these movements: and that is why they do not approach the truth.

However, even should one succeed in making an accurate calculation and taking account of all the causes of error, it should be acknowledged that the division of public spending cannot, in its arithmetical expression, serve as a basis for those political deductions which are often made. A fortress in a province of the Alps, the Moncenisio works, the institutes which exercise control on public spending serve not only the province in which they are situate, but all the state. They provide services of general utility.

But it is equally evident that every province or region has the greatest interest in ensuring that the expenses of general utility take place in its territory; these expenses in fact lead to a bigger series of local benefits.

The 11,000 soldiers in Cuneo province undoubtedly render a service to the entire peninsula, as they guard the border. Thus, the province of Campobasso, which has only 400 soldiers, also benefits from the big number of soldiers at Cuneo. But while the utility obtained by Campobasso is limited to a fact which could take place and which will be, in any case, common with Cuneo, Cuneo obtains a enormous series of certain benefits. The Naval Academy of Livorno, which is a very heavy burden for the state, also benefits the province of Salerno, in the sense that it too can send its youngsters to learn the arts of naval warfare and benefits from the existence of a navy. But these benefits are also scarce and in large part virtual: if the Military Academy were instead in Salerno, the benefits this province would receive would be of different nature, i.e., present and real. The fortresses in the Alps are undoubtedly useful to all of Italy; but all of Italy has for them, vice versa, channelled a very large amount of wealth into only a few towns. When a fortress which costs a million lire is built in a town, locally there is high demand for labour; there are therefore higher wages, higher consumption, and, from the landowners, who sell foodstuffs, to the producers and speculators, everyone benefits. But the benefits are confined to a specific zone.

A university can act in the same manner. If the state spends 300,000 lire and the university has only 300 students, who each spend a further 1,000 lire, there will be a demand for products and consumption which there was not before, amounting to six hundred thousand lire. Thus a court, a vocational school, an infantry regiment have, from the point of view of consumption and demand for local products, an identical action.

None of this takes account of the indirect benefits: the greater ease of obtaining education and finding a job, the greater probability of establishing profitable industries where there is already a consumption market, finally the higher level of civilisation which is the consequence of this. Contact with new people often elevates a small town, it engenders new needs, spurs the spirit of initiative, raises the level of life.

Modena and Benevento are without doubt two provincial cities at quite different levels of development; but it is not only the local energies which have determined this difference, but rather quite different causes. The small city of Modena has a large military academy, it has a university, it has a court of appeal, a fine arts academy, a fine arts institute, a technical institute, finally it has many other institutes of great importance and which cost many millions and give rise to large movements of outsiders, big outlays, the possibility of almost free education and training. If the city of Benevento were to have all these things, of which it has none (it has only just over 300 soldiers and none of the institutes of Modena), it would probably take only a few years to rise to the same, if not a higher level. Modena's music academy undoubtedly works for the artistic culture of all of Italy; but it is doubtful whether the city of Benevento is very interested in its maintenance and consequent outlays.

In general, if a province gives to the state 20 million lire and the state spends in it 8 million lire, the difference will constitute an annual deficit which will have to be made good by a bigger output. The 69 provinces can be viewed as a series of small economies: the same holds for states.

When a province is in the conditions indicated, if it does not wish to exhaust itself in a short time, it has to sell 12 million lire of products more than it buys. The net surplus can only be made good by exports which are higher than imports; of by the province itself being the creditor of other provinces for a amount of interest which is at least the same. This cannot even be supposed of southern Italy which is always a debtor.

Italy's political order and geographical configuration endows this problem with an intensity not found in any other country. In federal countries such as Switzerland and Germany, the expenditure is divided broadly; in unified countries such as France, the geographical form ensures that the division, although not uniform, never tends to concentrate itself in a single zone, as is the case in Italy. Eminent statisticians have shown that France has 26 departments in which the state spends more than it receives; but these departments are generally the least rich. In Italy the opposite takes place, it is in the poorest regions, Basilicata, Apulia, Calabria, where the state spends proportionally less.

Where disagreement exists, as between Austria and Hungary, the burdens are proportioned not only to the wealth and population, but also to the benefits the state's spending produces.

Moreover in Italy the state budget plays a much more important role in the national economy than in any other country.

The annual production of England has been calculated by some (Bowley, 1891) in £1,611 million. The state budget, which totals just over £100 million, amounts to a sixteenth of it.

But in Italy, where it is unlikely annual production exceeds 8 billion lire, the state budget amounts to just under a quarter.

Now the history of Italy's budget has still to be written: and furthermore, we have still to study what action it has exercised on the life of each region.

On 12 December 1871 Quintino Sella stated in the Lower House: «I was saying, sirs, that a study of the Treasury service will allow us to draw most important lessons concerning what has happened for our finances, and which should be done in the future.

«Let us examine this spending of 10,400 million lire made in the past decade; let us break it down by category.

«The so-called intangible spending amounted to circa 4,500 million lire; the spending of the Ministry of War and the Navy amounted to 2,800 million lire; the spending of all the rest of the administration, which I will call the civil administration spending, amounted to only 3,100 million lire.

«Even more important is the study of the trend of said categories of spending... — And after having examined the reduction made and the economies achieved, Sella asked: — But, sirs, what is the use of all this, if the intangible part of the budget, which has risen from the 197 million lire it was in the year 1861 to 718 million lire in the budget for 1872, in other words if the intangible spending has more than tripled?

«In this part of the budget there has been an increase of 500 and more millions; two fifths of the budget!»

The situation as regards the state's outlays has become much more serious since 1871.

And now anybody who wishes to write the history of Italy's public finance should pose above all two questions: — How much has the Italian state taken from taxpayers since its establishment and in what form has it done so? How much has Italy spent since its establishment to date and for what purposes has it spent it?

These two questions, for those who wish to penetrate the causes and not confine themselves to mere numerical exercises, would entail a considerable series of studies.

But the mere exposition of the figures also has a real importance, even more so considering that we believe the calculation mentioned by Sella has never been made.

Since 1862, which was the year of our tax unification, to 1896-1897, the state has taken from the taxpayers 41,284 million lire in taxes and duties of every kind; it has moreover obtained 7,045 million lire from the movement of capital and 2,195 million lire from that for the construction of railways.

The property tax, which thus includes the tax on land and that on buildings, which were originally combined, accounts for 12.12% of all receipts, and 14.14% of real receipts.

Without entering into detail, if one bears in mind that in Italy the annual capitalisation, i.e., the amount the nation saves each year, oscillates at around just 500 million lire, and, vice versa, the population quickly grows; only if one thinks of the weakness of national saving will one realise the importance of the state's financial policy in the nation's economy.

But when wishing to calculate the action of the state in the life of the single regions one should take into account not only the revenues, but above all the spending.

Most of the spending has been absorbed by interest to serve the debt, military spending and the collection of taxes. This is a harsh necessity which hangs over almost all the states of Europe.

One of the most illustrious writers on public finance, Ricca-Salerno, perceptively noted that: «A comparison of the budgets of the various states of Europe shows that a considerable share of public spending consists in the payment of interest and the annual allowance for amortisation of the public debt ... Thence the primary needs of political existence, defence and offence, the needs of security and the purposes of power absorb the most conspicuous share of public spending of modern states, a share which increases from year to year ...

«However, abstracting from the sum employed in works of public utility, and principally in the building of railway lines, most public spending is destined for the purposes of security, law and power. In this aspect, the budgets of the more civil states are very similar to those of individuals belonging to the lower classes, in which the primary needs of existence absorb by far the greatest share of their spending, and leave quite a relatively small margin for the purposes of civilisation and culture».

Although this fact is not specific to Italy, it is more evident and acute in Italy.

The principal categories of spending in Italy clearly indicate that the state has spent the greatest part of its resources where government annuities are concentrated and where the land and sea garrisons and naval shipyards are situate.

From 1871 to 1896-1897, real revenues (disregarding capital movements and railway construction) increased from 1,013 to 1,684 million lire and spending from 1,175 to 1,679 million lire.

The revenues which saw the greatest growth were indirect taxes: customs duties yielded a revenue of 3.90 lire per inhabitant, and in the last year studied 7.84: tobacco which yielded only 2.77

now yields 6.01 lire; excise duties have risen from 0.04 to 1.44 lire. Only revenues from internal sales duties have decreased.

Except for the tax on land, direct taxes are now also more onerous than they were in 1871: from 1871 to 1896-1897, revenues from the tax on buildings rose from 1.93 to 2.82 lire; and those from the tax on personal non-property income increased from 5.34 to 9.21 lire per inhabitant.

The items of spending which have increased the most, also in order of importance, are those which regard public-debt interest,

STATE REVENUES IN ITALY FROM 1862 TO 1896-1897
overall revenue: 50,525,190,307.

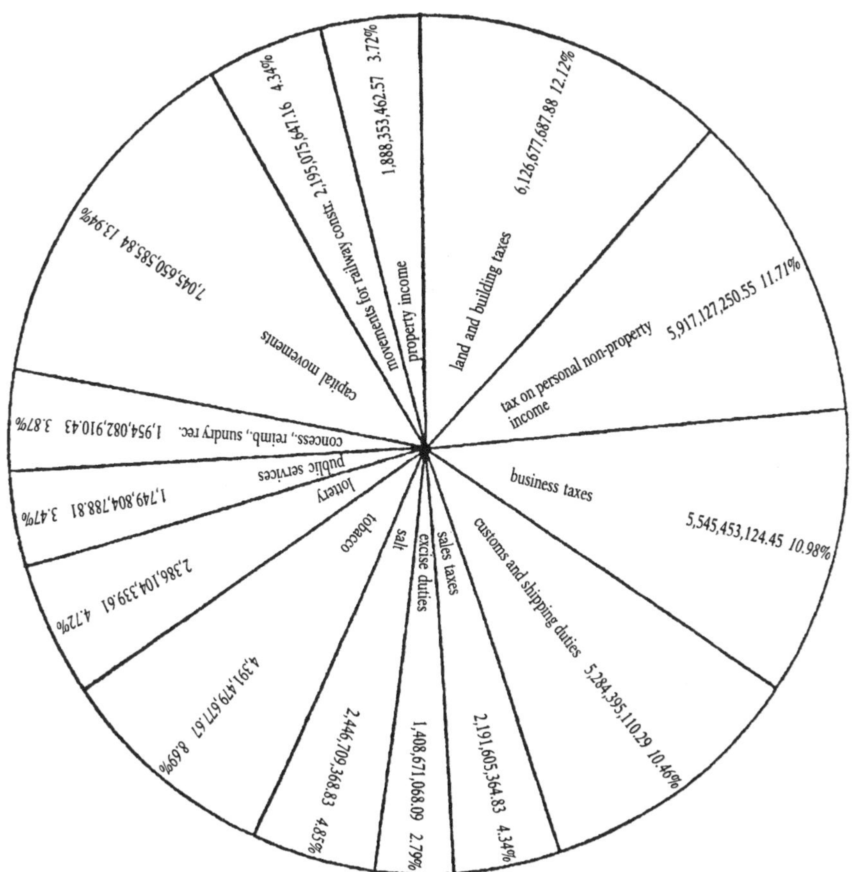

the army and the navy. Spending on the navy saw the strongest increase, rising from 0.84 to 3.16 lire per inhabitant, that on the army rose from 5.37 to 8.19 lire while debt-service expenditure rose from 16.77 to 21.95 lire per inhabitant.

The increase in intangible spending and military spending was such that the budget, as it is now, has no margin and no elasticity at all.

It has been justly noted that if the real resources of the budget amount to 1,600 million lire, the Treasury's commitments to-

STATE SPENDING IN ITALY FROM 1862 TO 1896-1897
overall spending: 50,877,704,622

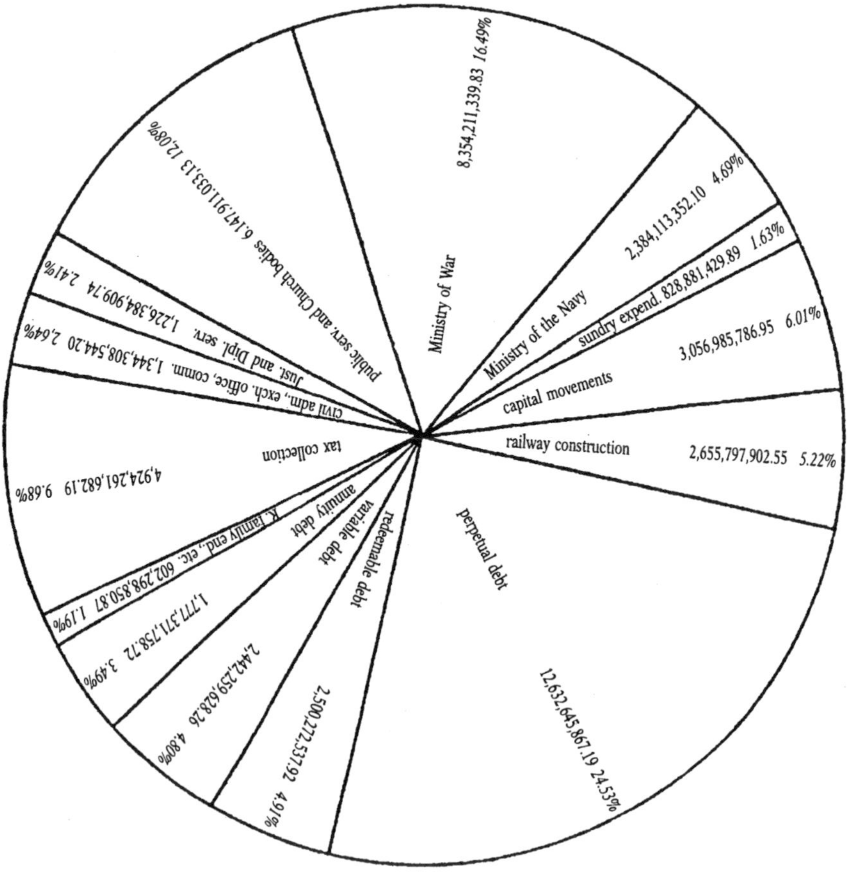

Ministry of War 8,354,211,339.83 16.49%
Ministry of the Navy 2,384,113,352.10 4.69%
sundry expend. 828,881,429.89 1.63%
capital movements 3,056,985,786.95 6.01%
railway construction 2,655,797,902.55 5.22%
perpetual debt 12,632,645,867.19 24.53%
redeemable debt 2,500,272,537.92 4.91%
variable debt 2,442,259,628.26 4.80%
annuity debt 1,777,371,758.72 3.49%
R. family end., etc. 602,298,850.87 1.19%
tax collection 4,924,261,682.19 9.68%
civil adm., exch. office, comm. 1,344,308,544.20 2.64%
Just. and Dipl. serv. 1,226,384,909.74 2.41%
public serv. and Church bodies 6,147,911,033.13 12.08%

tal 800 million, while a further 100 million of Treasury commitments are hidden in other budgets. Hence there are some 900 million lire of unavoidable commitments.

Hence the 'true' budget, that which is actually discussed, does not exceed 700 million lire. Just under half this amount is dedicated to army and navy spending: which amounts to 48% of the available budget.

From 1862 to 1896 the Treasury's commitments increased from 200 to 800 million lire; in other words they rose by 600 million lire. Six hundred million lire which capitalised amounts to an enormous figure. As Hon. Rubini, Chairman of the General Budget Commission noted «From 1862 to 1896 we have incurred one million lire per day of debt».

This is one of the few things on which the governments which have succeeded one another have agreed.

It is quite difficult to specify with any precision the financial situation of each of the old Italian states when annexed. Pasini first attempted this in 1863. In a diligent study published in *Annuario statistico italiano* he sought to indicate the revenues, expenditure and debt of each of the states. These figures however, particularly those for the Kingdom of the Two Sicilies, should be viewed with considerable reservations.

What is certain is that the Kingdom of Naples was in 1859 not only the most respected in Italy for its financial solidity — and this is proved by the quotations of its bonds, which were higher than those for French consolidated stock — but also that which, of the leading states, enjoyed the better conditions. There was little debt, taxes were not onerous and well harmonised; all the state's fiscal and treasury services were of great simplicity. This was the very opposite of the Kingdom of Sardinia, where taxes had reached very high levels; the fiscal regime consisted of series of continuous overlaps largely introduced without any criteria; it had an enormous public debt and was menaced by the spectre of bankruptcy.

Without diminishing any of the great merits Piedmont had for the unity of Italy, which was in very large part its work, it should equally be recognised that, without the unification of the various states, the Kingdom of Sardinia was necessarily condemned to bankruptcy as a result of its abuse of spending and the poverty of its resources. The financial depression before 1848, compounded between 1849 and 1859 by an enormous quantity of unproductive public works, had led to a situation with only two possible outcomes: either bankruptcy or merging Piedmont's finances with those of another large state.

Piedmont was the last of the large Italian states to build a railway.

The first railway, as is known, was built in the Kingdom of the Two Sicilies; the short line Naples-Portici, which entered service on 4 October 1839, was followed only a year later, in 1840, by the Milan-Monza rail line in Lombardy.

Between 1842 and 1848 no railway line was built in Piedmont, neither by the state nor by private players, while railway lines had been opened in Lombardy, Veneto, Tuscany, Kingdom of the Two Sicilies, etc. The first railway line built in Piedmont was the Turin-Moncalieri line which was only 8 km. long and commenced operation on 24 September 1848.

But between 1848 and 1850 there was a veritable building fever in Piedmont and the state which was the last to pursue the path of building was also that which abused it the most. Reading the debates of the Turin Parliament from 1850 to 1859 one can see that the great political struggle in which Piedmont was engaged was overshadowed by financial concern.

Now it is strange that the finances of the various Italian states have never found a serene judge. If this had been the case, the judgement would be quite different from that proffered at present, according to the publications of Scialoja and other Neapolitan refuges who fought for a great political cause, but who were far from being impartial judges.

In 1857, the exiled Antonio Scialoja published in Turin a proud attack on the Bourbon government entitled *The Budgets of the Kingdom of Naples and of the Sardinian States*. This book was the focus of much discussion and worried the King of Naples and received a correct rebuttal by Magliani: those of others were less worthy.

What was Scialoja's book? A political statement, equal to that made by P. S. Mancini when he proclaimed the principle of nationality in Turin. Neither one nor the other concerned himself perhaps with historical precision and scientific truth: both however harboured a great and noble passion which did not allow them to judge with that serenity which is due now, forty years later.

A range of judgements can be passed on the Bourbons of Naples: they were weak, they did not sense the new times, they wholly lacked any vision; many times they broke their promises, many times they sinned; always out of timidity, never perhaps out of anger. They were not dissimilar to most of the princes of the peninsula, including the Pontiff.

But whatever one's judgement, it should not be denied that their administrative arrangements were often excellent; that their public finance was good and, in general, honest.

Scialoja's book should today be included among the most important political documents: however no partial technical study can fail to take account of the parallel between the finances of Piedmont and those of Naples.

To now judge the finances of the Kingdom of Naples we have two elements of great value, in addition to the numerous historical and political monographs.

June 1860 saw the publication of the situation of Naples' finances, edited by the Ministry of Finance; this publication contains all the budgets from 1848 to 1859. It is the first authentic document with undeniable historical value.

The second element of great importance is the report published by Mr. Vittorio Sacchi in 1861. Sacchi was a friend of Count Cavour: director until 1860 of the taxes and land register of Sardinia, Sacchi was sent to Naples by the Piedmont Ministry with a mandate of absolute trust to govern and regulate the finances of Naples. He himself confesses that he did not have, nor could he have had, favourable prospects. Indeed, doubtful whether to accept, he illustrated the difficulties of the undertaking to Cavour; and Cavour replied: «Go, go, if you do not succeed, you can console yourself with all those who have encountered the same fate». Sacchi was general secretary of finances in Naples from April 1 to October 31 1861 and he enshrined his work in a report, which is a document of inestimable value.

Although there was a constitutional regime in Piedmont, the Piedmont finances are no easier to examine than those of Naples, which was under an absolute regime. In 1862, the final budgets only went up to 1853: there was considerable disorder in the collection of taxes and in spending and even today many elements of judgement are lacking.

The finances of Naples, organised by a man of genius, Medici, were perhaps the most suited to the country's economic situation.

Revenues were few and large and easy to collect.

The base of the fiscal arrangements was a swingeing property tax. It was so well organised that it was a complete contrast to that of Piedmont, where it was much more onerous and difficult to collect.

In his report to the Secretary General of Finances, Sacchi notes that: «The collection system for the property tax, the first and most important of the state's resources was unarguably probably the quickest, simplest and most certain of those in Italy.

The state, without that detailed interference to be found in France and in the old Provinces, where the legislative power intervened even in the sending of the payment notices, had ensured at set and clearly determined periods the collection of taxes with the solidest guarantees against any malpractice on the part of the accountants».

There was almost no tax on personal non-property income. As this was just coming into being, Medici and his continuators deemed that any attempt to tax it was fraught with danger. Internal trade enjoyed a host of facilities: «personal non-property income and trade in particular — Scialoja says — were exempt in Naples from any form of direct taxation, while property was hit by a tax which was much more onerous relative to the state's general revenues».

Registration and stamp duties, which were very onerous in Piedmont, were quite modest in the Kingdom of Naples. The Banco di Napoli's arrangements for credit certificates, admirably simple from this aspect, made registration superfluous. «The admirable financial organism of the Neapolitan Provinces — Sacchi notes — was seen above all as regards the Banco's functioning».

«The Banco — Sacchi writes — accepted cash from whomsoever wished to deposit it, it held it at its own expense and returned it at the depositor's request in equivalent money.

«On receipt of the money it issued a piece of paper called credit certificate, for amounts from ten ducats upwards; a policy for smaller sums. Both one and the other had to be handed back to the bank when the money was returned.

«The depositor could have opened in his name a credit ledger to record there the sums of money which were subsequently deposited and this was called a *madrefede*.

The amounts deposited can be withdrawn in full or in part, and one could pay third persons, by means of a proxy which was called a bill.

«The credit ledger showed the movements of the deposits and withdrawals; the certificate and the policy were exchanged at sight on signature by the payee. They serve for private negotiations with the signature of the payer and the payee. They are unseizable like the money deposited at the Banco.

«Private persons hold the credit ledger even when it has been closed; the Banco the bills or certificates paid.

«These are the advantages of this institution, which has made it so dear and popular to the population.

«Firstly, there is the conservation of the money of private persons with the computation of their dealings in the credit ledgers. The certainty of the date and the authenticity of the transactions which can be noted on the bills or certificates, there sufficing the delivery and acceptance of them without any cost, and also with the payment of the stamp and registration duties.

«There is the check by the person to whom the money should be paid, whether he receives it for himself or under proxy from others. Finally, there is the means to ensure that he who receives the money fulfils his obligations, as these obligations are noted down on the bill and the money is not paid out until these obligations have been fulfilled. This is how the dotal and pupillary capital should be employed, as well as that of public establishments or non-profit bodies, and the bills are not paid if the courts have not deemed such useful.

«Finally the archive holds a copy of all the bills and certificates whenever they were issued».

These simple arrangements facilitated contracting. There was a single, fixed register and all the very onerous taxes that existed in the other states were almost unknown in the Kingdom of the Two Sicilies.

Together with the land tax, most of the revenue derived from customs duties and indirect taxes: above all from the fiscal monopolies. Tobacco, salt, gunpowder, playing cards, lotto were all government monopolies.

The budget of Naples can therefore be deemed as based on the following principles: a hefty tax on land property collected in the most economic manner; some important monopolies; the almost total exemption from taxation of personal non-property income; very low taxes on transfers of property and exchanges. If the government's policy had not been inspired by an almost paranoid fear of any innovation, and if it had not stood in the way of industries and kept the provinces in almost a state of barbarism; if the police had not been blind and corrupt and had not constituted a state within a state; the financial order of the Bourbons was most suited to the development of wealth in the south.

In Piedmont, on the other hand, the financial order, which was then extended almost wholly to the rest of Italy, was most onerous. Even when the genius of Cavour sought to simplify it, it shed none of its original defects.

From 1848 to 1859 the Kingdom of the Two Sicilies, despite the internal differences, introduced no new taxes neither did it increase existing taxes.

In the same period in Piedmont, all the existing taxes were increased, and many new ones introduced, and the price of powder and tobacco and official stamped paper was increased, inheritance duty, the mortmains, the taxes on property transfers were all increased, new taxes on industries and advance tax deductions on pensions were also created.

In 1861, the General Secretary of the Ministry of Finances, noticing these enormous differences between the taxes of Piedmont and those of Naples believed it difficult to subject the southern people to the Piedmont taxes; a long period of study was necessary before the salutary sacrifice could be achieved.

«It is very difficult, — said Sacchi — that the multiform system of taxation of the old provinces could be applied here.

«The inaccuracy of the cadastre would make fair distribution of the taxation of property wealth long and hard.

«One will have to turn one's attention to studies of property wealth, of trade and of acts entailing transfers of property as well as stamp duty.

«Parliament shall deal with these issues and decide their solution.

«These are necessary sacrifices, on which the health of the motherland depends. Who would dare to refuse them?»

Almost all the taxes which were more onerous in Piedmont, were not to be found in Naples; to extend them appeared a difficult task, necessary sacrifices as the General Secretary of the Ministry of Finances said.

The revenues of the Kingdom of Naples, calculated in Italian lire, were for the year 1860 (those which we indicated in *Il bilancio*, p. 43)[1].

The costs of collection amounted to 14,200,000 lire and were calculated separately. Sicily's budget contributed more than 17 million lire to the lgeneral costs.

Calculating the costs of collection and merging the budgets of Naples and Sicily, the ordinary revenues of every nature, patrimony receipts, taxes, duties did not even total 175 million lire.

On the other hand, the revenues of the Kingdom of Sardinia, whose population was less than half that of the Kingdom of the Two Sicilies, totalled 91.4 million lire in 1853 and 144,332,371 lire in 1859.

---

[1] See NITTI F.S., *Il bilancio dello Stato dal 1862 al 1896-1897. Prime linee di una inchiesta sulla ripartizione territoriale delle entrate e delle spese pubbliche in Italia*, Napoli, Società anonima copperativa tipografica, 1900, pp. VI-454 (printing ended on 8 May 1900, it was published in an edition of only 100 copies as an excerpt from «Atti del Reale Istituto d'Incoraggiamento di Napoli», 1899-1900).

It is quite easy to imagine the difference in the tax burden in the two states. If we take Tuscany, the Duchy of Modena, that of Parma, the Church State we see that everywhere taxes were more onerous than in the Kingdom of the Two Sicilies.

Neither was the cost, in its proportions, different in the Kingdom of Naples than that of the other states. The civil list, taking account of the population, was identical to that of Piedmont; expenditure for public order was less than in the other states; expenditure for religion much lower than that of the Kingdom of Sardinia: finally, expenditure for the army and navy more or less identical to those of the other states of the peninsula, taking account of the number of inhabitants.

Between 1848 and 1859 the budget deficits in the Kingdom of Sardinia amounted to circa 370 million lire: those of the Kingdom of Naples less than 139 million lire. The Kingdom of Naples did not sell off its assets; the Kingdom of Sardinia sold state land, railways and also industrial plants. The Kingdom of Sardinia contracted a large debt: between 1848 and 1860, the Kingdom of the Two Sicilies contracted only a small debt.

It is always said that Piedmont prepared the war of independence: this is true and to its glory.

But it should always be borne in mind that, for opposite reasons, the other states, principally the Kingdom of Naples, made similar preparations for war.

To suppress the internal revolutions, the Kingdom of the Two Sicilies spent enormous sums: the Austrian occupation and the reorganisation of the army in 1820 cost 80 million ducats; the revolution of 1848 more than 30 million ducats. Between 1855 and 1860, enormous sums were spent for the army and navy.

The financial ruin of Piedmont in 1859 did not depend, or at any rate solely, on the preparations for war. To combat Piedmont in the opposite sense, the other states, which had an equal or higher number of soldiers, also made considerable sacrifices: some of them, to repress the unification movement, spent more than Piedmont to support it. The political historian will bear the difference in mind. But, from the point of view of public finance, it should be borne in mind that in 1860 Piedmont had an extensive road network; numerous railways and canals and public works of considerable importance. These causes, largely extraneous to the war, were the true agents of the financial depression.

«In 1848 — Bonghi wrote — Carlo Alberto had declared war on Austria, quite well supplied with what is called backbone. It had been setting money aside for considerable time: and used it for an expected occasion. In 1859, on the other hand, although Piedmont had waited for a new occasion to present itself, several circumstances forced it to wait for it in rags».

Why then, nonetheless, did a man of such high intellect as Antonio Scialoja, one of the true geniuses Italian public finance has ever had, extol the virtues of Piedmont's public finance, so disordered, and compare it with that of Naples, which was in many aspects superior to the present arrangement? For a quite simple reason. Public finance was for Scialoja merely a pretext to judge the policies of the Bourbons of Naples, which, in reality, could not be more weak, more soft, more timid, and, on some occasions, more violent. Violent out of fear and not cruelty.

It suffices to read Scialoja's book to see the political prejudice which inspires it on every page.

The direct taxes, above all the land tax, were in the Kingdom of Naples much less onerous than in Piedmont, where, moreover, the surtaxes were very harsh. In Piedmont, however, Scialoja writes, there are numerous roads: the value of the land will increase. «The surtaxes, following the flawed division of the main tax, only compounded the inequalities. The new cadastre will right the problem» (p. 46).

The Kingdom of the Two Sicilies was an agrarian country in which, in order for industry to form, there had to be tax exemptions for personal non-property income. The Neapolitan finance officials had wisely all but exempted commerce from duties and taxes. Scialoja found that «commerce is by its nature more querulous (p. 51), — and that one is afraid to introduce taxes on personal income — the absolute governments, which appear fearless, put on the mask of courage, as actors in the theatre, but are in reality guided by fear in almost all their resolutions» (p. 52).

The inheritance tax, which was very onerous in Piedmont, was much more tenuous in Naples: «it is much less onerous than would be thought at first glance» (p. 53), notes Scialoja. And the reasons are quite unconvincing, the heir, if he pays the tax with the capital inherited, considers the value of the inherited assets diminished by so much that it is as though the deceased left him nothing; when he pays the tax with the income, his loss is as if he from whom he inherited had died later» (p. 53).

In Piedmont as in Naples, the lottery was one of the important sources of revenue: «an immoral, albeit voluntary tax ... in Piedmont as in Naples it is deplorable — says Scialoja — but in Naples it deserves being more deplored because there is less culture and the people are more imaginative». In Piedmont however the lottery indicates the desire to progress; while in Naples it is proof of decadence. «The experienced and great political and economic changes raise hopes and engender emulations, which are effective stimuli for carrying out distinguished facts, but which often spur inexpert people to risky undertakings and generate in their soul too ardent a desire to improve their proper condition» (p. 55). In Naples, vice versa, «the unbridled love for the lottery and the interest of the government to maintain it alive as a financial and political resource simultaneously — (p. 54) — has prevented any progress in foresight and has depressed the people».

We have already noted the excellent arrangement for registration and stamp duties in Naples, hence the light taxes and duties. Stamp duty being fixed and registration fees very low; thus with a much greater number of inhabitants, the Kingdom of Naples received from registration and stamp duties three times less than the Kingdom of Sardinia. The tariffs in Naples were so low that they amounted to a third or a quarter those of Piedmont. The high taxes of Piedmont should have generated serious concern. Scialoja noted only: «The quite high and increasing fruit they produce in Piedmont, without wholly justifying it, is however a sign of the advancement of public prosperity» (p. 58).

Neither are the criteria by which the spending judged different.

The civil list, given the number of inhabitants, was almost identical in the Kingdom of Sardinia and the Kingdom of the Two Sicilies: in Naples it amounted to 8,289,000 lire of which Sicily accounted for 1,740,000 lire; in Piedmont to 4,500,000 lire. The Piedmont monarchy, at least in cost, did not differ from that of Naples. But, according to Scialoja, it should be judged differently. «A constitutional government, in which the king is not the first feudal lord of the kingdom, but the first representative of the state, entails outlays which concern less the splendour of the reigning house, but the decorum of the entire nation» (p. 66). And finally, the absolute prince, spending, can make spending an «instrument of oppression»; the constitutional prince «can increase the state's importance».

The public debt was very high in the Kingdom of Sardinia and low in that of Naples. Scialoja wrote that «if all the Italians were called to choose between the Sardinian government with its debts and taxes and that of Naples, I will not say with less debt and with lower taxes, but without taxes and debt, I do not believe anyone would doubt the outcome of the ballot« (p. 73).

Pensions were in absolute terms much lower in Naples than in Piedmont; the tax collection costs were almost identical: 14.9% in Naples and 14.4% in Piedmont. «This is very remarkable — adds Scialoja — and testifies to the simplicity of the taxes of Naples and the multiplicity and complication of those of Sardinia» (p. 75). One can add that it is no less remarkable because the Kingdom of Naples covered an extensive area without roads; while the Kingdom of Sardinia on the other hand was less extensive and had a large number of railways.

Although the magistrates were paid much better and were in general of a higher level, the administration of justice cost less in Naples than in Piedmont, taking into account the area and population.

We could adduce many other examples if they are needed.

It is now evident that the political concern was sovereign, and the high intellect of Scialoja had public finance serve only to confirm his thesis, which found its reason in the historical need of the moment.

But, once the political concerns were over, the Bourbons hounded, the general secretary of finances of the new Kingdom of Italy, sent to Naples by Cavour to facilitate the work of General Cialdini, gave an opposite opinion of the finances of Naples to that of Antonio Scialoja, and admired the simplicity and moderation of the financial organism of the Kingdom of the Two Sicilies.

If the Italians, as Antonio Scialoja said, had to chose between the taxes and debts of Piedmont and the flourishing of the Kingdom of Naples, they would have opted for Piedmont. One should say, if the most elect part of Italy. It is a serious wrong to believe that the unification movement started from popular conscience: it was the consequence of the new needs of the more educated middle classes; and it was more than anything the consequence of a great artistic and literary tradition.

But from Ferdinand II onwards, every time the popular masses of the Two Sicilies have had to chose between a Neapolitan and foreign monarchy, between the king and the liberals, they have always plumped for the king: in 1799, 1820, 1848 and 1860, the popular classes, even badly guided or put to the service of nefarious purposes, have taken the side of the monarchy and the king.

This popular concept (which I have studied in detail elsewhere) is not, as is claimed, the effect of ignorance or chance.

The Bourbons feared the middle classes and opposed them; but they were also concerned with assuring the people with the greater possible prosperity. In their conception, narrow and almost patriarchal, they were concerned only with satisfying the people, without bothering about the future, without looking ahead. It suffices to read the instructions to the Intendants of the Provinces, to the state-property commissioners, to the tax agents to see that the monarchy sought to base itself on the love of the popular classes. The king himself wrote to the Intendants to listen to anyone from the people: he warned them not to trust the most powerful persons; he incited them to satisfy with every love the needs of the population. Reading these reports, these letters, these circulars, one is often overcome by that warm sense of popular affection that exudes from every phrase. But every phrase also reveals the idea that the people can be content only if ignorant, if living in love of the altar and the throne.

Between 1848 and 1860, economies were sought everywhere so to avoid the introduction of new taxes: taxes on goods of everyday consumption were particularly avoided. No schools, but no unjust taxes; few public works, but few taxes. The king set a good example, reducing his civil list spontaneously by more than 10%; something of an uncommon fact in the history of the European princes, whether in absolute or constitutional regime.

It was often a corrupting, vulgar «paternalism»: it was sought to keep everyone satisfied. Undemanding jobs, most of which of little import and without pension rights; but enormous crowds of state employees. If they did not become a liberal, those who could read often became a state employee. The children of state employees were often employed at the age of ten, as at Banco di Napoli; sometimes even before the age of ten. The quiet life, the flow of traditions and admiration of the past were liked. And when the past was not glorious, there were always the obliging poets; and the historians were even more obliging than the poets. The Mezzogiorno, which has never had neither great art, nor a great literature, was depicted as the centre of European history in those emphatic publications. From Archimedes, who was a Greek from Syracuse, to Pythagoras, who was a Greek from the Magna Graecia, everything was aimed at speaking of past glories; and when the countries had no glories of any kind, they took pride in the fact that small and large battles had taken place on their territory, or that their lands had been dominated by one feudatory rather than another. Even today the old ideas of those times have far from disappeared, and talk continues of past greatness rather than of present duty.

The bourgeoisie did not like struggle, and the monarchy liked it even less.

It was the old Europe, with all its aversion for everything new, with all its weaknesses.

Industrial concessions were avoided; the formation of joint-stock banks and companies was avoided; the penetration of speculation, and with it the desire for novelty, was feared. A monastic quietism was loved: a people contented by a tranquil life; a bourgeoisie to be held at bay by jobs and the clergy; a obsequious nobility tied to tradition. Enjoyment and leisure were much loved; the great individual energies were feared; the old Europe, with all its prejudices. Masses of monasteries, the career of easy priesthood; banditry as a perennial danger; a very large city as capital with a large number of almost impenetrable provinces.

But a prudent, perspicacious administration was sought.

Public finance was rigid, the bank honest.

From 1818 to 1861, on an annual average of 69 million lire of advances and discounts, Banco di Napoli lost only 65,000 lire per year, less than the Bank of England, less than the Bank of France, less perhaps than any large bank in the world.

With a much greater wealth, the Kingdom of the Two Sicilies stayed in a static phase; between 1848 and 1868, Piedmont was always in a dynamic phase. The enormous imbalance made it necessary to accelerate the movement.

What was the situation of the various states at the moment of annexation? When unification came into being, what burdens did each state bear? What were the advantages?

It is without question that the taxes in Naples were, given the wealth of the inhabitants, at least three times lower than in Piedmont; undoubtedly much lower than those of the other states of the peninsula.

In 1800 the situation of the Kingdom of the Two Sicilies, compared with that of the other states of the peninsula, was as follows, given its wealth and number of inhabitants: 1) the taxes were lower than those of the other states; 2) state and church property amounted to an immense wealth, and, together, totalled more than similar such assets owned by the other states; 3) the (very slight) public debt was four times lower than that of Tuscany; 4) the number of state employees, calculating on the basis of pensions in 1860, was half that of Tuscany and almost half that of the Kingdom of Sardinia; 5) the quantity of circulating specie, later withdrawn from circulation by the state, was in absolute terms twice that of all the other states of the peninsula combined.

The present arrangement is not the result of any pre-established plan.

In general, the architectural designs in which the authors of public finance delight are divorced from reality. There is perhaps no country in the world, not even among the new countries, in which the tax system has been co-ordinated by a new concept. It is indeed very often the case that some minister or other has introduced profound reforms and sought to harmonise the taxes around an informing idea; however, not even from this angle is there a complete work, neither has there ever been one.

How could an organic tax system arise in Italy when the Italian state came into being amidst so many difficulties? There were the needs of the moment, imperative and supreme needs which had to be met; there was no time to engage in extensive discussion on how to meet them. Debts were contracted at onerous conditions, old taxes exacerbated and new taxes introduced without any economic criterion, often with no other criteria than the fiscal criterion. On some occasions, prodigality is a duty. As in the life of a man, in a supreme moment, the loan-shark also becomes a benefactor, thus also the most disastrous loans were, for the Italian state, in some moments not only useful but necessary. There is also the example, we believe unique, when all the taxes and duties in Italy were increased at one go, proportionally, with concern neither for their nature, nor for their burden.

Hence continuous modifications, additions, re-orderings, as the needs of the moment imposed, as appeared most opportune to increase the revenues or not to see them diminish.

The two big nuclei which in 1860 formed the Kingdom of Italy were the Kingdom of Sardinia and the Kingdom of the Two Sicilies. The economic importance of the first was much less, with an area and a population more or less half, its finances in disorder; as it was a movement of unification, i.e., of merger and not of conquest, it had to take second place.

Since 1860 the problem of which fiscal order should be preferred, that of Naples or that of Sardinia, came to the fore.

The Neapolitan order, less costly and more harmonious, best suited to an agricultural country, appeared by far the best from an economic point of view; the Sardinian order on the other hand, with a large number of taxes and duties, appeared the least suited to a new kingdom which had to facilitate the birth and expansion of new energies.

Neapolitan public finance had given, moreover, the best and most audacious financiers, Ludovico Bianchini, later Agostino Magliani, there was perhaps nobody after who could equal their intellect. Bianchini had been the continuator of Medici's work, and was a man of considerable erudition and experience.

The secretary general for finance sent by Cavour in 1861 held a high opinion of the financial administration, whose lower-level staff was poor but whose higher level staff were excellent: Sacchi found the tax system less expensive than in Piedmont, he admired the simplicity of the means of collection; praised the treasury system; he thought the public debt stance so good that he wanted to «base the national public debt service on it».

The financial bodies «excellent as regards the administrative mechanism, left very little to desire as regards the personnel».

In general, in Naples' finances, according to Sacchi, «many fine intellects stood out. And whatever one might wish to say to the contrary, there were men of great culture. The economic sciences, elsewhere generally unknown by the class of state employees, were here generally practised. Easy and ready the concepts, purged and elegant the language, the writings of the offices differed from that amalgam which elsewhere fills out official correspondence.

«In short, in the various branches of the financial administration of Naples one finds capabilities which would honour the most enlightened of governments».

Not only was Naples' financial order more organic and less expensive, but in the administration there were, as we have seen, men of great value.

Why was it not preferred?

The political reasons are evident. The politicians of Piedmont, who dominated the government, ignored Naples' financial order, indeed they were for the most part agreed in believing that there was only disorder in the Bourbon administration.

On the other hand, constantly, victorious countries tend to impose their laws and orders on the defeated countries. And although this wasn't the case, as it was a union and not a conquest, it was undeniable that Piedmont should consider itself as victorious. The administrative and financial arrangements of the Kingdom of Sardinia, the legal order, inferior in every aspect to that of Naples, were replaced wholesale. It was believed that the Piedmontese systems were akin to the complement of freedom, the corollary of the constitution.

But a fact of general nature also helped ensure that the financial laws of the Two Sicilies were not accepted. The finance of Naples, simple and inexpensive, was more suited to a country with moderate taxes. In 1860 and 1861, with many new needs, with ever-increasing outlays one had necessarily to plump for the more onerous, but more remunerative system. The general conviction was then that Italy, above all southern Italy, hid treasures; only tyranny had prevented it from revealing them. It was thought that the land hid immense wealth: freedom of trade would suffice to ensure prosperity.

The southern Italian politicians, overwhelmingly very ignorant (and even the best were guilty of excessive presumption), compounded the erroneous ideas on the Mezzogiorno's wealth, and spurred to those errors which underpinned the entire financial policy.

The financial system of the Kingdom of Sardinia was extended to the rest of Italy. It was Batogi, between 1861 and 1862, who carried out the work of transformation.

With five government bills, which were the base of the subsequent laws, Bastogi extended the Piedmont fiscal system to all the old states which were now part of the new kingdom. Thus, as a result of the new order, the Kingdom of the Two Sicilies suddenly found itself, without any economic transformation having taken place in it, indeed losing all its army and many of its institutions, promoted from the category of countries with low taxes to the category of countries with very onerous taxes.

It did not even seem useful then to discuss if it was not more convenient to allow each of the old states to retain its old financial system.

There is a plethora of facts which prove — Bonghi wrote — that there was no other way of inducing in the many parts of the country so recently joined together, the conviction that each would bear an equal portion of the burden the creation of the new kingdom imposed on all. And without this conviction it was evident — and the facts, which despite the fact that they have taken place, have proved it to those who did not wish to believe it then — that we Italians would have come to blows and have ended up by turning our backs.

It is an elementary canon of finance that new taxes are always more onerous than the old taxes; or at least that two equal taxes are borne quite differently according to whether they were introduced long ago or recently. Just think therefore what profound disruption the application of a tax system which was not only different but almost opposite caused in the Kingdom of Naples. While other regions eased or stayed with their old systems, or enjoyed reductions, the Kingdom of the Two Sicilies, in just a few years, saw taxes which it had either not been known before or had been known in a much less onerous form: the tax on personal non-property income, the registration and stamp duties, in large part ignored, the legal taxes, the tax on inheritances, that on buildings, everything was profoundly disrupted. Inheritances, which earlier were exempt from any tax, trades and transactions which had been facilitated by the Banco di Napoli's system, everything was changed and disrupted.

Reading the Neapolitan newspapers of that time, one sees the fright the new tax systems engendered, behind the superficial enthusiasm.

The financial systems of the Kingdom of Sardinia, which replaced the simple and almost elegant organism of Neapolitan finance, made it necessary to increase the number of state employees excessively, and to increase the collection and operating expenses.

It is incredible what the bureaucracy was in Piedmont between 1850 and 1860: a state within a state, an excessive number of agents of all levels.

In 1852, in the Subalpine Parliament, Hon. Farina reported on the reform of the central administration, relating the stages needed to approve a public work recognised as necessary.

The Provincial Council's engineer — Hon. Farina wrote — who recognised the appropriateness of a new work along the royal road which runs in the province where he exercises his office, informs the chief engineer and the province intendant, who inform the division intendant, who reports the matter to the General Internal Agency which, either directly or via notification to the Ministry of Public Works, orders the preparation of a project. This decision is notified to the general intendant and the chief engineer who forward the necessary provisions to the province intendant and the engineer who is to draw up the formal project for the work. The prepared project is revised and corrected by the chief engineer and, either through the general intendancy or directly, forwarded to the internal Agency which obtains an opinion of it from the Standing Committee of Water, Bridges and Roads, which approves it or prescribes modifications or variations, for the inclusion of which the project is once again sent to the internal Agency and from it, either via the Intendancy's procedures or directly forwarded to the author with an invitation to adopt the suggestions and prescriptions of said Standing Committee. The project amended by the author is, via the usual channel, again forwarded to the Standing Committee which, having approving it, forwards it to the General Internal Agency which, following the ministry's authorisation, includes the cost in the budget.

We have seen the judgement concerning the Neapolitan treasury by one of the highest officials of public finance of the Kingdom of Sardinia, General Secretary Sacchi. It appeared to him as a truly admirable service. He thought there was nothing simpler, more economic and more certain.

Instead there was nothing more complicated than the Piedmont treasury: a payment on behalf of the state gave rise to a series of long and costly operations.

A Piedmont official, Lencisa, thus described in 1853 the operations to be carried out for a payment by the state: a minister, by virtue of the king's authorisation, when laid down by the law, orders the sending of a order on the funds available in a category of his budget. Now the minister has to write an official letter to the relevant General Agency, which is situate two paces from the ministry, for it to release the order in question. The General Agency, having drawn up the order, sends it to the ministry from which the order signed by the minister originated, and he has to once again sign the order. Having done this, the order is remitted to the same General Agency, which has to forward it to a neighbouring audit office. Here the order goes first to the registration office, where it is registered, as is certified by the signature of the clerk delegated to such task, and then passes into the hands of the general comptroller, who also has to sign it. After this, the order returns from the audit office to the General Agency which issued it, and this General Agency has to submit it to the General State Inspectorate, where it has to be registered and signed by the general inspector. Now it returns from the general inspector for the fourth time to the General Agency from which it started out, and should be registered once again in said Agency's ledger.

These facts and these judgements refer to the years 1852 and 1853; i.e., when, after the proclamation of the *Statute*, Thaon di Revel, Ricci, Nigra and briefly Cavour had been ministers of finance from 20 April 1851 to 22 May 1852. Now Cavour, who was truly the greatest politician of his time, and whose glory will always increase, was re-appointed Minister of Finance on 5 November 1852 and remained such until 15 January 1858. In more than five years of administration with his perspicacious mind, he changed many things and corrected many others. He considerably reduced the central administration, modified the provincial offices. Absorbed by other matters, he could not, however, complete the work started, and the Piedmontese order remained rigid, onerous, and costly.

As a result of the new arrangements, the regions of the north, Piedmont, Liguria, Lombardy saw their tax burden lightened. The unity of Italy had still to be completed and Minghetti stated in the Turin parliament: «Since the Kingdom of Sardinia has transformed itself into the Kingdom of Italy, I believe its financial position has much improved».

Naples was then not only by far the most populous of Italian cities, which have now become more or less equal, but it was above all the great centre of elegance and luxury. But the amount of savings in the south was exaggerated in the north and it was thought there was considerable margin for new taxes. Above all one started out from the erroneous belief that the Mezzogiorno was rich.

Hon. Depretis, in a much commented speech, found it strange that it was believed that «the productive forces of Lombardy are superior to the productive forces of all the mainland provinces of the former Kingdom of Naples». Naples was, according to Sella, who had then visited it, Italy's conspicuous city; according to Depretis, the southern provinces were «the rich provinces of the Kingdom of Naples».

When in 1863 the parliamentary commission, whose members included Lanza, Sella, Allievei, and of which Pasini was proposer of the bill, reported on the bill and tax on personal non-property income, which was applied by contingents, assigned to the province of Naples 1,806,604, to Genoa 1,153,081, to Florence 1,005,729. Naples was thought not only the most populous, but also the wealthiest city of Italy.

While therefore the Mezzogiorno was asked to pay more taxes, it was thought almost a right for the north to have more participation in the state.

Sella, who always spoke with excessive rough sincerity, asking for a lyceum for his native Biella, at Biella which he described as poor and skilful, said:

«I'll go even further, the agricultural population (I do not speak of the industrial population) has been in these last years so afflicted by ills, that it is truly forced to live off its wits, as the land no longer provides a living. It is forced to find a way to send the youngsters to school modestly, pettily, when this is needed, so that they can find there a way of procuring their bread, but it absolutely cannot send its youngsters to other cities. Now, this population, which fights so nobly, so stubbornly, if one can say thus, to earn its living, entrusts itself to your indulgence...»

In its apparent roughness, in its modesty, in its simplicity, this language was much more nobler, because it was much sincerer, than the rhetorical tirades of which the southern Italian deputation gave example, which decided to leave the flights of rhetoric only to descend to personal gossip.

The tax system of the new Kingdom was therefore merely the extension by subsequent laws of the regime of the Sardinian state; it was formed in the conviction that the Mezzogiorno, which paid the lowest taxes under the Bourbons, was vice versa the richest, most prosperous, most conspicuous country, as was said at the time during almost all the sittings of Parliament when taxes were discussed.

3. - The Present Tax Burden

3.1 *How the Mezzogiorno is Hardest Hit*

Which regions of Italy are hardest hit by taxes? The Italian state spares no caresses for any, such that no region can say it pays little. But it is unarguable that Lombardy, given its wealth, pays much less than Calabria and Basilicata; perhaps half as less, but undoubtedly much less.

Revenues are offset by spending. If a city pays 10 and the state spends in or for it 20, then one can say that the tax burden has been generously compensated.

No study of state spending has ever been carried out; neither has a detailed study of revenues.

To study thus both revenues and spending one cannot take a single year. It is evident that there may be causes of great distuption. The state has built a railway, or carried out large-scale army manoeuvres: the spending is therefore exceptional. And thus the revenues may seem less than in reality. For example: if a zone for special causes has been exempted in whole or in part from the land tax or from that on buildings, one risks considering as definitive a fact which is merely temporary.

And hence for both revenues and spending we have chosen the period from 1894 to 1898. The choice was not random, neither only because these are the most recent years.

The period 1893-1898 saw no wars, except that of Africa. As a result of which state spending in Naples and Campania appeared greater than it is in actual fact in normal periods: there were no significant shifts.

There were few railways built.

Since 1862 there has been no year in Italy in which less railways were inaugurated than in 1896, when only 10 km of line were opened for service. Undoubtedly, in the other years many railways were opened for service and totalled 507 km of line in 1893.

But when one thinks that in the previous years there were years such as 1886, with 818 km., 1888 with 764 km. it is clear that one couldn't have chosen a better period.

It is not possible to know whom all the taxes hit, above all from the territorial point of view. A sugar producer in Liguria pays excise duty; but in actual fact it is not Liguria which pays, but the cities which consume the sugar. Thus with customs duties. Nobody can say to whom the luxury hats from Paris and cleared from customs at the border, in Piedmont or Lombardy, go and hence who pays the duty in actual fact.

There is a third of all the state's revenues which nobody can say which regions actually pay: the state estate revenues deriving from the railways and the taxes for railway movements, customs revenues, foreign legation and consulate fees, revenues from prisons, from the deposits and loans bank, etc.

Even if a calculation could be made, it would only be fallacious.

But there remains the overwhelming majority of the revenues, two thirds of total revenues which amount to circa one billion lire; the three most important direct taxes, the business taxes, excise duties (if one wishes to include them), internal sales taxes, industrial monopolies (salt, tobacco, lottery), the public education tax, the postal and telegraph taxes.

Who pays this spectacular set of very differing taxes, which makes Italy something of a tax museum?

It should be clear that each of these taxes imposes a different sacrifice: and this too should be borne in mind.

If a zone pays one million lire by way of land tax, it in actual fact pays such amount for services of general utility; but if a zone pays one million lire for tobacco, it instead receives a certain amount of products to consume, said products being worth more or less a quarter of the sum paid. Vice versa, when a country contributes one million lire for the consumption of postal services, in actual fact it receives from the state little more than four fifths of that which it gives. The latter case is an example of a true tax.

He who spends one lire to obtain postal or telegraph services gives to the state, in actual fact, 19 cents. But if a town gives one lire as a duty fee, it gives the entire one lire and not a cent less.

There are some taxes which cost less to collect, others which cost more; in any case one should hold that the sacrifice differs according to the taxes.

Each tax should be studied separately: it will suffice, without entering into technical details, to mention the effect of each on the economy of the single regions.

From 1866 to 1896-1897, the land tax produced 3,680 million lire for the budget. But it is among the few taxes which, as regards the state, far from being exacerbated, was diminished by the war arrears. From 130 million lire, which is what it produced in 1872, it fell to 107 million lire. And while in 1871 the average contribution of each inhabitant amounted to 4.88, it fell in 1896-97 to 3.40 lire. Only the surcharges of the local administrations have weighed down on the burdens of land property, for which the state has shown itself unwilling to impose new burdens. It has imposed them however by other means, above all by increasing the business tax, which to a large extent falls on land.

He who says sundry tax — wrote Hon. Allievi, the proposer in 1863 of the bill for the provisional settlement of land tax — says miscellaneous production expenses, says imbalance of competition, protectionism, domestic monopoly in favour of some and to the detriment of others. No, when the tradesman in Naples pays no tax on licences, while the tradesman in Turin pays a very hefty one, when a hectare of land of equal fertility pays in Lombardy a third more than that which is paid in Tuscany, there can no longer be equilibrium of force and of economic relations, there is no longer any justice, there is no integrity of freedom.

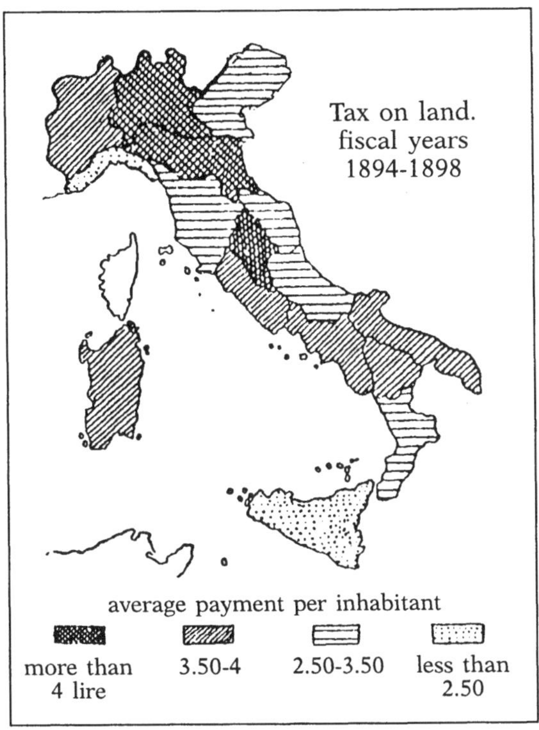

It was the concern of the time: it was thought that the Mezzogiorno, much richer, paid less.

The provisional settlement of 1864, and all the subsequent laws up to the equal distribution law of 1886, were all made in the conviction that the Mezzogiorno paid little and that it should, vice versa, pay more.

The motivations which determined the law of 1886 were clearly indicted in all the publications and Parliamentary acts.

Now the year after the law was enacted, in 1887, the protectionist phase began, this sacrificed the agriculture of southern Italy to the new industries of northern Italy. As a result of the country's geographical configuration, in addition to wine and citrus fruits, southern italy could not export to the north of Italy, except in very limited quantities: and the railway tariffs acted in many cases as protection duties. Such that it cost much less to send a good even to distant countries from any part of the Mezzogiorno than to send it by rail to Lombardy or Piedmont.

The current manner of implementation of the land tax means that it tends to hit the size rather than the owners' actual income; if some region of the south has not been harshly hit, there are others which are among the hardest hit.

In the five fiscal years from 1894 to 1898, the annual average of tax paid by each inhabitant of each region for the land tax was as follows:

Piedmont	3.78	Lazio	3.56
Liguria	1.35	Abruzzi and Molise	2.61
Lombardy	4.36	Campania	3.58
Veneto	3.18	Apulia	3.87
Emilia and Romagna	4.52	Basilicata	3.60
Tuscany	2.66	Calabria	2.96
Marches	3.36	Sicily	2.15
Umbria	4.22	Sardinia	3.53

And if we divide Italy into 5 big zones, we will have:

Zone	Tax
northern Italy	3.68
central Italy	3.88
southern Italy	3.39
Sicily	2.15
Sardinia	3.53

It may appear strange that the land tax was calculated according to the number of inhabitants and not according to area.

But it should be borne in mind that in southern Italy the landowners' incomes were, given the very nature of the agrarian contracts, proportionally higher: that, after 1887, there was little possibility of export, on the other hand, the wealth and hence consumption power of the north did increase; and finally the taxes faced by landowners in the Mezzogiorno were, for many reasons, much higher.

The tax on buildings, perhaps the most onerous of the direct taxes, has a pressure which is perhaps unequalled anywhere else.

It is no secret that in countries where wealth, industry and general property are scarce or remain stationary, not only is the tax on buildings much more onerous, but it also tends to be shifted onto the tenants. There is no stimulus for new buildings and vice versa the growing population leads to higher rents. This was the case in Italy, even more significantly than in other countries.

But a fact which is insufficiently felt, and which vice versa has the greatest importance, is the tendency of the tax on buildings to become more onerous in the towns with agglomerated populations.

Taking account of the single disruptive causes, one can almost deem a constant fact that in Italy the tax on buildings tends to hit more harshly the inhabitants of the zones with the greatest agglomeration of the population.

Let us take some provinces which have more or less the same population and we will note that the tax is harsher where the scattered population is more rare (see the illustrative scheme in *Il bilancio*, p. 83)*.

The building development of Udine province is undoubtedly far superior to that of Potenza province, which has no large cities, has little trade and is one of the poorest in the Kingdom.

Alessandria province is one of Italy's most prosperous provinces, while only a part of Bari province has a considerable development of agricultural and industrial wealth.

No less evident is the contrast between Campobasso and Arezzo, Lecce and Cuneo. It appears barely credible that Milan province, which is more populous that that of Naples and is much wealthier and with a much larger building development, pays vice versa considerably less.

---

* See footnote 1.

Although there lack precise criteria for distinguishing the agglomerated from the scattered population, we can accept the criteria adopted by Italian statistics.

Now if we adopt this criteria, we can distinguish three large zones in Italy: minimum agglomeration, from 40 to 50% Veneto, Marches, Emilia, Tuscany; average agglomeration, from 50 to 76% Piedmont, Liguria, Lombardy; maximum agglomeration, from 76 to 93% Lazio, Abruzzi, Campania, Apulia, Sicily, Calabria, Basilicata.

Except for some small zones, southern Italy is a large area of agglomerated population. But the existence of large towns, dependent on historical or climatic causes, far from being considered a factor of prosperity, is almost always proof of agricultural poverty and development difficulties.

In the five fiscal years from 1894 to 1898 the average contribution per inhabitant of each region for the tax on buildings was:

Piedmont	2.78	Lazio	9.61
Liguria	5.35	Abruzzi and Molise	1.28
Lombardy	3.15	Campania	3.87
Veneto	1.91	Apulia	2.64
Emilia and Romagna	2.16	Basilicata	1.63
Tuscany	3.16	Calabria	1.08
Marches	1.49	Sicily	2.00
Umbria	1.38	Sardinia	1.89

And if we divide Italy into 5 big zones, we will have:

northern Italy	2.89
central Italy	3.39
southern Italy	2.56
Sicily	2.00
Sardinia	1.89

Therefore, although the North is by far much richer and the cities are more numerous and more prosperous, the tax on buildings hits the northern and southern provinces almost to the same degree: indeed, all too often, the provinces of the South are the hardest hit. If we disregard the revenues from the tax on buildings for cities with more than 60,000 inhabitants, Bari and Naples for the South and Alessandria, Brescia, Genoa, Milan, Padua, Turin, Venice and Verona for the North, we see that the buildings pay almost three times more in southern Italy than in northern Italy.

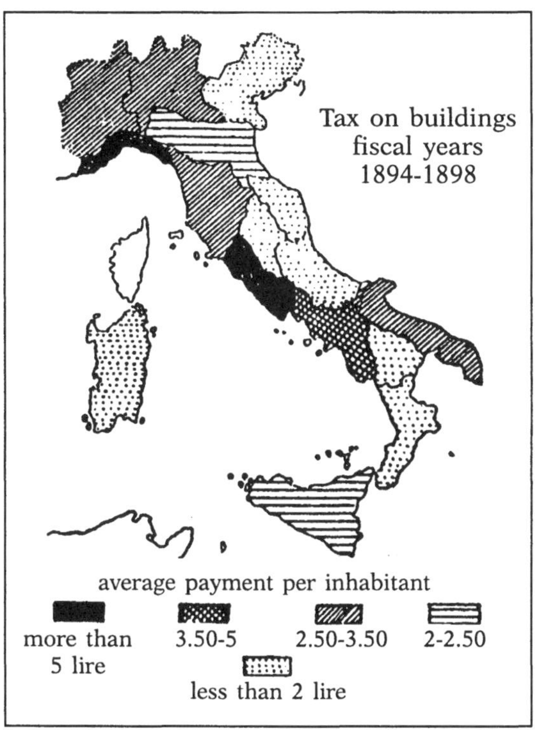

How can it be that two provinces, such as Udine and Potenza, the first with considerable development, the second in great poverty, with almost equal populations, show the strange case that it is the poorest province which pays most?

The reason lies in a very simple fact: as the land tax currently hits the size of the land rather that the net income of the landowner harder, thus the tax on buildings, exempting almost all the regions with scarce population, hits the regions with agglomerated population much harder taking account neither of the size of the property income nor of its value.

According to the 1881 census, in Udine province the scattered population amounts to 16.50% of the total population and to 6.80% in Potenza province.

Bari province, with a population more or less equal to that of Alessandria, but undoubtedly less wealthier, has just 33 towns and overall no more than 66 inhabited centres; while Alessandria has 343 towns and 935 inhabited centres. The scattered population in Alessandria province amounts to 35% of the total population, and to 6% in Bari province.

Cuneo and Lecce are almost more or less in the same conditions. While Lecce has but 130 towns, Cuneo has 263; but the population, while it is very scattered in Cuneo, where it amounts to 42.50% of the total population, barely amounts to 10.50% of Lecce's total population.

It would appear, at first sight, that the provinces of Campobasso and Arezzo have a different situation: as while the former has 133 towns, the latter has just 40. But this fact is only apparent. While the scattered population amounts to 77% of Arezzo's total population, it amounts to barely 12.5% of that of Campobasso.

Just twenty years ago, southern Italy paid more than northern Italy not only in relative, but also in absolute terms.

In 1877, with a population (in round figures) of 9,847,000 inhabitants, Piedmont, Liguria, Lombardy and Veneto produced a total 19,862,000 lire, that is to say 2.01 lire per inhabitant. In the same year the quota per inhabitant was 2.17 lire in southern Italy (excluding Abruzzi).

Twenty years later, in 1897, the quota per inhabitant in northern Italy is 2.97 lire compared with 2.74 lire in southern Italy. But, on the other hand, the ratio of wealth between the two large zones had shifted considerably.

The tax on buildings is a typical example of what is the true cause of a profound imbalance and of some striking injustices.

Parliament has always believed that the small towns, or the results of numerous aggregates of scattered population, were poor towns. Thus not only the tax laws, but also the laws on education, on public works, in general all the administrative laws, far from recognising that the agglomerated population, when not the result of industrial development, is the effect of adverse natural or social conditions, at the same time sanction a continued injustice and a most dangerous inequality.

The personal non-property income tax, such as it is now, was almost unknown in the Kingdom of Naples.

When it was introduced, the first steps were hesitant and it was dared to apply it only by contingents.

For 1864, the contingent was set at 30 million.

It was commonly held that southern Italy should pay less: first of all because it had received fewer economic benefits from unity, and then because it was a new tax for it.

On 2 August 1862, discussing the sale of state assets, Minghetti stated the following as regards personal non-property income: «And here I am pleased to assure that in some central provinces of Italy and also in Lombardy I have heard many times illustrious capitalists and tradesmen who stated they accepted, indeed they desired this tax (jeers from the left). This is a statement which perhaps appears strange, but I have heard it from more than one. I have heard tradesmen and industrialists who said: we have benefited from the new order of things, and because of the abolition of the customs borders, and the opening of new railway lines, and the increase in business of every type, so why should we not be taxed? In truth we all feel the justice of contributing proportionately to the needs of the state (murmurs from the left). These speeches generate in me a great sense of satisfaction, because they show me that public opinion was formed, the terrain ready and prepared for the tax...

«I don't know whether my honourable colleagues from the southern provinces can say the same, indeed I believe they cannot, because the growth of wealth, which should arise from the new order of things, has yet to take place in those provinces afflicted by extraordinary calamities...».

And on 3 July 1863, when Lanza complained that the contingent was not calculated in an equitable manner for the Mezzogiorno (it was 1.70 for the northern provinces, 1.40 for the central provinces and 1.20 for the southern provinces), Minghetti reaffirmed the same concepts.

Lanza supported criteria which, had they been adopted, would have made the tax very harsh in the South. Sella himself proved to him that the North had to pay more than the South because personal non-property income was actually being formed in the North.

Minghetti's and Sella's concept was that the personal non-property income tax should principally hit the North; where, since the first years, the economic and financial policies of the state had engendered the greatest benefits and given rise to much spending and very lively trade.

Now, if we stop a moment to compare the personal non-property income tax payments recorded in the tax rolls (that by withholding not being a sufficient criteria and often denoting not a true contribution, but a larger quantity of public services and public expenditure), we shall see that the provinces whose population was more or less the same, but whose wealth was quite different, paid more or less in the same manner.

How this was the case, given a uniform arrangement, would appear almost inexplainable.

Potenza province was among the poorest in Italy: it had almost no industry: and yet it paid almost the same as Udine which was rich, fertile, at the borders of Italy, with more developed industries and buoyant commerce.

Como is an admirable centre of activity; the development of the industrial factories reminds one of the affluent regions of Saxony and Switzerland. Moreover, it has a flourishing hotel industry and the prosperity is general. Salerno, apart from the northern zone, is a province in quite mediocre conditions, with few, nascent industries and no great revenue from outsiders. And yet the difference with Como is minimal.

The contrast between Naples and Turin is even more striking.

Leafing through the numerous reports of the General Office of Direct Taxes and the special studies on personal non-property income has not helped us understand how this is possible.

Table 1

Provinces	Population at 31 December 1897	Average personal non-property income tax paid in the five fiscal years 1894-1898	Comments
Naples	1,116,717	8,865,476	Ministry of Agriculture data indicate Turin had 60,601 industrial workers in 1892, in 1893 49,592. After, the growth of Turin was strong, while Naples stagnated.
Turin	1,128,507	7,847,329	
Salerno	576,897	1,279,812	In 1898 Salerno province had 160 steam boilers and in 1888 15,885 workers. Como is one of the Italy's richest cities. In 1897 it had 68,391 industrial workers.
Como	580,061	1,847,099	
Reggio Calabria	405,371	765,403	There is almost no manufacturing industry in Reggio di Calabria province: in 1898 there were just 127 boilers, mainly for mills.
Treviso	416,164	734,684	
Potenza	549,771	1,071,119	Ministry of Agriculture data indicates Potenza province had 5,744 workers in 1891; in 1889 Udine already had 21,793 workers. After, Udine saw strong growth.
Udine	536,734	1,391,165	
Bari	815,618	2,436,801	The number of workers in Alessandria province is much higher than in that of Bari.
Alessandria	803,402	2,869,365	
Lecce	660,443	1,643,373	Not only is the number of workers much lower in Lecce, but the trade is also much lower. There were only 187 boilers in the whole of Lecce province in 1898.
Cuneo	664,570	1,741,551	
Campobasso	269,659	707,423	These two provinces, essentially agricultural, have a very different productivity. Arezzo is a fertile region, Campobasso is mainly little fertile. It had only 59 steam boilers in 1898.
Arezzo	245,429	544,713	

A high official, who has been superintendent of finance in a province of Lombardy for many years, maintained that currently most of the industries of Piedmont, Lombardy and Veneto elude the tax, in part if not in whole.

We should also note another fact, which the statistics and reports of the general offices of direct taxes prove and underscore. In the south, those exercising the free professions are mainly hit: and they do not produce material wealth. Living in agricultural towns, they live directly or indirectly on the agricultural populations. Thus the clients of the lawyer, of the doctor, etc., are solely farmers. While in the provinces of the north, the big and increasingly booming development of industries distributes the burden more broadly on the less homogeneous classes of population, and the tax is thus more bearable.

In southern Italy, both directly or indirectly, it is almost solely the land which bears the burden of all the taxes.

The current law on personal non-property income hits the income of the agricultural industry when it is exercised by tenants on the land of others but not when it is exercised by the owners themselves. The regions in which lease prevails — namely all of

TABLE 2

Quota per inhabitant for direct taxes		Comments
Piedmont	11.85	1st example Even if we disregard the half a million (more or less according to the year) of personal non-property income tax paid by Banco di Napoli, the direct contribution per inhabitant is higher in Campania. Now the greater wealth of Piedmont is common knowledge.
Campania	12.16	
Veneto	9.08	2nd example In Veneto there are big companies which operate throughout the state (it suffices to think of the insurance companies and banks): the real contribution is therefore less. Conversely, the personal non-property income by withholding is larger. It is unexplainable why Veneto, which is much richer than Apulia, pays less direct taxes.
Apulia	9.72	

southern Italy — are subject in actual fact to a new tax, which is avoided by all the regions which practice direct production and almost all those which practise sharecropping, which pay barely 0.5% of the land tax.

While the wealth is quite different, southern Italy pays by way of direct taxes not only relatively, but also absolutely, often as much as and more than the very prosperous regions.

There are regions with quite different levels of propserity which pay the same, and often it is the poorest which pay more.

Basilicata, which is impoverished, pays by way of direct taxes (7.45), more or less the same as Marches (8.23) and as much as Umbria (8.86); from the point of view of the affluence of their inhabitants, these regions are in quite different situations.

The item 'business taxes' in the Italian budget indicates a series of taxes and duties which are grouped as follows: *a)* inheritance tax; *b)* mainmorte tax; *c)* registration duties; *d)* stamp duties; *e)* registration and stamp substitute taxes; *f)* mortgage taxes; *g)* government licence taxes; *h)* sundry taxes and receipts from public services.

They did not exist in most of the Kingdom of Naples and when, after the laws of 1862, they were introduced, there was general consternation.

Between 1860 and 1870 the army, the big state construction and the big consumption markets had been transferred to the north. The important railways lines hurriedly built for defence reasons; the big low-priced issues of government bonds artificially stimulated the volume of business and augmented the imbalance. At the same time, either the old tariffs people were used to paying when business was not flourishing, were maintained or even reduced when business increased.

Vice versa, southern Italy saw a reduction in personal non-property income, a reduction in business, a smaller volume of trade, but also a very steep increase in taxes and duties on business which either did not exist previously or else were very small. Hence when slack, business generated a higher burden, to which not only were people not accustomed, but which one had to get used to when business was paralysed.

Where the exchange of wealth flourishes the most, it is there that these taxes should produce more. Now the comparisons of some provinces only suffice to show that the opposite is true (Table 3).

Now in the years 1892-1893 to 1896-1897 there took place a strange fact that Apulia paid much more than Veneto, and, in general, while southern Italy contributed with 5.43 per inhabitant, Sicily with 5.03, northern Italy, in such superior conditions, gave just 6.43.

How is it that at Como the number of deals and transactions concluded every year are at least twice as many as in Salerno but then, vice versa, it is this latter province which pays more for the business tax? This fact is unexplainable unless we examine the mechanism of our laws. The manufacturing North and buoyant trade eludes numerous taxes and duties. The values recorded for inheritances are far smaller than those in areas which are almost wholly agricultural by vocation, where nothing can be hidden. While in trade transactions are completed in the quickest manner, often by a mere telegraph, and bargaining, even for considerable amounts, is carried out by letter; in the agricultural towns the registration and stamp duties are much harsher.

Moreover, the inheritance tax in Italy hits more directly real estate, which cannot elude them. And since the land tax and that on buildings hit the South considerably harder, sometimes not only in relative but also in absolute terms, the inheritance assessment criteria are quite different.

It is, to say the least, strange that the business taxes yielded 7.04 in Campania and just 6.70 in Piedmont and 6.55 in Lombardy. If one also calculates the virtual stamp duty paid for the circulation tax by Banco di Napoli (and one should bear in mind much more for Lombardy and Piedmont) the constrast still remains considerable. It is wholly unexplainable why Apulia pays much more than Veneto; indeed, why Veneto and Basilicata are hit more or less to the same extent. There should be and there is in all the taxes and duties on transfers of wealth some reason why the mass of wealth transferred is not hit to the same extent; but some forms bear the brunt.

TABLE 3

Provinces	Population at 31 December 1897	Average business tax payments	Comments
Naples	1,166,717	13,645,382	Taking account of the population the revenue is more or less the same. Milan has three times the number of industrial workers; twice the amount of government bonds; its area is more than triple; and the length of its rail network is almost triple, its volume of business is three times greater.
Milan	1,307,091	15,030,519	
Potenza	549,771	2,213,930	The volume of business is quite different. In 1898, in Potenza, Banca d'Italia granted 1,561,151 lire of discounts and advances (Banco di Napoli also granted a slender amount); at Udine Banca d'Italia granted 19,980,971.
Udine	536,734	1,992,226	
Bari	815,618	4,604,848	Discounts and advances granted by Banca d'Italia in 1898, Bari 18,593,759; Alessandria 40,630,399. At 31 December 1896 Alessandria has 21,686,164 lire in post-office accounts, Bari 6,553,672.
Alessandria	803,402	4,788,937	
Lecce	660,443	3,165,385	In 1897-98, 5,218,832 lire was paid at Cuneo by way of government bond interest; at Lecce 1,552,984. At end-1895, post-office accounts amounted to more than 17 million lire in Cuneo and just over 6 and a half million in Lecce.
Cuneo	664,570	3,396,942	
Salerno	576,897	2,686,773	Discounts and advances by Banca d'Italia in 1898 were circa four times more in Como. In 1896, post-office accounts were almost double in Como. Government bond interest paid in Como in 1897-98 was more than double that in Salerno.
Como	580,061	2,178,280	
Cosenza	472,505	2,047,588	Brescia was 14th in 1897-1898 of the provinces of the Kingdom for government bond interest payments. Cosenza was 43rd. Deposits are much lower at Cosenza, bank transactions of every kind are considerably fewer in number.
Brescia	497,464	2,274,432	
Campobasso	265,559	1,524,579	Campobasso is one of the provinces of Italy with a low level of trade, the number of bank transactions is small, and there are few deposits. No big industry.
Piacenza	229,830	1,131,101	

Most authors wrongly repeated that in Italy indirect taxes form the base of the budget. Often, also in moments of political struggle, it is stated that Italy is the country in which indirect taxes have reached their highest limit. These two statements are equally far from the truth.

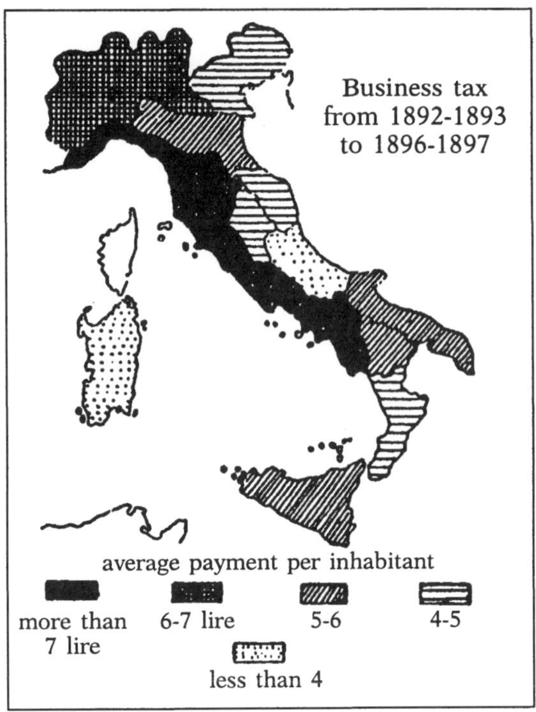

The base of the budget, if we can put it thus, the backbone of the Italian tax system, consists of three big direct taxes and the business taxes, which from 1862 to 1896-1897 accounted for more than a third of all the ordinary and extraordinary receipts; and 42.61% of all the real receipts.

If we eliminate the monopoly rights, the customs duties, the maritime rights, the consumption taxes and the excise and sales duties, they represented only 17.56% of overall tax receipts. And even if we add those for salt, tobacco and the lottery do we obtain a sum more or less equal to that given by direct taxes and those on the transfer of wealth.

The proportions are quite different in almost all the other countries. It is the three monopolies which push Italy to the top, vice versa the direct taxes, if one does not take them into account, are higher in France, the Netherlands, Germany, Portugal, Great Britain, Austria-Hungary, Russia and Spain. And if, instead of looking at the average revenue per inhabitant, we instead look at the ratio between direct and indirect taxes in the budgets, we would see that Russia, France, England, Austria, Germany and several other minor states were considerably ahead of Italy.

It is said that the Italian ruling classes are much worse than elsewhere, because they tax popular consumption disproportionately. There is considerable exaggeration in this statement and above all there is much ignorance of the truth.

It is unarguable that, above all after 1876, there was frequent recourse to indirect taxes, but it should also be said that the land and personal non-property income are hit, in Italy, by a much more greater proportional burden then elsewhere, and it is not at all true that popular consumptions lie at the base of the budget. If the tariffs are harsh, it is the blame of the entire tax system, too onerous, which restricts consumption, but which equally restricts the increase of land or personal non-property income.

Excise duties would appear to be mainly paid by northern Italy, in reality by the towns which consume and which, given the customs regime, cannot bring some provisions in from abroad.

The internal consumption duties are distributed, if not in a uniform measure, at least almost so; but it should be clear that they are much more onerous where consumption is scant and poverty greatest.

The state monopolies have such a considerable importance in the budget of the Italian state that only in the budgets of Austria or France do they have more importance, and then not by much.

The three fiscal monopolies alone — salt, tobacco and the lottery — produced in 1896-1897 receipts amounting to almost a sixth of all the ordinary and extraordinary revenues: and the tobacco and lottery monopolies together produce a gross revenue greater than that of the two taxes on land and on buildings.

The revenues from the monopolies totalled as follows in the fiscal years 1893-1894 and 1897-1898:

TABLE 4

Region	Salt	Tobacco	Lottery	All three fiscal monopolies
northern Italy	2.56	6.61	1.60	10.77
central Italy	2.69	7.31	1.92	11.92
southern Italy	2.41	4.66	2.88	9.95
Sicily	–	3.85	2.41	6.25
Sardinia	–	4.84	–	4.84

Southern Italy pays more or less the same for salt and more for the lottery: the basic difficulties of today and the improbable hope of tomorrow. It pays less only for tobacco, i.e., for a voluptuary consumption, which should indicate a greater affluence.

The postal and telegraph taxes produce much more in northern Italy where business is buoyant, and in central Italy, which has large cities and the capital, than in southern Italy, which has much worse economic conditions.

The taxes on the postal and telegraph services therefore produce much less in southern Italy and in Sicily.

	Average per inhabitant for postal taxes in five-year period 1893-1894 — 1897-1898
northern Italy	2.45
central Italy	2.59
southern Italy	1.31
Sicily	1.35
Sardinia	1.26

Where there is the greatest growth of wealth and traffic, where the public services are concentrated, there is also the greater revenue for the postal and telegraph taxes.

But for every lira of postal and telegraph taxes raised, the state spends more than four fifths for the service it renders.

The importance of school fees in the state budget is so small that it is almost not worth taking them into account.

They yield overall only circa 7 million lire per year and are absolutely inadequate to the spending on education, above all on secondary and high school education which is generally given to rich or well-to-do persons, or at least to persons belonging to the middle classes.

Teaching in Italy, because of a preconception which can never be sufficiently deplored, is almost free in the secondary and high schools run by the state; just as it is free in the primary schools run by the local councils.

As we shall see below, school institutions are almost wholly concentrated in the north and centre of Italy: vice versa, the school fees are paid in large part in the south.

In 1897-1898, the average yield of the school fees per inhabitant was:

northern Italy	0.21
central Italy	0.24
southern Italy	0.21
Sicily	0.25
Sardinia	0.22

The province of Naples alone accounts for circa a seventh of the total receipts for school fees and mainland southern Italy accounts for circa a third. Vice versa, while in the north there is a high school every 1,155,186 inhabitants and in the centre one every 558,153 inhabitants; while there is a secondary school every 47,343 inhabitants in the north and 41,227 inhabitants in the centre; in southern Italy there is a high school every 2,782,207 inhabitants and a secondary school every 68,414 inhabitants.

Among the inhabitants of the Mezzogiorno, the desire for education appears so great, that while they have a very low number of educational establishments, they pay for school fees on the mainland as much as northern Italy and in Sicily even more than in all the rest of Italy. A contribution to this perhaps comes from the dangerous trend of universities to beckon the middle classes which, having lost their ancient simplicity, and desirous of a better life, are still deprived of the possibility of an industrial education and the knowledge of a more modern life.

Even though it is much poorer than northern Italy, southern Italy is hit as though it were in the same conditions; at times as though it were wealthier.

It has been said: solatium miseris socios habere penantes; but nothing is worse than when everyone suffers a little, being forced to bear the greater burden and to have less force of resistance.

4. - State Spending

4.1 *How Much Each Region Gives and How Much the State Spends in Each*

But one should not see — which is what is almost always done — just one side of the question. It does not suffice to know how much a province gives: one also has to know how much the state spends in its territory.

If we disregard the interest on the national debt and the payments of the central treasury, the state, through its provincial treasuries, spends circa one billion lire per year for public services and spending of every kind.

How is this spending broken down? How much takes place in each province? How much in each region?

A complete study of territorial distribution has never been carried out. Vice versa, it can be made much better than that of revenues.

There are, as we have seen, some taxes and some duties which cannot be divided by territory: some by their very nature, others because they are paid only in some places.

Vice versa, for state spending, a very exact study of its distribution by provinces or regions can be made.

We have a central treasury and sixty nine provincial treasuries.

The central treasury effects not only the payments for the national debt, both domestically and abroad, but also all the payments it is ordered to make.

The orders the central treasury pays concern principally the civil list, the expenses for Parliament, missions abroad and all the payments for the national debt which the provincial treasuries debit to the central treasury.

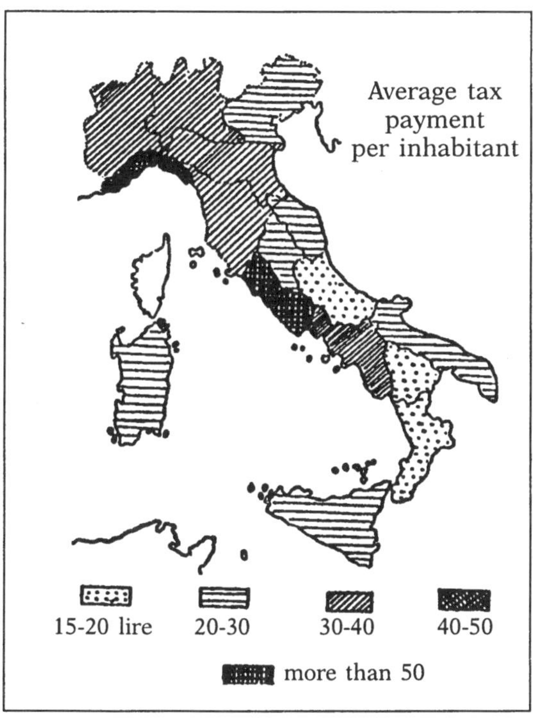

As the distribution of government bonds will be studied in depth below, and the other expenses for establishment and representation abroad can be considered by their nature not to have taken place in any specific region, thus the payments made by the provincial treasuries have a great importance and furnish an approximately exact indication of the distribution of public expenditure.

The state spends in many ways: by direct orders, with vouchers in orders available, according to rolls or schedules for fixed spending, under the special form of the costs of justice, etc. Although the forms via which it spends are much less varied than those via which it receives, they are nonetheless quite numerous. But whether it spends in one guise or another, the form is of little consequence: what is important is whether a lot or a little is spent by the state.

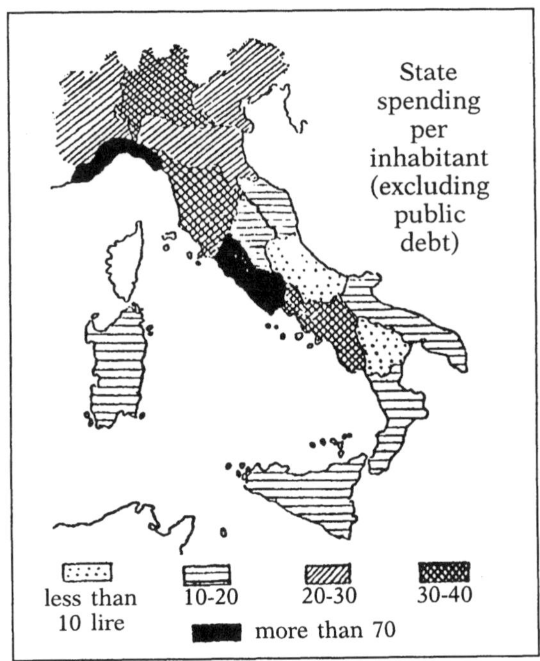

Brescia province undoubtedly pays a large sum; but it must be of some comfort to know that in it the state spends more or less as much as it receives. Foggia also gives a lot; it gives, in proportion to its wealth, much more; but it must be the source of some anger to know that the state spends in it, I am afraid to say it, for it, less than half of what it receives.

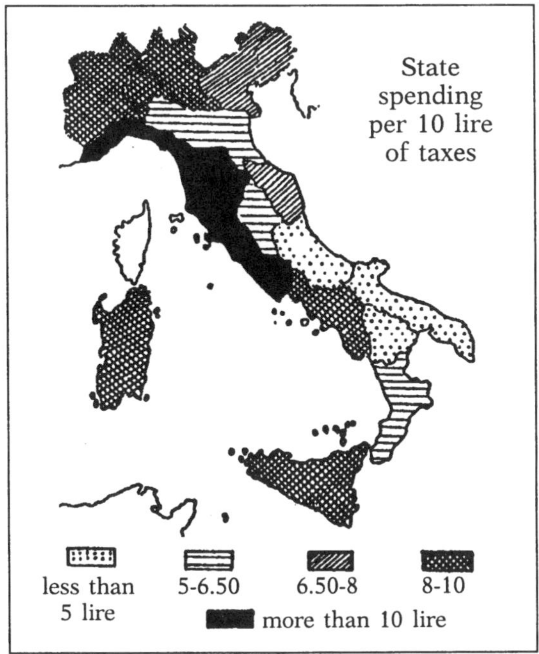

There are some taxes and some spending which figure in some provinces, and vice versa are made for others or for all.

There are big joint-stock companies (railway companies) which pay many millions of lire by way of tax, and which vice versa receive many millions of lire by way of subsidies. The state's revenues and spending in Lombardy and Tuscany therefore appear higher than they are in actual fact.

In Lazio, in addition to the personal non-property income tax withholdings, which should be almost wholly subtracted, the revenues also include the taxes paid by Banca d'Italia, and the collection of Rome Council's duties. moreover, some joint-stock companies pay their taxes in Rome, even though they operate throughout the Kingdom.

The revenues for Naples include not only the receipts from the consumption duty, but also the taxes paid by Banco di Napoli, which vice versa, operates throughout Italy. And the spending includes the amount the government pays, for the duty it exercises, to the city council.

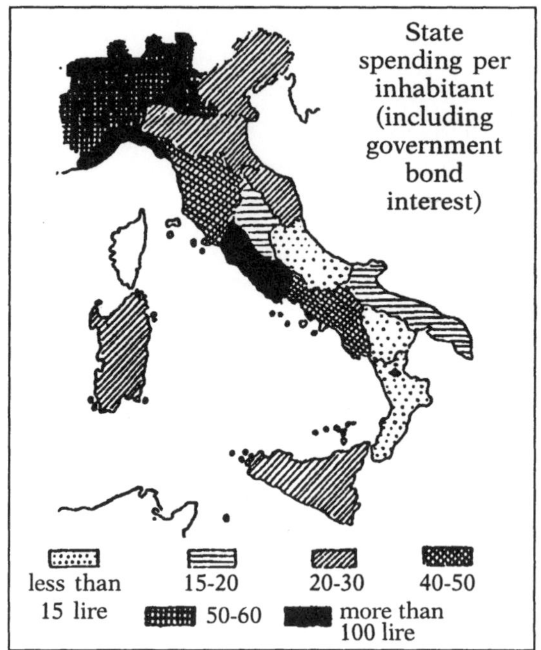

But if all these causes are borne in mind and one excludes from the revenues and spending those mentioned in this and the foregoing section, either because they cannot be broken down or because they will be taken into account later, the situation appears as follows for the five years in question:

	Average contribution per inhabitant	Average spending per inhabitant		Average contribution per inhabitant	Average spending per inhabitant
Piedmont	34.99	29.71	Lazio	77.31	93.00
Liguria	52.71	71.15	Abruzzi and Molise	17.92	8.64
Lombardy	39.50	32.87	Campania	37.45	33.00
Veneto	29.17	21.90	Apulia	28.79	12.54
Emilia and Romagna	32.06	20.78	Basilicata	18.55	8.77
Tuscany	37.15	37.56	Calabria	18.54	11.26
Marches	23.21	17.59	Sicily	21.86	19.88
Umbria	24.79	14.81	Sardinia	20.23	19.08

For Sardinia and Sicily the criterion applied is not the same as for the other regions: hence we have not disregarded (precisely because they are banks and companies which operate in the circumscribed territory) the taxes paid by Banco di Sicilia and the taxes and operating dues paid or received by the railway companies.

But, if we employ the same method of calculation for all the regions, also for Sicily and Sardinia, the result is that for every 10 lire collected from the taxpayers of the billion we are considering, the state has spent, disregarding the payments of the central treasury, as follows (indicated in *Il bilancio*, p. 183)*.

These figures show that almost all the regions which not only give, proportionally to their wealth, more but also those which receive less compared to what they give are in the Mezzogiorno.

And yet the state spending excludes payments for government bond interest. If we include that too, as it is recorded for 1897-1898, then the state's spending is almost complete, as it includes most of the payments of the central treasury, and proves that, while the Mezzogiorno's contribution is very high, it is vice versa the north of Italy which receives a much larger number of benefits.

In France and in many other more advanced states it is the poorer regions which receive more than they give: in Italy it is the poorest regions which give much more than they receive.

And here lies the principal, I shall not say the sole, cause for the depression which would appear to have afflicted all of southern Italy.

5. - Where the Billions for the Army and Navy Have Been and Are Spent

On doit solliciter doucement les chiffres was the process of which politicians have made liberal use, and which I would hazard they continue to abuse considerably.

---

* See footnote 1.

Even when they are the fruit of diligent studies, the excessively general figures often fail to dispel the public's doubts.

The comparisons made on the basis of treasury payments furnish only an approximate idea of the distribution of the public services.

But when the considerable spending of the state for the army, for the navy, for cultural institutes, for judges, for public works is studied separately, then one can reach very precise conclusions.

From 1862 to 1896-1897 the state spent by way of interest on the consolidated debt no less than 12,632 million lire and 2,500 for redeemable debts. Where did these two sums, which represent more or less a third of real spending, end up? In which regions? And to what measure?

8,354 million lire were spent for the army and 2,384 million lire for the navy, i.e., just under a quarter of all real spending. Where did these sums go? How? To what regions?

The same questions, and in no less serious a measure, spontaneously arise for public works, above all for the railways, for spending for the civil administration, etc.

It is unarguable that the spending made in one region does not benefit it alone when it is of general utility. But it is equally true that it is the inhabitants of a specific zone which derive the most benefit.

Thus nothing is more useful than to study one by one the distribution of all the large items of spending from 1862 to 1896-1897. And this is what we shall do in summary form.

Proportionally to the amount of private wealth and the public revenues, the old Italian states spent much more for their armies than Italy does now.

In some states, military spending absorbed not only most of the revenues, but its importance in the budget was far from that it has now. It was the supreme necessity of conservation: and the smaller one was, the more one felt the need to sacrifice everything for defence.

It is very wrong to believe that the Kingdom of Sardinia, to prepare the war to defend unification, spent more than the other states to fight against unification.

The Kingdom of the Two Sicilies spent enormous amounts; its army was so numerous that it was superior to that of all the other states of the peninsula together, except for Austria. It never carried out any acts of heroism, not even when Ferdinand II attempted to reform it or when its leaders included men of great doctrine and great value. Not even in this was and is there any fatalism, the same persons, led by Joachim Murat, proved themselves valiant and carried out acts of heroism.

The armies of the old states were between 1856 and 1850 (distributed as shown in *Il bilancio*, p. 187)*.

In Lombardy and Veneto, the serious and compact Austrian discipline reigned, Piedmont had great military traditions, albeit a dearth of leaders. In the Kingdom of the Two Sicilies the army lacked both one and the other.

But, as regards spending, it was the Kingdom of Naples which outdid all, and it was the city of Naples which had the largest number of soldiers in Italy.

And as in Sicily there was relatively few number of soldiers, at Naples above all there was a very large number. The city of Naples lived almost solely on the spending of the landowners from the provinces, the Bourbon court and the army. Hence the development of all the forms of parasitism which still survive and the terrible imbalance which took place after 1860.

In addition to the royal guard, which was numerous, there was a large number of special corps. More than 30 thousand soldiers were permanently stationed in the city of Naples and nearby.

1860 changed all this.

After the disbandment of the armies of the old states, there remained only the Piedmont army which formed the nucleus of the present army. The almost one hundred thousand men who comprised the army of the Two Sicilies were dismissed on the spot. The officers of the Tuscan army nearly all joined the national army; but only a few of those of the army of the Two Sicilies did. Many of them lacked sufficient culture: many believed in resign-

---

* See footnote 1.

ing out of loyalty; many because they believed in a return to the old order. The cause of banditry lies in large part from the enormous mass of soldiers who were out of house and home; the bandit chiefs were in large part dismissed soldiers and non-commissioned officers of the disbanded Bourbon army.

But there took place a fact which was even more serious and which was necessary.

After the war with Austria it was believed that there would be another war with that country. Between 1860 and 1866 large numbers of soldiers were sent to Lombardy. Except for the few soldiers charged with repressing banditry, the garrisons of the south were all empty.

There was no deliberate intent; there simply was no alternative.

Military spending increased, that on weapons doubled, the building of railways was speeded up; but always in Lombardy and where it was thought the theatre of war would be.

The Parliamentary Left found the Right also timid; more railways had to be built than was the case, and the same held for arms.

Billions were spent in a few years, almost entirely in the Po plain, where earlier there was a lack of money and which saw almost all the budget resources flow there.

In 1862 more than 300 thousand men were under arms, almost all of them in the Po plain.

The masses of wealth which in this manner shifted from the south to the north were enormous, by the very necessity of things and for the supreme obligation of defence.

Neither are things any different now.

If one does not follow the puerile method which some newspapers follow when they wish to prove that everything proceeds regularly in the best of manners, one cannot confine the study to seeing how many army corps or how many divisions are stationed in each region.

It is a calculation which tells us nothing.

First of all, the military divisions have a varying number of soldiers; and then the distribution of the soldiers does not close-

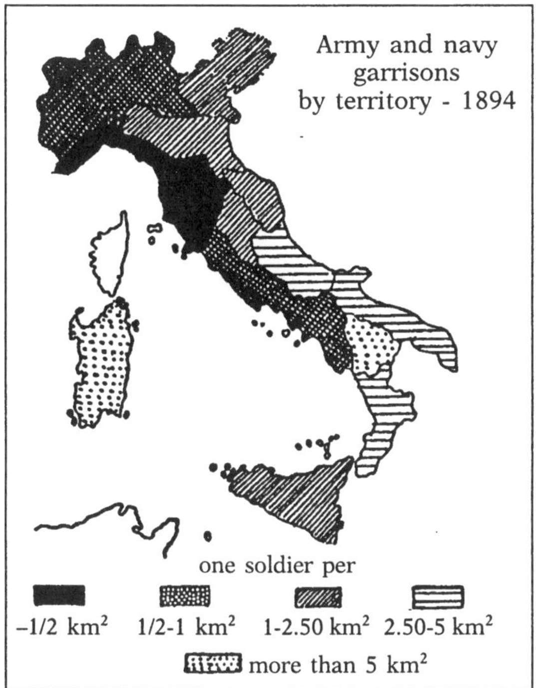

ly follow neither that of the army corps, nor that of the division commands, and not even that of the brigade commands.

Hence, we have to calculate it directly.

The Ministry of War, for political and strategic reasons, refuses to give any information in this regard. But this refusal does not prevent one from carrying out research.

In 1893, the Ministry of Finance, for fiscal reasons, wished to see the benefit the single regions obtained from the army and naval garrisons. A fact of strategy this too; but directed against the taxpayer, who finds it more difficult to defend himself than the foreigners.

Now in 1893, according to the official data of the Ministry of Finance, Piedmont and Liguria together had many more soldiers than the entire old Kingdom of the Two Sicilies, such that the ensuing situation is that Liguria had the most and Basilicata the least.

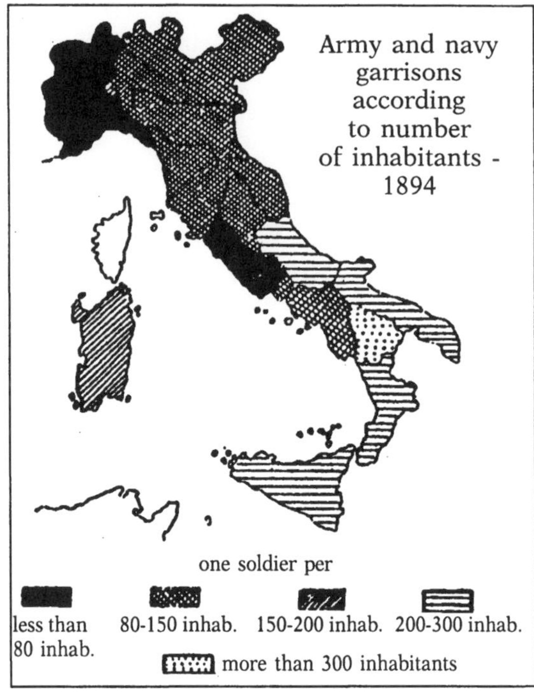

In ratio to area (the Mezzogiorno is so poor and scarcely populated) the garrisons were distributed thus:

	Km² per soldier		Km² per soldier
Piedmont	0.59	Marches	1.41
Liguria	0.30	Abruzzi and Molise	2.85
Lombardy	0.85	Campania	0.61
Veneto	1.04	Apulia	2.97
Emilia and Romagna	0.72	Basilicata	10.19
Tuscany	0.39	Calabria	2.88
Lazio	0.72	Sicily	1.56
Umbria	2.14	Sardinia	5.07

Neither was the situation any different with regard to the number of inhabitants:

	Inhabitants per soldier		Inhabitants per soldier
Piedmont	67	Marches	140
Liguria	56	Abruzzi and Molise	237
Lombardy	139	Campania	117
Veneto	129	Apulia	282
Emilia and Romagna	80	Basilicata	350
Tuscany	133	Calabria	253
Lazio	60	Sicily	206
Umbria	132	Sardinia	196

I have studied the distribution of the army very recently (28 January 1899) and found that the situation has not changed at all since 1894. Most of the soldiers are still stationed in northern Italy, in Emilia and in Romagna.

Hence for many years billions of lire have flown into the same zones, in which there was the largest number of state institutions of every type.

There is no doubt that the army can be distributed only with solely military criteria. But the military establishments and schools satisfy no tactical need, at least in the majority of cases, and can be situated indifferently in one or another region.

It would not damage the army if a military academy was located in one region instead of another. If the military academy of Turin, was, let us suppose, in Caserta; if the military academy was at Palermo instead of at Turin; if the military academy was at Reggio di Calabria instead of at Modena and the medical corps academy at Salerno, one would suppose the army would not be damaged in any way.

Military academies cost the state roughly 3 million lire per

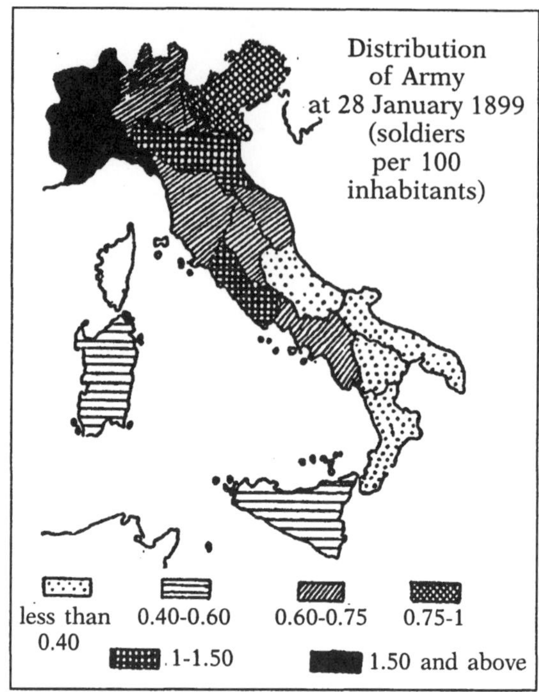

year; but in the places where they are situate, they determine considerable spending.

Now the war academy, the artillery and engineering academy, the military academy are in Turin, the military academy is at Modena, the medical corps academy in Florence, the fencing academy in Rome, the infantry academy in Parma, the cavalry academy in Pinerolo.

In other words they are all situate in northern and central Italy, southern Italy only has a dying military college which might be closed, as it has no importance and no utility.

The military artillery and engineering plants and factories are also almost wholly in the north of Italy.

The reasons for the location of some of them is perhaps explainable; but it is not clear why the military fittings factory, the central military pharmacy and other institutions, which are of great importance for spending, should be located in the same places as the military academies.

But the concentration of the army is of little import compared with that of military spending.

Calculations made in 1897 by the Ministry of War showed that most of the military budget is spent in the north of Italy: more than twice as much being spent there as in the south.

Now, if we bear in mind that from 1862 to 1896-1897 8,354 million lire have been spent, we can appreciate the extent of the benefit enjoyed by the regions of the Po plain.

Neither are things any different for the navy: indeed, they are worse, because almost all the spending is concentrated along the Ligurian and Tuscan coast to the south of Livorno.

Before 1860, only the Kingdom of the Two Sicilies had a proper navy. In 1856 it consisted of 98 vessels, of which 32 were steam-powered (14 frigates, 4 corvettes, 14 vessels of various classes) with 832 cannons.

At the start of 1858 the fleet consisted of 121 vessels with 820 cannons.

In 1859 the Sardinian navy consisted of 29 vessels and 436 cannons. The 29 vessels included 6 steam frigates and 4 sail frigates; 3 steam corvettes and 4 sail corvettes; 3 steam and 4 sail escort vessels or brigantines; 3 steam freighters; a steam tug. There were just 16 steam vessels, against 32 in the Neapolitan fleet.

The Tuscan and papal navies were almost non-existent, so scant was their importance and small their number of vessels.

Now southern Italy has an increasingly minor importance as regards spending on the navy. Genoa province, alone, has half of the coastal sailors.

The largest number of war vessels, as a consequence, is stationed in the waters of Liguria, and it is between La Spezia and Genoa that the most naval activity is concentrated.

All this is of much more interest than might be thought.

Naval officers are the best paid of all state employees; the superior officers receive wages and allowances which appear barely believable in a poor country such as Italy.

General naval officers receive, between wages, position indemnities, official expenses, servants, etc. two to three times more than a chief justice of the court of cassation; the superior officers receive twice as much as a state councillor.

Concentrating almost all the activities of the navy in one point means determining a flow of several million lire per year in a single region.

The naval academies, in turn, are concentrated in the same zone.

One can perhaps understand the reasons of defence which explain why most of the army is stationed in the north; but however much we strain our acumen, we cannot understand why the navy shipyards all have to be in the same zone, and the naval academies should all be in the same point.

Livorno naval academy is one of the state's most expensive institutions. While Turin's military academy accounts for only a slight burden on the state budget, the Livorno naval academy, which has just 163 cadets, costs more than 600 thousand lire, and generates for the state a debt of more than half a million, not taking account of the costs for the education campaigns and ships kept at Livorno for the cadets' training.

A cadet of the Livorno academy costs more than 5,400 lire per year; of which barely circa 1,600 are provided by the cadet: the rest is provided by the state!

The costs for the maintenance and reproduction of fleet is, in turn, concentrated in the Liguria-Tuscany zone.

Now, when unification took place, the shipyards of Naples and Castellammare were the most important in the new Kingdom.

Immediately after 1860 one started on the other hand to say that it would be better to spare Naples the danger of a bombardment, and transfer elsewhere all the shipbuilding. Naples, it was said, was too beautiful a city to expose it to such a serious danger.

In his famous financial statement of 1870, Sella said: «It is not ill-will against Naples: I confess that if I was a Neapolitan and if I had had the fortune to be born in Naples, I would wish to carry out a full-blooded crusade on this argument against the naval port. In fact, sirs, have you the conviction that Naples can ever be a naval port? (Good!) In this case it is necessary to fortify Naples such that an enemy group, in the event of war, cannot approach it; otherwise, under the present conditions, with those military establishments what have you? Nothing more than an invitation to the enemy to wreck damage to your city...».

It was feared for the city of Naples; but since then one has sought to transfer the shipbuilding. There was even a ministerial crisis over the question of whether or not an arsenal should be established at Taranto.

After, without daring to abolish the arsenal of Naples and the shipyards of Castellammare, they were left to decay while large amounts of work were being given to the private Ligurian industry. Together Naples and Castellammare have little more than half the personnel of La Spezia and Venice; but there is a fierce competition to reduce the number of contracts entrusted to them so as to underscore their lack of utility.

And at the same time as the shipyards of Naples and Castellammare were being left to decay (and the decadence engenders the bad customs which are then deplored), large orders are being given to the private industry artificially created in Liguria and in Livorno.

Of the completed vessels built for Italy's navy in the twenty-year period 1879-1898, work worth 31 million lire has been entrusted to companies in Liguria, work worth 56 million lire to companies in Livorno, and work worth 11 million lire to companies from southern Italy.

But most of the orders awarded to private shipyards are for torpedo boats and floats and for motor and boiler equipment; almost 75 million lire in the ten-year period 1886-1887 — 1896-1897. These orders have only served to artificially create the so-called Ligurian industry.

The billions of lire spent for the army and the navy, all or almost, in the same zone, have led to the first great formation of capital in some regions and have allowed, as in almost all of northern Italy, the formation of big industry.

6. - On the Difficulty of Obtaining Education and Justice in Southern Italy

In southern Italy, obtaining an education costs much more than in northern Italy; obtaining justice is much more difficult, as a result of the lower number of judicial institutes.

The concentration of the armed forces in a single zone was a necessity.

But our comments in this and the following chapters on the distribution of spending for education, judges, public works, etc., should be considered from a very different angle. There is no way the existence of such strident contrasts can be explained.

The existence of a technical school in a small inhabited centre should not be considered only in relation to the spending to which it gives rise, but also to the results it produces in a specific population. More education heightens the desire for a broader life; where there are more schools, there arise new activities, new energies for the country's industrial life or, at least, a bigger contribution to the state's commitments. One can say that the distribution of state employees follows that of the schools.

All the educational institutes are unequally distributed.

We cite the case of universities, undoubtedly it is serious, but it is still minor.

Of the 17 state universities, 4 are located in northern Italy, 7 in central Italy, 1 in southern Italy, 3 in Sicily and 2 in Sardinia. Higher educational institutes are distributed in accordance with more or less the same criteria.

The four free universities are in turn all located in central Italy.

It is common knowledge that in some of the minor universities, the average cost per student amounts to an enormous sum.

In 1897-1898 the University of Naples alone had at least 5,888 registered students, taking account also of the engineering and veterinary schools, well over a quarter of all the university and higher educational students in Italy.

While there are universities in central Italy which have less than 300 students, in southern Italy there is only one university.

In 1898-1899, the number of university students was as follows:

University	Students	University	Students
Naples	5,536	Catania	986
Turin	3,344	Messina	626
Rome	2,258	Parma	584
Bologna	1,812	Modena	450
Padua	1,495	Cagliari	230
Pavia	1,385	Siena	220
Genoa	1,297	Sassari	152
Palermo	1,068	Macerata	196
Pisa	1,062		
Total			22,701

Hence Naples University accounts for one quarter of the students of all Italy's universities; and while in central Italy there are state universities with less than 300 students, or with little more than 200 students, southern Italy has only one large university, «one, but important», says Ferraris. However, its «importance» does not stop one spending less for it — the only one in all the Mezzogiorno —than for others which are much smaller, such as that of Rome, which has barely one third the students of that of Naples.

Scarcer educational institutes mean not only a scarcer possibility of education, but also higher outlays to obtain professional academic titles or degrees. The inhabitants of Emilia, Tuscany, and northern Italy obtain education more easily, more cheaply than those of the Mezzogiorno. This explains not only the higher level of education; but their prevalence among state employees; but the greater action exercised in state policies.

A large number of university faculties, moreover, produces an increase in the figures of persons who are employed in higher education: a single faculty, even though the number of its students is higher than that of ten small faculties, never gives rise to the same movement of study as two or three small faculties.

It is said that higher education is quite irregularly distributed because, after the establishment of the Kingdom of Italy, one had to respect the institutes which already existed; and as there were already too many, rather than distribute them more rationally, it was decided to conserve the existing state of affairs.

Nothing is less true. Many universities of central and northern Italy were not worth between 1848 and 1860 much more than those of Aquila, Bari, Salerno and Catanzaro. They were dying institutes which could have been suppressed without any difficulty; instead they were transformed first into secondary universities and then into primary universities, while, vice versa, in southern Italy one wished to suppress even that little which already existed.

In Piedmont, in Liguria, in Lombardy there was a rapid creation of lyceums, of gymnasiums, of technical institutes. We saw the words used by Quintino Sella, already an eminent parliamentarian, when asking for a lyceum for his native Biella. In 1864, according to a report by Minister Amari, only eight provinces had more than one lyceum and two more than two. The latter were Milan and Turin; of the other six, two were also in Piedmont, one in Lombardy, one in Liguria. Under the law of 16 February 1861, in southern Italy lyceums were limited to the provincial capitals.

Now, the classical and technical schools and the normal schools are distributed even more unequally than the universities.

Mainland southern Italians find it very difficult to obtain an education as a result of the distance of all the educational institutes.

It should be added that the lyceums and secondary schools in the Mezzogiorno are considered almost as places of punishment, to which young people at the start of their career are sent; or professors who are being punished. The schools of southern Italy are full of teachers on annual contracts and deputy teachers, in unjustifiable proportion.

But there is a fact of exceptional seriousness which reveals the entire orientation of our domestic policy.

It is known that in Italy the local councils are responsible for funding primary education. However the state intervenes to assist the councils which, on their own, are unable or do not know how to meet all the costs; such as to promote the construction of school buildings which are healthy and meet the requirements of hygiene.

It is clear that these laws of subsidy are directed in particular to helping the poorer provinces. And since, by unanimous con-

Number of km² for each institute in the single regions assuming the number of km² for each institute throughout the Kingdom to be 100.

Number of inhabitants for each institute in the single regions assuming the number of inhabitants for each institute throughout the Kingdom to be 100.

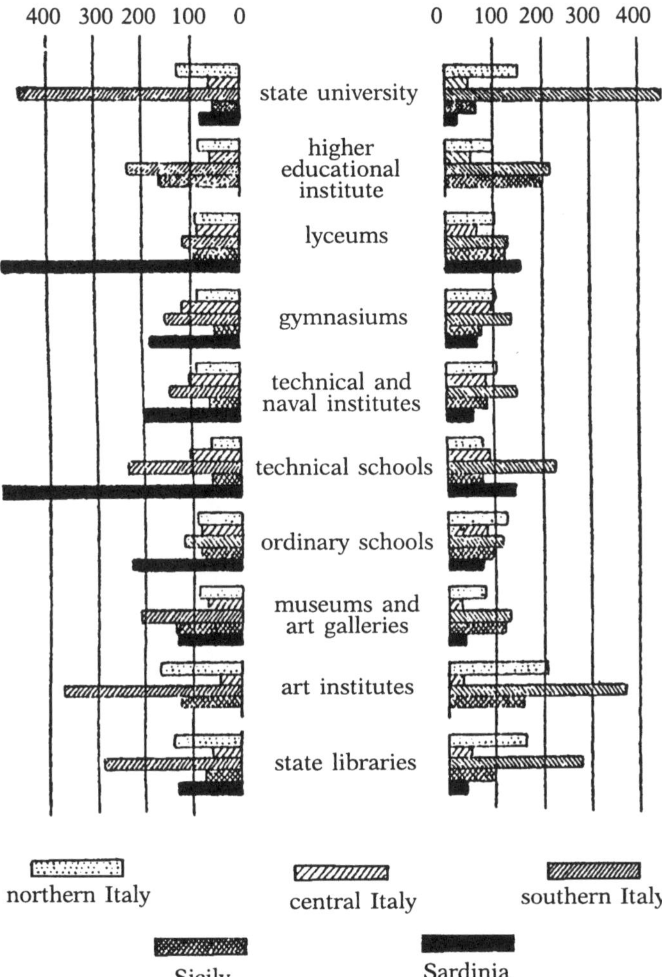

sensus, they are in southern Italy, such spending should take place in the Italy of the Mezzogiorno.

The authors of the law believed one should help the poor councils, and above all the smallest among the poorest.

As is often the case, in Italy it was believed that small town means poor town. The towns with agglomerated population were therefore, immediately considered as such as not to be taken into consideration. And so Piedmont, Liguria, Lombardy and Veneto, for circa thirteen years, saw the inflow of those millions of lire destined for the towns of the poorest regions. With the law of 1886, the state, which had already helped towns with a population of less than 1,000 inhabitants, channelled a considerable part of its educational budget to the more prosperous regions.

The author of a report on the public education budget recently asked: «What distributive justice, whatever the letter of the law and the interpretation it should be given, has overseen this distribution of state funds for primary education to four fifths of the towns of Italy? Why has the other fifth been excluded?

«The justice is indicated by the list, where we see, just to give a few examples, extensive provinces, of more than 100 towns, in which, as already said, all the towns which comprise it have been allowed to enjoy this state aid; other provinces of from 200 to 400 towns, in which 80 or 90% and more of them have benefited with the issue of sums which approach 100,000 lire per province; while in Trapani, for example, only two of the province's 20 towns had until 1896-1897 benefited, and for the total of 139.98 lire; and only 7 of Caltanisetta's 133 towns benefited; only 12 of Bari's 53; 4 of Ferrara's 16; 40 of Palermo's 76, 9 of Siracusa's 32, and so forth».

We have not confined ourselves to studying the distribution of the subsidies in a single year. There may have been in some cases some exception which should not have been generalised. We have instead extended our study to the period from 1890-1891 to 1897-1898: and it emerged that the subsidies destined for the poor towns went to the richest regions.

The loans for new school buildings were also distributed unequally.

In the two laws which concern the granting of loans, there was not, nor could there be, any idea of distinguishing between different regions. Indeed, in the Mezzogiorno where the regions with the greatest agglomeration and the more densely-populated towns are to be found, the benefits of the law could have been more significant.

But accepting a loan means being able to repay it. And the towns where the councils are not even able, in many cases, to meet their mandatory outlays, cannot take out any loans, even those on good terms.

The school inspectors agree that, in most of the southern provinces, the schools are unhealthy hovels. But they add that they have not taken advantage of the law. In one province of the Mezzogiorno only 1 of 133 councils has built a specifically-designed school building.

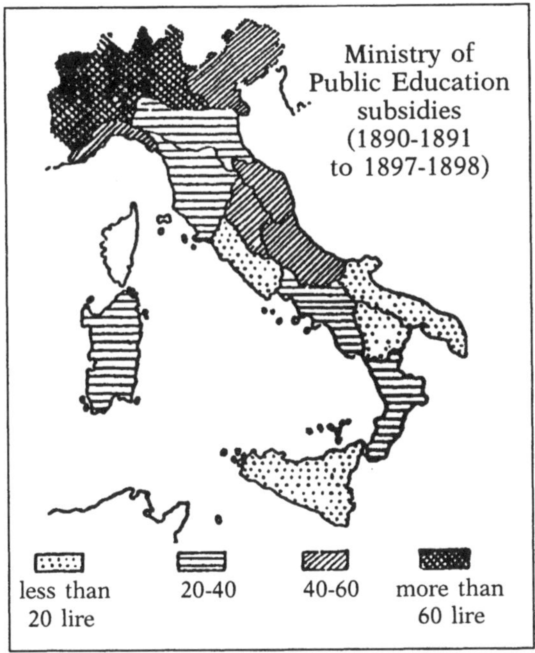

The inspectors and directors of education of southern Italy, who know nothing of public economics and even less of public finance, are unable to explain the reason for the modest applications in their reports to the ministry. A director of education adds: a special law is needed.

The forest of laws is thick: it has been said that it is the thickest forest left standing in Italy. And the more one sees the lack of utility of many laws, the more one demands others; and when the ordinary laws are inadequate, special laws are demanded.

The spending for technical and industrial education, borne by the Ministry of Agriculture, is also distributed such that Piedmont, Lombardy and Veneto receive the largest share.

Even the state's archives are almost all situate in the north.

There are 19 state archives in Italy: namely 1 in Piedmont, 3 in Lombardy, 1 in Liguria, 1 in Veneto — hence 6 in northern Italy; 4 in Emilia, 1 in Rome, 5 in Tuscany — hence 10 in central Italy; 1 in all the Mezzogiorno at Naples; 1 in Sicily in Palermo; 1 in Sardinia in Cagliari.

Undoubtedly, numerous and most evident historical causes have determined the present distribution. And there is no doubt that a traditionally centralised country such as the Mezzogiorno is in much different conditions than northern and central Italy.

But it should also be borne in mind that the unification process, when it came up against even small interests, came to a halt in northern and central Italy.

Our foregoing considerations make it clear that the educational and cultural institutes are not only distributed quite unequally, but that they tend even today to be increasingly concentrated in northern and central Italy.

This fact was known for higher education, indeed it had been pointed out many times. But what is serious is that it is not only confined to higher education.

Secondary, classical and technical education is in a much striking situation.

A person who in northern Italy wishes to send his son to a classical school finds a lyceum every 2,088 km^2 and every 288,796 inhabitants; in southern Italy he finds one every 2,850 km^2 and every 309,134 inhabitants. If he has the fortune to be born in central Italy he finds one every 2,061 km^2 and every 196,108 inhabitants.

The difficulties will be even greater should the person wish, going to live in the Mezzogiorno, to give his son a technical education. He will find a technical school every 3,760 km^2 and every

397,458 inhabitants. Vice versa, if he has the fortune to live in northern Italy, he will find a technical school every 1,018 km^2 and every 140,876 inhabitants. Southern Italy will be even more put to shame as regards technical institutes.

Having completed his secondary studies, the difficulties will increase even when he has to obtain a degree. The degree, as is known, is worth little in Italy because everyone has one; but precisely because it is worth so little he who wishes even the most modest of positions cannot do without it.

Artistic and musical education is almost prohibited in some regions: the needs of such nature, given the present set-up in Italy, can be satisfied only when one lives in northern and central Italy.

When it comes to finding a library, the inhabitants of southern Italy can find only a few at Naples. There are 7 in northern Italy and 16 in central Italy.

Finally, as it is difficult to think of new things in the Mezzogiorno, he who wishes to fall into decadence, thinking only of his forefathers (an idle, but sometimes agreeable occupation,) will find it much more difficult to go to a state archive to discover even imaginary nobilities.

Southern Italy, as anyone knows, produces quite a large contingent of criminals; and as there are still many controversies regarding the limits of rural property, and there are many contentious traditions and a very large number of lawyers, the judicial institutions should be large in number.

In southern Italy, under the Bourbon regime, when wages in general were not high, only the judiciary had very high wages. The old Neapolitan order of 29 May 1817 awarded many magistrates wages which were much higher than those paid today.

According to Scialoja, the expenditure for the judiciary in the Kingdom of Naples amounted to 4,403,826 lire; in Piedmont in 1857 to 3,537,889 lire. But while in the Kingdom of Naples there was a small number of judges with high wages, the opposite held in Piedmont, where there was a large number of judges with much lower wages.

«The total number of courts and judges — Scialoja wrote — is greater in Piedmont than in Naples and the wages are lower.

Now, if I had to express my opinion on this detail, I would frankly say that I do not side with those who prefer a large number of courts and lowly paid judges, but rather few courts and well paid judges».

In 1860, however, the opposite criterion prevailed. And since it was desired to satisfy all, instead of reducing the judiciary, it was decided to increase, and in some areas, such as Piedmont and Liguria, to transform the small, local magistracies into magistrate's courts, such that magistrate's courts spawned everywhere. It suffices to point out that now — after the reductions — the average extension of the jurisdiction of each magistrate's court is 91 km^2 in Liguria, 136 km^2 in Piedmont and 195 and 237 km^2 respectively in Apulia and Basilicata.

When the bill to reduce the number of magistrate's courts was being discussed, one fact was not taken into account: the population.

Now as regards judicial institutions, two things should be borne in mind: the average workload of each, on the one hand, and the size of their jurisdiction on the other.

As regards offences, Italy always achieves something of a sorrowful place in international statistics. But it is above all in southern Italy that some crimes take place in a very high proportion. The general total of offences in the two-year period 1897 was highest in Lazio, Sardinia, Calabria, Campania and Molise. Northern Italy and most of central Italy remained below the general average for the Kingdom of Italy. The harsher conditions of existence, the greater poverty, the distressing traditions of the past mean that throughout the Mezzogiorno crime is generally much higher than in northern Italy.

In the period in question, Sicily had the highest number of murders (27.90 per 100,000 inhabitants), Sardinia followed with 26.22, Campania with 24.53, Calabria with 22.64. The minimums are found in Tuscany with 6.58, in Piedmont with 5.38, in Emilia with 5.37, in Veneto with 3.18 and in Lombardy with 2.92.

The highest levels of personal injuries are recorded in Calabria with 602.80, in Abruzzi with 487.14 and in Campania and Molise with 480.27; the lowest levels are recorded in Veneto with

114.51, in Emilia with 117.92, in Piedmont with 124.73 and in Lombardy with 126.31.

Offences against public morality are generally more numerous in northern Italy; although in this case the statistics' value is quite relative.

The highest level of theft is recorded in Sardinia, Lazio, Abruzzi, and in Basilicata; the lowest in Piedmont and Veneto.

The judiciary, particularly the magistrates, therefore represents for southern Italy not only a need, but also a means of defence, and should be proportionally much higher than elsewhere.

If however we take the reports of the judicial authorities, we see that the judicial institutions are more numerous where the need is less.

Magistrate's courts which issue less than 50 sentences should be undoubtedly considered as of little evident utility: now they are all situate in northern Italy and in Emilia. There are some such as Godiasco, Villanova Mondovi, Frabosa Soprana, Perrero and Zavattarello which issue almost always less than 10 sentences; they are in general in Piedmont or Lombardy; some of them issue only 5 or 6 sentences. Disregarding the town magistrate's courts which almost everywhere in the big cities have a large number of cases to deal with, almost all the magistrate's courts which issue a higher number of sentences are in the Mezzogiorno. And it is in the Mezzogiorno that, as a result of the law which modified the areas of jurisdiction, that the number of magistrate's courts was reduced even further.

There is also a surplus of courts in northern Italy, to the extent that they issue just 258 and 385 sentences per year in Piedmont and Lombardy; compared with 1,125 sentences in Sicily, 1,506 in Campania and 1,555 in Apulia. The courts which issue the largest number of sentences are (excluding those of the big cities) all in southern Italy; vice versa, those which have issued a lesser number of sentences are in northern Italy, indeed all in Piedmont or Lombardy and some in central Italy: Breno with 73 sentences, Pontremoli with 61, Varallo with 60, Castelnuovo di Garfagnana with 44, Borgotaro with 43 and even Bobbio with just 31! No court of southern Italy issues less than 200 sentences for criminal offences, there are on the other hand 12 in Piedmont, 6 in Liguria, 9 in Lombardy, 4 in Veneto which could be abolished or reduced without any damage.

The unjust distribution is even more evident for the appeal courts. While Campania's sole appeal court has issued 6,115 sentences, 2,015 the appeal court of Trani, 2,193 that of Catanzaro and even 595 the division of Potenza, many appeal courts of central and northern Italy have had almost nothing to do. That of Perugia has issued only 368 sentences, that of Macerata 329, that of Parma 169 and that of Modena 166.

Equally striking are the differences for the court of assizes circuits. Their lesser number in the Mezzogiorno, like that of the courts, means that preventive detention is longer, much longer, that the accused wait for a longer time, whether they are innocent or guilty. The circuits of Naples, Palermo, Catania, Catanzaro, Potenza issue a number of orders and sentences which ranges from 192 and 102, that of Rovigo issued 1, that of Cremona 2, those of Sondrio, Grosseto and Reggio di Calabria 3 and those of Mantua and Lecce 4.

If this is the distribution of criminal justice, that of civil justice is no better. The judicial order, which lies at the base of each, means that there are no significant differences.

It appears, at first sight, that southern Italy has, vis-à-vis the population, a greater number of magistrate's courts. In fact, of the 1,535 magistrate's courts (excluding the town courts) 484 are in northern Italy, 312 in central Italy, 501 in southern Italy, 159 in Sicily and 79 in Sardinia. But, as we have said, in respect of judicial institutions, the criterion of population has a minimum importance and there can only be two criteria: the size of the jurisdiction and the workload. Now in central and northern Italy a large number of magistrate's courts have nothing to do. Those of Chiusa di Pesio, Borgo Ticino, Busseto, Casola Valsenio have issued 9 sentences in civil suits; Cuggiono, Vilminore, Pisogne, Barga, Chiusdino, Loiano 8; Biandrate, Borghetto Lodigiano, Bormio, Isola del Giglio, Sogliano al Rubicone 7; Paullo Lodigiano, Bovegno, Castiglione delle Stiviere, Salò, Asciano and Castelfranco Emilia 6; San Nazzaro dei Burgondi and Valdieri 5; Asso, Volta Mantovana and Radda 4; Piadena, Pienza, Campana and Ustica 3; Crodo and Moretta 2 and Perrero 1.

All these magistrate's courts are in northern Italy, in Emilia and in Tuscany. Campana alone is in Calabria and Ustica in Sicily; but both have a heavy workload of criminal cases. Campana issued 69 sentences in criminal cases in 1897 and Ustica 110, and it needs a magistrate's court in view of its specific situation. Many magistrate's courts of northern and central Italy, on the other hand, have no reason to exist. And yet, disregarding the criterion of the population (which was not followed in other laws which benefited the Mezzogiorno), in Basilicata, Calabria and Apulia magistrate's courts, which represented a true element of civil progress, have been abolished.

For the civil courts, not even the population has been taken into account. In northern Italy there is a court every 105,311 inhabitants, in central Italy one every 208,697 inhabitants and in Sicily one every 209,511 inhabitants. When one thinks of the lower density of population and the large number of cases, then it is clear how expensive justice is in the Mezzogiorno. The courts which pronounce a larger number of sentences, excluding those of the big cities, are all situate in the Mezzogiorno: vice versa, the 22 courts which in 1896 issued less than 100 sentences are, except for one in Sicily and one in Sardinia, all in northern and central Italy: Varallo, Bassano, Como, Sondrio, Mistretta, Domodossola, Lanusei, Pontremoli, Castelnuovo di Garfagnana, Civitavecchia, Pavullo, Camerino, Castiglione delle Stiviere, Salò, Orvieto, Bozzolo, Borgotaro, Rocca San Casciano, Portferraio, Bobbio, Montepulciano and Breno. This last court issued only 23 sentences.

Appeal courts are much more numerous in central Italy: 1 for every 745,287 inhabitants; vice versa, taking account of the division of Potenza, there is one every 1,544,360 inhabitants in southern Italy, one every 1,818,416 inhabitants in northern Italy and 1 every 1,977,718 inhabitants in Sicily. While the number of sentences of each appeal court averages however 1,133 in southern Italy, falling to 633 in northern Italy and to a minimum of 271 in central Italy!

Thus the institutions of justice are distributed almost no better than those of education, and ensure that between persons who, by tradition and need, are more quarrelsome and more ready to commit a crime relations are more virulent and the difficulties of existence greater.

And so, while in the Mezzogiorno the judicial taxes yield more than in all the rest of Italy, the state spends proportionally much less for civil and criminal justice.

7. - Spending on Public Works

7.1 *How Most of the Spending Takes Place in Northern and Central Italy*

The most discussed topic, indeed, the most tormented is that of public works; as the new Italy has had to sacrifice much for them, what fruit have these sacrifices borne?

The north believes that southern Italy, wholly lacking in roads and means of communication when annexed, has to a large extent drawn on the state budget for the costs of roads. Later, it not only induced the state to build unproductive railways; but through the constructions made only for political or electoral purposes, considerably contributed to the state's financial problems.

The south, on the other hand, believes that the sea coasts are neglected, that the river works are scarce and the torrents devastate the countryside: then that the immense regions have not even seen the smoke of a steam engine or have just seen it recently; then that malaria still kills and the reclamation works have been slow; it is believed that the Mezzogiorno has obtained little and that vice versa the state has sacrificed much to the north.

To date the debate has never come to anything nor proved anything; newspaper articles, timid hints in parliamentary speeches.

The thick jungle of laws on public works is so impenetrable that if frightens even those endowed with the most audacious spirit. Vice versa, even if one knows the legislation perfectly, it is not possible to reach precise results, nor to fix in figures how much each region has received from the state for public works of every nature, by direct, protracted and fatiguing research.

Indeed, until very recently, this research was absolutely impossible, and the official budgets and publications lacked any element for assessing the territorial distribution of the state's public-works spending.

But that which was until very recently impossible, is no longer so. The Ministry of Public Works, thanks to Hon. Lacava, who takes the merit for one of the most notable studies ever carried out by the Italian administration, has published in three thick volumes, for the 1900 Paris Exhibition, his report on state spending for public works in the fiscal years from 1862 to 1896-1897. Employing this as our guide, taking into account also the many and numerous special publications of the Ministry of Public Works, collating the elements scattered in ministerial and parliamentary reports from 1862 to 1896-1897, and drawing on our direct research, we believe we now have all the elements to assure that the controversy leaves behind it the field of statements and can be made concrete in certain figures.

Moreover, if we take as a point of departure, the report which Stefano Jacini presented to Parliament on 31 January 1867 as Minister of Public Works, and also take account of the excellent studies by Ferrucci and of others as regards the railways, we can reach precise conclusions.

For roads, it is unarguable that more has been spent for southern Italy that for northern Italy; and it is this that is looked at, even excessively so, forgetting that the spending on roads is not the only public-works spending.

In 1860, the conditions of the new Italy were very different as regards roads and communications of every kind.

In northern and central Italy there was a considerable number of railway lines; however, Sicily and Sardinia had a considerable shortage of them, and in mainland southern Italy communications were very difficult.

The Bourbons really believed that the roads opened for the populations not only new needs, but dangerous trends such that not only did they not encourage their construction, but at times they hampered it.

The famous Commission of Inquiry into Banditry whose members included Saffi, Sirtori, Bixio, Castagnola and others, and whose report was written by Giuseppe Massari, described to a secret session of the Lower House in May 3 and 4, 1863 the terrible scourge then tormenting the Mezzogiorno of Italy thus: «The lack of good roads abets banditry, we believe this so evident that there is no need to demonstrate it. This deplorable lack was one of the elements of the Bourbon system and consequence of a preconceived design. The Bourbons built magnificent roads in the proximity of Naples to deceive foreigners, to procure for themselves the appearances of a civil government; they knew that most, if not all, of the foreigners stayed in the capital, and did not bother to go and visit neither the Capitanata region nor Basilicata. This the intent was achieved: at Naples a veneer of civilisation, in the provinces, barbarianism without any kind of veil. Basilicata is a province which, in size, equals or at least approaches, that of Tuscany; one can say that it is totally lacking in usable roads; the only roads it has are that from Melfi to Potenza, that from Potenza to the province of Salerno and to Naples, that which passes through Lagonero to link the provinces of Cosenza and Salerno. The road from Potenza to Matera stops at Grottole. There is no way of communication towards the Ionian Sea.

One travels for ten and fifteen and twenty miles for steep paths, with dangerous slopes, without coming across a village. The trade routes are therefore precluded to those inhabitants, communications are impossible, the beneficial contacts of civilisation prevented. The many advantages the configuration of the terrain gives the bandits are thus flanked by that deriving from the difficulty, often insurmountable, that the lack of roads poses to their pursuit and capture. The long space which separates Abruzzi from Capitanata is equally lacking in roads. Quite a few Abruzzi landowners have holdings of considerable importance in Foggia province, but when they intend to visit them themselves, they are obliged to make a very long detour, to go first to Naples and from there to Foggia. Every year the shepherds who come down from Abruzzi travel the so-called *tratturo*, to reach Capitanata, but, except for them, that route is not accessible to others, and in the winter it is almost wholly impassable. neither is there any decent road from Capitanata to the other adjacent province of Benevento.

Of the 124 towns of Basilicate, 91 have no roads; the same holds for 92 of the 108 towns in Catanzaro province, 60 of the 75 of Teramo province. In the province of Naples itself 24 towns are without roads. Bari is the privileged province, for each square myriametre it has eleven kilometres of road where in Abruzzi, Capitanata, Calabria and Basilicata the proportion is only three kilometres. Overall, of the 1,848 towns around Naples, 1,321 lack roads. Now this lack of roads only benefits the bandits who come into being, show themselves and prosper everywhere the works of civilisation are not to be found.

These were the conditions in which the Neapolitan provinces found themselves when the political upheaval of 1860 took place! and here we are naturally led to discuss the near and immediate causes of the present banditry, because, it should not be forgotten, those we have taken into account up to now are only the general causes which predispose the cruel scourge».

It was, therefore, not only an economic necessity, but a supreme necessity of defence to build decent roads in southern Italy.

However, it was not only the south, as is said, which lacked roads.

In northern Italy, as a result of the political division of the various states, there were no general connecting roads through above all the Alpine and Apennine passes. The Po river formed a border line, so scarce and uncertain were the passes and, almost everywhere, there were few river crossings.

In general, however, northern Italy's road system was already very developed.

Given its area, Sardinia also suffered from a lack of roads.

If southern Italy lacked them, there were however many more than Massari's words might have one believe.

Around the capital was a big road network built, maintained, Jacini says, «with Roman magnificence at the expense of public finance». Apulia, particularly the Terra di Bari and Terra di Otranto areas, was generously equipped with roads. From 1848 to 1885, according to the same author, the Bourbon government allocated, for the upkeep and construction of roads this side of the Faro, the annual sum of 600 thousand ducats, which was increased from 1856 to 1859 to 800 thousand ducats (3,400,000 lire); while in 1860, for ordinary bridge and road works, 947,076.86 ducats (4,025,076.25 lire) of spending was envisaged. Perhaps a considerable amount was spent, but the entire system of construction was bad, slow, inefficient. Even in Sicily the roads were not in good condition. Maintained on the island's budget with an annual allocation of 300 thousand ducats, the roads stretched for 2,080 km.: but were generally poorly upkept.

Thus it was that the spending for roads, as a result of the various laws which succeeded one another, totalled 174 million lire in northern Italy, 101 million lire in central Italy, 280 million lire in southern Italy, 100 million lire in Sicily and 62 million lire in Sardinia.

Undoubtedly therefore, southern Italy, Sardinia and Sicily were the major participants in the 718.5 million lire spending made by the state.

While southern Italy and Sicily accounted for 38.9% of the Kingdom's population, they received circa 54% of all the spending for roads.

When one speaks of roads one believes that is the whole story; but one forgets the water-defence works.

Is water perhaps silent also in public finance?

If for southern and island Italy from 1862 to 1896-1897 political and economic necessity forced the state to make great sacrifices for the construction of roads, the 457.9 million lire spent to date for water-defence works went wholly to northern and central Italy: 266.9 million lire to northern Italy, 187.8 million lire to central Italy, 1.6 million lire to southern Italy, and 1.3 million lire to Sicily.

The biggest amounts spent were 58.4 million lire in the province of Rome, 49.2 million lire in that of Padua, 45.9 million lire in that of Mantua, 29.8 million lire in that of Verona, 26.6

million lire in that of Ferrara, 20.6 million lire in that of Venice, 20.3 million lire in that of Bologna, 18.6 million lire in that of Ravenna, 18.2 million lire in that of Milan, etc.

Hence more than 450 million lire went on water-defence works in northern and central Italy.

Rome province saw the great masterpieces of works for the Tiber river, Padua the works for the Adige, Brenta and Gorzone rivers, the many canals built in a few years entailed the spending of some 50 million lire.

In Mantua province, the works for the Po, Mincio and Oglio rivers, the construction of numerous water-defence works lifted the spending to 45.9 million lire. Nearly everywhere in northern and central Italy the state spent generously for water-defence works.

In southern Italy on the other hand, the rivers which had changed into torrents continued their work of destruction, without obstacle or shelter.

If therefore southern Italy and Sicily which, apart from their size, have together a population of slightly more than northern Italy, have had, as is always recalled, much more spending for roads, 205.7 million lire more; northern Italy has had 263,9 million lire more for water-defence works.

Spending for land reclamation, which totalled 111 million lire from 1862 to 1897-1898, went mainly to the Mezzogiorno: 53.3 million lire, and to central Italy: 44.7 million lire: while in northern Italy the spending amounted to only 9.6 million lire and in Sicily to 3.6 million lire.

But the 53.3 million lire spent in southern Italy consists almost exclusively of the 27.7 million lire spent in Caserta province, 12.9 million lire in Salerno province, 4.7 million lire in Naples province, 4.3 million lire in Foggia province and 1 million lire in Lecce province.

Now it should be borne in mind that this spending was in very large part the effect of laws which dated from before 1860. In fact, the land reclamation works which cost most were those of the lower basin of the Volturno and Bagnoli, in the provinces of Caserta and Naples. These works were ordered by the royal orders of 23 October 1840 and 24 November 1852 and by the Royal Decree of 11 May 1855. And it is only thanks to these works that southern Italy is generously represented in the spending for land reclamation.

But the laws made after 1860 have in this as in many other things tilted the balance in favour of northern Italy. And it can be held that at the end of 1922-1923, the state administration will spend more in northern Italy than in southern Italy and Sicily.

The sea coasts of southern Italy are more or less, by length, four times those of northern Italy, and more than twice those of central Italy.

Nevertheless, the port works of southern Italy have been very scant: 142 million lire in northern Italy, 72 million lire in central Italy and 86 million lire in southern Italy.

Calabria has almost no ports, even where with a modest outlay one could create advantageous traffic conditions; in Apulia and on the Abruzzi coast, there have slightly more port works, but again they have still been scarce.

In general, one can say that, not only in proportion to the length of the coast, but in proportion to the needs of the traffic much less has been spent in the Mezzogiorno than was necessary.

But the public works which have had the most importance have been the building of railways, which demand a separate examination.

The Kingdom of Naples, as is known, had its first railway line in 1839; it was the first line built in Italy, and one of the very first built in Europe.

The first railway in Europe was built in 1821 in England; the second, in 1827 in America; the third, of 18 km., in France in 1828; the fourth in Belgium in 1834. Five years later, in 1839, the Naples-Portici line, Italy's first railway line, was opened.

Settembrini notes that the Neapolitan government never considered the railway other than from the military point of view and that of leisure. «In 1839 there was built, the first in Italy, the railway between Naples and Castellammare where there is the royal residence of Quisisana and a branch was extended to Nocera, where there is an army garrison. After, the other line from Naples to Caserta was built to link the two palaces, as is written on the

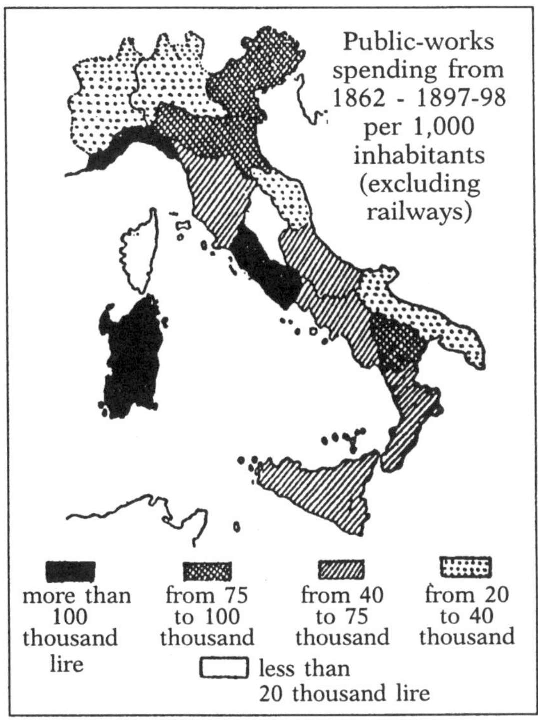

medal struck to commemorate the fact; and it was extended to the fortress of Capua, with a branch line to Nola, another army garrison. Thus King Ferdinand did not hate the railway as did the Pope, but he built few of them and short lines solely to move his troops and to ensure his domination, not for any utility for the people. There was much talk of a railway for Apulia, but it came to nothing. No thought whatsoever was given to Calabria, Abruzzi and Sicily; and now we still do not have all the lines, even though we were the first to have one».

There is perhaps a pinch of exaggeration.

When the Naples-Portici railway line was inaugurated on 3 October 1839, it was, as we noted, the first in Italy, King Ferdinand, replying to the delegate of the French company which had built the line, said, according to a contemporary historian: «I am overjoyed to see French and Neapolitans join their industrial forces in a useful enterprise. The rail road will undoubtedly boost

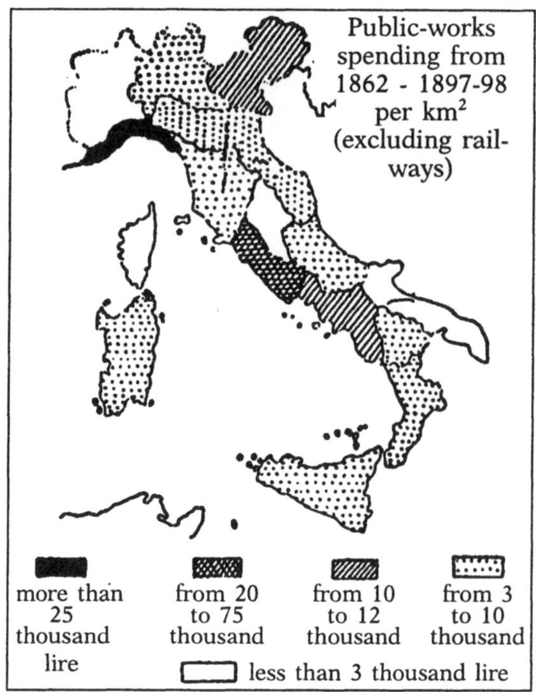

trade, which was why he had protected in every possible way this initial stretch which had been built this side of the Alps. While bearing in mind that this new road should be of utility to his people, he was much more pleased with the thought that once the works to Nocera and Castellammare were completed he could see it extended via Avellino to the Adriatic sea resort».

It was the period when the penultimate king of the Bourbon royal house was truly inspired by a liberal spirit, after 1848 he saw things very differently.

Having inaugurated the first railway at Naples, the Kingdom of the Two Sicilies, of the great states of the peninsula, later however lagged behind all as regards the building of railways.

An official document indicates that in April 1859, that is to say at the start of that war which determined the constitution of the Kingdom of Italy, the situation as regards railways was as follows:

TABLE 5

RAILWAYS IN ITALY IN APRIL 1859

Provinces	Km. in service	Km. under construction	Total	Km. under licence
Subalpine	807	59	866	—
Lombardy	200	40	240	180
Emilia	33	147	180	276
Marches and Umbria	—	—	—	360
Tuscany	308	16	324	362
Naples	124	4	128	128
Sicily	—	—	—	—
Totals	1,472	266	1,738	1,306

According to an excellent survey by Senator Roux, by 1860 the length of railway lines in service totalled 2,139 km. All the lines had cost a total 641,013,024 lire.

Once the new Kingdom had been proclaimed, it was necessary to quickly build military lines, those which most served for defence and they were almost all in northern Italy; and at the same time it was necessary to give the regions which were most deficient (and this was also a political necessity) railway lines.

But initially, the urgency of defence was almost disregarded; it was a supreme necessity, but sometimes even the necessity was overstated.

When the railways were not useful for defence, the criteria did not change. Speaking of special treatment granted to Liguria, Sella said: «It is desired, it is worthwhile repeating, that it should never serve as a precedent and model for other similar contracts».

On 1 January 1898 the length of railway lines in Italy totalled 15,470,070 m.

At the end of 1899, the total length of railway lines was 15,546 km distributed as follows:

TABLE 6

Zones	State-owned railways km.	Railways run by private industry under licence km.	Total km.
Northern Italy	3,377	1,736	5,113
Central Italy	3,350	735	4,085
Southern Italy	2,161	1,754	3,915
Sicily	1,083	377	1,460
Sardinia	—	973	973
Total	9,971	5,575	15,546

In northern Italy, of the lines operated by private industry, a total of 1,056 km., are now run by Società Mediterranea or Adriatica. The other 600 km. are run by other special companies

The *Report on the Exercise of Italian Railways*, published by the General Railway Inspectorate, contains, in its volume for 1895, which was released only in early November 1899, a cost schedule of all the railways built by the state and their rolling stock at 31 December 1895.

Grouping the data contained in that publication and adding those regarding the two subsequent years, it turns out that state spending for railways it owns amounted to 4,076 million lire at 30 June 1898, comprised as follows:

Northern Italy	1,584,825,197
Central Italy	1,148,316,518
Southern Italy	863,776,073
Sicily	479,248,752
Total	4,076,166,540

The majority of state railway building took place, therefore, in northern Italy: however, this ratio conceals the prevalence of central Italy which, with more than 4,085 km., has 3,350 km., while northern Italy, with 5,113 km. has 3,377 km.

The forms and methods followed in the building, the technical arrangements, everything played in favour of northern Italy.

Without going into details, which would take too long and which I have given in my work *Il bilancio dello Stato dal 1862 al 1896-1897**, it suffices to note that the contractors, chief engineers and also the workers, even in the Mezzogiorno, were almost exclusively from northern Italy and some regions of central Italy.

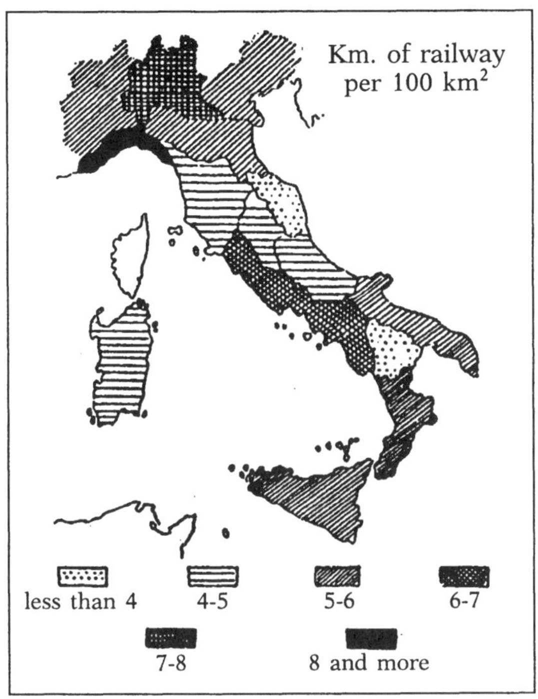

According to recent studies, the net spending of the Ministry of Public Works incurred by the state from 1862 to 1896-1897 amounted to 6,031 million lire, composed as follows:

Payments from 1862 to 1897-98 from the budget of the Ministry of Public Works for all branches of service which depend on it	4,690,963,521.41

* See footnote 1.

Payments from 1862 to 1897-1898 from the budget of the Treasury Ministry for sales of public-debt securities for the execution of public works	1,614,879,399.09
	6,305,842,920.50
less payments to Treasury from 1862 to 1897-98 for shared costs and reimbursement of interested local bodies	353,598,328.73
thus net cost borne by state totals	5,952,244,591.77
adding however 141,424,255.10 lire of residual liabilities and subtracting 62,210,448.56 of residual assets, i.e., extra net spending of	79,213,776.45
gives the total spending for public works, namely	6,031,458,368.22

It would be desirable to see how these 6 billion lire have been spent. But it is not possible to obtain a precise breakdown of the 1,614 million lire spent to service debt by the Treasury Ministry. One can hold, without fear of error, that most of this sum was spent for northern Italy, and in general for those regions where the railways were mostly built in the period prior to the law of 1879.

Taking into account also the outstanding amounts to be paid at 30 June 1898, the spending for public works is as follows:

category I.	ordinary costs	1,036,646,893.45
	extraordinary costs	1,137,227,399.28
category II.	construction of track	2,628,592,906.51
category III.	movement of capital	21,038,115.71
category IV.	clearing entries	8,882,431.56
	total	4,832,387,746.51

Of these 4,832 million lire, a relatively precise calculation can now easily be given.

According to recent studies in which, above all for the calculation of the railways, it was preferred to consider Emilia and Romagna as belonging to northern Italy, [and] taking account of the railway lines, all the public works for the sum of 4,832 million lire were comprised thus: 1,965 million lire were spent in northern Italy, Emilia and Romagna included, 793 million lire in central Italy, 919 in southern Italy and 545 million lire on the islands.

As regards spending per-capita, central Italy leads the way: 159,606.75 lire per 1,000 inhabitants, followed by northern Italy with 141,016.51 lire, and Sicily and Sardinia with 124,909.47 lire. Southern Italy is last with 109,552.73 lire while the average for the Kingdom is 152,595.56 lire.

From the point of view of area, the situation is not fundamentally different. For every square kilometre 18,865.37 lire were spent in northern Italy, 14,254.81 in central Italy, 10,956.48 in Sicily and Sardinia and 11,947.93 lire in southern Italy. The latter remains far behind the average for the Kingdom which was 16.858.26 lire.

If we now use the foregoing criteria to give a proportional average $\sqrt{ab}$ (a = 1,000 inhabitants, b = 1 km^2) the result is that much less was spent in mainland southern Italy than elsewhere. While the general average for the Kingdom is 50,791.78, that of northern Italy amounts to 51,578.27, central Italy to 47,698.66, Sicily and Sardinia to 36,719.78, and mainland southern Italy to only 36,179.12.

As regards population, as also for area, or that of a proportional average between one and the other, everything considered, railways, roads, water works, land reclamation, port works and those for the sea coasts, taking everything into account, the result is still that less was spent in southern Italy.

This belies the legend that the Mezzogiorno of Italy has benefited most from public works, to the detriment of the state and unjustly vis-à-vis the other regions; a legend which is not only untrue, but is above all immoral, an almost cruel irony for populations which have certainly not been favoured by all the laws of present-day Italy[2].

---

[2] Remarkable imbalances are also found for the postal and telegraph services, these were pointed out in *Il bilancio* (see footnote 1).

8. - On Some Shifts in Wealth from South to North

From 1860 to the present, there has been a continuous drainage of capital from the South to the North as a result of the state's policies; several billion lire have been transported in this period from the southern part of the peninsula, which was already the poorest, to the northern part, which was already the richest. Through many channels, created by the laws, much wealth by unknown or little known routes has emigrated from the Mezzogiorno.

If it was possible (we have attempted the calculation only in part and for given years) to put on one side all that which southern Italy has given by way of taxes and duties of every kind, and on the other all that which the state has spent in it for the army, navy, justice, public order, works, in short for all the public services, it would turn out that there is a difference of several billion lire which has moved from southern to northern Italy.

It has been a true channelling, a work of annual and hence continuous drainage; a slow, but never interrupted work.

Having moved the border and the big consumption markets to the North, the movement was precipitate between 1860 and 1880, slower afterwards.

That which southern Italy has given above that which it has received represents a series of non-material benefits: the entry into civilisation, greater security in domestic order, finally the biggest potential possibility for development the Mezzogiorno has ever had.

But in addition to this continuous drainage, there are some facts which, in view of their importance, should be studied separately, and which have contributed to determine the present-day situation in a truly exceptional manner.

In order to assess the importance of the facts which have taken place, we should study separately: *a)* the monetary situation of the old states; *b)* the situation and sale of Church and state assets in each region; *c)* the public debt of the old states and the issues made in the Kingdom after 1860; *d)* the principal state procurement, public works and distribution of the shares of the joint-stock companies subsidised by the state, or exercising privileged or monopoly industries; *e)* participation in the public jobs of the state and number of state employees in each region.

It is above all the facts listed in letters *a)* through *d)* which will receive the closest scrutiny for this study.

There was in the Kingdom of Naples a great abundance of specie, above all of silver specie.

The Bourbons' economic policy was such that money had to flow in, even if there was little general wealth. It was a true mercantilist policy, except that the sale of raw materials abroad also engendered serious concern.

Scialoja, with manifest aversion for the Neapolitan government, which truly merited so much disdain and not for one matter alone, wrote: «those who know anything about economic laws and their practical effects understand how and why the money had to flow toward the Kingdom of Naples as water toward a lower place. Undoubtedly, if it had been possible to degrade that kingdom in whole and fully toward the Middle Ages and, in the middle of the XIX century, to take it back to the conditions in which it was in the XVI century, when Mons. Mascitelli sold his grain at 8 coins per *tomolo*, and Giuliano the sillkmaker wrote that with 12 carlins he could buy a pig; much more money, in this hypothesis, would have flowed in from all the civilised world, because it would there have acquired a much higher value than that it currently has. I say this only because it should be clear that, if the wellbeing of a people was measured in this manner, the conclusion could only be that this hypothetical return to the sixteenth century would be the height of prosperity of the Neapolitans.

«In any case, silver was in abundance at Naples. And last year there was a surplus; such that, after much hesitation, the government allowed the export of biscuits and pasta, as well as of grain, maize, barley, oats, broad beans and other similar foodstuffs, and reduced the duty on the extraction of oil. Such that the exports of this product led to the almost doubling of the inflow of silver.

«These are the principal causes for the Naples mint's coining of a prodigious quantity of money. According to the official journal of 18 June 1857, the value of the money coined in these last years was as follows: (1852) 1,818,193 ducats; (1853) 2,228,168 ducats; (1854) 7,766,537 ducats; (1855) 6,939,247 ducats; (1856) 13,628,628 ducats».

However, these criticisms were not very founded, and, with considerable skill, Magliani cut them down to their proper worth.

However, it cannot be denied that the Neapolitan government followed a limited economic policy. Many of its measures recall the old rationing whims. It was a system of prudence and fear, which suffocated many energies which otherwise would have awakened. But that increased the monetary wealth, which was truly enormous.

COINS OF THE OLD ITALIAN STATES
WITHDRAWN FROM CIRCULATION

Parma and Modena	millions	1.7 =	0.3%
Lombardy	millions	8.1 =	1.2%
Venice	millions	12.8 =	1.9%
Kingdom of Sardinia	millions	27.1 =	4.0%
Grand-Duchy of Tuscany	millions	85.3 =	12.9%
Rome and the Papal State	millions	90.7 =	14.0%
Kingdom of the Two Sicilies	millions	443.3 =	65.7%

The monies of the old states amounted overall to 668,926,140.14, of which the Kingdom of the Two Sicilies alone accounted for 443,281,665.23 or 65.7% of the total; Veneto 12,761,333.39 or 1.9%; Parma and Piacenza 1,209,135.09 or 0.2%; the Papal state 90,726,142.14 or 14%; the Duchy of Modena 456,152.51 or 0.1%; the Grand-Duchy of Tuscany 85,263,102.51 or 12,9%; and finally the Kingdom of Sardinia 27,096,268.09 or 4%.

The greatest monetary wealth was therefore to be found in the Kingdom of the Two Sicilies: 65.7% of the total. Taking into account that after 1860 and for some time, gold was a depreciated metal as a result of the discovery of new gold fields in Australia and America, it is easy to comprehend the wealth represented by 424 million silver coins.

Between 1820 and 1860 we can say that the Mezzogiorno only saved money; and this alone explains how it could account for such a quantity.

The southern country had no economic culture and not even an industrial education: it saved in the primitive form. This mass of money was however drained in a short time; it served either to pay the new, very harsh taxes or to buy state assets.

Southern Italy has contributed with its state assets, of the so-called old property, and with its church assets to the tune of much more than half a billion lire to the budget.

It should be borne in mind that in the Mezzogiorno, the church owned an enormous number of assets, the state a large number. The badly-realised disposals of one and the other, the pressing needs of public finance, did not raise that income it was hoped and presumably should have been raised. But those huge sales of assets, which lasted many years, which have still not finished to this date, have had a considerably effect on the entire orientation of our public finance.

What in actual fact caused the sale of state assets? Nothing more than a transfer of monetary wealth, from each region to the state.

When plots of land were sold for tens of millions of lire in Apulia, it was always the Apulian citizens who bought. Hence the wealth of Apulia diminished because the monetary capital available went elsewhere. And while one was doing no more than transferring property from a collective body to private citizens, the personal non-property income disappeared. The state in turn destined it to those regions where spending was higher, Lombardy, Piedmont, Liguria.

The so-called old property, consisting of public land for the most, land which the state put up for sale under new laws (21 August 1862) or the application of old laws, was almost all situate in southern Italy and in Sicily; a small part in Sardinia for former common land and in Tuscany for the Maremma assets.

Large amounts of property were quickly sold during the first years of the new Kingdom either directly by the state or by a joint-stock company. The highest income from said sales was obtained in 1865.

Sella and Minghetti discussed at length the importance of the sale of the former state property, formed in large part by the public assets of the Kingdom of the Two Sicilies. One hazarded a certain amount of income raised by said, the other another amount.

Undoubtedly, one could not have sold worse, or in a more damaging way, for the state and for the agrarian economy of the Mezzogiorno: extensive woods were destroyed, land was sold for a pittance or became the instrument of immoral speculation.

There is no break down of the sales of the so-called old property.

But from 1861 to 31 December 1898 the state sold directly (54,866 plots for 130,078,226.11 lire) or by joint-stock company, during the time it operated, from 1861 to 31 December 1885 (43,124 for 239,868,052.89) 299,995 hectares of land for a total 369,946,279 lire.

This sum came principally from southern Italy.

There was, in turn, much more Church property in the Mezzogiorno than in the rest of Italy.

The Bourbons had sought, above all with Charles III and, in the first years of his reign, with Ferdinand II, to contain the church's power.

In 1786, the population of the Kingdom of Naples amounted to just 4,800,000 inhabitants which included 100 thousand clergy, of which 13,500 were monks.

In 1789, in the same kingdom, the church property generated a revenue of 6,373,000 ducats per year. According to Galante, the bishops and prelates received no less than 524,000 ducats; the 800 hospices 160,000; the 3,700 parishes 740,000; the 9,000 chaplaincies and benefices 180,000; the 14,000 holy places 580,000, which arranged for the maintenance of the churches, 80,000 the Order of Malta and more than 4 million the monasteries of landed friars.

According to a recent document, the region of Italy which generated the most income from the sale of church property was Apulia: 79.8 million up to June 1898; that which generated the least revenue was Liguria with 11 million. Only two regions, Apulia and Basilicata, generated more revenue than Liguria, Lombardy and Veneto combined.

Hence the calculations which put the revenue generated from the sale of the old-state and Church property in the Mezzogiorno at more than 600 million are somewhat less than the actual figure.

But the biggest cause of drainage, the most greatest of all, not only in view of its importance, but also of its effects, was the public debt. It led to a shift of wealth which has perhaps not been equalled by any other country of modern Europe.

In 1860, after the establishment of the new Kingdom, the economic and financial situation of all the states of the peninsula which comprised it was very different. No attention was then paid to interest: what was the point of discussing it when one was to remain united? The union of everything appeared the most natural: union of debts, union of taxes, union of burdens. And then it was thought that in the Mezzogiorno it sufficed to stamp one's foot on the ground for the wealth to come out! Only the work of tyrants had prevented the Two Sicilies from becoming an enchanted land: it was a country too favoured by nature (sic!), Bonghi wrote in a missive to the King. Massari, Spaventa, Pisanelli, De Sanctis, Mancini, all more or less the leading southern politicians of 1860, who lived outside their country, or had lived in books when in their country, were politically ideologues and did not know the Mezzogiorno's economic situation. Too favoured by nature was southern Italy, with almost all the provinces afflicted by malaria, with large zones of low productivity, with bad distribution of water, with quite few natural resources, at least in eight or nine provinces!

In other countries of Europe, union was not conceived as here in Italy; but here one did not wish, in a moment when any discussion which re-awakened regional passions, to discuss interest was deemed dangerous even though it was of vital importance.

As one had to live together, it was better, or so it appeared, not even to tolerate any disputes of such nature arising.

Thus it was that the debts were united without discussion.

And the debts were quite different in their nature.

According to an official publication of the General Office of Public Debt, the figures of the debts of the various states recorded in 1862 were:

Consolidated debt and interest included in the public debt register:

Sardinia	61,615,255.05
Lombardy	7,531,185.53
Modena	794,534.42
Parma	610,453.95
Romagna, Umbria, etc.	121,500.00
Naples	26,003,633.50
Sicily	6,800,0000.00
Tuscany	8,093,284.00
Total	111,569,846.45

Taking into account the population recorded by the 1861 census, the average cost of the debt inherited from the various states was therefore:

	Annual quota per inhabitant
Kingdom of Sardinia	13.93
Grand-Duchy of Tuscany	4.43
Kingdom of the Two Sicilies	3.58
Lombardy	2.68
Duchy of Modena	1.32
Duchy of Parma	1.21
Romagna, Umbria, etc.	0.08

Subsequent variations led to further changes in these situations; the big debt of Veneto was included, as was the large mass of the Papal debt, roughly 22 and a half million of interest; some corrections were made.

Southern Italy therefore had a small number of debts and, as a ratio of the population was last, of the large autonomous states of the peninsula, as regards debt and also trailed well behind the others in said respect.

The Bourbon government was equally averse to debt and taxes; and as it introduced the latter unwillingly, fearing unpopularity, it resorted to the former as rarely as possible.

The public debt of Naples and the mainland Mezzogiorno, when the Bourbon monarchy fell, was quite modest, if one takes into account the size of the state and the number of its inhabitants. The law of 4 August 1861 recognised in fact an interest of 26,003,633.50 lire equal to 6,118,502 ducats, i.e., 25,6438,376 lire of 5% consolidated debt and 335,275.50 of 4% consolidated debt.

It was a very small debt and weighed on the budget in very limited manner only. Its first nucleus dated back to the re-organisation of the finances undertaken under the law of 25 June 1860, which again entrusted the state treasury with collecting the so-called *arrendamento* taxes which had been collected by private bodies from July 1st of said year, and laid down that the creditors of said, known as grantees or consignees or sub-grantees, were recorded in a public register for an annuity to be calculated on the average of the product obtained in the ten years from 1 January 1796 to 31 December 1805.

The first loan of 12 July 1808, which led to the law of the subsequent August, was a forced loan and amounted to 1,200,000 ducats. One could almost say that the debt reared its head again only during the unrest of 1820, when the national Parliament took out a first loan. After there were others, but the sums involved were always not large. They abused the principles of paraphernal and primogeniture (18,000 ducats per year in 1850 as extradotal to Princess donna Maria Carolina Ferdinanda; 15,000 to Prince don Giuseppe Maria; 26,000 to don Pasquale Maria, count of Bari, etc.); but the majority of the new debts served to pay the old ones; some were made after periods of revolutions; others, but few, for the construction of roads or for public works.

Between 1850 and 1859 the issues totalled only 620,000 ducats, of which 70,000 for allowances to princes and princesses.

This explains the high prices of the Neapolitan bonds which, despite the political errors, were always above par.

The public debt of Sicily, recognised by the law of 1861, amounted to 6,800,000 ducats. Of very old origin, it had a specific nature, which meant it represented a contribution by the island to the monarchy rather than a true state debt to private citizens.

Sicily's old debt derives from the donatives the parliaments granted to the king to meet the needs of the state, and from the taxes decreed for the same purpose.

Donatives and taxes were distributed among the various classes of private and bodies corporate each of which was assigned its own contribution rate, payable at specific annual deadlines called *tanda*s. The government, in order to have more ready money, issued bonds, called *soggiogazione*s, with lien on the *tanda*s of the donatives and the tax receipts of the private citizens and bodies corporate which administered the capital.

It is said that the Kingdom of Sardinia contracted its enormous debt for the wars of 1848 and 1860. The reason is true to only a very limited extent. It should always be borne in mind that if a state spent to facilitate the unification movement, others spent to combat it. It should also be borne in mind that if the war of 1848 was prepared with considerable financial sacrifices, that of 1860 was carried out without money. It should finally be borne in mind that Piedmont already had a big network of roads, navigable canals and railways; and all this had cost no less than the war, indeed, even more.

«In the meanwhile — Minghetti told the Chamber of Deputies on 27 June 1860 — adding to these the last loans taken out for the war of independence, if I am not mistaken, I believe I can calculate that the state of the public debt of the old provinces, abstracting from what he obtained from Lombardy, was 850 million, which amounts to circa 170 francs per head. I know that the reasoning on these calculations to find arguments has no absolute value; however, they do not appear to lack all efficacy.

«Let us now look at the changes brought about by the annexation of the new provinces. When the Kingdom of Sardinia transformed itself into the Italian Kingdom, I believe that its financial situation much improved ... — and then added — see, sirs, how Piedmont, during the period in which it increased its debt, lifting it from 67 million to 850 million, not to the detriment of the public wealth, indeed, production was increasing, agriculture was advancing, trade was flourishing, the traffic on the railways brought everywhere activity, industry and a general improvement; and we, at the same time that the state's debts and deficits were increasing, saw the country's wealth increase and as a result there was no reason to be worried. Now, who can doubt that the same might happen in the other provinces, which have so many sources of wealth which have been little productive to date because of bad government, but which thanks to freedom and a wise regime will quickly become most flourishing? If we were to compare our Kingdom and the other countries of Europe, I believe we would once again have reason for comfort. Let us disregard England, which has 20 billion of debt, let us disregard Holland, which has two and a half billion (a very large debt with regard to the country's small size); let us disregard Belgium, which also, if I am not mistaken, has more than 700 million of debt, let us look only at France: it has 8,600,000,000 of debt, which, taking the population into account, amounts to 240 francs per head. It will be argued that France is richer than us, and I agree, but I do not believe however, that France is more than twice as rich as us, and if France's finances are believed flourishing, why should we believe that our state is any less so, is less sufficient to its needs, to its future destinies?

«If before leaving these arid figures, I am allowed with a daring flight to review the whole of Italy, I would say that, given that our state has 1 and a half billion of debt, Rome has 360 million, Sicily 85, Naples 425, Venice, as much as Lombardy, namely 250, there are circa 2,600,000,000 of debt for the 25 million inhabitants in the most beautiful and fertile country of Europe, which amounts to just over 100 francs per head, without taking our state assets into account, without calculating the government railways, without calculating the plentious *Tavolieri* of Apulia, without calculating the church assets in the Roman state (Ah! Good!)».

The consolidated and redeemable public debt in every form amounted to 12,908,324,496.81 at 30 June 1899.

The 5% consolidated debt consisted at the same date of 113.8 million of interest inherited from past governments, 322.3 million of interest on debts contracted since 1862. Eliminating from this 35.3 million for redeemable debt conversion laws, the consolidated interest amounted to 400.8 million, equal to a nominal capital of 8,017,063,893.80.

We already know that the first big nucleus was formed by the debts of past governments, and above all by northern Italy.

But the enormous mass of debt was contracted later, in various forms and was often contracted under the most serious of conditions. In the period from 1860 to 1870, above all, the state issued securities with very onerous conditions.

In his famous financial statement of 12 December 1871, Sella, after having spoken of the pensions, which continued to increase, said: «But this is not the most serious increase; the increase of pensions is explained by political causes which can only give satisfaction; but the increase in the public debt, for a timid man such as me (laughter) is frightening.

«Public debt interest amounted to 113 million in 1861, and 380 million in 1870, in other words the public debt interest has increased by 270 million! Sirs, these are frightening figures!

«The various ministers of finance have never spoken to you of the increase in nominal capital so as not to dishearten you, but one should at least glance at the facts: from 2,300 million we have reached 8,200 million, we have increased the capital of our public debt by almost six thousand million.

«To give you an idea of the terrible effect of this increase in the public debt interest, please be so kind, sirs, to reflect on the figures I have laid before you and those which I am about to inform you of. And note that the increase in the public debt has come about despite the sale of the railways and of much state and Church property, selling which, it is a good thing we have deamortised it, is a good thing from the economic point of view, but on the other hand, we have sold off quite significant assets.

«And so, to raise 2,619 million in real terms, we have committed ourselves for a nominal debt of 3,852 million, and in this very same decade we have carried out these transactions: we have paid 1,369 million for interest and premiums and for repayments (however only 150 million) in addition to very transactions which generated 2,691 million. This is the history of the improvident son of the family; and we cannot continue at this pace. Considering that between losses on the nominal capital and that which we have paid in this decade for these transactions we have lost 2,530 million. And we have only received 2,691 million! And it is thus that the increase in the public debt interest I mentioned is explained».

The state therefore made 3,852 million worth of commitments and obtained in actual fact from its debt 2,691 million. The regions which bought in the first period of our unity and which either retained or resold the bond when it was around par, earned an almost similar amount. Neither after did the conditions change for many issues, made, in general, with the most unfavourable of conditions.

Piedmont was accustomed to issue at low prices.

In 1857, to obtain 95 million of credit, it indebted itself to the tune of 122 million of recognised capital and 6 million per year of interest. This was the opposite of the Kingdom of Naples which exaggerated in the opposite direction.

Thus the habits already acquired, exacerbated by the new needs, led to low-priced issues.

146 million at 80.50% in 1860 cost 186 million of capital and 9 of interest; 496 million in 1861 at 70.50%, 715 of capital and 35 of interest; 699,900,000 in 1863 part at 71, part at 68, part at 65, a billion of capital and 51 of interest; 418 million in the middle of the same year 1865 at 66% yielded 60 million of capital and 33 million of interest.

It is now calculated that the annual capitalisation of Italy amounts to circa half a billion per year.

Between 1862 and 1873 there were years when the deficit rose to 600 million. the imperious need for arms had to be met whatever the cost.

«One will perhaps forgive — Sella told his voters — the inexperience of provisional governments, which diminish or abolish existing taxes without replacing them. But I fear history will pass a severe judgement on the fact for several years the debt annually contracted by the state remained equal to, or approached, private citizens' savings.

«In 1863 very authoritative persons stated to me in France, that the annual savings of this most wealthy of nations amounted then to no more than 1,000 million per year. Do you believe that the savings of poor Italy reached or was perhaps ever greater than half, namely 500 million? And yet, the state sought 400 million of loans mainly as a result of the unhappy rate of our loans.

«The foreign markets could absorb only a part of our bonds: the remainder, given the meagreness of the national market, had to be placed on the domestic market at very low rates».

Southern Italy did not buy; it could not do so.

Its taxes had been doubled without any change taking place in production.; banditry was rampant in five or six provinces and made the harvests difficult and uncertain; public debt was almost unknown and there was no tradition of investing one's savings in bonds.

On the other hand, the state had thrown an enormous mass of state and Church property onto the southern market. Land was offered for a value of hundreds of millions, and investments in land were preferred by a country which knew almost nothing of public debt.

The purchase of state assets, in the economy of a region, amounted in reality to a tax. As, while the general wealth did not increase, indeed it diminished, the monetary capital went elsewhere.

And in the case we are studying it went in general to Lombardy and Piedmont and Liguria for the big military works and for the new widely spread institutions and the old ones which had been generously conserved.

The Mezzogiorno could not buy.

Between 1863 and 1870, government bonds saw brusque fluctuations: they fell to below 40 and were above 70 only in 1864 and 1867 and for a short period in 1864. Now in these years state issues amounted to circa 3 billion.

Between 1860 and 1870 the price of government bonds on the Naples stock exchange was always below that of the Turin and Milan exchanges. The average annual price during 1864 was on the Naples stock exchange 67.57, and on that of Turin 67.64; in 1864 the difference was even greater.

Southern Italy wholly lacked any tradition of stock-market speculation: above all as regards public notes. Instead, in 1859, the war allowed many fortunes to be made in Piedmont, Liguria and Lombardy.

The Mezzogiorno was accustomed to high bond rates and also to their relative stability: those brusque variations engendered worry.

It suffices to point out that before 1860 the Neapolitan bond was priced not only much higher than that of Austria, but higher than that of Belgium and of countries deemed prosperous.

On the Paris stock exchange, between 1853 and 1860, the various consols were generally quoted lower than that of Naples.

The Neapolitan bond appeared to be unshakeably safe, even in 1860, after the overthrow of the Bourbon dynasty, it was always higher than those of Piedmont and Austria.

Magliani, then a Bourbon official, in 1858, after having spoken of the financial conditions of the Kingdom of Naples and of the abundance of numeraire in it, said: «This is not the last reason for the high price of government bonds, which have risen to the almost incredible price of 114 and 114¾».

Almost everywhere, in the other Italian states, the population was accustomed to low rates of return, but not at Naples. Hence the initial reluctance to buy Italian notes.

But after 1870 and until 1886, the consols enjoyed an almost uninterrupted ascent, if one disregards the fluctuations of 1877 (Turko-Russian War) and the minor perturbations.

After 1870, the Mezzogiorno, initially averse, had grown used to the new order to things, and followed the opposite path: it started in the years when the high price of grain and wine allowed some provinces to flourish again, to buy bonds again. The grain-bearing lands enjoyed years of prosperity; the wine industry transformed for several years some lands of Apulia into a true California. Until, that is, the new orientation of customs policy turned the entire national economy on its head to the sole benefit of the industries of Lombardy.

From 1872 to 1886 the Mezzogiorno bought back off the north around par or at high prices those consols which had been bought for lower prices.

In 1872, on the Naples stock exchange. the average price of the consols was higher than in the rest of Italy; in 1874 the average annual price was 73.04 in Florence, 73.01 in Turin, 73.27 in Naples. With almost constant regularity, this situation continued until 1888.

Thus a considerable mass of wealth emigrated from the south to the north of Italy again and compounded the differences between them which had been caused by other facts.

The payments for public-debt interest amounted to a very considerable figure in Italy; given the scarcity of national savings we can say that government bonds played a significant role in the distributive processes.

Never as for twenty years now, have government bonds been held so proportionally in Italy.

Calculations made directly from the reports of the General Office of Public Debt indicate that in the three fiscal years 1881, 1891-1892 and 1897-1898 government bond interest was in the following proportions:

	1881	1891-1892 (millions)	1897-1898
Government-bond interest paid in Italy	240.52	202.37	359.44
Government-bond interest paid abroad	85.19	185.14	106.22
Total	325.71	387.51	465.66

If we make the totals 100, the respective position of government bonds in Italy and abroad appears, therefore, as follows:

	1881	1891-1892	1897-1898
Government-bond interest paid in Italy	73.84	52.22	77.19
Government-bond interest paid abroad	26.16	47.78	22.81

Disregarding any considerations as to whether this is wholly good, it is unarguable that never before has such an amount of government bonds been held domestically.

It is commonly held that the southern Italians, either because of their scant providence or feeble spirit of enterprise, invest their capital in government bonds. Indeed, it is said that the barons of the Mezzogiorno, when they are not latifundists, are at least receivers of government-bond interest. Unfortunately we have to point out that this idea is very far from the truth.

The Mezzogiorno had never owned many bonds and having generally bought them at high prices, now only owns but a few.

If we group the figures for the 69 provinces in the report of the General Office of Public Debt for 1897-98 and compare them with the population calculated for 1897, we have the result indicated in *Il bilancio*, p. 348*.

If we eliminate the figures for Lazio, which do not express a real situation, all the others perfectly respond to reality. Now the government bonds appear to be mainly held in Liguria, Piedmont, Lombardy and Tuscany; to a lesser extent in Umbria, Abruzzi and Molise, in Calabria, Sardinia, Apulia and Basilicata. The figure for Campania is relatively high only because it includes payments which concern other regions of the Mezzogiorno.

The proportions have not changed for the fiscal year 1898-1899. Indeed, the figures of the last report indicate that consols have returned to Italy: 365.34 million were paid at home, and 95.50 million abroad.

But if the situation of all the nation is respectively more

* See footnote 1.

ITALIAN GOVERNMENT BONDS HELD IN ITALY
AND ABROAD IN 1881, 1891-1892, 1897-1898

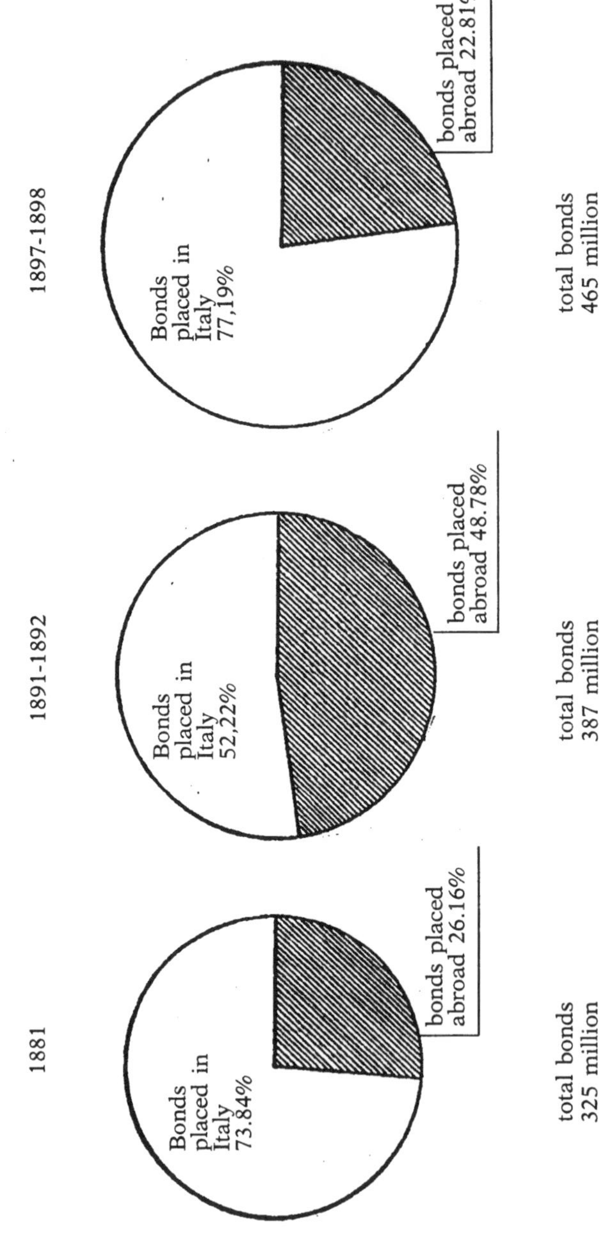

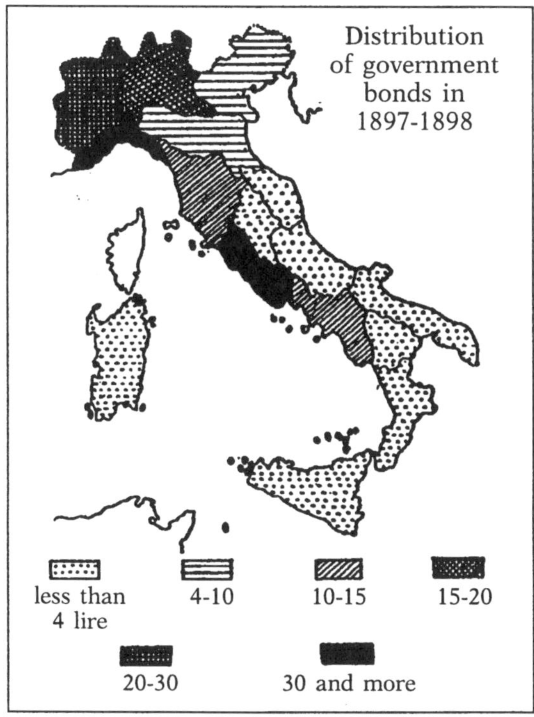

favourable, another fact has also accentuated itself: the lower ownership of bonds in the southern provinces.

The foolish idea that the Mezzogiorno has immense, idle monetary wealth derives from the most absolute ignorance or at least from lack of knowledge of the Mezzogiorno's economic life.

All the trading companies which have had privilege or monopoly, all those who receive subsidies, all the plants which collect premiums are entirely or almost in northern and central Italy. The big contracts, the most profitable concessions are, or were, in large part in turn in the same zone.

There was a time when public works worth hundred of millions were awarded per year: there were contracts for railways, the supplies were hurried, and everything was concentrated in the same points, in part out of necessity, in part because the origins of the government or the administration exacerbated or created the necessity.

The hundred of millions for subsidies to shipping companies, for construction and shipping premiums to shipping companies, for privileged banks, etc., were spent in the same regions, everything was concentrated.

When anyone expressed surprise or complained, even the most cautious and honest of politicians satisfied themselves with denying the matter or toning it down.

Banca Nazionale, now Banca d'Italia, for shares issued at a face value of 1,000 lire, and which in the years of forced circulation exceeded 4,000 lire, distributed in 1865 a dividend of 196 lire per share and in 1868 of 215 lire and for many years sums of between 100 and 200 lire. Between 1864 and 1870, Banca Nazionale's shareholders received by way of dividends, paid by the nation, more than they had spent to buy the shares.

In 1870, discussing some measures on July 14th which the government wished and which would have created a situation of privilege for Banca Nazionale, Sella even went so far as to deny the evidence, namely that there were more shareholders in northern Italy than elsewhere: «Hon. Castellani and several other of his colleagues tell us that this parity is a chaotic jumble, it is a banner which should cover a good, which should ensure approval of the convention with Banca Nazionale: that the Commission and the ministry have no other purpose, they only want to ensure this convention is passed, but no break-even will be reached.

«Hon. Toscanelli goes even further, he says I sought to frighten the country and the Chamber. And do you know why, sirs? Again to ensure the convention with Banca Nazionale was approved. He even went so far as to say a phrase which could be an insinuation, if I felt it was aimed at me, namely that the aim of said is to enrich northern Italy at the expense of central and southern Italy, because in northern Italy he *believes* the Banca d'Italia has more shareholders than in the other parts of the Kingdom».

However, it was not a case of *believing*; almost all Banca Nazionale's shares were held in Piedmont, Liguria and Lombardy, and because the convention proposed was approved, a situation of privilege under which all the nation paid hundreds of millions of lire to those regions was maintained and augmented.

What Sella said was so untrue that even now the distribution of the bank's shareholders (after the merger with the Tuscan banks and the greater intervention of southern elements) remains the same.

At present, the companies which exercise banking in conditions of privilege, or receive subsidies for construction; the subsidised factories; the industries with a more artificial nature and which live on protection or state purchases, are wholly or almost so, in northern Italy.

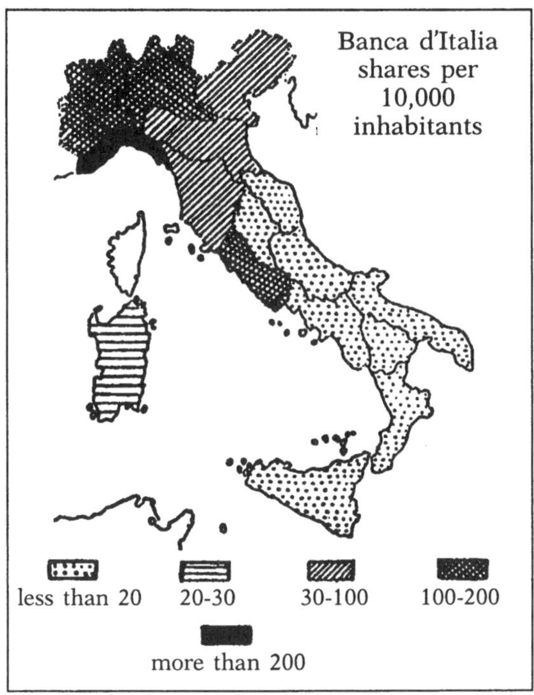

If four fifths of the shares are now in northern Italy, before the merger of the banks of issue of central Italy, the proportion was even greater. And if now 1/15th of Banca d'Italia's shares are held in the mainland Mezzogiorno and in Sicily, there were then much less.

And yet Sella's affirmations were not even challenged!

Now the big companies which sold off the Church property, which were granted enormous railway concessions, for which often (as in the case of a large company) without advancing almost anything found themselves in receipt of astounding profits; the companies which operate monopolies wre almost wholly composed of elements from the north. For some fifteen years now, above all since 1890, control has increased and the greater difficulties have made it more active and experience more efficient; but that which has been done in an inexpert country, after 1860, at times strains the credibility.

Between 1860 and 1870, for the afore-indicated reasons, there was a significant movement of capital toward the north of the peninsula. this movement, for differing reasons, continued to varying degrees, as indeed it still does.

Now when after 1870 Lombardy above all had a big road network and found itself the market of all Italy and the centre of Italian business with central Europe, there gradually emerged in it the trend toward a transformation of the customs policy. The first nuclei of wealth, or rather, the biggest had been formed by the big subsidised companies, with the enterprises for public works, with supplies to the army and navy; in general, in the most part, as a result of the state's policies.

Southern Italy, which had seen its personal non-property income diminish, did not have the capital to transform itself into an industrial country. On the other hand, its principal products, wine, olive oil, grain, citrus fruits, sulphur, etc., were simple products which did not require complicated transformation processes.

The trade policy initiated in 1861 by Cavour (and of which the treaty concluded with France on 17 January 1863 was the maximum expression), aided the development of the agrarian regions. Italy remained an exporter of raw materials and importer of manufactured goods.

After 1870, as there was a considerable mass of available capital in the North, there began the movement toward the formation of an industrial nation. The customs survey, which was carried out between 1870 and 1874, recorded the highest point of this trend, which was initially asserted in the customs tariffs which came into force on July 1, 1878.

Although the customs tariffs of 1878 made possible the emergence of some big industries in Lombardy and other regions of northern Italy, they did not assure them a solid formation.

Vice versa, to consolidate them, a final effort had to be made. The customs tariffs of July 15, 1878 marked a profound revolution throughout the national economy.

It suffices to indicate the shifts which took place in some products to comprehend the breadth of the protection granted. The protection enjoyed by cotton and wool fabrics was greater than that of almost all the other states of Europe; and the iron industry obtained even prohibitive tariffs for many products. Thus for many other industries.

The effects of these customs tariffs in the economy as a whole are not measurable; but it cannot be denied that the enormous benefit was limited, above all in an initial period, to some regions, and that, vice versa, all the rest of the peninsula and the island functioned in the same manner as colonies in general functioned, as a consumption market, assuring ultra high profits. The southern areas, on the contrary were dealt a mortal blow: they saw their field of export limited and, simultaneously, they had to acquire industrial products at very high prices.

Neither did the conditions change so suddenly such that the northern regions, above all Lombardy, were able to purchase the south's agrarian products.

On the other hand, the effect of the transport regime on the Mezzogiorno's agricultural products was to defend the north's agriculture as a true protection system. It cost as much and more to send agricultural produce from Calabria or from Apulia to Veneto or Lombardy by land as by sea to America.

But as it was always possible to transport them by sea, the shipping tariffs completed the work of domestic protection. Even now these tariffs are such as to make it quite difficult for the Mezzogiorno's agricultural products to make their way to the markets of northern Italy.

For some time the agricultural products of northern Italy had almost no competition, and in any case that modest competition it did have was largely compensated by the increased wealth deriving from the formation of big industrial centres.

Thus the work of transformation proceeded.

Now industrial transformation has been completed, above all in Lombardy, and some products can even hold their own under competition, indeed they are now being exported.

But it would be of considerable interest to study the sacrifice this transformation entailed.

9. - Whether the Civil Service is Invaded by Southerners or Northerners

If we disregard military spending and spending for the public debt, it is unarguable that the largest part of the budget — there remains so little for a country with 32 million inhabitants! — is spent for state employees. The spending for the central administration and for the provincial administration amount to a very considerable sum. Moreover, the costs of many budgets, even without appearing so, are spent for personnel; thus, for example, the budget for posts and telegraph is destined in large part for personnel.

Now, for the argument we are to deal with, it is of great interest to study the distribution of the state employees, above all with regard to their native region. It is a study which has never been attempted before and which will not lack interest.

It should first of all be noted that the state bureaucracy in Italy has increased much less than one might think; or rather, compared with past governments it is less numerous than is said.

It is almost impossible to compare the bureaucracy of the various states, in view of the range of functions in each of them. In some countries the railways are state-run, in others not; in some primary education is entrusted to the state, in others to local administrations (Italy, Spain, Austria, etc.); in some countries such as France or Italy the state is charged with many functions which in others, such as England and Holland, are entrusted to the lower administrative bodies. Hence it is impossible to lay down comparisons which have a relative precision, except on a service by service basis.

In any case, the figures gathered by Turquan, which refer to 1896, give an approximate idea. According to these figures, the number of officials and the average amount of wages are (those indicated in *Il bilancio*, p. 359).

The mirror cannot lead to exact comparisons. The officials in France include, for example, not only the primary-school teachers, but also the 20,000 workers of the tobacco factories, etc. This is also why the average wage appears so low. In any case the simplicity of the Austrian administration is remarkable, while France, Belgium and Romania have a bureaucracy which is perhaps too numerous. It can be said that Italy occupies an intermediary position in such a classification.

In 1892 the General Office of Statistics, with praiseworthy thought, published *Ruoli organici delle amministrazioni civili e militari del Regno al 1° luglio 1891, confrontati con quelli degli antichi Stati italiani* (Staffing Lists of the Civil and Military Administrations of the Kingdom at 1 July 1891, Compared with Those of the Old Italian States). It is of interest to compare the staffing lists of 1859 with those of 1891 and 1898 using said guide.

Such a comparison indicates that the bureaucracy in Italy has increased much less than is thought; its general conditions have improved; but the numerical increase has been relatively small.

It is obvious that the division of Italy into many states led to a complication and a multiplication of all the services. Where there is now one ministry, there were seven; where one State Council or Court of Audit there were many. If each office had a small staff, often the number of staff of seven was higher than at present. Furthermore, the customs officers, who served at the border, the borders being much longer than now, were greater in number.

The central administration staff, for example, is now almost half what it was in 1859 in the old states. And thus the State Council and the Court of Audit.

Now it is quite obvious that the increase in the number of employees is more an exaggeration than a reality, that it is also useless to cite the figures of publications known to scholars.

On the other hand, wages have increased and also to a considerable extent.

Wages averaged 1,194 in the Kingdom of Sardinia, 1,006 in Lombardy Veneto, 1,215 in Tuscany, 1,028 in the Two Sicilies, they were already 1,729 in the Kingdom of Italy in 1891.

The annual average cost per inhabitant, excluding the army, navy and Ministry of Foreign Affairs (was indicated in *Il bilancio*, p. 361)*.

From 1891 to 1898, the number of the state's civil employees decreased from 64,185 to 62,630 and wages from 135,265,987 to 134,424,780.

The army and the navy too, taking account of the population, have also seen an extraordinary growth. In the old states they depended on the Ministries of War and Navy, in 1859, military, administrative and service personnel amounted to 188,174 persons, in 1891 the number had risen to 309,222 persons.

The military personnel, who had totalled 303,889 persons, had however risen to 311,763 persons in 1898, an increase of 7,874 soldiers.

More than the number of men, it was the costs which had increased in the civil and military administration.

A truly big bureaucracy (at least as regards the number) existed above all in Piedmont.

In southern Italy there was, as we have seen, a large number of employees; but so poorly remunerated, in such precarious conditions, that they could not form a true administration. Moreover, if the financial administration, and up to a certain point, the judiciary were good, the rest was worth little.

The large number of state employees in Piedmont had to form the nucleus; there followed, by necessity, Tuscany, Lombardy, Liguria, Veneto and the regions of central Italy.

---

* See footnote 1.

Minghetti deceived himself in 1863 that the number of state employees would decrease. He, with an image repeated so many times and so little truthful, stated the bureaucracy was a form of socialism.

Who is not surprised when they see that the budget allocates 110 million lire for civil employees; that we pay out 33 million lire for pensions, that we pay out 10 million lire by way of leave! (Cries of outrage). If you add to that the expenses for lodging, representation, conversion of offices, you will find another 30 million lire, and obtain the more than 180 million lire the bureaucracy costs us! (Unrest).

Now who would not agree that if we changed the organic laws of our administration, we could simplify all this, and obtain at least a further 30 million lire of savings? (Bravo! Well said! from the left).

The present-day bureaucracy, sirs, is a form of socialism. That socialism that the bourgeoisie so feared some fifteen years ago, when it presented itself bloody and sordid on the public squares, it has welcomed and embraced when it appeared as an instrument of public order and government interference (Signs of approval from the left and centre).

May God grant that the Kingdom of Italy has the glory of showing that one can govern strongly and orderly without the state interfering in every branch of the public administration (Applause)».

That of the state employees appeared, from the very outset, as an intangible expense: nobody could be sacked without a scandal breaking out.

«A colleague of ours — Sella said — who is not only competent, but also a sociable person, told me recently that, for him, the truly intangible part of the budget, i.e., which cannot be reduced, is that part of the spending which regards the civil administration. There is undoubtedly much truth in this proposition. I do not deny, for example, that there are here and there schools and universities which can be closed, but has everything that could be been done for public education? And moreover, are our officials sufficiently remunerated?»

The Bourbon bureaucracy, which transferred to the new government, remained suspicious and diffident. Many old state employees believed the old regime would return and hurried to tender their resignation; others refused to serve the new order of things; lastly, quite a few were dismissed.

A multitude of schemers in the Mezzogiorno itself asked for their positions; and when they failed to gain them, they discredited everything and everyone.

Replying to Hons. Massari and Paternostro and to the remarks of Hon. Ricciardi, Hon. Minghetti, then Minister of the Interior, thus stated in the Chamber: «Hon. Massari has described the inveterate scourge of the petitioners; Hon. Ricciardi the corrupting habits of the Bourbon bureaucracy. Now, if this is true, do they believe it is possible to uproot these ills immediately?

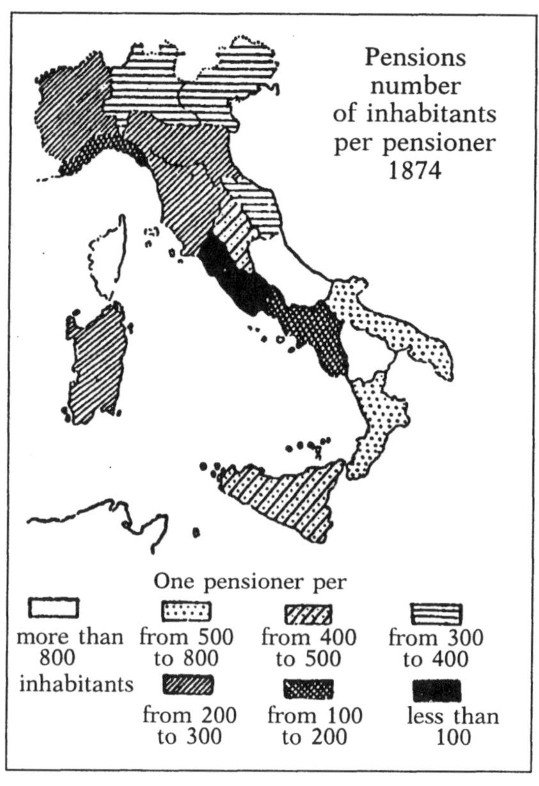

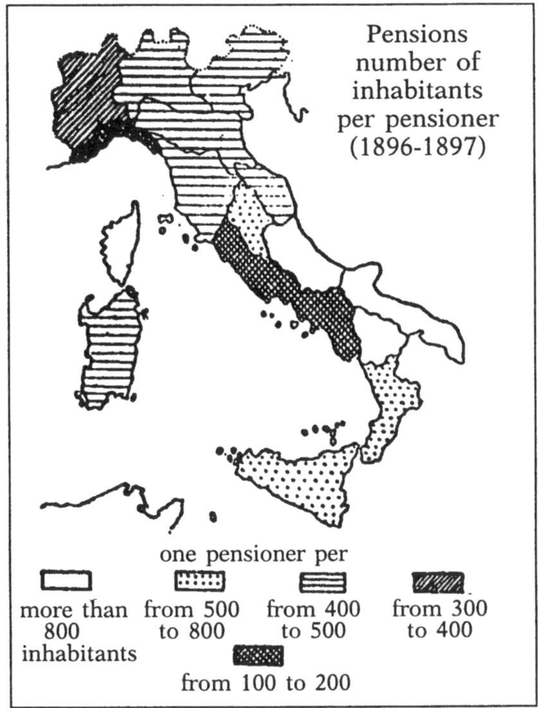

«I believe the government should and can attentively watch over its employees, gather with much solicitude all the facts which are specifically reported; I believe that it should severely punish the prevaricators, but I cannot truthfully imagine a method for uprooting suddenly all those customs which the two honourable members have mentioned.

«Moreover, in moments of revolution, we should not forget that slander is very easy to launch, and even easier to be heard and repeated. Neither would I speak of this frankly with regard to the Neapolitan provinces if I had not recently seen accused in the public newspapers honourable men, whose name alone should have sufficed to prevent such slander ever gaining currency (Well said!).

«There has also been talk of the excessive number of state employees and here also I do not disagree that there is some truth.

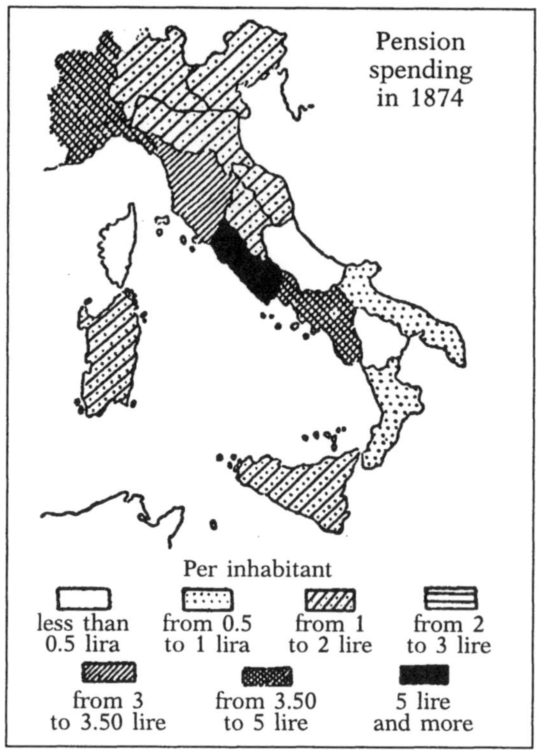

But I would beg the Chamber to consider that up to the Bourbon era this number was excessively large, add to this a very low wage which was almost an incitement not to work well.

«There was, as I have mentioned, the transition from the absolute Bourbon system to the constitutional period, from this to the dictatorship, from dictatorship to the royal government and to deputyship. It is natural that, at each of these changes, a large group of petitioners presented themselves to the victors and governors; it is natural that certain men of trust of one government were not wholly so of another; it is natural that, having an infinite amount of matters to handle, no thought was given at that moment to a reform such as that of reducing the number of employees which supposes not only precise laws which determine the wages and staffing levels, but also a regular administration in the public offices».

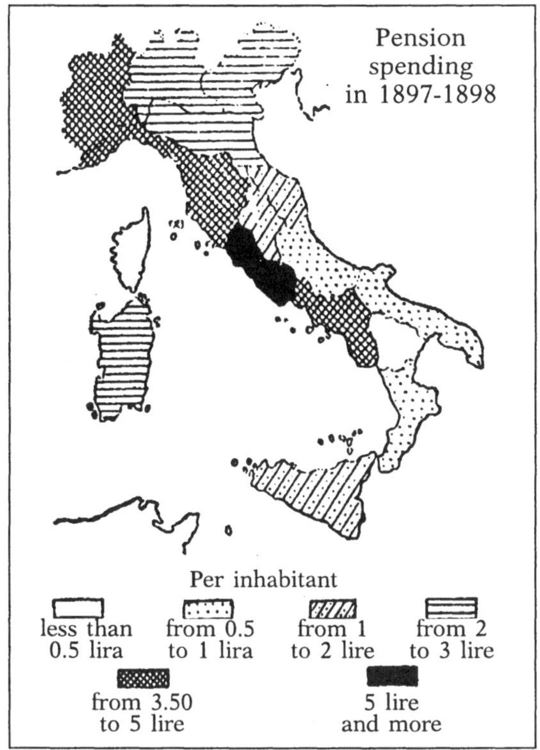

On another occasion, Minghetti said in the Lower House: «it should be remembered that the Neapolitan provinces have seen six or seven governments and deputyships and unfortunately each of these has introduced a new series of employees in the administration, placing the previous ones on leave or on call.

«This series of employees in the Neapolitan provinces, if I am allowed to make the comparison, are akin to the series of geological strata (laughter). Each government which came left behind it a stratum of employees on top of the previous such strata. I would say that one could almost recognise the passages of the various governments from the number of these strata. Now however much we wish to use the employees available, I doubt very much that they all can be.

«The best will be chosen, and as regards the others, I say that when the law has been passed, when the Commission has completed its task, their destiny should be decided. This is one of the trials which are inevitable in revolutions, in changes, but we should be deaf to these trials so as not to ruin the state's finances».

The old Bourbon employees were dismissed as unreliable, the new ones who proclaimed themselves liberals violently invaded the offices and often were expelled because of their incapacity.

Southern politicians, little prepared for the free life, often believed that having been a Bourbon was a requisite for expulsion, and presented veritable lists of prescription. Fortunately, not all the summary executions were carried out, but many still were.

Hon. Depretis, replying to Minster Nicotera, said: «In respect of the generic allegations regarding the bad administration of this or that service, regarding the number of employees denominated Bourbon in this or that administration, I naturally have had to put to Hon. Nicotera the question which would furnish me with the means to know who exactly were those employees whose previous conduct could absolutely no longer be tolerated in the state's service.

«The eve, if I am not mistaken, of my departure for Naples, Hon. Nicotera gave me a list of names which he indicated as respectable persons who could have enlightened me on the matter; but Hon. Nicotera will allow me to point out to him that when I went to speak with those very same persons he had indicated to me as those who could have furnished me with certain information, I found the most differing opinions on their authority, on the trustworthiness of their judgements such that I am very doubtful whether through them I could conclude a certain criterion for the determinations to be made. Hon. Nicotera should see that in the eight days I was at Naples, it was impossible for me to satisfy his desire, and I therefore believe his reproaches are undeserved».

Thus the old employees were squeezed, from every side, by the numerous bureaucracy of the other states which wished to invade everything; by the southern politicians who had crowds of acolytes to satisfy. it is no surprise therefore that the Mezzogiorno's role in the administration was scant and not always the best.

Civil and army pensions and the wages for civil employees and land and sea commissioned officers amount to 287 million lire per year: one can calculate that they exceed 300 million lire, taking into account allowances and special indemnities.

Now to participate in the state's administration implies not only having a direct action in directing the country's administrative life; but participating to a large measure in a considerable part of the budget spending.

Pensions are a first guide for calculating each region's participation in state careers. Then that the provincial treasuries make the payments in the respective provinces and one should suppose that the employees, having completed their career, mostly retire to their native region, the distribution of the pension payments is an almost certain index for calculating the number of employees from each region.

There are some cities in which the pensioners prefer to retire: Naples, Rome, Florence and Venice above all. Many from Piedmont and Lombardy stay in Naples; many Neapolitans in Milan or Turin.

However, these accidental variations do not modify the results obtained from the study of pensions as regards their distribution.

Pensions, which amounted to 40.98 million in 1868, rose to 81.8 million in 1898-99 of which 34.8 million for the army and 5 million for the navy.

The pensions, which each state contributed at the moment of annexation, were quite different: Tuscany led the pack, followed by the Kingdom of Sardinia, Lombardy and Veneto.

The two tables below which group all the data regarding pensions and pensioners in the years 1864, 1874, 1883 and 1897-1898 show how all the regions of southern Italy are in a state of significant inferiority with regard to the number of employees (See Tables 7 and 8).

But the respective situation of the various populations from the point of view of pensioners, and hence from that of the employees, is obtained by taking into account the proportion of each zone.

In 1871 the census indicated that the population totalled 26,801,154 inhabitants, in 1881 28,953,480 and in 1887 it was estimated in 31,479,217 inhabitants.

STATE PENSIONER

Regions	1864			1874		
	Population in 1863	Number of pensioners	Number of inhabitants per pensioner	Population as per 1871 census	Number of pensioners	N inh pe
Piedmont	2,762,263	11,090	249.07	2,899,564	12,642	2
Liguria	771,473	3,780	204.09	843,812	4,470	1
Lombardy	3,104,838	6,455	480.99	3,460,824	9,001	3
Veneto	—	—	—	2,642,807	7,422	3
Northern Italy	6,638,574	21,325	311.34	9,847,007	33,535	2
Emilia and Romagna	2,005,834	7,453	269.13	2,113,828	7,993	2
Tuscany	1,987,367	7,611	274.32	2,142,525	8,797	2
Marches	883,073	2,629	335.89	915,419	2,959	3
Umbria	513,019	967	530.52	549,601	1,248	4
Lazio	—	—	—	836,704	9,426	
Central Italy	5,389,793	18,660	288.83	6,558,077	30,415	2
Abruzzi and Molise	1,212,835	1,251	969.49	1,282,981	1,582	8
Campania	2,625,830	20,344	129.07	2,754,592	21,225	1
Apulia	1,315,269	1,390	946.24	1,420,892	1,897	7
Basilicata	492,959	297	1,659.79	510,543	457	1,1
Calabria	1,140,396	1,519	764.59	1,206,302	1,881	6
Southern Italy	6,787,289	24,792	273.77	7,175,310	27,042	2
Sicily	2,302,414	4,322	532.25	2,584,099	5,743	4
Sardinia	588,064	1,371	428.93	636,660	1,804	3
Kingdom	21,706,134	70,470	308.02	26,801,154	98,724	2

TABLE 7

64, 1874, 1883, 1897-1898

1883			1897-1898			Comments
opulation as per 1881 census	Number of pensioners	Number of inhabitants per pensioner	Estimated population at 31 December 1897	Number of pensioners	Number of inhabitants per pensioner	
3,070,250	12,579	244.08	3,362,288	15,224	220.85	The total for the Kingdom does not correspond exactly to that for the 16 regions because in 1874 there were 184 pensions, 62 in 1885 and 19 in 1897-98 not registered at any provincial office and paid mainly by Austria on behalf of the Italian Treasury and reimbursed by said by direct order under the convention agreed by Law no. 137 of 23 March 1871.
892,373	5,028	177.48	988,695	5,921	166.98	
3,680,574	10,298	357.41	4,082,716	10,504	388.68	
2,814,173	6,876	409.27	3,118,169	9,357	333.24	
0,457,370	34,781	300.66	11,551,868	41,006	281.71	
2,183,432	7,367	296.24	2,306,858	6,832	337.65	
2,206,869	7,844	280.83	2,324,499	7,400	314.12	
939,279	2,895	324.45	978,738	2,619	373.71	
572,060	1,162	491.52	609,952	1,130	539.78	
903,472	9,495	95.15	1,035,731	8,365	123.82	
6,805,112	28,763	236.59	7,255,758	26,346	275.40	
1,317,215	1,398	942.21	1,393,950	1,428	976.15	
2,896,577	19,712	146.94	3,161,275	16,171	195.49	
1,589,964	1,877	846.06	1,891,875	2,106	898.32	
524,504	383	1,369.46	549,771	398	1,381.33	
1,257,883	1,703	890.77	1,349,750	1,796	751.53	
7,585,243	25,073	302.12	8,346,621	21,899	381.14	
1,927,901	6,406	300.95	3,563,582	6,184	579.63	
682,002	2,044	333.66	761,148	2,036	373.84	
8,459,628	96,162	295.95	31,479,217	97,454	323.02	

PENSIONS PAID BY THE S

Regions	1864			1874	
	Population as per 1861 census	Amount of pensions	Average spending per inhab-itant	Population as per 1871 census	Amount of pensions
Piedmont	2,764,263	6,686,206	2.42	2,899,564	10,322,156
Liguria	771,473	2,038,810	2.64	843,812	3,269,611
Lombardy	3,262,312	3,511,099	1.07	3,460,824	5,615,049
Veneto	—	—	—	2,642,807	4,494,569
Northern Italy	6,798,048	12,236,115	1.79	9,847,007	23,611,385
Emilia and Romagna	2,005,834	3,164,864	1.78	2,113,828	4,120,619
Tuscany	1,987,867	6,229,594	3.13	2,142,525	7,354,013
Marches	883,073	1,012,253	1.14	915,419	1,198,177
Umbria	513,019	404,019	0.78	549,601	555,455
Lazio	—	—	—	836,704	5,947,502
Central Italy	5,389,793	10,810,730	2.01	6,558,077	19,175,766
Abruzzi and Molise	1,212,835	407,100	0.33	1,282,982	646,431
Campania	2,625,830	10,471,392	3.99	2,754,592	12,778,842
Apulia	1,315,269	579,407	0.44	1,420,892	865,187
Basilicata	492,959	106,037	0.21	510,543	199,439
Calabria	1,140,396	514,814	0.45	1,206,302	778,215
Southern Italy	6,787,289	12,078,750	1.78	7,175,311	15,559,114
Sicily	2,302,414	2,139,124	0.93	2,584,099	3,504,191
Sardinia	588,064	766,685	1.74	636,660	1,137,786
Kingdom	21,865,608	38,031,404	1.74	26,801,154	62,988,242

TABLE 8

I 1864, 1874, 1883 AND 1897-1898

1883			1897-1898			Comments
pulation as per 1881 census	Amount of pensions	Average spending per inhab-itant	Estimated population at 31 December	Amount of pensions	Average spending per inhab-itant	
,070,250	11,336,187	3.69	3,362,288	14,280,900	4.24	The total for the Kingdom does not correspond exactly to total spending for pensions, as one should add the sums paid by Austria under the convention of 23 March 1871 which concerned almost all the pensions in Veneto. In 1874, the amounts paid for said reason totalled 216,761 and in 1883 121,262.
892,373	3,990,303	4.48	988,695	5,333,600	5.39	
,680,574	6,444,346	1.75	4,082,716	9,375,400	2.29	
,814,173	4,189,590	1.48	3,118,169	6,283,400	2,01	
,457,370	25,960,426	2.47	11,551,868	35,273,300	3.05	
,183,432	3,301,721	1.51	2,306,838	5,883,800	2.55	
,206,869	6,843,740	3.11	2,324,499	8,243,200	3.54	
939,270	1,240,233	1.32	978,738	1,678,600	1.70	
572,060	542,536	0.95	609,952	746,300	1.22	
903,472	5,473,711	6.05	1,035,731	7,035,600	6.78	
,805,112	17,401,941	2.56	7,255,758	23,587,500	3.25	
,317,215	644,399	0.48	1,393,950	939,000	0.67	
,896,577	11,170,098	3.85	3,161,275	11,740,400	3.71	
,589,964	969,755	0.61	1,891,875	1,632,400	0.86	
524,504	173,141	0.33	549,771	230,000	0.43	
,257,883	799,677	0.64	1,349,750	1,258,800	0.81	
,585,243	13,757,070	1.81	8,346,621	15,810,500	1.89	
,977,901	4,001,532	1.34	3,563,582	4,724,700	1.30	
682,002	1,542,400	2.26	769,148	1,815,400	2.38	
,459,628	62,663,468	2.20	31,479,217	81,211,400	2.58	

If we make these three sums equal to 100, the population of each of the big geographical zones was proportionally as shown in Table 9.

TABLE 9

Regions	1871 (26,801,154-100)	1881 (28,953,480-100)	1897 (31,479,217-100)
Northern Italy	36.7	37.0	36.8
Central Italy	24.5	23.8	23.0
Southern Italy	26.8	26.7	26.5
Sicily	9.6	10.1	11.4
Sardinia	2.4	2.4	2.3
Kingdom	100	100	100

Now in 1874 and 1897-1898, making the number of pensioners equal to 100, the participation of each zone was (that indicated in *Il bilancio*, Table 89, p. 374).

It therefore turns out that in 1897-1898, while southern Italy accounts with Sicily for 37.9% of the Kingdom's population, it has just 28.7% of the pensioners; vice versa northern Italy has 42.1% of the pensioners, while it accounts for 36.8% of the population.

Comparing the pension spending yields an even more serious result. Northern Italy, with a smaller population, now accounts for 43.5% of pensions; southern Italy and Sicily account for only 25.3%.

Hence the mass of employees, contrary to what is said, have always been from northern and central Italy; southern Italy and Sicily have always had scant importance in the administration of the state.

The southern Italy which lives through state employment as it has been depicted, has never existed: it is nothing more than an immoral legend.

It has been said that some ministries — above all that of public works — were invaded by southern Italians; well then, the distribution of pensions in 1897-1898 shows that also of the pensioners of the Ministry of Public Works, most are from northern and central Italy.

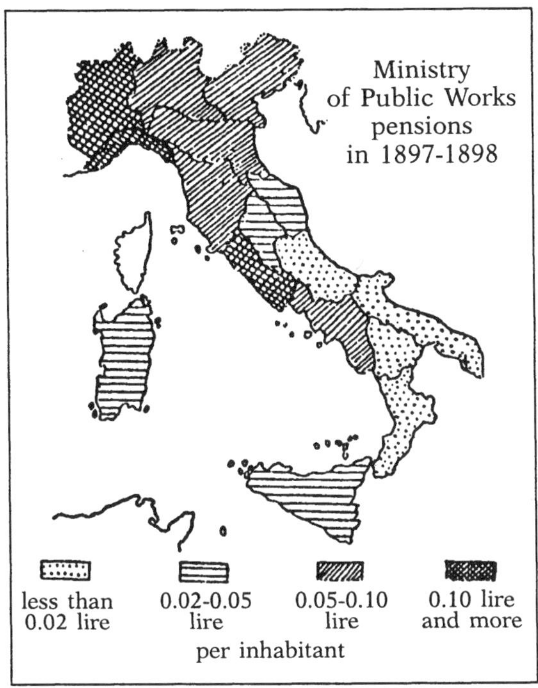

Now in France the opposite is the case.

It is the poorer départments which have the greater number of pensioners. While the general average of withholdings on pensions, divided by the number of male inhabitants aged from 20-60, is 52.50 those leading the classification, in addition to the départments in which Paris, Marseilles and some other city are to be found, we find those of Basses Alpes with 68.50, Hautes Alpes with 67.50, Belfort with 66, Herault with 65, Lozère with 61, Ardennes with 60, Corsica with 58, Calvados with 57, Vendée with 53, etc.[3].

But it is of more interest to study which areas currently provide the largest contingent for the bureaucracy. The present pen-

[3] The situation for each zone with regard to the number of pensioners in 1897-98 is evident from the following diagram:

STATE PENSIONERS IN 1874 AND 1897-1898

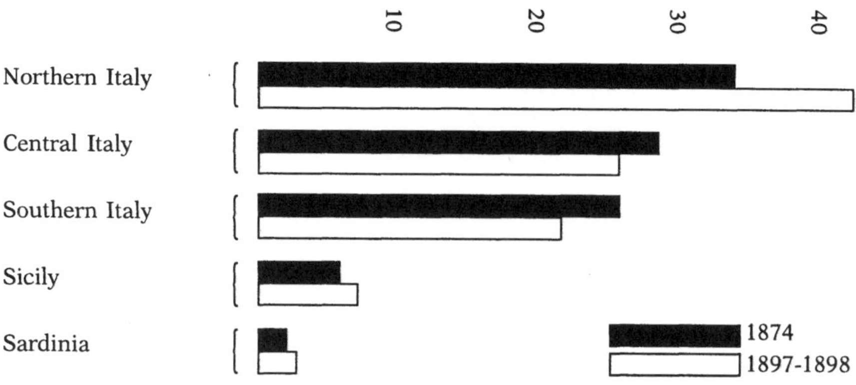

The diagram of the increases and reductions which took place in 1897-98 compared with 1874 shows that if there has been a slight improvement in Sicily, the number of pensioners in southern Italy has diminished considerably.

INCREASE OR DECREASE IN STATE PENSIONERS IN 1874 AND 1897-1898

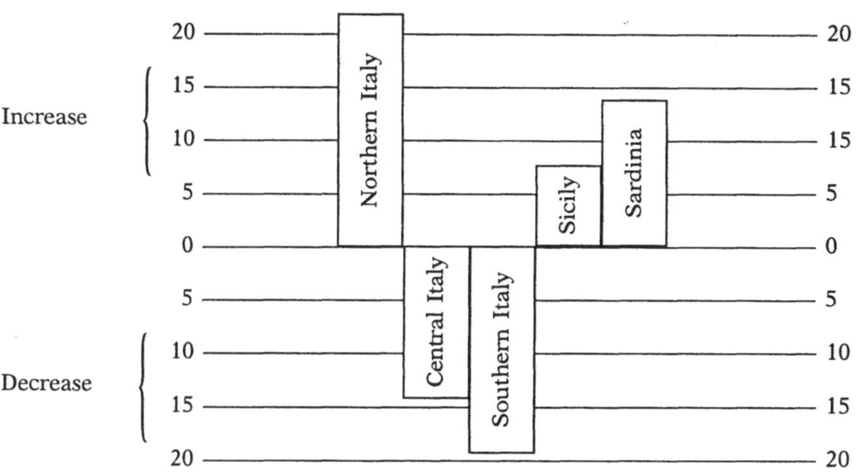

sioners represent the bureaucracy between 1860 and 1875. It is unarguable that after 1875 there has been a slight shift in favour of the Mezzogiorno.

Now such a study can only be carried out by direct investigation by the state which, for political reasons, has no interest in doing so. Scholars can only attempt it by approximation: it is research which is circumstantial and by analogy. And such research still presents enormous difficulties.

In 1897, Dr. Rodolfo Livi published in *Riforma Sociale* some important studies under the title «Saggio di geografia del militarismo in Italia» (Study of the Geography of Militarism in Italy) in which he attempted, on the basis of elements never previously studied, to ascertain each region's contribution to the commissioned officers and non-commissioners officers of the army. Studying the recruitment of the last eight years and deducting those who were called up, Livi calculated, as shown in Table 10, thus the proportion on 10,000 soldiers of cadets and commissioned officers taken together and ordinary volunteers.

The highest proportion of non-commissioned officers was found in Emilia and Romagna; the smallest in Basilicata. The re-

TABLE 10

COMMISSIONED AND NON-COMMISSIONED OFFICERS

Regions	Proportion per 10,000 conscripts		Regions	Proportion per 10,000 conscripts	
	of officers and cadets	of ordinary volunteers		of officers and cadets	of ordinary volunteers
Piedmont	21.4	81.0	Lazio	21.7	119.7
Liguria	15.1	42.6	Abruzzi and Molise	3.3	52.4
Lombardy	9.9	60.0	Campania	13.2	83.9
Veneto	7.3	70.9	Apulia	5.5	56.5
Emilia	12.7	132.4	Basilicata	4.4	41.1
Tuscany	16.9	71.0	Calabria	3.5	53.3
Marches	6.1	65.9	Sicily	5.2	60.8
Umbria	4.2	69.2	Sardinia	6.6	54.7

Total for Kingdom		
	officers and cadets	10.7
	non-commissioned officers	72.2

gions with the largest number of commissioned officers are, in addition to Lazio (where the sons of state employees dominate), Piedmont and Tuscany; the regions with fewer are above all in the Mezzogiorno; Abruzzi and Molise, Calabria and Basilicata. The proportion of commissioned officers for Piedmont is almost six times that of Abruzzi and even Lombardy, antimilitarist in parliamentary speeches, has three times as many.

But even in the big cities there is a large number of state employees; and there are from each region: disregarding the districts of the large urban centres Turin, Florence, Bologna, Naples, etc., each region's contribution to militarism is shown in Table 11.

There is therefore a true and proper abyss between the regions of northern Italy and those of southern Italy: for the commissioned officers, while Liguria where it is said, at least in its newspapers, that they do not like militarism, gives 14.6, Piedmont 13.3, Emilia 11.1, the southern regions fall like Abruzzi and Molise to 3.3, Calabria to 3.5 and Basilicata to 4.4.

TABLE 11

Regions		Proportion per 10,000 conscripts	
		of officers and cadets	of ordinary volunteers
Piedmont	(excluding the district of Turino)	13.3	69.9
Liguria	(excluding the district of Genoa)	14.6	40.8
Lombardy	(excluding the district of Milan)	6.7	51.5
Veneto	(excluding the district of Venice)	6.5	70.3
Emilia	(excluding the district of Bologna)	11.1	127.1
Tuscany	(excluding the district of Florence)	10.7	64.1
Marches		6.1	65.9
Umbria		4.2	69.2
Lazio	(excluding the district of Rome)	4.4	68.9
Abruzzi and Molise		3.3	52.4
Campania	(excluding the district of Naples)	6.0	75.0
Apulia		5.5	56.5
Basilicata		4.4	41.1
Calabria		3.5	53.3
Sicily	(excluding the district of Palermo)	4.2	56.7
Sardinia		6.6	54.7
	Total of Kingdom	7.2	65.6

No less serious is the contrast of the non-commissioned officers for whom Basilicata represents proportionally a third of Emilia.

«In southern Italy and the remaining .part of central Italy — Livi writes — the tendency to military life appears much scarcer than elsewhere».

This it happens that while the Mezzogiorno is deemed the author of militarism and its deputies vote for military spending more than those of the other regions, it is the provinces of northern and central Italy which as regards the distribution of the army, the supplies and finally also the origins of the commissioned and non-commissioned officers enjoy the benefits militarism produces.

We have not wished to attempt a study of the geography of the bureaucracy. As we could not ask all employees where they came from, we have confined ourselves to those for whom it was possible to have information as they are in the higher levels.

There is something akin to a general staff of all the civil and military administration: in the ministries there are the office heads upwards, in the provinces above all the prefects and the finance superintendents. For the army and the navy we have limited our study to general officers and admirals.

Now, if we group the ministries by affinity, we have:

a) political ministries. These are the Ministry of the Interior and the Ministry of Foreign Affairs, which have a prevalently political nature. Some public services, such as prisons and state archives or charitable institutions, depend from the Ministry of the Interior. But the two ministries' functions are mainly political. We have extended our study to the prefects of the Kingdom and those administering the prefectures and ambassadors, extraordinary envoys and plenipotentiary ministers;

b) military ministries, these are the Ministries of War and Navy. Our calculations have taken into account also the general officers and admiral officers. So as not to count the same persons twice, we have only taken account of the civil personnel on the staff of the central administration of these ministries;

c) financial ministries, these are the Ministries of Finance and the Treasury. But we deemed it useful to include the Court of Audit which also has financial functions and is closely related to them;

d) ministries which regard public services and are, in general, all the others.

Now, when one knows the native region of the higher officials, two things should be assumed:

1) either the career is the same for all, there being identical laws, and then the distribution of the higher officials is also that of their lower counterparts;

2) either the career is different and this means that some regions are, or were, prohibited from advancement.

As this second hypothesis is unlikely, one can and should accept the first. More or less then, the central staff of the bureaucracy will be a trace because we know the geography of the mass of the employees.

The situation is therefore this: while northern Italy accounts for just 36.8% of the Kingdom's population, it has 52.8% of all the higher officials: the old Kingdom of the Two Sicilies, representing a greater mass of population, has just 19.7% of the higher central administration.

The intrusiveness of the southern Italians is spoken of as a dangerous fact: with the exception however of the small zone of Campania, one can say that the rest of the Mezzogiorno is almost absent in the state administration.

The policies, whether good or bad, are entrusted, as regards the higher officials, almost wholly to northern Italians, who amount to 52.8%.

In the period we studied, the 75 prefects and prefecture governors were 39 in northern Italy and 18 in southern Italy and Sicily: 15 in mainland Mezzogiorno and 3 in Sicily.

Small Liguria and Lombardy have 10 and 9 prefects respectively: Piedmont has 13 and Veneto 7.

If the mainland Mezzogiorno, taking account of the inhabitants, had given as many prefects as Piedmont it would have 32 and it would have 83 in proportion to Liguria. The staffing limits would not even suffice to contain them.

In the senior diplomatic and consular service, the Mezzogiorno is hardly represented at all.

The state of affairs as regards the army is even more serious.

Of the 149 generals whose native region we have indicated, 114 were from northern Italy, 69 from Piedmont, 5 from Liguria, 34 from Lombardy (which hates militarism) etc. Southern Italy and Sicily managed to scrape together only 11.

Taking also into account the senior staff of the Ministry of War and Navy and the admiral officers, northern Italy which claims to combat militarism accounts for 63.9 of all the personnel indicated, southern Italy and Sicily, which have a larger population, just 13.5.

If, given its population, mainland southern Italy had as many generals as northern Italy, it would have 82 instead of 10: it would have 69 in proportion to Lombardy, 42 in proportion to Liguria, 171 in proportion to Piedmont.

The financial administration is in turn prevalently, 49.3%, entrusted to officials from northern Italy; 22% represent on the other hand the inhabitants of the old Kingdom of the Two Sicilies.

The ministries of agriculture, of the posts, of public works, of justice and education are said to be full of southern Italians; but the higher officials are instead composed no differently than that of the other ministries.

Throughout the state administration, while the population of the old Kingdom of the Two Sicilies is greater than that of northern Italy, the latter accounts for 52.8% of all higher officials and southern Italy and Sicily just 19.7%.

The respective situation of northern Italy, central Italy, southern Italy, Sicily and Sardinia is indicated quite clearly in the diagrams where the largest circle indicates the ratio of the population and the smallest circle the ration of the number of state employees.

Southern Italy has never a number of employees proportional to the population; that of northern Italy on the other hand, is always much higher.

In the 69 provinces of the Kingdom the prefects, who have administrative and political functions are in charge of the administrative services; the superintendents of finance are in charge of the financial administration. The military services are headed by the generals of the army of which the overwhelming majority reside in the provinces.

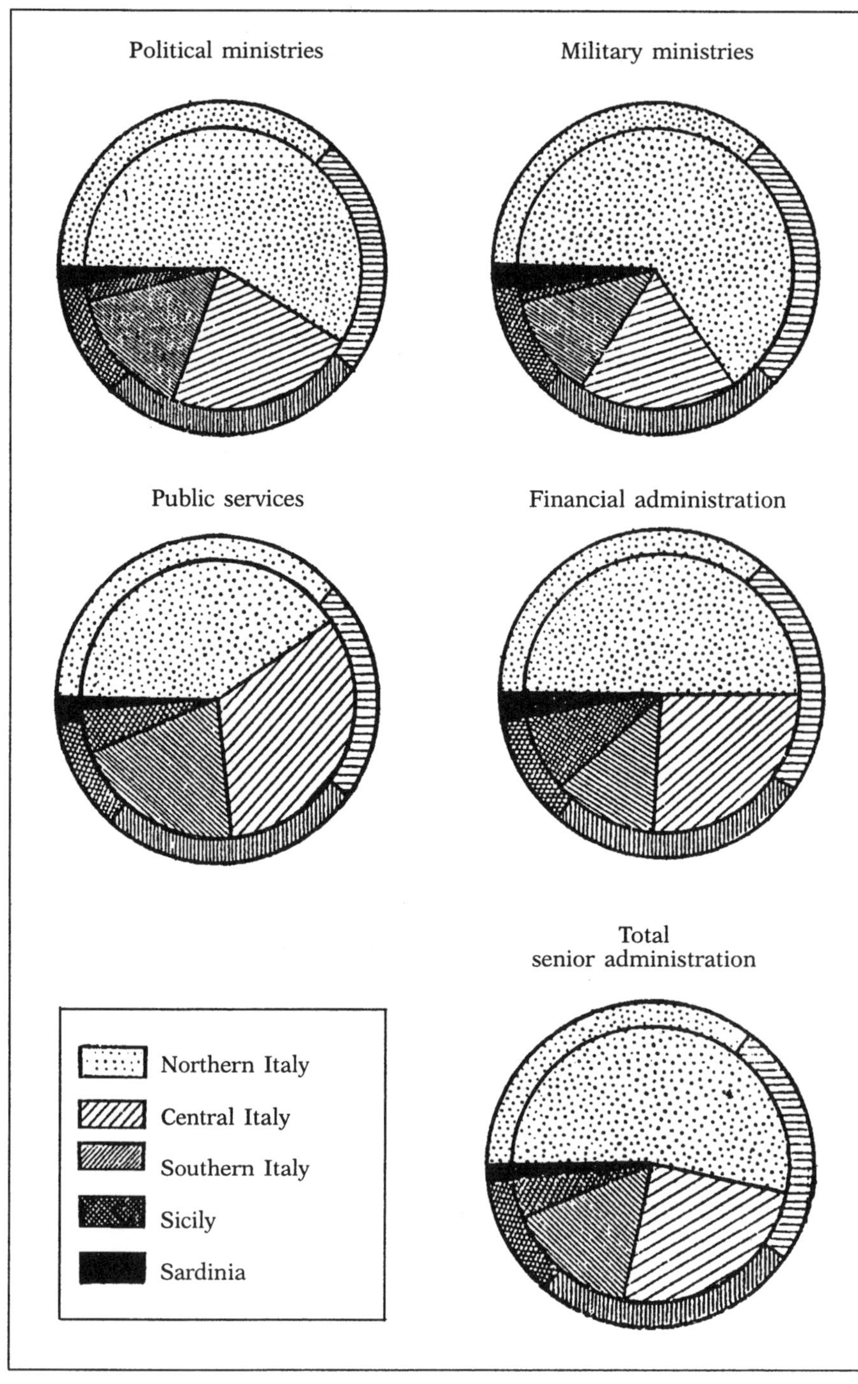
Political ministries
Military ministries
Public services
Financial administration
Total
senior administration
Northern Italy
Central Italy
Southern Italy
Sicily
Sardinia

This administration, which we can call provincial, and which concentrates the largest powers, consists of 293 officials, of which 189, namely two thirds, were born in northern Italy, which represents just 36.8% of the population, while there are only 43 from southern Italy and Sicily, just over a seventh, while the proportion of the population is 37.9.

Thus the legend that the southern Italians dominate the public administration is groundless.

Between 1860 and 1870 there were whole ministries which hardly employed a single southern Italian: after the proportions changed, but as in any case, the southern Italians always remained in a situation of considerable inferiority.

And not because they have no propensity to become state employees. For some years now, indeed, in the public examinations they show all too much such propensity; but it is because the overall set-up does not make it easy for some regions to even advance in the bureaucracy.

10. - The Growing Prosperity of Northern Italy: The Slowness of Growth in Southern Italy. The Present Conditions

Under the impact of the customs legislation, the economic legislation and the entire internal arrangements of the state, all the regions of northern Italy and several of those of central Italy have rapidly developed. Lombardy, after have formed a considerable mass of capital, has succeeded in completing its industrial transformation; Piedmont, Veneto, Emilia are following in its steps. Liguria has in forty years absorbed a large part of the benefits of the new Italy. Tuscany too has enjoyed several benefits.

Southern Italy, which before 1860 was in large part closed to civilisation and which, except for some small zone around Naples, was almost impenetrable, has benefited considerably from unification. The average level of education is much higher: customs have improved; there are many more roads; agriculture, particularly in Apulia, has improved; the wind of new civilisation is begining to make itself felt. But the benefits have been in large part ethical: there where quite a difficult economic situation has been created.

The mainland Mezzogiorno is not wealthy nor has it ever been.

The politicians, who do not know it (and were mainly from the south), spoke of it as a naturally wealthy country: too favoured by nature, Bonghi said; conspicuous, Sella said: rich, stated Depretis; prosperous, sentenced Minghetti.

It was instead a land in which the land, except for Campania felix and some zones in Apulia and Avellino, is naturally poor and where the resources are scarce.

In forty years this country has given what it could and what it could not; it has received very little, above all it has received badly.

It can be calculated that, as a result of the state's policies, of the difference between the contribution of the citizens and public spending, of government bonds, of state and Church property, of the form of the Mezzogiorno's annexation, several billion lire, four or five perhaps, have been transferred from the south to the north.

All this without taking into account the customs tariffs, whose effects cannot be measured.

Thus that in the Mezzogiorno, despite the progress which has or is being made, some symptoms of depression are already clearly manifesting themselves.

It is evident that the less onerous the taxes, the easier they are to collect; on the other hand, when they exceed certain limits of bearability, they become very onerous to collect.

Since January 1, 1873, direct taxes have been collected in a uniform manner, before then there was a broad range of arrangements. In some regions (Piedmont, Parma) collection was entrusted to government employees; in others (Tuscany, Modena) they were collected by the local councils; in others (the southern and Roman provinces, Lombardy, Veneto) they were collected by contracted tax collectors.

At present, as is known, direct state taxes and provincial and local surtaxes are collected by council or consortium tax-collectors remunerated by a collection commission.

The tax-collectors are paid a commission; and this, although paid by the local councils and provinces, weighs solely on the taxpayers, being added to the surtax.

And so those who cannot pay, have in actual fact to pay more; and the increases in the collection commissions are merely exacerbations of the old tax.

The tax is exacerbated inversely to prosperity; and, given the present system, the poorer one is and if one lives in a town with difficult communications and little trade, the more the taxes increase as a result of all the collections.

In 1898, tax-collection commissions averaged as follows:

Piedmont	0.99	Abruzzi and Molise	3.29
Liguria	1.09	Campania	2.11
Lombardy	0.91	Apulia	2.66
Veneto	1.41	Basilicata	4.02
Emilia and Romagna	1.37	Calabria	3.87
Marches and Umbria	1.97	Sicily	2.83
Tuscany	1.55	Sardinia	4.86
Lazio	1.68	Kingdom	1.78

All the regions of the north are, therefore, below the general average for the Kingdom, and the southern regions well above said.

It is easier to collect taxes in Lombardy then all the other regions: closely followed by Piedmont and Liguria. On the mainland it is most difficult to collect taxes in Basilicata with 4.02, closely followed by Calabria with 3.87, Abruzzi and Molise with 3,29.

The maximum collection commissions in some provinces of the Mezzogiorno are such as to appear unlikely.

Hence poverty gives rise not to an attenuation but instead to a harshening.

Where the difficulties of collection and poverty are greater, where the taxes are collected with the greatest difficulty, it is there that one often reaches that limit in which the taxpayers, being unable to pay at all, allow themselves to be expropriated.

The number of transfers to the state of property expropriated from taxpayers who owe direct taxes (as a result of the provisions of section 54 of the law of 20 April 1871) is, in relation to the population, highest in Calabria and Basilicata, and lowest in Lombardy and Piedmont.

In almost fifteen years from January 1, 1885 to June 30, 1897 the following expropriations of property have taken place:

Piedmont	128	Lazio	2,323
Liguria	226	Abruzzi and Molise	6,153
Lombardy	148	Campania	4,798
Veneto	210	Apulia	2,079
Emilia and Romagna	423	Basilicata	2,356
Tuscany	2,051	Calabria	11,773
Marches	113	Sicily	18,637
Umbria	449	Sardinia	52,060

There is therefore a white zone and a black zone. There are regions which know almost no expropriations and others which see a large number of them every day.

Basilicata, which in terms of population represents barely a twenty first of southern Italy, alone has a number of expropriations three times higher.

Calabria has much more expropriations than central Italy and northern Italy combined.

If we disregard Sardinia, where for already known causes and for the fragmented nature of land ownership, the phenomenon is different in form and proportion, nothing equals the torment of the Mezzogiorno.

If we relate the number of expropriations to the population, the latter have the following proportion of increase in the period January 1, 1885 - June 30, 1897:

	Inhabitants per one expropriation
Lombardy	27,416
Piedmont	26,906
Veneto	14,757
Marches	8,639
Emilia and Romagna	5,435
Liguria	4,350
Umbria	1,352
Tuscany	1,050
Apulia	900
Campania	655
Lazio	309
Basilicata	232
Abruzzi and Molise	225
Sicily	189
Calabria	114
Sardinia	14

Moreover, another serious fact should be borne in mind.

If the study is limited to the more recent period, that which runs from 1893-1894 to 1896-1897, the contrast is even more striking. this means that while comparatively the conditions of a part of Italy have much improved, those of another part, vice versa, have remained bad, if indeed they have not worsened.

In the four years between 1893-1894 and 1896-1897 seven provinces did not see a single expropriation for non-payment of direct taxes and they are all, except one, in northern Italy: Belluno, Bologna, Cremona, Mantua, Milan, Novara and Vicenza; Arezzo and Siena saw only one expropriation each; Como and Sondrio two; Macerata, Pavia and Turin three; Alessandria, Brescia, Modena, Padua, Parma, Pesaro, Reggio Emilia, Treviso, Udine and Verona less than ten.

Of the 25 provinces which saw more than 100 expropriations, only two were in central Italy, none in northern Italy: twenty three in southern Italy and the islands. The mainland Mezzogiorno is almost fully represented in this map of expropriations. The provinces which have had more than 100 expropriations in the 4 years are all in Sardinia and the Mezzogiorno, except for Rome and Grosseto.

If one bears in mind that ownership in the south is very concentrated, much more so than in the north, the impact of this fact can be properly appreciated.

Somebody has said that there is in the Mezzogiorno a custom of being expropriated. He is a somewhat macabre spirit; and not much dissimilar from advice proffered in some old recipe books: the rabbit likes being skinned alive.

Although it does not have a scattered and relatively small population, the Mezzogiorno lacks populous cities, which abound on the other hand in Emilia, Lombardy and also in other regions of northern and central Italy. In the land of Bari there are large urban centres of population; but they are agricultural masses which

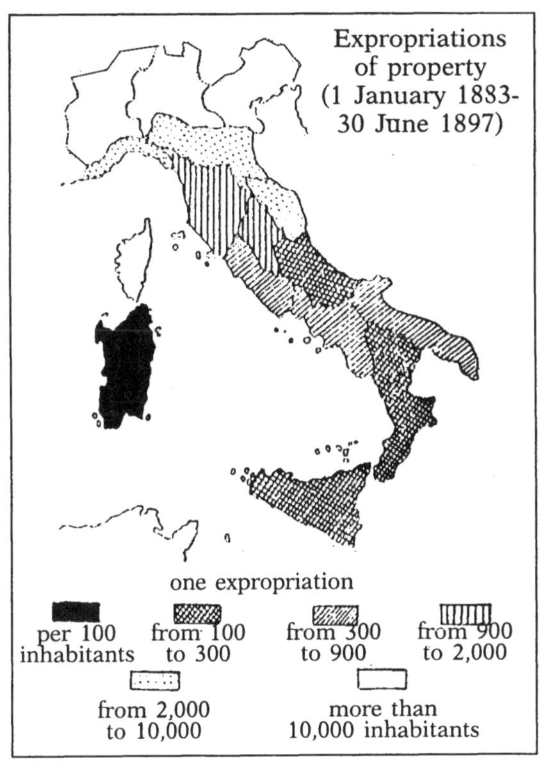

cannot live in the countryside, either because of traditions or local conditions.

It is common knowledge that in general southern Italy has the highest birth rate of the peninsula: Apulia, Calabria in particular have very high birth rates: on the other hand Piedmont, Liguria, etc., have very low birth rates. The birth rate in the south is always higher than that in the north of Italy.

Now, taking the largest city of the Mezzogiorno, Naples, it is instructive to compare its growth to that of other cities.

Between 1820 and 1860 to the present, there were two periods which were more or less the same. What growth did Naples, Genoa, Turin, Milan and Venice see in the first period? in short, what organisation allowed a greater growth? Between 1820 and 1860 there was the old regime: now there is the new regime. By how much more has each city grown?

The movements of the population show that the relative importance of Naples (even without taking account of the strong growth of Rome) has, since 1860, been on the decline.

In 1862 it had almost double the population of Milan and now Milan has only 89,000 inhabitants less; it had between three and four times the population of Genoa and now it has just over double; more than double the population of Turin and now it exceeds it by a third.

If we represent the 1860 population as 100, the situation in 1820 and 1898 was as follows:

	1820	1860	1898
Naples	80.9	100	134.8
Turin	43.6	100	174.8
Genoa	61.3	100	182.5
Venice	81.6	100	135.8
Milan	58.2	100	201.6

Naples has therefore grown after 1860 by little more than between 1820 and 1860. But its relative growth has been scant compared with that of Turin, Genoa, Milan, above all compared with that of these last two cities. If it had grown in the same proportion as Turin and Genoa, it would have a much larger number of inhabitants; it would have nearly a million inhabitants if its growth had resembled that of Milan.

Until 1860 the city of Naples lived almost wholly either on the bourgeoisie of the provinces and the agricultural rent of the big landowning families; but it above all lived on the state employees.

In the city and surroundings there were from 30 to 40 thousand soldiers and there was a rich court, with a large number of ministers and with sumptuous diplomatic representations. Anybody who had anything of a large fortune lived in Naples.

After 1860 public security increased in the countryside and the population of all the Mezzogiorno no longer irresistibly headed toward the big city which was previously their capital. Life in the provinces — and this was a good thing — started to develop; many nuclei of urban population in the provinces achieved, as regards building, considerable progress. Hence the relative importance of Naples diminished.

Now Lombardy has seen the city of Milan double from 1860 to the present; but life in the provinces has grown even more rapidly.

The big city, the political capital of a Kingdom, or the historical and intellectual capital of a region, is the very soul of the life of every community. It is to it that the best intelligence, the most combative spirits flow: it is the focus of culture, renews ties, maintains traditions. All Lombardy's business pivots around Milan, but so do all the traditions, all the aspirations, the entire intellectual movement. Thus Turin for Piedmont, Genoa for Liguria, etc.

Now the city of Naples, which before 1860 lived on the army, the court, the public administration, after 1860 had to renounce all these. It was the head of a Kingdom almost equal in population to the Kingdom of Sardinia and Lombardy Veneto together, in other words it saw flow in from the provinces and spend for the public administration as much as Turin, Milan and Venice combined.

After 1860, having lost the court, having lost the large central administration of the Bourbons, Naples had no alternative but to transform itself into an industrial city.

But it lacked the education, which could be formed only slowly. Above all it lacked the possibility.

Under the Bourbons the taxes had been very light, now some doubled, other tripled; many other new ones were introduced. The hasty sale of state and Church property took away on the one hand money, and on the other caused the transfer of considerable amounts of wealth from the south to the north. Enormous amounts of public debt were thrown on the market. In a country which almost knew no debt, the purchases took place not when the prices were low, but when they were high.

Later, quite a few governments considered the Mezzogiorno which had still not educated itself in the ways of freedom, as a country suited to form ministerial majorities: after 1876 it launched itself, and above all Naples did, into that electoral patronage which should instead have been fought. Even now entire cities are in the hands of true political bandits, whose infamous function is to form the praetorians for all the ministries. Hence instead of achieving an improvement in the administration, there came about that condition of things which is known to everyone and which prevents any development of industrial life.

The customs tariffs of 1887, which reduced the purchasing power of the entire Mezzogiorno, did the rest.

The general conditions of southern Italy are undoubtedly considerably improved, in the sense that the population has increased. But it is also unarguable that in the development of northern and central Italy on the one hand, and southern Italy on the other, there is a significant difference. Southern Italy was much closer to northern Italy, above all economically and demographically, after 1860 than it is now.

An obvious example is that of mortality.

Mortality has decreased throughout Italy because the general conditions have improved; but it has not decreased equally everywhere.

In the five-year period 1865-1869, mortality per 1,000 inhabitants was 29.00 in northern Italy and 31.86 in southern Italy; in the three-year period 1895-1897 it was 21.62 in northern Italy and 26.73 in southern Italy.

In 1895-1897 mortality in northern Italy has decreased vis-à-vis 1865-1869 by 7.44; that of southern Italy by 5.13.

It is equally interesting to note the number of rejected conscripts.

We have chosen the drafts for those born in 1842, 1852 and 1876 because they represent the first the draft of a year which gave the soldiers immediately after unification (1862), the second the draft which give them after the annexation of Lazio (1872) and the third a quite recent year, 1896.

Now, the path followed by the Mezzogiorno of Italy is quite different from that followed by the north as regards this phenomenon.

In Lombardy, of every 100 conscripts, those rejected as a result of illness and imperfections totalled 26.38 in the 1842 draft, 22.67 in 1876; in Basilicata 7.64 in 1842 and 12.65 in 1876. In Liguria those rejected because of illness totalled 12.32 in 1874 and they have risen to 17.93; in Apulia their number has increased from 10.38 to 23.51. And in general, the movements of those rejected because of illness and imperfections take quite different guises in the three drafts studied.

If we now compare how much some provinces pay with what the state spends in each of them and see what financial action the state exercises, it will be evident how there exist not only different situations, but opposing situations.

It being impossible to embrace all the taxes, we have chosen those are definitely paid by each province: moreover, they are those taxes which constitute the very base of the budget.

Alongside the taxes we have indicated the symptoms of the fiscal pressure: the average of the direct-tax collection commissions and the expropriations of property for non-payment of direct taxes over a considerable period of time.

We have indicated some facts which better serve to clarify the state's action:

1st example: Potenza and Udine.

The province of Potenza covers an area of 9,942 km^2. Its population, according to the census of 1881, totals 539,258 inhabitants: at 31 December 1897 it was calculated in 549,771. There is no trace of big industry in the province. There were only 5,744 workers in 1891; this number has probably subsequently decreased rather than increased. The land has a very tenuous productivity: farming is almost everywhere extensive; and above all as a result of malaria, the population is strongly agglomerated. In a few years, Basilicata has reached the maximum mortality for malaria among all the regions of mainland Italy. In 1899, Banco di Napoli discounted just over half a million lire and granted just over 134,000 lire of advances on securities, so scarce is the business activity. Banca d'Italia in turn in 1898 granted only 1,561,151 lire of discounts and advances. Saving, whatever its form, is very scant.

The province of Udine covers an area of 6,582 km^2; the population amounted to 528,559 according to the 1881 census; in 1887 it was estimated in 536,734. The land is very productive; the climate salubrious, the scattered population abundant; the distribution of the waters rich. In 1889 there were 21,793 workers; but this number has subsequently increased considerably. The movement of trade is so active that in 1898 Banca d'Italia alone granted just under 20 million lire of discounts and advances.

Hence, although the population is more or less equal, the conditions are very different.

Here now is the situation as regards the state of each of the two provinces, without pointing out that Udine contributed only a small number of state and Church assets while Potenza contributed a considerable number.

Some taxes: state tax on land in the five-year period 1894-1898: Potenza 1,980,625 lire — Udine 1,267,352 lire; state tax on buildings in the five-year period 1894-1898: Potenza 898,631 lire — Udine 614,530 lire; personal non-property income tax in the five-year period 1894-98: Potenza 1,071,119 lire — Udine 1,391,165 lire; turnover tax in the five-year period 1892-93 and 1896-97: Potenza 2,213,930 lire — Udine 1,992,226 lire; salt tax: Potenza 1,271,138 lire — Udine 1,110,622 lire.

Tax pressure: average collection commission in 1898: Potenza 4.02% - Udine 1.49%; expropriations from 1 January 1883 to 30 June 1897: Potenza 2,356 expropriations — Udine 48 expropriations.

The action of the state: average state spending from 1893-1894 to 1897-1898: Potenza 4,821,740 lire — Udine 5,630,500 lire: military garrisons in 1893: Potenza 977 soldiers — Udine 1,723 soldiers; annuities in 1898-1899: Potenza 1,753,888 lire — Udine 1,509,356 lire; state pensioners in 1874: Potenza 457 pensioners — Udine 682 pensioners; state pensioners in 1897-1898: Potenza 398 pensioners — Udine 962 pensioners: pensions paid by the state in 1874: Potenza 190,439 lire — Udine 354,240 lire; pensions paid by the state in 1897-1898: Potenza 230,000 lire — Udine 684,000 lire.

2nd example: Bari and Alessandria.

The province of Bari covers an area of 5,350 km^2; in 1881 it had 683,496 inhabitants. At 31 December 1897 it was estimated in 815,618 inhabitants. It has a population density of 152 inhabitants per square kilometre. It is the most advanced of the provinces of southern Italy. But even now agriculture is the principal source of its wealth. In 1892, according to Ministry of Agriculture data, it had 12,175 workers employed in industries; there has been no significant increase since. Post-office savings accounts amounted to just 6.5 million lire in 1896. The population is very agglomerated. At the start of 1898 there were only 232 steam boilers, of which 103 fixed, in the province.

The province of Alessandria is one of the most advanced in Italy.

The province of Alessandria covers an area of 5,052 km^2 and had, according to the 1881 census, 785,566 inhabitants, of which almost half, 373,900 inhabitants, are scattered. The province's population was estimated in 803,402 inhabitants at 31 December 1897. In 1892 there were, according to the Ministry of Agriculture, 17,148 workers; it is calculated that they now exceed 25,000. In 1898, Banca d'Italia granted 40,630,399 lire of discounts. There is a considerable diffusion of local banks, Post-office savings accounts amounted to more than 21.6 million lire.

Some taxes: state tax on land in the five-year period 1894-98: Bari 2,759,908 lire — Alessandria 3,135,312 lire; state tax on buildings in the five-year period 1894-98: Bari 2,324,503 lire — Alessandria 1,362,146 lire; personal non-property income tax in the five-year period 1894-98: Bari 2,436,801 lire — Alessandria 2,869,365 lire; business tax in the five-year period 1892-93 and 1896-97: Bari 4,604,848 lire — Alessandria 4,788,937 lire; salt tax: Bari 1,911,069 lire — Alessandria 1,855,063 lire.

Tax pressure: average collection commission in 1898: Bari 2.73% - Alessandria 1.24%; expropriations from 1 January 1883 to 30 June 1897: Bari 324 expropriations — Alessandria 59 expropriations.

The action of the state: average state spending from 1893-1894 to 1897-1898: Bari 11,000,760 lire — Alessandria 18,022,580 lire: military garrisons in 1893: Bari 2,268 soldiers — Alessandria 11,538 soldiers; annuities in 1898-99: Bari 2,210,258 lire — Alessandria 6,745,629 lire; state pensioners in 1874: Bari 781 pensioners — Alessandria 2,530 pensioners; state pensioners in 1897-98: Bari 964 pensioners — Alessandria 2,863 pensioners: pensions paid by the state in 1874: Bari 397,925 lire — Alessandria 1,040,314 lire; pensions paid by the state in 1897-98: Bari 456,308 lire — Alessandria 2,284,400 lire.

3rd example: Avellino and Verona.

The province of Avellino had 392,619 inhabitants in 1881; in 1897 it had 421,162 on an area of 3,037 km^2. The district of Avellino has quite an advanced agriculture and advantageous natural conditions of agricultural production, such that the population, almost solely agricultural, reached the enormous figure of 248.99 inhabitants per km^2. But the districts of Ariano and Sant'Angelo dei Lombardi are in quite different conditions. Except for a small sulphurous zone, there is no trace whatsoever of big industry. The Ministry of Agriculture calculated in 1889 that it had 8,117 workers. Local ordinary credit has seen a very weak development. In 1898, Banca d'Italia granted 3,499,948 lire of discounts and advances, Banco di Napoli 2,489,534 lire. At 31 December 1898, post-office savings accounts amounted to less than 3 million lire.

The province of Verona, which covers an area of 3,077 km^2, more or less the same as Avellino province, had 394,065 inhabitants in 1881 and 440,078 in 1897. The province of Verona has a very advanced agriculture, rich distribution of water, considerable natural conditions of development. In 1889 the Ministry of Agriculture calculated the number of workers in 8,658. But, following the protectionist tariffs, the manufacturing industries have also been developing. Now the number of industrial workers has almost doubled. The local banks are very developed and some quite prosperous. In 1898 Banca d'Italia granted 1,898 discounts and advances totalling 11,103,718 lire. There is much saving and there is a good smattering of local co-operative banks and local banks.

Some taxes: state tax on land in the five-year period 1894-1898: Avellino 1,701,692 lire — Verona 1,654,077 lire; state tax on buildings in the five-year period 1894-1898: Avellino 578,783 lire — Verona 1,009,545 lire; personal non-property income tax in the five-year period 1894-1898: Avellino 791,794 lire — Verona 1,861,319 lire; business tax in the five-year period 1892-1893 and 1896-1897: Avellino 1,805,284 lire — Verona 2,123,998 lire; salt tax: Avellino 919,225 lire — Verona 1,081,577 lire.

Tax pressure: average collection commission in 1898: Avellino 3.40% — Verona 1.64%; expropriations from 1 January 1883 to 30 June 1897: Avellino 1,112 expropriations — Verona 18 expropriations.

The action of the state: average state spending from 1893-1894 to 1897-1898: Avellino 3,042,940 lire — Verona 10,950,340 lire: military garrisons in 1893: Avellino 592 soldiers — Verona 8,336 soldiers; annuities in 1898-1899: Avellino 610,214 lire — Verona 3,027,403 lire; state pensioners in 1874: Avellino 554 pensioners — Verona 768 pensioners; state pensioners in 1897-1898: Avellino 479 pensioners — Verona 849 pensioners: pensions paid by the state in 1874: Avellino 243,800 lire — Verona 469,580 lire; pensions paid by the state in 1897-1898: Avellino 338,700 lire — Verona 821,200 lire.

4th example: Salerno and Como.

The province of Salerno covers an area of 4,964 km^2 and had a population of 550,1217 inhabitants in 1881, in 1897 it had 576,897 inhabitants. Except for a small zone near Salerno, the population is almost solely agricultural. The number of workers in 1898 was calculated by the Ministry of Agriculture in 15,855, mainly craftsmen. In 1898 Banca d'Italia granted 10,243,989 lire of discounts and advances. In 1895 Banco di Napoli 6,540,623 lire of discounts and advances. There is a very limited number of local banks. The population is generally agglomerated and there are vast zones of malaria. At 31 December 1896 post-office savings accounts amounted to just over 7 million lire.

The province of Como is one of the richest in Italy: it has considerable development of agriculture, large manufacturing industries, an active trade, and flourishing tourism industry. The climate is very healthy, the population very scattered. On an area of 2,826 km² it had 1,881 inhabitants in 1881 and 580,061 inhabitants in 1897. Although local banks are very common and prosperous, in 1898 Banca d'Italia granted 40,352,912 lire of discounts and advances. Ministry of Agriculture data in 1897 indicate that there were 68,391 industrial workers; the number continues to increase. At end-1896, post-office savings accounts amounted to almost 13 million lire.

Some taxes: state tax on land in the five-year period 1894-1898: Salerno 2,005,714 lire — Como 1,269,609 lire; state tax on buildings in the five-year period 1894-98: Salerno 1,029,658 lire — Como 1,023,560 lire; personal non-property income tax in the five-year period 1894-98: Salerno 1,279,862 lire — Como 1,847,862 lire; business tax in the five-year period 1892-1893 and 1896-1897: Salerno 2,686,773 lire — Como 2,178,280 lire; salt tax: Salerno 1,408,392 lire — Como 1,607,702 lire.

Tax pressure: average collection commission in 1898: Salerno 2.44% — Como 1.13%; expropriations from 1 January 1883 to 30 June 1897: Salerno 1,377 expropriations — Como 3 expropriations.

The action of the state: average state spending from 1893-1894 to 1897-1898: Salerno 8,475,360 lire — Como 6,562,500 lire: military garrisons in 1893: Salerno 3,595 soldiers — Como 761 soldiers; annuities in 1898-1899: Salerno 1,776,183 lire — Como 4,326,791 lire; state pensioners in 1874: Salerno 1,181 pensioners — Como 1,031 pensioners; state pensioners in 1897-1898: Salerno 1,093 pensioners — Como 1,231 pensioners: pensions paid by the state in 1874: Salerno 544,974 lire — Como 563,724 lire; pensions paid by the state in 1897-1898: Salerno 733,100 lire — Como 1,042,600 lire.

And so this book ends.

It was written with a great desire for truth, for a great purpose of good. I will be pleased to correct any errors I may have incurred, whatever their number; above all I shall be glad if I can mitigate what I have said.

The readers who have followed me in this arid study (shall I also incur the hypocrisy of the twenty five?) have seen that the facts enunciated prove two things: that the policies followed to date have been more favourable to the development of the north than that of the south of Italy; that the present differences have no nature of need or fatality. We have made many mistakes, perhaps; but there are none that the present difficult situation makes necessary.

The terrible philosopher of the *Leviathan* wrote, at the end of the seventeenth century, that when man is against reason, reason is against man.

I hope instead that if there are some truths in this book, they will be welcomed by those very persons against whose interests they go.

As the future of Italy lies in the close and larger union, in the growing tendency toward unity, those who will hear how much the new Italy has done for them will be more just toward that Mezzogiorno of Italy in which there lies the solution not only of the problems of unification, but also of the very existence of the liberal regime[4].

---

[4] Those bibliographical and statistical references which are not strictly necessary have been omitted, as has any history of the single questions.

I would only thank those who sought to help me in this study and, not being able to do so to all, would mention in particular Hon. Colajanni, who was one of the first to deal with this problem in depth, Professor A. Bosco, Dr. R. Livi and A. Torresin.

Sicily in 1876. Political and Administrative Conditions*

Leopoldo Franchetti - Sidney Sonnino

1. - Remedies

1.1 *Summary of the Effects of the General Conditions of Sicily. Duties which These Conditions Impose on the Italian Government*

All the phenomena we have sought to describe and analyse in this volume boil down to this: that in Sicily private authority prevails over that of society. The upshot is that on the one hand private interest prevails where that of society as a whole should prevail in accordance with the spirit of modern societies in general and in particular of the entire political and administrative order of the Kingdom of Italy, and on the other, that in general the law's sole criterion is force, and not those which determine it in modern societies. And thus, he who can makes liberal use of violence, the public assets and the work of the public authorities are aimed at the profit of a few, the rights recognised by Italian civil legislation have no redress against private arrogance.

Unarguably, this is a state of affairs like any other. And for centuries it was that of Europe as a whole; in some countries it

* From: Franchetti L. - Sonnino S., «La Sicilia nel 1876», book 1: *Condizioni politiche e amministrative*, Chapter VI: *Rimedi*, Firenze, Vallecchi, 1925, pp. 285-310. [Cod. JEL: N 43].

still persists, and contains the buds of that further social development which has manifested itself in a part of Europe itself. It is probable that with the course of time these buds will also produce their fruits in Sicily, perhaps gradually and almost imperceptibly, perhaps by means of a violent revolution or by a foreign conquest, nobody can predict. In the meantime, however, the island would remain in a state similar or little different from that which has reigned for a long time.

But if Sicily is to be governed by the same criteria as the rest of Italy, the continuation, even for a short while, the persistence of this state of affairs should be considered an unhealthy phenomenon, as a disorder, and consequently Italy is charged with suppressing it as quickly as possible.

However, nothing proves that suppressing it is possible, as *a priori* solutions are not possible in political and social questions. It is however unarguable that Italy should seek to eliminate it whatever the effort or cost entailed. On this condition alone has it the right to remain united with Sicily. It is therefore worthwhile employing every means, first to diagnose the illness, then to experiment the remedies suggested by said diagnosis and to act according to this experience.

But the Sicilians, considered in general, are not suited to contribute to this undertaking, as it is precisely their way of feeling and seeing which constitutes the illness to be treated. The opinions, judgements and suggestions of the Sicilians should be solicitously sought if one wishes to know the conditions of the island and the effects of the remedies applied. But these judgements, these opinions should be considered as phenomena, as symptoms of capital importance for he who wishes to discover the nature and process of the illness, not as guidelines for the treatment. For the doctor, hearing the patient complaining of thirst is often a reason for not giving him anything to drink. For the doctor, the sensations the patient complains of most relentlessly are often the sign that his remedies are effective and lead to recovery. Often a momentary relief and an apparent improvement are the sign that the illness is worsening and death is nigh. The Sicilians, or rather that limited class which in Sicily constitutes public opinion, holds, it is true, that some of the phenomena which manifest themselves on the island are unhealthy, but although on the one hand they are immediately materially damaged by them and on the other know by reputation that these phenomena can be suppressed because in other societies their manifestation is prevented; they do not however realise how and why they are. If they did not know by reputation that elsewhere they are eliminated, they would necessarily consider them as necessary and normal, albeit harmful, phenomena, like the pouring rain which rots their harvest as an ineluctable force of nature which they can complain about, but cannot accuse anyone, nor seek to remedy. Moreover, these phenomena are indissolubly linked with others which those Sicilians who constitute public opinion do not consider as anomalous, because they benefit from them, they would suffer as a result of their suppression and, ignorant of the nature of that state of things whose final effects they envy, they cannot understand how said phenomena are a necessary companion of that which they consider as an ill: this is proven by the bitter complaints on the state of public order by the very same persons, who, when a criminal is arrested, intercede on his behalf. Now, in order to cure those which even they consider ills, it is first necessary to eliminate that which they deem a good, it is necessary, as we had occasion to illustrate in the previous chapter, that they judge the remedies with criteria which are not only different, but opposite to those who wish to reduce them to the state of the rest of Italy, and the more effective these remedies, the more they will deem them bad and inappropriate, and will ferment complaints and opposition. This is as concerns those who currently make public opinion in Sicily. As regards the remaining well-to-do or educated class, which does not yet contribute to constitute public opinion, except when its opinions and interests are identical to those of those who stand over it, the immediate advantages which could be obtained from the remedies would perhaps compensate their harm, and it would be right to hope that they would not oppose them, above all when the moral influence which those who dominate them at present have over them. It would be mistaken to expect even directly useful advice or suggestions from it, as it too, as we have already noted, would be unable to comprehend the final aim of the measures taken or to be taken. As regards the overwhelming majority of the population, in its present economic, moral and intellectual conditions, it is absolutely incapable of judging whether a measure in the public interest is good or bad, neither can one for the moment expect from it anything other than uprisings and tumults caused by an increase of material suffering.

1.2 *If the Italian State Wishes to Right the Ills of Sicily, it should Avail itself of the Elements Provided by the Nation with the Exclusion of Sicily to Govern it*

Consequently, if Italy wishes to effectively seek remedies to the ills of Sicily and to apply them in the hope they succeed when it has found them, it should first avail itself of the moral and intellectual resources furnished by the nation except the Sicilians, or rather of almost all the Sicilians, as they will be better instruments than any other of those very few among them who comprehend the state of the island and that of modern societies.

Now, the sole body which can re-unite all a nation's forces, order them, discipline them and direct them to a given end is the state, that is to say the government. We shall spare the reader idle talk on the theoretical limits of the state, and merely observe that if in ordinary conditions one proceeds to govern a country, a region, a province with the combined work of its citizens and of the state, in Sicily, as long as it is part of Italy, these two elements are (at least in our opinion) incompatible. One or the other should dominate exclusively. If we opt for the citizens, then the state should step to one side; leaving Sicily totally at its own mercy, in the hope that there will spontaneously arise a social authority which will derive from its natural forces, and consequently be capable of governing it by means of said. But if Sicily is to be governed by the Italian state, it is inadmissible that, in governing one of its provinces, it renounces its own principles; these should be wholly and in toto substituted for those on which Sicilian society is based; neither should one attempt to reconcile one with the other. Otherwise the Italian state intervenes merely to disrupt the natural play of forces of a society, it prevents them from achieving a stable equilibrium in accordance with their inherent nature, without substituting this with another; and this engenders an element of disorder, as all governments in Sicily have been, particularly since the reforms of 1812; as is above all the Italian government. Which prevents the bandit from conquering land, from ending up, like the mercenary knights of the Middle Ages, lords of feuds and baronies, and from becoming an element of order; it puts down the rebellions of those villains who demand the lands which are theirs by law and who do not wish to be the only ones to bear the weight of local taxes, but it does not succeed in suppressing the bandits, nor forcing the well-to-do classes to administer in the interests of all. In short, in a society ruled by the supremacy of material force, the government removes from said the sanction, the faculty of exercising its rightful authority, the means to become the foundation of a stable order, but not to replace its own authority.

1.3 *How the State in Sicily Should, Before any Other Goal, Ensure that Private Force is Replaced by That of the Law*

The Italian state's mission in Sicily is therefore to ensure that its civil, penal and administrative law prevails over that which is presently in force. Its mission is to ensure the authority of the law prevails over private authority with whatever means and at whatever cost. Every other end should be subordinated and sacrificed to this, because this is the indispensable means for assuring the others. It should, at the cost of every effort, every sacrifice, at the cost even of suffering temporary setbacks, of worsening the apparent conditions of the island, employ the material force at its disposal to ensure respect of the law and to fight those who have broken it, without ever weakening or compromising. When it succeeds in ensuring this with a preponderant material force, its moral authority will be established in a country in which material force constitutes the law, and it will thus have banished the first of the obstacles to be overcome to ensure Sicily enjoys the social condition of a modern people. If it does not succeed, it should try as long as it has the means, and when convinced it has exhausted them all, it should conclude that there exist no artificial means for changing the social state of Sicily, or at least that, if they do exist, they are superior to the forces of the Italian state; it should abandon the island to its natural forces, and proclaim its independence. But if it does not wish to betray its first duty, and go against its most pressing interest, that of its existence, it should never compromise with those who break the law to obtain a false appearance of order or prosperity.

Ensuring that there prevails in part of one's territory a new law which contradicts the social conditions and consequently the moral state of the inhabitants, said is for every state, but above all for the Italian state, a most difficult task, which can be achieved only partially, and even then at the cost of the greatest effort and sacrifice of every kind. It entails detailed knowledge of the material and moral conditions of this part without the help of its inhabitants, of inferring from this knowledge what should be changed in the military and administrative arrangements and in general, in that part of legislation which aims to ensure the application of the rest of the laws. This entails applying the changes made, to verify in practice whether they are effective for the destined end, without being distracted in this assessment by other criteria, without being frightened by temporary deteriorations in the apparent conditions, and this always without the help of the inhabitants, indeed contrary to their assessments; in the midst of the complaints, of the threats of public protest, perhaps in the midst of fears, ignorant and unfounded criticism of public opinion of the rest of Italy, finally, in the face of the opposition by the Sicilian members of Parliament.

Because the Italian government is in the difficult position that to govern all of Italy it has to ask the help and approval of those who represent the interest of that very class against which it should ensure the laws prevail in Sicily.

1.4 *What Immediate Effects the Italian State should First Obtain to Then Achieve the Aim of the Supremacy of Modern Law in Sicily*

The question of the remedies to those disorders described in this volume for us boils down to that of the means the state can find to defeat the difficulties we have just mentioned. The question is twofold: first: how can the state find instruments capable of furnishing it with an exact and complete knowledge of the conditions of Sicily; of inferring from this the measures to be taken; to apply them according to their spirit, to judge their effects? Second: how can it resist the forces which will arise in its very bosom against the general thrust it has chosen? In other terms, the first is a question of personnel; the second of parliamentary politics.

1.5 *On the Personnel to be Deployed in Sicily*

The qualities required in Sicily for personnel of every level and order, both administrative and legal, are much superior to those which would be demanded in ordinary circumstances from more perfect personnel.

We have already had occasion to mention how an ordinary prefect is ill placed to know the phenomena to be found in Sicily and to ascertain their causes. However, as regards the preliminary study of the island's conditions, nothing obliges the government to confine itself to using officials resident on the island by way of duty. As it is a temporary work, they could call on all the country's intellectual forces to carry out surveys and investigations. Moreover, such a system has just been employed with the sending of the Parliamentary Commission of Inquiry, appointed following the discussion of the Law on Exceptional Public Order Measures.

But the question changes radically when talking about the application of the remedies, and the assessments as to their effects, in short, everyday government. This necessarily entails the use of permanent personnel. One has to find among these not conscientious and ordered employees, good at following a path which has already been traced and at applying the laws and regulations as the cases they envisage are encountered, but men capable of analysing complex social facts, of seeking out their causes, capable of knowing what to do in particular cases, in accordance with criteria which are precise and determined, but also general. A pedantic and unsophisticated bureaucracy would cause incalculable damage to the task of regenerating Sicily.

In order to be able to reasonably demand such qualities from the personnel, the government should first of all have clearly realised the conditions of Sicily, decided the policy it intends to pursue to remedy them and be irrevocably resolved to pursue them at any cost. Only then can it endow all the administration with unity of purpose and concept; only then can the officials endow their efforts with a determined and clear purpose, only then will it be possible to find the way to give the entire civil and legal administration uniformity in spirit and direction, and to infuse in all such a sentiment that, at least in the higher grades, every employee is conscious of the mission in which he is participating, understands the common purpose to which the work of the single officials should be directed, and feels for it that same love which every intelligent man feels, even without wishing it, for a great and difficult purpose. Then every employee, both in and outside his office, would always bear in mind that public interest which it is his task to promote and represent. We shall not dwell again here on the specific remedies we have already proposed for the single disorders described in this volume which were suggested to us by an examination of the island's conditions. The importance of said remedies is, in our opinion, wholly secondary and subordinate faced with the need for the representatives of the government and law to possess the qualities and spirit we have just outlined.

But to obtain such a spirit in employees, to enable them moreover to deploy their qualities of character and intelligence, the present system of continual transfers should be abandoned, and once an employee has been assigned to a place he should remain there for a long time. The difficulties a person from the mainland faces in getting to know the persons, customs, languages of Sicily have been much exaggerated; these difficulties do exist and if, as we are profoundly convinced, Sicilian employees are to be excluded from the administration of Sicily in every order and level, with but a very few individual exceptions, those from the mainland should be given time to fulfil their duties and then to put the knowledge acquired to work. The conditions offered to employees in Sicily should be such as to prevent them from viewing the island as an exile.

To achieve this, the special benefits for employees of every kind in Sicily should be very generous as regards both pay and promotion, so as to compensate on the one hand the considerable expenses which they incur, and on the other the discomforts and dangers of the office[1]. This applies in particular to magistrates. We already mentioned the importance we deem should be given to their office in Sicily. But we do not hide that any reform along the lines of our proposals would be fraught with danger and that it would be more worthwhile to introduce one in the opposite sense, as long as their conditions do not considerably improve; as long as the pay and prospects of promotion for magistrates in Sicily remain those currently in force, they will remain as they are now, and any office, however mean, will be for them too important, any responsibility too serious. To cover Sicily's 178 magistrate's courts, at least as regards the penal branch, one should send from the mainland a similar number of young magistrates, educated, intelligent, incorruptible and endowed with tact and courage for any trial. Such men cost dearly and wish to advance. It would not suffice to assure them a hearty pay, but rather to find a way to reserve for them a certain number of positions in the public prosecutor's offices after they had held their office in Sicily for a certain number of years. The public prosecutor's offices could only profit from persons who had undergone such a harsh and difficult apprenticeship.

---

[1] See the afore-cited report by Hon. Gerra of 31 October 1874 (Camera dei Deputati. Sessione 1874-1875. - *Documenti* no. 24 bis, p. 46).

Moreover, if the complete change of magistrates in Sicily would only raise problems of practical implementation, that of the irremovability of the judiciary would encounter such also in the legislation currently in force. The short time available does not allow us to study how to overcome this; we can only say that without a purge, any attempt at general reform in Sicily would only be a waste of time, energy, money and blood.

Furthermore, although we have only spoken of the higher offices when dealing now with the question of government personnel in Sicily, it nonetheless exists for all levels down to the last magistrate's court usher.

1.6 *The Difficulties of Finding in Italy a Sufficient Number of Personnel with the Qualities Necessary for Sicily*

However, when one has assured the special benefits for the personnel sent to Sicily, where will one find personnel endowed with the qualities needed for success? Undoubtedly, the administrative and legal personnel in Italy include numerous persons above all praise; but if one sends to Sicily all that which is needed, what remains in the provinces of the mainland, particularly in southern Italy, which in this as in many other aspects, has the same needs as Sicily? The question of personnel is common to all of Italy, which has pressing need for the average of the officials of every order to be far superior to that of present as regards intelligence, doctrine and morality; and we believe that the solution of all the other questions in Italy is subordinate to that of this question as it is little use making laws when it is not known how they will be applied. It is a question of set-up, remuneration, discipline and repression. However, our opinion on the importance would not appear to be generally shared, such that, as regards remuneration, measures were recently taken for those who are in the least need, deferring to a later date measures for the others; as regards the general reform, there is absolutely no intention at the present. A proposal to reduce the number of courts, and consequently the personnel employed therein, vanished without trace some time back in the face of threats by offended local interests. In any case, Sicily will have to wait for remedy to its ills, and this makes us fear all too greatly that for the time being reasoning on Sicily's ills is a purely theoretical exercise.

1.7 *Attempts to Repress only One Category of Disorders cannot Produce any Result in Sicily*

Whatever the case, one cannot think that the disorders described in this volume will be remedied until such time as the all the orders and levels of administrative and legal personnel have the necessary qualities; as one would attempt in vain to assure the supremacy of the law in one alone, letting the others proceed along their path. The disorders of every type which Sicily has derive from the same cause, private arrogance. Now, the arrogant derive their authority from points which are so different from one another that if one does not combat it on all sides simultaneously, in its relations with both the lawless and the local administrations and the societies, associations and persons of every kind, they will find a way to fend off the assaults, availing themselves of the means of which they are allowed free use. The wish to suppress only one of the manifestations of arrogance is akin to seeking to squeeze with one hand a large bladder which is half full of air. The air escapes to the free part, and one remains with the membrane in one's hand. But on the other hand, although the multiplicity of the points of support opens more ways for the arrogant to elude the authorities, it is, on the other hand, also the reason for them having a greater number of vulnerable points, when the authority assails them from every side. Who managed to avoid being convicted of ordering a killing can be sent to prison for misdoing in an local administration, and where for the first crime there will have been nobody willing to testify, perhaps for the second there will be no lack of tip-offs which will help uncover the factual proof. The reader will perhaps have noted that after having expounded long theories on the difficulties of distinguishing the forced accomplice from the voluntary abettor who profits from his abetting, we have indicated no criteria for distinguishing one from the other; in fact we do not believe an a priori criterion exists, and we have already sought to show this. An intelligent official, with much experience of the places and persons, has a thousand ways of distinguishing those persons whose principal purpose in abetting the criminals is to acquire authority and money, but it is very rare that he can find sufficient proof against them to bring them to justice. This difficulty will never be overcome directly. Abetting is the effect of the general social conditions, and it can be defeated only by combating the latter. This is the way to certain victory. He who is not an accomplice merely out of fear, is necessarily arrogant, and as a result the official who knows what he is has only to keep an eye on him to find in a short period of time ten rather than one reasons other than abetting for bringing him to court. In this manner, one will hit not only the accomplices, who enjoy material benefit, or monetary profit, from their abetting, but also those who receive only moral benefit when, in the overwhelming majority of cases, it would be absolutely impossible to obtain a conviction in a court of law.

1.8 *On the Government's Parliamentary Policy*

Furthermore, the work of the more excellent personnel always depends in the final analysis on the direction and support of the central government, in short on its parliamentary policies. It is evident and natural that, as soon as a government gave merely a hint of wishing to govern Sicily against the island's dominant class, it would raise a storm in the Sicilian Deputation, which would ally with any group or party in order to bring about its fall. Those among the members of Parliament from the island who were too demure in their opposition would not be re-elected, and so the fall of the government would, in the best of hypothesis, be merely a question of time. Unless, however, the question of Sicily and of the provinces of southern Italy in general does not acquire in public opinion, and consequently in Parliament, the importance it deserves, and then the members from northern and central Italy would eschew their numerous petty rivalries, interests and grudges to ensure its solution. Unfortunately, at the moment this is nothing more than a pipe dream and coalitions are forged in Parliament for wholly different reasons. In any case, much would be done to encourage public opinion to realise the true importance of the question of the southern provinces if a government had the courage to raise it in Parliament and the ability to fall on the issue.

In this question of the southern provinces, every Italian government finds itself torn between interest and duty, and up to now they have sacrificed duty to interest. To gain a few more votes at elections they have compromised with the very abuses it was their duty to end; the appointment and transfer of civil servants are disciplined not by their utility for the administration, but by electoral self-interest. On numerous occasions, when investigating crimes or their authors they have halted and even retreated before powerful guilty persons or accomplices. In short, the government has been the first to let itself be corrupted by local interests. Not for money it is true, but for votes, for newspaper articles, for demonstrations of so-called public opinion. Now, as long as things continue thus, it is evident that not even the highest qualities of the personnel can place them in a position to go against the wishes of the central authority which directs them and which they serve.

Under the conditions listed in this chapter, the specific remedies we proposed in the preceding chapters would suffice to establish the supremacy of the law. This could moreover undoubtedly be flanked and perhaps even replaced by others, when one analyses the single disorders in more detail. For us the question of special remedies for the single disorders is accessory and secondary. If these remedies exist, finding them is a matter of time and experience, when the general policy we have sought to describe in this chapter is adopted in Sicily. If this is not followed, even the most ingenious and studied of detailed remedies will be ineffective by virtue of their inherent flaw, at best, with considerable effort and with sacrifices disproportionate to the effect that will be obtained, it will be possible to temporarily procure an apparent improvement, which will last as long as the extraordinary effort from which it derives; a reduction in offences which will serve, more than anything else, to provide arguments for some government in a Parliamentary debate.

1.9 *The Unfounded Nature of the Assertion that Sicilians are More Difficult to Govern than Other Peoples*

After fifteen years of failure in governing Sicily, many claim that the Sicilians are ungovernable. We personally believe this assertion to be untrue; in any case it is unjustified; as any people one wishes to govern with means that are contradictory among themselves will necessarily appear ungovernable.

The difficulty in governing the Sicilians has also been ascribed to something enigmatic which distinguishes island-dwellers in general from the rest of mankind. We believe this explanation is slightly too similar to that given in Molière's comedy of why opium sends one to sleep «quia est in eo virtus dormitiva quae facit dormire». In any case, if it is very convenient for those who wish to spurn the responsibility they should bear, we believe it cannot hold up against a serious observation of the facts. If we compare the Sicilians for example with the English, and with the natives of the island of Tahiti, we believe it very difficult to find even the remotest similarity in the relations of each of these peoples with the public authority. Although it is true that if we confine our horizon to the large islands of the Mediterranean, there is a considerable similarity between them, not only in the specific aspect just mentioned, but in everything; and the explanation of this is, we believe, very simple and clear. From the Middle Ages to recent times, Sicily, Corsica, Sardinia, remained outside the mainstream of European civilisation. Undoubtedly their situation as an island contributed much to this, but this reason is flanked by many other special ones, which did not manifest themselves, by way of example, for England. The large islands of the Mediterranean resemble one another not because they are islands, but because they are all equally similar to the rest of Europe as it was four centuries ago.

1.10 *On Exceptional Public Order Measures*

Let us once again return to the question of the specific remedies, particularly as regards public order. Only experience, we said, can decide whether all those of normal or stable nature which one can imagine are effective. If, contrary to our expectations, they turned out to be impotent in establishing the supremacy of the Law, it would be worthwhile to resort to exceptional and provisional measures to clear and prepare the ground; in other words, to destroy that system of intimidation which prevents the action of the regular laws. What should such measures be?

Of those which we propose now, if some (such as for example the pure and simple abolition of the armed land wardens) are not definitive, they should be maintained for quite a long time and be considered as permanent. Moreover, they do not imply derogations to the Statute, except for our proposals regarding the jury. As regards this latter, we would say that in our opinion, in Sicily, its abolition within the afore-indicated limits cannot be an extraordinary and provisional measure, but a lasting one and such as to be considered normal; because we believe that the jury cannot exist in Sicily as long as there persist not only the present state of public order, but also the present social conditions. If one does not deem practicable the abolition by law of the jury in Sicily, one should make its work superfluous by referring, as a matter of course, all the serious criminal cases to the mainland Court of Assizes; and one should bear all the cost and administrative complications such a system would entail. Its disadvantages, however large, would be nothing compared to its advantages.

Having clarified this point, we still have to study as regards the extraordinary and provisional measures true and proper, namely: first, the institution of military courts; second, the means to remove those who are clearly the authors and instigators of crimes and have avoided a trial because of the exceptional state of public order. As regards the military courts, our analysis of the conditions of public order in Sicily indicates that the few advantages they would produce would not compensate their disadvantages. One would execute on the spot a bandit, a rogue, perhaps some accomplice, but one could not undermine the vast matrix of complicity which covers most of the island.

We believe it would be very efficient to exile suspects, on condition however this was implemented as it should be, without hesitation or misplaced pity. All suspects, whatever their rank and influence, should be removed from the island and they should remain outside the island not for a short time and as though provisionally, but for many years, for whatever time necessary to rend their relations, their ties, whatever their nature, with the island. Before resorting to exceptional measures, one should hesitate a lot and try every other means; but once the decision has been taken, being inexorable, cruel is a virtue and duty; compassion is a crime because if one does things only by half the measures will produce the great public and private damage which are inherent, but not the benefits. Compromise in these cases is to do as those who, out of great pity, do not have the courage to cut a dog's ears at one go, but cut a small piece off every day.

Moreover, even when it is clear that exceptional measures are indispensable, the re-ordering we propose in the administration of the police and justice would still be necessary, because to uncover and hit the authors and instigators of crimes without a trial, entails comprehensive and perfect knowledge of the smallest local details; otherwise one risks not hitting innocent people at random, but also becoming instruments of vengeance and arrogance of the inhabitants against the rest, thus falling even deeper into that abyss out of which one desperately sought to climb. On the other hand, as the operation is prepared in advance and the lists of the persons to be deported determined, it would suffice to suspend the ordinary laws for a very short time, sufficient to lay hands on persons in question, and thus reducing to the minimum possible the enormous damages to which a state of violence, such as that of summary law, gives rise.

1.11 *How Italy is Bound to Make Enormous Monetary Sacrifices to Improve the Material Conditions of Sicily*

Up to now we have spoken of government reform, of rigour, of exceptional measures; but Italy's duties toward Sicily are not confined to this. As it came to the island to impose a new social order, it is obliged to ensure the island enjoys the material conditions which would make this possible. Has it fulfilled this obligation? We believe not. Italy found Sicily with very few roads and without railways[2], and the sacrifices it has made to date for public works on the island are nothing in comparison to those due. Sicily, and with it the other provinces of southern Italy, certainly have no right to demand that Italy runs up a deficit; but they have that of asking it uses to their benefit all those forces on which it can draw, they have the right to ask priority over other regions in the construction of public works. Moreover, the delay here will not be wholly detrimental if the direction of government in the island will be changed, and if this henceforth will revolve around the interests of the entire population of Sicily, not around the needs and outcries of that part of it which predominates. Thus much of the money destined for the good of the island will not be wasted unprofitably in the future and end up in the hands of influential contractors in the form of scandalous earnings, which have in part been buried under the landslides and in the swamps to satisfy the clamorous caprices of some city or clique. The excerpt from the Commission of Inquiry's Report we cite in the Appendix gives an idea of the immense and painful losses which Sicily has thus experienced.

---

[2] As regards the question of ports and their particular importance for an island, sec page 314 of the *Relazione della Commissione d'inchiesta per la Sicilia*, reproduced in the Appendix to this volume.

1.12 *Why the Government is Obliged to Study in the Southern Provinces More than Elsewhere the Effects of its Taxes on Wealth*

Moreover, if the government needs to carefully study the effects produced in Sicily by its civil and penal laws, it still has the duty to ascertain with the most conscientious care the results produced by its taxes. If this duty is incumbent for all of Italy, it is more pressing than ever for Sicily and in general for the southern provinces, where a mistake which obstructs the economic activity makes he who committed it the advocate and accomplice of all those forces which check that part of Italy in its present social condition[3]. Unfortunately, for taxes as for everything else, the southern provinces are the last to be studied, and thus laws and regulations adapt to conditions which are de facto different from theirs, observed in other regions.

1.13 *How Repression of the Ills Described in this Volume are Suited for Making Possible the Preparation of a Permanent Improvement in the Conditions of Sicily, but not to Operate it*

Finally, when the government has found the most effective means to ensure the supremacy of the force of the Law over private arrogance, the results it obtains will be incomplete and precarious. Incomplete, because most of the non-violent private arrogance is the domain of civil law and cannot, even with the maximum of effort, be known and suppressed by the state, until such time as those offended do not go of their own accord to report it and to invoke its help. Precarious, because the laws will be backed by the artificial force of the state and not by the natural force of the social elements interested in their maintenance. The state, with the measures mentioned in this volume, can allow these elements, if they exist in embryo, to rise and gain strength, but not create

---

[3] See page 23 of the *Relazione della Commissione d'inchiesta per la Sicilia* for the effects in Sicily of the alcohol tax law. See also on p. 100 ff the comments on the collection of taxes.

them. The ills of Sicily derive from its social state, i.e., its economic conditions; the latter will last as long as the former, in substance if not in form, and will cease only when the latter have changed, in other words when a numerous middle class has come into being in Sicily. Now, in an almost wholly agricultural country such as Sicily, the overwhelming majority of the middle class can only arise from agriculture, and consist only of well-to-do farmers. The problem of the remedy to Sicily's ills therefore, in the final analysis, consists in this: If and how one can put the Sicilian peasants in a condition to acquire if not the ownership of the land they work, at least a certain affluence and independence. This problem will be dealt with in the second book of this work.

2. - Conclusion

If our analysis here of the phenomena to be found in Sicily is not wholly wrong, we should conclude that they have nothing abnormal, but are necessary manifestations of the social state of the island. We would add that if there is something abnormal in Sicily, it is the intrusion of a different civilisation which seeks to impose itself and disrupts the play of the natural forces which the regular and spontaneous development of Sicilian society would otherwise have operated.

However, if we leave the historical and philosophical aspect of the question to one side, and consider the political aspect, it changes face. Sicily is part of Italy and it is not admitted that it can be separated from it. The co-existence of Sicilian civilisation and that of central and northern Italy in the same nation is incompatible with the prosperity of this nation and, in the long term, also with its existence, as it produces weakness as a result of which it risks collapsing at the slightest shock from outside. Those parts of one of these two civilisations which are incompatible with the other should therefore disappear. Which should be that which has to give way is not, we believe, the subject of any doubt for any Sicilian of good faith and average intelligence. Of course, the social conditions of central and northern Italy leave a lot to be desired from every aspect, but unarguably belong to a state of civilisation which is subsequent in time to that of Sicily. Which has to pass through a similar state if it is to progress along the same path of those societies which, according to the criteria generally accepted in Europe today, are considered the most civil and superior in condition to that of the rest of mankind. We said a similar and not identical state, as civilisation, even though equal in species and level in various countries, can also be in each of them very different in its external forms and details.

Hence, if Italy has the right to exist, it also has that of using all the means at its disposal to bring Sicily to the level of civilisation of its most advanced parts. We do not know whether such a change is possible; but if it is, the most powerful means in themselves will prove to be miserably ineffective if the Italian nation does not feel this its duty and the obligations which it imposes. We said that to save Sicily, the state should govern it without the co-operation of the Sicilians, but it cannot govern Italy without the Italians, it would therefore do best to find support in the remainder of the nation.

Which up to now has not had the feeling of its duties and its mission toward Sicily and the southern provinces in general. We have received these our younger sisters who, without thinking of the future, have thrown themselves trustingly in our arms. They were emaciated, hungry, covered with sores, and we had to treat them with love, feed them, seeking with every means, also with fire, where necessary, to re-endow them with health. Instead, without even glancing at their wounds, we put them to work, hard and fatiguing work, to realise Italy; we asked them for men and money, we gave them in return a cheap freedom, of foreign origin, and we said to them: grow and multiply. And then after fifteen years we are surprised because the sores have become gangrenous and threaten to contaminate Italy.

Now the experience of these fifteen years suffices to teach us that in the state of the southern provinces there is something unknown to us which would explain the ineffectiveness of the means of government adopted to date. It is up to the educated class of central and northern Italy and to those few of southern Italy who realise the state of their country, to seek to know what is now ignored, to impose on the government that system which such knowledge indicates as necessary. Of course, a government too could attempt by itself that which we are now asking of the nation's educated class, and spur it instead of waiting for a spur from it. But we cannot reasonably demand that ministers sacrifice the interests of their party and so-called parliamentary expediencies to the general good of Italy. This may well take place: and as in private business, so even more so in politics, it is an elementary rule of prudence not to rely on exceptional cases. While left to itself, the government, whatever its colour and party, will continue to live day by day by empirical and unprofitable remedies and, without being able nor wishing to know the ill in itself and cure it, will lose heart around some phenomenon external to this, and every time a recurrence in the symptoms of the ill threatens it with some parliamentary questions or some newspaper articles, it will show its zeal by increasing the sacrifices of money and blood, again with the same profit. And those men who on the mountains, in the woods and cities of Sicily fall under the bullets of the criminals defending a Law which does not have the means to ensure its observance, do they not have the right to ask Italy why their blood was shed in vain, why Italian politicians lack the courage to call things by their proper names in Parliament, and to shake off the yoke of that cheap doctrinairism which all adore and in which nobody believes, because the educated classes of Italy, forgetting the mission which our political order gives them, are slothful or else concern themselves and disrupt the country for paltry local interests?

Italy can certainly survive for a long time still in those same conditions in which it has lived for fifteen years. There are many organic diseases which do not lead to immediate death. But in a weak organism, full of germs of decomposition, those same reasons which in a healthy body would produce hardly perceptible effects, generate general ruin. And when this happens, the first to suffer cruelly shall be the members of that class which now does not wish to understand what responsibility and duties are imposed on it before the rest of the nation by the fact that it is almost alone in profiting from the freedom of Italy.

III - EMIGRATION

Capital Lost to Italy by Emigration Abroad*

Alberto Beneduce

The problem of the cost of emigration for the single states is of the greatest importance and recognised as such by all scholars of political economy and statistics.

For Italy it has never treated directly, nor with sufficient precision. Professor V. Pareto, based on calculations made by Dr. Engel for German emigration, believes that from 1887 to 1893 Italy lost from 400 to 450 million lire per year[1] as a result of emigration. We believe this figure exaggerated.

In view of the variations which have taken place from 1893 onwards in the biometric conditions of the population, the increase of the latter and the different composition by age of emigrants, we deem it useful to treat the problem *ex novo*.

1. - The Economic Value of Human Life

Let us start by determining the economic value of human life in Italy, in the various years of age, considering two large classes of the population of the Kingdom, namely that employed in agriculture and that of craftsmen and workers.

---

* From: BENEDUCE A., «Capitali sottratti all'Italia dall'emigrazione per l'estero», *Giornale degli Economisti*, December 1904. [Cod. JEL: N 33].

[1] See *Cours d'Économie Politique*, p. 152.

Dr. E. Raseri, based on the budgets of some families of agricultural workers and on physiological observations, has calculated[2] that the unit of consumption[3] for the agricultural population averages 50 lire. To determine the value of the unit of consumption for craftsmen, we consulted the budgets of some families of workers resulting from surveys carried out by the General Office of Statistics on the living conditions and particularly on the diet of workers and from *Cent Monographies de Familles* gathered by E. Cheysson[4] for Italy. These budgets give an average of 11 units of consumption per family against an average wage per family of 822 lire. We therefore deduce that the cost of a unit of consumption for a craftsman's family is 75 lire. Let us take these values for the units of consumption as our base and allow, as Dr. Engel states and as the observations of Professor Flügge on the average food rations for subsequent ages, that the cost of an individual increases annually by a tenth of the initial cost, such that, considering the isolated individual, by the end of age x said costs $75 + 78.75x + 3.75x^2$, or $50 + 52.5x + 2.5x^2$ according to whether he belongs to the crafts or agricultural class.

It should also be noted that the capital spent in the single years for the raising of a child could have been invested and that those surviving beyond a given age, of a given generation, should bear the costs incurred to maintain that part of the generation which has been destroyed by death before it could become economically active. Hence, if c_0, c_1, c_2 are the costs of raising at birth, during the first and during the second years of life, and if of l_0 of those born, there survive l_1, l_2 at one and two years, and we allow that for the dead $l_1 - l_0$, $l_2 - l_1$, respectively in the first and second years of life one spends 2/5 c_1, and 2/5 c_2, one has the

[2] See Raseri E., «Valore economico della vita umana in Italia calcolata per varie classi di popolazione», *Rivista d'Igiene e Sanità Pubblica*, year III, Roma, 1892.

[3] According to Engel, unit of consumption is a man's economic value at birth (the more care the mother requires during pregnancy, costs of childbirth, etc.): having chosen this value as a unit of measure, the cost of the individual in the year of age x is $1 + (x/10)$; and this until the complete physical development, namely up to 25 years. From the age of 26 onwards the cost of maintaining an individual remains constant and amounts to 3.6 units of consumption (Dr. Raseri E., *op. cit.*).

[4] See *Bulletin de l'Institut Internationale de Statistique*, Roma, 1890.

cost of a generation considered at the end of the second year of life, namely:

$$l_0c_0(1+r)^2 + \left[l_1c_1 + (l_1 - l_0)\frac{2}{5}c_1\right](1+r) + \left[l_2c_2 + (l_2 - l_1)\frac{2}{5}c_2\right]$$

and the cost of a survivor at the second year is:

$$C_2 = \frac{l_0c_0(1+r)^2 + \left[l_1c_1 + (l_1 - l_0)\frac{2}{5}c_1\right](1+r) + \left[l_2c_2 + (l_2 - l_1)\frac{2}{5}c_2\right]}{l_2}$$

Similar formulas are obtained for subsequent years of age.

Taking the aforementioned costs of units of consumption and the number of survivors in subsequent years of age, given by the survival tables calculated by the General Office of Statistics[5] on the basis of the results of the census of 10 February 1901 and the records of deaths in the period 1898-1902, we have calculated the values indicated in Table 1.

Table 1 shows that at 12 years, a person belonging to the agricultural population costs an average 1,389 lire, and at 15 years of age a person belonging to the class of craftsmen and workers costs 2,933 lire.

Let us suppose that in the agricultural class a man from the age of 12 to 22 years is economically active and produces on average as much as suffices for his raising; similarly for the class of craftsmen from 15 to 22 years of age.

Given then the aforementioned cost of raising to 22 years, we have:

$$\frac{l_{12} \times 1389 \times (1+r)^{10}}{l_{22}} \quad \text{and} \quad \frac{l_{15} \times 2933 \times (1+r)^{7}}{l_{22}}$$

5 See *Movimento della popolazione secondo gli atti dello stato civile per l'anno 1902.*

TABLE 1

Age	Annual cost		Mortality tables	Average cost from birth to single years	
	rural population	artisan population		rural population	artisan population
	lire	lire		lire	lire
0	50	100	100,000	50	75
1	55	110	83,283	122	183
2	60	120	76,908	199	299
3	65	130	74,149	281	422
4	70	140	72,695	369	554
5	75	150	71,711	464	696
6	80	160	71,065	567	851
7	85	170	70,528	680	1,020
8	90	180	70,120	802	1,203
9	95	190	69,792	932	1,398
10	100	200	69,512	1,074	1,611
11	105	210	69,256	1,226	1,839
12	110	220	69,030	1,389	2,084
13	115	230	68,802	1,565	2,348
14	120	240	68,578	1,753	2,630
15	125	250	68,320	1,955	2,933

namely 2,157 lire and 5,148 lire respectively, which is the personal capital of a person belonging to one of the two classes considered, at the start of their useful return to society.

Assuming the individual is economically active up to the age of 60, we have calculated the fixed annual quota X which each individual from 22 to 60 years of age should yield on average to society in addition to the costs of his raising. We employed the formula:

$$C_{22} = \frac{x}{l_{22}} \sum_{1}^{38} l_{22+y}(1+r)^{-y}$$

and have thus obtained that to compensate society for the costs incurred by his raising, a person from the agricultural class should contribute on average, between 22 and 60 years of age, an annual quota of 120.30 lire, and that of the craftsmen class an average annual quota of 287 lire.

2. - Emigration

There are two types of annual emigration abroad: the one consists of persons who go abroad in search of work for a period of varying length, normally no longer than one year; the other of those who go abroad in search of a job for an indefinite period of time.

We shall not deal with the first type of emigration, called periodic or temporary, here as the individuals who comprise it not only deprive the motherland of capital, but in addition to finding the means of subsistence abroad for a year, bring on their return home to their family a small nest egg, the fruit of their saving.

The second type of emigration, called proper or permanent, in 1903 consisted of 26,522 persons aged less than 14 and 204,319 persons over the age of 14.

To calculate the cost of raising these emigrants, these data were insufficient, and to obtain classes of emigrants by more restricted age brackets, we assumed, in the absence of data regarding Italy, that the distribution by age group of Italian emigrants is akin to those of the German empire for whom there is a more detailed classification[6].

As a result, we have classified the emigration from Italy in 1903 as follows:

TABLE 2

Less than 10	10-14	14-20	21-29	30-49	50 upwards	Total
21,488	5,034	48,136	89,847	53,890	12,446	230,841

The Emigration Commission[7], with the elements at its disposal, gives a further classification of Italian emigrants aged less than 10 and thus we were able to divide the group of 21,488 emigrants below that age limit in proportion to the data published in the Commission's *Bollettino*, as in Table 3.

[6] See *Statistica dell'emigrazione*, 1903.
[7] See *Bollettino dell'emigrazione*, no. 3.

TABLE 3

Less than 1	1-4	5-9	10-13	14-20	21-29	30-49	50 upwards	Total
2,638	9,293	9,557	5,034	48,136	89,847	53,890	12,446	230,841

We could have employed interpolation to derive even more limited age groups, but the problem's nature allows only approximate solutions and we therefore retained the classification by age in the groups indicated in Table 3 only.

We attributed each individual of each economically passive group the average cost of that of the years included between the group's bounds.

For the groups 14-21, 21-30, 30-50 years, we chose 18, 25 and 38 respectively as the starting age of the emigrants.

We took no account whatsoever of the group of emigrants aged over 50, assuming that the duration of their economic activity suffices solely to compensate the country to which they emigrate for the costs incurred for their maintenance when older, when they will once again be economically passive. Finally, we assume, as indicated by official statistics, that 80% of Italian emigrants consists of farmhands or peasants, and the remainder of craftsmen, workers and small traders.

Classified by condition and age, the composition of Italian emigration in 1903 was as shown in Table 4.

TABLE 4

Age	Rural population	Artisan population	Total
Less than 1	2,110	528	2,638
From 1 to 4	7,434	1,859	9,293
From 5 " 9	7,646	1,911	9,557
From 10 " 13	4,027	1,007	5,034
From 14 " 20	38,506	9,630	48,136
From 21 " 29	71,877	17,970	89,847
From 30 " 49	43,110	10,780	53,890
From 50 upwards	9,956	2,490	12,446
			230,841

The average cost of each individual of each group considered, taking into account the greater value of raising for the interest paid on the production capital for the 14-21 year group, and for the 21-30 and 30-50 year groups, the annual quotas of benefit (in relation to that of the generation to which they belong) already given to society, in Italy, are shown in Table 5.

TABLE 5

Age	Rural population average cost lire	Artisan population average cost lire
Less than 1	86	129
From 1 to 4	287	432
From 5 " 9	811	1,218
From 10 " 13	1,389	2,085
From 14 " 20	1,758	3,252
From 21 " 29	1,804	4,305
From 30 upwards	774	1,848

And so the approximate cost of raising those Italians who emigrated in 1903 is as shown in Table 6.

TABLE 6

Age	Emigrant rural population	Unit cost lire	Overall cost lire	Emigrant artisan population	Unit cost lire	Overall cost lire	Total of the two classes lire
Less than 1	2,110	86	181,460	528	129	68,112	249,572
From 1 to 4	7,434	287	2,133,558	1,859	432	803,088	2,936,446
From 5 " 9	7,646	811	6,200,906	1,911	1,218	2,327,598	8,528,504
From 10 " 13	4,027	1,389	5,593,503	1,007	2,085	2,099,595	7,693,098
From 14 " 20	38,506	1,758	67,693,548	9,630	3,252	31,316,760	99,010,308
From 21 " 29	71,877	1,804	129,666,108	17,970	4,305	77,360,850	207,026,958
From 30 " 49	43,112	774	33,368,688	10,782	1,848	19,925,136	53,293,824
						total	378,738,910

In round figures one can say that the average annual cost of Italian emigration, as personal capital, amounts to 380 million lire.

To the personal capital lost to Italy by each emigrant one should add the personal goods and chattels he takes with him.

This element is difficult to determine; but as the sad economic conditions in which almost all our emigrants find themselves at the moment of departure are well known, no significant error would be committed if we were to conclude that they took with them the minimum indispensable to reach the United States or Argentina, the states to which our migratory flow is at present strongest.

Taking account of the average cost of the passage and the amount of dollars which each emigrant should have with him so as not to be declared a pauper and therefore sent back by the Amercian Confederation, we can estimate that on average each emigrant of any age entails the loss of 200 lire in goods and chattels for the homeland. It should be borne in mind however that many leave because they have been summonsed by relatives or friends, who buy the emigrant's ticket in America; such emigrants are known are 'prepaids', and are those most exploited by the shipping companies, as there are no provisions protecting them in the law of 31 January 1901 which regulates relations between carriers and emigrants in Italy.

In the General Commission for Emigration's report to the Ministry of Foreign Affairs[8], Senator L. Bodio calculated that in 1903 prepaids amounted to 27% of total emigrants and, bearing in mind that they are exonerated from the obligation to own 10 dollars as mentioned above, we calculate the loss of aforementioned goods and chattels only on the remaining 73%. We therefore estimate the annual loss of goods and chattels in 33,702,786.34 million lire in round figures.

Hence, if all those who have applied for a passport for transoceanic countries or have stated they are leaving for an indefinite period were never to return to their homeland, or, in other words, if the permanent emigration was truly such for Italy, it would cost our country 414 million lire per year, if the flow recorded in 1903 was to continue. But the classification of emigration into permanent and temporary has an uncertain and relative significance and even the General Office of Statistics has renounced maintaining it in the surveys it has carried out on this social phenomenon start-

[8] See *Bollettino dell'emigrazione*, no. 7, year 1904.

ing from 1904. Many individuals who stated that they were leaving indefinitely when the passport was issued, after a stay abroad of varying duration, returned to their homeland, induced by both the changed economic conditions of the country to which they emigrated[9] and as they had put together a small nest egg and perhaps also as a result of nostalgia for their homeland, even though it does not know how to feed them. Neither is there any shortage of individuals who in the same year go to and return from America, collecting the harvest in Argentina during the winter season when in their homeland they would find only cold and hunger - thus managing to better provide for their families' needs.

If we examine the statistics on returns from transoceanic countries, we find that in 1900-1903, after a long passage in third class, 376,929 individials disembarked in the ports of the Kingdom, while in the same year 1,001,150 persons left. As the majority of those who returned to the Kingdom by sea travelling in third class were undoubtedly Italians returning home, thus their number can be calculated as 37% of those leaving. We will not stray too far from the truth if we say that a third of those who leave each year, for different reasons and in different conditions, return back to Italy. Hence from the amount of personal capital calculated above we should deduct that which, in little different conditions of economic potential, returned. Carrying out said reduction, we reach the conclusion that Italy loses the round figure of 287 million lire per year as a result of emigration abroad.

3. - Benefits of Emigration

While it was possible to reduce the economic loss from emigration to figures we believe sufficiently approximate, given the complexity of the problem we are studying, it is not similarly possible for us to determine with sufficient accuracy the economic benefits of emigration itself. Their nature is such that they elude

[9] The number of emigrants who have returned to Italy from Brazil was in 1903 nearly triple the number of departures, namely 274%.

a statistical survey. We shall seek, to the extent such is possible, to enumerate and quantify them.

4. - Remittances from Emigrants

It is commonly held, and confirmed by everyday life, that most of the money which arrives and is traded in the agricultural centres, particularly in southern Italy, derives from remittances from transoceanic countries. Families of peasants who have never before seen a gold coin, now own a small plot of land, a house, and promote that division of land which should be the primary source of southern Italy's agricultural and economic resurgence. The money reaches Italy by a multitude of paths: and it is this diversity of the means and also the complication of the phenomenon due to commercial bills, which make it impossible to furnish an accurate estimate of remittances from emigrants.

It is true that the post offices gather the savings of emigrants and that for two years now Banco di Napoli has offered a transfer service, but it is also common knowledge that, given the extraordinary number of grabbing bankers who infest the centres most populated by Italian emigrants, the money handed over to them is paid in Italy by various banks or trading houses. Neither should one disregard the money which is remitted monthly, included in registered letters, nor that which the emigrants bring with them on their return.

At the end of 1903, our emigrants had deposited circa 56 million lire of savings at post offices and remittances through Banco di Napoli amounted to circa 24 million lire; but when one takes into account all the other paths by which money immigrates into Italy, the figure of 200 million lire per year, which those competent estimate is the overall amount of sums which enter Italy as savings made by our emigrants abroad[10], appears quite feasible.

Thus the direct loss for Italy would be reduced from 287 to

[10] See the *Report* of the Parliamentary Commission on the Emigration Fund (Prepared by Hon. EDUARDO PANTANO).

87 million lire: eschewing any assessment of the beneficial influence of this movement of capital on the trend of the exchange rates in particular and in general on the improved conditions of the national economy.

5. - Increase in Sea Trade

One of the most striking phenomena, a beneficial effect of emigration, is the progressive and considerable increase in the sea trade of our principal ports. Steamships flying foreign flags compete with those flying the Italian flag in the industry of transporting emigrants, offering Italy direct means of fast communication for the human good, and, more importantly, cheap means of transport for all imported, exported and transit goods. This is unarguably a far from negligible coefficient in the conditions which the port of Genoa wields against the port of Marseilles in the struggle for the supremacy of sea trade in the Mediterranean. One should also note the greater knowledge of products and markets, the spirit of entrepreneurship of our fellow countrymen who have settled in distant regions, the usages and habits which they have transported there: all these circumstances help explain, to cite figures, how Italian exports to the United States and Canada, which amounted to 73 million lire in 1891, rose to 118 million lire in 1902[11]. And one should particularly note the very significant growth of exports, particularly to United States, of popular consumption goods demanded by those markets almost exclusively by our compatriots, such that Italy exported circa 40 million lire of wines, spirits, alcoholic drinks, pasta, legumes, cheeses, fruit, tobacco, medicines in 1902[12]. Neither are the direct revenues, for paid freight, which emigration generates for Italy's merchant navy, by any means negligible. However, despite the efforts of our shipyards, only 41% of emigrants are transported by steamships flying the Italian flag, and of the 55 mil-

[11] See *Annuario statistico*, 1904.

[12] See *Statistica del commercio speciale d'importazione ed esportazione* - Direzione generale delle gabelle.

lion lire of fees which the movement of Italian emigrants to and from transoceanic countries generates for the means of transport, circa 23 million lire return to Italian traffic.

6. - Indirect Benefits of Emigration

Emigration is of exceptional importance for Italy's demographic trend, principally with regard to the country's economic conditions.

The increase in the population, its civil progress, the progressive increase in workers' needs has not been matched, at least for some regions of Italy, by a more suitable cultivation of the land, a development of the industries related to said, a more equitable distribution of the profits between capital and labour, and yet there have been plethoras of discontented workers, seized by the fever of emigrating across the ocean, attracted by the mirage of higher wages, which in those more industrious countries are offered to those with strong arms and the habit of work.

One repercussion, however, has been that as the supply of labour has fallen in many provinces of the Kingdom and in particular in southern Italy, wages have increased and the owners have been spurred also by this to adopt more rational rotation in the cultivation of the soil, to introduce the use of agricultural machinery and to put that small amount of capital which had to date had been idle in state notes to better use.

It is to be hoped that soon everyone will be convinced that the worker of the land should be considered not as a mere instrument, but as a valid co-operator in the production of the land, and that said co-operation will be more efficacious the more the labour is intellectually advanced.

7. - Conclusion

From the balance sheet of Italian emigration which we have illustrated without any preconceived notions and with the greatest possible accuracy, one can draw the conclusion that emigration is, in Italy's present conditions, economically beneficial. When one then considers that the annual surplus of births over the dead is constant in Italy (averaging 10.50 every 1,000 inhabitants from 1893 to 1902); that the density of the population of 113 inhabitants per square kilometre, at 10 February 1901, was less only than that calculated for England, Belgium and the Netherlands, whose industrial and commercial development is incomparably superior to ours; that the number of agricultural workers has not decreased in the Kingdom since 1882, despite the strong movement of emigration abroad and internal migration to the big cities, which has been recorded particularly in this class of the population[13]; and when one considers, finally, that the aforementioned benefits of emigration are almost exclusively the natural effect of this phenomenon, as the government has to date done almost nothing to increase it, then we do not believe it misplaced to express the hope that the state, with the funds of its budget and with those taken from the misery which is disappearing to endow us with wealth, is more efficient in protecting our emigration, indicates the path to follow and offers its material and moral aid in the lands which Italian blood helps make fertile and populate.

[13] On 1 January 1882 8,566,467 persons of both sexes and aged 9 upwards were employed in agriculture, on 10 February 1901 9,611,003 persons.

The Cost of Production of Man and the Economic Value of Emigrants*

Francesco Coletti

1. – The article «Capital Lost to Italy by Emigration Abroad» published in the December 1904 issue of *Giornale degli Economisti* revived in me an old intellectual rancour, if I can thus express myself, against the theory which is applied in that article and which consists in determining the losses suffered by a country as a result of the emigration of adults or death of children according to their respective cost of upbringing. My rancour originates from the sharp contrast the theory caused in my mind as a result of the fact that while I saw it developed and applied with such certainty by numerous and famous economists and statisticians, I nonetheless was unable to shed my radical objections against it[1].

I am therefore unable to resist the opportunity I now have to expound a part, at least, of my observations. In view of the complexity of the argument, which, contrary to what would appear from the simplistic theory here confuted, is linked to some of the most profound questions of political economy, I have to confine myself to points which more directly lie within my critical purpose.

---

* From: COLETTI F., «Il costo di produzione dell'uomo e il valore economico degli emigranti», *Giornale degli Economisti*, March 1905, pp. 260-91. [Cod. JEL: N 33].

[1] A voluminous bibliography of the works which deal with the theory of the valuation of man is given in RICCA-SALERNO, *La teoria del salario, etc.*, Palermo, Reber, 1900, pp. 216-8. One should add: MARSHALL, *Principles of Economics*, last edn., note 313; BENINI, *Demografia*, p. 61; RASERI, «Valore econ. della vita umana», *Rivista d'Igiene e Sanità Pubblica*, year III, 1892. See also several issues of the *Bulletin de l'Inst. Inter. de Stat.*

2. - In treating the theory in question, modern authors generally refer to Ernst Engel, who more than any other developed it *ex professo* and used it widely in his country, Prussia[2]. We shall therefore call it Engel's theory, even though, in reality, it is not only theory, but method and theory combined.

It would be pointless to re-expound Engel's theory here, also because it is outlined in the cited article in the latest issue of *Giornale degli Economisti*. We should however immediately indicate the point which is of particular interest to us. The calculation of the cost of production of man, even though it is sometimes applied to industrial, bureaucratic, groups, etc., is usually however referred to that which Engel calls the «most numerous class»[3].

This sort of partiality is explained by the purpose for which the subtle survey is often attempted, namely to determine the loss a country suffers as a result of emigration, which mainly takes place among that class. The calculation which one undertakes to ascertain the loss caused by child mortality, particularly of the poor classes, can be said to derive by analogy from the first topic of investigation, which impacts the interests of the capitalists, landowners and the state more directly, above all as could be inferred from it for the emigration policy.

However, although the calculation of the worker's cost of production and the application of it to emigration (which is the application to which we shall confine ourselves) are as though born together, it is necessary to resolutely distinguish and separate one from the other.

The most radical objections made concerning Engel's theory refer not so much to the first operation, separately considered, as to the application of the second and the conclusion which is drawn.

---

[2] See ENGEL, *Der Preis der Arbeit*, Berlin, 1866 (Collection dell'Holtzendorff): «Der Preis der Arbeit im Preussischen Staatsienste in Jahre 1875», *Zeitschrift des k. preuss. Statist. Bureaus*, Berlin, 1876.

[3] In the first of the studies cited in the previous note, Engel calculates the cost value of the labour of an ordinary worker, of the superior industrialist, of the public official, etc. But basically his attention is principally directed to the ordinary worker.

3. - In view of the target of my objections, I shall dwell on the scientific possibility of statistically surveying the cost of upbringing, education, and training working-class children only to the extent that suffices to show how I wish to consider the matter.

The difficulty, or main shortcoming of the survey in question consists, as in many other surveys and in many other statistical calculations, in this: that we cannot take account of a certain number of elements which in actual fact are part of the phenomenon studied, and we cannot do this for two principal reasons, namely that the need to isolate the phenomenon implies the need to abandon some elements which in reality are linked to it and that several other elements, by their nature, elude the investigation and the numerical expression.

I will furnish two proofs or specific illustrations which I believe quite characteristic of this distinct order of reasons.

Firstly, statistics indicate the subsequent annual costs of the child, young man and adult man, resorting to various elements which are at times heterogeneous, such as the data of monographs on families and the computations of physiology and chemistry laboratories, etc. on the average quantities of materials consumed by the specific bodies. Thus one calculates the liabilities side of the balance sheet of raising a human being. On the asset side, one usually includes the contributions of work and earnings (the two contributions are sometimes inappropriately assimilated, as I shall explain below), which the young worker will begin to generate more or less prematurely, depending on whether he is a peasant or a craftsman.

Now, my question is this. In the reality of social life, does not the birth of children, which entails new outlays, give rise to other phenomena? Statistics cannot always show them; but direct observation, either simple or by survey, uncovers and indicates them. The growth of the family (here is the popular phase we hear repeated many times) reacts on some, at least, of the components of the family which are capable of working, inducing them to take some job, or else to employ themselves in more productive work, furthermore, it generally determines a more healthy and useful distribution of the expenses of the household budget, through the forgoing or limitation of certain voluptuary consumptions. Many will have heard it said of some worker that he is no longer seen, suddenly, drinking out: «He's got wise, he's got a growing family to think about».

Should the greater employment and the greater production determined by said reason, the no longer unproductive use of a certain part of the income not be included among the assets of the balance sheet of man's production, for the same substantial reason for which we see «the capital spent in the single years» and which «could have been put to profit» included among the liabilities? We are not talking, it should be noted, of isolated cases; but rather of a phenomenon of general importance which is now well ascertained by means of statistical deductions, surveys, papers on families: when the children reach a certain number, the work of the women and youngsters is necessary to augment the insufficient earnings of the father; indeed, this new supply of female and child labour is also related to the introduction of machinery, one of the capitalistic methods of struggle with the working classes[4]. Does this wish to isolate so unilaterally, for the sole reasons of statistical techniques, so broad and complex a phenomenon such as the social cost of human production by branches and connections not imply, in truth, disregard of the interdependence of these phenomena?

An important kind of elements which statistics does not succeed in recording is given by the care the mother and the other

[4] Numerous documents, such as monographs on households, surveys, etc., indicate that the employment of a family's women and children is often contemporary to the increase of the children, which (as appears from the budgets of 600 worker families in Alsace and Lorraine) «at the birth of the third child incur debts and poverty and the subsidiary earnings of the wife become indispensable». (See: CHEYSSON - TOQUÈ A., «Les Budg. de Cent Mon. de Fam.», *Bull. de l'Inst. intern. de Stat.* (Vol. V, p. 82 ff); SINGER, *Untersuchungen über dei socialen Zuständein den Fabrikbezirken*, etc., Leipzig, 1885, pp. 130-2; RICCA-SALERNO, *op. cit.*, p. 158 ff, replete with data confirming our assertion in the text. Noteworthy, also because it comes from a professional statistician such as G. Rümelin, is the following observation: «The cost of upbringing and, in general, the education of the growing generation are not borne by the social wealth, but rather by the social income; it is arbitrary to hold that where they did not have to be made, the respective sum would have been saved and the social wealth would have been increased. One was forced to work more and to enjoy less, that is all». («Teoria della popolazione», *Bibl. dell'Econ.*, series III, vol. XIII, p. 1062).

family members dedicate to the upbringing of the children. This care is, economically, pure services. In the homes of the well-off and rich, some of them, starting from wet-nursing, have a quite specific price which can be included among the costs without any trouble. But can this usually be done for the working class? We believe not, unless one of the children is brought up in the foundling hospitals, etc., where everything can be said to be listed and priced.

The size of the influence of this cost element, i.e., of the varying degrees of care and love employed to bring up the children, is indicated to us, albeit as part of other concurrent causes, by the all too well known higher mortality of illegitimate children as compared with their legitimate counterparts. There sounds here one of the sentimental notes of statistics[5].

There are, furthermore, several technical faults in said calculations of the cost of man, which derive from the very complexity of the phenomenon.

In deducing the single elements of the cost, if I am not mistaken, the expense which the upbringing of children entails for the family budget, i.e., from the subjective point of view of the family unit, is not always clearly distinguished from the true and proper outlay or social cost, that is to say the consumption of wealth which said upbringing entails, objectively, for the national economy. The same holds for the earnings of the children because there would appear to be some confusion between the earnings corresponding to work or a service actually provided by the child and a mere shifting of wealth which it causes in its own favour (by way of public or private charity, by theft, etc.).

The same reasons lie behind the lack of statistical accuracy of the average of the costs in the first, second, third years of age, and so forth. Such general averages, as those which are offered, suppress the characters and measure of the costs, differing by place, trades, family conditions, number of children, and other

[5] As MARSHALL (*op. cit.*, n. 313) notes with exquisite delicacy: «The most precious of all capitals is that invested in human beings, and of that capital the most precious part is the result of the maternal care and influence...».

and very varying circumstances. These elements would instead be of importance to us if they were conserved. The number of births, higher in one village than in another, and hence, perhaps, the correlative greater number of emigrants or dead infants can depend on those characters and that measure of the cost of upbringing which are eliminated. It follows that the homogeneity of the elements assembled for evaluating the emigrants or dead children is impaired.

Not by way of easy criticism, but only to draw attention to a fact which supports my doubts, I would point out that quite a few of the writers who have applied to other villages the calculation of the cost of production of the workers have availed themselves, *faute de mieux*, as one of them confesses, of the same cost figures (100 marks before and during the birth) and same proportion of annual increases (10% per year) that the old director of Prussian statistics had used for his country[6].

An even more various and numerous series of theoretical and technical difficulties would arise if we wished to extend the principle of calculating the economic value of human life to the periods of life which come after the first. There would be little objection to such an extension. Once admitted, the principle should not suffer restrictions in its application. The difficulties to be overcome can only be technical.

If we develop Engel's theory, we see that the first phase should be followed, in a typical worker's life path, by at least six other phases: that in which a part of the individual's cost of production is compensated by the labour or services he supplies; that in which the cost of the worker and his production equal one another; that in which the individual produces more than he consumes and thus the social capital invested in his person is amortised more rapidly (this is the phase in which the worker usually starts a family and saves for when he is older); that in which the individual, declining in age and health, once again consumes more than he pro-

[6] It should be noted that RASERI (*art. cit.*) has very appropriately calculated for Italy special units of consumption for workers of both the countryside and those of the cities.

duces; that which completes the cycle and which touches the other extreme from where the cycle started, when man no longer produces and lives on the social wealth (disregarding the private distribution of this, a part of which can be the savings fund created by the worker during the period of maximum production).

Each of these phases should theoretically and technically have a special treatment, as regards both the cost or the individual's function in the national economy, and the loss or otherwise the emigration of persons belonging to one or the other category would cause to the country of origin. The interdependence of one phase on another would complicate and broaden enormously the problem, much more (as is evident) as would appear to he who confines himself to considering only the first period of human life. For example, to what extent would the expectation of old age serve to stimulate more work and savings in the productive age? How do the fiscal revenues which the state allocates for the aged and those unable to work, such as those in favour of technical education, etc., react and affect a country's economy and those of the single individuals?

Now we believe that quite a few of these and numerous other elements which should be included in the balance sheet would elude not only the statistical knowledge of the cost of the individual, taken in isolation, but would be difficult to distinguish and measure also by an analysis which confined itself to verbal and qualitative expressions and considered the phenomenon in its objective connections in space and time.

Let us therefore conclude our observations on this first of the Engelian operations, which is not technically impossible by itself, but certainly more complex and manifold than would appear if we satisfied ourselves with units of consumption and the other expedients which we see used. Some of the practical difficulties can be overcome, it is legitimate to assume, thanks to the progress, now so rapid, in gathering data and technical elaborations. But it would always be one of those statistical operations in which the figures by themselves do not shine, but have absolute need of limitations, specifications, qualifications, precisely as is the case of some books in which the text is well exceeded, in length, by the notes.

4. - What however can be stated as disputable and denied is this: that one can survey the economic value of emigration and the consequent economic loss to the country of origin on the basis of the emigrants' cost of production, indeed, more radically, that this problem can be proposed and resolve itself in the terms and according to the logical scheme adopted by the followers of the theory under question.

My criticisms are therefore not of a statistical nature, as some of those mentioned above, but relate back to the more general principles of economics: they tend to deprive the statistical construct of that base it uses as a support and cannot disregard.

Engel's theory is wholly founded on these two presuppositions: that the loss to the mother country from emigration is related to the economic value the emigrants represent, that this value corresponds to the cost of production of the emigrants themselves.

The two propositions are considered as two inseparable parts of a reasoning. And it is in this relationship, in this interdependence that I espy the equivocation or fundamental flaw of Engel's theory.

The equivocation consists in considering the worker, the personal capital, as nothing more or less than the compound capitals of wealth which, solely for reasons of brevity, now and henceforth we shall call material capital (chattels and property). The former are talked of as though they were the latter, imagining, as shown that the general laws of value do not apply in the group of phenomena considered by us and are not implemented with special forms and attitudes in the former and the latter case.

In material capital, value is directly related to cost and return. On this point, as on others, we can only speak within the limits of the maximum generalisation, without distinguishing the diminishing from the increasing costs, etc., we mention the theories for that part which they are involved in the economics of the proof. It is competition, with a well-known series of actions and reactions, which relates the phenomena of value, cost, return. Capitalising the return allows one to deduce the capital value of the capital good, just as from the capital value, considering a specific market at a specific time, one can obtain the return. The psychological measure of the cost (physical and mental effort) is not known: given the egoistic or hedonistic nature of man, the cost of capital will proportion itself to their value. It should be noted however that Engel intended by cost the sum of the outlays or goods employed to obtain the capital considered. This does not matter. With one or the other notion of the cost concept, we can state indifferently that Engel's theory would not encounter any obstacles if applied to the evaluation of the export of given quotas of material capitals and not to the exodus of men.

In free men, considered as personal capital, the phenomena are more complicated and we shall not quickly finish if we wished to highlight and contrast them with those of material capital[7]. The worker (to speak, brevitatis causa, of this) does not sell himself, he sells the useful manifestation of his physical-mental force, labour. By means of this and with this he enters into combination with the other complementary and capital goods of economic complexes.

---

[7] Material capital (to point out some differences) is formed and maintained with the direct and sole intent of obtaining an economic advantage (overlooking the exceptions). Man however enters this world without the parents, generally speaking, considering him as a good to be exploited: the personal capital is exploited by that very individual who incorporates it, when one considers a man's entire productive span. The Sicilian sulphur miners and certain categories of farm workers who procreate with the idea of almost immediately profiting from the work of the children are exceptions: they represent a phenomena of supply and demand. The parents who spend for their children and invest their savings in the children, with an eye of the remunerative jobs to which they are destined, are another phenomenon of supply and demand, but the imaginary equation between cost of education and future earning is undermined by the variability of the type and value of the elements which comprise education and by the variability of the economic circumstances from the period of formation of the personal capital to the period when it is put to work. The aims of the parents who spend for their children and those who spend for their own education are not solely economic, because satisfying certain needs can be an end in itself, it is one of the manifestations of physical and psychological life, both individual and of the family. In the other sphere of goods, the mentioned moral forces should be considered as unnatural and disruptive circumstances. Material capital is amorphous and can run from one pole to the other of the world either physically or in its economic equivalence. Labour cannot be separated from who produces it, and the latter can decide on his home, on emigration out of sentiments and individual criteria which differ from the purely utilitarian and economic criteria which reign in the field of non-personal capital. Personal capital forms slowly, remains always what it is, namely labour, as it is not always transformed into its productive qualities (special skills or trades, etc.). For all these and other similar reasons, the correspondence between cost of production, value, return, cannot be assumed as an *a priori* rule in personal capital. There are also all the other reasons which are developed in the article, in the third and subsequent sections.

It is labour therefore, which will have a utility, a value. It is in this distinction between the worker's labour and personality, between the value and cost of the labour, and the value and cost of this personality, that there lie the difficulties, the unknowns of the problem which we should resolve in the criticism of Engel's theory.

This point in fact gives rise to a whole series of problems, of which the following are the most important. Assuming that the worker does have a value in himself, is the norm by which one establishes the value of the worker equal to that with which one establishes the value of the labour? Do the worker and labour have two different costs? Is it the worker who imposes, by reason of his value, the value on labour, or vice versa?

Engel resolved the complex question very simply, as the assimilation made of man with the material capital immediately suggested, indeed imposed the solution: the value of man is related to the cost of his upbringing and education, the value of labour to the value of man. Basically, he did not resolve, but rather eluded the fundamental problem, considered in the terms in which we have proposed it, as he did not economically distinguish labour from the being which produces it.

Here are the propositions which we can put forward in support of our thesis.

If it is the labour (or man as he works, not as merely a living being who consumes) which enters in the productive contract with a country's economic combinations, it is the labour, we repeat, which has a value. Its value can only be given by its efficiency, by its productivity, meaning by efficiency or productivity the concrete, not potential, expression of man's physical-mental energy (labour force). But its productivity only manifests itself when associated with other goods (so as to consider only the fundamental cases, disregarding the cases of labour not associated to other elements). Its value will therefore be included in the total value of the economic complex to which it contributes and, if it were possible to measure in isolation the productivity of one or the other of the goods of said complex, the labour's share of the total productivity would be related to this productivity.

But, as it is a value, labour should have a corresponding cost. This will consist, in accordance with the concept previously applied to material capital, in the exertion, the effort which labour in itself implies.

Let us therefore summarise on the basis of the scheme of the problems posed.

Of the worker and of labour, it is labour alone which has a value. The worker, if he did not produce labour, for us, economically, would not have a value, unless he was considered a negative value. If one wished to hypothesise the capitalisation of the return, i.e., the value of the labour, one could conclude that the value of the man would be no more or less than the result of this very hypothetical capitalisation. The first fact (value of labour) would transform itself into a second fact (value of the worker). The deduction could not go beyond this exterior, extrinsic, contingent relation or parallel of equivalence.

5. - But is it not possible that Engel's theory and that we have opposed to it, albeit starting from different points, would meet in the same effect, namely that the value of man, determined as equal to the outlays which he has cost, corresponds to the similar value, determined as equal to the productivity of the expressed labour?

It is of no import that in this quick parallel, we have not opposed the precise figures of the cost of human production which Engel places before us thanks to his calculation, with anything but mere verbal expression. It is possible to prove, all the same, with greater certainty, that the two theories cannot reach a common point, and to prove it with three differing and heterogeneous orders of reasons: those regarding the logical and technical concept of the two theories, for economic-social reasons and for physio-psychological reasons.

Firstly, of the asset and liability side of the worker's balance sheet, Engel considers only the liability side in as much and to the extent this is still not amortised by the productive industriousness exercised by the worker, while we consider the opposite side, the asset side, which can reveal itself in the productive combinations, in which the labour participates, in a given moment of the national economy. The nature of Engel's method is therefore antithetic to ours.

It suffices for us to note that what appears a paradox to us is inherent in the method, that the loss caused by emigration is greater the less the emigrant produced, and the less the more the emigrant produced. The paradox, indeed, would find itself bounded by these two extremes: that the maximum damage to the native land would derive from the emigration of those who have still to start producing, while there would be no loss if the emigrant was a worker in the prime of his vigour and industriousness, should he already have repaid the capital of upbringing, etc., accumulated in his person. Neither is it worthwhile insisting and pointing out other numerous and blaring incongruities and contradictions with reality which, if I am not mistaken, clash even with that kind of economic common sense which is so alive and widespread among the common people, particularly the peasants, where the real individual is, in many aspects, similar to the abstraction of the rigid economic man[8].

The productivity of labour (and here is the economic reason) which determines the value of the latter, cannot be assumed, a priori, to be related to the cost of production of the personal capital. It depends on the quantity and intensity with which the human labour is employed in the single productive combinations and in the complex of national production, comparative to the quantity and intensity of the other associated complementary and capital goods (land and other natural goods, raw material capital, technical capital, etc.). This proportion of employment is, in turn, determined (to express it in the most succinct, and hence most approx-

---

[8] As here I have insufficient space to develop the observation, I take the liberty of referring the reader, whose curiosity may have been aroused, to a short paper of mine: *La psicologia del contadino e il progresso nell'agricoltura*, Piacenza, stab. tip. Porta, 1905, p. 8 ff. I note, among other things, that the peasant, particularly in countries which practise sharecropping, considers the family as a true economic association, in which everyone is valued according to what they produce. Children are often desired because they produce an early return. The disappearance of the unproductive old is little regretted. They are a useless mouth which no longer eats, this is sometimes the funeral oration heard at the tomb of some old peasants.

imate, formula possible) by the constant effort of the entrepreneur to produce at the least cost and by the indirect effects of the struggle for the highest remuneration fought by the classes which own the goods which are not productive unless jointly associated and co-ordinated. These two types of causes are interdependent on one another: the progressive exploitation of the natural forces and the increase of increasingly perfected technical capital makes it possible to restrict the quantity and function of human labour and, by means of said restriction, to contend with the workers' demands. It is in the vast and eventful ambit of these phenomena of the distribution of wealth which are, in effect, but special attitudes of the general law of value and economic equilibrium, that there lies the objective reason for our rejection of Engel's system.

The third order of reasons lies in the physio-mental nature of men, which has the widest variety from individual to individual, as regards physical force, aptitudes, intellect, moral resistance, adaptability, etc. It is of no consequence to note the differences of sex, as Engel's theory could calculate a cost of production for the male and one for the female. What is of interest to us however is this, that the same dose of cost will develop degrees of productivity (muscular, intellectual, moral) which differ according to the physical-mental endowments of the individuals in which they are invested. We can therefore deduce that the scale of costs of production of a series of individuals will not correspond at all, by virtue of this fact, regardless of the other causes, to the scale of real productivity of the individuals themselves, to their single value, which should manifest itself in the productive complexes, and to the damage of their emigration.

It cannot be said to what extraordinary series of combinations this differentiating cause gives rise in the reality of life. Tizio will not have become what he virtually could have become because the doses of capital (quantity, type of education and upbringing, availability of books, instruments, comforts, etc.) invested in him were not sufficient. The public, who sees the completed fact, will say that Tizio is less strong, intelligent, able than Caio, who, furnished with sufficient means, will have the fortune to develop his aptitudes to the full. Tizio's cost and return will not have any proportionality with

Caio's cost and return solely, precisely, because (again disregarding the other general reasons) that which was spent for Tizio did not combine with his natural assets or faculties in the necessary proportions and direction). Alongside the many persons of the so-called upper classes, which are worth little even though they cost a lot (which is almost a popular saying, and can serve as a spontaneous confutation of the equation between the cost of production and the value of man), how many persons on the other hand will be counted, particularly in the lower classes, who die taking with them very powerful moral, intellectual energies which remained latent and were not rendered fertile and appropriately elaborated by certain forms of capital (upbringing, education, etc.)!

The combinations to which the investment of capital in individuals differing by faculty (I was about to say by fertility) of different degree, from a given maximum to a minimum, had elegant connections, as regards the phenomena of value, with the theory (Marshall) of producer's surplus, whose classical case is David Riccardo's theory of land rent[9].

A mention of the phenomena which will be determined by the natural diversities of the labour forces, of the ability of the slaves themselves in a slave economy finds a rightful mention in our arguments. It will be seen that Engel's theory is applicable, in the normal cases, to the cost of production and the value of the salves, and this because economically the slaves can be assimilated to material capital, e.g., to the capital from which Engel deduced the norm to be applied to free men.

---

[9] We would point out immediately, for reasons of clarity, that the connections, which we mention are only indirect when they refer to the concepts we developed in the theory of the value of labour and of the worker. We believe, in fact, that the value of labour is determined by its efficiency in the productive combinations with the other goods, and said value cannot be considered directly dependent on the wage with which it is remunerated. We shall see this better in the text (section VI). The producer's surplus (we shall not speak of the producer's quasi-surplus so as not to complicate the digression) referred to the workers' aptitudes and abilities, only manifests itself, on the other hand, in an exchange economy, through the wage, which is the term with which the cost of labour will be compared, which here we assume as varied, on equal return, from one to another group of workers, differing by ability. I would cite, as regards Marshall's producer's surplus, JANNACCONE's «Prefazione» to vols IX and X of *Bibl. dell'Econ.*, series IV, page 63 ff.

We can reason on the basis of two distinct hypotheses.

If the supply of slaves runs below that of the demand, if the market is capable of absorbing also the slave with the lowest physical and acquired qualities, this unfortunate slave will be sold according to the cost of production. It is to be assumed, therefore, that if the labour and services of this slave were not valued according to the outlay borne by his raiser, the latter would not have incurred them.

If instead the supply of slaves is not less than the demand and the profession of slave raiser is open to all, then the raiser will find himself forced to renounce the Ricardian surpluses received under the foregoing hypothesis. If he did demand to receive them, he would receive from the complex of the enterprise a profit superior to that of the capital invested in other industries. But then he would soon find himself exposed to the competition of the other entrepreneurs, who would crowd in the slave enterprise, such that the conditions needed for the continuity of the surplus would disappear. The raiser therefore, in the foregoing hypothesis, would be satisfied with giving the slaves he owns a price, one by one, such that the sum of the single sales gives a total which corresponds to the overall cost of production incurred and to the current profit of a country's industrial capital.

If therefore in the first hypothesis Engel's theory could not find application, except in the extreme slave, in the second, on the other hand, it appears applicable as soon as one considers, as one should, the series of slave enterprises. This is an indirect proof of what was said above regarding the origin of the fundamental equivocation of the confuted theory.

But before concluding on the study outlined in this section, we should note the influence actually exercised by the capital which is spent to educate the working classes, to develop them and to specialise their aptitudes and technical skills.

Above all, man without any labour skill would not be an economic good. The untrained horse does not belong to the category of economic goods. In a civil society, the quality of personal capital is the same as owning the admission ticket to the world labour market.

The specialisation of the skills produced by the corresponding outlays with which some individuals (skilled workers) are trained in certain work unlike others are of the same nature as the foregoing. Thanks to these skills and the relative cost (it is of no consequence for the moment whether or not there is any proportionality between the latter and the former) there arise, in the great mass of workers, secondary groups which one can penetrate only if one owns the skills which characterise them.

While the first and more general influence mentioned almost mingles with that determined by the quantity and by the increases in the working population (as almost every man has some work skills however small), the second is instead specific and reflects upon the quantity and manner with which human labour is called upon to participate in the productive combinations. The given skill and given efficiency of human labour can, in a specific place, keep that position which elsewhere, in the absence of work having these specific qualities, could be held by machines.

But the capital invested in skilled workers, Engel's cost of production, will never determine, as we shall better see in the following section, the value of labour of said expressed in the productive combinations. It has only made these possible and might have given opportunity to said. The value of the workers' labour will be determined, as we know, by other elements, specific to the combinations mentioned several times above.

6. - In parallel with the criticism against Engel's system the elements of another theory have assembled themselves: this is the difference between scientific criticism and literary or artistic criticism, namely while the former, demolishing, generally has to substitute a new doctrine, the others demolish without creating anything.

We can now ask ourselves if, on the basis of the principle advocated here, we can obtain the marvellous effect Engel pursued with his method, in other words, if we can concretely measure the value of the worker and hence of the emigrant.

It is not possible to outline, in this article, anything other than a tentative response.

To the preliminary question, already mentioned, namely whether the efficiency of human labour employed in the economic complexes together with the other complementary goods can be discriminated, isolated, hence measured just as any other item, we know, as has been more or less implicitly said, that the reply can only be negative.

Inductive confirmation of this conclusion comes from labour surveys. The thirteenth annual report of the Commissioner of Labour of the United States of America includes a detailed comparative analysis of manual processing and machine processing[10]. The conclusion is that in all 672 cases examined, machine processing is much more productive than manual processing. But on the question posed by the American legislator in deciding the survey «whether the changes of the original cost of products are due to a surplus of labour or else to the introduction of mechanical energy», as on other similar such questions, inherent to the productivity of the single goods of the complexes, the report's author confesses that the facts gathered can be employed as arguments or as reasons, but not as conclusions in this respect.

If therefore the value of labour cannot be directly recognised from its specific efficiency, let us move to a second problem. Can such value be considered indirectly measured by the pay with which the labour is remunerated? It is evident that whatever the reply to the question, one can speak only of real pay, calculated, for example, with the accurate methods of which a very recent survey of the Federal Bureau of Labour of the United States of America has given us an exemplary paper[11].

Some of the more rudimental elements for the solution of this question are also to be found in the pages above.

Wage and value of labour are two clearly distinct concepts, as they represent two phenomena which form and develop as a result of different causes and with different elements.

---

[10] See *Thirteenth Annual Report of the Commissioner of Labour*, 1898; *Hand and Machine Labour*, vol. I; *Introd. and Analysis*, Washington, 1899.

[11] The results of the surveys carried out by the said Bureau of Labour are summarised in the November 1903 and July 1904 issues of *Bull. of the Bureau of Labour*.

Wage is established on the labour market: the profound and multiform activity of the capitalistic process manifests itself on this market with well known phenomena, such as the proportions of supply and demand of workers, both overall and in the single categories (skilled or unskilled, female and male, children and adults), the capacity of mutual resistance possessed by the working classes and the capitalists or, in general, the entrepreneurs, one in the face of the other. The value of labour, as we said, depends instead on the degree of productivity (in progress) that it, by its proportions and for the types of employment, has in the productive combinations of a given economy. It therefore varies with the varying of the proportions or efficiency also of one of the other complementary capital goods with which human labour is co-ordinated.

The wage's actions and reactions in respect of the function exercised by labour in the productive complexes are active and continuous, of this there is no doubt, but not such as to allow us to proportion the latter, the function, from the former, the wage. The raising of the wage and the amount of human labour employed in a complex can be considered as in antithesis. The entrepreneur substitutes the workers with technical capital as soon as the capitalist cost of the former is higher than the cost of the machines whose productive force is greater than that of man. Function and value of man will thus be immediately altered vis-à-vis the complex's other goods.

We should, indeed, in this respect, avoid a confusion into which it would appear at first glance that we could fall as a result of the equivocation of words and things.

Demography, assisted by other disciplines, such as biology and political economy, has shown that, particularly in the big industries, the wages of the workers, considered by age brackets, rise or diminish in direct correlation to the growth or decrease of the physical and mental productivity of the workers themselves[12]. That this correlation tends to take place is easy to allow, at least in those productive systems in which the worker's physical and men-

---

[12] See Benini, *Demografia*, cited, p. 57. Proof of said tendency can be found particularly in detailed professional statistics or those of single cities (Berlin, Leipzig) of the German Empire.

tal potential have space to sufficiently develop itself, as a result also of the numerous levels of skill in which human labour is technically distributed. Free competition, where it is possible to compare the units or quality of labour supplied by the single workers, ensures that the wages are proportionate to the efficiency which Tizio's work will have vis-à-vis that of Caius. But, as is clear, we are talking in these cases only of an individual phenomenon, better developed through the external comparison of the quantities of operations, of objects, of concrete services, which the individuals belonging to a group of workers, let us assume from 15 to 50 years of age, provide under the eyes of the interested parties.

However, the noting of such a correlation between the worker's potential and wage one cannot lead to deductions which, penetrating within the productive complexes, presume to estimate the efficiency exercised by the labour good according to the wage capital with which the labour is remunerated. This would be confusing two profoundly different phenomena. The words potential, productivity, efficiency of labour of the individual worker establishes a relation between the force, the capacity of this worker and the units of labour which he produces and these are compared with the units of other workers. When one talks instead of productivity of the labour good in the productive combination one intends to establish a relation between this good and the other complementary goods with which the former is associated, fixing above all the final overall yield of the combination itself.

Now who is to say, for example, that the highest wage achieved by the strongest and most skilled worker really measures the efficiency which the labour will deploy in the given productive combination? On the basis of what proof can it therefore be deduced that the set of all the wage capital of a industry corresponds to the actual contribution made by the mass of labour?[13] It could be

---

[13] We can imagine a case in which an entrepreneur determines, with the wages he will pay to his workers, the value which the workers themselves will have in his specific industry, taking into consideration however all the individual or subjective circumstances of the entrepreneur and industry (organisation of the company, quantity and quality of the other capital and complementary goods owned, market prices, clientele, etc.).

said, to cite one case, that the extraordinary skill of a group of engineering workers, remunerated with an adequate salary, increases the efficiency of the machinery which said use more than proportional to this salary, thus determining a correlative relation in the proportion of value between that work and the technical capital. And it is precisely in the sense and for the end indicated in this example that the entrepreneurs can be interested in using expert and skilled workers even though, however, the progressive mechanisation of the industries and the corresponding ordering of the company allow, above all in countries with expensive labour, to increasingly implement the new capitalistic trend of substituting skilled workers for unskilled workers as the former are generally better organised and accustomed to higher wages[14].

Concluding on the problem posed, it is clear that if it is not possible to deduce the value of the labour from the measure of the salary, neither can one obtain the worker's social value from the capitalisation of the wage. If we thought we could carry out such

---

If our imagined entrepreneur has given an exact price to all the factors of his industry (capital, machines, raw materials, other floating capital, natural forces, etc.) and if he knows the exact revenue which he will obtain without the addition of labour (or to make a more likely case, without the addition of a further and specific quantity of labour) he can know the maximum he can pay the labour to be added so as to obtain a higher income, which his goods, with the new labour good, would be capable of yielding. The difference between the first and second income will indicate the maximum of wage capital that the entrepreneur will believe he can pay for the new labour he needs, and this wage capital will indicate the value of labour in the industry in question.

But this is an extreme case. The same conditions in which the workers find themselves vis-à-vis the entrepreneur tend to prevent them from being normal. «The effects of the worker's disadvantage in bargaining – Marshall says – are cumulative in two manners. It lowers his wages and this lowers his efficiency as a worker and hence lowers the normal value of his labour. And moreover it reduces his efficiency as a contracting party, and thus increases the probability that he sells his labour for less than its normal value». (*op. cit.* p. 316).

[14] As proof that, thanks to the introduction of increasingly new machines and of special technical organisations of industries, capital tends to replace the natural productivity of the worker with artificial productivity, lower and less skilled, I shall confine myself to citing the results of the last census of the United States of America (1900) viewed from our viewpoint by WALLING W. E. in the September 1904 issue of *The Annales of the American Academy of Pol. and Soc. Science*. This capitalistic procedure strengthens the phenomenon which, in the previous note, we indicated with the words of Marshall. For the explanation of similar phenomena, from the point of view of value, see: PANTALEONI, *Principii di econ. pura*, Florence, 1889, p. 163 (note).

capitalisation we would also fall into the same most evident paralogism as some advocates of Engel's theory, when they admit that as the wage measures the labour, so the capitalised wages (illogically presupposing with this the distribution relation being sought as already established) measures the economic value of man[15].

Engel would appear, superficially, to avoid the paralogism by introducing an artificial logical presupposition in the mentioned deduction. He does not deduce knowledge of the value of the labour and of the worker directly and simply from the wage, but says it is the elements of man's cost of production, which vary in nature and cost, according to the categories of worker, which do or should determine that which he calls the natural wage. But this aprioristic and teleological conception, sullied also by preconceptions of natural equity, is not backed by convincing proofs and hence does not succeed in eliminating the original paralogistic flaw; it therefore has to fall before the doctrine which relates wage and the value of labour to the special laws of the capitalistic process and to the more general laws of economic equilibrium.

We therefore do not see how the efficiency of labour or the size of the wage can be considered autonomously and individually to resolve the problem which we posed above regarding the possibility of measuring the value of labour in the productive relation in isolation.

7. - If however we had succeeded in measuring, by some ingenious operation, the average value of labour in a country's productive combinations, this does not mean we would have resolved our initial fundamental problem (the loss to a country as a result of emigration and, more generally, the economic value of the worker) and which is normally, as we know, the principal purpose to which the calculators of the cost of human production tend.

Labour has a value as it is usable and is actually useful in the productive economy of the country considered. The workers who

---

[15] See on Engel's natural wage, the cited work of RICCA-SALERNO, p. 217 and in general, on the natural wage, LORIA, *Analisi della prop. capitalista*, pages 170 and 730 of vol. I.

cannot sell (for whatever reason) their labour good lose, at least pro tempore, the quality of economic goods, of personal capital[16].

It cannot be excluded that, in given circumstances, a value can also be attributed to unemployed workers. Disregarding also their use to the capitalists in the struggle to lower wages, etc., we can confine ourselves to considering them as a necessary stock or reserve for future production eventualities: the outlays employed to maintain them are akin to an insurance premium against the damages of a feared lack of labour. But, in general, considering *a priori*, as though it were normal or as though it were proven, that all emigrants have always a value (it being unimportant whether ascertained) and that the economy of their country of origin suffers a subtraction of wealth corresponding to the sum of said values is both a logical and an economic absurdity. Such a capitalisation of single personal values would be incapable of furnishing any data, neither real nor fertile, of any veracious inference for our studies.

The specific problem we have raised regarding emigration cannot be formulated around the individual units, that is surveying the value of labour and the personal capital of the single workers belonging to a given country and extending this value to the emigrants, but should be proposed by considering all the national productive economy objectively, i.e., in the economic combina-

---

[16] Our Ferrara, since 1855, has lucidly pointed out that «whatever wealth, if it is inert, paralysed, impotent to produce, loses first its character of capital, then its character of wealth. What the emigrant takes away from the country is precisely that portion of capital which for whatever reason did not produce or produced so little as not to merit its time and effort» («Prefazione» to vol VII, series I, p. XCIV of *Bibl. dell'Econ.*).

Even these elementary considerations indicate with greater clarity the difference between Engel's theory and ours. According to the German statistician, the country of immigration would become more wealthy (taking the simplest case) according to the cost of production of the emigrants (it is unimportant for the moment whether this cost should be calculated on the basis of the prices of the country of origin or of that of destination), according, that is, to the loss of personal capital suffered by the native country. We however believe that this gain can only be measured by the increase in value and return caused in the new productive combinations which will necessarily come into being and hence in the very same single goods with which the labour associates itself. The general gain for the social community, outside the divisions of the national markets, will correspond to the difference between that which has happened in the economy of the country of immigration and that which has happened in that of the native country.

tions of labour with the other goods and in the ensuing total return. It is the same concept on which we have based some of the criticisms aimed at the calculation of the cost of upbringing of the single workers (Section 3).

We know that production is effected through the combination of the complementary capital goods which appears most economic. For the country of origin, emigration diminishes the quantity and supply of the labour good; this reduction, according to the amount of capital prepared to be invested in wages (but this condition is evidently changeable, particularly in relation to the variation in the labour supply), can lead to an increase in the price of labour, this increase, which would represent the increase in the capitalistic cost of labour, would tend to determine a general change in the productive combinations, as it would alter the proportion of labour vis-à-vis the other complementary capital goods and hence the value of labour itself vis-à-vis both the other goods and the final yield of the respective enterprises.

Given this, our fundamental and complex problem — to consider it in its broadest approximation — can be posed with these subsequent questions. Does the alteration in the proportion of labour have the effect, in the economy of the given country, of forcing it to new productive combinations? Given this, are the assumed new combinations such that they yield results which are economically less profitable than the preceding combinations? Given this, can the reduction in the return be compensated by other benefits of an economic nature (reduction of unproductive consumers, decrease in private and public spending for the maintenance of the unemployed, less state spending for public order, etc.), and of a moral and political nature (more influence abroad, in the countries of immigration, less public unrest, decrease in crime, in illiteracy, etc.)?

The reply to the first and second questions, which are preliminary, will be negative, for example, when the emigrants in question were either unemployed or, if employed, can be substituted with either unemployed with the same productive efficiency who have not emigrated, or else, if this is not possible, or is not to one's liking, by machines which produce for at least the same cost of surrogate human labour. On the other hand, it will be positive when emigration gives rise to an increase in the cost of labour, which the capitalists or landowners do not discount only by a reduction of profit, rent, etc., but, through the new productive combinations which will have to come into being, leads to a reduction in total income.

Secondly, other questions will have to be formulated, such as the following. Will the new productive arrangements indirectly determined by emigration, given that the general productivity of the country considered is not affected, produce nonetheless damage to the owners of some of the other goods with which labour combines? Or given, similarly, that a general damage takes place, on whom will it bear or weigh most?

This first order of studies is related to others which, in importance, we shall deal with separately, those of demographic and biological order. Will emigration, we should ask, alter the composition and vital force of the population which has not emigrated such as to impair the overall physiological and economic power of future generations? Here we are merely projecting into the future our questions above regarding the productivity of the economic combinations we then referred to the period in which the emigration takes place.

It is therefore clear to us that a reply, as far as such is possible, which satisfies the questions posed in the terms barely outlined above, can come only from the study of the productivity of the given national economy, analysed and measured directly in its essential elements, i.e., in the relations of the goods from which various association and co-ordination is established, and controlled by the multiple phenomena which are impacted by and reflect the fundamental productive relation. Determination of the effects of emigration on the economy of the country of origin is thus immediately traced back to the larger sphere of the phenomenon of value.

Indirect confirmation of the principle advocated here, that the damage or otherwise brought about by emigration can be deduced only from the general economy of the country, is furnished by Marshall in a particularly evocative manner.

The eminent economist, who would appear to suffer these questions of the calculation of the cost of emigrants with gentlemanly indifference, concedes them only a few words of theoretical development, stating that the various schemes of estimates put forward are all rough and evidently flawed in their principles[17].

According to Marshall, two norms are available for calculating the value of emigrants, two norms which can be converted one into the other if one allows that the net production of an average individual and the consumption during the life are equal: or «we have to discount the probable value of all the future services which the emigrant would render, add them together and deduce from them the sum of the discounted values of all the wealth and direct services of other persons which he would consume, and one can note that in calculating thus every element of production and consumption at its probable value, we have incidentally taken into account the probabilities of his premature death and illnesses, as also of his success or failure in life; or else we can also estimate his value at the money cost of production which his native country has sustained for him and which, equally, would be found by adding the accumulated values of all the various elements of his past consumption and deducing from them the sum of the accumulated values of all the various elements of his past production».

Although we do not believe it necessary to dwell on what has been said regarding the second question, we would, however, dwell on the first question, because, while apparently contradicting it, it actually confirms the principle we have sought to prove.

With this first estimate scheme, Marshall basically proposes the compilation of nothing more or less than a complete and detailed advance balance sheet. However, he who is charged with assembling the various credit and debit entries of this balance sheet of the future should possess the gift of prophesy. the advance balance sheet, in this case, would be worthless if it did not have the degree of accuracy of a final balance sheet.

---

[17] Op. and place cited in the first note of this article. MARSHALL also gives a mathematical formula for the calculation of the value of the emigrant, It is note XXIV.

In truth it entails calculating not the accumulated values of expenses and services of the past, in itself so difficult to quantify, as in the second of the proposed schemes (which is then that of Engel), but to forecast future expenses and services, for the entire period of the emigrant's life in the hypothesis that he, vice versa, had stayed in his native country. Now, these forecasts are at least of triple order: those which fall under the sphere of needs and will of a average man of specific category, those which refer to his physical nature (illnesses, invalidity, more or less premature death), those which depend on the future developments and concrete future circumstances of economic life, as regards both that which concerns most closely the social class, industry, trade, place, etc., to which the individual belongs, and for those general phenomena which have have repercussions on the more limited circle in which the individual's life takes place (profound transformations in the technical systems of labour, crises, population growth). The simple exposition of these elements to be translated into concrete and precise figures in the emigrant's economic balance sheet is the clearest possible proof of the temerity of merely attempting such an undertaking. Marshall himself, in the text to which the note refers, of which I have cited the excerpt of most importance for our purposes, shows how even the simple forecasts of educated persons on the appropriateness of directing their children toward one or another profession or industry are extremely difficult and fallacious.

But proceeding, in view of the purpose, let us turn our attention to the third order of forecasts, which in the mind of the balance sheet's hypothetical calculator should have a keen influence for the determination of those of the first order. These are forecasts of a general and objective nature, to make which it is necessary to synthetically imagine all the economic movements reserved for the emigrant's native land. But what does this mean from our point of view? It means that Marshall is forced to seek the essential elements he needs to determine any damage brought about by emigration not in the individual in himself, but in the social complex: how will he be able to know, according to what was proposed, of the future success or failure of the emigrant (i.e., whether or not he will be employed, what wage he will receive, etc.), if he does not consider objectively the labour in relation to the other capital goods and does not calculate the economic effects of emigration on the value of the national labour, observed in all its various productive combinations?

Hence the valuation of the value of the emigrant, made from the point of view of the individual, taken autonomously, would only be apparent: it would always presuppose that general, objective valuation. The scheme proposed by Marshall is hence a valid indirect proof of our concept.

8. - I shall end this article with two conclusions, one which can be viewed as psychological rather than economic, the other methodological.

Why, I ask myself first and foremost, has a calculation such as that criticised, which turns out to be so unreal, unilateral and erroneous, continued to be tranquilly applied for so many years, I was about to say since the times of the old political arithmeticians up to our days?

This is, I believe, a strange phenomenon, also because of the following two compounding circumstances: first, that the calculation lends itself to being exploited for capitalistic purposes, that is to say to justify the bans on emigration, which is said to cost the native country so much wealth and capital[18]: secondly, that several of the writers, who employ quite a long time to establish the laborious accounts, then set out, one alongside the other, the principal elements as a result of which we should deem the theory unfounded and the calculation inapplicable?

What more? An educated, subtle and shrewd writer in the recesses of economics such as Vilfredo Pareto also shows a weakness (if I may be forgiven the sentimental expression) for Engel's method as that which I shall now mention.

In the first volume of his *Cours d'econon. Pol.* (sections 253-255), Pareto expounds Engel's method and then states that: «it is im-

[18] See, for example, the perceptive observations of COLAIANNI N., *Man. di Demogr.*, Naples, Pierro, 1904, p. 439.

portant to consider the value of man to realise the importance of the capital which a country loses as a result of emigration» and then applies Engel's calculations to Italy, concluding by stating that «we are not far from the truth if we calculate the amount the country loses annually as a result of emigration at 400-450 million lire». There is no doubt: Pareto speaks of the value of man on the basis of Engel's cost of production and loss suffered by a country for the capital lost as a result of emigration, valued according to the value of man, understood as above. And yet, in the second volume of the work (section 950) when the accounts have to be drawn up (this is a play on words which is significant), i.e., to calculate in concrete terms the amount of wealth of a country, he again finds himself faced with personal capital and confutes with incisive brevity that very method of Engel which he earlier applied. «Engel — writes the illustrious economist —, takes the cost of production of the personal capital for their value, but this calculation is far from being exact as it is the productivity of the capitals which should be borne uppermost in mind. Statistics do not currently furnish us with any means for resolving the problem thus posed». Why then consider it resolved in the applications made in the first volume? Perhaps this was so (but I briefly mention this as a mere and timid suspicion) because of the tendency, which some economists would not appear to eschew, to place personal capital on the same footing with chattels and land capital too absolutely?

But let us return to our initial question. The reply which we should perhaps give it is this, that in our age, avid of facts and precise and synthetic data, we are anxious to prepare also for many economic phenomena an elegantly simple and brief expression, such as that represented by the number. When the complexity and nature of the phenomenon do not allow this, man has not always the courage to stop: he attempts to give something. But at times, as in Engel's calculations for emigration, this something is not a part of the truth, but an error.

This hypothetical explanation leads me to the conclusion regarding the method mentioned above, which in actual fact is very simple.

It is absolutely necessary that the applications of statistics to economic phenomena should not be at the expense of a suitable examination of them, which alone can indicate to us the possibility and limits of the analysis and the statistical representation. It does not suffice, as do many authors who avail themselves of Engel's method, to add, in no particular order, observations which limit and at times verbally annul the value of the calculation made: it is necessary, as a preliminary and indispensable condition, to ascertain the nexus and theoretical relations of the observations themselves and to subordinate them to the delimination of the object and the statistical technique[19].

If we do not employ these positive and prudent criteria, how shall we, in cases such as those examined, give the lie to those who continue to repeat the malicious motto attributed to Thiers that statistics is the art of specifying that which one does not know?

---

[19] This concept of the subordination of the logic and technique of the method, etc., to the economic nature of specific phenomena, to which the former is applied, is general in nature. The pure statisticians, the pure jurists, etc., often do not follow such an evident concept. I have had occasion to prove it on several and various occasions: for example, for the jurists, in certain legislative formulations of agricultural contracts and compensation for rural improvements, and for statisticians, in many questions of statistics of foreign trade (particularly in the question of whether temporary imports and exports should be recorded under special trade). Certain convenient and academic separations of competences should now dissolve before the recognition of the complex nature of the phenomena and of the indissoluble co-ordination or subordination of the aspects by which the phenomena manifest themselves.

The Cost of Production of Man and the Economic Value of Emigrants (Regarding an Article by Professor F. Coletti)*

Vilfredo Pareto

There was once, in Rome, a shopkeeper who found it worth his while to go to Paris for some business of his. When back in Rome, he told his bookkeeper to calculate how much he had spent on that trip. The undertaking was not easy, as the shopkeeper had not noted down his expenses; and yet the bookkeeper did his calculations and found that his employer had spent from 400 to 450 lire.

Shortly afterwards, the employer started talking about his trip again with his bookkeeper and said: «How much do you think I lost or made overall on that trip? By how much, because of that trip, has my worth diminished or increased?»

«I do not know — replied the bookkeeper — how can I know whether you struck a good or bad deal in Paris?»

«My dear bookkeeper, you contradict yourself; I fear you show a penchant for the Engelian method, which considers something's cost of production its value. Today you are unable to resolve the question I pose to you; why then, just a few days ago, did you consider it resolved?».

Another day, that shopkeeper had the key to his safe stolen.

«How much have they stolen?» he asked his bookkeeper.

---

* From: PARETO V., «Il costo di produzione dell'uomo e il valore economico degli emigranti. (A proposito di un articolo del Prof. F. Coletti)», *Giornale degli Economisti*, April 1905, pp. 322-7. [Cod. JEL: N 33].

«You would do best to consult a locksmith. I suppose a new key would cost from 4 to 4.50 lire».

«But in the safe I had some documents which I need for a deal. By the time the locksmith has made the new key, it will be too late for me to use those documents. By how much do you think the loss of the key has diminished my worth?»

«You tell me. I do not know».

«Once again you contradict yourself. Why, if you are unable to resolve the question, did you deem it resolved when you replied that the loss of that key would cost me from 4 to 4.50 lire?»

This is my reply to the charge made by Professor Coletti in an article, which is moreover learned and perceptive. And I would add nothing more by way of polemic.

But it is worthwhile spending a few more words on the nature of the economic problem.

As Professor Coletti excellently puts it: «What however can be stated as disputable and denied is this: that one can survey the economic value of emigration and the consequent economic loss to the country of origin on the basis of the emigrants' cost of production». Indeed, he is more right than he suspects: that proposition is general and holds when one considers any economic good and not emigrants.

Professor Coletti, who has interpreted in a different sense my calculation on the cost of the emigrants, has been too generous toward me. He should have written: «This author, who asserts the doctrine which measures value by the cost of production is erroneous, then wishes to measure the value of man by his cost of production! This author, who deafens our ears, repeating in every possible manner that all the unknowns of economic equilibrium should be determined together; tries then to determine one of these unknowns, namely the value of emigrants, separately from the others. Find, if it is possible, a man who contradicts himself more».

I wish to make myself clearly understood and do not succeed[1].

---

[1] See *Cours*, I, p. IV: «The study of the three types of capital allows us to know the elements which, when they combine, give birth to economic phenomena».

I, alone, cannot find a way to explain myself more clearly; if somebody wishes to teach me this way, I will be more than grateful to him.

There was a critic who said that in my *Cours* I had become boring as I always repeated that to solve an economic problem, one had, in practice, first to analyse and then to synthesise. I believe he was not wholly wrong: and yet many have interpreted what I said without wishing to take account of this observation of mine. Hence, in my *Manuale,* which is about to be published in Milan, I will try another path to better illustrate that concept, but I do not know whether I will succeed.

The problem of emigration, as posed by Professor Coletti, is but a specific case of the general problem of economic equilibrium.

Let there be in a country an economic state which we shall call *(I)*, which differs from another economic state, which we shall call *(II)*, only in that to pass from *(I)* to *(II)* a certain item *A* has been removed from the country.

We are faced with two problems, namely: 1) what is the selling value, the price in money, of *A*; 2) what change in the state of the country does the subtraction of *A* entail, i.e., how do states *(I)* and *(II)* differ.

In practice, this second problem is the most important, and we are interested in knowing whether men in state *(II)* are worse, and to what extent, than in state *(I)*.

A rigorous solution of this problem entails knowing the amounts of ophelimity which men in state *(I)* enjoy, and those which they enjoy in state *(II)*, and then comparing them[2].

This cannot be done; and so the problem is, strictly speaking, unsolvable.

Moreover, better little than nothing, and if one seeks one manages to find some imperfect solution.

It is this type of solution that is put forward by Professor Coletti, who succeeds in taking into account the greater number of facts why states *(I)* and *(II)* differ; but he does not succeed in recognising them all and nobody in the world would succeed in doing so; he does not value, as would be necessary, the effects in

---

[2] In the case of emigration, we should also take into account that man's production is stimulated by emigration; and of other infinite circumstances which modify states *(I)* and *(II)*.

ophelimity and here also we repeat that nobody in the world would succeed in doing so.

A problem of economics or sociology can never be resolved with the rigour and certainty given by the solution to a problem of mathematics; one can only obtain approximate solutions with varying degree of probability. Hence one should resign oneself either not to deal with the matter at all, or to reason in the sole manner allowed by its nature.

As we are unable to accurately evaluate the ophelimities, let us make an exception. Instead of ophelimities, let us compare the cash revenues of the community in state *(I)* and in state *(II)*; or else, let us compare the capital, valued in cash, in these two states; or else, let us compare that ill-defined and nebulous entity which is given the name of «national capital» in state *(I)* and state *(II)*. And if we can't even do this, let us proceed with exceptions to the rule; is there absolutely nothing that one can know and that can give us an idea, even very rough, of the difference between state *(I)* and state *(II)*? At worst, there may be the price of *A* or its cost of production.

A Japanese battleship sinks. How much does Japan lose? A worthy admiral could hold forth quite well, studying the extent to which the Japanese navy is weakened by such event. But can we really say nothing without going and looking for that admiral? Here then: the Japanese ship cost so many millions, we have at least a vague idea of what Japan has lost.

Somebody might object, as Coletti does, that this is only a part of the truth, that it is an error. Who's to say that Japan lost something when the vessel sank? Indeed, it was a big gain, because Japan has agreed to make peace with Russia as its navy is now weakened; if war had broken out, it would have been defeated, it would have had to pay an enormous sum by way of repatriations to Russia.

Thus one can no longer reason about anything; and not only political economy, but the entire science of government of society lies on a blank sheet.

There is a pinch of truth in this; and we should note that all our deductions regarding social phenomena are merely approximate and probable; hence they should be employed with great prudence and appropriately, with practice, to correct the theoretical deductions.

If one wishes to record a country's receipts and outlays, it is unarguable that the expenses borne for human beings which the country raised until they were adults, and then emigrated should be included among the outlays. And let Coletti believe that his is not at all an idle calculation, and disregard whether it is «exploited for capitalist purposes»; as we shall disregard whether his article might be «exploited for socialist purposes»; because all this is digression and has nothing to do with science.

There is room for all research and all studies. Coletti does excellently to show once again, in a concrete case, that a thing's cost of production is not the value of that thing; and he also does well to observe that the cost of production of emigrants does not in the least represent the loss which, overall, the country suffers as a result of emigration; while at times there may be, overall, a gain instead of a loss. Neither is this flogging a dead horse, as there are still many persons who commit the same error. But Beneduce also did well to take the time to correct and improve the calculation of the loss caused by emigration. And anybody who increases our knowledge of both the single elements of the problem and also of the overall solution will also do well.

That item which we said above should be recorded in the outlays is flanked by other items which should be included among the revenues, and there are also other items to be included among the outlays. Each is worthy of being diligently known and calculated; and the time spent doing so is not lost, indeed it is excellently spent.

If we knew all these items, or at least the principal items, we would have the actuarial result of the operation; but it would not be the economic result, and by no means the social result.

A shopkeeper does not carry out his trade by reading only his books and ledgers; but this does not mean that these are not useful to him.

The statesman who condemned emigration solely because there is an expense to be recorded under the outlays would be foolish; but he would also be imprudent if he voluntarily closed his eyes and ears to neither see nor hear the size of that expense. If he is sensible and provident, he will take account of it as one of the elements of the problem which he has to resolve: he will seek to know as many other elements as he can and then draw his conclusions.

The path for solving any practical problem is no different: it is always necessary to analyse it, to study its elements separately; and then synthesise them, to combine them all and find the desired solution.

Personal Capital and the Economic Value of Emigrants*

Alberto Beneduce

The problem of the cost of production of man in relation to the value of the worker and that which is commonly deduced as corollary, the economic value of emigrants, is closely related to the fundamental principles of political economy, such as the theory of capital, and that of wage. It would therefore be best to fix the terms of the discussion so that one can proceed with logical reasoning from opposing definitions to deduce the parallel theories which represent, in every stage of their development, a different angle from which to perceive the same phenomenon; error arises only when logic is lacking. It is also best to fix the subject of the discussion in the essential quality which one considers and in the environment vis-à-vis which one studies it and man is such a complex subject, he has interdependent relations with many other players, that it is necessary to disregard his multiple, if not innumerable, intrinsic and exterior qualities (of relation with the outside world).

Let us start from the man who, in the limited economic environment, we shall consider as a living machine, as a capital good, capable of reproduction (α); we refer therefore to man as a being capable of accumulating in the potential state a certain quantity of physical-mental energy, which will transform itself

* From: Beneduce A., «Capitali personali e valore economico degli emigrati», *Giornale degli Economisti*, July 1905, pp. 3-44. [Cod. JEL: N 33].

into kinetic energy when, and only when, specific pressures of the environment act such as to allow the expression of that potential energy; and explicitly, we wish to here state that we believe the aim of the expression, the partial recovery of the conditions of the original good before the motion, is the reproduction of the good *(a)*. We shall then consider man in relation to his similars, capable of his same qualities and in relation to the other goods.

The use of the services of man's physical-mental energy determines the wage, measured in that quantity of consumption goods which allows the attainment of the aim of the afore-indicated expression.

Capital is for us, as for Walras and Pareto, «every good which can serve more than once for production» (β); a definition which appears to us broader than the other, of «wealth which serves to produce an income», or again that more limited definition given by Marx and Lassalle, «wealth which serves to produce an income, independent of the owner's labour» (γ).

Given this, we ask: Is man a capital?

If we allow (α) and (β) the reply is necessarily affirmative; if we allow (γ) it is negative.

However, in hypotheses (α) and (β) personal capital exists; it should be measured: one therefore has to fix the unit of measure. Will this be the infinitesimal element μ of natural force (economic good) whose consumption in space and time has determined the acquisition of the energy at the potential state, or else will it be the infinitesimal element ε' of the kinetic energy which expresses itself in time so as to achieve the end *(a)*?

In abstract, we can choose one or the other of the two infinitesimal elements; integrated, one could give us the labour achieved by the system in passing from one position of equilibrium to another, the other the corresponding increase in living force; and the dynamics of natural systems tell us that «when a system passes from one position to another, the increase in living force is equal to the sum of the forces' labour».

In particular, then, referring to the phenomena of economic science, the results of the two integrations would be equal only virtually: one would give the expression of the potential acquired by the good to satisfy (combining with other complementary goods) the needs; the other, the expression of the concrete manifestation of the energy acquired which enters, under the pressure of the economic conditions of the time and place considered, in real combination with the other complementary goods. If the two elements can be reduced to a common denominator, in other words if one can obtain their quantitative expressions in numeraire, the aforementioned results would furnish us with the expressions, in said unit of measure, of the cost of production of the potential of the good (C_p), of the economic value (V).

To the latter corresponds a production cost (C) (outlay of productive energy to achieve the given economic act), to the former a value (V_p)[1] (estimate of the expected utility, according to Jevons). We therefore have four expressions (C_p, V, C, V_p) which pair off such that the elements of one couple (C_p V_p) are to those of the other (C V) as potential energy is to kinetic energy; the corresponding elements of the two couples refer to concomitant concepts, the heteronymous elements to antithetic concepts. The relation between C_p and C is generally not unity, while that between V_p and V tends to unity. We also note that if the market conditions in two given periods of time, for a given good are little changed, we can assume C_p as an approximation of V_p; but however (the foregoing facts existing) if for a given problem it is necessary to measure V and this, in view of the complex nature of the variables of which V is a function, cannot be done, by way of a first approximation we could substitute V by the expression C_p (δ).

Turning now to the specific phenomenon being examined, we can state: 1) the quantitative production of the good man in relation to its yield, in two quite distant periods of time, has not significantly changed[2]; 2) while for the quantitative expression of

---

[1] V_p would equal zero when there was no degree of probability of the use of that good. Can this much be stated for the good man considering only the present state of unproductiveness in a single market?

[2] The absolute number of those born in the period 1879-1883 averaged 1,047,125 each year; in the period 1899-1904 it was 1,069,774.

the element ε, physiology and statistics furnish us with data which, if not mathematically accurate, are sufficiently approximate to the nature and scope of the problem being studied (and we would also add, the data are a priori reliable because they refer to observations of phenomena which took place), for the element ε' which should find its quantitative expression in the measure of the efficiency of the work of the value of the product, no experimental science nor mind whose power of investigative foresight was even as great as that of Vico can tell us anything.

Given this, to estimate the good considered, the essential data noted in proposition (δ) are needed and hence we are legitimate in considering C_p as an approximation of V.

But we also note that to obtain the quantitative expression of the element ε' it is necessary not only to fix the measure of the efficiency of labour in the time when the calculation is made, something which is of extreme difficulty if not indeed impossible, but to also envisage the measure of its variations in time; and this is not all, it is also necessary to fix the present standard of living and envisage the future, without overlooking the fact that one phenomenon is also a function of the other. When all this extraordinary calculation has been made, the difference between the two elements, and not just the first, would give us the quantitative expression of the element ε'.

This is basically one of the methods recommended by Marshall for calculating the real value of the emigrants' personal capital, «to discount the probable value of all the future services which the emigrant would render, to add them together and deduce from them the sum of the discounted values of all the wealth and direct services of other persons which he would consume».

These future services are actually something different from the probable value of the efficiency of labour in time, as the measure

---

The (nominal and real) wage of workers in the various industries for the two periods of time considered increased overall. One could for this purpose compare the wages given in the classical work by ROTA and those published in the Labour Office's *Bolletino*. The same conclusion was reached by GEISSER in the appendix to the translation of CAUDERLIER *L'evoluzione economica nel secolo XIX* and in GEISSER - MAGRINI's note in *Riforma sociale*, November 1904 on the same subject.

of this is something different from the measurements of the wage whatever meaning one wishes to give to such word. It cannot, however, be denied that the measure of the wage is a function both of the efficiency of the labour on the value of the product and of the so-called circulating capital and even more so of the sum of the potential energies which the workers enjoy. Although we are not against admitting a certain proportionality between the efficiency of labour and wage or the worker's yield whichever term one wishes to use, and so someone would propose, subordinately, capitalisation of the yield as a measure of man's value.

In the light of our foregoing consideration, we believe it unnecessary to dwell on this to show that this value would be erroneous.

De Foville, who has dealt with the important argument since 1875, applying a method of calculation little different from that indicated by Marshall, finds that in the rural population, a youngster of 17 years has a value of Lire 3,370, and at 45, an agricultural worker is not worth more than Lire 1,500. At 45, an agricultural worker is certainly in the prime of his forces, and even de Foville, therefore, who is not a follower of the method of measurement (ε) which is basically that of Engel's, falls into the paradox that the least harm to the country of origin is caused by the emigration of a worker in the prime of his vigour and activity, who has already repaid in full or in part his raising capital, rather than a worker who has not started to produce (we add, if the emigration takes place close to the age when he is about to begin to produce)[3].

Even recent[4] calculations by de Foville on the value of human capital confirm that when one takes wage as the measure of the worker's yield and applies Marshall's method in the calculation, the economic value of man obtained is almost identical to that obtained using Engel's method.

Furthermore, Marshall himself acknowledges that the results of the two methods of calculation are identical: «The increase in

---

[3] See COLETTI F., *Giornale degli Economisti*, March 1905.

[4] See *Bulletin de l'Institut International de Statistique*, vol. XIV, troisième libraison, 1905.

wealth which an immigrant causes to a country can be estimated by the excess of the value, discounted at the present moment, of the wealth he will earn and that which he needs for his maintenance. This estimate gives results which are quite similar to those obtained by the method of estimating the value of immigrants at an average age, obtained with the sum of the expenses needed for his raising and education»[5].

Now, if the practical results are also the same, why ostracise Engel's method, whatever its degree of approximation? It is after all based on more positive data, such as those gained from experience, to juxtapose them or an expression of the wholly abstract

---

[5] See MARSHALL, *Principles of Economics*, Book II, Chapter II, note, pp. 143-4. In note XXIV (*op. cit.*, p. 748), Marshall synthesises in two formulas the two methods of calculation, and gives first the value, discounted at the present, of the sum of the infinite probable elements of infinitesimal pleasure which a good can procure in time

$$\left[H = \int_{T'}^{T} wR^{-t} \frac{\partial h}{\partial t} dt\right]$$

and then the value, also discounted at the present, of the sum of the infinite probable elements of infinitesimal pain which can be experienced from the formation of a good from the start of such formation to the instant in which the good starts to be productive.

$$\left[V = \int_{T'}^{T'} w'R^{-t} \frac{\partial h}{\partial t} dt\right]$$

PARETO (*Giornale degli Economisti*, November 1893) avails himself of an integral more or less of the same form for calculating the cost of raising a man from birth to various ages [$\int_0^n y_x \, d\, C_x$, where y_x is the function of x which gives the number of those living at age x and C_x is the expression of the cost of raising from birth to age x]. We deem it proper to point out that in a previous article (*Giornale degli Economisti*, December 1894) we used the equation:

$$C_x = \frac{x}{l_{22}} \sum_{1}^{38} l_{22+y} (1 = r)^{-y}$$

to calculate the average quote each individual should repay to his country of origin to recompense the cost of upbringing. The quota x should be nothing more than the surplus of wage received on the overall cost of the consumption goods needed and on the annual quota of savings, necessary to satisfy the needs of the body in the age in which it becomes unproductive once again; the second member of the equality is the symbolic expression, in finite terms, of the value of a phase of human life, according to the first method of calculation advised by Marshall.

value or else another method which is based on data almost wholly aleatory, such as those which one has albeit pure, from a provident induction?

Of course if, from the results obtained on observations of masses, one wishes to descend to individual assessments, a host of other reasons of very different nature from those which political economy takes into examination should be analysed and weighed.

Who could have a priori determined the economic value of the shepherd boy who was later to become Giotto?

The single individual eludes and should elude political economy as statistics.

We still have to clear the discussion's terrain of another objection which tends to deny that the problem can be posed and resolved as we said above. It is true that with the considerations above and which refer to man as we have taken and examined them, as we believe they combine with the other complementary and instrumental assets which contribute to production; personal capital has the same economic efficiency as non-fixed and land capital. We do not insist on economic science's faculty to measure the value of the worker as an instrument of production, when applied mechanics considers him in any case as just another engine or just another dynamo, and measures his power in ergs or dines, and this principally, if not exclusively, for industrial purposes.

And does not the entrepreneur in any contingency of production compare the value of the use of the services of man's personal capital to the cost of machines?

«The entrepreneur replaces the workers with technical capital as soon as the capitalist cost of the former is higher than the cost of the machines which have a greater productive force than man»[6].

De Foville moreover has replied masterfully to this preliminary objection in two articles of 13 November and 4 December 1875 published in *Économiste Français* and in his most recent work cited above.

[6] See Coletti E., afore-cited article.

Continuing then, we could reply that Pareto[7] has efficaciously shown that the movement of the population (by way of marriage or births) depends on the variations in the economic state of the country considered; and that personal capital, like all other capital, is formed and transformed under the action of economic forces so as to ensure the maximum ophelimity.

We would add two further considerations. The source of the return of personal capital, like material capital, lies in the hire of the use of its services, neither should one dwell on the differences which are to be found in the market in the specific expression of supply and demand; these differences are not specific to personal capital, but merely contingent to the present capitalistic order of society; and any discussion of them would entail much time.

Personal capital is transported in time and space through the use of savings, as is the case with material capital; neither should it be objected that «Labour cannot be separated from who produces it, and the latter can decide on his home, on emigration out of sentiments and individual criteria which differ from the purely utilitarian and economic criteria which reign in the field of non-personal capital»[8].

This observation, in destroying economic man, would deprive economic studies of their raison d'être; and we would respond with Gide[9]: «the only thing that we are concerned with is the behaviour of men considered as a mass». Finally we do not wish to end without replying to another argument, however painful this may be on a human plane. Of course, we cannot affirm that personal capital is formed and maintains itself with the sole intent of gaining economic advantage. However, the phenomenon noted by Colajanni for the provinces of Girgenti and Caltanisetta, where the raising of children has become almost an industry, is much more extensive than thought. This was noted by Professor G. De Molinari[10] also in some regions of France, and he expresses it thus: «In the branches of agricultural industry where the children can be used early and above

[7] See *Cours d'Èconomie Politique*, p. 187.
[8] See COLETTI, afore-cited *article*.
[9] See *Principes d'Èconomie Politique*, Paris, 1905, p. 8.
[10] Cited by PARETO.

all in the factories of manufacturing industry where they replace economically the adults in a large number of jobs, it is advantageous to increase them. It is not uncommon to encounter families of workers where the women and the children employed in factories feed the father of the family addicted to drunkenness and debauchery (p. 40 of original) who exploits them like slaves».

Neither in Italy is the phenomenon confined to Sicily; until quite recently was not a base trade of children aged from 10 to 15 carried on in many southern provinces, the children being sold for some hundred or so lire to speculators who sent them to southern France where they almost always found death after several years of deadly work in the glass factories?[11].

Let us leave these painful investigations, even though they are an important aspect of the problem we are examining, but state, however, that while the intent to gain economic profit may not be present in the costs of subsistence, it is never absent, expressed in its various forms, though albeit not the sole inspirer, in the costs of education, upbringing and apprenticeship.

With regard then to the manner of formation of the personal capital, every objection we believe groundless: the costs of upbringing come from the social income and by limiting voluptuary expenses[12], or by an overall increase in the assets of the family budget as a result of the economic pressure which the «growing of the family» exercises on its components, all this does not invalidate the existence of abstinence in the consumption of economic goods and the formation of savings and consequent consumption of them in the formation of that specific capital; if then the costs of training the growing generation come from the transformation of some of the other capital into personal capital, in this case the personal capital shows its nature as an element of the social assets.

Those who compare the variations of social assets which took place in two different countries in a specific period of time would

---

[11] I am very sorry to say it, but does not one still exercise clandestinely, as far as I can tell, such as trade in some areas of Caserta province?

[12] We believe it useful to point out that it is useless to speak of voluptuary expenses for the class of population which in Italy furnishes the biggest contribution to emigration.

make a serious error if they did not take account of the part of converted savings or assets in bringing up a certain number of persons[13]. One can discuss whether a given investment is more useful than another, but it should nonetheless be acknowledged that this capital was formed, which assured in that given time and to those given owners the maximum of ophelimity.

Let us now turn to the corollary. Engel's method is applicable to the calculation of the economic value of emigrants. First and foremost, let us state that it is not right to compare the calculation of the losses suffered by a country because of emigration with that of the losses suffered because of the death of children, that the objections made to the results of this latter calculation are justified and it has been proven[14] the fallaciousness of the belief of several economists that: «countries with a low rate of child mortality have an economic advantage over those with a high rate». But we do not believe the objections of a purely statistical nature which are made regarding the results of the other calculations are proven in any way, «Death would eliminate that very capital which emigrates»[15]. When, how? Is it possible to grant that the worsening of a country's economic conditions, disregarding all other considerations, increases the number of adult deaths by an average of 240,000 per year? We do not believe that for the various districts of the same town the greater or lesser number of emigrants can depend solely on the greater or lesser number of births, and from the size of the cost of upbringing[16]. This latter may appear to have an influence: but only because the higher cost of upbringing is related to the greater wealth of the district, and hence lesser number of emigrants: as regards the birth rate[17], it cannot be denied that it influences the quantitative phenomenon of emi-

---

[13] If one does not take account of this element, one finds (Bertillon's calculations) that the assets of France increased more than those of Germany in the period 1850-1870, this would not appear to be confirmed by the political and economic history of the two countries (See BODIO, *Indici misuratori*, p. 9).

[14] See PARETO, *op. cit.*, and *Giornale degli Economisti*, November 1893.

[15] See COLAJANNI, *Statistica*.

[16] See COLETTI, *op. cit.*

[17] More than from birth rate, the quantitative phenomenon of emigration depends on variations in the growth in population (surplus of the number of births over the number of deaths); but this also represents only one of the function's variables.

gration; it is however useless seeking cause and effect relations between birth rates and percentages of emigrants in the various regions of Italy. Anyone who wishes to compare the two phenomena will soon be convinced of this: for example, in the two respective periods 1881-1883 and 1901-1903, he will find that the birth rate in Puglia (43.8) exceeds, and by a considerable amount, that in Marches (36.9), Campania (37.8), Calabria (38.1) Abruzzi (40.8) and Sicily (41), while in Puglia the number of emigrants per 1,000 inhabitants (5.94) is less than in Sicily (8.5), Marches (8.99), Campania (16.86), Calabria (23.47) and Abruzzi (30.70).

Apart from the objections above therefore, let us consider the liabilities side of emigration (indeed, if we wish to be more exact, we should say. Let us consider the element of greater efficiency of the liabilities side; if then to this we juxtapose the assets – benefits of emigration – in the few elements which can be calculated and in the many whose expression cannot be reduced to numbers, and we add them up and if the accounts close in the black, it is this which lets us judge the economic effects of the emigration phenomenon).

We find ourselves here faced with an accomplished fact of the raising of a given number of persons; what share of the social income or assets have been converted into capital for their raising? The answer to this question can only be given by a calculation made using Engel's method. The other assessments proposed could give only a probable profit for the country of origin, but would not give the real loss of personal capital it suffers as a result of emigration. And we would add: the cause of error of such a calculation could lie in its very foundations[18]; a worker who was temporarily unemployed would be worth zero, while this same capital transported in space through the consumption of modest savings (travelling expenses) would acquire a value much different

[18] The objections which can be made to the determination of the economic value of personal capital, through the capitalisation of yield, also hold, albeit in a very different measure, for the determination of the values of some material capitals. To give an example: Can one exactly calculate the value of a field used for growing wheat, under a protectionist regime, from its real yield? Can one exactly calculate the value of a stock-market security from its actual yield, if the security's price derives from a country's specific economic and political contingencies?

from zero. But there are further reasons of an economic nature which lead us to prefer Engel's method for the afore-indicated calculation. The workers who emigrate are certainly in sad economic conditions; but the share of them which emigrates solely as a result of an extended, total unemployment is very small. Overall, we do not believe we are far from the truth when we state that for the most, the workers who emigrate manage to obtain in their homeland only that limit, natural or necessary wage for which that minimum of pay necessary for the goods indispensable for subsistence is allowed.

So why not ascribe on average, to each, that economic capital value which furnishes the base for the natural wage? This concept has been much criticised and discussed in economics[19]; but here, we believe, is justified by the facts of real life. We agree that Engle's method is not immune from technical faults due principally to the insufficiency of statistical data regarding household budgets. The surveys themselves should follow the households in their budgets, from constitution to break up; but much water will flow under the bridge before statistics can furnish us with such precise elements!

The physiological and statistical material of observation, even imperfect as it is, always however provides us, and with approximation sufficient to the complex problem being examined, with the value of the variable with the greater weight in determining the cost of raising man in the individual years of age; and the results which are obtained, based on such data and on the discussed method of calculation, give the problem something which is, considered as a whole, sufficient for a first and perhaps also for a second approximation of the phenomenon in question (whose exact measure should be found in the «study of the entire national productivity!»).

Certainly, they furnish more than simple phrases which each mind can weigh, according to its own imaginative potential.

---

[19] See RICCA SALERNO, *La teoria del salario*, p. 212 ff.

Again on the Cost of Production of Man and the Economic Value of Emigrants[*]

Francesco Coletti

1. - My article with the same title as that above (published in *Giornale degli Economisti,* March 1905) has had some good fortune, including a refined and kind reply by Pareto (April issue) and a comic adventure. Until today, I was hesitant whether to reply or not. I now decide I shall, as I believe it appropriate to clarify in particular the concept and logical order of my proof.

In my article I dwelt on these three problems: 1) whether it is possible to statistically record man's cost of production; 2) if man's cost of production corresponds to his economic value; 2) if the calculation can serve to obtain the economic value of emigrants and hence of the loss to their homeland because of emigration. I shall proceed here in the same order.

2. - I do not believe any significant objections have been made against the critical observations regarding the first problem[1]. On-

---

* From: COLETTI F., «Ancora del costo di produzione dell'uomo e del valore economico degli emigrati», *Giornale degli Economisti*, August, 1905, pp. 179-89. [Cod. JEL: N 33].

[1] Dr. BENEDUCE (*Giornale degli Economisti*, July 1905, p. 42), referring to me says that he does not believe the number of emigrants can «depend only» on the number of births, etc. But why ascribe me such an affirmation which, so absolutely expressed, would be a foolishness. I wrote: «The number of births, greater in one village than another, and hence, perhaps, the correlated number of emigrants or dead children may depend» on the size etc. of the cost. Nothing absolute, therefore: I expressed my doubts regarding a possible case, which only the Lord can exclude in an absolute manner that it can ever happen.

ly that any objection was deemed «lacking in any foundation» regarding the manner of formation of personal capital, it being indifferent for the purpose of Engel's calculation whether the costs of raising a man came from capital or social income, increased or not by the greater production the «growth of the family» stimulated in the single household budgets[2]. And I instead observed that, if one did not wish to break the interdependence of the phenomena in determining man's balance sheet one should take account of the circumstance that the birth of children gives rise, in the family, to more employment and production and a more healthy and useful employment of the family income.

To defend myself, I have no need to resort to the opinion of those economists who, in cases similar to ours, deem it convenient to take as a unit not the individual but the family as a whole, so as not to overlook those collective phenomena internal to the family which might perhaps escape our knowledge and explanation if the analysis was carried out individual by individual. But it suffices to pose a simple question. Given as a fact that births cause more production on the part of the family, etc, given that some of those born then die or emigrate while young, could a resuscitated Engel state that if the deaths or emigrations and hence, with even more reason, those births had not taken place, the country would have saved a sum equal to that spent for those born up to their deaths? He could not. One should not limit oneself to seeing that the expenses have been actually incurred, but should instead reflect that part of them was paid by higher production, etc., and that this, by premise, derived specifically from the very fact which determined the expense. It would be illogical to consider only one of the two necessary and parallel effects, the negative one, and not place one in correlation to the other.

All this to show, and this was my intent, that the interdependence of phenomena creates serious technical difficulties for those, as in Engel's calculations, who have to isolate and measure one only and to then consider it (for the calculation not to be sterile)

[2] See BENEDUCE, article cited.

in a given relation with the social whole, i.e., with the ambit in which the interdependence acts and manifests itself.

3. - The second problem to which most of my article was dedicated is of truly fundamental importance.

I sought to show that the greatest equivocation of Engel's method consists in considering the worker, personal capital, as nothing more or less than the compound capital of wealth which, for brevity, we call material capital.

II believe it is worthwhile insisting on the proof of this proposition. Clarity will benefit by drawing a parallel between cost and value in material products and cost and value in the product man.

Referring first to material products, we see immediately that there are outlined before us four items of data or elements: cost (effort, sacrifice) and value of the product in itself, cost and value of the use of the product. What correlation and proportionality relations exist between these four items of data? If we suppose, on the one hand, that the goods we are talking about are easy to reproduce (because, for the purposes of the parallel, we need reproducible goods) and, on the other, that society consists of perfect hedonists and the market and competition are perfectly free, it will not be difficult to find the following formulas here expressed in terms of cost but which are expressible, with equal accuracy, in terms of marginal utility: *a)* that the value of each product, as such, should be proportional to the cost incurred to produce it; *b)* that the product's use value should be, similarly, proportionate to the cost or sacrifice of who has profited from such use for a given period of time; *c)* that the product's value, as such, should be in a given correlation and proportion with the use value, as the cost of the former should be in a given correlation and proportion with the cost of the latter.

These formulas, to which one could, as is obvious, add other developments or combinations of the third, are nothing more than simple applications of the Ricardian theorem according to which given the known presuppositions, the values of the products of each producer should be proportional to the cost incurred to produce them[3].

The upshot of this is that, for given material goods, proportionality and correlations are acknowledged between the four terms, and that hence, whenever necessary, one term can be substituted and exchanged with another, and more specifically, the expression of value can be replaced by the expression of cost. In short, if we allow the afore-indicated premises, if I know a cost's size I can deduce the size of the value.

Now, this reasoning cannot repeat itself, according to me, with regard to the product man, personal capital.

It should first be noted that of the four data examined above, personal capital only offers us concretely three. There exists a cost of production of man, there exist a cost and a value of the use of man, i.e., of the concrete expression of his potential psycho-physical energy, but there does not exist in actual fact a value of man, i.e., of that potential energy and this is simply because, in present social economy, man is a free player and, as such, he is not in himself subject to valuation in the product market.

Hence, what enters said market is the aforementioned expression, the labour which man really performs. The item of value will therefore be labour. And also the value of the labour can be determined, in general, either in terms of cost or in terms of marginal utility.

Given these positive differences between the economic conditions of personal capital vis-à-vis material capital, the problem is now formulated somewhat differently and certainly more simply, with fewer number of elements: what relations will there be between the value of the use of man and the cost of production of man for himself?

Subordinated to his first problem, or rather, to its solution is a second problem, which I (despite the reality of present economic life, in which man is not subject to exchange) can propose for reasons of ideal and synthetic representation of the living, human social energies which a country enjoys. Basically, we are talking of

---

[3] See Pantaleoni M., *Principii di Economia pura*, Barbèra, 1889, pages 205-26 ff.

the research to which Engel intended to respond with his calculation. And here lies the problem: to determine the economic value of the body man, should I confine myself to a formal capitalisation of the value attributed to the labour carried out by man, or else can I resort to the cost of production of said? If in replying to the first problem, I stated that there is a relationship of correlation and proportionality between the value of labour and the cost of production of man, then I can make use of the recording of the cost of production: if instead I denied such type of relations, I will be forced to the formal and hypothetical capitalisation mentioned and will have to forgo a similar representative expression[4].

The reader knows that I solve the first and second problem with this last part of the dilemma. According to me, therefore, the theory of cost is not applicable when one relates the cost of production of man and the expressed labour, as the value which corresponds to this cannot be presumed to be neither correlated nor proportional to the cost of production of the man.

I sought to illustrate, as best I knew, the specific reasons for my conclusions in my article. They received an axiomatic rebuttal, based on statements and formulas void of content[5]. It is neither to my nor the reader's benefit that I repeat myself. Only when I have further clarified the problem, whose formulation is perhaps

[4] I spoke of «formal and hypothetical capitalisation». When one says, for example, that as x is the value of the labour, its capital value, i.e., the value of man, will be x, all one is doing is developing and expressing in a different manner the sole data ascertained and known, the value of labour. If to the capital value, so ideally known, one wished to give a meaning, an importance in itself, one would fall in a parologism similar to that of he who capitalises the wage believing that in doing so he can find a pre-existing data, the capital value of the labourer.

[5] In his formulas, Dr. Beneduce, if I too am not mistaken, follows a vicious circle. He tacitly presupposes as a fact that which should be shown, that is to say that consolidated economic relations exist between the elements before us. To be able to conclude, in fact, that the expression Cp can take the place of that of V, when one does not succeed in obtaining the size of V, it is necessary to show first that between Cp and V there is that certain relation of correlation and proportionality which I deny. The egregious scholars of mathematics should convince themselves, I believe, that the mathematical expression given to an economic demonstration always presupposes the economic demonstration, for the same good reason that a hare stew presupposes a hare. This is said without in the least diminishing Beneduce's merit for this diligent calculation (*Giornale degli Economisti*, December 1904) which gave rise to this discussion.

more precise and clearer than on other occasions, will I return to some ideas indicated but cursorily in a long note (on page 269 of the article cited many times) and which I believe, all said and done, worthy of consideration no less than other ideas which, with sufficient breadth, are developed in the text.

To prove that the equation between the cost of man and the value of said does not exist, we can consider the question from the point of view of the individual, subjectively, or else from the point of view of the social economy, objectively. We will thus see that from both the individual and the social economy there derive causes which, as they are jointly determined and combine, give rise to the same result. In the note indicated above, I briefly mentioned the first order of causes.

It suffices to consider the difference of origin, of formation and use, of transformation of personal capital vis-à-vis material capital to realise that the theory of cost, although applicable to the latter, cannot be applicable to the former.

Who, above all, saves to form material capital does so with economic criterion, referring, one understands, to the average of individuals. Who instead brings children into this world generally does so for the persuasive reasons which the Biblical serpent is supposed to have whispered to Adam and Eve. On the other hand we have the example of the sulphur miners, of the sharecroppers, etc., amongst whom proliferation is said to be higher than the average because the parents can immediately benefit from the employment of their offspring. Nobody would dream of denying the possibility of such a simple phenomenon. It is a phenomenon which will tend to be found in all those environments in which children are relatively scarce vis-à-vis demand and this and the remuneration are, correlatively, very high. But what does this prove? It proves that even the production of children, given specific conditions, is influenced by the law of supply and demand: the hedonistic instinct spurs the parents to profit from the difference that exists between the costs of raising the offspring and the pay, which is presumably high, that they will soon earn. But all this proves nothing with regard to the thesis of he who cites the phenomenon in his favour, as though it was some great argument; indeed, on closer examination, it proves precisely the opposite. In fact, the value of child labourers should be thought much higher than their cost, as otherwise the economic stimulus to procreate would not exist. The death of these children or their emigration would entail, hence, for the family, a much higher loss than that resulting from application of Engel's theory of the cost of production.

Let us deal with the second point. The choice of the form and use of material capital derives from purely economic views and norms. It cannot be claimed that this is the case for all the expenses which individuals accumulate for their raising, educating and maintaining, etc. The reason for this is very clear.

Man is spurred by a series of feelings and needs, a conspicuous part of which lies outside the economic sphere, even when to satisfy them it is necessary to resort, as means, to the economic element. The satisfaction of these needs is life, it is (if the metaphysicians will forgive me) the real purpose of life. Now, all together the expenses made to satisfy the needs of a person constitute the cost of that person, but not the cost of production in the sense this expression has when directly related to the concept of economic return, economic utility, value. Hence, in order to make the concepts of cost for both personal and material capital homogeneous, there has to be a point of juncture between the expenses accumulated in the former, considering only those which have direct or indirect pertinence to the productive work to which the person has dedicated himself. But is this possible, given the complexity of the effect which every type of satisfaction and expenses can have determined in a man, given the possibility each of us has to profit, for economic ends, of the habits that in us have been, unconsciously, determined by a broad-ranging series of expenses?

Let us shift our discussion to a less hazardous terrain. It is a fact that a part of the expenses incurred for an individual (it does not matter whether the individual decides them on his own behalf, or whether others do) are destined to procure him a skill which can then be economically exploited. Thus operate the bourgeois classes. Thus is also the case among the working classes, above all for skilled trades, because for unskilled workers the cost of professional education is almost non-existent, is relatively very small. It would be revealing and useful to know whether the calculations made on the person of an individual, between the cost of professional education and the gain correspond and are proportionate such as to be able to actually state that from the value assigned to the labour which the individual performs one can deduce the cost which the preparation of it has entailed or whether the former can be deduced from the latter.

In my article, I sought to give the reasons which led me to respond negatively. I also refer to the refined observations of Marshall[6]. The forecasts as regards future professional gains, for which one today spends, are disrupted by the variability of social events, this variability is compounded by the length of what I would call human investment. That which, in the more favourable hypothesis, relatives and the individual can expect is that, in the single trade or professions, comparatively considered, there is a certain broad proportionality between the price in practice attributed to the given professional work and the specific (not general) expenses incurred to acquire the corresponding habits or specific skills. But for how many professional groups and in how many cases is this the case? And this without taking account of the preliminary question, namely that the remuneration is not a priori the measure of the value of the work performed by man.

Some considerations, thirdly, on the transformation of capital, the possibility or facility of which, considered in the two types of capital, serves to characterise them.

Material capital, from the viewpoint of he who owns it, can, whatever its nature, be realised in cash or by the sale of the object which it represents or with the lease of its use. This exchange re-establishes from time to time the equation between the marginal utilities or between value and cost. Considering then material capital in itself, objectively, one sees that circulating capital transforms and renews itself in each production cycle while the periods of depreciation or reconstitution of fixed capital is not, in

[6] See MARSHALL, *Princ. of Econ.* Last edn., n. 308, 318 and passim.

the overwhelming majority of cases, so slow and long as the average life of a man, as the duration that is of the average personal capital. The mentioned equation therefore re-establishes itself in the afore-indicated cases automatically.

Man on the other hand, ordinarily finds himself in quite different and even opposite conditions. Subjectively, man cannot sell his own personal capital, i.e., himself, neither in general does he lease for long periods (except in some milieus, such the bureaucracy), the use of himself, i.e., his own work, as in this case he would remain even more tied and enslaved economically and morally to the special nature of his productive capacity.

Man retains the abstract possibility either to transform his productive capacity or to take it elsewhere by emigrating, adapting himself in both cases to the indications of the market. But in real life, not everyone is capable of transforming themselves, of learning another profession. The many reasons which stand in the way of this include those of a technical nature and those in respect of psychological adaptation. One should not be deceived by the many-coloured crowd of people of no trade and, at the same time, of all trades. I have read, for example, that when in Milan the trams were transformed from horse-drawn to electrically-drawn most of the personnel which drove the horses had to be dismissed because they were unable to adapt themselves to the new system. Undoubtedly, men, above all manual labourers, can emigrate, transporting their personal capital, consolidated in the given technical skills to where there is most demand. But here we should refer back to our observations above regarding the criteria with which one spends funds for oneself or for others. Labour cannot be separated from he who produces it and in he who produces it there exist, against emigration, obstacles of various nature, of which the most serious are those of an affective nature, prejudices, etc. I sought to demonstrate this and to elaborate a theory of this in one of my recent writings. The worker does not always succeed in getting the best of this set of sentiments which constitutes, all said and done, his moral personality, which makes him what he is. This means that this personality prevents the rigid expression of the economic self-interest, as this does not correspond to the overall self-interest. Of the two orders of self-interest, that which is the weightiest wins, which concerns all the man, and this by virtue of the very same general law of self-interest.

For having made, with few and modest words, these observations in the previous article, I have been accused (by nothing less than a legal expert's opinion by ... Gide) of having killed economic man. But if I am guilty of this homicide (moreover bloodless as it is an abstraction!) the classical economists are equally guilty, starting from our father David Ricardo, who founded the theory of international trade on data one of the most important of which is the imperfect mobility of personal capital, said imperfect mobility being ascribed to causes such as those which I briefly mentioned.

The deduction from all the foregoing observations is that the strictly economic criterion, dominant practically in material capital, also as regards the form, etc., of their use, encounters obstacles which are at times insurmountable in the other sphere of goods.

To conclude with regard to the three orders of differences now examined and to other such similar, which is it easy to add, I will limit myself to repeating that the reality of economic life and of one's complex personality will induce man to a valuation of which labour, not on the base of the cost of the productive potential which he represents, but on a more immediate and concrete item of data, the greater marginal utility or lower cost of one or the other expression of those which, in a given moment, are accessible to him.

Of the objective conditions which we above acknowledged as concatenated with the subjective conditions, I should add nothing, brevitatis causa, to what I noted in my previous article. It suffices to bear these two concepts in mind: that labour is a complementary capital asset and that its value cannot be determined separately from the economic body to which it is applied; that the value of the body is related to all the elements of which the given social economy consists. Now in this irregular and vast ambit, in which so many forces deploy their multiple action, should not the original cost of productivity be recognised as more than diminished in its directing and informational efficiency?

4. - The third problem asks whether Engel's calculation can be applied to the economic value of emigrants. I refer to Section VII of the old article. The application of the calculation to emigration uncovers best and greatly aggravates the intrinsic shortcomings of the calculation itself. It has not been proven to me, as I stated, that these two concepts inherent in the method contended are not absurd: — that the expatriation in the prime of his industriousness and vigorousness of the emigrant, who has repaid in whole or in part the capital spent on raising him, leads to less loss that the expatriation of he who has not yet started to produce, — that constantly supposing every emigrant represents always, for the economy of his homeland, a positive value is to go against the most evident reality.

5. - All the observations I have made induce me to reach the conclusion that the something given to us by Engel's calculation, applied to emigration, is not a part of the truth, but an error. Some however respond, and their number includes Vilfredo Pareto in the front ranks, that, in the absence of anything better, one should content oneself with that something and one should not be so hard to please and absolute in one's condemnation.

However much I have reflected on this, as Manzoni advised, and the superior and dear authority of our illustrious economist has weighed heavily on my spirit, I have not been able to convince myself of the scientific rather than evangelic reasonableness of this satisfiability.

I could justify this only in one case, that the data which Engel's method furnishes us was a first, and, to the extent one wishes, extremely broad approximation. But can one really talk of a first approximation when the concept which, in the case of personal assets, we have of the value, when the principle and the method of study which we repute correct, are intimately and irremediably different, indeed opposed to those from which such first approximation is derived? What value, whatever its degree of airy-fairy, can represent for me a datum which, because of the method by which it was obtained, is forced to speak to me always of an economic loss to the country of origin, when even analytical and positive studies, increasingly approximate, show me that a certain emigration is instead beneficial for said country?

I therefore do not believe it excessively ingenuous to hold, as some do, that if we forgo Engel's calculation, we would be forced to gratify ourselves with 'mere phrases' of varying degree of fantasy.

But then, before an item of data, simply because expressed, indeed disguised, in a figure, many of the economic and financial studies which are carried out every day should appear as 'mere phrases'!

But in truth do I not pose a logical problem regarding the size of the loss or gain produced by emigration when I intend to study the favourable or unfavourable effects of protectionism or free trade, of a given tax system, of a given industrial regime, of a given trend of workers' legislation and so forth? And does not the very fact that governments have alternately banned and encouraged emigration show that those governments, even without Engel's data, had, more or less roughly, intuited the size of the loss or gain of emigration to the national economy or the interest of a class? Who undertakes the aforementioned studies or do not the governments who halt and let free the migratory flows, not draw inspiration ordinarily from the opposite method to Engel's simplistic method, to the method which I acknowledged as necessary, to recording the effects of the phenomena from direct and indirect data on the entire complex of the national economy?

6. - And what of the comic adventure to which I alluded at the start. Here it is.

Mr. Emilio Macquart, who published a long review of my article in the July 15 issue of *Journal des Économistes*, ascribes me a curious expedient, an expedient which, in the economic field, it is claimed I do not know the example.

He confuses me with Dr. Beneduce, who as the reader is well aware is the author of the article on the value of Italian emigrants which inspired my theoretical observations, and he writes blithely that my article «is particularly original in that it tends to demonstrate the inanity of conclusions which the very same author had reached with much effort several months previously, to calculate and establish with an entire world of developments, with laborious care to affirm as rigorously as possible that truth which today he himself charges is nothing other than an error!».

I can well understand how with this most strange preconception in his head Mr. Macquart perhaps did not take the effort to read my equally arduous article with the necessary effort. I would thank him, in any case, for the flattering praise of the literary elegance and beauty of my discours. But as regards the substance of his criticisms, is it not true, kind and intellectual brother, that it is not the case to stop and examine them, also because you will find them in large part confuted in this article, which I dare entrust to your benevolence but (let us be clear!) to your patient benevolence?

IV - INFRASTRUCTURES, PUBLIC WORKS AND ENTERPRISES

A State Within a State[1]

Luigi Amoroso*

1. - There has already been that of the Praetorian Guard in ancient Rome and of the Huguenots in the France of Louis XIV; of the Jesuits in the XVIII century Church; of the mercenaries in Renaissance Italy.

Now in Italy the railwaymen tend to form a state within a state.

The causes of this fact are:

1) railwaymen form a homogeneous group of 150 thousand men, which in number is slightly less than the military - (the armed forces today in Italy total - excluding the officials - 250 thousand men) but is a much more selected and intelligent group than the military (soldiers);

2) unlike all the other classes of workers, railwaymen know no distances: they can, availing themselves of means which are impossible for other workers, maintain direct contact between themselves so as to form a compact bloc. On the other hand, they are aware of their force and united in a few organisations (four main ones), each of which can count on the blind and absolute obedience of its members;

3) railwaymen control one of the most difficult and important public services; the only one whose lack immediately brings

[1] These are the Sindacato dei ferrovieri italiani based in Milan; the Unione movimentisti based in Rome; the Unione nazionale fra gl'impiegati ferroviari based in Turin; the Sindacato operaio based in Florence.

* From: AMOROSO L., «Uno Stato nello Stato», *Giornale degli Economisti e Rivista di Statistica*, Roma, Atheneum, June 1913, pp. 554-66. [Cod. JEL: N 43].

the nation's economic life to a halt. In the event of war, the importance of their role is only just exceeded by that of the armed forces;

4) despite all these favourable circumstances which endow the railwaymen with a primary political force, they (the railwaymen) have received quite a middling economic treatment from the state[2]. Neither – given the present constraints on the railway budget – has the state been in a position to significantly improve these conditions.

A sign that these causes act on a fertile terrain is the eternal and continuous industrial unrest by the railwaymen which started in 1890 against the companies which ran the private networks, and which, after a few years, forced the government to order the Gagliardi Inquiry. The railwaymen subsequently obtained wage increases, and thousands of temporary employees became permanently on the payroll, employees' representatives sat on the Pension Fund Committees (which for the first time sanctioned the railwaymen's right to representation in the management of the railway company): they imposed without discussion, by means of obstructionism and strikes, the management of the railways by the state from which they obtained in eight years economic improvements worth more than 80 million lire per year, which raised the average pay of each employee from 1,300 lire per year in 1903 to circa 1,800 lire which is the present figure: they de facto obtained the right to insult and discredit their direct superiors in their periodical publications in particular, and the General Direction of the Rail-

[2] Public opinion does not realise this fact. And proof of it is that the number of workers who aspire to enter the railway administration is always big. Except - a few years after - when they regret their decision.

It is impossible, in the short space of a footnote, to provide statistical comparisons: moreover, they have been given many times in railway journals. We only note that this fact can be appreciated (qualitatively, if not quantitatively) from that modicum of personal experience each has.

An engine-driver who loses four nights out of seven and travels in the open with the fire in his face and the wind at his shoulders (engine-drivers have a very high mortality rate vis-à-vis the rest of the population) earns considerably less than a chauffeur or a mechanic: the pointsman who hundreds of times in a day can with a momentary distraction cause the death of hundreds of persons, earns less than a bricklayer, etc.

ways in general[3]: to negotiate directly with the Minister, circumventing the General Direction: and finally, to institute a railway parliament in which all the categories of personnel are represented and whose first parliamentary crisis we are seeing at this moment[4].

History teaches that when a state is constituted within a state a position of unstable equilibrium is always created and this sooner or later tends to produce:

1) either the ruin of the principal state. This was the case of the Praetorian Guards in Rome;

---

[3] In order to prove that there is no exaggeration in our claim, we cite from the journal *In Marcia* (Pisa, April 1913) and *Tribuna dei ferrovieri* (Milan, 8 April 1913), the following two articles:

Iniquity and Dissolution in the State Railways. The empty chatter of the Minister of Public Works has not persuaded us otherwise. The Director General can be compared to him. He is surrounded only by careerists, cronies and thickheads. It is the most bureaucratic and inquisitorial phalanx of any administration, etc.

«Iniquity and abuse are the system. The bonuses are the latest example of this.

«Against them powerless meetings, vibrant protests, loud demonstrations against the Director General have been held. The beggarly mass grumbled.

«Against the violence and malversation, nothing. The humbug of the reordering is passed over in silence, instead of shouting aloud: You have added two departments to the ten, and a new service to make room for cronies.

«It is an administration of pirates. Etc. (We believe it right to omit any insinuations against specific persons).

«His Excellency speaks. The thirty two protesting representatives note that if during these two years they have become all too familiar with the taste of empty phrases, the blame is not of Direction General, nor of 'father' Bianchi, no, but rather of His Excellency the extreme-radical Sacchi. Here is what the "horse-breaker Ettorre" stated recently to the House:

«The delay in the convocation (at which the known protest took place) should in no way be ascribed to the Director General; it is I who did not deem it appropriate to do so earlier. If there was any delay, I assume full responsibility for it and am tranquil, because that delay was used to gather and introduce in the preparation of the bill, the personnel's views, with which I was well acquainted even without the formality of the convocation and which were fully satisifed".

«Can we put just three questions to His Excellency?

1) why at the plenary conference of August 1912 was representative Pecoraro interrupted by the Director General, when he blamed Sacchi for the delay in convocation and the lack of importance of the items then on the agenda with these words: "The blame for the delay lies not with the Minister, but solely with me", when on the other hand it is now the Minister himself who exonerates Bianchi from this responsibility, he assuming it in full? In clear Italian which of the two is lying: Bianchi in August 1912 or Sacchi in February 1913? etc."

[4] Public opinion has remained unmoved by this and this is quite natural. It is the same story as that of the centurion Romano (in Rostand's *Samaritaine*) who, talking of Jesus Christ, to a passer-by says «It will not be he who will disrupt the world».

2) or the breakdown of the state which tends to form within the state. This was the case with the Huguenots in France, with the Jesuits in the XVIII century Church;

3) or the transformation of the state which tends to form within the state: a transformation which eliminates the former's capacity to produce harm. This was the case of the mercenaries in sixteenth century Italy: their place was taken by the citizen's militia, of which the permanent armies are the continuation to this day. This force which in the hands of a few was a social danger for a long time became a guarantee of social peace when it became the property of all citizens.

2. - What is the nature of the transformation which can take place in the railway body? There is an entire current of public opinion which, faithful to the old ideology of the French revolution and of humanitarian socialism, believes that renewal can take place through a moral transformation. The overwhelming mass of railwaymen – this is the opinion of the most authoritative representatives of this current of ideas, of Hon. Luzzatti and Minister Sacchi, for example – is by nature good: the blame is wholly of a few instigators: eliminate them, and all the railwaymen will not hesitate to feel bound to cease threatening the state which pays them, which looks after them and to whose fortune their own is increasingly linked.

We do not hesitate to categorically state that our opinion is precisely the opposite: the relations between the state and the railwaymen are determined by a set of forces, among which the sense of duty and justice (on both one side and the other) are wholly extraneous, or but slightly relevant. This opinion is founded on the experimental observation of that which has always happened. We do not know how better to clarify this than by citing the speech which Machiavelli places in the mouth of a Florentine during the wool carders' uprising in book III of his *History of Florence*.

«If we were to decide now if we should take up arms, burn and steal the houses of citizens, despoil the churches, I would be one of those who would be far from thinking so, and perhaps I would opine that tranquil poverty is better than a dangerous gain.

But as the arms have been taken up, and many ills have been done, and I believe we should reason that they will not be put down and that ill will be done. I believe certainly, that when others do not teach us, need does. You see all this city full of regret, and hatred against us; the citizens are disappearing, the Signoria always sides with the magistrates. It is certain that nooses are being prepared for us and new forces are preparing to move against us. We should therefore seek two things, and have two aims in our deliberations; one not to be punished for the things we have done in these days; the other to be able to live with more freedom and satisfaction than in the past. It is therefore worth our while, I believe, to ensure our old errors are pardoned by committing new ones, by doubling the ills, and by increasing the arson and theft, and to ensure that we are in many to do so. Because where many err, nobody is punished, and if small faults are punished, the big and serious ones are not. For when many suffer, few seek revenge, as universal abuse is borne more patiently than small-scale abuse. Hence the more our ill deeds, the easier it will be to obtain pardon and it will give us the way to have those things which we desire for our liberty, and I believe we will achieve some gains and those who could stand in our way are disunited and rich; and hence their disunity will give us victory and when their wealth has become ours we will not relinquish it. Neither should you be dumbfounded by those ancient ties of blood with which they reproach us. Because all men having had the same origin are equally ancient, and by their nature are made in one way. Undress us all and you will see we are alike: let us put on their clothes and they ours: we shall undoubtedly seem noble and they lowly: because only poverty and wealth make us unequal. I am truly sorry that I feel that many of you repent in your conscience of the things you have done, and wish to abstain from new such deeds. And undoubtedly if it is true, you are not the men I thought you were; as neither conscience nor infamy should dumbfound you; because those who win, however they win, are never ashamed of this. And we should not heed our conscience; because where there is, as there is in us, the fear of hunger and of prison, there cannot nor should be that of the infernal flames. But if you notice men's way of proceeding, you will see all those who attain great wealth and great power either dishonestly or by force; and to hide the ugliness of the acquisition of those things, usurped either by deceit or by violence, they justify it as honest by the right of earning. And those who either by way of lack of prudence or of excessive foolishness eschew these ways, always drown in bondage and poverty; because faithful servants are always servants, and the good men are always poor; and they never escape bondage unless they are unfaithful and audacious, and poverty if they are not rapacious and deceitful[5]. Because God and nature have placed in the midst of them all the fortunes of men, which are susceptible more to robbery than industry, and to the bad than the good arts. Thence men devour each other, and those who are least able are always the worst off. Hence force should be used when we have the opportunity, which cannot be offered to us by greater fortune, as the citizens are still disunited, the Signoria hesitant, the magistrates dumbfounded: such that those who come forward are united, and stop the easily oppressable spirit of courage. Hence either we shall remain lords of the city, or we will own so much of it that not only will our past errors be pardoned, but we will have the authority to threaten new abuses. I confess that this undertaking is audacious and dangerous; but where need forces daring is judged prudent and courageous men never take heed of danger in large things. Because those undertakings which start with danger, end with reward, and one never leaves danger without danger. And I also believe that when one sees the prisons, the torments and the deaths being prepared, that more fearful is the being there rather than the assuring it, as under the former the ills are assured and in the other doubtful. How many times have I heard you complain of the avarice of your superiors, and of the injustice of your magistrates? Now it is time not only to free yourself of them, but to become so much their superiors that they will have much more cause to complain and fear you, than you them. The opportunity that occasion furnishes us flies and in vain when it has fled does

---

[5] «I remind my reader that here as below it is my hero, who speaks, etc...» (De Musset, *Numouna*, Chapter I, verse XXXIX) and I have too much respect for him to allow myself to omit a single comma from this text.

one seek to recapture it. You see the preparations of your adversaries. We are foremost in their thoughts, and whichever of us will first take up our arms will undoubtedly be the victor with the ruin of the enemy and his own exaltation; thence for many of us honour, and security for all».

No populist, no socialist, no trade unionist has ever spoken in this manner. But is this not the force of the great psychologists (Aristotle, Titus Livius, Machiavelli, Montesquieu, Pareto) capable of succeeding in specifying that which everyone feels, but nobody is capable of expressing: and thus succeeding in refinding the intimate, latent, profound and instinctive origins of human actions?

3. - A moral transformation cannot therefore right the railway body. To see what could be the nature of the transformation which would be the most efficacious, let us seek whether history does not present – among the facts which we recalled at the start of this paper, as typical of those which represent a state within a state – something, which allows us to find our bearings. This orientation – we believe – is obtained when one considers the transformation, already mentioned, of the bands of mercenaries into permanent armies.

And once again we have to refer to Machiavelli. It is well-known that he on various occasions insisted on the need for a state to have citizens' armies: the bands of mercenaries, which are hired when one fears an external danger or one wishes to carry out a war of conquest, sooner or later – this is his thought – become the ruin of the state which hires them.

Machiavelli's thesis has ended up triumphing completely. Today throughout the world there exist not groups of mercenaries, but permanent armies.

When one is faced with a phenomenon of such general breadth which regards four centuries of history, which gives rise to institutions accepted by all civil nations, this means that there is some essential reason by which it corresponds to some profound need of nature or human society.

Why in 1500 was Italy in the hands of bands of mercenaries while the other nations had permanent armies instead? Perhaps the cause of this phenomenon consists in the fact that at the time Italy was economically by far the most advanced of all the nations of Europe. Admitted, and it would be difficult not to admit such, that a state needs to protect itself by means of armed mercenaries against any aggression or to proceed to useful conquests, the institution of bands of mercenaries is the most economic satisfaction of this need.

It in fact corresponds to one of the most accepted principles of economic policy, namely to the principle of the division of labour. It is much more advantageous economically for society that a few individuals dedicate themselves to the martial trade and make it their sole occupation, rather than oblige the citizens to dedicate a period of their life to said trade. Military (and also profane) technicians know that victory is more the fruit of military habits and the exercise of these habits than the number of soldiers: an army of veterans has always gained the upper hand against new troops under fire. At parity of result, the number of working days society has to pay to obtain the purpose of safeguarding of its external interests is infinitely less if it were to hire a band of mercenaries than if it set up a permanent army.

But then, if it is true that the bands of mercenaries correspond to an economic solution of the military problem, how is it that the modern European nations, which are masters in adapting the means to the achievement of economic ends, have ended up by adopting the diametrically opposite solution?

The reason for this lies essentially in that which we noted above, and which all said and done is that which Machiavelli noted, namely: «the economic advantage which society enjoys by having individuals specialised in military services is considerably less than the political harm which arises from the possibility that these individuals might abuse the power which lies in their hands».

In economic language, if one adds to the cost of the bands of mercenaries the price which individuals continually armed in the midst of a crowd of unarmed persons make the latter pay by way of imposition and privileges, the balance is more than tilted in favour of permanent armies.

Nonetheless, the solution of permanent armies, despite its

enormous political advantage, could not have been adopted by the civil societies, and the latter would have had to continue to bear the imposition of the military element if it was not for the fact that for all the functions of the overwhelming majority of the armed men (privates) the military profession requires no particular specialisation. The ratio between the necessarily specialised functions (of the commissioned and non-commissioned officers) and those with little specialisation (privates) is very small.

And basically it is because this condition is satisfied that the politically more advantageous solution (of the establishment of permanent armies) can be adopted; moreover, the same condition reduces the drawbacks deriving from the lack of division of labour. The effects of this being much more noteworthy and important, the more specialisation the labour requires.

4. - Reasoning by analogy leads us therefore to a conclusion: the same causes produce the same effects. It may be a question of time: if the state does not become the prey of the railway oligarchy (which we all hope), if the railways continue to develop so as to become increasingly linked to the nation's economic life (which is probable if the nation continues to advance economically and no invention is made which leads to a revolution in the means of transport), the power which the railwaymen today have at their disposal and which threatens, if held but by a few, to fell the social body from its foundations, should be sooner or later re-introduced into circulation. All this the sooner the railwaymen with their threats place the state in serious danger.

What does re-introduced into circulation mean? If we take as our base that which held for military power, this means that of the 150 thousand railwaymen, which is how many there are in Italy today, the overwhelming majority of them will be railwaymen for a very short period of time: just as one is a soldier for only three years, today's railwaymen will for the most be different from the railwaymen in ten year's hence, etc. A small group (of those who will be entrusted with the most delicate and difficult and special functions: skilled workers, stationmasters, management staff, etc.) will be railwaymen for all their life.

Only the future will say whether this will be the future solution. Undoubtedly, whatever the form, its nature will be an organisation of the service such that the functions of most of the railwaymen charged with operating the service become increasingly less specialised, and can be substituted by persons who have no special skills, while on the other hand the functions which are specialised by nature will be concentrated as far as is feasible in that part of the railway staff which is not charged with operating the service, and which therefore does not hold any political power, neither can it impose itself with obstructionism and strikes.

At this point, we should pose a question. Do the technical requirements of the railway service allow an organisation such as to reduce the specialised functions and concentrate them in that part of the personnel which is not charged with the running? Or is not every railway service by its nature a service which – to be performed – requires special skills and knowledge?

We hold that such an organisation is possible, and that even in railway services the specialisation can be reduced to a minimum. Nonetheless, the nature of this paper and limits of space do not allow us to develop this question: we shall therefore confine ourselves to considering that which is generally held – and quite rightly – to be the most difficult, the most delicate, the most special of the railway services, namely the engine-driver service.

There are two systems of engine-driver service which can be adopted to organise the shifts of the locomotives and personnel: the English system, which is adopted by almost all the European railway administrations; and the American system, which in Europe is adopted by most of the tramway companies. Under the first system each locomotive is assigned to a pair of employees (engine driver and stoker) which is responsible for it. The locomotive follows the pair's shifts: there are long periods of pause during which the locomotive remains inactive, and periods of rest, during which the locomotive is parked and is washed and repaired. Under the American system, on the other hand, the locomotive is not assigned to any specific pairs of employees, the employees work indifferently on any locomotive: and each locomotive is handed over to various pairs of employees, thus travelling very long distances and staying out many days before returning to the depot. Under the English system a locomotive lasts for many years, thus reducing the interest and capital amortisation allowances. Conversely, under the American system:

1) the service can be provided with a much lower number of locomotives: hence plant and maintenance costs are lower.

2) the short life of a locomotive, barely ten or fifteen years, allows the company to always own the most modern type of locomotive.

In short, therefore, from the technical point of view, the American system is not inferior to the English system, which has the enormous political advantage that the engine-driver is such rather than a mechanic. The engine driver is charged with no task other than that of driving the locomotive: he does not have to carry out any repairs. The repairs are carried out in the workshops by skilled workers who have nothing to do with the locomotive personnel. Hence the locomotives require a much less specialised personnel, as regulating the pressure and stoking the fire can be easily learnt by any person after even a brief period of practice.

The political power of being able, should one wish, to bring the nation's economic life to a halt lies with the engine-drivers (non-specialised personnel), not with the workers in the workshops who carry out the repairs (specialised personnel). But the engine-drivers, precisely because they do not carry on a specialised work, even though they do not form a mass which continuously renews itself (final solution), can easily be replaced in their functions (provisional solution): any political threat has therefore vanished.

5. - The state has a regiment of railwaymen (VI Regiment of the Engineer Corps). It currently deals not so much with railway services[6], as military services related to railway services. Evidently this could be the base for the forthcoming transformation; it could start with the increase in the number of these regiments;

[6] As railway service it currently does no more than run the Turin-Torre Pellice line!

with the assignment to them of continuous and well defined railway tasks. Experience would show whether it was feasible in practice, and if there were any drawbacks it would also indicate the means for remedying them.

The problem with which we are dealing is, to a certain extent related to the entire military problem of officer cadets and one-year voluntary privates. The one-year voluntary privates include a large number of persons with technical knowledge and special diplomas: engineering degrees, diplomas from polytechnics or from naval and professional institutes, etc. It requires little perspicacity to recognise how little the state today profits from these forces it has at its disposal!

It should also be noted that a practical application of our concept would also profit those concerned who at present obtain no profit from military service in its current form, and would be quite pleased, if it could enable them to acquire a certain number of skills which are not acquired at school and even more so if it would help (and why not?) them as a means for entering the railway administration permanently.

It is obviously useful for the state itself to choose its fixed agents from among this continually renewing flow, just as it is undoubtedly useful to recruit non-commissioned officers from among privates. The function of non-commissioned offices is so delicate that it cannot be carried out by merely anybody, but demands an entire set of qualities which reveal themselves in the first year of military service. Now is it not precisely the same for the railway service? If it is true that control of this service is a primary power, is it perhaps not useful for all to know the psychology of those who are entrusted with this power? Should not all those who ferment unrest, are unwilling to submit to discipline, all those, in a word, who in one way or another can be a danger for the community, be excluded?

And would one not obtain precisely this result if the state were to choose its railway engineers, its stationmasters, its workers, its engine-drivers, in short all the railway workers who have fixed or most important tasks, recruiting them from the railway corps of the Engineering Corps?

Without considering that the large mass which renews itself (railwaymen with non-specialised tasks) would gain a powerful stimulus for remaining attached to the service. Everyone knows how in all social conditions it is often difficult, at the start of a career (and this regardless of personal value), to find employment. If it became known that the railway military service gave the best employment, would there not be therefore a spur, and a powerful spur, to be counted among the best?

6. - If the transformation does take place, it will do so in the face of the hostility and perhaps the outright opposition of the overwhelming majority of railwaymen: this is because it runs against their ideology. And yet it will benefit the railwaymen, as it will allow the state to resolve the railway question also from the economic point of view, granting the railwaymen living conditions which are better than those, unfortunately unhappy, which they enjoy today.

We disregard the forms of the transformation: we have now indicated how it could take place; whatever - moreover - the manner, it can always not offend the existing interests: the railway body is renewed at the rate of circa 5% per year, and hence within circa some twenty years one could achieve a balanced solution.

On the other hand, precisely because the Treasury would achieve a saving, paying part of the railwaymen as army personnel and not as free workers, the afore-mentioned transformation would allow an economic solution of the question of the fixed railwaymen (i.e., those with specialised functions). The fact remains that, as we have already noted, on the one hand the economic conditions of railwaymen today are certainly not that of privilege, while on the other the state sees the revenues it obtains from the railways diminish with each year. Said amounted to circa 70 million lire in the last years of the private management: now that the traffic has more than doubled it oscillates around 35 million lire (and even if one takes into account the amounts paid for amortisation of the extraordinary works carried out during the period of state management, it does not total 100 million lire). The consequence: as things stand, new, significant improvements for the railwaymen can only entail a serious burden for the Treasury such that it would completely wipe out the present operating surplus and perhaps soon even transform this surplus into a deficit, with the result that the railways would be supported by the Treasury.

Italy today has an army of circa 250,000 men; with the new law it will soon total 300 thousand men. France, with a population more or less the same circa 700 thousand, and Germany, with a population which is less than double, circa 850 thousand men. Italy can therefore, without an excessive economic burden on free labour, ensure peace in the most important of public services.

'Related' Costs and the Economics of Transport*

Enrico Barone

R40

1. - Introduction

1.1 *'Related' Costs and 'Joint' Costs*

The economic theory of transport gives rise to many applications of the theory of supply to related costs: let us say, by way of emphasis, related costs and not joint costs.

It is known that, some English and American writers (Pigou and Taussig for example) in particular have discussed at length whether the expression 'joint costs' should be ascribed with a more limited meaning, reserving it for the case only in which two or more goods – products with a single process in which the costs cannot be separated – are such that the production of one can-

---

* From: BARONE E., «I costi «connessi» e l'economia dei trasporti», *Giornale degli Economisti e Rivista di Statistica*, Roma, Atheneum, 1921.

This study is a brief introductory chapter to a broad course of the economics of transport which the author is reading this academic year to the students of the Royal Superior Institute of Commercial Studies of Rome. It is the author's intent, in this course, to summarise the most salient results of the studies on economics and transport, and moreover to order and co-ordinate this part of economic science according to some overall guiding concepts which he believes can give rise to a very comprehensive synthetic theory. These guiding concepts are briefly expounded in this text.

As these are essentially quantitative studies, it was not possible to expound them with some precision without resorting to symbols. But as far as was possible, the author has confined these symbols to some footnotes, aiming in the body of the text, with the help of some graphs, to make the substance of what he says comprehensible also to those who do not possess the little analytical knowledge needed to follow the notes. [Cod. JEL: R 40].

not, in general, increase without the production of the other or other goods increasing (mutton, sheep hides and wool for example); or else whether the expression 'joint costs' should be given a broader meaning, extending it to many other cases of goods or services produced with a single process, whose quantities are constrained by other types of conditions (for example, the tonnes of goods and number of passengers which can be carried by a ship, by a railway train). There is, in truth, some similarity between the facts of one and the other category; but the similarity is purely formal and boils down to the existence for one and the other of a certain 'constraint' between the quantities of the two (or more) goods or services which can be produced: such that the nature of this constraint is in one substantially different than in the other; and the economic equilibrium and dynamics are also substantially different. This is why we deemed it appropriate not to confuse them, and to distinguish them by different names, employing the expression 'related costs' for the specific order of facts which we shall deal with in the economic theory of transport[1].

2. - Equilibrium at 'Related' Costs

2.1 *The Characteristics of this Order of Facts*

Transport companies are producers of various categories of services at 'related costs', each of which has its own demand.

The circumstances characterising this order of facts of related costs regarding transport are as follows: 1) that in the pro-

[1] In both the phenomena of joint costs, in the narrow sense, and in those of 'related' costs, there is a certain 'constraint' $\vartheta(x_a, x_b, x_c ...) = 0$ which links the quantity x_a, x_b, x_c ... of the goods and services produced, such that in both one and the other the cost of x_a cannot be separated from that of x_b, x_c ... because the goods are part of a single production process, such that one can speak only of a cost $\Phi(x_a, x_b, x_c ...)$ of the goods and services taken together: but the similarity does not end here: the differences of the economic equilibrium and dynamics are substantial and depend above all on the fact that when referring to joint costs, the partial derivatives $\vartheta x_b/\vartheta x_a$, $\vartheta x_c/\vartheta x_a$ ... are generally positive, and generally negative when referring to 'related' costs.

duction of the various services *(A)*, *(B)*, *(C)*... there is no possibility of specifying the cost for the quantities produced x_a, x_b, x_c but there is an indivisible overall cost; 2) that in this overall cost there is a considerable part, which in certain limits – that is up to a point which we shall call 'plant saturation' – which can be deemed constant, while the other part varies with variations in x_a, x_b, x_c ...; 3) that the overall cost of x_a, x_b, x_c ... can be held, by way of approximation, to be represented by $k + c_a x_a + c_b x_b + c_c x_c + \ldots$ In this expression k is the constant part we mentioned above; c_a, c_b, c_c ... are what we will call the 'partial unit costs' of *(A)*, *(B)*, *(C)*... Strictly speaking, this is inaccurate, because the partial unit costs are not constant, but variable quantities; and they generally diminish as the output increases: but in a first approximation such as this we can consider them as constant. When, however, deeming them thus can alter the conclusions of our reasoning, we shall take account of their variability and the diminishing with the increase in output; 4) that the quantities x_a, x_b, x_c ... cannot be varied as one wishes: they are tied to a certain quantitative relation, which we shall call a 'constraint' and which for transport is generally of a linear form; we shall give it the form $x_a/a + x_b/b + x_c/c + \ldots = 1$. For example, the 'constraint' for a steamship which divides its available space between goods, which occupy different spaces for each tonne of weight, and passengers of various classes is linear: and similarly so is that for a railway train. The linear constraint means that if the company limits itself to producing only *(A)*, the maximum quantity it can produce with the plant it owns is a. Similarly, b for *(B)*, c for *(C)* and so forth.

2.2 *The 'Standard Combination'*

In view of its great importance for our study, it is here worthwhile putting forward the notion of that which, to be clear, we shall call the 'standard combination'. It is thus defined (Graph 1): the combination, of the various with full saturation compatible with the constraint, which maximises the sum of the hatched areas. This sum of areas represents the total utility, expressed in money, of x_a, x_b, x_c ... diminished by their simple partial cost. The curves are those of the demand for *(A), (B), (C)*... [2].

GRAPH 1

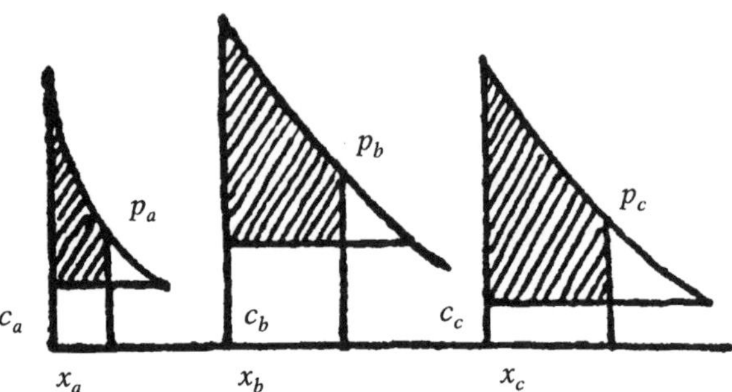

2.3 *Equilibrium in the Case of Competition*

Given this, we can express the equilibrium of the prices of *(A), (B), (C)* ... with related costs in the case of competition, in the case of private monopoly and in the case of collective monopoly. For private monopoly we shall distinguish between two subcases: unlimited monopoly, in which no limit is posed as regards the quest for the maximum profit; limited monopoly when a limit is posed to this quest (for example with regard to the capital employed in the company) as is generally the case in practice.

Here also we shall reason on three goods *(A), (B), (C)* for the sake of simplicity so as not to complicate the symbols; but any reasoning, here and below, is general and applies to any number of goods.

---

[2] This standard combination is unequivocal and perfectly detemmined. If we suppose three goods (we suppose three for the sake of simplicity, there could be n, and the reasoning would be the same) we have six unknowns x_a, x_b, x_c, p_a, p_b, p_c. And we have six equations Three are given by the demand $p_a = F_a(x_a) = F_b(x_b)$, $p_c = F_c(x_c)$ One is given by the constraint $x_a/a + x_b/b = x_c/c = 1$. The other two obtained by maximising $U_a(x_a) + U_b(x_b) + U_c(x_c) - (c_a x_a + c_b x_b + c_c x_c)$, whose maximum gives rise to two equations:

$$a\,(p_a - c_a) = b\,(p_b - c_b) = c\,(p_c - c_c)$$

If the common values of these products are made equal to M, we will have $p_a = c_a + M/a$, $p_b = c_b + M/b$. $p_c = c_c + M/c$, The quantity M is, evidently, the surplus of the income over partial costs, because we have $p_a x_a = c_a x_a + M\, x_a/a$ and the two similar ones; and summing the three $p_a x_a + p_b x_b + p_c x_c = c_a x_a + c_c x_c + M$.

In the case of competition, at prices p_a, p_b, p_c, which are assumed to be temporarily given, each single company produces the quantities x_a, x_b, x_c, with a certain profit g, these four quantities are determined by four conditions: one is given by the constraint; one is the equality between the revenues on the one hand and the costs plus the profit on the other; the other two express the condition that the profit, i.e., the difference between income and costs, is maximum. Hence, for a given series of prices, a x_a a x_b, a x_c for each company: hence a x_a, a x_b, a x_c overall. The prices p_a, p_b, p_c will be in equilibrium, when these overall x_a, x_b, x_c are those which in the demand of *(A)*, *(B)* and *(C)* correspond to the temporarily given prices p_a, p_b, p_c.

It is easy to analytically reach the following enunciation, which represents the general law of the trend of related cost prices with full saturation of the plant, under free, perfect competition (when the constraint is linear as in transport): the price of *(A)* is equal to the unit cost the company would incur if it produced only *(A)* in the maximum quantity a allowed by the constraint; the same holds for *(B)* and *(C)*[3].

The analysis also clearly shows: 1) that under perfect competition the equilibrium solution is none other than the standard combination which we discussed in 2.2 above; 2) the under perfect competition, if $c_a > c_b$ it in no way follows that $p_a > p_b$; as also if $c_a = c_b$, it it no way follows that $p_a = p_b$[4].

---

[3] It is appropriate at this juncture to clarify some expressions we shall frequentiy employ. The company (Graph 2), spurring its production to the maximum compatible with its present plant, can even produce *OS*. Let us call *S* the point of saturation of its present plant. Let us consider the amount produced *OA*: its overall cost *AM* consists of a constant overall cost *AC*, and of a variable overall cost *CM*. For the amount produced *OA*, *cd* is the unit cost, *ef* is the partial unit cost. If in addition to the amount *OA*, one produces also the amount *AB*, the increase of cost *ab* we shall call the supplementary cost of *AB*. Generally, to simplify, we shall assume that the cost of production of X_a is $K + c_a X_a$, in which c_a is a constant: i.e., by way of approximation, to the curve of Graph 2 we shall substitute the straight line of Graph 3.

[4] Here is how. For each company the constants a, b, c of the constraint have a specific value; and thus also for k, c_a, c_b, c_c. These constants do not have the same value at the various companies except in the state of extreme competition, or perfect competition (when, that is, this has annulled the profits and reduced the companies to a few of the same type). Let us consider one of the companies.

Graph 2

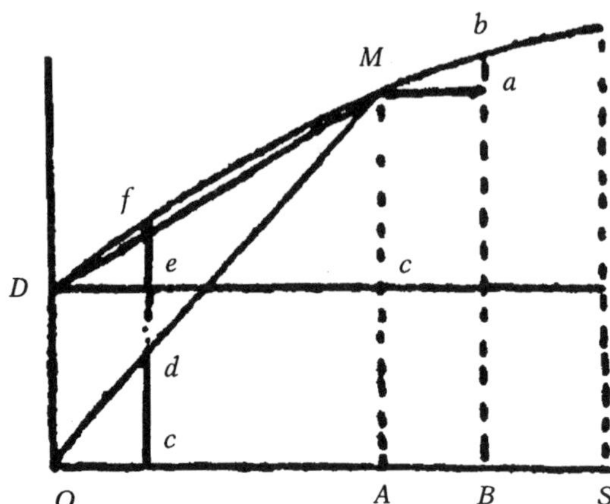

The equations which, assuming the prices p_a, p_b, p_c as given, determine the quantity x_a, x_b, x_c and also the company's profit g are the following four:

$$p_a x_a + p_b x_b + p_c x_c = c_a x_a + c_b x_b + c_c x_c + k + g$$

$$\frac{x_a}{a} + \frac{x_b}{b} + \frac{x_c}{c} = 1$$

plus the two equations of the maximum profit (here for the maximum one differentiates, considering the *ps* as constants).

$$a\ (p_a - c_a) = b\ (p_b - c_b) = c\ (p_c - c_c)$$

From them we have:

$$p_a = c_a + \frac{k+g}{a},\ p_b = c_b + \frac{k+g}{b},\ p_c = c_c + \frac{k+g}{c}$$

which says that under a regime of perfect competition, the constant part of the overall cost plus the profit, tend, in each company, to be divided out in addition to the partial cost in the ratio of $1/a$, $1/b$, $1/c$.

On the marginal company, which makes neither a profit nor a loss — and also in those premarginal companies in the state of extreme competition — one has $p_a = c_a + k/a$, $p_b = c_b + k/b$, $p_c = c_c + k/c$ which is precisely the analytical expression of the proposition eunciated in the text.

One can also see: 1) that in perfect competition the equilibrium solution is the standard combination; 2) that in perfect competition if $c_a > c_b$, it does not follow that $p_a > p_b$. It suffices to recall that $p_a = c_a + k/a$, $p_b = c_b + k/b$ to see that however, one should take account of the quantities a and b conceded by the constraint.

GRAPH 3

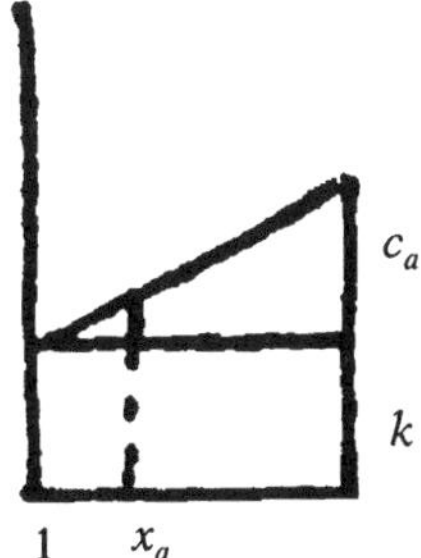

2.4 *Equilibrium in the Case of Private Unlimited Monopoly*

The solution prechosen by the private unlimited monopolist is that x_a, x_b, x_c of those possible within the limits of the constraint in which (Graph 4) the sum of the hatched areas (which contain k plus the monopoly profit) is maximum.

This solution, which is univocal, is obviously different from the standard combination[5].

Let us consider for a moment the values of x_a, x_b, x_c which each maximise their respective hatched triangle. Then if, by pure chance, this solution saturates, nothing more or less, the company's plant, the monopolist will adopt it; if it exceeds the limits of saturation, the monopolist will have to stick with the general solution we have just seen (and which we analytically specified in a footnote) and satisfy himself with maximising, as he

[5] The six equations are: first and foremost the three usual ones of demand and that of the constraint, which make four; but instead of $a\ (p_a - c_a) = b\ (p_b - c_b) = c\ (p_c - c_c)$, these others (having, when differentiating, to consider the ps as variables):

$$a\left(p_a + x_a \frac{dp_a}{dx_a} - c_a\right) = b\left(p_b + x_b \frac{dp_b}{dx_b} - c_b\right) =$$

$$= c\left(p_c + x_c \frac{dp_c}{dx_c} - c_c\right).$$

Graph 4

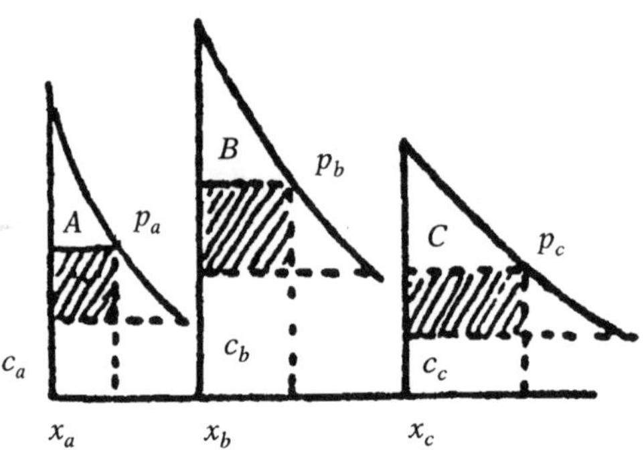

best can, not each area, but the sum of the areas. But it may even be that the solution which maximises each area is outside the constraint, such that it leaves him available a certain production potential: then it is worth his while to procure other demand, even though to attract it he has to quote a price which is just above the partial cost.

2.5 *Equilibrium in the Case of Private Limited Monopoly*

In the economics of transport, even when it is in the hands of a monopolist, it is rare that he can exact a tribute as he wishes from senders and travellers and is not subject to constraints which limit his profit in one form or another. There then arises the problem of seeing how, the monopolist, according to his plant and with the attainment of a given profit G can regulate prices so as to obtain the maximum possible consumer's surplus.

The problem, again referring to the example of only three goods, for the sake of simplicity (the reasoning is general, we repeat, and holds whatever the number n of goods) is posed in these terms.

Prices should be determined such that (Graph 4): 1) x_a, x_b, x_c are compatible with the constraint; 2) the sum of the hatched areas furnishes the constant part of the overall cost and the given profit, namely $K + G$; 3) the sum of the three white areas $A + B + C$ is the maximum possible[6].

To resolve the problem we can start from the standard combination, which, as we know, enjoys the property that the sum of the hatched areas such as indicated in Graph 1 is the maximum possible, of all the combinations which, within the limits of the constraint, and compatible with this, can be imagined. Hence this standard combination would be the most fitting solution, except that in it the sur-

---

[6] The problem is determinate, because there are six unknowns and one has six equations. Of these: α) ...three are given by the demands; β) ... one by the constraint; γ)... one by the condition that the sum of the areas should be $K + G$.

$$(p_a - c_a)\, x_a + (p_b - c_b)\, x_b + (p_c - c_c)\, x_c = K + G$$

δ) ... and finally, one is given by the condition of the maximum of the sum of the unshaded areas:

$$U_a\,(x_a) + U_b\,(x_b) + U_c\,(x_c) - (p_a x_a + p_b x_b + p_c x_c)$$

which is like maximising:

$$U_a\,(x_a) + U_b\,(x_b) + U_c\,(x_c) - (c_a x_a + c_b x_b + c_c x_c)$$

The maximum gives a single equation, because the three unknowns x_a, x_b, x_c are already bound by two conditions, (β) and, (γ).

It is superfluous to point out that, although the expression of the quantity to be maximised is in this case the same that we saw in the standard solution (note to Section 2.2), the values of x which give the maximum required in this case, are different from those of the typical solution, because then the xs were bound by a single condition, that of the constraint, while here they are bound by two conditions, that of the constraint and that of the recovery of $K + G$ The single equation which in this case expresses the maximum, is found quite easily with the determinants: but it is somewhat complicated, because it results from equalling to zero the sum of the three terms for a, b, c, similar to the following:

$$a\left(p_a - c_a\right) = \left(b.x_b \frac{dp_b}{dx_b} - c.x_c \frac{dp_c}{dx_c}\right).$$

Hence the convenience, as we shall see, in resolving the problem of the tariffs for the limited private monopoly, of taking our cue from the simpler standard solution and modifying the values of x increasing some and decreasing others, within the limits of the constraint, until we obtain the recovery of $K + G$, disrupting as least possible the consumer's rent furnished by the standard solution.

If, in the most general manner, the goods numbered n, one would have $2n$ unknowns with $2n$ equations: α) n given by the demands; β) one by the constraint, γ) one by the condition that the sum of the areas should be $K + G$, δ) $n - 2$ by the maximum of the sum of the unshaded areas, because between the n quantities of x there are already two equations of condition, β) and γ).

plus of income over partial costs does not allow the monopoiistic company to recover $K + G$. Hence this $K + G$ has to be recouped by disrupting the typical combination as little as possible.

Of the goods which can be produced by the company with the same c_a and the same a — for which hence the standard combination produces the same price $c_a + M_a$ — there are those which have different utility (or demand); and to be clear, let us suppose them classified into superior goods (A_1), average goods (A_2) and inferior goods (A_3). The latter are such that (Graph 5) at the price $p_a = c_a + M/a$ of the standard combination, they would not find any consumers. If we maintain the typical price p for the average category, raise this price for the superior category, which restricts the production of *(A)* by Δx, we can then, without altering the constraint, produce an equal quantity Δx of (A_3) and sell it at a 'substandard' price, just as (A_1) will be sold at a 'supra-standard' price, while (A_2) will maintain the standard price. What we have done for good *(A)*, we can repeat for good *(B)*, for good *(C)* and so forth. The problem of disrupting the standard combination as little as possible lies in the fact that under the condition of constituting a sum of hatched areas (Graph 5) equal to $K + G$, the utility given by the standard solution should be altered the least possible; or, which is the same, the sum of the upper blank areas in Graph 5 should be the maximum possible.

There is an arbitrary part in this solution which depends on how the various categories to which the supra- and sub-standard prices should be applied are constituted: and this depends on the number of categories it is wished to make, and on the goods it is

GRAPH 5

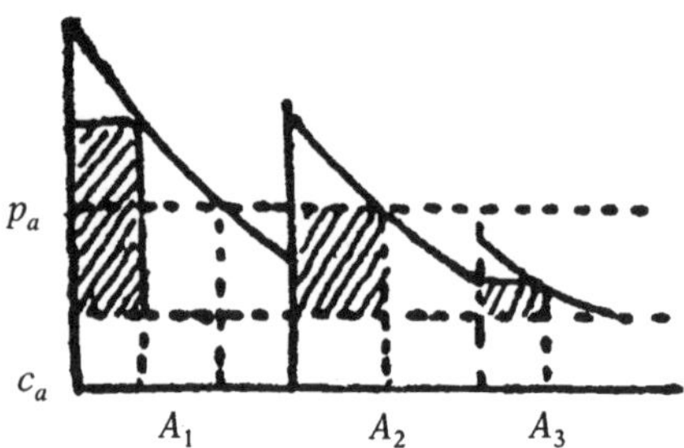

decided should be included in each of them (the monopolist takes advantage of this arbitrary act to satisfy certain practical needs and to take account of the other utilities which are not the 'sender's surplus' as we shall see in due course); but once the classification into categories has been established, according to their demand, between the various goods which have the same price in the standard combination — in other words which have the same c_a and the same a, and hence the same $p_a = c_a + M/a$ — the problem of the standard, supra-standard and sub-standard price is perfectly determined[7].

---

[7] To see that the problem is perfectly determined, we have only to repeat the same general reasoning made in footnote 6.

As we noted in the text, the arbitrary act lies solely in the fixing of the categories, i.e., the number of them and how they should be composed.

If (A_1), (A_2), (A_3) .... (A_n) are the goods for which the partial cost c_a is the same and have the same constant a in the constraint (we shall see the significance of this a in the applications to transport) and we suppose to make, for example, not a price only $p_a = c_a + M/a$, but three different prices, the arbitrary part is above all in these three, and then in the manner in which the 1st, 2nd and 3rd categories are constituted with the various goods. But having established this, the problem of prices and of the quantities is perfectly defined by the demands, by the constraint, by the condition to recover $K + G$, and to maximise the sum of the unshaded areas compatible with these conditions.

For a given $K + G$ this maximum of the sum of the unshaded areas will differ according to the number and constitution of the categories. One could do a general analytical treatment to see how this obtainable maximum, given a $K + G$ to recover, varies as the number of the categories and their composition varies; but the study would lead us to use too many symbols and the result would not be adequate to the fatigue, as it is one of those many problems which practice resolves more easily by trial and error. It is practical necessity which counsels the number of categories not to be exceeded; and it is practical experience, which, having resolved this number of categories, resolves by trial and error the assignment of a good (or service as we are talking of transport) to one or the other category, according to the demand.

Nonetheless, one can gain a rough idea of the analytical problem, by simplifying it and proceeding as follows.

Let us suppose, for the sake of simplicity, a single category of goods, producible, given the constraint, in the quantity: a let the partial cost, by hypothesis, be the same for all, c. As the goods have the same a, one can vary the production as one wishes, on condition that the sum of quantities produced and consumed be always a. Let us start from the typical solution (Graph 6) with a price equal for all, $p = c + M/a$. As we know,, $M = a\ (p - c)$ is the sum of the shaded areas.

Let us increase the quantities: this gives rise to an equal number of increases in the prices: one has to combine these increases so as to recover $K + G$ with the minimum reduction of the sum of the unshaded areas.

If there are n goods, there are $2n$ increases to determine, i.e., the Δxs and the Δps.

GRAPH 6

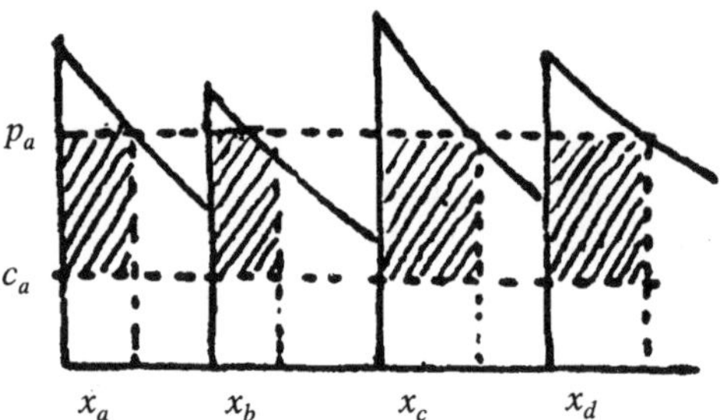

2.6 *Equilibrium in the Case of Collective Monopoly*

The collective monopolist aims to make neither a profit nor loss, but compatible with this condition (and with the constraint, it is understood) wishes to assure the maximum benefit for the community.

The reasoning is wholly similar to that in 2.5 above, only that we no longer have to recoup $K + G$ but only K. If the col-

---

Now there are, as is easily seen, $2n$ equations:
n are given by the demands $p + \Delta p_a = F_a(x_a + \Delta x_a)$, $p + \Delta p_b = F_b(x_b + \Delta x_b)$ ...
1 by the constraint $\Delta x_a + \Delta x_b + \ldots = 0$
1 by the recovery $(p + \Delta p_a)(x_a + \Delta x_a) + (p + \Delta p_b)(x_b + \Delta x_b) + \ldots = ca + K + G$
$n - 2$ by the maximum of the unshaded areas

$$U = U_a(x_a + \Delta x_a) + U_b(x_b + \Delta x_b) + \ldots - (ca + K + G)$$

and as the quantity in the last brackets is a constant, one has to maximise:

$$U_a(x_a + \Delta x_a) + U_b(x_b + \Delta x_b) + \ldots$$

This maximum gives rise to $n - 2$ equations, because the xs are already bound by two conditions, namely that of the constraint and that of the recovery of $K + G$. The problem is determined.

Now let us suppose that having found the expression of the maximum of U we can group the n goods into categories, each of which contributes so that disregarding the differences between the respective Δps, this exercises little influence to vary U. The greater the number of categories, the less one will lose of U; but the lower this number, the simpler will be the price system in practice. This is the problem of the number of categories and of their composition which practice resolves by trial and error.

lective monopolist makes the community bear $M - K$, he can stick to the standard combination, thus achieving an increasingly simple price series; but if he does not want this, and instead wishes to realise $K - M$, he too is forced to supra- and sub-standard prices; which are achieved with the same reasoning which saw above.

2.7 *The Dynamics of the Standard Combination*

Let us now examine the dynamics of the standard combination.

In these dynamics we should distinguish a pre-saturation phase and a saturation phase. Disregard of this distinction and having reasoned as though one was always in a presaturation phase has often been the source of erroneous conclusions and idle controversy. We restrict our study to only two goods: this limitation is convenient for us to make the exposition more perspicuous, but our reasoning is general and applies to any number n of goods.

We call, unambiguously, the presaturation phase that in which demand at price equal to the partial cost, *OA* and *OB* (Graph 7) does not saturate the plant's potential. It is easy to see that in this case, both for the purposes of the company' interests and for social purposes, it is more advantageous to renounce exploiting all its potential and to limit oneself to producing *OA* rather than exceeding points *A* and *B*.

GRAPH 7

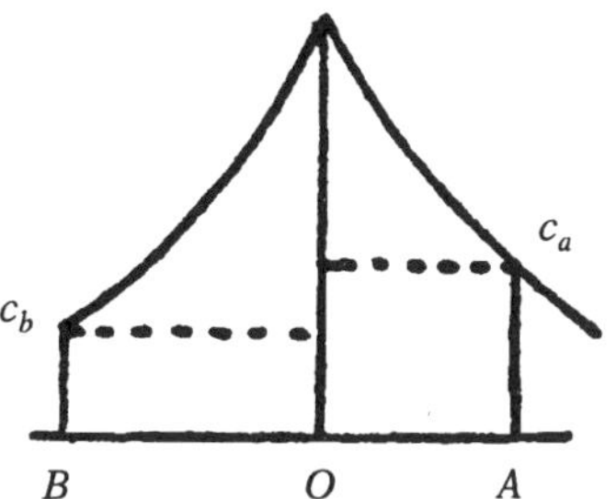

Now, limiting ourselves to *OA* and *OB*, the action of the constraint still does not make itself felt, the extreme prices are equal to the respective partial costs, but the prices have also to be higher — and significantly so than the lower prices — because the sale of all the quantities produced at prices equal to partial costs, would mean that the company lost *K* and *G*.

Let us now start (Graph 8) from a presaturation phase 1.

As one or both the demands rise (which takes the concrete form of what is called the increase of traffic when speaking of transport) we will reach situation 2 in which the demands at partial cost will saturate the combination. In the transition from 1 to 2 there will be no change in the extreme prices, but the higher prices introduced for each of the categories *(A)* and *(B)* can be less severe, if the monopoly is limited or collective.

If the rise continues, then the constraint starts to function (Graph 9). The standard prices, i.e., the prices of the standard combination, will both increase above the partial costs: this already gives rise to a partial recovery, of $K + G$ (or of *K* in the collective monopoly) represented by the hatched area, such that the limited monopolist and the collective monopolist will have to ask less help for the supra-standard prices; hence said tend to mitigate the gap with the sub-standard prices, such that, as the demand continues to increase, one reaches a point in which the hatched area, growing, equals $K + G$ (or *K* if a collective monop-

GRAPH 8

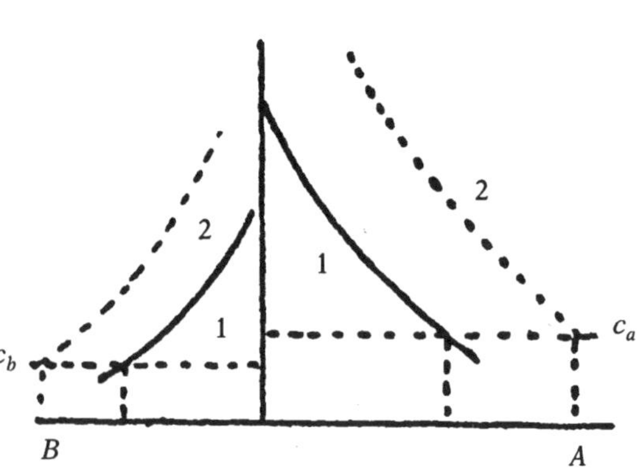

GRAPH 9

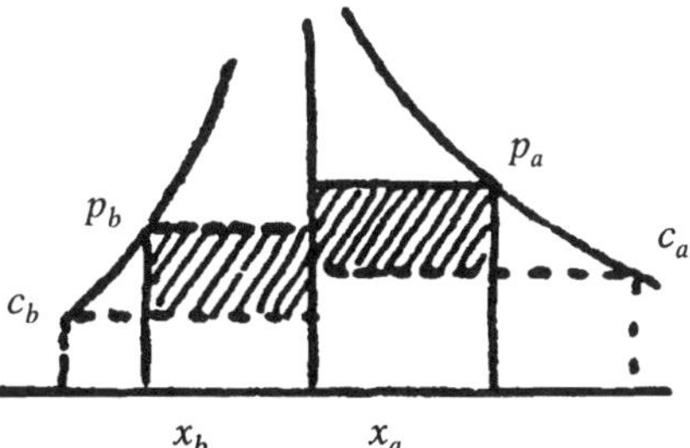

olist) and there is no longer any need for supra-standard prices and the standard combination can easily be wholly applied. Hence the complication of the supra-and sub-standard prices and the accentuation of the latter over the former, are specific to presaturation and tend to disappear as the demands gradually increase (as the traffic gradually increases in the economics of transport).

Naturally, all this does not apply to the unlimited monopolist. He too in a presaturation phase has no interest in practising extreme prices which are less than his partial cost; but in a saturation phase neither his prices are those of the typical combination, nor does the gap in prices tend to close, because as the demand gradually increases, so does the consumers' surplus, which he then can seek to appropriate. These observations on the dynamics of prices according to whether one is in a presaturation or a saturation phase, and according to whether the monopoly is limited or collective or else unlimited, explain and illustrate, as we shall see, many facts regarding the economics of transport and resolve many important points of issue.

2.8 *A Controversy is Resolved*

And it is here, to give an example, that we will resolve one of such points of issue.

There has been much discussion as to whether (Graph 10), as F_a is different from F_b and $c_a = c_b$ whether p_a can differ from p_b.

GRAPH 10

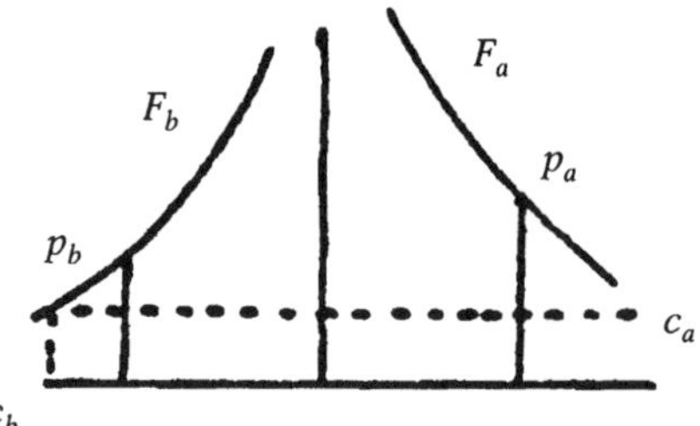

And if it can, is this because of the fact of monopoly or could it also be so under a competitive regime.

In a monopoly regime, obviously, if F_a differs from F_b, there is no reason for $p_a = p_b$ just because $c_a = c_b$. The question relates only to the regime of competition (a long and fierce discussion, for example, between Pigou and Taussig).

Now, for the perfect competition regime we have seen that, giving the constraint, assumed to be linear, as is almost always the case in transport, the form x_a, x_b, x_c $/a + x_b/b = 1$, competition tends to make $p_a = c_a + k/a$, $p_b = c_b + k/b$.

For p_a and p_b to be equal, not only do c_a and c_b have to be equal, since the partial costs could also be equal and the prices not be at all equal; but a and b also have to be equal: in other words, the constraint should take the form $x_a + x_b = c$, in other words, again without any variation of cost for the company, it is possible to produce a certain amount extra of *(A)* and a equal amount less of *(B)*.

Then — and only then — is Pigou right; because c_a and c_b equal can give rise to p_a and p_b unequal, also under perfect competition if the constraint does not have that very specific form.

The discrimination between the price of transport of a tonne of *(A)* or of a tonne of *(B)* when they occupy the same space, and is wholly indifferent as regards costs, to load one or the other, which is precisely the meaning of that specific form of the constraint, this discrimination on the basis of the different value of the absolutely identical transports cannot take place under perfect competition. It is an effect of the monopoly. Neither can one —

as some writers maintain — attribute the fact not to the monopoly, but to the different demand F_a and F_b; since it is clear that, under a competitive regime, if $c_a = c_b$ F_a and F_b are also different, P_a and P_b are equal when the constraint has that specific form for which $a = b$; and if F_a and F_b are identical, they will have different prices, even if the partial costs c_a and c_b are equal, if a is different from b. It is therefore the form of the constraint which decides the matter.

All the muddled controversy, which we believe we have resolved with the few words said above, derives from not having considered the essential fact in related costs: the constraint.

Differing prices for the very same service with the same partial cost can be made by the monopolist, not by perfect competition. But these discriminations according to the so-called 'transport value' or according to 'that which the transport can pay' should not always be ascribed to the rapacious aims of the monopoiist: as we have clearly seen, he can be induced to make them not to increase his profit, but to make possible, compatible with a given profit, the maximum consumers' surplus: indeed the collective monopolist who aims to make neither a profit nor a loss, is necessarily forced to this discrimination, if, compatible with this condition, he wishes to maximise said consumer's surplus.

3. - Some Applications to Rail Transport

3.1 *Introduction*

In transport economics we find ourselves faced either with monopolies (private — usually limited — or collective) as is the case for railways, i.e., in competing companies with more or less mitigated competition, by conferences, as is the case with shipping. We therefore should examine above all the standard combination; which, when there is competition, gives us the prices of the single types of traffic and the division of the means of traffic among them; when there is a monopoly, it gives us the typical prices which, as we know, cannot be final, because at these prices the monopolist would not recover $K + G$ (or only K if the monopolist is collective and hence does not intend to make either a profit or a loss).

3.2 *The Standard Combination in Rail Transport*

Let us therefore start with the standard combination for the railway monopoly. The elements which determine this standard combination are: demand, partial costs, the constraint. For transport there are demands which differ according to the distance, speed and type of goods (we shall disregard passengers for the moment). From the company's point of view, there are differing partial costs according to the distance, speed and type of goods, as, essentially, each type of good requires a greater or lesser dead load for each tonne of useful load transported: the different values of the goods transported, the dead load necessary for each tonne of useful load being the same, only impacts costs in a secondary manner in view of the greater sum of the company's liability in the event of loss or faults. But we shall, for now, set this discrimination of costs by the value of the goods to one side.

Let us say that a good *(A)* has a dead load coefficient π_a, when the transport of a tonne of it, the vehicles being fully loaded, requires the towing of a dead and useful weight $1 + \pi_a$.

The equations which determine the standard combination are, as we know:

$$p_a = F_a(x_a),\ p_b = F_b(x_b)$$

$$\frac{x_a}{a} + \frac{x_b}{b} = 1$$

$$a(p_a - c_a) = b(p_b - c_b)$$

which give rise to a unequivocal solution with which we are well acquainted. (For the sake of simplicity, we have assumed two goods only, but we know that the reasoning holds for as many related goods as we wish, subject to the constraint $x_a/a + x_b/b + \ldots = 1$).

In the standard combination, M (Graph 9) being the symbol of the shaded areas, i.e., the surplus of revenues on partial costs, (hence M will differ, generally, from K) will be:

$$p_a = c_a + \frac{M}{a},$$

$$p_b = c_b + \frac{M}{b}, \ldots$$

Let us apply these notions to rail transport.

Let us suppose that the capacity of dead and useful load of the material available is P tonnes[8].

Let the two series of transport be: that of a good *(A)* with a dead load coefficient π_a, distance d_a, speed v_a; and that of a *(B)* with a dead load coefficient π_b, distance d_b and speed v_b. x_a is the number of tonnes of *(A)* which are transported at price p_a per tonne; similarly, x_b for *(B)* at the price p_b. It is assumed that the demands are those of a given period of time t which is expressed in hours, as the speeds are also expressed in hours. Let p_a be the rolling stock used in the first transport, p_b that for the second, such that:

$$P_a + P_b = P$$

which is the constraint; whose linear form we will shortly see.

It is superfluous to note that we disregard secondary circumstances to focus on the substance.

For *(A)* the length of a journey is d_a/v_a; the rolling stock can be used to make tv_a/d_a journeys in time t; P_a will be able to transport each time $P_a/1 + \pi_a$ tonnes of *(A)* and hence, in time t, $tv_a/d_a \cdot P_a/1 + \pi_a$ tonnes. Hence:

[8] In actual fact, a given set of rolling stock, when fully loaded, represents a quantity which is greater or less than the dead and useful load, depending on whether the goods in question are loaded, in other words depending on whether they require a lot or little space, i.e., a little or a lot of dead load for each tonne of useful load. But let us disregard this circumstance, and refer to an experimental average value, according to the average load. Although this considerably simplifies our study, it in no way influences its general conclusions.

$$\frac{tv_a}{d_a} \cdot \frac{P_a}{(1 + \pi_a)} = x_a$$

Similarly we have:

$$\frac{tv_b}{d_b} \cdot \frac{P_b}{(1 + \pi_b)} = x_b$$

But $P_a + P_b = P$, hence:

$$\frac{x_a d_a (1 + \pi_a)}{tv_a} + x_b \frac{d_b (1 + \pi_b)}{tv_b} = P$$

which is a linear constraint between x_a and x_b; the constants $1/a$ and $1/b$ of the general form $x_a/a + x_b/b = 1$ are:

$$\frac{1}{a} = \frac{1}{Pt} \cdot (1 + \pi_a) \frac{d_a}{v_a}$$

$$\frac{1}{b} = \frac{1}{Pt} \cdot (1 + \pi_b) \frac{d_b}{v_b}$$

and hence the prices of the standard combination are:

$$p_a = c_a + \frac{M}{Pt}\left(1 + \pi_a \frac{d_a}{v_a}\right)$$

$$p_b = c_b + \frac{M}{Pt}\left(1 + \pi_b \frac{d_b}{v_b}\right).$$

To simplify the theory of the tariffs; let us carry out a small transformation in these formulas; i.e., let us include in it, in the term which refers to the partial cost, not the partial cost of the transport distance d and speed v_a of a tonne of the good with a dead load coefficient of π_a, but instead, in general, the partial cost of transport distance d_a and speed v_a of a tonne of dead and useful load. The formula thus becomes, in general:

$$p\pi_{dv} = (1+\pi)\left(c_{dv} + \frac{M}{Pt}\frac{d}{v}\right)$$

in which we repeat c_{dv} indicates the partial cost of transport for distance d and speed v of a tonne of dead and useful load.

We shall see below how we determine M to fix these typical prices.

3.3 *A Digression: What Prices would be in a Extreme State of Competition and Plant Saturation*

Let us digress. If one were in an extreme state of competition (with but a few companies, of the same type, of the most economic size, and no profits) the prices of the competition (then $M = K$) would be:

$$p\pi_{dv} = (1 + \pi)\, c_{dv} + \frac{K}{Pt}\,(1 + \pi)\,\frac{d}{v}$$

This formula says that the price of each transport would be equal to its partial cost, plus a share of the constant cost K, according to the tonne-hours required by said transport. In fact, d/v is the duration of the transport, which has entailed for each tonne of good $a + \pi$ tonnes, i.e., $(1 + \pi)\, d/v$ tonne-hours of the Pt tonne-hours available in time t.

As the c_{dv} — partial cost of the transport distance d, with speed v, of a tonne of dead and useful load — increases with the distance, but slower than the latter, and as with the increase in v, starting from a certain value of v c_{dv} increases; one has, again under perfect competition: *a)* distance influences the price of transport, the second term increasing proportionally, and the first term (partial cost) less than proportionally; *b)* speed has a dual influence in the opposite sense, as when it increases beyond a certain limit, it causes the first term (partial cost) to increase, but proportionally diminishes the second term[9]; *c)* the dead load coefficient influences the set of the two terms, causing both to increase, but less than proportionally[10].

This can be called the general law of transport prices under extreme competition, assuming the complete saturation of the rolling stock. It is clear that when we are talking of different iines and one wishes to make the computation separately for each, one should distribute the K among them, and assume the P is also distributed. Then each line has a formula with its respective $(c_{dv})_1$, $(c_{dv})_2$... and K_1/P_1t, K_2/P_2t .. where K_1, K_2 are the fixed costs of the lines 1, 2... and P_1t, P_2t ... the labour, for each, of the rolling stock used in the time t: namely the traffic; hence also in a case of extreme competition, the price of transport of a tonne of a given good, with given speed at a given distance, can differ from line to line; and it is entirely feasible that there arises the case — which some writers describe as an anomaly and attribute to the effect of private monopoly — that the price of transport is lower on one line which required a higher installation cost than on a line which required a lower installation cost: this is due to the additional term: it is very possible that a bigger K can have a smaller p, because the traffic Pt is bigger. And this, evidently, is neither an anomaly, neither do its origins necessarily lie in private monopoly. It could be found also under a competitive regime. This also explains what some think is an error, namely that a light line, which has cost less per kilometre, can practice lower tariffs, because — it is said — the extra needed to remunerate the capital is lower. But one should take into account not only the lower capital, but also the traffic; if K

[9] For a given distance d, there is a most economic speed for the cost of transporting a tonne of dead and useful load c_{dv}, i.e., a certain speed which minimises this c_{dv}, but this is not the speed which minimises the price p; as (Graph 11) the added temm diminishes as the speed increases (the greater the speed, the more intensely the material works). But when the speed becomes very high, the mitigating influence of the added term on the total sum decreases: which explains why high speeds have, overall, a higher price than slower speeds.

[10] If π for example is $^1/_2$ and becomes double, the factor $1 + \pi$ does not become double, but less than double: from 1.5 it increases to 2.

GRAPH 11

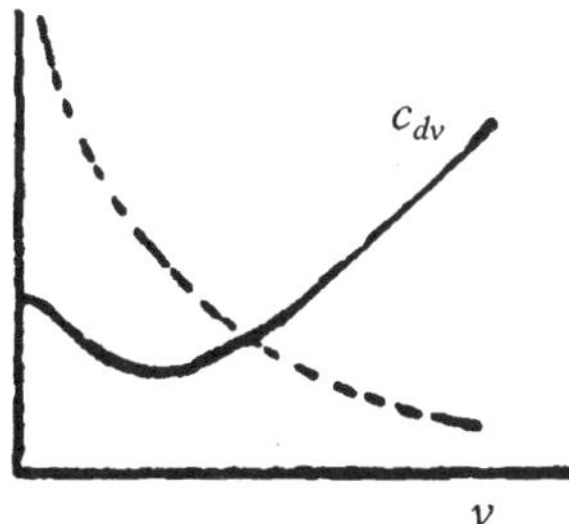

is small, but Pt is also small, K/Pt can be big. And this is often the case: the fact that it was deemed opportune to build a light rather than a heavy line presupposes that one expected only a low level of traffic on the line.

To conclude this brief digression on the prices in the extreme case of competition, a few words on transport of passengers of differing classes.

As a first, rough approximation, we can treat the question in a general manner, viewing the travellers as goods with different πs, according to the classes, and then the usual formula:

$$p\pi_{dv} = (1 + \pi)\, c_{dv} + \frac{K}{Pt}\,(1 + \pi)\,\frac{d}{v}$$

gives us the price: or rather the price of the transport, as we can put it, of a tonne of passengers (live load) of 1st, 2nd and 3rd class, transported at speed v for a distance d.

However, we should bear in mind not only the different xs, but a further two circumstances: that the carriages for the 1st, 2nd and 3rd classes are furnished differently, and hence weigh on K differently; and that, moreover, for passengers there are, according to the classes, as many different ancillary costs as the services which are offered to them; but these are details which, if we wish, it is easy to take account — as we shall in due course. We shall leave them here, this first and rough approximation sufficing for the moment.

3.4 *Returning to the Standard Combination: Conclusions on Railway Tariffs*

Let us return to our standard combination: we determined the prices for the standard combination for each type of traffic characterised by the quantities π, d, v; namely:

$$p\pi_{dv} = (1 + \pi)\left(c_{dv} + \frac{M}{Pt} \cdot \frac{d}{v}\right)$$

We deferred saying how M is determined because, as we know, it is different, - in general, from K. Let us assume (it will be convenient for us below) $M = \gamma K$; we have to determine γ. Now this γ is an experimental datum. It depends on the knowledge of the traffic demand curves that operating experience allows us to acquire. The value of γ is that which saturates the plant. And by trial it is obtained when:

$$X_a (1 + \pi_a) \frac{d_a}{v_a} + X_b (1 + \pi_b) \frac{d_b}{v_b} = Pt$$

or, in general:

$$\Sigma\left[x (1 + \pi) \frac{d}{v}\right] = Pt$$

in which, as is clear, each of the terms of Σ indicates the number of tonne-hours required by the respective traffic.

It should not be thought that γ is suddenly determined at a table: γ shall be too small when the demand for traffic at prices which derive from said exceed Pt the number of tonne-hours available; it will be too large when at these prices a part of Pt remains unused.

Here therefore is how by this we resolve also the question of the determination of M — in other words of γ — for setting the prices of the standard combination.

With the determination of the prices of the standard combination (the 'standard prices' as we have called them), the theoretical problem of the tariffs can still not be said to be resolved — in general, at least — because these typical prices, as we well know, do not allow the limited private monopolist to recover $K + G$ (or only K for the collective monopolist, who makes neither profit nor loss): it would leave the undertaking with a loss of $(1 - \gamma) K + G$ or of $(1 - \gamma) K$ respectively.

As we are talking of transport, we should not talk of multiple prices (in the proper sense of the term) as some authors do, engendering considerable confusion. We are not dealing with multiple prices here: we are dealing with the fact that there are traffics which have the same π, d, v, hence the same partial cost $(1 + \pi)\, c_{dv}$, but different demands, which are made to pay different prices.

We can only repeat, to reach the concept of supra- and substandard prices, and to the classification into categories, for the specific case of rail transport, the reasoning which in general we made in Section 2.5 and which was illustrated by Graph 5.

Let us consider three different traffics — here also the reasoning is made on three traffics, but it is general and applied to any number — whose traffics have the same π, d, v and hence the same typical price:

$$p\pi_{dv} = (1 + \pi)\left(c_{dv} + \frac{\gamma k}{Pt} \cdot \frac{d}{v}\right)$$

Let this price be prohibitive for traffic A_3. Diminishing the traffic A_1 by a certain quantity by increasing its price, there remains available a certain amount of tonne-hours which can be employed for the transport of a corresponding quantity of A_3, on condition the price is lowered to below the standard price.

It should be noted: every time that we, starting from the standard solution, move a certain quantity of tonnage hours from A, to A_3, we evidently reduce the overall utility given by said standard solution. Hence these movements should be made in the sole measure that is strictly necessary for the attainment of $K + G$. But do we, in actual fact, with these movements draw closer to the attainment of $K + G$? Yes, generally, because — also disregarding that the new traffic A_3 helps to recover $K + G$, this help is represented by the small hatched rectangle of Graph 5 which corresponds to A_3 — raising the price of the traffic A, above the standard price p_a, although it naturally restricts this traffic, increases the corresponding hatched area, because when we are talking of high-value traffic, the standard price is generally lower to that corresponding to Cournot's point; and so by raising it, within certain limits, the hatched area increases. In other words, the recovery of $K + G$ is achieved by the limited monopolist by starting from the common price p_a of the standard solution to draw closer to the respective Cournot's points of each demand, rising for the transports with the higher value, such as A_1, and falling for those of least value, such as A_3.

We have assumed a group of πdv and consisting of only three goods. The work can be done for all the goods of the group πdv, and for all the groups of πdv; and knowing the demands for the various traffics, i.e., of the change which certain given altemations of the typical prices engender in them, to reach, by way of trial and error, the result which, by increasing the price for the high-value goods above the standard price and reducing below this the price for the low-value goods, makes it possible to attain $K + G$ (or only K for the collective monopolist) with the minimum possible loss of return, vis-à-vis that which would have derived from the standard price, for the senders.

Here the quantitative theoretical problem of the setting of the tariffs ends. This need to raise some prices above the standard price and to lower below such so as to satisfy other needs of a practical order and to attain other utilities which are not only those of the senders, narrowly understood, because it is not at all true, as we shall see, that there is an absolute coincidence between the utility of a transport and the senders' surplus.

Those who superficially examine the path taken by our study to reach a first approximation of the problem of tariffs may believe that it is much more simple and direct, without passing through the standard combination, to follow another path: this involves, taking account of the various demands for transport, to basically determine (Graph 4) the prices p_a, p_b, p_c ... such that, while the sum of the hatched areas gave $K + G$, (or only K for the collective monopolist) and the tonne-hours do not exceed those allowed by the existing plant, the sum of the white areas A, B, C ... are the maximum possible. And in this, in actual fact, consists the problem of tariffs. Except that when we sought not only to merely enunciate the problem, but also to resolve it — or rather to trace a rational method for its solution — we would have run into all those difficulties which we gradually dealt with and sought to overcome.

Of course, following the facile simplism of some authors — who take no account of the 'constraint', who take no account of the differences of the partial costs, who take no account of the different demands, and sum in overall demand elements which are really heterogeneous, such that these overall demands become void of any economic meaning — the problem would have taken on a character of elegant simplicity. According to these authors, the curve *MN* (Graph 12) is the demand for *TK*; i.e., the ordinate represents the price *BC* per tonne-kilometre at which the demand for a quantity of tonne-kilometres is represented by the respective abscissa *OB: OA* is the partial cost: the area *MAN* represents the senders' surplus, when one eliminates $K + G$ from it: the *TKs* most to the left correspond to the higher-value goods and lesser distances: the *TKs* most to the right correspond to the lower-value goods and greater distances: hence, on condition that the extreme prices *N* are made equal to the partial cost *OA* of

GRAPH 12

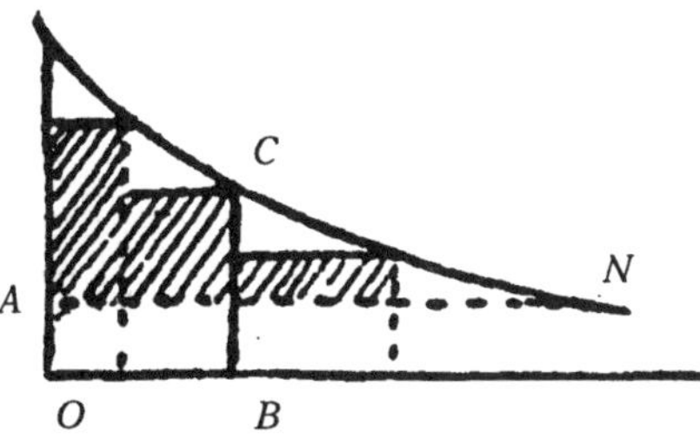

the *TK*, the problem is resolved, however one established a classified list of multiple prices to obtain the hatched area $K + G$; because, in whatever manner, the senders' surplus will be the curvilinear triangle *MAN* diminished by $K + G$. After all we have seen to date, it is superfluous to waste words to prove that this series of propositions — which endow the question a false simplicity is nothing other than a series of assertions void of any truth; and hence of no value whatsoever for deducing aid for the concrete problems.

4. - Some Applications to Sea Transport

4.1 *Introduction*

This problem is fundamental in the economics of sea transport: a steamer, of given size *L*, plies the route *AB* which is *D* miles long at a speed *V* when fully loaded. How much does it cost to transport each register ton? How does this cost vary with the size of the vessel, the distance, the speed? Knowledge of this cost then, with the aid of the related costs, allows one to obtain a first approximation of the final equilibrium to which freight charges, at full load, tend assuming perfect competition. This can be used as the starting base for subsequent approximations, so as to take account, for the theory of freight charges, of the many circumstances of reality neglected in the first approximation. To reply to the problems posed below, we shall avail ourselves of a quantitative expression of this cost, roughly approximated: which serves only to draw attention to how the size of the vessel, the distance and speed influence that cost. We said above 'size of the vessel' in the singular: we should have said 'size of the vessels': but assuming that the vessels are similar solids — and this assumption considerably simplifies the exposition and does not influence the general conclusions — let us call the size of the vessel (for example the length) *L*.

Another brief premiss: the amount of fuel needed is that necessary to overcome the opposing resistance of the water to the vessel's submerged main section; and for each unit of time it varies according to this main section — which in turn varies according to the square of the vessel's size — and a function of the speed which, by way of approximation, we shall deem to be the cube of said.

The Greek letters are experimental numerical coefficients, or given quantities: in short, quantities which in their differentiation from *L, D, V* can be considered as constants.

4.2 *The Cost of Register Ton at Full Load for a Given Route* AB, D *Long, at Speed* V, *of a Vessel of Size* L

Let L be the size of the vessel, D the distance in miles of the itinerary, V the speed in knots per hour. Let φ (in days) be the sum of stopovers for each voyage.

The time t, in days, of sailing for each voyage will be:

$$\frac{D}{24V}$$

the length of each voyage in days: $\frac{D}{24V} + \varphi$

the number n of voyages per year: $\frac{365}{\left(\frac{D}{24V} + \varphi\right)}$

the register tons occupied by fuel: $\alpha L^2 V^3 t$

the gross register tonnage: βL^3

the net register tonnage: $\beta L^3 - \alpha L^2 V^3 t$

Let us deal with the costs: let the cost of the vessel (variable, roughly according to the area, and hence to the square of the size) be: γL^2.

Let λ be the overall coefficient of interest and depreciation, maintenance, insurance for the year; such that the amount of these three items of expenses per years (1, 2, 3) shall be: $\lambda\gamma L^2$.

The amount of the wages for the crew per year (item 4 of expenses) varies according to the size of the vessel, but less quickly than the tonnage: let us assume, by way of approximation, it is variable only according to the squares of the dimensions[11] L^2.

If ρ is the price of the amount of fuel which occupies the space of one register ton, the total cost of fuel in the year (item 5 of expenses) will be: $n.\rho.\alpha.\ L^2.\ V^3.\ t$.

The port fees (item 6) do not all increase in proportion to the vessel's tonnage; let us assume they too vary with the cube of the size: $n\theta L^2$.

The general operating costs (item 7) do not all increase in proportion to the vessel's tonnage: let us assume they too vary with the square of the size: εL^2.

Adding all these expenses and dividing them by the net tonnage in the n voyages which is:

$$n\ (\beta L^3 - \alpha L^2 V^3 t)$$

one obtains the cost c_{dv1}, of the register ton (at full load) transported distance D at speed V by a vessel of size L; this cost, removing the factors common to the dividend and the divisor, is:

$$C_{dvl} = -\frac{1}{\beta L - \frac{\alpha}{24}V^2 D}\left[\frac{\rho\alpha V^2 D}{24} + \left(\frac{D}{24} + \varphi\right)\left(\frac{\lambda\gamma + \delta + \varepsilon}{365}\right) + \Theta\right]$$

[11] This item of expenses (4), as the subsequent items (6) and (7), we deemed, by way of approximation, variable in proportion to the value of the vessel; and hence, again by rough approximation, variable according to the square of L.

The reader should note that we do not intend to expound all the relations, which would be quite complicated, to express the cost in question, but only to obtain a determination of it, roughly approximate, which suffices to clearly understand how it varies with the size of the vessel, the distance and speed.

The formula appears complicated, but reuniting in a single expression with small Latin letters the sums or products of the Greek letters (constants), that cost can be held to be approximately as a function of *D, V, L* of the form:

$$C_{dvl} = -\frac{1}{aL - bV^2D}\left(cV^2D + d\frac{D}{V} + e\right)$$

in which *a, b, c, d, e* should be considered as constants. It should be noted, in view of our remarks below, the price ρ of the fuel is in the constant *c*, which increases as this price increases.

4.3 *How* C *Varies with the Size* L

How c_{dvl} varies with *L, V* and *D* remaining unchanged, can be represented with a curve of the form shown in Graph 13: namely diminishing and with a upward concavity: this means that as *L* increases, *C* diminishes, but a given increment of *L* corresponds to a decrease in *C* which is smaller the larger *L* is. Moreover, the reduction of *C* with the increase in size is quicker the higher the price of the fuel; in other words the high price of fuel is a greater incentive to increase the size of the vessel to diminish the cost of register ton at full load[12].

4.4 *And with the Distance* D

As *D* increases, so does *C*. But to see how it grows, it should be recalled that the denominator of *C* indicates the tonnage which remains available, when one loads the fuel needed for the entire journey: and it is natural that when the problem is posed thus, the

[12] The partial derivative $\vartheta C/\vartheta L$ is negative; the second derivative is positive; and as regards the price of the fuel, $\vartheta C/\vartheta L$ becomes larger in absolute terms, the greater *c*. Hence the conclusions of the text.

GRAPH 13

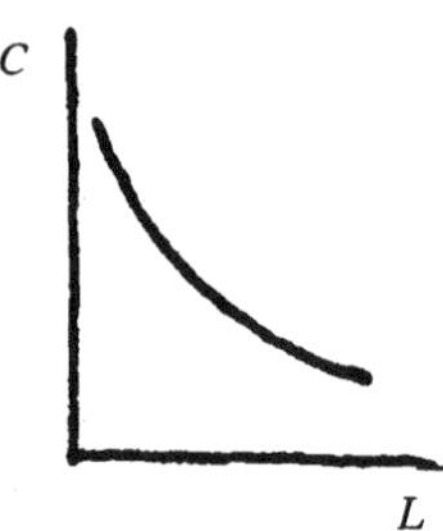

cost C should tend to always increase when, as the distance increases and hence the amount of fuel needed, the space available for the useful load continues to decrease, tending toward zero.

But the problem should not be posed thus: one should assume that as the distance increases, the stock of fuel renews itself, such that the available tonnage for the load does not fall below a certain limit; and then the first factor of C can be held to be constant as the distance varies, and the second for a double distance does increase, but by less than double. This is a factor of great importance in sea shipping.

Furthermore, bearing in mind that the price ρ of the fuel is in the constant c, the higher price of fuel tends to accentuate the increase in the cost of register ton as distance increases.

Finally: at a given distance, the increase of the cost corresponding to a given ΔD is smaller, the smaller is C; in other words, graphically (Graphs 14 and 15) the cost curve, as the distance varies, grows much slower the smaller the cost, i.e., as the costs gradually diminish in time (change from 1 to 2) the cost curve tends to settle on the horizontal. This explains a fact of special importance in sea transport: with the decrease, in time, of the freight charge costs, the tendency of the freight charges to equal one another even for considerably differing distances[13].

[13] If, for the reasons given in the text, one allows that the first factor of C can be considered as a constant, the $\vartheta C/\vartheta L$ is positive; it increases as c increases, that is to say it increases with the increase in the price of the fuel. If we consider the first factor of C as constant, this takes the forrn $C = 1/M\ (RD + S)$, the quantities M, R, S are to be considered as constants; and then $\vartheta C/\vartheta D$ can be put, evidently, under the form $\vartheta C/\vartheta D = C \cdot R/RD + S$. Hence the conclusions of the text.

GRAPH 14

GRAPH 15

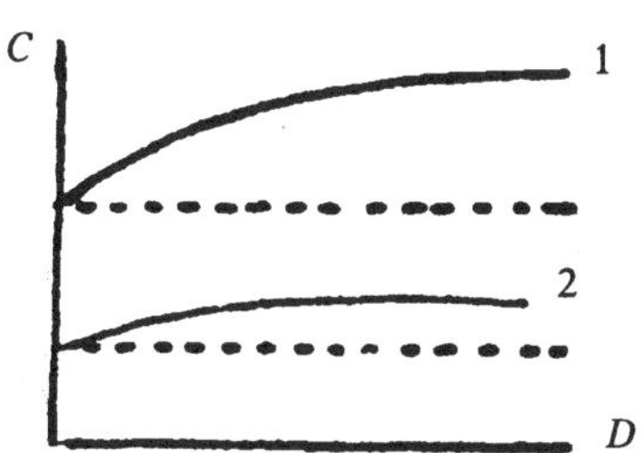

4.5 *With the Speed* V: *the Most Economical Speed*

We can deal with the question in the same manner as in the previous two cases. But it is better to see the thing with a much simpler, albeit rougher, procedure.

The costs of the vessel for the journey can be divided: into a daily fixed part S_f, which it has to meet, regardless of whether it actually makes the journey; in a daily part for the days in which it does travel, and which, as they regard essentially fuel, varies like the cube of the speed, and finally, the port charges, S_p; hence the journey costs are:

(1)
$$\left(\frac{D}{24V}+\varphi\right)S_f+\frac{D}{24V}aV^3+S_p.$$

The days in port φ and the port charges S_p for the journey *AB* of distance D we can consider as independent of the speed, and hence *(1)* can take the following form:

$$\frac{D}{24} \cdot \left(\frac{S_f}{V} + aV^2 \right) + b \tag{2}$$

The cost per net register ton at full load is seen in *(2)* above divided by the net register ton.

$$\frac{\frac{D}{24}\left(\frac{S_f}{V} + aV^2 \right) + b}{T_n} \tag{3}$$

Let us now see how this cost varies with changes in speed.

We should really consider *Tn* variable with the speed, because T_n diminishes with the increase of said in view of the greater space occupied by the coal. This means that, considering T_n as invariable with the speed, the simplified procedure will give us an increase of C, with an increase in V, certainly less than that which would have been recorded if we had also taken account that as V increases, the net available tonnage diminishes: basically, considering T_n as invariable with the increase in speed does not alter the drift of our conclusion, which is that the cost C rapidly increases with the increase in speed, as can be seen from the evidence of the formula. Furthermore, the increase in cost for a given ΔV is greater the higher V. This, however, starting from a certain point, because there is a more economic speed, i.e., the trend of the cost with the variation in the speed is that shown in Graph 16.

GRAPH 16

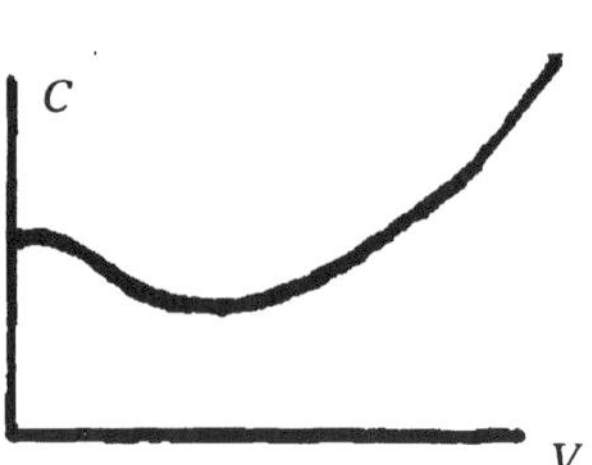

The price of fuel enters in the constant a, which increases as this price increases[14].

It is easy to verify these deductions: 1) The most economical speed is higher the higher the fixed costs (and hence also higher the greater the size of the vessel); 2) The most economic speed is smaller the higher the price of fuel; 3) The increase in cost per register ton corresponding to a given increase in speed is higher the greater the speed; 4) The increase in cost for a given increase in speed is greater the longer the distance (bigger D); 5) the increase in cost for a given increase in speed is greater the higher the price of fuel; 6) The increase in cost for a given increase in speed is smaller the larger the size of the vessel (the higher T_n, the greater S_f).

Such that summarising: *a)* the most economic speed increases with the increase in the size of the vessel and decreases with the increase in the price of fuel; *b)* the increase in cost for a certain increase of a given speed, increases with the increase of the speed, of the distance and of the price of fuel; and decreases with the increase in the size of the vessel.

Finally, it should be noted that this cost of the speed vis-à-vis its utility which, for each knot of increase in speed, the saving of time on the route AB becomes always and quickly smaller the higher the speed[15], while instead the cost of the register ton transported in B becomes always and quickly greater: such that one

---

[14] The partial derivative $\vartheta C/\vartheta V$ takes the form *(4)* $\vartheta C/\vartheta V = D/24T_n(2_aV - S/V^2)$ which shows that as V increases, while the first positive term in brackets increases, the second, negative, term decreases rapidly; i.e., as speed increases, the cost increases rapidly; and as the second derivative is positive, evidently, the increase in cost for a given DV is the greater the bigger V. The most economic speed corresponds to $\vartheta C/\vartheta V = 0$: i.e., with a very rough approximation:

(5)
$$V_e = \sqrt[3]{\frac{S_f}{2_a}}.$$

Hence the conclusions of the text; those which follow in the text are immediate deductions from *(4)* and *(5)*.

[15] One has $t = D/V$ and hence $dt = -D/V^3\,dV$; in other words the time saved for a given increase in speed decreases rapidly with the increase of the latter.

can say, by analogy with other economic theorems, that the speed has a rapidly increasing marginal cost and a rapidly decreasing marginal utility.

4.6 *The Partial Unit Cost of Register Ton at Full Load*

We have seen what is the cost at full load of a net register ton for a given vessel of size L which goes a distance D (miles) at a speed V knots. We have also seen how this latter cost varies with changes in L, D, V.

With this study, carried out in sections 4.2-4.5, we determined for a vessel of size L, which travels a distance D at a speed V, the quantity ST, total cost of the journey at full load, and OS of net available tonnage (Graph 17). If we now imagine ST to be divided between fixed cost K and variable cost AT we can find in c_r, the partial unit cost of transport of a register ton, at full load, at distance D and speed V in the given conditions of the vessel's size.

We will make similar use of this notion to that which, when dealing with the railways, we made with the partial cost of the transport of a ton of dead and useful load distance d, with speed r.

4.7 *The 'Register Coefficient' of a Good; the Partial Cost of a Ton of Chartered Freight*

The various types of sea traffic which are carried out over distance D with speed V have only, from the point of view of cost,

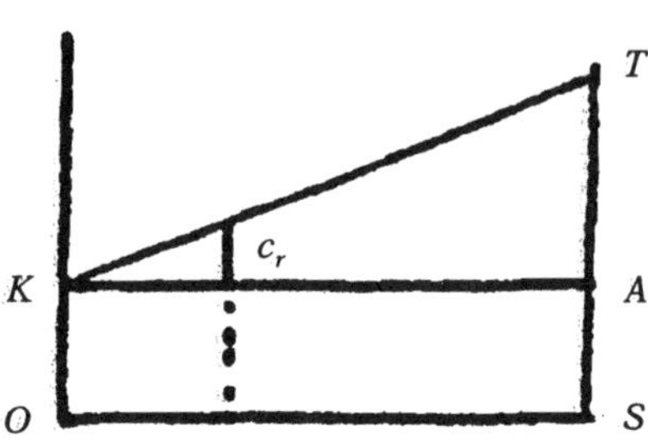

this circumstance which differentiates them: the number of register tons needed for a ton of freight. (We shall deal with passengers shortly). As the insurance for the freight is paid by the sender and not by the carrier (unlike the railways), for goods of great value, one does not even have to take account of this difference as regards partial cost, and everything reduces itself to the slightly more care they require: an element which can be disregarded in our study.

For the railways let us use π_a to indicate the dead load coefficient of good *(A)*, meaning that to transport a ton of weight of good *(A)* one has to tow $1 + \pi_a$ of dead and useful load. Here, for sea transport, we introduce a similar concept: we use π_a to indicate the register coefficient of the good *(A)*, meaning that to load a ton of freight of it one has to occupy π_a of register tons.

Generally, π_a is a fraction less than 1 (under average circumstances it hovers around 1/2 because it is 1.44/2.83). Hence, c_a being the partial cost of a chartered ton of good *(A)*, $c_a = \pi_a c_r$ as c_r, is the partial cost of the register ton at full load of which we spoke in the previous section.

4.8 *The Price of Transport per Ton of Chartered Freight*

Let us now suppose that two goods *(A)* and *(B)* with register coefficients π_a and π_b (let us make the example of two goods, but the reasoning applies in full to any number of goods). Let us proceed here much quicker than for the railways, as the reader is now familiar with the studies and calculations. Let the prices — which the entrepreneur should consider as given, as in a competition regime they do not depend on him alone — be p_a and p_b per chartered ton. Let x_a and x_b be the quantities of transport which he offers of *(A)* and *(B)*, dividing his available tonnage between them. The two unknowns are determined by two equations, that of the constraint: $\pi_a x_a + \pi_b x_b = T_n$ ... and that which maximises the difference between the revenue $p_a x_a + p_b x_b$ and the cost $K + Cr\ (\pi_a x_a + \pi_b x_b)$.

The usual constants a and b of the constraint $x_a/a + x_b/b = 1$ are $a = T_n/\pi_a$, $b = T_n/\pi_b$; hence:

$$p_a = \pi_a c_r + \pi_a \frac{K+g}{T_n}$$

$$p_b = \pi_b c_r + \pi_b \frac{K+g}{T_n}$$

in other words the constant cost and the profit are divided, in addition to the partial costs, in direct proportion to the register coefficients.

The formula and theorem are similar to those already encountered elsewhere.

If the company is at the margin:

$$p_a = \pi_a c_r + \pi_a \frac{K}{T_n}$$

$$p_b = \pi_b c_r + \pi_b \frac{K}{T_n}$$

How then are the prices p_a and p_b which the single entrepreneur should consider as given determined?

Let us suppose as given — if in short we cry out at random p_a and p_b — there are three unknowns for each company x_a, x_b, g and there are three equations: the constraint; the revenue equals the costs plus profit; that which maximises the profit; hence an x_a and x_b for each company; and hence, for all $\Sigma x_a = X_a$ and $\Sigma x_b = X_b$. The prices will be equilibrium prices when:

$$p_a = F_a(X_a),$$

$$p_b = F_b(X_b);$$

the difference $p_a X_a + p_b x_b - \Sigma\,(c_a X_a + c_b x_b + k)$ will be the sum of the profits of all the companies.

4.9 *The Price of Transport of Passengers*

Let us now deal with the passengers. Let us start by considering only one class of them: let us see immediately below the case of several classes.

Let us suppose two demands: of the good *(A)* and of passengers *(V)*. The reasoning, as we shall now see, is general and applies to as many goods as one wishes and to several classes of passengers.

Each passenger, according to the greater or lesser comfort he is given, is assigned a certain number of register tons. This is the passenger's register coefficient. Here π_v is the considerably greater than 1. When all the register tons are saturated, the costs included those in excess which we can call of floating hotel for the passengers - let us suppose s for each of them along the journey - but one has less, vis-à-vis the vessel which transports only goods, the less effort of traction needed. For the $\pi_v x_v$ of register occupied by the passengers, one transports only a_{xv} tons of weight and not the weight corresponding to $\pi_v x_v$ register tons, a being the weight of the passenger and his luggage expressed in tons (and hence a is a fraction considerably less than 1 and also of $^1/_2$). And hence the cost for the journey is:

$$K + \pi_a c_r x_a + (\alpha c_r + s)\, x_v$$

Recalling that the constraint is $\pi_a x_a + \pi_v x_v = T_n$ one reaches, — following the entire foregoing procedure of maximising the profit of each company, considering p_a and p_b as constants, — at a supply x_a and x_v of each company, the sums, supplied overall:

$$\Sigma x_a = X_a, \quad \Sigma x_v = X_v$$

will be in equilibrium when they shall be such as to satisfy the equations:

$$p_a = F_a\,(X_a)$$

$$p_v = F_v\,(X_v)$$

And one has similarly at 4.8:

$$p_a = \pi_a c_r + \pi_a \frac{K+g}{T_n}$$

$$p_v = (\alpha c_r + s) + \pi_v \frac{K+g}{T_n}$$

Here the theorem is similar to the usual one: the constant cost and the profit are divided, in addition to the partial costs, in direct proportion to the register coefficients.

If the company is at the margin:

$$p_a = \pi_a c_r + \pi_a \frac{K}{T_n}$$

$$p_v = (\alpha c_r + s) + \pi_v \frac{K}{T_n}$$

The reasoning is general; it applies, as we have said, to as many classes of goods as we wish and to several classes of passengers.

If these classes, for example, are two and the goods are two, for the passengers each class will have a different π_v, a different s, and perhaps a different a (for different luggage concessions), all larger for the superior classes.

And then one will have (as the constraint is always represented by a sum of terms which should equal T_n):

$$p_a = \pi_a c_r + \pi_a \frac{K+g}{T_n}$$

$$p_b = \pi_b c_r + \pi_b \frac{K+g}{T_n}$$

$$p_{v1} = (\alpha_1 c_r + s_1) + \pi_{v1} \frac{K+g}{T_n}$$

$$p_{v2} = (\alpha_2 c_r + s_2) + \pi_{v2} \frac{K+g}{T_n}$$

from which g disappears for the marginal company.

One sees that the price for the 1st class passenger is greater in view of the more luggage he can take, the more expensive board (expenses of floating hotel) and the higher register coefficient.

4.10 *Conclusions*

It is superfluous to point out that these prices — which are those of a definitive equilibrium, under a regime of perfect competition, and for vessels which sail fully loaded — allow only this discrimination: for the goods, that deriving from the different register coefficient (we have disregarded the greater partial cost which goods of value can entail in view of the greater care they require); for the passengers, that deriving from the different register coefficient, from the different *a* and from the different *s*s.

But in fact there are provisional and not definitive equilibria — we would say dynamic and not static — competition is never perfect; ships never travel fully loaded.

These circumstances and others modify this first approximation which we have reached regarding freight charter; as circumstances of other types modify the first approximation we reached regarding railway tariffs.

We shall deal with all these circumstances in detail and fully in the following chapters with an attentive eye on the facts.

But, as will be seen, this first, rough, approximation on tariffs and charter fees will help us considerably to coordinate, relate, explain all the complicated jumble of facts which we shall examine.

The Telephone Industry and State Exercise of Said*

Antonio De Viti de Marco

Two circumstances hamper an objective examination of the question of telephones in Italy: the example of other countries, which have resolved it in the sense of state management, and the recent creation of the Ministry of Posts and Telegraph, whose bureaucracy is biting on the bridle to take the place of private industry.

But if these two reasons have succeeded in asserting themselves, and almost sufficed to gather in favour of state exercise a majority of members of Parliament in part indifferent and in part unprepared to discuss a problem of such special and delicate nature, they should be eliminated to resolve it in the real, objective interest of the national economy and tax service.

The issues can be grouped into three basic groups: 1) whether it is true that the telephone competes with the telegraph and thus forces the state to assume its exercise, to defend the revenue from telegraph taxes; 2) whether the telephone is truly a public service by nature like the post and telegraph services; 3) whether the extension of telephone communications, promised with state exercise, will be an advantage for the national economy.

It will be useful to see if the reasons which explain the government exercise of the post and telegraph industry, and up to a certain point of the railway industry, lead to the same result for the telephone industry.

* From: De Viti de Marco A., «L'industria dei telefoni e l'esercizio di Stato», *Giornale degli Economisti, Rivista Mensile degli Interessi Italiani*, September 1890, pp. 279-306. [Cod. JEL: N 43].

1. - After the invention of the telephone, its analogy with the telegraph appeared so evident that our Council of State, following the opinion of magistrates of all of Europe, defined it as «the application of the same principle to the transmission of thought and word» and deemed the law which regulates the telegraph monopoly wholly applicable to the telephone.

Hence the government granted the exercise of said service to private companies, in return for the payment of a fee and with infinite conditions and cautions, and now hints that it wishes to exercise the service directly, just as it does for the telegraph service.

But the formal analogy and the legal arguments adduced cannot lead to this extreme consequence, by ignoring the substantial economic differences which exist between the telephone and the telegraph.

This point merits attentive consideration in view of the light it throws on all the economic and financial questions concerning the telephone industry.

It has now been proven that technically the telephone can be exercised at great distances and not just only within the limits of the town and city. Hence it cannot be claimed that a given kilometric distance can give the general criterion of a division of functions between telegraph and telephone, such that licences are granted for the latter within a priori determined kilometric radiuses of territory[1].

If instead we view the quality of the service the telephone and telegraph are each capable of providing, it is immediately clear that the telephone is by far least suited than the telegraph in all the cases when the thought transmitted should leave a written trace or a document. This its inferiority is the cause of a considerable reduction in its use, because the public administration cannot and will not be able to use it to transmit orders, instructions, questions and replies, which commit the responsibility of the of-

[1] This is an erroneous criterion, also because what counts is the economic distance, and from this viewpoint, the limit of 100 kilometres, proposed by some, can be a big distance, where there are no rail services, and a little distance where these are easy and quick!

ficial, and which in any case should be conserved, to judge at any moment, without interruption, the acts undertaken by the administration.

The same holds for the big private companies, particularly the rail companies[2].

This is a first limitation of the useful employment of the telephone, in which there is practically no competition with the telegraph.

In the field of private correspondence, the telephone can efficiently serve to facilitate, with savings of time, personal relations, and hence can truly extend itself in those distances of space which are not obstacles to the customs of personal relations. Thus one explains how the telephone service — technically capable of large distances — has de facto established and developed inside the city, or between this and neighbouring centres, with which contacts are daily and the means of communication quick and frequent. This fact, which is general everywhere the telephone has arisen and is exercised as a private industry, proves that this is the true and proper need the telephone can now cheaply satisfy. It presupposes, prepares and facilitates the more or less immediate meeting of persons, but does not normally eliminate the need for the meeting, in the sense that one can negotiate, discuss and conclude the business in question by telephone. Within these limits, in which one usually does not use the telegraph, but the letter, the messenger boy, the servant, the errand boy, it is obvious that here too the telephone poses almost no competition to the telegraph.

There remains long-distance mail. Here the competition is undoubtedly effective, but it does not go beyond certain limits, as moreover is proven by the fact that on the Paris-Brussels line the income from telegraph has decreased, but not considerably. The reason for this lies in that although the telephone can better prepare business, while waiting for the written letter or telegraph to intervene, it cannot wholly replace them.

[2] I can, cite, among others, this fact, that a director of railways, quite willing to accept that which is innovation and progress, refused to assume responsibility for the operations if telephones were laid along the lines.

Business people, with the telephone, will save on the use of the telegram, but cannot wholly do without the latter.

It should also be noted that the use of the telephone is not always more useful, even in transmitting preparatory business information or that of a personal nature only.

It greatest utility lies in the fact that the telephone places the correspondents in the presence of one another, and hence makes more rapid their intelligence, and makes it depend on them alone, and it saves them any delays of office and errand boys. But at the same time, telephone correspondence is conditioned by the presence of the persons who correspond in the places which are corresponding. In the event of absence, even temporary, from the city or home, the telegram remains the most sure and certain means of correspondence. Such that the telephone will usefully be employed by trading companies, and by persons who have offices which have fixed daily opening hours; it being evident that it cannot penetrate in the use of the public at large, also because, as one will say, it is more expensive than the telegraph and hence, all other conditions being equal, less suited to replace it in general consumption.

This can be said, technically and given the present state of the industry, regarding the reciprocal use of the telephone and telegraph, and one sees within what modest confines there can be true competition of one with the other. But we do not wish to make absolute forecasts for the future, nor deny that future improvements and expedients, of which there is no trace at the present, can make this means of communication more complete.

The decisive factor in the present question of state exercise in Italy is the de facto state. The Parliamentary Commission and the Minister, to prove the fact, inform us that the revenues from telegraph have decreased on the Paris-Brussels line along which the telephone runs!

Apart from the fact that in Europe there are many other inter-city lines, which are not mentioned, and hence that single item of data would prove nothing even in the question of principle, it would be more practical, in this concrete case, to know if in Italy the telephone network goes beyond, and to what extent, the town boundaries; and if these lines, the only ones which can compete with the telegraph, have seen any reduction in revenues from post and telegraph; and then one would have to calculate whether the fee for the licence does not or is unable to compensate the state for that loss.

Only when this is proven to be impossible on the basis of concrete facts would it be appropriate to try another more radical solution of the problem.

Now the fact is that in Italy neither inter-town lines exist, except for some rare exception, nor do the telegraph taxes yield less than before.

Yet it is useful, to eliminate any equivocations, to immediately initiate this hypothetical study.

Let us therefore allow that the competition of the telephone is real in Italy, that the revenues from telegraph taxes have diminished and are even more threatened in the future.

Even in this hypothesis, the argument that the industrial exercise of the telephone should be monopolised to defend the telegraph revenues is absurd.

The increase or decrease in revenues depends solely on the consumer's preferences.

If the public now de facto prefers the telephone, it is inevitable that the telegraph revenues will decrease. This means that the telephone industry becomes remunerative and that of the telegraph ceases to be so. And it is not clear how the state, by taking the exercise of the telephone on itself, can avoid the result of seeing the revenues from the telegraph tax gradually diminish in its budget.

It would be like saying that Tizio, who has invested 100,000 lire in the trade of wine, which he does not sell with profit, thinks of defending this his bad business by investing another 100,000 lire in the production of beer, which he sells with profit, instead of divesting the first 100,000 to invest all his capital in the productive industry. The mere fact of owning two companies, one remunerative and the other not, does not authorise us to say that the latter defends and sustains the former!

In this case the state should behave as any private player would behave. As the revenues from the telegraph decrease, the state should disinvest the telegraph capital, reducing the plant, the material, the number of employees and offices and raising, where necessary, the tariffs to bring supply into line with the new conditions of reduced demand.

If, having reduced the telegraph plant to the minimum required by the own and exclusive need of the public administration, revenues do not cover costs, a supplement to the taxes will have to be demanded.

Hence it is not a question of defending the telegraph taxes from the competition of the telephone, but of monopolising the exercise of the telephone industry to obtain, in its profit, a tax compensation.

The new monopoly, derived and sustained by that argument, would have the character and purpose of tax monopoly, and should be discussed as a tax measure to be adopted and not as a public service to be assumed by the state[3].

One could speak of defence of the telegraph taxes in a single case, namely if competition by the telephone was suppressed, its use banned, or else made de facto impossible by means of prohibitive tariffs. And should this policy, also moulded by narrow criteria of fiscal monopoly, end with evident damage to the country's general economy, it was sought to achieve something similar with the clause included in the licences that the concessionaires should guarantee the state the present telegraph revenues. This has considerably hampered the installation of telephone lines between towns where the telegraph taxes would have given a lower revenue and the entrepreneur's risk would be too high and the tariffs would have to be excessively high, to pay not only the telephone service, for which there was a real demand, but also the telegraph services for which there was no longer any demand.

This constitutes in every manner an anti-economic use of national capital and produces damage which can be avoided only by a suitable reduction of the capital invested in the state telegraph.

---

[3] This is one of the equivocations played on during debate in the Lower House: state exercise of the telephones was indicated as a means to compensate any losses of telegraph taxes; and the measures were defended with the reasons usually adduced to maintain that telephones are a public service.

Moreover, the case is not wholly new.

Post was a government monopoly for the transport not only of letters, but also of persons and luggage, when the railways came onto the scene. Nonetheless, to defend the revenues from the post service, it was proposed to extend the monopoly to the railways.

Instead, gradually, the state gave up transporting persons and luggage and indeed ended up availing itself of the railways for the transport of mail, simply because, under the changed de facto conditions, this was the most inexpensive system for organising the postal service.

Similarly, when alongside the post, which was already a state monopoly, there arose in England the telegraph as a private industry, the government did not concern itself about defending the postal tariffs by hampering the development of the telegraph or rushing to redeem them. And when later leading English economists and politicians discussed the problem of redemption, it did not lead, as far as I know, to the unsteady terrain of the defence of mail taxes, but was discussed with wholly independent arguments.

Two consequences derive from the above observations. The first is that, given the competition of the telephone as real, the government is first and foremost called upon to restrict the supply and production costs of the telegraph service. The second, that the telephone in any case — public service or mere fiscal instrument — is an independent economic problem.

But the *Report* which precedes the bill presented to Parliament excludes state exercise being proposed as a fiscal expedient, in the same manner as the monopoly on salt and tobacco; — an analogy against which the Minister of Posts and Telegraph protested with impartial indignation.

It is common knowledge that the post and telegraph were also absorbed by the state for reasons which were more fiscal then economic in origin; but it is still certain that with time the first fiscal reason disappeared and now the post and telegraph are conserved by the state not as private property, not as fiscal monopoly, but rather as a public service, i.e., as a productive function of the state.

And if one wishes the government to operate the telephone service, it is because it appears to have the characteristics of a public service. This is all said and done the sole and true question in play and which we should examine here.

2. - We need an exact definition of public service, and this is not only absent in the ministerial and parliamentary reports, but is still debatable in science. This is not a drawback, but it is a drawback that it has been reasoned and one continues to reason as though the definition exists and is known to all, because the consequence of state exercise derives from the premise, assumed as axiomatic, that the telephone is a public service[4].

As we cannot, dealing with telephones, deal in depth with the question of public services, which pervades the entire set-up and the tasks of the state, it will suffice to mention their essential characteristics.

---

[4] Here are some examples: «The telephone has conquered in economic and social life a privileged position to which it is entitled in view of the importance and range of services it renders. This instrument of perfect docility increases the points of contact, extends the circle of business and increases the extent of general production. The more immediate and timely relations help a more active and flourishing life circulate in exchanges and transactions.

Given this, it is evident that the telephone service has the nature of a public service...» (*Report* of the Commission, p. 5).

The Minister's *Report* totally lacks any rudiment of definition, and insists only in the concept that the telephone, being a public service, can only receive from the state that complete organisation and expansion which is desired by all. (*Report* of the Minister pp. 2 and 5).

In his speech the Minister said: «the present-day state tends to increase its tasks because it tends to protect the collective life, taking on those services which are of general public utility». (Sitting of 4 July 1890). This is still the most precise phase in the entire speech. To give an idea of the confusion of ideas which reigns as regards this issue and the absolute lack of logic, here is another excerpt: «The telephone has entered in that period of time, when it has become of general and not local use; and I am surprised that it is compared to the bakery and the drinking water service, in which at the most the municipal authority can intervene to regulate, as these are not general, but local services». Elsewhere: «The telephone service is similar to the telegraph service, and as a service similar to the telegraph service should be regulated and exercised in accordance with the same provisions». Elsewhere: «as long as you maintain that the operation of railways is an industrial service we can discuss it; I too considered it thus. But is the telephone service industrial? No, it is an service eminently of public interest, like the telegraph. Otherwise the telegraph too is an industrial service...!».

Neither does the Minister believe it necessary to add anything else to prove the things which are asserted in these excerpts.

The public service is a product of the economic activity typical of the state. The legislative provision which makes it a government monopoly with the exclusion of private players is the sanction of an economic predominance already acknowledged and acquired by the state.

To investigate the reason for some present public services and to argue the possibility, that some other services, left to date to private industry, become such, one has to show that the state's production was or is or is about to be more useful to the consumers than private industry.

But the state, however conceived, is always a collective enterprise, and as such is, as a rule, less capable than individual enterprise, and, at best, as capable as a private collective enterprise.

Hence it is quite arduous to show — today above all when it is very easy to establish powerful joint-stock companies — that the state is technically more capable than private industry.

This is not the path that leads to a solution.

Before reaching government industry true and proper, the state generally proceeds through a growing system of intervention in the field of private economic activity which is progressively reduced. The state industry should logically be considered as intervention in the relative private industry, taken to its extreme limit, in which the latter is de facto suppressed and the former takes its place. Thus we should start by investigating the reasons for this intervention to explain the final and eventual fact of a state monopoly.

Now the first reason for state intervention lies in the formation of large private monopolies, which are the characteristic phenomenon of present-day economic organisation, and the natural result of three causes: the division of labour, competition and big industry. The variously combined action of these forces leads in the market to the triumph of the most powerful and best organised company, which has reduced its overhead costs to a minimum and is thus able to offer its products at the best price and banish the small competing industries. The more difficult and long the struggle fought in an extended market, the more powerful and difficult the resulting monopoly will be to undo.

But this monopoly realises the principle of maximum useful effect more rigorously through a more economic use of the productive elements (economies of production) which is wholly to the benefit of the consumers, who have enabled it to triumph and have an interest in its continuing to do so. The only danger is that the company, having become a monopoly, discontinues the policy which ensured it victory in the competition, and abuses its new position and the powerful organisation acquired, and inaugurates a monopoly policy raising prices, worsening the quality of its goods, etc., etc.

This is the first economic reason for the state's intervention, in the interest of all the consumers, who are represented and have the majority in the government. The purpose of the intervention is to guarantee, as far as such is possible by law, those advantages that were naturally acquired with the formation of the private monopoly.

But the most characteristic and decisive case of private monopoly, which has moreover immediate application to the problem of telephones and the means of communication in general, is that which realises the principle of the maximum useful effect through a more economic consumption of the item produced (economy of consumption).

This case is found when a same unit of good produced can satisfy at the same time the identical need of many persons. For example, music can satisfy simultaneously the need of 1,000 persons who are gathered in a theatre. If two theatres with the same music and in the same conditions are open, each can count on the presence of 500 persons, but the capital employed in one of the two is less. When one of the theatres wishes to attract the public from the other, it can without loss lower the prices up to half, but the other in turn can lower them by more than half and in growing proportion as it sees its public of 500 persons diminish.

Whether the competition continues or whether an agreement is preferred, the result of the struggle will be the monopoly, and with regard to the national economy there has been a waste of capital and labour; the maximum effect is achieved when the unit produced is exploited by the greater number of persons in the simultaneous satisfaction of the need of each.

This simple economic principle, of immediate intuition, explains the monopoly, which ends up establishing itself in the railway, in the telephone, and in the telegraph service where they are not exercised by the state.

With the growth in foreign and domestic trade, communications form a system whose every part is more useful, the closer its connection with everything. A single road network suffices for the exchanges and communications of all the individuals who live in that given village. The monopoly's, but also its social advantage, is seen here. In intervening, the state should aim to conserve the benefits, preventing only the monopolist from exploiting the consumer by imposing monopoly prices and a poor quality of service.

Now when two companies build two competing networks where one would have sufficed, they are led, by the calculation of their interest to reach an agreement, but then it is inevitable that the tariff to remunerate a double capital, should be higher than that which would have sufficed to remunerate the capital of only one of such companies. Hence state intervention is in such a case necessary more than ever.

But a second condition is generally needed, namely that the need in question is common to all the components of the community, as then they are all consumers, and as such all interested in state intervention. The intervention is the more to the general advantage the more general the need to be satisfied.

Having established the conditions of the intervention, there then arises the question of the limits.

Now the condition of the general nature of the need, combined with the other of the monopoly of the industry, acts on the determination of the limits. In fact, state intervention will be as a rule minimal or none when the monopoly damages or threatens a small class of consumers, unless these are the masters of the government.

Only when the class of consumers embraces all the citizens, and this, in view of the essentially democratic political constitution, is master of the government, does state intervention aim at the total absorption of private industry. This is because the true consumers of the industry exercised by the state are all the taxpayers, and if all the taxpayers are also the consumers of the service produced, the personal identity between rulers, producers and consumers naturally leads to the solution to eliminate the effects of the monopoly price which everyone should pay to a private company, thanks to the replacement of the monopoly by state exercise.

Indeed, this solution at first appears more natural and economic than that of intervention, which often requires often difficult legislative work and an expensive surveillance, and constantly causes friction between the administration and the private monopolist.

But while government production, which has the complex economic nature of a production and consumption co-operative, offers the advantages of consumption co-operatives — as it imposes only the cost price on the consumer — it encounters all the difficulties of production co-operatives, which, as they are not founded on the principle of maximum profit and individual responsibility, are unable to sustain the competition of similar private companies.

The exceptions are those when the nature of the industry entails little risk and hence requires neither much capital nor special and difficult attention on the part of the partners, neither complicated accounting and when the responsibility of the individual officials is clearly delimited and surveillance on the part of those interested is easy and inexpensive.

Thus, when these conditions and others similar, which should be ascertained on a case by case basis, act in favour of an monopolised industry, it is foreseeable that one will prefer monopoly and state exercise; when on the other hand they are absent one will prefer the system of control, which prevents the private monopoly from exercising itself to the detriment of the consumers, and at the same time leaves private initiative with the task of organising and exercising the industry in question with the maximum economy.

It is known that these conditions are encountered in the postal service and not in the railways, one understanding that the former has become almost wholly a public service while in the latter the state is charged with acting as a watchdog, a role which has gradually increased, and has entrusted its exercise to private companies. For the telegraph service the question was debated for much longer, and it was initially resolved in favour of state exercise instead of mere control and believed that the state could have organised the service more economically, using the postal service's plants to a large extent[5].

However, this solution has not triumphed everywhere, neither, where it has triumphed, are all the telegraph lines exercised by the state.

Now we shall turn to the telephone.

It has not been shown that the need for telephone correspondence is generally felt in Italy, nor can it even be presumed it will be in the near future. It suffices to consider, accepting the statistics presented by the Minister, that in Italy with 19 companies operated urban networks in little more than 70 cities, the number of subscribers totals 11,780. Germany has 30,000 subscribers, Great Britain 21,826 and France 10,837. We are ahead of France and this lead increases in weight if one relates it to the size of the population, as the Minister has done. But the fact is that the absolute population has no importance in the question; it would have if in all the states it was equally distributed over the territory, equally agglomerated in the cities or spread in the countryside. This method yields data which obviously cannot be compared, form Luxembourg, which has a subscriber every 412 inhabitants, to Austria Hungary which has one every 7,577 inhabitants.

If we take account of the population density and the number of large cities, we conclude that the relative value of the 11,780 subscribers, compared with the other countries, is much less than the absolute value.

Instead we should hold that need in Italy is saturated more than elsewhere and that the consumption is not destined for a

[5] Thus it was thought and sought to show in England before the redemption of the telegraph, as can be seen in the article by JEVONS, *On the Analogy Between the Post-Office and Telegraphs, etc.*, reprinted in *Methods of Social Reform*, p. 277 ff.

rapid and imminent expansion. We speak here of that need which is able to pay by itself the price of the service which it demands, and suppose that the cost of production does not reduce significantly in the near future.

Now in Italy some towns which have a telephone service have less than 10 subscribers; the tariffs are among the lowest in Europe; the telephone companies' life is difficult, as is shown by their balance sheets, and they have just started to distribute some dividend to their shareholders[6].

These clues allow one to legitimately argue that the telephone industry has enjoyed an impetus superior to the country's true need. This is borne out by the following comparative table of the extension of consumption of the postal, telegraphic and telephone services in the principal states of Europe:

	No. of letters per inhabitant	No. of telegrams per inhabitant	No. of inhabitants per telephone subscriber
United Kingdom	33	1.3	1,700
Germany	27.5[7]	0.38	1,300
France	16.1	0.72	3,199
Austria Hungary	13.8	0.25	7,577
Italy	5.1	0.3	2,521

The table shows that Italy was last in postal correspondence and telegrams, but is one of first as regards telephones. This level was reached from 1885 onwards.

According to some data furnished by Neumann Spallart, at the end of 1885, Great Britain had 180 cities with telephones, Germany 112, France 20 and Italy 18. Hence over the span of a few

[6] These data are to be found in the Appendices to the *Relazione* of the Commission (14 May 1890, N. 117 A) and of the Parliamentary Bill (10 February 1890, N. 117).

[7] This total includes postcards, hence the average should be slightly reduced for Germany and Austria-Hungary. But the gap between Italy and the other states is so considerable that subtlety is a waste of time. The data for the railway network and transport and passengers see Italy even further behind. They are not given, because the analogy between the railways and telephones is even more distant.

years we achieved the figure of 67 cities. Consumption has reached its highest expansion; the tariffs are at their lowest limit, neither is a further lowering possible, as the cost of production of the telephone service tends to grow with consumption. This is an important point.

The use of the telephone, conditioned by the fact, as we noted, that the two correspondents are one in the presence of the other or that they can by themselves put themselves one in the presence of the other, lies essentially in the home subscription, and it is only exceptionally that one, who has not a telephone, acting as proposer, can correspond with who has a telephone. Hence normal correspondence can exist only between two subscribers at home; and hence, as consumption extends, the cost of production of the service for the part which refers to the price of the actual telephone, grows proportionally to the number of subscribers. The overhead costs and the cost of materials also grow considerably as the network of wire extends and becomes denser.

This circumstance, which the telephone shares with the telegraph, becomes an obstacle to the lowering, beyond certain limits, of telephone tariffs, as it was and is for the telegraph, where Rowland Hill's principle could not be applied. Hence, if we allow that the revenue from telegraph taxes should cover the cost of production, it is practically absurd to count on an expansion of the consumption which normally follows the lowering of prices, and on which it appears the Minister so greatly and surely relies. It should also be borne in mind that the telephone, as a means more costly than the telegraph, will be consumed primarily by the affluent classes. Given this, the present tariff in Italy is relatively modest, being one of the lowest in Europe, and hence cannot be in itself considered an obstacle to a normal expansion of consumption. For the well-to-do classes it still remains too high: and hence a moderate lowering — which is what perhaps could be conceded — would not allow the telephone to become part of their habitual consumption. Both these reasons lead one to believe that the demand lacks elasticity[8].

---

[8] See MARSHALL A., *Principles of Economics*, London, 1890, p. 162 ff.

But to judge if the need for telephone communications is general, one should bear in mind not only the number of subscribers or consumption vis-à-vis the population, but also the connection of the various lines with each other or consumption on the territory. One should see whether they form a co-ordinated system of communications, extended throughout the territory of the state.

Now it is a fact that to date the telephone in Italy has, as a rule, not ventured outside the city walls, but has remained essentially a local service[9].

If we reason with preconceptions here, we have to admit that in a country where lots of companies function and all the principal and many secondary cities have a telephone service, the lack of inter-city communications only proves that there is no need, either because it is too expensive to satisfy it or because the telegraph suffices to satisfy it.

Here it should be noted that the expansion of inter-city communications lacks the first and principal reason: the need of the public administration, which we discussed above.

This is how the posts and telegraphs have historically become state industries. The administrative need in itself and for itself and independent of the need of the public, this is the first reason for state exercise. For a long time, public industry co-existed with private industry; but either for tax reasons or for economic reasons or the opportunity of adopting a uniform tariff regime on all the networks run by the state, the latter was gradually induced to decree the legal monopoly.

It should be noted that the administrative need of the state was already in itself a general need, because it was to the benefit of all those administered, and because it required the entire territory be connected in a co-ordinated network of postal and telegraphic lines.

The problem was therefore posed, by the natural play of the economic forces, with the following dilemma: either the state or

---

[9] The inter-city service is operated by Società telefonica ligure to link the towns of S. Pier d'Arena, Cornegliano and Quarto al mare with Genoa. This is the most important example; and yet the life of these and many other towns of the Ligurian riviera is so merged with that of Genoa that they can be considered one with it.

a single concessionaire, and the decision was made for exercise by the state.

But for telephones, the question cannot even be put in these extreme terms, because the state does not have the same need and interest in connecting all the local administrations to the centre by the telephone, as the public is satisfied with the service confined to the city and short distances. This demonstrates the present sufficiency of private industry in meeting the public's need.

Rather, if one wishes to foster the expansion of telephone communications, as they are deemed advantageous for the national economy, as soon as the budgetary conditions allow such, one should grant greater freedom of action to the private companies, abolishing the proviso that they should guarantee the present revenues from telegraph taxes on the inter-city networks.

Because this is the sole circumstance whose excessively aleatory nature makes one suspect that the development of long-distance communications has been shackled.

The second essential condition, which would justify state intervention, is that of the monopoly, as we have already seen. Now the reasons with which one proves that the monopoly benefits consumers when talking about satisfying a collective need hold for the telephone as they hold for all the means of communication in general. They hold both if we are talking of a national network vis-à-vis all the population, and of a local network vis-à-vis the local population.

Hence it is certain that in the city the telephone service tends to be a monopoly. The consumers enjoy a utility which is greater, the greater the number of subscribers with whom they can communicate when necessary, while the subscribers of a company cannot, as a rule, communicate with those of a competing company. The producers for their part can always, all other conditions being equal, grant price facilities as the number of subscribers increases.

The state therefore intervenes to guarantee the good results of the monopoly and prevent the bad ones. To this end it has already implemented some effective measures and others can be adopted, without achieving the complete absorption of the private industry.

In fact, when the government has allowed private companies to install and exercise a telephone service in Italy to date, it has not guaranteed them an exclusive privilege; but has reserved to right to grant new licences in the same city.

This is a first limit placed on the monopoly of the service. If the tariffs are too high, if the service is bad, a new licence can be granted; it is therefore in the interest of the present concessionaires to avoid competition. Moreover, messenger boys, servants, the telegraph itself compete with the telephone within the same city. It is in the company's interest to defeat these its natural competitors, offering the service at the lowest price.

This is the second limit to the monopoly; and since the state owns the telegraph service, it can always exercise a brake on any monopoly by the telephone companies by improving the transmission of domestic telegrams and lowering their charges.

Finally, at the expiry of the contract, the new licence should be granted to the highest bidder, taking as a rule, the tariffs and conditions of the previous contract as a base for the tender, to improve them. It is during the exercise of this service that competition benefits the public of consumers and should be exploited.

From this point of view, the problem was better resolved in one of the previous bills, which introduced the condition, accepted by the companies, that at the expiry of the first licence — granted naturally for quite a long period of time — the state retained, without indemnity, ownership of the telephone installations.

However many objections may be made to this measure, it is still in the direction in which the policies of the state should go: increasing its intervention in the construction of competing telephone networks, to promote the competition of exercising concessionaires.

And if, after all these guarantees, the telephone service does not improve and the tariffs do not decrease and consumption does not increase, it has to be concluded that the public does not need such service.

In conclusion, the telephone industry lacks the characteristics to become economically a public industry, a productive function typical of the state, a public service.

3. - Thus it has been generally proven that, given the present state of the telephone industry and the need of the public and the needs of the budget, state exercise of the telephone service is not justified: *a)* because the private service does not provide true competition to the state telegraph service; *b)* because any reduction in revenues from the telegraph service entails, first of all, the reduction of the capital employed, and then has to be compensated by the telephone licence fee or any other tax measure; *c)* because the state cannot be itself the consumer of the telephone service as a means of administrative communication throughout the Kingdom; *d)* because the public need is not general, but confined to the well-to-do classes and localised in the more populated centres; *e)* because the monopoly of the private companies is practically zero, and can also be reduced with the system of bidding for the operating licences.

In actual fact, when the government and the supporters of state exercise have spoken of monopoly of private companies and universal public need, they believe they are predicting the future and preventing it. In fact, it is feared that the present operating companies in Italy will merge but it is certain that such a coalition does not exist today. Thus one speaks of the need to extend telephone communications to all the territory of the state, the Minister promises this and it appears that everyone expects this of him, but an extended network, which shows the present general need, does not exist.

In this manner of argument there is an equivocation, because the 'need' is that which de facto the consumer feels, not that which the producer attributes to him out of interest or fantasy.

The government, which wishes to exercise the telephone service, supposes that there exists a general need, which remains unmet because of the responsibility, incapacity or rapacity of the private companies: and this latent need should be fully satisfied by extending telephone communications throughout the state.

The latent need undoubtedly exists, because there is no need that, at the state of desire, does not exist in the soul of each person, and it is also certain that if the means of satisfaction becomes cheap and free, everyone will consume it.

The Minister and the Commission confuse the desire which everyone has to correspond by telephone with the real need which is limited by the cost. This is the crux of the question.

Faced with the fact, which we have mentioned on several occasions, that the telephone industry has seen an extraordinary expansion in Italy, and that the concessionaires have distributed dividends, which are on average much lower than the current rate of interest, the promise to extend the telephone networks throughout Italy, i.e., to centres or between centres which are less remunerative than the present, and to furthermore lower the tariffs[10] includes the claim that the government will exercise it more economically than the private companies.

To date convinced worshippers of the state have attempted to show that in collective enterprises the state's aptitude equalled that of private companies, because both one and the other had to avail themselves of the work of salaried workers. It was for them a desired maximum, which moreover the adversaries did not grant for the reason that the employees of private companies are already the fruit of selection, and paid according to their utility, with a rigour unknown to the public administration.

Hence the government's claim is of a wholly new audacity and it should rather be held that the greater extension promised by the Minister will either not take place or will be an anti-economic expansion as there will be a lack of consumers, and the tariffs will have to be lowered to below the cost of production to create them.

In this case the difference not covered by the tariffs will then be covered by taxes, just as with the railways. But the strategic reasons which justify, at least in part, the construction of railways, which a private industry would not undertake, do not hold for the telephone whose utility is determined solely by the single consumers, and according to the price said are prepared to pay.

---

[10] The Minister of Posts and Telegraph, in his speech to the Lower House at the sitting of 7 July 1890, calculates and promises to reduce the present tariffs by one sixth!

If private economic revenue alone does not suffice to measure the useful effect of the railway and post and telegraphic networks, it should for the afore-indicated reasons alone measure that of the telephone network.

If today the private companies overall lose or do not earn, the state will certainly lose as an industrialist. This is why it puts forward and artificially inflates the argument of public interest; it will be the broad public of taxpayers who will cover the operating losses of the state's telephones.

This would still not be a very large loss, if the loss of this anti-economic production was distributed over all the taxpayers, which would be the case only if all the taxpayers were normal consumers of that service. But it has already been seen that the class of consumers is very limited, hence the operating deficit will be to their benefit and to the detriment of the taxpayers, who will pay a part of the price of a good which they consume neither directly nor indirectly. This is an iniquitous distribution of the cost of production which is compounded by another reason.

Exercise by the state will give rise to a single administration inspired in its behaviour by the interest of the citizenry as a whole, and hence the tendency towards a system of uniform tariffs for all the state.

At most, taking account of the greater or lesser cost of production required for the network in a large or small city, the tariffs can be divided into two or three categories and applied to the various centres according to the number of inhabitants. If the state now extends the telephone networks to smaller centres than those which are today served, and by way of hypothesis wishes to cover the total cost of production with the revenues from taxes, it will be forced to raise the average tariff of the higher categories. The large centres, which could enjoy a comparatively lower tariff, will pay for the small centres, which should have a comparatively higher tariff. This compensation is justified when the service is of truly general utility, because then in the long term the compensation takes place de facto in the consumption each makes of the good in question. But when the utility of the service is wholly local, that compensation takes the form of a finally unequal distribution of the cost of production[11].

These predictions are susceptible to more detailed proof.

The balance sheets of the principal telephone companies[12], which provide the elements necessary to make them compatible to formulate a quite sure overall judgement, show the following results:

Total value of telephone network	Lire	6,200,000[13]
Gross income	Lire	1,083,869
Total costs	Lire	890,543

Hence the capital invested would be remunerated, between interest and profit, in the ratio of 3.12%; and costs amount to more than 82% of gross income.

This is, in the best of hypotheses, the actual state of the private industry. Now if the government with its management were

---

[11] The provisions, contained in section 9 of the *Bill* approved by the Lower House, that the tariff (within the maximum and minimum limits laid down by said section) is fixed place by place by Royal Decree will prove to be ineffective and damaging when implemented.

It contradicts the principle on which the entire project rests, that telephones are a public service and hence cannot resist for long the assaults of the cities, which will demand the preferential treatment. Personal and electoral influences will take the place of economic criteria in determining the local tariff.

The system is furthermore contrary to the evolution already undergone by postal and telegraph tariffs and also by the railway tariffs; and the argument of the analogy, with which erroneously one wishes to now classify the telephone as a public service, will be very valid after, to combat the system of different tariffs when the growing general trend is towards a uniform and single tariff.

[12] Which are: the telephone company for central Italy, that for southern Italy, the Roman and general, the Lombard, the Brescia and Ligure companies. Others could not be taken into account as their balance sheets are neither complete nor clear. We are speaking not of the original balance sheets, but of those published in the Appendix to the *Report* of Hon. Balestra, the only ones we could verify.

[13] The total value should rightly be Lire 6,605,027 which I reduced to the round figure of 6,200,000, to take account of the capital for related subsidiary industries, which give a gross income of Lire 63,925, circa one seventeenth of the gross income of 1,083,869 due solely to telephones. It may be that the assessment of 6,605,027 of the telephone network already excludes the capital of the subsidiary industries. I preferred to exclude it, to reason with more certainty on the hypothesis least favourable to my thesis.

to obtain the same income and not incur greater costs, it would not basically incur a serious loss[14].

But the Minister believes that state management will be more economic, because one can use the installations and senior personnel of the postal and telegraph services for the telephone service.

Certainly, if the technical difficulties which hamper the use of the telegraph wires for telephone communications were to be overcome, a powerful reason would be gained for state operation. But to date all attempts have failed.

It is moreover extremely instructive to recall that the same reasons were put forward in England at the time of the redemption of the telegraph in support of state operation. It was claimed — and the claim was based on detailed technical calculations — that use of the installations and personnel of the post service would enable the state to organise the telegraph service more economically than the private companies.

But should de facto a part of the running costs of the post service be shared with the telegraph, these predictions would completely collapse. It should be said that the lower efficiency of labour of public employees compared with private employees made the envisaged reduction in personnel impossible.

What happened in England for the telegraph would happen in Italy for the telephone. State operation would lead to an extension of the network and increase in the correspondence, but at the same time would increase the percentage of costs[15].

---

[14] Without discussing the inappropriateness of weighing down the balance sheet with the amount needed for the redemption, the capital would be remunerated at the rate of 3%, and the income, which the state receives today for fees, circulation tax on shares, movables and for the discount of 50% which the company grants on public administration subscriptions would not be lost (as has been erroneously claimed by adversaries of the Minister's project) as it is included in the company costs and therefore is part of the net income in the state's accounts.

[15] According to JEVONS (*The Post Office Telegraphs and Their Financial Results*, *Op. cit.*, p. 293 ff) from 1870, the year of the redemption, to 1875, the number of telegraphs increased from 8,000,000 to 42,000,000 and thus the length of the network and offices, but the cost year by year increased to 57%, 78¾%, 89½%, 91½%, 96⅔%.

The reason is that for the telegraph, as for the telephone, the cost of production grows with the extension of production, while for the post the correspondence can increase, with broad limits, without this increase engendering higher costs.

Hence the government's promised extension of the telephone service cannot circumvent this elementary economic principle of productivity or of diminishing returns, which was and is operative in the telegraph and railway industries.

It will not even produce the financial results of the private companies[16].

But it is precisely these reasons of anti-economic production and iniquitous distribution of costs which have engendered the majority in favour of state exercise in the Chamber of Deputies.

It is an hoary observation that in a large number of questions parliamentarians represent specific interests — of class or regions — and that in these cases the majority comes into being from agreements and reciprocal concessions, such that the final result does not coincide with the general interest of the country. This is especially true always when talking about national public works, because then each is prepared to vote for the entire planned system of constructions if it includes that in which he is most interested.

Each fights all the more energetically to obtain a port, a road, a station, a post office, a telegraph office, the more he is convinced that the cost will be borne by the country as a whole. If each town was to truly pay the price of the thing asked, they would abstain from asking for it most of the times.

---

[16] The provision of section 8 of the *Bill* approved by the Chamber of Deputies, which gives the government the right to accept advance payments by towns for the installation and exercise of telephone networks has no value, as it — even when it is in force — will exonerate the accounts of the state and similarly weigh on those of the towns. In relations between the state and the town it only proves that, in spite of the phrases employed to baptise the telephone as a public service, there has in fact been a refusal to acknowledge that it is an essentially local service. But in relations with the national economy and finances it matters only that, to calculate the capital that will be invested anti-economically in telephones, one will have to add the burden on the local budgets to that on the state's budget.

But when all reason in this manner, the calculations and hopes of each remain deluded in the total sum, which cannot fail to highlight the anti-economic use of the national capital.

It is a vicious circle which originates from an elementary fact, namely that in the bills for public works, the cost, budgeted overall, represents a sacrifice for the country as a whole, while each single work is a more immediate and special advantage for a centre or class of persons.

The single member of Parliament, in his specific interest, to which he feels closer and more interested, loses sight of the final result, which embodies the general interest of the country. Instead of comparing the overall cost with the overall utility of the constructions proposed, or else first calculating the unit cost for each region, or group of those with the most interest, to enable a comparison between this and the unit utility, the single member of Parliament, as a rule, compares an overall cost, of which he has a distant and vague awareness, with a unit utility of which he has a clear and immediate perception.

It is a phenomenon of psychological mirage eluded only by those few endowed with superior character and intellect.

In the concrete case of telephones, most have flirted with the idea of the telephone office in the main city of his more or less rural constituency, without weighing the cost which said city has to bear to pay that advantage.

Each has preferred to persuade himself that in the 8 million and then 3 asked of the Minister, there was capacity at least for his provincial or constituency capital.

And when most openly cede to the evidence, that the 8 or 3 million should be set against the sum of provincial or district capitals, tacitly each hopes and prepares to wrest the initiative from one's colleagues and obtain the telephone office before the others. Those who do not win in the competition will shout out after that they and their cities have equal and more right to the telephone network. How can one rebut them when all this becomes a struggle of special interests and a race by the majority to achieve them first?

The Municipalisation of Public Services: Theory, Debate and Practice. Various Papers

Giovanni Montemartini

1. - The Economic Theory of the Municipalisation of Public Services*

1.1 The premisses on which one should erect the construct of the theory of the municipalisation of public services are those on which the entire public-finance doctrine is founded. They can be summarised as follows: *a)* the town council is a political enterprise, an enterprise whose purpose is to coercively distribute the costs of some productions (supply of goods or services) among all the members of the municipality; *b)* the sole function of the town council is to coercively distribute certain costs. The sole need of the town council is to procure the coercive force to achieve its purpose; *c)* the productions for which the town council is responsible are contingent to the time, place and economies which, in a given moment, constitute the political enterprise. The hedonistic calculation to determine the economic expediency of having the town council bear the costs of a production is made by the economies which comprise the enterprise; *d)* a production is called municipal (and

---

* From: MONTEMARTINI G., «La teoria economica della municipalizzazione dei pubblici esercizi», *Giornale degli Economisti*, February 1901, pp. 180-7.

Excerpt from a work by Professor MONTEMARTINI G., *La municipalizzazione dei pubblici servigi* (Part 2, Chapter 1). [Cod. JEL: N 43].

inappropriately spoken of as a municipal need) when the procurement of the products takes place by distributing the costs over the municipalities. It is the method of production which constitutes the nature of the costs known as municipal needs; there are no a priori private needs and municipal needs.

1.2 Given these premisses, let us suppose that, in a given moment and in a given municipality, all the needs, or better, all the productions whose costs should be borne by the community are established by means of struggles and economic calculations of varying degree of elaboration. We can also suppose, to facilitate our treatment, that the costs are expressed objectively in specie. This then means that the municipality is coercively induced to hand over to the political entrepreneur — the town council — the amount of specie needed and sufficient for the provision of some goods or of some services.

The town council then proceeds to the expenditure, namely to the provision of those goods and services that satisfy the needs of the enterprise and of the political entrepreneur.

These goods and services can be provided under two systems: *a)* either the town council resorts to exchange; it buys products on the commodities market or spends there the amount of specie it has had handed over by the municipality; *b)* or the town council resorts to the direct production of those specific products which it needs; in other words it spends the amount of specie obtained from the municipality on the production factor market.

Economically the two transactions have the same base: a revenue is transformed into consumption goods; one can resort either to exchange or to production. Exchange entails production just as production entails exchange. The economy will adopt that system which maximises the profit obtainable by a given revenue.

1.3 This direct production by the town council which we now consider should not be confused with other forms of direct production which the political enterprise can undertake. The town council — just as the state and any other political body — can engage in production to produce a revenue. When the town council cultivates a piece of land or a wood which it owns, when it rents its own accommodation, it is exercising a state enterprise. When the town council — as is the case in Italian political law — constitutes legal municipal monopolies: it exercises the monopoly of public weights and measures, it holds the monopoly to lease stalls for fairs and markets (paragraph 4 of article 147 of the provincial and town law), then one has a fiscal enterprise. In both these cases, in the state enterprise and the fiscal enterprise, there is a way of acquiring a revenue, and a means is adopted to distribute the costs of future products over the municipality. On the other hand, in direct production, which we wish to study now, the revenue is already formed, and all that has to be done is to apply it in the most economic manner to the procurement of specific products. This form of direct production corresponds to the following purpose: «to procure specific products at a lower price than that obtainable with exchange under free competition». In this case, and only in this case, does one encounter the phenomenon of the municipalisation of public services.

Municipalisation therefore consists in a passage from a form of exchange to a form of production in the procurement of certain goods. Or else it can also consist in the adoption of the form of production, without first adopting the form of exchange. The municipalisation of public services can thus be defined as: «a direct production whose costs are borne by the municipality, and whose purpose is to obtain products at a unit price lower than would be obtained if one resorted to private producers operating under free competition».

1.4 The economic problem in the phenomenon of municipalisation can therefore be formulated thus: «is the direct exercise by the town council of an industry which offers products suited to satisfy certain needs more advantageous, or better, cheaper — or is it preferable that the town council procures the necessary amount of said products from private entrepreneurs?».

The advantage in municipalising can be political and economic. The political advantage deriving from the different composition of the political enterprise is studied in a political theory of municipalisation, the economic advantage finds its natural seat of treatment here.

1.5 When we say that the town council produces, we adopt an elliptical expression which should be clarified to avoid confusion with the financial theory of production. Taken literally, the expression would appear to imply that the town council has other industrial functions in addition to that of the coercive distribution of the costs. But the town council is not a true producer, it is nothing other than a spender of the revenue obtained from the municipality. A part of the revenue shall be spent on the commodities market, another part on the production factors market. Here the town council procures the producer services — land, capital, labour, executive force; the money from the municipality is destined to create a sector of producers, to give life to a set of production factors, to an enterprise which produces only for the town council. Production, as regards its technical aspect, the transformation of the materials, the creation of the utility and products is truly the work of the enterprises commanded and brought into being by the town council. This production is not a function of the political enterprise. The municipality, under the spur of coercion, pays, offers the political entrepreneur the means to procure the factors of production and to give life and movement to a productive arrangement. The risks of the arrangement are borne, as are indeed all its costs, by the municipality. The town council's action, principally, lies in ensuring that this aim is achieved. Moreover, the political entrepreneur: *a)* decides what productions are to be undertaken; *b)* regulates the methods of production with norms which are more or less fixed; *c)* appoints the technical directors of these production companies. These companies are the delegated companies, their directors do not work as independent entrepreneurs, but in the name and on behalf of the principals. Some make the town council a delegated company; while the town council is an autonomous enterprise, with its own political function. The representatives of the political enterprise are the delegates, but the company is not delegated. While the production companies, commanded by the town council, are fully-fledged companies; they only produce; the town council is not a producer in the proper sense of the word, but only of the coercive forces which have to distribute the costs of certain of its products over all the municipality.

1.6 There are different kinds, or rather, different degrees of direct municipal production — in the sense of production ordered by the town councils according to the use the town council intends to make of the goods produced. We therefore have: *a)* production directed at the procurement of goods which will serve the enterprise's needs. To achieve its political object, a town council will need specific goods: buildings, lighting, furniture, insurance, etc., etc. These goods will be necessary for the functioning of the company: the costs of their procurement can be viewed as a production cost, with regard to the town council's objects, and an administrative cost, with regard to the enterprise's progress. In general, the town council representatives procure goods employing the tender system. Here however there arises the problem of whether the goods in question can be obtained more economically by direct production; *b)* production directed at the procurement of the goods which will serve the needs of the political entrepreneur. In this case these are the consumptions pertaining to the entrepreneur; the production's purpose is the satisfaction of the needs proclaimed as public by the entrepreneur himself. In case *a)* one produces capital goods for the political entrepreneur, in case *b)* one produces consumption goods. Here, if direct production is cheaper than buying on the private market, it will decrease the costs which weigh on the municipality; *c)* production directed at the procurement of goods which will then be sold on the common market, in competition with other private producers.

1.7 These different phases of direct production can be encountered simultaneously in the satisfaction of some needs which can be common to the political enterprise, the political entrepreneur and to a more or less extended group of private consumers. Let is take, for example, the need for lighting. The town council has to arrange for the lighting of its premises, its offices. The town council can subsequently think about lighting the entire city, assuming that the satisfaction of this need is declared public by the political entrepreneur. Lastly, the town council can sell lighting to the citizen who may request such. The same holds for insurance. The town council may have an interest in directly arranging for the insurance of all its premises, of all its employees; it can also cumulatively take on the service of insurance for all those citizens who request such.

1.8 Given this analysis of the various phases of the direct municipal production, we see that this economic procedure takes on two distinct forms which are differentiated by their nature and the differing objects it is desired to achieve. We shall also see that the causes which give rise to these forms are different. We have: 1) simple direct, or economic, production. This form aims to procure goods which serve the needs of the enterprise and entrepreneur. The cost of this production is wholly borne by the municipality; 2) complex direct, or industrial, production. The municipal company produces to sell at cost price and produces in competition with private entrepreneurs. The production costs borne by the municipality are therefore only the costs which represent the business risk. Care should be taken not to confuse these enterprises with state and fiscal enterprises. The two differential natures of industrial municipal enterprises are clearly formulated by Maltbie: *a)* they sell at cost price, *b)* they produce in conditions of free competition. If the company produces a loss or goes bankrupt, the municipality is forced to bear the losses. Thus the municipality advances and risks all the plant costs which are sometimes very high. If on the other hand the enterprise succeeds, if all the units produced are sold at cost price, then the real cost of production is borne by the consumers. Some claim that here the town council presents itself as a production co-operative, but it should be noted that here the real consumers have joined forces to force the town council to start the enterprise. The co-operative enterprise is established by the consumers and not by the town council; and we know that one cannot encounter needs common to all the municipality and on whose municipalisation the entire community agrees.

1.9 Causes provoking a lower cost of municipal products. If the town council finds it to its advantage to directly produce goods or services — and if the citizens find it advantageous to resort to the municipal enterprise rather than to the private enterprise, this means that the town council produces at a lower cost than the private entrepreneurs because we have postulated that the municipal enterprise sells at cost price, and lives by bearing alone all the production costs. This means then that the municipal enterprise has given rise to a new combination of the economic forces, which entails the creation of a production cost or a replacement value which previously did not exist. The new enterprise has to establish a superior and better industrial organisation which succeeds in shifting previous conditions of production.

The changes to the previous productive conditions brought about by municipalisation can be classified into two types: *a)* economic changes; *b)* physical or technical changes.

1.10 *a)* Economic changes are those which act on the production factors and can change the production coefficients. Pareto has clearly distinguished two ways in which the change is obtained (*Cours*, § 75). It may be that a class of economies which owns production factors, can directly impose some production coefficients on the society of which they are members. This can be the case also with municipalisation: let us suppose that the working class obtains protective measures as regards wages and working hours. In this case, the imposition will take place in the political struggle reflecting the conditions of the enterprise. In a second case on the other hand, let us suppose that a class can only set the price of the services of which it has the monopoly, which modifies the production coefficients only indirectly. This is the case in particular of land owners, of inventors of technical innovations, of skilled workers, etc., who all find themselves in conditions of monopoly.

In these cases we note that free competition no longer functions, and that the state of monopoly has replaced the state of freedom. A state of equilibrium comes into being. To exit from it, the previous production conditions have to be shifted; only thus will one have a new and more advantageous state of equilibrium. This involves destroying the conditions of monopoly, and re-establishing the conditions of free competition in their place. If the municipal enterprise succeeds in this intent, it becomes more economic than the previous productive forms, and completely triumphs. But one has to wrest the power to directly impose some production coefficients from some classes, and the upshot will be a political struggle. It will also entail removing the monopoly of certain forces from the hands of other classes, to prevent them from setting prices at the typical point of monopoly, and to set the price back at the cost of production.

The various cases of monopoly which give rise to municipal enterprises will be examined when we deal with the various forms of municipalisation.

1.11 *b)* Physical or technical changes are those which cause an expansion of the enterprise, hence the municipal enterprise can enjoy the advantages of big industry in the competition it has to sustain with private companies. Here we can find the following cases: α) higher and more constant sales than the private companies. If the amount of consumption varies with changes in prices, it is certain that the town council will foresee a higher consumption, either by itself or by the citizens, and hence the need for more production, by selling at its cost price, which is less than the real market price, as it comes from a more extended enterprise. It should be added that in the cases when the companies are set up, it is important to be able to accurately calculate the future clientele, and the oscillations of this clientele. Under some circumstances and for some products, the town council can rely on the custom of certain institutions and the employees of the town council itself. β) The use of more capital. As the town council can easily resort to borrowing, and find credit, it will be more inclined to undertake initial, improvement and equipment costs. It is certain that as the risks of capitalistic investment are spread over the entire municipality, and as the capital can be found with greater ease and at lower cost, the trend will be toward big investment of capital. γ) The possibility to procure the production factors at a lower cost. This is because the town council may already own large areas of land or of other natural forces. These assets will probably have a use value which it is worthwhile calculating, but the new productive use will be carried out only in the event of a greater productivity. Thus also the labour force necessary for a new undertaking can be had at a very low cost, because the control costs and the other administrative costs regarding the new services can be distributed over a workforce already employed by the town council and already used for similar public services.

2. - The Trend Toward Municipalisation in Italy. The Danger of Excessive Legislative Intervention*

The reason behind *Giornale degli Economisti*'s decision to institute a special section dedicated to the phenomenon of municipalisation is not only that of opportunity, but is also determined by the need for legitimate defence.

The appropriateness of a section dedicated to the problem of municipalisation is clearly evident, as Italian town councils have already started out along that path of direct production that has already been effectively undertaken by councils in England and America. Our most important municipalisations include those in the cities of Padua, La Spezia, Como, Vicenza, Asti, Bologna, Voghera, which have municipalised the gas service; the cities of Milan and Florence, which have municipalised the drinking water service; the city of Milan again, which has in part municipalised the tramway service. And many small towns of the Apennines and valleys of the Alps, which have municipalised the electrical lighting service. All these are forms of industrial municipalisation, there are then innumerable cases of ordinary municipalisation, in which the town council operates one or another branch of services which have been declared municipal — funeral ser-

---

* From: MONTEMARTINI G., «Municipalizzazione dei pubblici servigi», *Giornale degli Economisti*, January 1902, pp. 72-4.

vices, fire service, watering service, waste and road maintenance services, etc. It would be no exaggeration to conclude that this question of municipalisation will become the most interesting, from the scientific and practical points of view, of all the questions which comprise the present municipal problem. To relate the entire movement, to examine the municipalisations which already exist, to see them in action, to record their results, to illustrate the political and economic conditions which have produced them, to study the new projects, the new publications, this should be our task, these are at least our intentions.

But our purpose is that of preparing the defences, to combat a danger which threatens the new institutions. The danger consists in the state's threat to intervene to regulate these new forms of municipal life which have to date developed spontaneously, the state dangles the threat of bills regarding direct production by councils. Of late, the fondness shown in the high spheres of government for the phenomenon of municipalisation has been increasing. After the Parliamentary Commission for the town and provincial council credit bill — which became law on 24 April 1898 — invited the government to study the question of direct municipal production, in 1898 Minister Pelloux set up a Commission charged with drafting a bill on the municipalisation of public services. At present we know that Hon. Giolitti is having the problem studied, with the probable intention of in turn presenting a bill. Parliamentary initiative too has no wish to remain on the sidelines, and there is talk of a bill presented by Luzzato in the present and moribund session. The Royal Commission of Inquiry for Naples proposed as a means of rescue for the overburdened finances of the Mezzogiorno's capital, the remedy of the municipalisation of gas, electrical lighting, tramways and Serina water (see *Relazione sull'amministrazione comunale di Napoli*, Rome 1901, vol. 2, pp. 798-803). The question would appear to have made considerable progress in a few years, if in 1898 the Minister of the Treasury, Hon. Luzzatti stated to the Lower House that the moment was not ripe to resolve the question of municipalisation by law, while of late bills have been flowing in and threatening from all sides.

The advocates of municipalisation have therefore changed tack: municipalisation was once demanded only in the programmes of extreme parties, brandished as an electoral platform in the programmes of the socialists and republicans; now it penetrates in the government's intentions. Municipalisation was once demanded by the consumers of special public services and by the taxpayers, now it is offered by the spheres of government. It remains to be seen whether it is the same good, if the quality of the product demanded coincides with that supplied, whether the correspondence of the purposes is real or purely nominal. Here lies the crux of the present question.

In any case, legislative intervention frightens us. The sole legislative intervention admissible is a negative intervention, if such an expression is admissible. Every law which seeks to channel and discipline town councils' new activities with constant and uniform provisions will only suffocate the development of municipalisation at birth. The phenomenon of municipalisation arises spontaneously when the political and economic conditions of the environment are favourable. The sole duty of a wise legislation should be that to remove all obstacles which impede the development of the institution, grant town councils a wider field of action, eliminate the useless supervisory authorities, allow the redemption of the old monopolistic contracts and the proper capitalisation of the concessions. This is the negative legislation of which we spoke, the only one possible, and the only one which is not harmful. The wish to impose municipalisation for, for example financial purposes, would distort the purposes to which the municipalisers of other countries tended, namely the abolition and crumbling of the monopolistic positions, the reduction of prices, the diffusion of some democratic consumptions. One should do everything possible to prevent the state intervening to make municipalisation a mere instrument of finance, a transformation of tax systems, a new body of indirect taxes. The institution should arise and develop spontaneously; the liberalists should protest against state intervention. Municipalisation already represents a form of intervention of the political enterprise in the field of production, let us let the demand for intervention originate naturally from the conditions of the environment, following in this the wise English policy and let us not hamper the fatal evolution of the new economic bodies by interfering.

And so the task of our section will also be to watch over the invasion threatened by the legislator — to champion the principle of liberty in this complex question of municipalisation.

3. - The Municipal Bakery. The Case of Cremona*

Those who have a mystical conception of the public service realise all the forms of municipalisation in the direct production and distribution of gas, electrical light, trams and water, and in some other article of common use. For those however who have a positive conception of the public service, this is but the distribution on the community of the costs of the given production, as it is in a given historical moment. And so public services will vary with the change in the composition of the political enterprise, and the forms of municipalisation will be various and multiple according to the needs of the classes which hold power at specific times.

In a democratic political enterprise, i.e., in the town councils, the productions in which the necessary and sufficient conditions for municipalisation prevail will be those which concern necessities, goods of general consumption for the proletarian and working classes. The most typical case of these productions lies in the breadmaking industry, and it should be no surprise if the working class prevails in a given political ambit, there immediately arises the problem of how best to procure a product, such as bread, of such common use and consumption for the economically inferior classes.

The problem is latent precisely at Cremona, one of the most advanced political centres in Lombardy, and hence in Italy. Indeed it appears that the problem will be definitively solved this Febru-

* From: MONTEMARTINI G., «Municipalizzazione dei pubblici servigi», *Giornale degli Economisti*, February 1902, pp. 165-8.

ary. But the problem has been further complicated of late in such a curious manner that it is worthwhile expressly relating; even more so as we are no longer talking about resolving an isolated case, but of the struggle of two systems which are now confronting one another: the co-operative system and that of municipalisation.

Here, in brief — because, as we have said, it is not so much the fact in itself as the significance of the arguments we wish to emphasise — is how things stand. After the economic perturbations of 1898, the democratic town council, struck by the excessively high price of bread and under the pressure of public opinion, appointed in early 1890 a Commission to draw up and study a project for municipal milling and breadmaking. After long study and elaborate research on the problem of breadmaking, the Commission entrusted the author of this column to prepare a report. The report concluded affirming four principles: *a)* free competition does not function efficiently in the bread industry and the systems of small private bakeries are expensive and at times dangerous and a health hazard; *b)* legal price control is neither a precise nor efficient form of municipal intervention; *c)* the co-operative bakery cannot function as a perfect price control and does not resolve the problem of the low price of bread for the community; *d)* municipal breadmaking is economically and technically the most suited means for resolving the question of bread «at least in cities which in size and population correspond to Cremona». The report ended with a concrete project for a municipal bakery which entailed an overall cost of circa 40,000 lire.

The Commission's discussion of this final project was long and at times interesting. The results were these. It unanimously accepted principles *a)* and *b)* of the report; on principle c) no agreement was possible, and there arose a question of principle. The Commission divided into two groups; the first, headed by the mayor and the council, maintained it was possible to resolve the problem of bread by intervening and promoting the development of the local co-operative bakery; the second, supporting the report's conclusions, opted for municipalisation. The question was put to the vote and the resolution tabled by the mayor in favour of intervention in the co-operative won the day.

Thus the question became one of principle — on the one side the supporters of municipalisation, on the other those of the co-operative. Charles Gide could not have been happier with this excellent triumph of his principle in one of Italy's most democratic and liberal administrations.

The debate between the two principles is so important for a scholar of economics, and for the importance it could have in subsequent applications, that we should dwell on the assertions of the contending parties.

The mayor's resolution contained this first objection to the municipalisation of the bakery: «under the present social, economic and legislative conditions, the only municipalisations from which the public benefit are of those industries which by their nature and conditions of exercise, such as transport, electricity, drinking water, are already almost a de facto monopoly; this is not the case for breadmaking carried out by numerous small bakeries». To which the advocates of municipalisation replied that the breadmaking industry has the characteristics of de facto monopoly as shown on pages 3 and 4 of the report, and as the council itself admitted when it initiated, and won, a famous lawsuit in 1898 against the organised class of bakers. They also pointed out that municipalisation has been carried out not only in cases of monopoly, but also in those of anarchical competition, and namely every time bad organisation of production augmented costs.

A second argument of the aforementioned resolution was that: «the creation of the municipal bakery of limited capacity would not resolve the problem of the price of bread better than a co-operative bakery». Here lies the crux of the question. But the advocates of municipalisation object: give us an example of a single co-operative bakery which sells its bread at cost price, and we will admit defeat. Or else give us the example of a single bakery in which co-operation is not a specific closed circle. Having achieved a certain level of development, each co-operative bakery either turns down new members or is unable to acquire more customers and to extend its sales. Refute this principle, with logical arguments or with one example, and we will support the co-operative solution».

The conclusions the mayor reached were these: «the town council, with the due caution and equal conditions, following the reforms to the by-laws of the local co-operative bakery, so as to assure the constant predominance of the object of public benefit, shall subsidise it with resources and fit premises to achieve its dual function of natural price control and a practical example of a modern and cheap industrial production». At this juncture, I believe, as a good liberalist, that the liberal council is in the wrong. The question has been shifted: it is no longer a question of co-operation or municipalisation, but of protection. A new fact is introduced in that fausse co-operation which so agitated Guyot. Why not protect also the other bakeries? Take care that carrying a co-operative bakery thus on your shoulders does not alienate the entire class of bakers. Also because it is whispered that the present co-operative bakery will soon have to write-down its investment capital and that without your intervention it will be in a bad state. Why protect only a single category of consumers, more specifically the most intelligent consumers who have a small nest-egg to invest in a co-operative enterprise? And finally we can ask: how big will the town council's subsidy to the co-operative bakery be? There is no way out: either the subsidy will be big, and then the members of the bakery will let the by-laws be modified as the radicals want, or the subsidy will be small, and then the partners will continue to do things as they wish. But if the subsidy is big, why does the town council not municipalise the service. Is it perhaps afraid of the word? Why then not adopt the proposal of one of the Commissioners, Dr. Locatelli, who wants to town council to build the bakery, contracting out its operation to a private company?

The question is in any case ripe, and in this month will probably be resolved. There is rumour of a possible referendum. Certainly, if there is a question which justifies the holding of a referendum it is that of the bakery. Before settling the issue before the town council, it would be advisable to resort to the popular judgement in a problem of such serious importance for the working classes. The municipal administration of Cremona, so imbued with true democratic spirit, will certainly not refuse to listen to the voice of all those concerned, of the consumers and taxpayers. And whatever the reply of the people, the administration, emanation of the people's will, will remain and co-operate in the implementation of those tasks which the voice of the referendum will proclaim.

4. - Giolitti's Bill on Municipalisation*

We are faced with a concrete bill, and we are also faced with the dangers which tend to derive from a legislative intervention. Here I confine myself to noting the overall impression deriving from a cursory examination of Giolitti's bill.

The bill has already received a warm welcome, and from various points of view. The ministerial workers say: see that the government is not afraid to municipalise. And the extreme parties comment: the bill has some flaws, but all said and done marks a step forward, we should support it.

I say: it is not perfectly right to claim the merit and sing victory because one has succeeded in receiving only twenty blows instead of forty; I would deem it more correct to fight the system of blows.

In any case, if the bill has some shortcomings, everything should be done to eliminate them, and to prevent these shortcomings from becoming law.

For me, the bill's biggest shortcoming lies in the fact that it gives more importance to the form than the substance of municipalisation. And in the present age, I am persuaded that all those who praise the bill are particularly struck by the word *municipalisation.*

I will confine myself to mentioning some of the probable effects a future law which drew on Giolitti's bill could have.

Section 20 of the bill lays down that town councils can also take on the direct exercise of public services, even if these are already entrusted to private industry, on condition that five years

* From: MONTEMARTINI G., «Municipalizzazione dei pubblici servigi. Il progetto Giolitti sulle municipalizzazioni», *Giornale degli Economisti*, March 1902, pp. 251-3.

have passed since the granting of a licence for the service. It appears impossible that Hon. Giolitti is so furiously against private initiative. It's best not to imagine what might be the results. I speak not of the concessions which have already been granted, but of the future concessions, what private entrepreneur would wish to risk large sums of capital in a company which will be immediately municipalised if it produces good results! Unless the entrepreneur thought of amortising his investment capital in a period of five years!

I recall the commotion aroused in England by the advocates of laissez-faire for the right granted to local corporations to redeem a concession, for electricity companies, after the period of 21 years. It was said and maintained that such a provision would hinder the development of the electricity industry in England. And Giolitti's bill reduces the period to 5 years. Hindrance to the development of private industry indeed!

And now the second point; the bill speaks of company profits which should be transferred to the local council budget. Here lies the greatest danger of the law, given the conditions of local finance in Italy, which gives a tax weapon to seven thousand indebted local councils in very poor financial condition. Just think how these poor councils will swoop joyously on municipalisation, which can become a new method for the collection of indirect taxes. The present forms of indirect taxation no longer suffice or become too odious; hence the need to find a better method for continuing in the cushy system of insidious taxation.

I repeat that the greatest danger lies here, and that one should in some way remedy this shortcoming unless one wants the future law on municipalisation to represent a mere fiscal body rather than the triumph of an important economic principle.

4.1 *The English Examples and the English Parliamentary Commission's Report on Municipal Trading*

Although the success of an institution in foreign lands is not a valid reason for proposing its introduction in other ambits which can have different economic, political and social conditions, it is nonetheless useful to study what experience has taught in other places, albeit bearing in mind the specific conditions of the environment of the country being studied.

Now, it is unarguable that we can obtain valuable tips on economic policy by studying in the cradle of municipalisation, in England, the great movement towards direct municipal production, which in this moment interests us.

I wish to draw the attention of scholars of the argument to a document of exceptional importance and to which, I believe, Italian economists have given scant attention.

I refer to the report of an English Parliamentary Commission charged by the two Houses with studying the problem of municipalisation[1]. We are truly faced with the last and perhaps greatest trial initiated against the municipalisation system. The Committee heard outstanding witnesses against the system and witness defending it; witnesses chosen in the field of science and in that of practical business in the field, in the public and private fields.

The Parliamentary Committee consisted of 5 lords and 5 members of the House of Commons and held 15 sittings from 22 May to 22 July 1900 at which it questioned a total of 38 witnesses. Deeming then that the inquiry was not yet exhausted, neither could it be exhausted before the end of the Parliamentary session, the Committee could not come to final conclusions, but confined itself to referring the evidence, which included 4,408 questions and to giving 25 appendices concerning the facts studied.

For those who wish to proceed with the positive method, the study of these documents is necessary. We hope that scholars in general, practical men and legislators can learn a lot by not ignoring the warnings which arise from facts and experience of things.

---

[1] See *Report from the Joint Select Committee of the House of Lords and the House of Commons on Municipal Trading*; London, Printed for Her Majesty's Stationery Office, 1900.

5. - Municipalisation of the Pharmacies*

The bill drawn up by Hon. Giolitti for the direct assumption of public services by local councils has reached us too late, and so we are obliged to defer detailed examination of the bill to a later issue.

We wish to speak today of a form of municipalisation which we were very surprised not to see mentioned in the demonstrative emuneration of the various cases of direct exercise of public services given in section 1 of Giolitti's bill. We do not understand how the municipalisation of the pharmacies has not been considered one of the forms to be recalled specifically in a bill; when one thinks of the questions to which the pharmaceuticals industry has given rise, and at the attempts which have been made in Italy and abroad for the direct municipal exercise of said industry.

We have before us the January issue of *Farmacista cooperativa* of Ravenna, the journal of the Pharmaceuticals Mutual-aid Cooperative of the Romagna region, which has forwarded a petition to the national Parliament for the municipalisation of pharmacies. The petition closes with a bill, consisting of 15 sections, which makes compulsory the establishment of pharmaceutical practices in all towns and lays down that every town should provide free pharmaceutical assistance for its inhabitants.

The underlying concepts of the bill derive from another bill, by Professor Dioscoride Vitali, which tends to authorise and regulate the acquisition by local councils of pharmacies in their territory, for reasons of public utility — and from the proposal of a Parliamentary Commission, which wishes to amend section 14 of the present law on public health and hygiene so as to make pharmaceutical assistance compulsory and free for all inhabitants.

The detailed provisions of the bill aside, some of which could be modified, its fundamental idea should be accepted. If there is an industry in which the causes which spur town councils to di-

* From: MONTEMARTINI G., «Municipalizzazione dei pubblici servigi (Municipalizzazione delle farmacie)», *Giornale degli Economisti*, April 1902, pp. 356-8.

rect production reign, this is the pharmaceuticals industry. This is an industry which in most places and particularly in the small rural centres, is exercised in conditions of monopoly. The price of the products is not related to the value of the raw materials, but depends rather on the value attributed to the medicine itself. And we note that in the pharmaceuticals industry, that if there is agreement as regards the determination of the prices between pharmacists for the raw materials, there certainly is in assessing the service for the sending of the prescriptions; a service which cannot be budgeted in advance, which varies from prescription to prescription, which eludes any control, which is the secret of the pharmacist's earnings. Finally, it is an industry in which the adulteration of the medicine, or at least the substitution of those prescribed with a similar, cheaper medicine, is frequent and difficult to control.

In addition to these reasons of a mainly economic nature, there are technical reasons which spur one to remove the pharmaceuticals industry from private speculation. The petition we have before us rightly notes that present-day science has revolutionised the field of pharmaceuticals. In fact, today antisepsis triumphs; but in order to reap the fruits of antisepsis special equipment is needed, in other words, considerable outlays, which the pharmacists, because of their specific conditions and because the public usually does not want or cannot pay, alone cannot bear. Hence the need for intervention by the local council. The action of co-operatives may also not suffice to resolve the problem, because co-operatives only give partial solutions for specific groups of consumers, and cannot be made general without risking transforming themselves into capitalistic companies. Co-operation's impotence is acknowledged by the very Petition we are studying.

Whatever bill made council pharmacies compulsory would only resolve a problem of simple municipalisation. But it is unarguable that the introduction of council pharmacies for the poor would quickly lead to industrial municipalisation. The taxpayers who have already had to bear the capital costs of a pharmacy would find it wholly to their advantage to be sold medicine directly by the council pharmacy. The expenses each household would have to bear for this need, which we can call general, would decrease in an extraordinary manner.

The municipalisation of medical assistance is a very common occurrence in our towns. It is incomprehensible why the pharmaceuticals industry whose products are an essentially complementary good to the doctor's services have still not been municipalised. To have a doctor and not the medicine is like displaying a good in a shop window, but banning anyone from approaching it.

We shall end with an observation. There is not, we believe, any need for a special law for the municipalisation of pharmacies. It would suffice for Giolitti's bill, to eliminate any doubt and any future controversy on such a controversial issue, to add to the list in section 1 the right for councils to municipalise pharmacies. Subsequently, the big and useful reform could be implemented by carrying out a humanitarian propaganda, particularly in the country towns, where the life and health of the poor classes are entirely at the mercy of private speculation.

6. - Again on Giolitti's Bill on Municipalisation*

It is unarguable that Giolitti's bill is timely and may be useful in the future life of Italy's town councils. The liberalist profession on page 4 — which states that the political enterprise should be allowed to intervene only to restore free competition — suffices to approve the bill on principle. What however is most important is to highlight the shortcomings of this future law, before it is enacted. I propose today to insist, anticipating some critical concepts which I have developed more thoroughly in a work of mine whose publication is forthcoming, on two fundamental points, on the fiscal concept behind the project and the method of capitalising the concessions proposed by Hon. Giolitti.

* From: MONTEMARTINI G., «Municipalizzazione dei pubblici servigi. (Ancora del progetto Giolitti sulle municipalizzazioni)», *Giornale degli Economisti*, May 1902, pp. 447-53.

6.1 Of the two economic systems which English councils follow in municipalisation, that of selling above cost and that of selling at production cost, Hon. Giolitti prefers the former system, and hopes to reform local finances with the profits which can be obtained by assuming direct exercise.

But every profit that an industrial municipal undertaking wishes to make is an indirect tax on consumption. Municipalisation then becomes a means for collecting a tax, in other words it becomes a fiscal instrument. The consumption tax will amount to the difference between the selling and production price of a given service.

Some wish to combat this concept, in other words, they would deny the tax nature of municipal profits. We also read in Giolitti's bill: «As regards relations between consumers and councils, it should not be thought that the public exercise of industries can be resolved by imposing consumption taxes on the products and services supplied ... The bill aims to prevent on the one hand the excessive decrease, and on the other the excessive increase of prices. As long as they remain the same as normal prices under a competitive regime, they cannot degenerate into taxes».

The confusion of economic terms is evident. It is not clear how why the state receives above the production costs is not a tax. It is the same as saying that an entrepreneur, who offers a good at a price lower than that of his competitors, does not make any profit. Selling more or less dearly, on condition it is above the cost, does not establish a tax nature, but simply its size. Evidently, the bill commits a deplorable confusion between tax and size of tax.

Let us now look at the special characteristics of this indirect tax which takes the form of profits in the municipal companies. We can view things from the point of view of the consumers and from that of the taxpayers — assuming that the profits are used to reduce fiscal pressure.

As all consumption taxes, that of municipal profits does not take account of the citizen's taxable capacity. Take for example the tax on passengers who use the tram, it is unarguable that the poorer consumers will be harder hit, while the rich can use other means of transport. And thus also for all the other services — gas, electricity, water — if the unit price of the services will be the same for every category of consumer, no account will be taken of the taxable capacity. Finally, if we grant that municipalisation has taken place for services of broad and general consumption, the tax in question will be also inversely progressive.

From the taxpayers' point of view, if there was a reduction in fiscal pressure, the reimbursement should be made such as to equitably compensate the various taxpayers. The sole method would appear to be to diminish the tax in fair proportion for all the taxpayers. This would mean that the benefits from municipalisation would be distributed among the taxpayers according to their wealth, the richer would receive a larger part of the profits, the poorer a smaller part. However, two things should be borne in mind: if the taxpayers have any right to have their taxes paid by new categories of taxpayers, and if the municipalisation does not benefit any of them in any way, why then should this last element also be borne in mind in the distribution of the benefits. We do not understand why a tax is imposed on a new category of taxpayers solely because they now consume specific goods. And as regards the benefits deriving from municipalisation, we should note that, in general, the classes of taxpayers that profit most from the tram companies, from the water, gas and electricity plants which the new councils are establishing, are precisely the owners of land and houses who see the value of their property increase. Moreover, even vis-à-vis the entire body of taxpayers, every municipalisation brings into being superior social and economic positions, determines greater opportunity for the enjoyment of citizen's life in thousands of forms. Hence it does not seem fair that those who most benefit from the introduction of the municipal enterprise should also enjoy a reduction in tax at the expense of specific categories of consumers; and it is in any case unjust that all taxpayers, who differently enjoy the benefits of municipalisation, should experience a proportional diminution of the tax burden.

When Giolitti's bill also proposes, among its other objects, a tax purpose, namely: «to spur councils to a rational transformation of their tax system», it places no limitation on the profits that a municipal enterprise can make. In this it eschews the practice of many English councils, which limit the profits to specific percentages; for example, the profits deriving from electricity plants, in excess of 5% should be used to reduce prices. But furthermore, in the Italian local tax system, this omission of limitation for a special consumption tax, is a flagrant exception in the system itself. All our local taxes are maintained balanced by numerous limitations, which seek to conserve a certain proportionality between local taxation and state taxation and between the various local taxes. Thus there are limits on the surtaxes and there are limits on personal taxes. There is a surfeit of limits for sales taxes; additional local duties cannot amount to more than 50% of state taxation, local duties are determined according to the value of the item being taxed; the maximum tax on retail sales is set down by royal decree. It is incomprehensible why, as these are new sales taxes, the usual provisions, which lay down a ceiling which can defend the consuming classes, have not been followed.

As they are sales taxes, this defence was even more necessary in Italy, where indirect taxation, an anonymous and dangerous form of taxation, has already triumphed in its worst manifestations. In fact, the sales tax has become one of the fundamental bases of the local tax system: it accounts overall for 45% of all tax receipts; taking account of the distribution of tax over the different environments, we see that in provincial capitals this tax accounts for 67% of total fiscal pressure, and 57% in district capitals and in small towns.

In Italy therefore the danger of allowing municipal enterprises to make profits, without even adopting the normal precaution of laying down limits on the new tax, — is very great, given the tendency and the possibility of the ruling classes resorting to indirect taxes. Probably, the Italian councils, burdened as they are with debt, will gleefully embrace this new tax, without thinking of renewing their tax system, indeed, finding a convenient means for exaggerating its shortcomings.

The reduction in indirect tax could be obtained by laying down, for example, that the profits of municipal enterprises be used precisely to reduce or suppress sales taxes. But here also, having to compare the consumptions which are currently hit and those which could subsequently be hit by municipalisation, it is doubtful if the law would be broadly applied in Italy. On the one hand we have rice, flour, drinks, fodder, fuel, building materials, furniture, soap, raw materials which are hit by the sales tax, - on the other Giolitti's bill would allow a tax on the consumption of water, gas, trams, bread, meat, baths. Many have already felt, from a social point of view, the importance of the diffusion of certain special public services of this latter category. In Italy, moreover, where the present municipalisations encompass almost wholly aqueducts and slaughter-houses, of 424 municipal enterprises, 151 are aqueducts and 171 are slaughter-houses — the first indirect taxes, obtained from the profits of municipalisation, would be on the consumption of water and meat.

Using municipalisation as a tax instrument could be defended only from the fiscal point of view, as a superior form of collection. Instead of the Mediaeval, oppressive and costly system of tariff barriers, one could resort to direct production, as the state does in fiscal matters. But a heavy tax regime, broadened to so much of productive life, also presents dangers and very serious shortcomings.

6.2 A second point, worthy of the maximum consideration, regards the method to be followed in capitalising the licences and plants. In general, unilateral points of view are adopted in this financial operation: either one is concerned only with the council, and resorts to the formula of reproduction cost, or one is concerned only with the private entrepreneur and wishes to consider only the production cost, or only the present income of the plant.

But the fiercest debate concerns the loss of anticipated profits of the enterprise; capitalising a licence, should one compensate the owner of the plant also for those profits which he will lose for the number of years when he can no longer exploit the licence?

The most frequent practice, in the United States of America, is contrary to the recognition of loss of anticipated profits, to take account, that is, of the future earning prospects. The law on lighting in Massachusetts, in disciplining the case of acquisition by the local council of private gas or electricity lighting plants, lays down that «the value of said plants will never include their future earning capacity». Also in the case of water plants, practice and case-law in Massachusetts is that «the value of the plants will be estimated without any increase due to the future earning capacity» and this stance is repeated subsequently in the Acts of 1894, 1895 and 1896.

Giolitti's bill, on the other hand, enshrines an opposite principle. Section 21 of the bill proclaims: «Should the town councils wish to revoke the licences they have granted, they should pay the concessionaires an indemnity to be calculated taking into account: *a)* the present value of the plant's movable and immovable assets; *b)* fair compensation to be paid on the profit which will no longer be earned for the remaining duration of the licence».

One could think that the reasons which spurred Hon. Giolitti to lay down provisions which are so different from the practice adopted in municipalising countries — also in England the loss of anticipated profits is not compensated — are reasons of exceptional seriousness. But in the report accompanying the bill we find no reasons which would justify such measures. And yet acceptance of the principle of loss of anticipated profit has a theoretical and practical significance of the maximum importance.

Let us see how things stand. A tram company obtains a dividend of 10%, earns a net income of 50,000 lire, is valued, at the current rate of interest 5%, at one million lire and has only invested 500,000 lire. The town council, which has made the redemption, can obtain 5% from its capitalistic investiture. Furthermore, the licence has ten years left to run and one wishes to indemnify the company for the profits which it will not now earn for this period. As we are talking of 50,000 lire per year which should be calculated for ten years, we are talking overall of 500,000 lire which the company should pocket. The upshot would be that the local council should now pay out 1,500,000 lire and assuming that it will succeed in maintaining, during its management, the earnings obtained by the private company, it will obtain from its investment an interest of 3.33%. As for the company, it will see its capital suddenly double.

Now, one cannot see how one can be entitled to a doubling of capital, for transferring to the local council that which belongs to the council. Revoking the licence does not damage the concessionaire, because he is repaid the invested capital in full — he is only deprived of a privileged position which derives not from his merit, but from the public will. To compensate him for loss of anticipated profit, one would have to assume that the capital repaid to him did not earn anything for a certain number of years, that his capital remained absolutely idle. But this is a gratuitous hypothesis and certainly far from reality.

Moreover, from what causes do the generous profits one wishes to reimburse go to the concessionaire? For the most they derive from social causes, from the increase in the population, from improved economic conditions, from the fact that certain industries represent local monopolies, and above all from the fact that the municipal authorities have allowed the concessionaire to take advantage of these monopolistic conditions. When the local council no longer wishes to grant licences for public property, it is fully entitled to withdraw the licence. Public property always belongs to the public, and nobody can claim any rights on it. A law which agreed compensation, for claimed loss of anticipated profit, in the case of expropriation, would destroy the rights local councils have on their roads, on public land, on all municipal property. To safeguard the claimed private rights, one would fight the more general and superior rights of the local council, of the community.

If denying loss of anticipated profit can eliminate any recompense the concessionaire who would find some problems in promptly re-employing his capital, would receive — this being the sole damage expropriation can bring about — it should not be forgotten that every economic transaction is subject to risks and that when a private entrepreneur takes on a public enterprise he exposes himself to the specific risk of municipalisation.

Finally, if we consider the issue from the practical point of view, we can only conclude that the provisions in Giolitti's bill regarding the compensation of loss of anticipated profit is of such significance that it would hamper any municipalisation movement in Italy. In all the cases in which the terms of the licence are still long, it will be impossible for a local council to amortise a large quantity of capital which will not yield, for a long time, any recompense. The recompense would already have been eaten away in advance, by he who has not contributed, in any way, to its formation.

7. - The Majorana *Report* on the Giolitti Bill*

The Majorana *Report* is a truly exemplary and balanced work which can be a precious aid to the Giolitti Bill; the *Report* is related to the Bill as the twin of the legislative provision, as academic work to purely legislative work.

The various technical and practical aspects of the issue in question are illuminated, thus bearing out the various conclusions the legislator wishes to reach. Majorana is far from being enthralled by the concept of municipalisation for the sake of municipalisation — he seeks to trace the conditions which should exist to give life to the phenomenon. Having recalled the trend of modern cities to grow extensively and intensively, he passes from this sociological substratum to the economic conditions of the municipality and finds them in the lack of efficacy of the freedom to combat monopolistic positions. This concept has already been vigorously affirmed by Giolitti and the social conditions for this order are constantly being proclaimed by the Italian liberal bourgeoisie.

This theoretical premiss leads Majorana to enunciate the principle that municipalisation «should always be separated from the various conditions of time and space». And the Report also feels obliged to study the attitudes of the various industries to see whether one can encounter in their evolution the social and economic conditions which presuppose municipalisation. If it is thus that the proposer can have the Commission accept the addition

* From: MONTEMARTINI G., «Municipalizzazione dei pubblici servigi. La Relazione Majorana sul Progetto Giolitti», *Giornale degli Economisti*, August 1902, pp. 173-5.

of some industries to those which Hon. Giolitti demonstratively listed in section 1 of the Bill, such as the breadmaking, ice, corn, and pellagra industries.

This treatment — whose theoretical need is exact — contains minor faults it would be useful to point out. In general, no account is taken of the laws of development of industries nor of the examples of municipalisation which foreign countries can offer. In some industries, no account is taken of the social and economic conditions which lead or should lead to municipalisation, as is the case, for example, for the gas and tramway industries. Hon. Giolitti's justification for bread at controlled prices is bereft of any study of the true effectiveness a controlled-price bakery could have on the determination of bread prices. In the praise attributed to the small Piedmont insurance companies there is no mention of the danger one is heading for in promoting forms of insurance which can only be based on small areas.

These — as we have already said — are the minor faults of the *Report*. Where however we dissent wholly from the order of ideas proposed by Majorana is in the concept which inspires the entire bill. The Commission has embraced the treatment Giolitti's Bill wishes to give to municipalisation. Municipalisation continues to be considered as a fiscal means to give new life to the exhausted local finances which, in the final analysis, only ends up in a new system of indirect taxation.

The Giolitti Bill and that of the Commission do not rise to a different conception of municipalisation because the Italian legislator considers the phenomenon treated as a special phenomenon, wholly distinct from all other phenomena of political and financial life. It also follows that the number of precautions and safeguards excogitated in the institution of municipal enterprises will undoubtedly hamper the municipalisation movement.

The proposers have forgotten their initial premiss. If the council proclaims that its new function is that of intervening every time private monopolistic production threatens the consumer — if the council includes in the series of public needs that of defending the consumer — there is no reason to give special significance to this new function. The industrial municipal enterprise is a case of the complex life of the political enterprise. If one wishes to sustain the safeguard with the usual argument that the local bodies of some regions should not be left to act autonomously, it is incomprehensible why there should be a more rigid system of safeguards for the new industrial enterprises. One would understand the contrary, when one thinks that control by the public is simpler for the new industrial enterprises because the consumer would have a sure and immediate index in prices for re-ordering the good progress of the enterprise. Hence the justifications of a purely Italian system one wishes to propagate, to surround the exercise of the future municipal enterprises with every possible guarantee, fall by the wayside.

In general, one could say that both the Giolitti Bill and the Majorana *Report* go out of their way to proclaim and justify the principle of municipalisation, while simultaneously creating obstacles to prevent the implementation of the principle. The crisis of freedom is proclaimed, and one would say that there is much fear of freedom. One allows, for example, the liberist form of the referendum, but does not surround it with extraordinary protection. The affirmation of the principles of autonomy is a moving formula — there is no faith in the beneficial and educational effects of freedom.

Furthermore, the system adopted for redeeming the licences creates new obstacles to the development of the municipalist principle.

The Majorana *Report* limits the period for which one should pay the fee to the redeemed private companies to 15 years, and also indicates the reasons presented for defending the interest of capitalistic private players which are not convincing. They are reasons of equity which clash with the introduction of a limitation of time in the exercise of a right; without also considering that no account is taken of a private right to impose a right of traffic.

These are the shortcomings which should be eliminated in the future law on municipalisation: the law should not have fiscal purposes; it should mark a true affirmation of the principle of autonomy; it should not hamper the natural and spontaneous movement of modern councils toward new functions.

8. - Apathy for the Giolitti Bill*

It is amazing how the bill on municipalisation, even though it aims to discipline one of the most controversial problems in the field of economics and politics, has aroused such little attention and has not been reflected in Italian public life. Professional politicians did not concern themselves with it, — the councils took no interest whatsoever in it, — only some association of capitalists lodged a protest with the Ministry. Then the bill was forgotten, and it will probably be talked about at the last moment when it is presented in Parliament for a rushed discussion and approval. Even the socialist party, the most interested in the theoretical question, has still to tackle the problem, and the Imola Congress included on its agenda the question of the nationalisation of the railways without mentioning Giolitti's imminent bill on municipalisation.

8.1 *A Regulatory Liberalist*

Only some rare theoretician has taken the bother, spurred by the good occasion, to examine the phenomenon of municipalisation which the Giolitti Bill wishes to make a fashion. And as usual two currents immediately surface: some, decidedly opposed to the minister's policy, criticised the spirit and practice of municipalisation, - others on the other hand sought arguments in favour of the bill, or of some of its principal provisions.

In the last issue of this journal, Mr. G. V., regulatory liberalist, stuck a blow for the regulation of industries by the local council. But, even though the author wishes to proceed inductively, examining some industries in which municipalisation predominates, the problem of control has not been studied at all. The author confines himself to stating that direct production has some drawbacks, and that free production regulated by the local councils

---

* From: MONTEMARTINI G., «Municipalizzazione dei pubblici servigi. Apatia intorno al Progetto Giolitti», *Giornale degli Economisti*, October 1902, pp. 378-80.

would be preferable, - but forgets to prove that the system of control is possible, easy to implement, inexpensive and reasonable. It is precisely in the industries examined, aqueducts and tramways, we have disastrous examples, in Italy, of municipal control. What is therefore the point of schematically enumerating — as was the fashion in economic monographs twenty years ago — the advantages and drawbacks of direct production, without at least adopting the same method for the opposing system proposed? In municipalisation, we are not talking of studying the advantages or drawbacks of the system, but of determining the conditions which give life to the system itself. We will certainly not have a classification of the industries in those which can and cannot be municipalised, - but we shall establish in what circumstances any industry will tend toward municipalisation.

8.2 *The Monopolistic Nature of Public Services*

In a first article on the municipalisation of public services published in *Nuova Antologia* of June 1, Professor G. Vacchelli dwells on the characteristics of municipalised public services and challenges the principal argument put forward by the Giolitti Bill to support the need to municipalise, namely the monopolistic nature of the services which should be directly produced.

But Professor Vacchelli has not sufficiently examined that which he calls the «social-financial exchange» which takes place in a phenomenon of municipalisation and which manifests itself in the economic determination of a political enterprise. The hedonistic calculation is always made by the political entrepreneur who holds power in that moment, without concern for the social utility, for the utility, that is, for the entire community. Hence the benefit of the municipalisation is always judged by a part of the community, which alone judges the monopolistic nature of the services to be municipalised. This is why at times industries which are only relatively monopolistic are municipalised, because such is the interest of the consumers, who in that moment are political entrepreneurs. Observing the history and evolution of the municipalisation phenomenon, is it certain that one of the most influent causes for deciding municipalisation was the defence of consumers against the abuse of monopolistic positions by privileged products.

8.3 *Profit or Tax?*

But the Giolitti Bill also has its defenders; the special provisions which mould the future law, the possibility for the councils to obtain profits from their industrial enterprises are defended in this very journal (the June issue) by a Mr. y who upholds Giolitti's principle that selling above cost is not a tax, but merely a profit. Mr. y satisfies himself with this verbal assertion, believing he has resolved the question with it; he does not reflect on whether an industrial profit can be a tax. I say tax because probably the writer of the article confuses tax and duty, and uses the term in the sense of tax. But I would be interested to know if he does not call indirect sales tax that which is obtained by a fiscal monopoly, e.g., that obtained by selling salt at 40 cents per kg. while production costs do not exceed 4 cents. And yet here also we are talking of revenues from sales in excess of the production costs, a surplus determined by the ordinary laws of exchange.

It is useless beating about the bush: if the council sells above production cost, local indirect taxation will see a new and vast horizon unfold before it. And this should be opposed to the bitter end.

9. - The *Times*'s Criticism of Municipalisation*

At the last minute, just before discussion of the Giolitti Bill, the Italian press, and particularly the conservative press, was howling about a series of articles which an anonymous author had

* From: MONTEMARTINI G., «Municipalizzazione dei pubblici servigi», *Giornale degli Economisti*, January 1903, pp. 87-91.

published in the *Times* in the months of August, September and October. The articles were very well done, full of details and also of gossip; they scandalised for example, the upright English public with certain revelations concerning the enormous quantities of champagne and cigars consumed by the various municipal commissions charged with studying direct production projects. Then it was discovered that the anonymous author was none other than an agent of some powerful societies engaged in the production of public services. The enthusiasm and trust in the articles diminished considerably — but in any case it was agreed that the writer had an uncommon skill as a polemicist.

The anonymous author painted a dark picture of the political danger the municipalisation projects could hide («The Socialist Idea», *Times,* 10 August). The intrusiveness of the modern council in all branches of economic life was illustrated in detail, with numerous facts («The Council as Comprehensive Supplier», *Times,* 23 August). The consequences were shown to be fatal as a result of the necessary transformation of the tax systems, which preferred to hit every productive activity, hampering growth («Local Taxes and Commercial Enterprises», *Times,* 2 September), - and the subsequent tightening up of taxes («Local Tax Pressure Increases», *Times,* 28 August). Direct production by councils was perceived as damaging to the development of private production, as a dangerous and artificial competing force («Municipal Industry against Private Industry», *Times,* 5 September). The author examined the results of some municipal enterprises in the corporation of West Ham, governed by the socialists («A Socialist Regime in West Ham», *Times,* 16 September), and in Battersea, which fell into the hands of the Labour Party («A Municipal Mecca», *Times,* 18 September). The statistics of the municipal enterprises of Birmingham and Glasgow were also subject to close scrutiny (*Times,* 25 and 30 September) seeking to show their errors and inferiority vis-à-vis private enterprises.

For the impartial reader, the anonymous author's criticisms might appear well presented and sharp — while not revealing any point further to those which had already been revealed and discussed in the famous *Report* which the English Parliamentary

Committee of Inquiry published on municipalisation. We summarised the findings of this inquiry in a previous issue. It is unarguable that all the charges, mentioned by the anonymous author, are given a total or partial defence in the replies of the witnesses who support the institution. This of the anonymous author is only a bell, more specifically the biased bell of the enemies of municipalisation. To give the proper weight to the opposing arguments, one should first hear ring also the bell of those in favour of municipalisation — neither can we deny that, through the English inquiry, it no longer rings in full peal.

9.1 *Hon. Bertolini-Sonnino's Precondition*

Given the conservative press's campaign against municipalisation, discussion of the Giolitti Bill in the Lower House was expected to be lively. Instead the opposition was half-hearted and hesitant and the bill was passed with very few amendments.

The opposition did not resort to their usual touching rhetoric to fight the new institution. Hon. Majorana could be satisfied that throughout the discussion the absurd fear of those who thought they saw in the Giolitti Bill a first step towards a socialist regime was not once broached.

Evidently the statements by Hon. Borciani — on behalf of the Socialist group - «that the socialists view the law as a first step towards the realisation of their ideals» was not taken seriously, neither by the opposition, nor by the government; the law as it was formulated allowed no room for such doubts.

But the opposition, instead of resorting to the usual arguments — which were repeated, in a cursory form, only by Hon. Scalini — preferred to avail themselves of a precondition. In other words they sought to show that rather than resort to the dangerous system of municipalisation, it would be more prudent to discipline the concessions granted by the councils to private companies. Hon. Sonnino attempted to restrict the sphere of direct production, putting forward and in good light the system of municipal control of monopolistic private companies.

The thesis was not new, and the attack was to be expected — after Hon. Bertolini had illustrated an additional Bertolini-Sonnino bill in an article in *Nuova Antologia*, based entirely on the efficiency of the system of controls. The trouble is that the shortcomings of this system are so serious that the drawbacks of the municipalisation system almost disappear in comparison.

In the United States, where municipalisation is very uncommon, so much so that this country is cited with satisfaction by the opponents of direct production — the system of control has fallen into general discredit as a result of the implementational difficulties it engenders.

It was therefore easy for Hon. Giolitti to eliminate Sonnino's thesis, while also enjoying some ironic taunts.

9.2 *Discussion of Giolitti's Bill in the Lower House*

The general discussion was not so much broad as lofty and serene. Hon. Fusinato's speech can be described as masterly in its command of the problem, less broad but much more profound in its economic concept was the speech of Hon. Alessio, equally instructive were the considerations of an administrative nature presented by Hon. Codacci Pisanello, while the speeches of Hons. Borciani and Majorana were very interesting.

Of Hon. Giolitti one can only admit that he was exceptionally skilful in defending his bill, its principles and the contradictions of his principles. We have already mentioned that the principle of intervention of the political enterprise at every case of monopolistic abuse — a principle proclaimed by Hon. Giolitti and accepted by all the speakers in the Lower House — was wholly contrary to that of a political enterprise enjoying industrial profits. The discussion revolved around this point, section 2, but Hon. Giolitti was able to uphold his contradiction, as it was formulated in the bill and accepted by the Report of the Parliamentary Commission, adding that a law such as this — introducing a new fiscal body — would help introduce the principle of social justice in our legislation!

It should not be thought that the Lower House embraced wholeheartedly the admission of industrial profits by municipal enterprises; Hon. Alessio criticised it surely and vigorously. Selling at above cost appeared to all, from Fusinato to Sonnino, from Frascara to Alessio, as a quick method for collecting an indirect tax. And faced with the new tax body new provisions to mitigate its consequences were called for. Frascara for example, logically maintained that the profits of municipalisation should be used either to reduce the price of municipal products or services, or to reduce existing indirect taxes. Alessio, on the other hand, struck by the possibility of an increase in indirect taxation, proposed that at least certain industries, and more specifically those which offer necessities, should sell at cost price. But all these provisions were rejected by the minister proposing the bill, by the Parliamentary Commission and by the Lower House — such that the law preserved its fiscal nature. There were some optimists, for example Hon. Fusinato, who prophesised the future prevalence of the social over the fiscal element in the practice of municipalisation, but experience will show with time which of these two criteria Italian councils will embrace.

The reasons advanced by the supporters of municipal profits have no weight —prejudice and banal argument was worth more than a serious and logical consideration of the facts and premisses. Hon. Giolitti said: but how do you wish to sell at cost? this is an inapplicable practical criterion. But how? Does not every private industrialist, before commencing production, make his calculations and budget the costs he has to sustain? There will be provisions for unforeseeables, for reserves — but the calculation should be certain and accurate. There is no need to resort to doctrinal revivescences as Hon. Majorana presupposed, to admit this fact. This is what the councils should do — and the English councils which follow the policy of prices in line with cost follow precisely and without difficulty the procedure of every private enterprise. Hon. Giolitti also said, supported by Hon. Majorana: that selling at cost would offend private industry. Here evidently there lacked a proper concept of the manner of calculating the costs — and this was seen in the duscussion on controlled-price bakeries.

But once the costs are calculated on the base of the same elements which a private enterprise should employ — one cannot see where and how municipal competition can offend private industry.

The Hon. Minister then deployed a portentous argument: don't worry about the profits — he preached — they will eventually return to the community. It was like listening to a financier of the first half of the last century. But, Hon. Minister, nobody believes any longer in this abstract community you invoke; real life is all strewn with struggles of interests and class. And moreover, profits represent an indirect tax, and then your very same arguments should be extended to the entire tax system. What would you say if one reasoned thus: let us not concern ourselves with how taxes are distributed — they will sooner or later return to the community. This is fine, when the taxes hit others, not when they hit us.

One last observation and I have finished. Hon. Fusinato found it little natural that prices be determined and profits limited for those industries which operate in competition with private players. But Hon. Fusinato did not remember at that moment what are the economic conditions which in certain periods call for the intervention of the political enterprise. There are industries in which there prevails a form of competition which is live but not efficient of good effects, an anarchical competition which prevents the formation of economic enterprises which can sell at diminishing cost. If the council can establish a superior enterprise, it should not however take advantage of it and enjoy the differential rent which it would obtain, sell at the prices of the marginal companies.

9.3 The second fundamental point of the Giolitti Bill consisted of section 25 of the scheme proposed by the Commission and regarded the redemption of the licence. Here also there was discussion, but the will of the proposers and the fear of excessively audacious innovations won the day. We can only appeal to experience and time — we shall see what redemptions the councils can implement given the onerous and obstructive provisions laid down by the legislator.

10. - Municipalisation Spreads*

Facts are worth more than theories: the phenomenon of municipalisation enters and affirms itself in the life of Italian councils. The municipalisation of the breadmaking industry would appear to have triumphed in Catania, and is being meanwhile studied in Bologna; the municipalisation of workers' housing is being forced on Milan council; the pharmacies are starting to be run by the councils; even the wine producers wish to be municipalised. From this great real movement, and from this set of facts, both the theory and practice of municipalisation can be learnt — it would be advisable therefore to closely examine and scrutinise the facts.

10.1 *The Municipalisation of Workers' Housing in Milan*

The most important question for the present city council of Milan is that of workers' housing. It has already claimed the councillor responsible for finances; and the position is still vacant, as nobody wishes to take responsibility for the position, as not even the council as a whole wishes to state its position on this controversial municipalisation. All the parties are alert and controlling the administration, while there is neither general agreement nor acceptance of the benefit of the new municipalisation.

Direct council intervention in the construction of the workers' housing was first called for by the trade union centre. We have two reports on the matter drawn up by a commission charged with studying the question. The two reports do not wholly agree on the final aims. While the first maintains that the council should, not only build and administer the workers' housing, but also immediately arrange for the acquisition of the land by expropriation of the land which is still undeveloped —

---

* From: MONTEMARTINI G., «Municipalizzazione dei pubblici servigi», *Giornale degli Economisti*, February 1903, pp. 181-3.

the second defers this operation and acknowledges the advantage of starting with the reduced programme of construction alone. The need for the council's intervention as industrial entrepreneur is inferred from the fact that the supply of workers' housing in Milan runs below demand, because private speculation always preferred to build for the upper and middle classes; because charity and philanthropy have proven themselves impotent and insufficient to resolve the problem; because co-operatives have not succeeded in raising sufficient capital, contributing only to a partial and negligible satisfaction of the need in question.

The clamour promoted by the trade union centre for its project ensured that the city council also dedicated itself to it. We have a first proposal made by the councillor responsible for finances Colli. The Colli *Report* proposes to encourage the construction of at least 5,000 housing units immediately. But for reasons pertaining to the sphere of public credit, it is deemed appropriate to establish a wholly autonomous institution, which would be charged with acquiring the land, building and administrating the housing. The loans needed for the operation would be furnished by this autonomous body, which would grant a mortgage lien on the land and buildings — in addition to this lien, the subsidisers would also have one from the council for the interest and amortisation. And as the council has the right to redeem and also to take over the institution, the report author's statement that he believes his proposal a remote municipalisation, i.e., after a specific test, is justified.

Colli's proposal was not deemed acceptable by the council, and the post of councillor responsible for finances was abandoned and is still vacant. Meanwhile the council drew up a municipalisation project which was illustrated in a report by councillor Pugno. It was decided that the council would begin the gradual construction of the workers' housing on its own behalf and on land to be acquired specifically for said purpose, within the limit of Lire 4,000,000, the funds being obtained by a loan transaction. For the construction and management of the housing, the *Report* proposed to appoint a special commission, comprising an autonomous company along the lines of the commissions introduced by the Giolitti law on municipalisation. This is the present state of the question. Meanwhile the various parties are not wasting time, and fighting for and against the principle and proposal of municipalisation, taking advantage of the period of rest and reflection into which the city council and citizens would appear to have fallen.

The Republican Party councillors have presented two Reports by Chiesa. One insists on the need for a statistical survey before taking a final decision on the question of the workers' housing, whatever said decision may be. We note, by way of aside, technically, the report has some shortcomings, because while the study proposed has the status of an inquiry, it is proposed to implement it with the methods of a census. The second Report is against municipalisation as a means of resolving the problem, and proposes instead that the council should intervene and promote a civil company between it, the council, the local savings bank, the congregation of charity organisations, the pawnbrokers' institution, the local co-operative bank and the Umanitaria charitable organisation. The council is to immediately provide, as a first contribution, the sum of one million lire to be allocated in 1903 and 1904.

The Conservative Party councillors have still not announced an official stance; however, interviews with some of the party's leading figures would appear to indicate that they are opposed to the principle of municipalisation, and that instead favour a protectionist intervention by the political enterprise. Namely, the state should arrange for exemption from the tax on buildings; the council should reduce the tax on building materials, and the costs of sewage systems and drinking water for housing units with one or two rooms, and the eventual freehold of the area. The intervention of the political body is in any case allowed also by the Conservative Party, thus acknowledging that private competition does not resolve the problem of workers' housing.

Certainly in this month, the council will decide on the question and we will keep the readers of this survey informed of developments.

10.2 *The Housing Question in Municipal Affairs*

Before leaving the problem of workers' housing, we would draw attention to the latest issue of *Municipal Affairs* which is dedicated to the housing problem. There are studies on housing conditions in Germany, France, England and the United States. All the possible solutions are mentioned and supported, by specialists: municipalisation, co-operatives, private initiative. Once again we have proof that the problem of municipalisation does not entail absolute solutions, but is instead a problem of limits.

Index